MORE HUMAN

MORE HUMAN

DESIGNING A WORLD WHERE
PEOPLE COME FIRST

STEVE HILTON

WITH SCOTT BADE AND JASON BADE

PublicAffairs

New York

PublicAffairs books are available at special discounts for bulk purchases in the U.S.
by corporations, institutions, and other organizations. For more information, please
contact the Special Markets Department at the Perseus Books Group, 2300 Chestnut
Street, Suite 200, Philadelphia, PA 19103, call (800) 810-4145, ext. 5000,
or e-mail special.markets@perseusbooks.com.

Library of Congress Cataloging-in-Publication Data
Names: Hilton, Steve, author. | Bade, Scott, author. | Bade, Jason, author.
Title: More human: designing a world where people come first / Steve Hilton with
Scott Bade and Jason Bade.
Description: New York : PublicAffairs, 2016.
Identifiers: LCCN 2016002227 (print)
LCCN 2016004482 (ebook)
ISBN 9781610396523 (hardback)
ISBN 9781610396530 (ebook)
Subjects: LCSH: Human behavior. | Practical reason. | Choice (Psychology) | Political
planning. | Social policy. | Social change. | BISAC: BUSINESS & ECONOMICS /
Government & Business. | POLITICAL SCIENCE / Public Policy / General. | BUSINESS &
ECONOMICS / Economic Conditions.
Classification: LCC BF199 .H55 2016 (print) | LCC BF199 (ebook) | DDC 320.6—dc23
LC record available at http://lccn.loc.gov/2016002227

Editorial production by Christine Marra, *Marrathon* Production Services.
www.marrathon.net

BOOK DESIGN BY JANE RAESE
Set in 10-point Utopia

FIRST EDITION

10 9 8 7 6 5 4 3 2 1

TO ROHAN

Roop!

CONTENTS

INTRODUCTION

ON JUNE 9, 2014, Jennifer Devereaux boarded a JetBlue flight from New York to Boston. She was traveling with her two young daughters. Everything seemed normal: the passengers found their seats, the announcements were made, the plane left the gate and moved toward the runway for takeoff. But then it all started to go wrong. The captain announced that there had been a delay and the aircraft would have to wait on the tarmac for around forty-five minutes. Jennifer's three-year-old daughter announced that she needed to use the bathroom. Because they were just waiting around on the tarmac, Jennifer thought it would be fine to get up and take her daughter to the toilet—they were sitting just a few rows away.

Big mistake. As soon as she started getting up, a JetBlue cabin crew member zoomed up and yelled, with that special kind of rudeness we all know and love: "Ma'am, you're going to have to sit down."

"But I'm just taking my little girl to the restroom."

"You need to sit down right now. The captain has the seatbelt sign switched on."

"Please, can you let us go? She's a three-year-old and she can't wait."

"Ma'am, I'm ordering you to sit down and fasten your seatbelts. You need to comply with my instruction."

That was just the start.

After another half-hour or so, the poor little girl couldn't hold it any longer and wet herself in her seat. Jennifer, upset and wanting to do anything to reduce her daughter's discomfort, called a crew member and asked whether she could have something to mop up the mess—a cloth, some napkins, anything. The flight attendant walked off—and didn't come back. After a few minutes of waiting, Jennifer couldn't bear it any longer. She remembered she had a sweater in the overhead bin and thought she could use that to dry her daughter's seat a little. So she stood up to open the bin and—you guessed it—a crew member raced down the aisle and screamed at her to sit down. Jennifer explained that because no one from JetBlue had brought her anything, she was just trying to get her sweater so she could mop things up and surely, as they weren't even moving, it would be okay to—

"It doesn't matter what it is—the seatbelt sign is on, and you have to sit down right now!"

In disbelief—remember the plane was just sitting on the tarmac—Jennifer kept going, reaching for her sweater.

'That's enough, ma'am. Sit down now!"

Defeated, Jennifer did as she was told. You can imagine how she felt. And worse, how her poor little girl felt.

Then the captain's voice came over the intercom.

"Ladies and gentlemen, I'm afraid that we have a noncompliant passenger on board and are going to have to return to the gate to remove them from the aircraft."

That "noncompliant" passenger was Jennifer, trying to look after her three-year-old daughter who needed to use the bathroom.

Rude, aggressive, lacking in compassion—even though, thanks to the last-minute intervention of an off-duty pilot seated nearby, the flight crew finally relented and allowed Jennifer and her daughters to remain on board, JetBlue's behavior toward that family was inhuman. Talking about it after the event, Jennifer said, "Why can't we just treat each other with kindness and decency, like human beings?"[1]

IT'S A GOOD QUESTION and one this book will try to answer. You could look at that story and say, "Well, that's just the way some of these airline employees behave. You see that kind of thing all over the place with officious bureaucratic-minded people. That's just life."

But it's not just life. Being inhuman is not the natural order of things. People don't instinctively behave that way: they're made to by the circumstances they're in and the structure of the world around them. And being inhuman is not just about bad behavior—it's actually a big part of our deepest problems. Economic problems: our efforts to end poverty, to deal with rising inequality, to make sure everyone has the chance to get a decent, well-paying job. Social problems: how our children grow up and are educated, how we organize the places we live and the health care we receive. Political problems too: the way we're governed and the way we make policy. We have designed and built a world that is inhuman. Government, business, the lives we lead, the food we eat, the way our children are raised, the way we relate to the natural world around us . . . it's all become too big and distant and impersonal. Inhuman.

In governments the world over, political leaders who mean well (and who are, if anything, underappreciated for the good they do) preside, frustrated and impotent, over vast bureaucratic systems that routinely disappoint and leave citizens enraged that they can't control what affects their lives. The schools we send our children to, the hospitals that care for us when we're sick, the very food we eat—we've allowed these intimate things, that matter so much, to be provided by anonymous, distant, industrialized machines. Business, such an awesome vehicle for human ingenuity and interaction, has become dominated by a detached and unaccountable global elite who think that the solution to the social and environmental problems *they cause* is to fly to Davos and pontificate on 'panels' and in 'plenaries.' Technology, with its incredible power to liberate and educate, has become unhealthily fetishized as an end in itself, while those who dare to question its remorseless rise are dismissed as mad—or, worse still, old fashioned. Nature? Who cares, let's conquer another planet.

We're told things are getting better. Growth is up! Big Government is on your side, along with Big Business and Big Energy and Big Food and Big Tech and Big Media, all giving us Big Savings! Big Value! But the problem is, we're not Big. We are quite small, actually. We tend to be happiest when we can relate to each other in a human way. We do best when things are organized on a human scale.

But size is not all that matters. Big is not always bad, and small is not always beautiful. Just look at a company like Airbnb, the website that allows people to rent out spare rooms, flats, or entire homes. It has enabled previously unimaginable new personal connections, showing that scale and technology don't have to be inhuman. There's an even more significant point about technology. The information revolution is giving us untold power: people talk warily about Big Data, but the truth is that big data is flowing into our own hands, giving us the chance to make decisions and choices as never before.

For all these reasons—the problems and the opportunities—it's time for a real shake-up. We need to make the world more human.

THIS AIM OF this book is to kick-start the debate. I don't have all the answers, but at least let's ask the right questions. In the summer of 2015 Hillary Clinton, in a revealing conversation with a Black Lives Matter activist, said, "Look, I don't believe you change hearts. I believe you change laws, you change allocation of resources, you change the way systems operate."[2] She's half right. Of course, in the end, in order to make a difference in people's lives, you do need to change laws, budgets, systems.

But the starting point—especially when the changes needed are really big—is to change hearts, and that's my primary aim in this book. *More Human* offers an argument, not a prescription. It is not a comprehensive survey of every problem out there; I've focused on areas where I have the greatest knowledge and experience and, frankly, on the things I care about most. I know there are important things left out.

Chapter 1 looks at politics. We all know our system is broken, beset by cynicism and corruption; we can see the rage at the political machine. But is there something constructive we can do with that rage? My answer is yes. I believe we can bring about the kind of revolution people are yearning for, but without yelling at each other—instead, getting involved, working together, crafting the radical reforms we need, as a community of people rather than a collection of positions. Politics is the starting point for government, and that's the subject of Chapter 2. We need to change priorities so government focuses more on real people than abstract numbers. We need to change the way policy is made so those who make it understand the lives of those who experience it. I'll look at how innovations in the way we design products have the potential to transform how we design government programs too. But we must also tackle the structure of government, a structure that too often impedes progress; the inefficiencies and needless centralizations of federal, state, and even local power that accentuate the worst of government while suppressing its best.

In Chapter 3 I take aim at our schools, where industrialized processes for cramming knowledge into children's heads are churning out young people equipped for the last century, not the current one—and making them miserable in the process. Similarly, in Chapter 4 I argue that the care has been ripped out of health care by bureaucracy and an obsession with 'efficiency' that undermines one of our most human instincts: looking after other people when they're not well. But we should also look after ourselves, an aim made more difficult by the vast culinary-industrial complex: our taxpayer-subsidized factory food system, which I'll investigate in Chapter 5.

Corporate bureaucracy is a common theme in this book, and I address it directly in Chapters 6 and 7, looking at the hotly contested arguments over capitalism and the role of business in society. In Chapters 8 and 9 I take on the topics of poverty and inequality and show how a more human way of looking at them—with a particular focus on families—could move us further forward than the somewhat sterile debates we've seen so far.

Children are humans too: that's Chapter 10. One of the most profound failings of the modern world is that it undervalues the needs of children. This may seem strange in an age when family life is celebrated, parenting advice is everywhere, and the imperatives of 'child protection' trump all other concerns. But as I will argue, we're getting it completely wrong. We are blasé about the impact of technology on children's lives and at the same time are undermining one of the most natural, human, and, above all, developmentally important aspects of children's lives: play. Finally, Chapters 11 and 12 examine the world around us: the spaces we design for ourselves and the way we relate to nature.

Throughout we'll meet people who, in their own way, are making the world more human—extraordinary people you may not have heard of yet. Nadine Burke Harris is a San Francisco pediatrician in the vanguard of reshaping how we see the effect of adverse childhood experiences on children's life chances. Jamie Heywood is an engineer who has used his brother's tragic death to change the way we see medicine. Paul Willis has made pig farming ethical on a large scale, and Jason Pittman has a vision of the classroom of the twenty-first century. We'll engage with some of the world's brightest minds who are helping lead the way to a more human future, like E. O. Wilson, perhaps our greatest living thinker on ecology, and Sebastian Thrun, the Silicon Valley technologist who is reshaping skills training for the digital age. I'll also introduce some of the people I've been lucky enough to work with, like Rohan Silva, my closest friend and former colleague in government, now creating the world's most in-novative creative work spaces; Sarah Stein Greenberg, who taught me 'design thinking' at Stanford; and Louise Casey, an amazing civil servant in the UK who is leading the program charged with turning around the lives of Britain's most troubled families.

THIS BOOK–THE ANALYSIS and the ideas—is the product of my experiences in government, politics, and business, most of them in the UK, where I grew up. At Number 10 Downing Street, as senior adviser to Prime Minister David Cameron, I had the incredible privilege of being in a po-sition to help implement policies and reforms that could tackle many of the problems addressed in this book—and you will find some of the lessons reflected in these pages. Prior to that I was part of the team that led the modernization of the British Conservative Party's political strat-egy and policy program. (As those familiar with British politics under-stand, the term 'Conservative' should not be seen as a direct parallel to

US ideological alignments. With a platform that favors marriage equality, action on climate change, and the introduction of a national living wage but equally: lower taxes, a tough stance on immigration, and deficit reduction, it's hard to plot today's British Conservatives on the US political spectrum.) Before that, with my firm, Good Business, I spent years working on social and environmental issues from a business perspective. In 2012 I moved to the Bay Area with my wife, Rachel, and our two children. I was fortunate enough to take up a teaching post at Stanford University and went on to found a political technology startup, Crowdpac.

When I served in the British government I was called a 'blue-skies' thinker, the government's 'ultimate radical.' Another way of putting it: I was the annoying, crazy person. So is this book, as some will suspect, basically just a list of all the 'crazy' things I wanted to do in government but they wouldn't let me? Well, yes, partly. But a much bigger part of *More Human* is based on the thinking I've done since leaving government and reflecting on what I got wrong as well as what went right. In particular, the book conveys what I've learned as part of the incredible, entrepreneurial community at Stanford, especially its renowned Institute of Design, or 'd.school.' At the d.school, students are taught to solve problems by starting with people—what they need, how they think, how they feel. Learning to teach there has been a transformational experience and has profoundly affected my point of view on almost everything. In Chapter 2 I look at how we might apply the d.school approach in government, but its principles of human-centered design are present in every chapter.

My experiences as a government veteran turned Silicon Valley CEO have profoundly changed how I view policy challenges. Unquestionably government can learn a lot from the tech sector, and harnessing some of California's entrepreneurial spirit could go a long way toward improving the sclerotic institutions that dominate our lives.

But I also aim to do something else: provide the view of an outsider to American politics. (To be clear, I am a bit of an outsider in British politics too: although I am a close friend and supporter of Prime Minister David Cameron, there are plenty of positions I take in this book that would fit more comfortably in the British Labour or even Green Parties. In fact, when the UK version of this book was published, more than one reviewer suggested I join the Labour Party leadership race! In the context of America's leadership race . . . perhaps Bernie Sanders meets John Kasich meets Rand Paul. Go figure.) Although I am a fan of markets and decentralization, as you will quickly learn in this book, I am also a strong believer in well-organized and well-funded state intervention to tackle social problems. I'm as anti-establishment as the best of them (or worst, depending on your point of view), yet I'm pro-immigration—not just because I'm the son of Hungarian refugees and a Brit now working in America but because I believe it's vital for America's future success. I strongly support marriage equality and generous parental leave for mothers and fathers; in fact, I believe in marriage equality so much, I even think straight people should get married if they're going to have children. Yes, I'm afraid this book will likely goad Democrats and Republicans in equal measure. And that's okay. (Not least because my political tech startup, Crowdpac, is nonpartisan.)

To be honest, goading the two old parties is precisely what I want to do. We live in a political system that is almost completely broken, ossified by money into a structure that a plurality of Americans don't identify with. (A Pew survey found that a record 39 percent of Americans identified as political independents, a much larger share than those identifying as Democrats or Republicans.[3]) While the cynical political insiders dismiss these findings, saying that come election time, there are very few real independents and that self-identifying independents usually break for one side or the other, this misses the point. The point is that when asked, they identify as independent. The lack of independent voting options is not their fault and doesn't undermine their stance. These independents eschew party—and often politics—because they feel the system ignores them, trapped in an era of 'workers vs. capital.' And it's no wonder, given the structural forces driving our politics: the Democrats, dependent on labor unions, and the Republicans, reliant on billionaire businessmen. They're stuck in a model that is now well out of date.

It's time for Americans to envision the country they want for themselves, not the country that politicians (and their donors) tell them they should have. I hope this book can challenge voters and politicians alike to think about solutions that cut across ideology and the narrow dogmas of American party politics. As shown by the introduction of the world's first national living wage law by my (Conservative) former colleagues in the British government, you don't have to be on the political left to be on the side of workers. But equally, you don't have to be on the political right to recognize that unleashing (reasonably regulated) markets is often the best solution to a given problem, even social goods like education and health care. Indeed, whole sectors can benefit from a judicious blend of government and market-based solutions that might appeal to and repel extreme bases in equal measure. But I hope my perspective as a Brit who has come to America, started an American business, and taught

American college students can help cut through the partisan obstinacy that—as the natives keep telling me—has made many aspects of American public life depressingly stale and stuck.

Although I'm critical of the way some things work in America, I want to make one thing clear: I write as a passionate admirer who simply wants the United States to fulfill its unmet potential. In fact, it is my faith in the American project and in America's capacity for greatness—and for change to fulfill that greatness—that compel me to write what I do. I love America; I think America is the greatest place on earth, a place where the ingenuity of its people—their ability to consistently break barriers, invent, and discover—is only matched by their relentless optimism. And although America sometimes seems broken, it is still making great strides. I hope I can help point the way in a few places.

I'm also in awe of the more human American virtues: kindness, community, faith. It's fashionable overseas to mock America's 'have a nice day' culture, the automatic disposition to be open, to smile. Why? It is, for a Brit, incredibly refreshing to live in a place where the cultural norm is to be positive. We talk a lot in England about 'community spirit,' but it seems to me that it is much more alive and well in the United States. And then faith: again, a deeply ingrained characteristic of American life that can be quite shocking for a secular person like me, from such a secular place as the UK. There was, however, a moment of epiphany for me: the aftermath of the terrible murders of nine people at a Bible study in Charleston's Emanuel AME Church in June 2015. In those events I saw and appreciated the worth and power of faith. The astonishing grace of the victims' families, as they came face to face with their loved ones' killer and declared, in those haunting cadences, "I forgive you." And then President Obama's eulogy for Reverend Clementa Pinckney, slain that terrible night: "Amazing Grace" the theme of his remarks; the electric moment when the president sang those words. I recall these scenes almost every day, and as I do I can barely prevent the tears from coming to my eyes. They say something profound and good about America.

As you will see in this book, I firmly believe America—and, indeed, the world—is on the cusp of great developments in a variety of fields. One of those is politics. Although the United States seems more partisan than ever before, the hyperactive, point-scoring politics we've grown accustomed to might well be the dying gasps of an antiquated system. There is a reason for the appeal of 'outsider' candidates like Donald Trump, Ben Carson, Carly Fiorina, Bernie Sanders, and Elizabeth Warren as well as Jeremy Corbyn in the UK. The Establishment, voters from all backgrounds agree, has failed—and failed badly. The political commentator Peggy Noonan put it well as she sought to explain the rise of 'the Donald': "When citizens are consistently offended by Washington, by both parties' leadership, they become contemptuous. They see Mr. Trump's contempt and identify. What the American establishment has given us the past twenty years is sex scandals, money scandals, two unwon wars, an economic collapse, an inadequate recovery, and borders we no longer even pretend to control. They think: What will you give us next, the plague?"

The wise men—and they are mostly men, still—of the political and governing establishment may scratch their heads in bewilderment at the rise of candidates they consider to be 'not serious'—but the public, I'm afraid, no longer trust the serious people to steward their interests. In a way, that's unfair. In my experience most politicians are good and sincere public servants. But the systems that have been built up over decades frustrate their efforts at accomplishing anything, let alone actually changing the systems. There is a famous series of comedy sketches in the UK in which every reply to a customer's request, however reasonable, by a bored and disdainful clerk is "Computer says no." That's certainly how government feels to the proverbial 'little guy.' But alarmingly, it's all too often how it feels to the people in charge too.

That's why changing the underlying systems—and not just the policies—really is so important, a priority I return to time and again in different contexts in this book. I believe it is eminently possible. Across the world we may soon see the birth of a new kind of politics that eschews left and right for engagement and transparency. Tony Blair wrote in his memoir that he believes the new axis of politics is 'open vs. closed' and that we will concern ourselves less with ideological purity than with which politicians and their methods work best.[4] We seek government that is effective and responsive, society that is orderly and fair. Those are values—intrinsically human ones, I might add—that no political movement can claim as its own.

THERE'S ANOTHER IMPORTANT POINT to bear in mind that makes the idea at the heart of this book more relevant and urgent than ever. In the last few decades great advances in science have given us new insights into who we are as humans: how we think, feel, and behave—and why. Neuroscience, social psychology, behavioral economics—work in these fields means we can now base our judgments about how to organize things much more soundly on what we scientifically know. These human insights don't just tell us more about humanity; they also tell us that making things more human is itself natural.

For example, evolutionary biology shows that in the course of human history we have become ever more empathetic. Scientific and economic progress has in part been accompanied by an expanded consciousness of the experiences of fellow human beings. We have in some ways become more human, even as the world we have built for ourselves pushes in the other direction. The expansion of our capacity to communicate and collaborate with each other has enhanced our capacity to understand each other's realities. As we've gotten to know one another better, we've extended basic protections and rights to ever-wider swathes of humanity.[5]

Although our capacity for empathy has evolved, it has always been one of our defining traits as humans. And there are other human values that define us and for which we should strive. Not everything can be quantified by data or captured on a spreadsheet. There are certain things that we simply accept make life worth living: purpose, happiness, beauty, compassion, laughter, love, joy. These are the things that dignify our lives and that every individual deserves the chance to experience. Another key part of our humanity lies in our differences. Fulfillment in life will come through different things for different people—whether it's faith, literature, work, friendship, music, children . . . even baking a perfect loaf of bread. The burden of society—specifically of government—is to provide the greatest chance for us to find what life means and then live it to the fullest.

Society has another burden, though: to protect us from and help us to overcome our inherent flaws, the troubling aspects of our nature. For all the good of humanity, there are plenty of impulses that are harmful, traits like avarice, malice, and intolerance. These also are human, and although we shouldn't forget that, we should do all we can to help people avoid the worst of their demons, especially when their weaknesses hurt others. There is evil and terrible cruelty in our world. We see it in the crazed, Islam-derived brutality of ISIS, but while we confront and defeat it militarily, ideologically, politically, financially, diplomatically—as we must surely resolve to do—we must remember that there will be no final victory in this, the defining war of our age, unless we triumph at the individual, human level too.

But we are both individual and social creatures. We work better, as I will argue throughout this book, in communities, families, social networks, and on small-scale levels. So how, then, if human nature is naturally inclined to be human, have so many of the institutions that shape our lives become so big, distant, and removed from the human scale?

Think of it in historical terms. (Spoiler alert: for those readers familiar with the speeches of David Cameron, especially "the early, funny ones" as Woody Allen might have described them, this is an argument you will recognize.) Before the Industrial Revolution, politics, government, and business were almost entirely local—because they had to be. Rulers simply did not have the information and reach to make decisions about individual people's lives or run centralized bureaucracies. Local governors or feudal lords were delegated almost all sovereign power, answering only nominally to the far-off capital. Bureaucracies existed, but even the most sophisticated ones in China and the Ottoman Empire relied heavily on provincial officials. Corporations were limited to the most complex of businesses-like banks, even then often in quasi-official roles. Companies like the East India Company or the Rothschild banking empire delegated wide autonomy to local officials; superiors at the center had only the most limited strategic control. This period we could call the prebureaucratic age.

As with many things, war, commerce, and technology changed the dynamic. With larger armies and more sophisticated warfare, the conflicts of the French Revolution and Napoleonic eras saw full-scale mobilizations that could only be managed through hierarchical and complex bureaucracies. At the same time, Napoleon applied these principles to the civilian part of his growing empire and created the first modern law code, the Code Napoléon, and an administrative state to implement it.[6] Meanwhile economic trends led to similar developments in America. The invention of the cotton gin in 1793 spurred a revolution in the American cotton industry, but it required scale to really be revolutionary, especially in the form of railroads to connect distant farms and merchants. Unlike maritime trading companies, the railroad companies upon which the American cotton industry relied needed centralized management to ensure safety and efficiency (sharing track and sharing the seas are two very different matters). Bureaucracy was the only way to accomplish the logistical feat of connecting entire continents with one system.

Just like the cotton producers, railroad companies also had to consolidate, as building rail infrastructure was, by definition, large scale and expensive. Only big firms could manage the undertaking, and as the demand for capital correspondingly increased, a new, centralized banking system sprang up to finance it all. Bureaucracy was a cycle that built itself, feeding back into its own further expansion and centralization. The new interconnected systems that enabled military and industrial growth soon spread to other aspects of life. Centralized governments were now able to build bureaucracies to run things on behalf of citizens, and government evolved into an accretion of massive hierarchies. Over the course of the twentieth century this model grew into the form of government that we have today. Along with its counterpart in the business world, it was—and is—the bureaucratic age.[7]

Bureaucratic modernization brought a whole range of benefits, from universal schooling to a professional civil service, to social security, to the rule of law. In America it built a national infrastructure and enabled a superpower. These same centralizing mechanisms that enabled growth in the public sector eventually conquered the rest of the economy. With efficient transport and technology, unprecedented quantities of raw materials flowed to factories that, powered by steam engines, could now produce and distribute manufactured goods. Firms adopted the administrative apparatus of the bureaucratic railways, and the modern corporation was born. As commercial empires emerged, a cult of management science soon dominated, whereby businesses—and, eventually, government departments—were run by those at the top applying principles of 'engineering' to the workers below. It was all about mass production, mass management, mass distribution—and as World War II mobilized the American economy on a national scale, the large corporation became a fait accompli. Coupled with automation and other improvements in technology, the process continued unabated; vast conglomerates were commonplace by the 1960s. The age of the independent local business wasn't over, but it was dealt a huge blow.

The inexorable growth of big business throughout the last century and a half has brought great benefits; in many respects someone on an average income in America or Europe today has a higher standard of living than even the very richest did a century or so ago. But the mostly national corporations of the mid-twentieth century that had at least some sense of connection to and responsibility for their local communities have given way to rootless global entities—private-sector bureaucracies—many of which have lost all sense of community, of perspective. The never-ending trajectory of mergers, consolidation, and growth has a cost—and not just a financial one (repeated studies have shown that corporate mergers generally destroy value for the acquiring firms' shareholders).[8] We are no longer driven by a human economy; we don't know where our products come from or how they are created, and too many of our corporate bosses have no conception of their workers' or customers' experiences. We live in an age when the effects of our decisions seem less and less important because we don't really know what they are. We 'love a bargain' but don't see the appalling conditions endured by the people who produce a product that can be sold so cheaply. We troop to the supermarket but don't see the small businesses and farmers whose livelihoods are wrecked by 'everyday low prices.' The human consequences of our choices are felt by people separated from us by time, space, and class.

In government too, we continue to live with a system that is a relic of the past. It did work once, but we're no longer in the age of either sail or steamship, so why are we still governed as if we were? Manifest Destiny is no longer relevant, and many of the services that government provides—education, social services, welfare—are well established and no longer require centralized bureaucratic systems, whether at the federal, state, or even local level, to run them. Simply put, the raisons d'être of centralized government no longer justify it. But its costs remain.

You can see it in the way that twentieth-century factory-style approaches—standardization, automation, mechanization—still infect intrinsically human areas like education, health care, food, and housing. We used to think factories equaled progress. They were sanitary, standardized, and quality controlled. They took urchins off the street while providing the middle and working classes with once-only-dreamt-of luxuries. Having tens of thousands of cows or chickens on a single farm seemed like the modern thing to do. But that vision is now out of date.

It's not just the arc of history, bureaucratic momentum, or mass standardization that has led us to this point; we need to apply a critical eye to our unrelenting quest for progress and how some of our leaders—in government, politics, business, and society—define it for us. Where I live now, in Silicon Valley, the goal is to be bigger, faster, cheaper. Does that equate to better? Much of the time it does. But too often the 'progress' we are offered is not an improvement; it's just more 'efficient' and, worse, more efficient for the producer, not the user. Astronauts used to consume Tang, a powdered orange drink, because it is compact and nutritious (a requirement on space missions). But should we substitute it for actual orange juice? Or oranges? Just because something is more 'efficient' doesn't mean it's better.

The misguided quest for efficiency has led to negative side effects that are only now being understood. As technology critic Evgeny Morozov points out in his book *To Save Everything, Click Here*, efficiency can undermine much of what makes us human: "Imperfection, ambiguity, opacity, disorder, and the opportunity to err, to sin, to do the wrong thing: all of these are constitutive of human freedom, and any concerted attempt to root them out will root out that freedom as well."[9] I would add that a world programmed to perfection is no longer a human world: without problems to solve and imperfection to inspire us, we would become complacent. We would not only lose our ability to innovate and be creative but, worse, our world would become sterile. If we never get lost, we will never go to unexpected new places. If we never have to repair things, we will cease to tinker and make anew. Without the spontaneous discoveries—and mistakes—that so enrich us, humanity stagnates. Mother Nature is often 'inefficient,' providing us with two kidneys, for example, where one is enough. Efficiency is not always bad, but we need the cultural confidence to say no, to reject efficiency for human priorities that matter more.

AS YOU WILL SEE, this book calls for dramatic changes in how we do things. Some might ask whether that is really necessary. They could point to America's economic growth, political stability, and social safety net; its dominance in science, technology, universities; the strength of our culture; and the growing vibrancy of cities like Los Angeles or Houston and say, "Things are pretty good. Sure, they can always be improved, but take it easy . . . we just need a touch on the tiller, not a change of course."

Really? Have you noticed that it tends to be the wealthiest and most powerful who say things like that? Life is certainly good for them. But look around: life isn't great for most people, and in many ways it is getting worse. With years of stagnating wages, people don't feel as though they're getting ahead.[10] They're underpaid and overworked (Chapter 8). They aren't gaining the skills they need (Chapter 9). They're unhealthy because nutritious food is not only more expensive than heavily processed, toxic junk (Chapter 5) but often inaccessible. And their children—without the built-in advantages of their richer peers—are falling behind (Chapter 9).

But the inhumanity of much of modern life—in schools, in hospitals, in urban planning—is no concern for the elites because they (we) don't have to experience it. Our children go to private schools, we live in the swankiest neighborhoods, and we shop at Whole Foods or the farmers' market. When life gets rough, we go on exotic holidays or to our tastefully appointed vacation homes. When things get busy, we employ nannies, housekeepers, and delivery people to buy ourselves more time.

For most people, though, the current system simply isn't working. Incremental change isn't working. When most people haven't seen a rise in living standards for over a decade and many have seen a fall, when daily life is often such a hassle, when people's quality of life is below what they see in other countries, when there is a massive underclass persistently poor in every way for decade after decade, I think this calls for a sense of urgency. It's a crisis, and it demands a big shake-up, not steady-as-she-goes. But our debates feel small, stunted, fiddling around the edges—and this fuels the dissatisfaction with politics and the political system, increasingly expressed in support for fringe parties and politics.

There is hope, however, small signs that things can be different and examples of the kind of change we need. I have seen them and learned from them over the last few years I've spent in California, and some are profiled in this book.

FOR ALL THESE REASONS I think we need a revolution, not evolution, and I want to show you in this book that it's possible. That we can heal America's malaise by putting power back in people's hands, taking back control over the things that matter to us from the anonymous, distant bureaucrats in government and business. We can move to something better: a postbureaucratic age, an age when things work on a comprehensible and controllable scale. An age that is more human.

Apart from any specific changes, however small, that might happen as a result of the people, stories, and ideas that follow, I also hope that they collectively help you to see the world a little differently. A little more humanly. And who knows where that might lead?

The modern world is a fantastic place full of excitement and ingenuity. But as we continue to invent and innovate and move forward, we should remember what makes us human: people, relationships, spontaneity, emotions. As we create and spread wealth and opportunity, build a world of technological wonder, remake our institutions, and push the boundaries of knowledge, we should try to do so in line with these essential human truths.

chapter one

POLITICS

PEOPLE LOVE TO COMPLAIN about government—and yes, there's plenty to complain about. (There is also much we can do to make government work better, as we'll see in the next chapter). However, before we even get to government, we have politics. Politics underpins government. If we want to make government more human, we need to start with politics.

Politics might seem like a weird blood sport, fascinating only to insiders, but it's much more than that. A healthy political system means that solutions to problems are debated, citizens' voices are heard, and society maintains a stake in how it is governed. Of course, American politics today is far from healthy. But instead of just railing against our broken political system, shouldn't we try to fix it? I agree with those who say that America's problems demand a revolution, not evolution. But I also believe we can harness the political system to achieve it, that we can have a revolution without yelling at each other, a revolution based on real reform. That needs politics—more human politics.

IT STARTS WITH engaging more people in the political process. It's not just America; in most democracies trust in politics is falling—and one of the main reasons is people's belief that their participation doesn't matter. But there's a more pronounced version of the problem here in the United States than anywhere else. American democracy no longer seems to serve 'we the people' but rather the interests of the wealthiest. It seems today that political legitimacy stems not from votes, but money: the more of it you have, the more government pays attention to your concerns.

We have, in some ways, regressed. Corruption used to be the norm in most countries, democratic or otherwise. Power was inherited and bought, political appointments traded for favors in a system where the elites literally owned the state. But although it is no longer so explicit, the ascent of big money and its lobbyists means that while there is no explicit quid pro quo, it is hard to mistake what donors intend when they

1

make political contributions. Or what businesses want when they take politicians to dinner, golf retreats, or the Super Bowl. We may not have aristocratic courts and inherited offices, but our democracy is increasingly captured by a ruling class who seeks to perpetuate its privileges. Our democratic system has, in the apt word used by political scientist Francis Fukuyama, "decayed."[1] America, where the rich and powerful literally buy the outcomes they want from the political system, is no longer in any proper sense of the word a democracy; it is a *donocracy*.

When the corporate bosses, the members of Congress, the journalists—and the authors of books like this—all go to the same dinner parties and galas and live in the same neighborhoods of Washington, New York, and San Francisco, an insular ruling elite precipitates. They flit and float between Congress and K Street, Washington and Wall Street. Regardless of who's in office, the same people are in power. It is a democracy in name only, operating on behalf of a tiny elite, no matter the electoral outcome. I recognize it because I was part of this class in the UK. Although there is no conspiracy—and I know from personal experience that almost all politicians and officials have good intentions—the assumptions, structures, and rules that govern daily life are not subject to anything as unpredictable as the will of the people. No wonder voters feel that others' voices are being heard more than their own. It's because it's true.[2]

In addition to the traditional fundraising and lobbying dominance of Big Business and Big Labor, wealthy individuals increasingly use campaign finance loopholes to directly and personally pick candidates and elections. There had been some progress on the problem of money in politics with reform efforts like the McCain-Feingold Act in 2002 (itself an inadequate response, merely limiting contributions to parties). But the Citizens United Supreme Court ruling in 2010 enabled unlimited political donations through independent expenditure-only committees, known as Super PACs. Super PACs, in theory, can't coordinate with official campaigns. But seeing as they mostly underwrite advertising—the most expensive part of campaigns anyway—coordination isn't necessary. In any case, the distinction between a candidate's campaign and a Super PAC supporting them, in a supposedly 'uncoordinated' way, is rapidly becoming a sham.

Here's a farcical, almost comic example. Super PACs that support candidates are prohibited, in line with the requirement not to 'coordinate,' from featuring the name of the candidate in their own organization's name. The Super PAC supporting Republican presidential candidate Carly Fiorina, "Carly for America," was therefore told by the Federal

Election Commission that it couldn't put Carly Fiorina's name in its own name. Oh, it's not her name, came the reply. It's an acronym: CARLY for America—Conservative, Authentic, Responsive, Leadership for You. "The FEC requested that we change our name and we complied," said Katie Hughes, a spokesperson for the Super PAC. Although you can't blame them—the rules and the almost total nonenforcement of them are at fault—this kind of thing just makes a monkey out of our democracy.

And it's getting worse: In 2014 around sixteen hundred Super PACs raised almost $700 million, spending some $345 million of it.[3] This in an election that cost well over $1.6 billion.[4] By comparison, *all* of the campaigning for *all* of the parties in the 2010 general election in the UK (in which I played a part and for which, unlike 2015, there is published data) added up to less than the equivalent of $50 million.[5]

Super PACs now give unprecedented power to donors, with politicians, like horses, chosen, bought, and nurtured by extremely wealthy individuals. Many of the 2016 presidential candidates had, from the outset, their own pet tycoon in their pocket—or is it the other way around? Hedge fund magnate Robert Mercer has given tens of millions of dollars to Ted Cruz. Marco Rubio is backed by Miami businessman Norman Braman. And Foster Freiss, an Idaho billionaire who funded Rick Santorum's campaign in 2012, is similarly following him around the country this time. He's even promised to make his donations as opaque as possible. "You'll find out my giving maybe if you work real hard," he told one reporter, "but I'm going to make it hard for you to find out where I'm giving and how I'm giving."[6]

Although Democratic candidates haven't been so clearly tied to single prominent donors, they have benefited from plenty of big money. Dozens of individuals gave more than $1 million to Priorities USA, the 2012 Super PAC that backed President Obama. And Democrats and Republicans have kept up with each other in terms of spending and fundraising. One leaked memo from Democratic Senate candidate Michelle Nunn advised she spend 80 percent of her campaign time fundraising.[7] Incoming Democratic members of Congress are advised by their party leadership to spend four hours of their day making fundraising calls *after taking office*.[8] New York Democratic Congressman Steve Israel, former head of the Democratic Congressional Campaign Committee, in announcing that he would not run for reelection said, "I don't think I can spend another day in another call room making another call begging for money ... I always knew the system was dysfunctional, now it is beyond broken."[9]

Even when not coming from 'super-donors,' these contributions overwhelmingly come from the richest people in America. In 1980 the wealthiest 1 percent of the 1 percent contributed around 15 percent of all the money in US politics. By 2012 it had risen to over 40 percent and is still heading upward, toward half.[10] So when Donald Trump says that the politicians who raise money are 'puppets' of their donors, that candidates like Jeb Bush and Hillary Clinton are '100 percent controlled' by their donors, it strikes a chord.[11] It is hyperbole to be sure, but at the same time, people know that there is some truth in his claim. The burgeoning cycle of money and politics has a real-world effect: the rich must be getting some return on their investment, and even if it's less than commonly perceived, the perception matters. It puts people off from getting involved in politics, assuming that the whole thing is a setup.

But the super-rich are backing more than just political candidates; many, especially on the left, are also adopting individual causes. Democratic super-donor Tom Steyer, for instance, created a Super PAC to support candidates fighting for climate change policy, spending $70 million in the 2014 midterm election cycle. He felt that it was the only way to make a difference: "We felt from the beginning that Citizens United was a mistake, that the way that money is used in American campaigns isn't good for democracy," he told PBS's Gwen Ifill. "It's just been a situation where we felt as if there's an immense amount of money on the other side, and as long as this is the system which the Supreme Court has put in place, there's got to be somebody on our side."[12] Although Steyer and, on the other side of the political divide, the Koch brothers have discussed their political financing openly, there is some irony, leading Republican campaign lawyer Ben Ginsberg tells me, that since the advent of caps on direct (and transparent) donations to candidates, money has flowed to the places where no transparency is required.[13]

Meanwhile, in states that have referendums, wealthy individuals and well-financed special interests like corporations and unions often create and bankroll their own pet ballot measures. In California it is epidemic. In 2006 real estate heir Stephen Bing gave almost $50 million to Proposition 87, a ballot measure that would have raised taxes on oil.[14] But it was in 2012 that things got out of hand. Six of the eleven statewide measures in California that November were each funded primarily by a single wealthy donor. Heiress Molly Munger disliked Governor Jerry Brown's tax measure, so she funded her own with $44 million. Meanwhile her brother, Charles, gave $36 million to defeat Brown's education measure. Proposition 33, an initiative that changed car insurance rates, was supported by Mercury Insurance founder George Joseph with $16 million. And Tom Steyer spent $9 million to support Proposition 39, a green-energy projects initiative.

POLITICS IS SUPPOSED to be a platform for people power, not plutocrat power. The role of money in politics risks fatally undermining this concept, but it's not the only big problem. Increased partisanship and polarization are leading to an increasingly fractured, fractious political climate that makes it harder to get things done—and also has an unintended negative effect on the propensity for regular people to get involved, whether as voters, donors, or candidates.

In 2014 69 US representatives ran completely unopposed.[15] Of course, it's not as though those who have competition face much of a challenge. According to the nonpartisan Cook Political Report, 377 House seats were safe as of summer 2015. That's 377 out of 435—87 percent. Only eighteen races—about 4 percent—are deemed to be 'toss-ups.' With more and more safe districts—and the pattern is repeated at the state and local levels of politics too—the incentives for political candidates are, more and more, to appeal to the extremes. Why? Because in safe districts the 'real' election is actually the party primary, in which turnout is typically derisory and limited to a party's core supporters, often those with the most extreme views.

Of course, there are some congressional districts that naturally are solidly Democratic or Republican. The San Francisco district of former Speaker Nancy Pelosi is not likely to elect a Republican in my lifetime, although I suppose you never know. But in many districts widespread gerrymandering, in which boundaries are artificially drawn to serve the party in control of the state legislature, which controls the redistricting process, gives undue and undemocratic precedence to incumbents from the majority party. "Partisan gerrymandering," writes legal scholar Sanford Levinson,

> makes the distribution of voters more consequential than their raw number. It explains why Republicans were able to win a 34-seat majority in the U.S. House of Representatives in 2012 despite trailing Democrats by approximately 1.4 million votes overall. Similarly, President Barack Obama carried Pennsylvania with 52 percent of the vote, and Democratic Sen. Bob Casey Jr. won more than 53 percent, but due to partisan gerrymandering, Republicans won 13 of the 18 congressional seats.[16]

Voters still get a say under gerrymandering, but by purposefully mini-mizing their impact, it is essentially a form of legal disenfranchisement. Political scientist Simon Jackman showed that following a 2010 partisan redistricting, Wisconsin became one of the most gerrymandered states in the country. In 2012 Democrats won only thirty-nine of ninety-nine seats (39.4 percent) in the legislature despite an estimated 51.4 percent of the vote; in 2014 they won thirty-six seats (36.4 percent) with 48.0 percent of the vote. "Few states," Jackman writes, "ever record EG scores [a way of measuring gerrymandering; the further from 0 the score, the worse they are] as large as those observed in Wisconsin; indeed, there is virtually no precedent for the lop-sided, two election sequence of EG scores generated in Wisconsin in 2012 and 2014."[17]

That's why nonpartisan redistricting commissions like the one en-acted by Republican governor Arnold Schwarzenegger in California or the one in Arizona upheld by a 2015 Supreme Court decision can help improve our democracy. Although critics contend that they aren't 'demo-cratic' because they're composed of unelected commissioners, that's sort of the point. How is it acceptable for a legislator to draw the lines of their own constituency—and to their own advantage? Every element of an election except the vote itself should be completely impartial.

Another promising reform was championed by former California Governor Arnold Schwarzenegger. In elections for statewide office, state legislature, or Congress, the two candidates who receive the most votes move on to the general election regardless of their political party. This not only has opened up primary elections to voters from parties other than the main two; it has also given voters a choice of more represen-tative candidates during the general election—candidates who may not have otherwise gotten through their own party's highly partisan prima-ries. While it's too early to see the full results of this particular reform, there are now examples of more moderate politicians (like Steve Glazer, an independent-minded Democrat, who took a stand against labor unions and was nevertheless elected to the California State Senate in a May 2015 special election) achieving success by appealing to a broader electorate.

Even if we make our electoral system fairer, our democracy has one more challenge: people's political views are more nuanced than the simplified two-party model that America's ossified electoral system forces onto them. Many of the ideas and proposals I will propose in this book would be at home in parties across the political spectrum; others wouldn't be welcome anywhere. In a true democracy this is fine. Hardly anyone is a 'dyed-in-the-wool' anything, anyway. And in today's age of nearly unlimited information, we can form a much more complex worldview. Yet in public life you have nowhere to go if you take Republican views on taxes, Green views on the environment, and Democratic views on social justice. Our opinions are as complex as we are, but our politics are not. Our views are not 'politician'; they're human. We need our politics to reflect this.

THERE ARE MANY well-intentioned efforts to change our political system for the better. Most observers agree that since the 1976 *Buckley v. Valeo* Supreme Court decision that equated political spending with free speech, money is constitutionally bound to play a big part in US politics. But Ben Rattray, the brilliant founder of Change.org, believes that he can reduce money's impact from the bottom up—by making personal recommendations, rather than campaign ads, the main influence in voting decisions. Law professor Lawrence Lessig has attempted a campaign for the Democratic presidential nomination with the sole aim of passing the Citizens Equality Act, an electoral and campaign finance reform package.[18] Run for America is using crowdsourcing to find and fund young, fresh political candidates to go shake things up in Congress. Democratic Maryland congressman John Sarbanes's Government by the People Act would encourage small contributions by matching donations under $150 at a rate of six to one and giving donors $25 tax credits.[19] The state of Maine has actually passed a similar reform, and early indications are that one of its results has been the emergence of more independent—and independent-minded—candidates. A committed group of political reformers in California have come together to advance the cause of independence in our politics—for example, setting up the Independent Voter Project and an associated news website, IVN.us. Organizations like the Bipartisan Policy Center, No Labels, Every Voice, the Pluribus Project, and more are, in various ways, tackling the deep problems with American politics. Even Hillary Clinton, the beneficiary of a well-oiled and well-funded campaign machine, has called for a constitutional amendment limiting the 'unaccountable money' in politics.[20] To his great credit, one of her primary opponents, Vermont senator Bernie Sanders, pledged at the outset of his campaign not to accept money from Super PACs, showing that individual leadership can make a practical difference.

But despite these attempts, the hurdles are immense. The system privileges the insiders, even when they protest. There is no consensus on reform, not by a long shot. And any constitutional change seems like an impossible stretch.

The truth is, many of the biggest problems with American politics today reinforce one another. People see the dysfunction in Washington and are put off from voting. So turnout drops. So the most extreme voters end up being decisive. So the candidates pander to them. So they have less incentive to compromise once in office. So less actually gets done. So the dysfunction gets worse . . . and so on around the depressing spiral downward, every twist and turn accelerated and amplified by more money from fewer people.

Some have argued that the solution to all of this is not political at all but economic. That in the second half of the twentieth century, steady and strong economic growth of over 3 percent meant that people were basically happy, incomes were rising, life was getting better, so citizens were less angry and the political climate, consequently, was less shrill. The answer, on this reasoning, is to prioritize a return to the kind of strong growth America was once used to and politics will improve.

I'm not so sure about that. Of course, strong economic growth is a good thing to have in its own right (although it's a little more nuanced than that, as we'll see in the next chapter). But I think we need something else, something more human.

The central problem with politics in America today is that it has been taken over by a tiny number of rich people and well-connected insiders. And the best way to solve *that* problem is to get more people involved.

That's why I started my company, Crowdpac.

CROWDPAC: GIVING POLITICS BACK TO PEOPLE

Crowdpac is designed to give people a practical way to improve how politics works within the system we have. We want to give politics back to people—in America and around the world—and give voice to more than just the rich and powerful. So we're building simple tools that make it easier for people to engage effectively in the political system: voting, funding campaigns, even running for office. In all these crucial areas we want to boost participation: Higher turnout at elections—especially in primaries, which are now so crucial, given the number of 'safe' districts. More small donors so we dilute the influence of big money, special interests, and party machines, and reduce the time candidates need to spend fundraising. More independent—and independent-minded—people running for office so we bring in new blood and give voters more options than the stale two-party duopoly. And for us at Crowdpac, all this starts with the thing that so much else depends on: good, objective information about politics and elections.

Our research shows that the best way to predict how a politician will behave in office is to look at their donations: who gives them money and who they give money to. It's a great way to cut through all the spin and negative ads and really see where different candidates stand. This is especially important in elections where voters have less information—for example, lower down the ballot and in primaries. Most of the decisions that affect people's daily lives in America are made far from the White House or Congress but rather in state legislatures or county government, for example. Yet with the protracted death of local and regional newspapers, the coverage of local politics and state legislatures is pitiful. And on the national level more and more is geared toward stories designed for social media impact rather than real social impact.

Improving the way our political system works—especially the role of money and elite influence—is essential. As Lawrence Lessig puts it, "It's not that mine is the most important issue—it's not. Yours is the most important issue. But mine is the *first* issue—the issue we have to solve before we get to fix the issues you care about."[21] This is the starting point: if we want to make our government more human, and our world more human, we first have to mend our broken political system and make politics more human too.

chapter two

GOVERNMENT

I ONCE WROTE a book called *Good Business: Your World Needs You*, which was based on a simple argument: business runs the world. The world needs changing. Let's use business to change the world.

Looking back, with the benefit of my experience since then, working with some of the world's biggest companies to try to solve social and environmental problems and then working in politics and government to do the same, I can see that I was—how shall I put this?—wrong.

Business does not run the world. In the end, government sets the rules by which business operates, and rightly so. Government is—at least notionally—accountable to people in a way that businesses are not. Businesses clearly make a huge contribution to society, both positive and negative, and they should try to improve it. But if we really want to change the world—if we want to make it more human—then we must use the mechanism designed for that purpose: government. As we saw in Chapter 1, we need to change the way we choose our governments by fixing our broken political system and getting more people involved. But we also have to change government itself: the priorities of those within it, the way policy is made and implemented, and the way the whole thing is structured.

MORE HUMAN PRIORITIES FOR GOVERNMENT

Sir John Cowperthwaite was the financial secretary of Hong Kong in the 1960s and the man widely credited with creating the conditions for its phenomenal economic success. When asked what advice he would give to a poor country trying to get richer, he said, "They should abolish the Office of National Statistics." Cowperthwaite believed that the collection of economic data simply encouraged governments and bureaucrats to needlessly and destructively interfere in the economy, so he refused. This infuriated his masters in London. When they sent a delegation to persuade him to change his approach, Cowperthwaite literally sent them straight back on the next plane.[1] I love that story for its wonderfully British rebelliousness. But that rather eccentric episode from the 1960s also highlights the big problem with government today: its prioritization of numbers over people. Of course it sounds obvious, trite even, to argue that government should 'put people first.' And yet it doesn't happen. Look at any government's priorities: the focus of federal, state, or even local government bureaucrats, the things that drive big decisions—it's actually about numbers, about economics.

The political world's focus on economics was most famously captured by Bill Clinton's 1992 election campaign strategist James Carville when he scrawled, "The economy, stupid" on the office walls of Clinton's headquarters. In government, money reigns supreme, and I don't just mean lobbying and political donations. The official calendar is dominated by economic events—job statistics, quarterly growth numbers, inflation, interest rates, what's happening in the stock market. In government it really is the economy, stupid.

You can understand why. Economic growth pays for progress in other areas—the human things that really matter. On an individual or family level the more money you have, the better life tends to be. Money doesn't buy happiness, but it can certainly eliminate many of the things that make us unhappy. Money provides security and opportunity. It is often those who have never experienced what it's like to have little or no money who say it doesn't matter. Try telling that to the mother of three who's working two jobs to feed her children and still can't afford to buy diapers.

So I don't have any problem with the idea that the government should concern itself with how to improve society's economic circumstances. Political leaders could have many worse aims, after all, than making their people more prosperous. Prosperity generally has brought us longer, healthier lives, with better education, more art and leisure, greater civic and political participation—all good things. Economic growth has been a decent enough proxy for these important human outcomes.

My argument is different: it is not about challenging the value of economic growth but about the *way* our government goes about it. We've made a narrowly defined representation of the economy—economic indicators—the priority while forgetting that 'the economy' represents something deeper: our actual lives as they are lived. Basing everything on numbers pushes government policy toward mechanical, bureaucratic systems rather than more organic approaches that put people first. Take a so-called economic issue like jobs. It's just as much—if not more—a social, human issue. Of course you can fiddle around with interest rates and taxes, and that will have some effect on unemployment rates. But the effects are far less certain or predictable than economic policymakers let on. The wiser and more self-aware of them know that there is very little they can do to 'improve the economy' or 'create jobs' in a general sense. If you want to see more jobs created and more people able to take them, the things that really work are specific, human things.

Help people get the skills they need. Help them gain the confidence and support to become entrepreneurs. Help make sure children are brought up in a way that gives them the character and the capacity to learn, to train, to hold down a job. None of the social policies required to bring about these ends are captured in the job numbers or the growth statistics. But they are critical to achieving the economic results we seek. On the surface economic issues are human issues at their heart. Social policy *is* economic policy, just more effective.

We know from the latest developments in neuroscience and evidence from long-term research that the conditions in which children grow up, especially in the first few years of life, have a crucial impact on the rest of their lives: whether they will work or be on welfare, a contributor to society or a cost. But government doesn't prioritize spending on the causes of social problems; it wastes money on the symptoms. This flaw is systemic. It's not because politicians and public officials are stupid or useless or malevolent; quite the opposite: they are mostly highly intelligent, dedicated, and public spirited. The problem is a system that forces every decision into a framework that is literally inhuman. It's one of the reasons citizens feel that so little of any real substance seems to change, regardless of what party or politician is in power.

To design a more human world, we must change the priorities of government. We have to start from the notion that certain things *must* be in place for people to lead a decent life, that government's overarching priority should be to lay the infrastructure, in its broadest sense, that will allow that to come about. Of course, there's physical infrastructure—roads and railways, energy grids, and utilities. But we need human infrastructure as well—education and health services, early childhood education, mental health, relationship and family support. Infrastructure's problem, though, is that it tends to need expensive upfront expenditure before the benefits flow. As a society, we already make a certain commitment to this idea. We subsidize our children's education, for instance, because we think of it not as a cost but as an investment that will enable productive lives later on.

Now we need to adopt that same mindset across the board. This isn't new. In Britain the Victorians thought like this 150 years ago. As economist Diane Coyle points out, so-called Victorian values aren't just prudish or conservative; they "also speak of hard work, self-improvement, and above all self-sacrifice for the future."[2] The Victorians had the forethought to build tangible investments in their communities like railways, canals, sewers, town halls, libraries, concert halls, and modern hospitals. Meanwhile, they strengthened society through the police, trade unions, mutual insurers, learned societies, and the nursing profession. At the same time in the United States, we saw similar investments in public libraries, hospitals, schools, and colleges. President Franklin Roosevelt marshaled such forethought to invest in great public works projects as a means both to spur the economy out of the Great Depression in the short term and to undergird long-term growth in the future. President Dwight Eisenhower channeled this impulse in the 1950s with the Interstate Highway System—while in the states, governors like Pat Brown of California established the three-tiered higher education system. This "sense of stewardship," as Coyle described it in the context of the Victorians, is what can fundamentally define success or failure for a society.

Today we have shirked our duties as stewards. Public universities are in a perpetual crisis (California's have faced years of budget deficits and tuition hikes). According to the American Society of Civil Engineers, the United States must spend some $3.6 trillion by 2020 to meet demand for and maintain essential infrastructure like roads, dams, schools, levees, bridges, railways, and water and energy systems.[3] America is the world's leading economy, yet the Internet speed in our technology hub, San Francisco, is no faster than Mexico City's;[4] our trains are no faster than Japanese trains in the 1960s,[5] and one of our airports, New York's La Guardia, made Vice President Joe Biden think he was in "some Third World country."[6] We have chosen the tyranny of a narrow short-term economic calculus over America's long-term future.

This approach to governing is flawed in another way: it causes decision-makers to focus too much on the symptoms of problems instead of their causes. Government massively underinvests in infrastructure—both physical and human—because government accounts treat it as a cost with no benefits. Consequently government, whether federal, state, or local, applies its energy to the symptoms of social problems (welfare, crime, etc.) rather than their causes (e.g., what happens in early child-hood). Art Rolnick, former vice president at the Minneapolis Federal Reserve Bank, has dedicated his career to this point. In Minneapolis, state and local government provided nearly a billion dollars over the last decade to subsidize new professional sports stadiums[7]—spending that tends to have low and sometimes even negative effects on eco-nomic development. Meanwhile early childhood education, which has been shown to generate high returns on public investment over time, has hardly been funded.[8] Thankfully Rolnick and his allies fought for and won an unprecedented $250 million from the Minnesota state leg-islature last year for early childhood development, from prenatal care to preschool (see Chapter 8). No other state has made such commitments.[9]

One way to think about it, as Oxford economist Dieter Helm suggests, is to distinguish between spending money on assets and spending money on liabilities.[10] Infrastructure is an asset. Yes, it costs money initially, but we can predict (and later record) its 'dividends,' such as the economic activity a new fiber-optic network produces or the money an early child-hood intervention saves later on. That money goes in the 'plus' side of the ledger and, in any sensible accounting system (like the one used by businesses), can be offset against the spending. Eventually it will pay for itself. But in government, infrastructure spending isn't treated any differently. Tackling unemployment by building a high-speed broadband network that would help in the creation of new jobs is counted as no different from handing out the same amount of money in welfare pay-ments. Tackling crime through parenting programs that could prevent offending in the first place is counted in the same ledger as keeping criminals in jail. Long-term human needs come second to the short-term imperative of the numbers; sensible, long-term policies are rejected be-cause their dividends come down the road. The numbers rule, in a totally irrational way, and we end up with budget-based priorities instead of priorities-based budgets.

The issue really centers on a process called *scoring*. When government, at any level, does almost anything, it is 'scored' by a nonpartisan budget office that assesses that action's fiscal consequences: How much will it cost? Will it make money that offsets some or all of its costs? Will it lead to savings in one part of government but more spending in another?

Currently the standard practice is *static* scoring. Static scoring consid-ers a policy's fiscal impact upon implementation. Although it's not *inac-*curate, it is often misleading. For instance, it's obvious that if you spend money or cut taxes, it will have some impact beyond the initial cost.

Say a tax cut or an infrastructure project stimulates economic growth. It follows logically that the economic growth will result in greater tax revenue, offsetting the initial cost. Yet static scoring fails to consider that eventuality, so the tax cut and investment look much more expensive than they really are.[11]

But there's another type of scoring: *dynamic*. Unlike static scoring, dynamic scoring considers the fiscal effects of legislation over time. Let's say a tax cut stimulates economic growth enough to bring in new tax revenues or a spending increase boosts the economy. Projections of those effects can be applied to offset the initial cost of the policies. Dynamic scoring helps us take a long-term view. And because infrastructure usually takes a long time to pay off, the long-term view is more human.

After winning congressional elections in 2014, Republicans did introduce dynamic scoring for some measures—namely legislation that affects tax bills. Republicans—including presidential candidate Jeb Bush—rightly argue that dynamic scoring demonstrates the long-term benefits of tax cuts. But that's only half the story. Yes, tax cuts can pay for themselves,[12] and it is absolutely right to show that. So can spending on infrastructure, however, but political partisanship has gotten in the way of applying dynamic scoring to that. Dynamic scoring needn't be used on all legislation (as some experts point out, it would be uninformative and simply too cumbersome in many cases[13]), but it should be used on significant revenue *and* infrastructure spending projects, whether that's physical infrastructure like roads and bridges or human infrastructure like early education and family support. "If dynamic scoring is truly about reflecting the on-the-ground impact of government action, it must be applied to both sides of the ledger: spending and revenue," writes Democratic congressman John Delaney. To use different accounting systems for different parts of the budget is "intellectually dishonest."[14]

I wanted to tackle this—frankly quite geeky—question of government accounting systems and their impact on policy priorities because it's a good example of something we will see over and over in this book. To really change things, we need to understand the underlying causes of problems, and more often than not they are structural and systemic. In election campaigns the candidates battle over this tax cut or that spending commitment. These aren't unimportant questions, but they fail to get at the fundamental factors that seem to leave many massive social and economic problems permanently unsolved.

In the 2016 election the animating issue on the left is inequality; Bernie Sanders and Hillary Clinton discuss it constantly. Yet instead of talking about the causes of inequality, they're debating how to treat its symptoms. Whether you agree or disagree with their solutions—taxing the rich, new rules for banks, wage hikes, and so on—the sad truth is that they are all, basically, tactical fixes. They might make a difference in the short term, but they won't solve the problem of inequality in the long term. We need to address the structural problems of capitalism that lead to growing inequality, not just tax more here or regulate more there. We need to invest in early family support, to address inherited cultural disadvantages. And we need to overhaul the economic regimes that have prevented people from escaping poverty and achieving upward mobility. But in our current political reality, many of these options are simply off the table. They don't all cost money, but the type of investment required to make some of them viable is dismissed out of hand as too expensive— and thus impossible to even contemplate.

It's the same kind of thing on the right. Republican candidates talk about how we need growth and jobs, proposing lower taxes and less regulation as a means to get there. But these responses are just as superficial: way out of kilter with the scale of what's needed to really address the problem, which is the chronic underperformance of the US economy for decades, dramatically illustrated by languishing productivity growth.[15] America's economy is not suffering because of any particular regulation or tax (although I would be the first to agree that many of both could usefully be cut or abolished), but because of underinvestment in the infrastructure that underpins it. Internet speeds, bridges, mass transit, energy all are areas in which badly needed investment would pay untold economic dividends. Again, though, the scale of investment required is impossible given a system that refuses to see such investments as fiscally sound.

Avoiding proper analysis of how to actually solve our problems— rather than just managing their symptoms—has become rampant in our politics: all the time, no matter the party. Our election campaigns might entertain us, even occasionally inspire us, but they are irresponsible. By failing to countenance bold, systemic policy changes, our shallow and insubstantial political debates prevent leaders from, well, leading. They don't talk about the long-term, underlying structural problems—or the solutions—and so have no real mandate to act for the long term when in office. Our politicians once understood the need to build for the future; instead, the system of government accounting has defeated them. If we want government to have more human priorities, we will need to change that system.

A MORE HUMAN WAY TO DESIGN AND IMPLEMENT POLICY

In 2000 then UK prime minister Tony Blair floated a new idea to clean up antisocial behavior on British streets. He proposed that offenders be made to pay an on-the-spot fine of £100 (about $150); if they didn't have the money, they'd be taken to an ATM to withdraw it. The policy was never implemented. One of the main reasons was because it turned out that the 'yobs' (British slang for young folks up to no good) targeted by this policy did not usually have £100 in cash 'on the spot,' or a bank account to withdraw it from; often they did not even have £100 to their names.[16]

Why did Blair make incorrect assumptions about those committing street crime? Come to think of it, how did anyone in any government anywhere conceive that dopey new tax, that waste-of-money antipoverty program, that white-elephant urban-regeneration plan, and so on? It's easy to blame 'useless politicians,' 'partisan aides,' and 'incompetent bureaucrats.' But that's simplistic; we need to go deeper. One reason for the failure of so many government programs over the years—and the dissatisfaction so many people feel with the public services they receive—is the fact that the people the programs or services are designed to help are too often an afterthought. The lives of average people—especially the poor or those interacting with social services—are simply unknown to policymakers. Blair and his advisers' daily reality was so far removed from that of the people who made trouble on the streets that no matter how right the theory, the policy could never work in practice.

Don't think that politicians don't care about people or the effects of their policies—they do, most of them, sincerely and deeply. It's just that by the time politicians are in their government offices, trying to find slots in their overfilled schedules to actually think about policy and its implementation, they're unable to do so on a human scale, in a human way.

It's not just the design of policies; it's the delivery too. Consider the New Enterprise Allowance (NEA), another well-intentioned UK government idea, this time from the administration of David Cameron. It was aimed at helping people get off unemployment benefits—and was in fact a policy I helped create and fought hard to introduce. The idea was that some unemployed people might want to start their own businesses, so if we could get each of them a loan and some advice from a mentor, they'd be on their way. The NEA loan would be administered through Jobcentre Plus offices, the British equivalent of work-placement offices, which were already in most communities. When the program was launched,

the initial uptake was disappointing and the Treasury officials in charge
of its funding wanted to cancel the whole thing. Rohan Silva (my closest friend and former colleague in government who you will meet a lot
in these pages) was curious about why the program, loosely based on
a similar one that had been extremely successful in the 1980s, wasn't
working. On a hunch that perhaps it wasn't being pitched in the right
way, he asked the officials running the policy what the staff at Jobcentre
Plus offices were trained to say to potential candidates and what their
reasons would be for granting or turning down a loan if the conversation
got that far.

The officials had no idea. They never gave it a moment's thought. They
just assumed that because the opportunity was available, anyone who
wanted it would sign up. A low level of sign-ups must have meant the
policy was defective. The government was about to cancel a potentially
effective program without any sense of how it was being implemented
where it really mattered: the human point of contact between two people.

THE D.SCHOOL AT STANFORD

In 2012 I came to Stanford University, where I taught a number of courses,
including some at its Institute of Design, or d.school. This required me
to reflect on how we did things in government—what we did well, what
we did badly, and what we could have done differently. That reflection
has been profound. I now realize why so many policies fail, why so much
money is wasted, why so many promises are never delivered, why this
happened in our administration—and in every government. It has to do
with a mindset, an attitude, an approach in which policymaking is much
more about theory than practice, where the people making the policy
and the people implementing it make no real effort to understand, in
detail, the lives of the people whom the policy is for. I have no hesita-
tion in saying to my students that the single biggest improvement we
could bring to policymaking in government is to make it more human,
to put people at the center of the process. That may sound platitudinous.
But I mean it in a very precise way, based on what I learned at Stanford
about the process of human-centered design—or, as it is known at the
d.school, *design thinking*.

Formally established in 2004 as the Hasso Plattner Institute for Design
at Stanford, the d.school is the academic home of design thinking. In the
late 1980s the software usability engineer Donald Norman put forward

his vision of user-centered design, and by the late 1990s and early 2000s designers at the Silicon Valley design firm IDEO (the company responsible for Apple's first mouse), started to realize that they could apply user- (or human-) centered design (by now also called design thinking) not just to objects, products, and software but also much more broadly. In the 2000s design thinking had been applied to entire business models, not to mention consumer experiences. By the time the d.school was founded it was clear that because innovators in almost any discipline are creating new things—whether business ideas, healthcare interventions, education policies, or consumer services—and that the act of creating is an act of design, graduate students from any university program would benefit from a design-thinking education. Stanford's d.school was established to give them that opportunity. It's now run by Sarah Stein Greenberg, my brilliant coteacher and the person who more than anyone else has helped me understand what design thinking is all about and how it could help improve policymaking and implementation.

At the d.school students are guided through a process that, though inevitably messier in practice, can be explained in a handful of straightforward steps:

Empathize with the user
Define the problem
Generate ideas
Prototype solutions
Test the prototypes
. . . keep testing, adapting, and improving.

Empathy is not a word you hear very much in government. But to understand a problem and imagine a solution requires an understanding of the people affected. This is an act of empathy, and human-centered designers put themselves in the shoes of those they are designing for. Empathy requires close, highly detailed observation of people in the context in which they'll be using the product or service in question. This borrows from the anthropological practice of ethnography, which assumes that observations and open-ended interviews reveal more about a person's beliefs, needs, emotions, and desires than opinion surveys and market research ever could. In the design-thinking process taught at the d.school this means talking to 'users' before doing anything else, which really means listening to users. Politicians, of course, will say they listen to their constituents all the time, either directly or through polls and focus groups. But this is different. The kind of empathy work required for design thinking is about deeply understanding the life of the person you're designing for, forcing yourself to be open-minded rather than selling your own ideas.

The first stage of the designers' process includes observing users in their day-to-day routines and immersing themselves in the users' environment for days, even weeks on end. The acclaimed urban theorist and writer Jane Jacobs captures precisely this sentiment in her 1961 masterpiece, *The Death and Life of Great American Cities*. She writes that the only corrective to ineffective, top-down city planning—generally by 'visionary,' egotistical architects and politicians—is to base policy on "true descriptions of reality drawn not from how it ought to be, but from how it is."[17]

These true descriptions of reality are the basis for step two: defining the problem. This might seem straightforward, but it's surprising how frequently policymakers can be found solving the wrong problem—a superficial one, a symptom rather than a cause—or a problem perceived in one way by the outside world but totally differently by those actually experiencing it. A great example comes from a student project that began at the d.school as part of a course called Entrepreneurial Design for Extreme Affordability. In "Extreme," as the course is popularly known, teams of Stanford graduate students come together for over six months to work on different problems facing the world's poor. Each group, which deliberately mixes up students from any field—law, medicine, business, history, computer science—is paired with an international NGO to solve a specific problem in an extremely affordable way.

One team was tasked with developing a lower-cost baby incubator to be piloted in rural Nepal (nearly 1 million children die each year globally from complications due to premature birth[18]). The team of four first met in January 2007 when the course began. They spent two and a half months researching incubators as well as infant mortality and the medical requirements of premature babies. It is customary with Extreme for one or two of the students on each team to visit their partners on the ground. For the incubator team Linus Liang, a computer-science student, traveled seven thousand miles to Nepal along with two other student groups working on similar health-related problems.

"We were very ambitious—we landed, got to the hotel, and went to the hospital that day," Linus recalls. "We did exactly what design thinking instructs—lots of interviews, observations, etcetera. We talked to at least twenty doctors and then went to the neonatal intensive care unit and observed all the different doctors and nurses, the amount of noise—everything."

Linus discovered one odd thing. There were incubators everywhere, but they sat empty. "There's this hospital with nothing, no resources—there's mold growing on the walls," Linus recalls, but "they had all these donated incubators. Some [of the instruction labels] were in Japanese, some were in German—there were all these different languages. And all of them were pretty damn good. So Linus asked the next question: given that Nepal had all these incubators, why did it have such a high infant mortality problem? It turned out that many of the country's premature births happened in rural villages, far away from the hospital and the life-saving incubators. The babies were dead on arrival.

It was clear that the d.school team needed to go deeper to understand the problem. So they got on a bus and went to a village outside Kathmandu. "It was kind of horrible what they had out there. There was no infrastructure." In the village they visited it became quickly apparent that the team's initial idea—a cheaper incubator for hospitals—wasn't going to get them anywhere. There was no running water, no local hospitals—just shacks with barely trained 'doctors' who did their best to serve the villagers' medical needs. The incubators they used were simple wooden boxes with light bulbs in them, most of which were burnt out anyway, some for as long as four years. They told Linus that they had no money to buy new bulbs, but in any case there was nowhere to buy them, nor electricity to power them.

"You slowly learn all the constraints. And then we started designing for that when we came back," Linus explains. "That's when we really understood the need." Back at Stanford the team used its findings to develop a new point of view. They were no longer looking to design a cheaper, simpler incubator for local hospitals: "We wanted to design for the mothers who have no actual healthcare system, no water, no electricity, no transport, no money." The team redefined the problem they were trying to solve based on the empathy they had gained. And it was at this point that they could start to generate ideas for what a solution might look like.[19]

This might sound familiar—who hasn't sat through a 'brainstorming' session to come up with something clever or creative? But this step in the design-thinking process, like the others, is usually given short shrift by politicians and policymakers, many of whom already have solutions in mind that they're trying to advance, based often on ideology rather than empathy with the people they're trying to help. One of my favorite teaching moments at the d.school is our demonstration of a bad brain-storm versus a good brainstorm. Take it from me—most of the ones you see in government are bad. The cardinal rule for getting good results? Defer judgment. Whether you're alone or with a group of colleagues, the best way to kill potentially good ideas is to point out their flaws at the moment you're trying to come up with them. That's not to say that "there's no such thing as a bad idea." Of course there is. But the time for evaluating ideas is not when you're trying to generate them.

For me, the part of the design-thinking process that offers the great-est contrast with how things are done in government is the final stage: prototyping and testing an idea. The key is to embrace experimentation, testing a concept with cheap and rough prototypes before investing more in its development. This is a world away from how government does things. Yes, there are pilot programs—but these typically cost many mil-lions of dollars and are launched with great fanfare. The incentive is to prove that they work, not to find out whether they do. Prototype testing is not piloting. For example, rather than building a website—still a costly exercise—you could literally sketch it out on pieces of paper, put it in front of people, and get feedback on how they would use it based sim-ply on asking them to point at boxes they would 'click' on and why. The methodology of rapid and low-cost prototyping and testing taught at the d.school is now the basic modus operandi for every tech firm in Silicon Valley, from the biggest names to the smallest start-ups.

And that's exactly what the d.school team working on the incubator problem did next. Based on insights gained from Nepal, they shifted their focus from the hospital and the clinician to the village and the mother. The team reframed the problem from "building a cheaper incubator" to "keeping premature babies warm." The result was a wrap like a sleep-ing bag, warmed by a special heated insert, all costing about 1 percent of the price of an incubator. When the course was finished, the team set themselves up as a company (called Embrace) and moved to India, determined to bring their concept to a stage at which it could actually be deployed. They continued testing new versions, each time gaining fresh insight from the mothers whom they watched using the prototypes. Small tweaks came from observation: a plastic window over the chest, allowing doctors to see at a glance if the baby was breathing, or a simple OK/Not OK indicator in place of the previous numerical temperature gauge that the mothers didn't trust (digital displays tend to malfunction so often that there's an automatic suspicion of them). From its humble origins as a student project, Embrace has now expanded its operations across Asia, Latin America, and Africa and has gone on to save fifty thousand lives—and counting.[20]

DESIGNING POLICY FOR WHO WE ARE,
NOT FOR WHO WE OUGHT TO BE

It's amazing what you can discover when you listen to people. But a more human approach to policymaking doesn't just mean paying attention to details on the ground; it's about understanding behavior too. Over the last thirty years psychologists, neuroscientists, and economists have systematically cataloged ways in which we consistently fail to live up to traditional expectations of how humans 'ought' to behave. This means that we now have a rigorous body of work, rather than just our hunches, that we can use to enhance the effectiveness of public policy.

For example, economics assumes that we value money objectively—that a dollar gained causes as much pleasure as the pain from a dollar that's lost. But in the late 1970s psychologists discovered that we tend to be much more averse to a loss than we are keen to have the equivalent gain. This work was so disruptive to traditional economics that its discovery by Daniel Kahneman and Amos Tversky earned the Nobel Prize in 2002.[21] An interesting application of the principle was an experiment in a Chicago school district. For many years school administrators around the world have tried to incentivize better teacher performance through bonuses awarded at the end of the year if certain targets are met. In Chicago Heights a group of University of Chicago academics tried an approach based on this behavioral concept of loss aversion. They gave the teachers their bonus at the beginning of the year and told them that at the end of the year, all or parts of it would be taken away if they didn't meet specified goals. Two control groups were also established: one in which teachers were given no performance incentive and one involving a traditional end-of-year bonus. The results were spectacular: the performance of the students taught by teachers in the two control groups was about the same, suggesting that the traditional performance bonus doesn't really make much difference. But in the group where the teachers were given an upfront bonus with a threat that it would be lost, the students' results improved two to three times more than the traditional bonus group.[22]

More human policy design would also recognize that we often neglect to do things that are in our own best interest—and that we even say we want to do—like put money in our pensions, exercise, and remember to go to doctors' appointments. But government policy has been designed and implemented for decades based on the assumption that people will behave with perfect foresight and self-control. Consider government's approach to fighting poverty: programs of the left traditionally consist of giving money, jobs, food, and other "free stuff"—as critics like to call it—to alleviate material deprivation, while programs of the right traditionally try to improve economic incentives so that poor people can 'lift themselves up by the bootstraps.' Both approaches, as the *New York Times* columnist David Brooks has pointed out, errantly "treat individuals as if they were abstractions . . . shaped by economic structures alone, and not by character and behavior."[23] The simple truth is that our actions don't always match our intentions. Human things like forgetfulness get in the way.

People also tend to do what they think other people are doing. One of my favorite examples comes from an experiment that psychologist Robert Cialdini carried out in Arizona's Petrified Forest National Park. He posted signs drawing attention to the high incidence of looting pieces of ancient wood. They backfired: letting people know that theft was frequent—normal even—actually increased theft.[24] Traditional efforts by governments to change people's behavior so often make this classic mistake—highlighting the negative behavior they want to *dis*courage rather than promoting as a social norm the positive behavior they want to *en*courage.

IN HIS 2015 State of the Union Address, President Obama highlighted a growing problem: many people are desperate for jobs and the requisite skills but are unable to afford college and obtain them. To that end Obama announced the expansion of a model tried out in Tennessee and Chicago: "that two years of college becomes as free and universal in America as high school is today."[25]

The idea of free community college sounds attractive, of course. It will likely boost enrollment and help those who can't afford college courses. But what about those who enroll but don't graduate?·In other words, what about *more than half of them*?[26] College affordability is no doubt part of the problem. But it's only a part—and may not even be the biggest part. For many, it's the seemingly insignificant barriers that defeat them.

A lost transcript, an unpaid fee, the difficulty of filling out a financial aid form—the maze of paperwork that students must navigate would be daunting for the best of us. Rich students—or students at rich universities, like Stanford—have layers of advisers, academic support, and material resources to help them through the pitfalls of college, but students at community and state colleges often don't. Even worse, many of those students don't come from backgrounds that prepare them for academic culture or the soul-crushing challenge of navigating college bureaucracies.

So although the policy of making community college free is undoubtedly well intentioned, it may not be so well designed. Instead of asking, "How can we make community college less expensive?" officials might have asked, "What can we do to help community college students succeed?" Free tuition is a reasonable answer to the first question. It isn't, necessarily, to the second.

That's because enrolling and paying for community college is relatively easy: signing up is straightforward, and poor students' tuition is often covered by Pell Grants and other government aid. "The important task," as again, David Brooks points out, "is to help students graduate."[27] That's where a human-centered approach might pay off.

In the summer of 2014, months before President Obama's State of the Union proposal, Howard Schultz, founder and CEO of Starbucks, announced that his company would work with Arizona State University to help Starbucks employees—many of whom have already earned quite a few credits—finish college. Two years of tuition would be absolutely free; those with more than two years to go would get a significant discount until they reached that point.[28] Although on the surface the two plans seem quite similar, Schultz's plan had a crucial difference from Obama's: it was designed in a more human way.

Starbucks assigns students an individual counselor who frequently calls to help students plan courses and, more importantly, to help them overcome practical barriers like signing up for classes or finding lost transcripts. Mary Hamm, a forty-nine-year-old barista in Virginia, had always wanted to go to college and jumped at the opportunity to attend online through Starbucks. But when she got her first quiz back, she was crestfallen at her seven-out-of-ten result. She felt like a failure. Her counselor asked whether she was allowed to use her notes on the test: it turned out that she was. But she didn't know that, inadvertently handicapping herself. After several decades out of the classroom, it turns out you can forget some of the tips essential to simply being a good student, and the presence of a counselor can be a simple, practical part of the solution. It also helps boost confidence. Students like Hamm "often have doubts about themselves being college-ready," says Dave Jarrat, an executive at InsideTrack, the firm that provides the counseling support for the program. "That manifests itself when they get into college, take a quiz, and get a C and say, 'See? I'm not college material.' Then they drop out."[29] The counselors' goal is not only to provide their students with helpful tools and point them to valuable resources but also to prepare them for the reality that they will have setbacks to overcome.

The Starbucks plan is a great example of human-centered design. It addresses real student needs, however trivial they may sound, and welcomes feedback so the program can continuously improve. When some students dropped out of the program, they were asked why; after telling their advisers that tuition was still too expensive, Starbucks made it cheaper.[30] It's still unclear how successful that fix will be. The Starbucks program certainly won't be the model for getting every aspiring college student on track, but it shows the value of empathizing with 'users' and adjusting big bureaucracies to *their* needs. That simple but profound change of perspective can improve the chances of any policy—and make the difference between a waste of money and a successful investment.

We need a more human approach at least in part as an antidote to policymakers' increasing overreliance on data. I'm not against using data as a policymaking tool; it can help us understand the extent of a problem's existence, scope, and distribution as well as its trend over time. Data can help us see whether existing policies are having the desired effect or if concepts that worked well in one place are effective in others. Perhaps data's most crucial function is helping us understand what has *generally* worked or failed before. But when it comes to the design of specific programs or the way public services are actually delivered, it's dangerous to make assumptions based on data, as if all people and situations were the same. Here's David Brooks again, on efforts to combat teenage pregnancy: "A pregnancy . . . isn't just a piece of data in a set. It came about after a unique blend of longings and experiences. Maybe a young woman just wanted to feel like an adult; maybe she had some desire for arduous love, maybe she was just absent-minded, or loved danger, or couldn't resist her boyfriend, or saw no possible upside for her future anyway. In each case the ingredients will be different. Only careful case-by-case storytelling can uncover and respect the delirious iconoclasm of how life is actually lived."[31]

POLICING: AN URGENT NEED FOR A MORE HUMAN APPROACH

At the height of the crack-cocaine epidemic in the 1990s, New York City police commissioner Bill Bratton instituted a program called CompStat in an effort to radically realign the department around a clear principle of accountability for crime reduction. Police officials were required to attend weekly meetings at which they discussed the key data of the week, with statistical trends analyzed across departments and over time. Although it was largely credited with reducing the specific measured crimes (muggings, murders, etc.), the program precluded tactics that might have been more effective in the long term but were less amenable to measurement, such as trust-building in communities. Events like the 2014 riots and overmilitarized police response in Ferguson, Missouri, or the brutal chokehold arrest and subsequent death of Eric Garner, an unarmed petty criminal in New York, are partly the result of such a targets-driven culture. Bratton, who advocates CompStat around the world, himself acknowledges that too much attention has been placed on "the numbers of stops, summonses and arrests" and not enough on "collaborative problem-solving with the community."[32] Jim Bueermann, president of the Police Foundation and a former police chief, admits, "If you ask a traffic officer how many tickets he wrote today, their emphasis is on writing tickets to meet a number, as opposed to a desired outcome, which is safer streets."[33]

This data obsession and the results it evokes are reasons why so many people in America are losing trust in the police. In Ferguson the public—in this case the African American minority—has been egregiously abused by the city government through its police and court system. A US Department of Justice (DOJ) report found that "Ferguson law enforcement practices disproportionately harm Ferguson's African-American residents" and that there was "substantial evidence that this harm stems in part from intentional discrimination in violation of the Constitution."[34]

The DOJ report is instructive for laying bare the insidious effects of a targets-based policing culture. The NYPD might have made errors with CompStat, but those errors were at least made with the intent to reduce crime and make New York a safer city. In Ferguson the police prioritized "productivity"—read: writing citations—and residents were seen "less as constituents to be protected than as potential offenders and sources of revenue." The municipal court, meanwhile, failed in its essential function to adjudicate legal disputes. "Instead," the report found, "the court primarily uses its judicial authority as the means to compel payment of fines and fees that advance the City's financial interests." In doing so, the court's practices "violate[d] the Fourteenth Amendment [of the US Constitution according "equal protection" under the law] . . . and impose[d] unnecessary harm, overwhelmingly on African-American individuals, and run counter to public safety."[35] The court mired citizens in red tape, issuing warrants over missed court appearances and unpaid tickets (some nine thousand in 2013 alone, in a town of twenty-one thousand), and erecting "unnecessary barriers to resolving municipal violation[s]," including "fail[ure] to provide clear and accurate information" about fines and court procedures.[36]

Justice may have been carried out to the letter of the law in Ferguson, but it was hardly according to its spirit. In Ferguson, targets undermined the effectiveness of the very services they are supposed to help improve. Take this example of a Ferguson man who ran afoul of Ferguson police:

> In the summer of 2012, a 32-year-old African-American man sat in his car cooling off after playing basketball in a Ferguson public park. An officer pulled up behind the man's car, blocking him in, and demanded the man's Social Security number and identification. Without any cause, the officer accused the man of being a pedophile, referring to the presence of children in the park, and ordered the man out of his car for a pat-down, although the officer had no reason to believe the man was armed. The officer also asked to search the man's car. The man objected, citing his constitutional rights. In response, the officer arrested the man, reportedly at gunpoint, charging him with eight violations of Ferguson's municipal code. One charge, Making a False Declaration, was for initially providing the short form of his first name (e.g., "Mike" instead of "Michael"), and an address which, although legitimate, was different from the one on his driver's license. Another charge was for not wearing a seat belt, even though he was seated in a parked car. The officer also charged the man both with having an expired operator's license, and with having no operator's license in his possession. The man told us that, because of these charges, he lost his job as a contractor with the federal government that he had held for years.[37]

Did racism cause the criminal justice system to abuse targets? Or did a targets culture lead to racist abuse? Probably both. Certainly there was truly horrific racism and corruption in Ferguson, and it is a fact that the African American population disproportionately bore the abuse of the criminal justice system. But the Ferguson scandal was also the consequence of how the system operated. Ferguson's police force was judged not by how safe the streets were but by how many tickets its officers could write, and the courts were judged not by how just their proceedings were but by how many fines they could levy. Racism may have led Ferguson's system to target African Americans, the town's most vulnerable and least powerful demographic, but any system set up to privilege citations and the revenue they produce over due process is destined to result in corrupt and unfair results. Targets disguised those injustices as the results of legitimate law enforcement.

Although the spark in Ferguson was, in retrospect wrong (Darren Wilson, the police officer who shot Michael Brown, prompting the initial investigation, was ultimately cleared), the flame of the Brown-related riots illuminated the injustices present in the criminal justice system: an often authoritarian police culture that is overmilitarized, underscrutinized, and at odds with the public safety objectives with which the police are entrusted. In the short time since the Brown shooting, Americans, especially white Americans, have become increasingly aware of police misconduct, especially misconduct that disproportionately hurts black Americans. A steady stream of deaths of African Americans at the hands of the police has given rise to the Black Lives Matter movement, most notably: Eric Garner, who died in New York after police put him in a chokehold for illegally selling cigarettes; twelve-year-old Tamir Rice, who was shot by police without warning in a Cincinnati park for holding an airsoft gun; Freddie Gray, who sustained fatal injuries while being transported by Baltimore police; Sandra Bland, who died in her jail cell (ruled a suicide by the coroner) after being arrested over a traffic infraction; and Samuel DuBose, who was shot by University of Cincinnati police during a traffic stop.

Police officers across the country have an inestimably difficult job, and we place a great deal of trust in them to carry out their duties. The vast majority of them are not simply good, honest, and decent officers; they are brave heroes for putting themselves in harm's way to keep us safe. Something is wrong, however, when they blindly follow targets; when they unfairly target the poor, the black, and the male; or when they bark out orders to people as if they were animals. When police officers put targets before people, rules before relationships, and revenue before community, they are not acting in the best interests of the people—whether they be black, Hispanic, Asian, or white.

We urgently need a culture of more human policing. As long as police officers work under a siege mindset in which they fear leaving their cars—or only do so when armed to the teeth with military gear—a disconnect will exist between the police and the communities they are sworn to protect. Police forces are not invading armies; they do not need tanks. Police officers are not soldiers; they do not need full-body armor and assault rifles. Instead, they need a more human approach in which they are integrated with their communities. They should heed the words of Sir Robert Peel, the British statesman who started London's Metropolitan Police, the world's first modern police force: "The police are the public and the public are the police."[38]

Overreliance on targets, on data, is certainly not the only factor contributing to the police becoming more authoritarian; indeed, data is a valuable tool to understand the policing needs of a community. But we have seen what happens when the police see citizens as data points: their actions become beholden to statistics, not good police work. It leads to a cycle in which the police dehumanize people and people dehumanize the police. In communities of color, where longstanding historical grievances and the legacies of racism persist, already tenuous relationships between people and the police are pushed to the brink in which abuse and civil unrest are all but inevitable. There are many steps to be taken to resolve the crisis between America's police and so many of its citizens. But the first is straightforward: let's not confuse measurable actions like stops, citations, fines, and arrests with the true goals of safer streets and citizens.

"GO OUT INTO THE REAL WORLD"

In the end, numbers are just not that helpful in actually designing or implementing policy in government and in public services like the police. For example, knowing whether a family is above or below the poverty line tells us nothing about *why* that's the case. And if we don't know why a family is in poverty, we can't know how to design programs to help that family out. No statistics or set of data can substitute for the intimate, nuanced knowledge that a policymaker should internalize by going out and experiencing the complexity of the world where the policy will have its effect.

In government in the UK we tried to move things forward. In 2008, while we were still in opposition, Rohan ordered ten copies of *Nudge* by Dick Thaler and Cass Sunstein, a book that sets out the case, in theory and with practical examples, for using behavioral economics to improve people's ability to make decisions. The book promotes a sort of 'libertarian paternalism': steer people in the desired direction without outright compulsion. David Cameron picked up a copy from the pile on Rohan's desk and shortly thereafter started referring to it eagerly. Within weeks of becoming prime minister Cameron gave the go-ahead to set up a 'nudge' unit of our own. Under the direction of social psychologist and Cabinet Office veteran David Halpern, the Behavioural Insights Team worked with government departments to help improve policy design, now replicated in the US federal government in the shape of the White House Social and Behavioral Sciences Team. Nudges aren't just cute tricks to tack on to existing policies. One of the most successful—and oft-quoted—nudges instituted by the Cameron government was to require large companies to auto-enroll employees in their pension plans, increasing pension savings dramatically.[39]

Design thinking, too, has started to make inroads in government. After Rohan's experience of the New Enterprise Allowance brought home to him how detached officials were from the actual people government policies were trying to help, he decided something had to be done to bring the users of government programs into the way programs were designed. "I was so frustrated by the officials' answers to these basic questions about the way this policy was presented to the people who might benefit from it. What is the script? What posters are up? What materials do people get if they're interested?" he recounts. "Just imagine the individual lives that could have been changed, the amazing businesses started, the jobs created, if there had just been this small change, if there had just been a moment's thought given to the actual human interaction. Why is there such a dislocation between policymakers and reality? And this is just a small policy in the overall scheme of things. Think about all the policies right across government and how much more effective they could be."[40]

Rohan initiated a process to bring design thinking into the heart of government. He met with experts at the Royal College of Art, Jeremy Myerson and Anthony Dunne, as well as Tom Hulme from the UK office of IDEO. From that came the idea to run a design-thinking course for top civil servants. "I wanted to devise a systemic response to this systemic problem," Rohan says. So in November 2012 he convened a group of a couple of hundred of the UK's top civil servants at Number 10 Downing Street for a design-thinking workshop. The venue, the State Dining Room, emphasized the importance of the enterprise: "I chose that room very specifically because it's the grandest room at Number 10," Rohan recalls. "Civil servants are a pretty cautious bunch, and Whitehall is not a particularly amenable place to new ideas, so I wanted them to understand that this was serious." Professors from the Royal College of Art's new Service Design program, who led the day-long crash course, made good use of the space, covering it in Post-its (the global medium of design thinking, I've discovered since teaching at the d.school). Cabinet

Office minister Francis Maude kicked it off; Cabinet secretary Jeremy Heywood and head of the Civil Service Bob Kerslake weighed in to make closing remarks. "The day was bookended by the people in charge," Rohan explains. "I did everything I could to frame this as legitimate and mainstream."[41]

In the United States, design thinking is even starting to reach the most bureaucratic of agencies. The Office of Personnel Management (OPM) is in charge of more than 2 million employees across the entire federal government—hardly an agency that is naturally at the forefront of anything. But with wheelable whiteboards, oddly shaped furniture, Post-it Notes, and Sharpies galore, the basement beneath its Washington, DC offices looks more like what you'd find in Stanford's d.school than a typical government office building. This is the OPM's Innovation Lab. "It's very different, believe me, from OPM's typical work," says Sydney Heimbrock, the executive in charge of OPM's innovation practice. Here, OPM staff use the space to teach design courses and workshops for government employees and to teach other agencies, like the US Department of Agriculture (USDA), how to build similar programs.

Among its many other responsibilities, the USDA is in charge of the nation's Food and Nutrition Service Program, which distributes free or reduced-cost school lunches to low-income students. Unfortunately far fewer students are enrolled in the program than qualify, meaning that many go hungry or undernourished every day. For ten years, despite trying every approach they could think of, USDA officials couldn't get to the root of the problem.

Enter OPM's Innovation Lab team. With their colleagues at the USDA, they embarked on the design-thinking process, including visits to schools and time spent talking to administrators and school lunch workers. The most valuable insights they gained were in many ways the most banal, things that nobody would think warranted the attention of top-level staff, and yet made a big difference. For example, it became quickly apparent that simply redesigning the application form could have a huge impact on enrollment. The box for the family name wasn't large enough for very long names, which many low-income immigrant families tend to have. Challenges with low literacy made it difficult for some parents to complete the form. It was also more complicated than it had to be: people regularly filled it out incorrectly or found its complexity too much of a barrier. Through the design-thinking process, the USDA learned and experimented enough to be in a position to implement changes on a wide scale. "It's an easy way to quickly address challenges to the program," explains Stephanie Wade, the Innovation Lab's director. "It's a really good example of the government working quickly to be better for the people."

Of course all this—the jargon, the Post-it Notes, the brainstorming—is easy to mock or portray as the latest management fad. In fact, however, it's much more than that; it's a fundamental reorientation of policymaking, from a focus on bureaucratic needs and priorities to the real lives of the real people government is supposed to serve.

But let's not get carried away. Although there have been steps forward—for example, Prime Minister David Cameron commissioned intensive 'mystery shopping' research so he could learn how policies were actually being implemented in the real world; Megan Smith, the US chief technology officer and a Google veteran, brought together teams of engineers and health experts at a day-long 'hackathon' to design a better Ebola suit[42]—the vast majority of government policymaking and implementation is still mired in a bureaucratic mindset. The number of politicians, policymakers, and other public officials who have even heard of human-centered design or behavioral economics, let alone experienced it, is minuscule. And although OPM has been somewhat successful, some of those trying to infuse design into government have run into trouble. When Karen Courington, a former congressional aide who took part in a class I taught at the d.school, tried to infuse the Capitol with a bit of design-thinking spirit, she met fierce resistance. After asking someone in charge whether she could set up a nonpartisan room with whiteboards where staffers could meet and brainstorm policy ideas—perhaps with a few Post-its!—he told her, "No, there'll never be a white board in the Capitol as long as I'm here."[43]

So although having specialist units, like the Innovation Lab or nudge units, is a promising start, the big benefits in terms of a much higher hit rate of policies, programs, and services that actually work will most quickly be realized if the principles of design thinking are integrated into the everyday habits of every government employee at every level. That means government officials regularly spending time with their 'users'— that is, citizens. Of course, elected officials and civil servants are busy, but it's really just a question of priorities. Instead of spending half their time in meetings being briefed on policy problems, they need to go out and actually experience them. Before designing a new parenting program while in government, I went along to parenting classes and talked to the parents about their experiences. Before implementing one of our government's biggest and most ambitious domestic policy initiatives— National Citizen Service, a kind of universal, nonmilitary personal development and community service program for teenagers—we spent years prototyping and testing the model.

A MORE HUMAN WAY OF ORGANIZING GOVERNMENT

But there's still a problem: scale. Too often the people making decisions are too far from the people affected by them. Government is too big, too distant, too complex, whether it's in Washington, state capitals, or county administrative centers, all of which can incubate their fair share of bureaucratic inanity. In Britain the problem is centralization: to an absurd and counterproductive degree, things are run from the center in London. But in the United States the problem is different. Size and centralization are part of the problem, but with cities, counties, states, and the federal tier, American government is one of the most fragmented in the world. More often its problem is complexity: layers of government that do the same task and ossified bureaucracies that are Kafkaesque in scope. Red tape has gotten so bad, in fact, that one respected scholar, Charles Murray, literally—and rather exhilaratingly, in my view—suggests *breaking* rules in the spirit of regulatory civil disobedience as the most effective approach to reform.[44]

Accountability in government is fuzzy, lying with endless obscure bits of the bureaucracy with multiple overlapping responsibilities that are not clearly defined, least of all to the average citizen. Adhering to regulation or interacting with government is a complicated obstacle course rather than a straightforward endeavor. In his 2011 State of the Union Address, President Obama colorfully illustrated the point:

> We can't win the future with a government of the past. We live and do business in the Information Age, but the last major reorganization of the government happened in the age of black-and-white TV. There are 12 different agencies that deal with exports. There are at least five different agencies that deal with housing policy. Then there's my favorite example: the Interior Department is in charge of salmon while they're in freshwater, but the Commerce Department handles them when they're in saltwater. I hear it gets even more complicated once they're smoked.[45]

The hubris of big, bureaucratic government has grown to the point at which its self-inflicted catastrophes are now clearly undermining support for government itself. It used to be said that centralized government is more efficient. Occasionally, yes. There are obviously certain public policy objectives that are best handled at the national level. Localizing our foreign policy doesn't make much sense. But many problems that beset government arise precisely because they are handled at the wrong scale. This is most obviously the case when it comes to the contracting out of enormous parts of the state to external organizations, often in the private sector. But the problem is not the contracting out: it's the size of the contracts.

In *The End of Big*, Nicco Mele identifies "nerd disease," in which technical experts make things needlessly complicated in order to justify their own maintenance services. He describes consulting for a business that had an online staff in one building and another team in a warehouse across the street shipping orders. The company wanted to integrate the computer systems for the two sides of the business, and the technical staff were advising the CEO to spend $1 million on a contract with an external supplier. Instead, Mele suggested something different: simply have someone walk between the buildings twice a day with the orders.[46]

As expensive as nerd disease is when things go according to plan, it is even worse when they go wrong. The ramifications tend to be massive. Instead of a small, local failure, it's national and affects everyone in the system, often all at once. And because bureaucrats and contractors are reluctant to inform superiors of problems (to protect themselves politically), they often only become apparent when it's too late. Consequently, big government contracts end up mired in waste, failure, fraud, and abuse.[47]

In America the implementation of the Affordable Care Act offers a cautionary tale. It all started with nerd disease. In order to take advantage of the healthcare market created by Obamacare, users had to go online to 'exchanges' to browse and apply for different insurance policies. But first the government had to build the website, which, given that it was meant to reform an industry the size of the entire French economy, unsurprisingly didn't go according to plan. There were several delays in launching the system, and once enrollment started, substantial problems with the interface plagued prospective users as they tried to navigate the site. The administration had underestimated the website's complexity from the start, hiring just one official with experience in healthcare IT, Todd Park of Castlight Health. Instead of managing it directly, the administration shuffled responsibility to the Centers for Medicare and Medicaid Services in Maryland, which didn't even have a permanent director because his appointment was blocked in Congress.

By taking on such a vast and wide-ranging initiative at once, the president and his staff knew that they were playing a bold political game with high stakes; Republicans would look for any glitch to try to torpedo the whole project. Consequently the pressure to keep everything on schedule was immense. Through fear of confirming the criticism of Obamacare's political opponents, problems went unreported to the White House; as a result, those with the ability to push back major deadlines or make significant changes were unaware of problems until they were too late to fix. Meanwhile the Health and Human Services Secretary, Kathleen Sebelius, was, according to one commentator, "out of her depth" and unable to properly oversee such a vast project.[48] In trying to do too much too quickly and with too little capacity, the Obama administration was left reeling. But honestly, how surprising is it that one single contract to manage one-sixth of the US economy should go wrong?

The trouble with bureaucracy running amok in this way is that it has the unfortunate tendency to keep running amok. During the twentieth century, as we turned to the state to organize vast new areas of activity—education, health, welfare—we tolerated bureaucracy in order to achieve scale and efficiency. But once the ball started rolling, bureaucracy begot more bureaucracy; government grew larger and more distant. To this day governments follow the same basic formula, choosing distance and centralization for the sake of assumed—but rarely demonstrated—efficiency, all at the expense of accountability.

MVG: MINIMUM VIABLE GOVERNMENT

In Silicon Valley there is an overused cliché about when to launch your startup that nevertheless contains an element of wisdom: *minimum viable product*, or "MVP." It means you should get your business idea out in front of real customers as quickly as possible. If you wait until your product is perfect before you launch it, you're too late. Hence, MVP: the smallest, simplest version of your idea that might possibly work. When it comes to public policy our rule should be MVG—minimum viable government. To avoid the pitfalls of big, bureaucratic, inhuman government, we should always aim to decentralize power. Ideally, this would be directly to people themselves so they can make as many of the decisions that affect their lives as possible. That is typically how the richest and most powerful members of society live, and we should want those same freedoms for everybody. Power—and budgets—should be devolved to the level that is just large enough to be practical.

That's why I've always been a huge fan of directly elected mayors, a form of government that, despite being commonplace in America and many other parts of the world, is rare in the UK. That's a shame, because a directly elected local leader is recognizable, accountable, and responsive. Mayoral government is more human. It is also more pragmatic and often nonpartisan—mayors are *doers*. They might nominally identify with one party, but their typical concerns are fixing street lights, not bloviating about political controversies. They focus on getting things done because they literally have to live with the results. Making the buses punctual, the parks clean, and the city center thrive might not inspire intellectual debate in newspaper opinion pages, but they're the stuff of everyday life: they are what matter to most people.

It's not enough simply to *have* a mayor, though. Mayors must have real power to get things done. And sadly that's not the case everywhere. In San Francisco, for example, the mayor has very little power to really lead change: responsibility for crucial parts of daily life in the city is split between the mayor, the school district, and even distant Sacramento. The Board of Supervisors exerts a powerful and generally unhelpful check on positive action, and mayors in San Francisco have shied away from taking control of public schools. All of this is completely counterproductive: fragmented public policy responsibility prevents the mayor from actually implementing the kind of fundamental reforms that are sorely needed in this astonishingly divided and poorly run city, with massive wealth and technological know-how next to entrenched poverty, inadequate social services, and almost comically shambolic public transportation, to name just a few of many egregious local government failures.

As well as having the power to get the basic things done, mayors must also be able to experiment. The decentralization of power is the best way to generate and test new ideas, and in the United States, experimentalism is seen as a critical part of localism. Governors at the state level and mayors at the municipal level pioneer fresh approaches and policies that get adopted elsewhere in America and sometimes the world over. At least in this respect San Francisco provides a positive example in the shape of former mayor Gavin Newsom. In 2004 he presided over the first gay marriage in America. It prompted years of public debate, referenda, and legal wrangling, but the result is one of the biggest social changes in history, with the legalization of gay marriage sweeping across the United States and the world. That incredible, liberating revolution began in earnest with the conviction of an assertive mayor. President Obama's healthcare plan was based on the reforms of Mitt Romney, Massachusetts's former governor. Angel Taveras, the mayor of Providence,

Rhode Island, won the Mayor's Challenge (a prize established by Mike Bloomberg) for his initiative Providence Talks, which helps poor children close the 'word gap' (poor kids hear millions fewer words during childhood than their more affluent peers, hampering cognitive development).[49] In areas as diverse as civil rights, education, the legalization of medical and recreational marijuana, environmental protection, assisted suicide, food safety, the regulation of drones . . . in America change often starts at the bottom and trickles upward. It's even true in Japan, where the most recent advance in gay rights has come from a *district* in central Tokyo, Shibuya Ward, which announced in February 2015 that it would give same-sex couples the same legal rights as married heterosexual couples, a major step forward in a country that, although tolerant of homosexuality, grants gay couples relatively few rights.[50]

For all the problems of US government and politics, America has at least one thing right: for the best results, policy innovation cannot happen in a vacuum, and it cannot all come from the top. This role of local jurisdictions as "laboratories of democracy," articulated by Supreme Court Justice Louis Brandeis and based on the Tenth Amendment of the US Constitution, is deeply American, and we should encourage even more creativity, innovation, and risk taking at the local level.

POSITIVE DEVIANTS

Sometimes, however, the most human thing government can do is realize that people can solve their own problems. One particular expression of this idea holds great potential: the power of positive deviance.

In 1990 Jerry and Monique Sternin, workers for the charity Save the Children, moved to Vietnam to set up a program to fight child malnutrition in poor rural villages. While conducting surveys to understand the scope of the issue they grew curious about the handful of children who, despite coming from families as poor as all the others, were perfectly healthy—*the positive deviants*. What were these kids doing differently? If they could discover behaviors that enabled even the most materially deprived parents to raise healthy children, the implications would be tremendous. They found that *all* the parents of the positive deviants collected tiny shell pieces from crabs, snails, and shrimp from rice paddy fields and added them to their children's diet along with the greens from sweet potato tops. *None* of the other families did. Both these ingredients, though free and available to anyone for the taking, were commonly considered to be inappropriate, if not dangerous, for children and so were generally excluded from their diets. In addition, in five of the six positive deviant homes, parents were abnormally hygienic. Another difference: parents would generally feed their kids twice a day (before and after work in the fields). Parents of the positive deviants, however, instructed caregivers to feed their children regularly throughout the day. Though total daily calories were no different, because of the small stomach size of children under three, those with multiple meals were absorbing up to twice the nutrition with the same amount of food.

These findings enabled aid workers to set up homegrown educational programs that passed on the lessons to other parents. The beauty is that the solution required no more resources than the villagers *already* had. The answers to the problem were right there in the community with the people who lived there.[51] Imagine if we designed our domestic policy programs with a 'positive deviance' approach. Imagine if policymakers went to the very populations they were trying to help to find not just problems but solutions as well. Near where I live, in Oakland, California, a project called the Family Independence Initiative (FII) is doing just that.

Part of the problem of poverty, according to FII's founder Mauricio Lim Miller, is that government defines poor people by their problems, neglecting—and even inhibiting—what they're already doing well. So at FII, staff are explicitly *forbidden* to advise families or give them ideas. For 'helpful' people (as social workers tend to be), this is a very difficult— sometimes impossible—impulse to control. But stepping back is essential, as it creates a vacuum that families fill with their *own* ideas. "The best and most culturally relevant solutions are embedded in community," Lim Miller explains, "and people build and strengthen their social networks when they look to friends and neighbors who have successfully faced similar challenges."[52] FII provides income support on the condition that its clients record and make steps toward achieving basic goals on issues like income, debt, health, education, and relationships and that families meet once monthly to discuss their goals. Staff are allowed only to ask open-ended questions like: "What do you think should be done?" and "Do you know of anyone who successfully did what you want to do? Can you ask them for help?"[53]

According to Lim Miller, "When we respect families to lead their own change and give them access to resources the way middle- and upper-class people access them, they begin to transform their lives." It wasn't easy: families used to the traditional (literal) give and take of welfare programs were looking for direction from FII staff. After they received none, they started to share goals, then ideas. Sometimes it was clear that families were on their way to making a mistake.

Jorge and Maria-Elena were a recent immigrant couple, refugees from El Salvador's civil war. After seven months of meetings, in which Jorge and Maria-Elena had mostly talked about their health and their children's education, they declared they were going to buy a home. A Spanish-speaking real estate broker had promised them they could buy a house in their neighborhood, and friends would help them meet the down payment. It took all the self-control Lim Miller and his staff could muster to stop themselves from 'saving' the couple from what was—obviously to them—not going to be a rosy situation. But rather than intervene, Lim Miller told his staff to track them and simply accept that people had to make their own mistakes. The house was purchased, and the broker made his commission. But Jorge and Maria-Elena were now saddled with a mortgage that was 65 percent of their income. Losing the house seemed all but inevitable. Lim Miller felt bad, and his staff was upset they had let this happen.

But that's when the couple surprised them. "We had assumed the family was clueless," Lim Miller recalls, "but at some point they had recognized that they were in over their heads. They had included a refinance clause in their mortgage."[54] With the help of their friends, they renovated it, increasing its value so they could refinance the house and bring their mortgage down to 40 percent of their income. "From that point on," says Lim Miller, "I promised myself that I would try to avoid underestimating people's ability to solve their own problems." (The couple still own their home, by the way).

What makes this story interesting is the ripple effect that an organic, human success story has on others in the community. Now Jorge and Maria-Elena's friends knew what to do—and not to do—to buy a house. Two months after the refinancing everyone started saving more because they wanted to buy a home too, just like their friends. Within eighteen months the four other families in their FII cohort had purchased homes, but without using the predatory broker. By helping families find other families who succeed in overcoming problems associated with poverty, Lim Miller is building a self-perpetuating platform from which the working poor don't just walk away with lessons learned but also inspiration.

The results are clear: household incomes of the initial twenty-five families increased by nearly a third after two years. Moreover, 40 percent had bought new homes within three years.[55] A year after the program's payments ceased, household income still increased (now 40 percent higher than baseline).[56] After extending the program to San Francisco, the numbers continued to impress: amongst families there, in two years household income increased by an average of 20 percent, half of school-age children showed improvements at school, and three of five households reduced their debts. The initiative has since expanded to Hawaii and Boston, where within one year of its operations incomes increased 13 percent.[57] "When you come into a community that is vulnerable with professionals with power and preset ideas, it is overpowering to families and it can hold them back," according to Lim Miller. "But the focus on need undermines our ability to see their strengths—and their ability to see their own strengths."[58]

Lim Miller found that when people—even if just at the neighborhood level—are given a bit of responsibility over their lives, a bit of power, they wield it well. It's a lesson we need to apply throughout our system of government. We need to find ways to give power back to the people who can use it most effectively.

WE'VE GROWN USED to government that doesn't seem to respond to our needs. It seems to worry about the problems of someone else, somewhere else. When it does touch us, it seems endlessly bureaucratic. Government is not and should not be the solution for every problem. But where it is necessary, there is no reason for it to be so aloof and unresponsive. The imperative to shake it up is urgent. Those who serve in the public sector have an awesome responsibility; most are genuinely public spirited and well intentioned. Let's unshackle them from the structures that inhibit them. Let's change the accounting structures so we design policy for the long term, solving problems at their root causes. Let's change the working structures so we design policy based on real people's needs. And let's decentralize power, bring it closer to people, and put it directly in people's hands when we can.

If we do all this, we will certainly make government more human. We might even make it more popular.

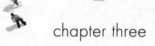

chapter three

SCHOOLS

SOUTH KOREA'S EDUCATION record is the envy of reformers around the world, with its students consistently topping international league tables. Korean students do well in tests, because preparing for tests is all they do. The competitive culture of Korean schools, in which all the students in a given class are ranked against one another, and the culture of Korean families, which equates academic success with family honor, means that when a student falls behind in class rankings, families pull out all the stops to ensure success. They might hire tutors or nag them to study. Or they might just send them to a *hagwon*. Hagwons are, according to Korean journalist and academic Se-Woong Koo, "soulless facilities, with room after room divided by thin walls, lit by long fluorescent bulbs, and stuffed with students memorizing English vocabulary, Korean grammar rules, and math formulas. Students typically stay after regular school hours until 10 p.m. or later."[1] According to Koo, who taught at one of these schools for a time, Korean students might succeed in the tests, but they suffer elsewhere. Koo remembers how his students lost clumps of hair, hardly slept, and were even suicidal (like half of Korean teenagers).[2] Suicide is in fact the leading cause of death for South Koreans aged fifteen to twenty-four.[3]

BY MOST MEASURES Palo Alto, California, is a stunning success story. One of the wealthiest municipalities in America, it lies at the center of Silicon Valley, is adjacent to Stanford University, and has some of the nation's best schools and recreation. But Palo Alto residents have another activity: volunteers patrol the railroad tracks. They aren't crossing guards, nor are they trying to stymie some crime epidemic.

They're trying to prevent the community's children from killing themselves.

"When it comes to tangible measures of success, I think a town's teen suicide rate is the better indicator than the number of kids with top grades or SAT scores."[4] Julie Lythcott-Haims is a Palo Alto parent with a unique perspective on our country's youth: for many years she was the dean of freshmen at Stanford. And although Palo Alto's children are amongst the brightest in the country, they kill themselves at an alarming rate.[5] "Here in Silicon Valley success seems to be admission to Stanford, a startup by the time you're a late teen or in your twenties, maybe a Tesla in your driveway," says Lythcott-Haims, who has now written a *New York Times* best-selling book on the subject.[6] "We have these trappings of success that we inadvertently ask our children to aim for when in fact it's the narrowest possible definition. And then we measure their accomplishment towards those goals by things like standardized tests. A score that is in the 99th percentile nationally is only in the 75th percentile in Palo Alto, and yet Palo Alto is a community that expects excellence of its kids. So even those who on a national scale are achieving on the highest possible level are made to feel mediocre here because it's virtually impossible for a child to distinguish themselves. This culture breeds in our kids a sense of hopelessness—that they'll never somehow make it from the 75th percentile into the 80th, 90th, and so on."

Palo Alto is obviously an extreme case, but it is not unique: the entire basis of America's school system is driving our sons and daughters to conform to a single, outdated version of education 'success'—and it's ruining their lives. "Colleges like Stanford seem to demand of a young person that they have a singular noteworthy achievement by age 17," says Lythcott-Haims. "It's become more and more of an arms race. Look at what we ask kids to do. And yet kids are chronologically the same as I was twenty years ago, and there's still only 168 hours in the week. . . . Kids try to do what they think is necessary in order to be successful, to meet their parents' approval and their community's standards. But to do so, they are mortgaging their childhood."[7]

This, it seems, is what it we are striving for. It is inhuman.

KHAN LAB SCHOOL

Jason Pittman didn't begin his professional life as a teacher. He started his own tech company, but when he found himself rushing home from work to get to his volunteer teaching gig, he realized it was time for a career switch. So he went to graduate school and soon afterward took a position teaching fifth graders at a public elementary school in Alexandria, Virginia, a suburb of Washington, DC. "I had such a wide variety of student need," Pittman recalls. "More than half our families lived below the poverty line. But we also had quite a few that were fairly well-to-do. We had first-generation immigrant families that were just getting started in the United States, and we had parents who were lobbyists on Capitol Hill.[8]

"I had a little girl from El Salvador . . . no English-language support at home. But she was reading out of a college geology textbook! She was so in love with understanding the earth better. I had another who was ten years old. He had left Somalia and was in a refugee camp in Kenya. He came into my classroom not having spent a day in school in his life. According to the school district I was supposed to be teaching him American history, fractions, reading comprehension . . . but none of it made any sense to him." What frustrated Pittman was the curriculum's absurd rigidity. "If I taught the fifth-grade lesson that was in the state's standardized curriculum, it was, no matter how hard I tried, the right lesson for absolutely nobody. I could make it an average lesson, but I could never really make it valuable to even one student in my class. There was such a wide variety."

One day he tried something different. "I pretty much threw up my hands and told the class: 'I'm so sick of disappointing you every day—what would you like to do? What would be something fun we could just do together?' A couple of kids wanted to build a robot, so we got some NXC chips [NXC is a programming language used with Lego robotics] and put them on robotics parts. We had a couple of kids who were into gardening, so we got them in the garden. The girl from El Salvador who was into geology, she ended up lecturing the class on types of rocks and how they were formed. All of a sudden it was fantastic—my students were doing well by every way I could assess them, even on standardized tests, and I didn't even teach to the test!"

Pittman then started to run a program aimed at preparing children for a science-orientated magnet school in the area. On a weekly basis he would teach science, math, and technology to all seven hundred students in his school, from pre-kindergarten to sixth grade. From the start Pittman diverged quickly from how science is typically taught. "The traditional science-lesson format starts with the teacher giving a concept, then explaining how it all works. You give a bunch of step-by-steps to prove that what I told you at the beginning of the lesson is true, and then I ask you to write a conclusion verifying what I told you at the beginning. There's no science in that at all, obviously. So I dropped the cookbook-recipe science format. I just said, 'Look, let's just rip out all the procedure pages from these lessons.' I basically said, 'Let's just play with this awhile—let's tinker with it.' And we used the question to actually get to the answer."

Pittman's lab quickly became a sanctuary for bored students across the school. "I left the lab open every day so they could come in and work on their projects," he remembers. "They could come down and work in the garden, work in the lab, and build their robot or their rocket or whatever it was they were excited about." Once again, it worked. Pittman's low-income students were closing the gap with their better-off peers. He was so successful that he's since won multiple national teacher-of-the-year awards. First Lady Michelle Obama visited his thirteen-thousand-square-foot educational garden, and he was twice selected as an 'educator-at-sea' for *National Geographic*, joining oceanographic explorer Dr. Robert Ballard (discoverer of the *Titanic*) on board his vessel E/V *Nautilus* to conduct lessons from maritime expeditions.

But then, out of the blue, Pittman's program was cut from the school's budget. Eliminated entirely. "It was so frustrating. I felt like I'd proven that we have a better way here, and we can actually serve kids and not serve tests." But that's not what the school was interested in. His methods couldn't be tested or quantified or regulated, so when the budget tightened, it was his program that was cut. Thankfully a group of local business owners and parents got together and started a charity specifically to raise money for his program. It was an imperfect solution, though. Pittman went from teacher to perpetual fundraiser. 'Every year I had to be a part of the advocacy, making speeches at fundraisers, raising my own salary. And I was still getting the same pressure to help kids practice multiple-choice tests."

So here was a teacher, recognized on a national level and achieving incredible results for low-income students, being forced to spend his free time raising the money to pay his own wages (which were, in any case, being systematically cut). He'd had enough. During an appearance on the public radio show *This American Life*, he described how he went to the Pentagon to receive a science-teaching award and then got back home to find another pay cut. "My frustration sort of hit a peak," he recalls. After talking to the host Ira Glass about what was going on, Pittman announced, on air, that he couldn't do it anymore. "As it turned out, making yourself available in front of 2 million people is not a bad way to find something else!"

A couple of months later the phone rang. It was Sal Khan, the hedge-fund analyst turned social entrepreneur who founded Khan Academy, one of the world's most popular online learning platforms. "I had been using Khan Academy in my classroom, so I thought it might be a joke." It wasn't. Sal wanted to start a school—a prototype for the school of the future, one that could literally help every school in the world teach children in a more human—and more effective—way. And Pittman would be just the right person to help it get going.

KHAN LAB SCHOOL is that prototype. Launched in September 2014 with a handful of children, it's a year-round, mixed-age, mixed-gender 'one-room-schoolhouse.' It is 'mastery-based' and free of grade levels and grade assessments, meaning that each child moves at a pace that's right for them. They aren't advanced just because the calendar says so. As Pittman explains, "We were trying to get kids to practice a certain skill until they can demonstrate it at a proficient level."

At Khan 'traditional' academic learning manifests itself in lessons by the teachers—sometimes one-on-one, sometimes in small- to medium-sized groups—as well as computer-based tutorials from Khan Academy and Udacity (whose founder we'll meet in Chapter 9) that mix videos and exercises students work through at their own pace. But this is combined with something much more radical. The students always seem to be building things. Like a giant ribcage made out of cardboard, paper, and papier mâché. They could have learned about a ribcage with a diagram or by passing around a plastic model, but these students learned by building one—big enough for them to stand inside. The project started out with students thinking about ways in which they were similar to one another. They used an online course from Udacity to learn about the human genome, discovering that our organs and internal systems are largely the same, which led them to zero in on the ribcage.

Pittman's philosophy as a teacher is that students should be 'makers' as well as learners. "There's a basic human desire to create things," he says. "If we can let that sit in the driver's seat, it will be much easier to get kids investing in their own education." One of the experiments at Khan Lab School was to devote the afternoon to creation time. "There's a high level of engagement because you're building these projects with groups of friends." Contributing to their own learning in this way also "eliminates the 'When will I ever use this?' question," says Pittman. "'Well, you'll use it this afternoon in the giant ribcage project,' I tell them." It's not just a free-for-all, of course: "We curate the content behind the afternoon projects in the morning. There's knowledge acquisition, direct instruction, and practice in the morning, and then you're putting those skills to work in the afternoon." For instance, to build the giant ribcage, his students applied the geometry they had been learning during morning lessons.

Self-directed projects like this aren't just a better way to engage students from hour to hour; they teach a broader set of skills that are essential to being a better learner overall, regardless of the subject. Traditional content areas—math, writing, reading, communication, art, music, and physical activity—are all important at Khan. But there's much more: teaching the skills that enable children to acquire knowledge themselves and, perhaps even more importantly, developing in them the intrinsic desire and motivation to do so. For over a century there has been a pervasive belief in education that you have to make children learn content in blocks of time, or 'lessons,' as we know them. Forty-five minutes of math, then English for forty-five minutes, and so on. The Khan Lab School philosophy is to turn this on its head—to replace the traditional 'extrinsically motivated' approach with a sense of independence and responsibility in the students themselves, with the freedom to choose what they work on when, what projects they choose to do, where to set things up, and so on. As Jessica Lahey writes in her book *The Gift of Failure*, "The quickest way to kill off your child's interest in a game, topic, or experiment is to impose your will on her learning."[9]

Although some students at Khan were at first not used to having so much ownership over what happens next or to having so much attention paid to things like 'perseverance,' 'cooperation,' and 'entrepreneurialism' alongside math and science, they bought into it pretty quickly. "Students have so much responsibility in everything—from setting up the furniture, setting up lunch every day, cleaning up . . . scheduling their own lessons if they think they need instruction. They're organizing around what the learning tool should be. And it's wonderful," says Pittman with a smile.

He is spot on. I know this firsthand. One of those kids he's talking about? He's my son Ben.

ACTON ACADEMY

If you want to see a school that is even more radically rethinking education, you should go—as Rohan and I did in 2012—to the Acton Academy in Austin, Texas. We were intrigued by this new school we had heard about and wanted to see what lessons it might hold for school reform in Britain.

Acton Academy, a school for five- to sixteen-year-olds, focuses on teaching character, not content. Started in 2009 by Jeff Sandefer, a Texas energy entrepreneur who later went on to found one of the top business schools in America, Acton uses the Socratic Method; its teachers are 'guides' who facilitate 'journeys' and 'quests' for the students, who work with each other to learn organically. Sandefer rejects the idea that students should be *taught* anything, reasoning that only a few teachers can be the best at teaching a particular subject anyway. In order to 'learn to know,' Sandefer uses games, activities, and technology to inspire children to seek out information for themselves, in the process holding themselves accountable for their own learning.

His curriculum also emphasizes 'learning to do.' Students take part in activities that build skills and give them real-world experience. In one instance, rather than read a storybook or hear a lesson on the American Revolution, students dressed up in eighteenth-century colonial costumes and simulated for three days the situation in the run-up to the War of Independence. By putting themselves in the place of the American revolutionaries, they didn't learn just history but also how to solve problems, negotiate, and empathize with others. Such character traits are central to the third part of the curriculum, 'learning to be.' Students take part in long 'hero's journeys' that have many steps on the way to an end goal, for instance finding 'the world's greatest treasure' stolen by an 'evil sphinx.' Each week the students have to overcome a new challenge to get closer to their goal. Along the way they act, perform role play, and practice public speaking, creative thinking, problem solving, decision making, and time management. These tasks inculcate honesty, patience, and gratitude.

Jeff Sandefer's ultimate vision is for a school with no teachers at all, where the students run the place entirely, the older ones taking responsibility for the younger ones, and all children collectively taking responsibility for the entire running of its community life. The level of responsibility and empowerment given to Acton students is far greater than in any university I have ever heard of, yet they are six, seven, eight years old and, as Rohan and I saw when we visited, thriving in this extraordinarily bold, innovative school regime. We looked on as a plan was being developed for the next school year: the ideas and themes that the students would be exposed to. They included Karl Popper on the scientific method and Nassim Taleb on 'antifragility.' Anyone who thinks that a more human, progressive, innovative style of education lacks intellectual rigor had better think again.[10]

Now there are fifteen Acton schools, with eight more in the pipeline. After his year helping to set up Khan Lab School, Jason Pittman moved on, but the experimentation keeps going, and Ben is still thriving. Chris Chiang, the academic director of Khan Lab School is in fact incorporating many aspects of the Acton approach in those experiments. As journalist Jason Tanz writes in his profile of the Khan Lab School in *Wired*, "The point here isn't just to build a better school but to refine a model that other educators can build on—to change education across the country and the world."[11]

FACTORY SCHOOLS

The terrible truth about our education system today is that it is more like South Korea's—children with hair falling out from stress and the highest youth suicide rate in the world—than the Khan Lab School, whose children negotiate with their parents to stay on at the end of the school day. We have dehumanized our children's education. Schools treat students like statistics, mandating lesson plans across regions—even countries—to hit specified test results. We obsess over how our children rank compared to their peers, both at home and abroad. If they aren't 'falling behind' the Chinese or the Singaporeans, they are falling behind each other or even themselves. The fact that Palo Alto—with its intense pressure, mental illness, stress, and suicides—is considered the pinnacle of our public education system is a harbinger of a serious problem.[12]

The regimented, top-down approach not only turns children off learning by treating them all the same; it also discourages teachers, the very people best positioned to respond to each child's learning needs. Industrialized, mechanized, centralized, today's education system is outdated and ineffective. Our children are mass produced in schools that are literally designed to resemble factories. This is a disastrous way to prepare children for their lives. It takes the creativity and individuality out of learning, forcing children into a common style instead of letting them evolve intellectually into independent-minded people. We need to leave behind the nineteenth-century mindset. It's time for more human schools.

THE ENTHUSIASTIC REACTION to the documentary *Most Likely to Succeed*, a damning indictment of our factory school system, shows that people are starting to understand how destructive it really is.

The culture of tests is a big part of the problem. Measuring students' success based on how well they do in an academic test is superficial. It

ignores the deeper learning that will actually help them thrive. Education policymakers' obsession with test scores, particularly in math, is in
part motivated by their own desire—need—to 'prove' the success of their
policies. It's also a way of evaluating teachers. But the price children pay
is relentless drilling and the neglect of unquantifiable skills that are actually—and increasingly—more important. Worse, if you examine the tests
forensically, they fail even on their own terms.

Consider PISA, the OECD's Program for International Student Assessment. It's the yardstick everyone uses. This might make some kind of
sense if it were an effective yardstick. But it isn't. Politicians trumpet
PISA scores as if they were a key factor in economic success, yet Germany and the United States, two leading global economies, lag behind
countries like Vietnam and Poland.[13] Many assume that the PISA rankings are based on rigorous, statistical analysis of educational data from
around the world. They're not. The scores are based on a one-off test
taken by a tiny sample of children in each country. And the test itself
is hopelessly flawed. It is long—two hours—and many students simply
don't finish.[14] Not all students are assigned all the questions or even all
the sections, so sometimes they are given a reading or math score without having answered a single reading or math question.[15] Considering its
international scope, the test obviously faces cultural challenges, but it
totally fails to address them: questions in different languages create in-
consistencies across countries, and some countries, particularly in Asia
teach directly to the PISA test, whereas other countries treat it as simply
something that is done casually once a year alongside whatever they're
doing anyway. Questions used in some countries are thrown out in others. The test also fails to take into account disparities within a country.
Using PISA tests to drive our education policy is the height of irresponsi-
bility. You might as well use some random opinion poll.

Perhaps its biggest flaw is the 'headline factor.' No matter the nuance
PISA notes within its reports, it is the league tables that get all the attention and drive headlines—and thus put pressure on policymakers. This
is the GDP of the education world, the metric that drives all yet includes
just a fraction of what matters. Yes, math is important. But because of
PISA, we focus on math excessively. To succeed in the twenty-first century economy, children need to learn to be creative and collaborative;
drilling them for tests fosters no skill except memorization, no character trait but individual ambition. Obsessing over math will not nurture
adaptable and entrepreneurial children but rather 'worker bots' who are
readily replaceable by technology. The culture of tests is a fitting symbol

for schools as factories, complete with bells, separate facilities, and batches of children. Yes, the basics of literacy, numeracy, history, and science—subjects taught and tested in factory schools—are important, but we also need to focus on developing the skills that will enable our children to succeed in a globalized, knowledge-based, rapidly changing world. Success is no longer just learning facts; it's about more human skills like empathy, self-regulation, conscientiousness, teamwork, resilience, problem solving, innovation, and critical thinking—skills that will give children a platform to build a successful, happy life.

These 'twenty-first-century skills' reinforce each other. Teamwork has been shown not just to improve output, communication, and planning but also—through increased engagement with others' ideas—to lead to even more learning and skills enhancement than going it alone.[16] Self-discipline has been shown to be more important than IQ in predicting academic performance.[17] And global CEOs consider creativity to be the most important leadership trait.[18] Factory schools that shame failure kill the impulse toward entrepreneurship and risk taking that we should most want to encourage. It also threatens the strength of our democracy: "In any complex society, differences of opinion are inevitable," Tony Wagner and Ted Dintersmith write in the book *Most Likely to Succeed*. "But consider how differently our country might approach these problems if most citizens were equipped with the ability to critically analyze, collaborate, communicate, and creatively solve problems."[19]

Our current education system is designed to ignore these vital skills. Creativity is consigned to art class. We say we're teaching critical thinking, but we test it with box-ticking exercises that have 'correct' answers, regardless of how thoughtful they are. Employers increasingly seek workers with empathy, but cognitive surveys of empathy among college students show steady declines since the 1980s.[20] We tell ourselves that students are allowed to plot their own intellectual journey, but really that just means choosing between chemistry and physics. And although we stress individual achievement, we forget the power of collaboration for success; humanity's most celebrated individuals almost all rely on (sometimes lesser-known) partners to achieve greatness.[21]

Schools have no incentive to think about social and emotional learning, character, or twenty-first-century skills unless they serve the very instrumental function of improving test scores. No student is graded on grit, no teacher evaluated on how entrepreneurial their students are. A study undertaken by psychologists collaborating across Oxford, Cambridge, and Exeter Universities shows that in schools, mindfulness, a calming technique based in Buddhism, reduces mental health problems, improves well-being, and makes children better students.[22] But it has no place in a factory school, in a world of tests.

All this is central to our arguments about inequality. "If you care about equity, schools are the only place where you can expose every child to the same chances," says Barbara Chow, the education program director at the William and Flora Hewlett Foundation. Children not exposed to social and emotional learning outside of school might not get it at all. This disadvantages them doubly: standardized tests have been shown to inherently disfavor less-fortunate students.[23] If those same students are also not gaining character skills, a test-based school system perpetuates inequality twice over. Indeed, the system seems insidious to Chow, who "suspects it produces what it is designed to produce: it's a sorting mechanism that perpetuates social order."[24] Every once in a while someone else gets through, and it's used as evidence that the system isn't rigged.

END THE TESTING MADNESS

We need to stop judging students and teachers by test scores. That doesn't mean abandoning tests entirely; used diagnostically, tests can help teachers track their students' progress, identify problem areas, and plan relevant lessons. They can also shed a light on inequity; civil rights leaders are strong supporters of standardized tests because they provide a way to compare poor black students in Compton or the Bronx to their wealthy white counterparts in Beverly Hills or the Upper East Side—test scores can identify and highlight injustice. But as soon as testing becomes a basis on which to sort students or, worse, judge them, we induce a damaging rat race.

Nowhere is this problem more acute than with the SAT and ACT, the bane of every college-bound high school student in America. Although these tests have improved—the new version of the SAT will focus more on analysis and less on vocabulary, for instance—and despite some progress through Congress's reversal in late 2015 of some of the worst over-testing aspects of the No Child Left Behind Act—the logic behind the testing regime in America's schools is still inherently counterproductive and the damage caused is still very real. These are standardized tests that rate on a curve. In the eyes of the test makers, America's high school students are there to be ranked. This approach, called *norm-referenced* by education wonks because students are graded relative to each other, is highly problematic and fundamentally doesn't work. Richard Atkinson, a former president of the University of California, and Saul Geiser, a scholar of higher education argue,

> Norm-referenced tests like the SAT and the ACT have contributed enormously to the "educational arms race"—the ferocious competition for admission at top colleges and universities. They do so by exaggerating the importance of small differences in test scores that have only marginal relevance for later success in college. Because of the way such tests are designed, answering even a few more questions correctly can substantially raise students' scores and thereby their rankings. This creates great pressure on students and their parents to avail themselves of expensive test-prep services in search of any edge. It is also unfair to those who cannot afford such services. Yet research on college admissions has repeatedly confirmed that test scores, as compared to high school grades, are relatively weak predictors of how students actually perform in college.[25]

No matter how academically proficient students might be, there are inevitable losers. If you don't do well on the SAT or ACT, the logic goes, you are not bound for success. What a ridiculous proposition—it's not as if those students simply leave the country. "It's just untenable," writes Frank Wu, the dean and chancellor of UC Hastings College of Law, "because 99 percent of us are not going to be in the top percent. If the choice is you must be *number one* or it's not worth trying at all, then none of us should even get out of bed. That's an insane standard to set; it wrecks people's lives when they feel that no matter what they've accomplished it will never be enough."[26]

If they are to become valuable contributors to our society and workforce, we need to rid ourselves of a system in which more than half our young people *must* be unsuccessful. Reformers like Atkinson and Geiser advocate a "criterion-referenced" test in which success is based on mastery of a subject, not speedy test taking or effective test-taking strategies and in which all students might theoretically do well if they have mastered the subject matter. Although this would be an improvement, it doesn't go far enough; ultimately students' academic lives would still depend on the results of a single standardized test.

Hampshire College, a liberal arts school in Massachusetts, stopped accepting SAT and ACT scores from applicants in 2014: "Standardized test scores do not predict a student's success at our college," explains Jonathan Lash, Hampshire's president. Instead, the school's admissions officers look for an "overarching narrative that shows motivation, discipline, and the capacity for self-reflection." As a result, the quantity of applications has decreased, but quality has gone up," Lash reports. "Applicants [give] more attention to their applications, including the optional components, putting us in a much better position to predict their likelihood of success here." Shifting away from standardized tests has had another, ancillary benefit: the percentage of students who are the first in their families to attend college has increased, as has the overall diversity of the student body.[27]

Instead of treating testing as the default method for organizing or evaluating learning, educators should have to justify every standardized test they administer. First, any standardized test whose purpose is to rank students, evaluate and compensate teachers, or admit students to a school or college shouldn't exist. Any test that does exist should only serve some valuable human function like individual student diagnostics or giving policymakers an idea of disparities between schools (in which case, results might be anonymized). Even then, educators should do everything in their power to find alternative ways of fulfilling those functions—standardized tests should *always* be a last resort.

TRUSTING TEACHERS

Putting tests back in their place is just the first step. We must also turn our attention to the school system's most human element. My friend and former colleague Michael Gove, the former UK education secretary, talks often about how the most powerful factor influencing the quality of education is the human part: the teacher. We have amazing people who enter the education world to share their gifts, and yet we shackle them, limiting their ability to do what they know is right, particularly through testing. "Exams are like limits for the teachers," says Sergio Juárez Correa, a somewhat rebellious—and, as a result, extraordinarily successful—public school teacher in Mexico. "They test what you know, not what you can do, and I am more interested in what my students can do."[28]

Correa teaches at the José Urbina López Primary School in Matamoros. A border city of half a million, it's a grim place, at the crossroads of an interminable drug war. The school is built next to a rubbish dump and has been nicknamed *un lugar de castigo*—"a place of punishment." Here children are lucky to survive childhood, let alone dream of careers and success.

As you'd expect, Juárez Correa's students were disengaged from the official curriculum, which bored even him, and their test scores were correspondingly low. He was desperate to try something different. According to writer Josh Davis, who profiled Correa and his students in the magazine *Wired,* he voraciously read educational materials online, trying to find something to stimulate both him and his students. It was on one of these searches that he discovered the work of Sugata Mitra, an educational theorist in Britain who experimented with giving computers to children in poor countries and letting them direct their own learning experiences through online material and lectures. Mitra's work, rooted in the methods of educational reformers like Maria Montessori and Jean Piaget, took hold of Juárez Correa, and he resolved to try it in his classroom. Perhaps, he thought, this was what would shake him and his students from their stupor?

On August 21, 2011, Juárez Correa walked into class on the first day of the school year. He told the children that they had potential and that "from now on, we're going to use that potential to make you the best students in the world." His approach would be completely radical: he didn't have computers, but he could pose open-ended questions and give his students as much autonomy as possible to work out the answers. For instance, instead of explaining fractions, he wrote on the whiteboard "1 = 1.00" and then wrote "½ = ?" and "¼ = ?". Although his training would suggest explaining the concepts of fractions, using Mitra's methods, he stayed silent and let his students stew it over. He brought various coins in to help them work it out; the students noticed that two half-peso pieces were the same as four quarter-peso pieces, prompting a debate on the nature of what one-half meant. One student, Paloma Noyola Bueno, quickly understood and helped convince the other students of how fractions worked, counting out the *centavos* for each side of the pile.

This streak of brilliance in Paloma, it would turn out, was not a fluke. One of the great tragedies in the world is the inequality of opportunity for the multitude of bright children who never get a chance with an education. It's not just tragic for them personally but for all of us: society will never gain from the gifts they have to offer. Whether through class barriers, infant mortality, or poverty, many don't get the opportunity even to go to school. The students in Juárez Correa's class had it better than most: they were at least there. And he was curious about Paloma: she excelled at relatively simple tasks like the basic fractions exercise and then others way beyond that. One day he raised the bar to a seemingly impossible height. He told the story of Carl Friedrich Gauss, an eighteenth-century mathematician, who, as a student, had famously answered an extremely difficult question in just a minute: Juárez Correa thought he'd try the same question, not expecting anyone—even Paloma—to solve it. So he asked the class: What is the sum of every number between 1 and 100? Within a couple of minutes Paloma raised her hand: "The answer is 5,050. There are 50 pairs of 101." It was so simple, so elegant, but so advanced for a child of Paloma's age. Juárez Correa, awed, asked Paloma, who had until then showed no real love for math, why she hadn't engaged before. "Because no one made it this interesting," she told him.

When national testing rolled around in June, Juárez Correa was anything but enthusiastic, but it had to be done. It was a good sign at least that his students breezed through it. Although Correa didn't put much stock in the results, even he was excited when he learned a few months later how good they were: the previous year 45 percent had failed math, and 31 percent had failed Spanish. Those numbers had now dropped to 7 percent and 3.5 percent respectively. But it was the highest-achieving students who proved a real shock. Three placed in the 99.99th percentile for Spanish, ten at the same level for math. Paloma had the highest score in the school: 921. When the school's assistant principal showed Juárez Correa the results, imagine his surprise when he moved the cursor over the high score for the region: it was 921. Then he moved it to the high score for the country. Paloma was the top math student in Mexico.

Without Juárez Correa's experimentation, his students would not have succeeded; instead of being feted in Mexico City and in articles read around the world, Paloma Noyolo Bueno might still be languishing next to a dump. Juárez Correa is the kind of teacher we need everywhere. We need to draw our most creative thinkers and doers from the rest of society into teaching as if it were the latest tech startup. We need our superstars to be teachers, our teachers to be superstars (even if fame is not the result).

ONE OF THE REASONS our system relies so much on tests is that we don't trust teachers. To see how successful a different, more human approach can be, we can look to Finland, home of one of the most successful—and decentralized—education systems in the world. In Finland schools are "small-scale democracies," according to Finnish education scholar, Pasi Sahlberg, with the only centralized aspects relating to professional requirements for teacher training and standards regarding learning outcomes (not teaching methods or test results). Teachers and school-level principals are given tremendous leeway in developing their own curricula, with the understanding that they know their own students and local conditions best.

In many circumstances policymakers would be concerned at placing such trust in education providers at a local level. Finnish officials solved this dilemma by putting only the very best people there to begin with. Good people don't need bureaucratic guidance to do what's right; they do what's right because responsibility lies with them and because they're good—and Finland is a land of unequivocally great teachers. Year after year Finland attracts all its new primary-teacher students from among the best graduates. To teach in Finland is so competitive that only one in every ten applicants is accepted for preparation. All Finnish teachers must earn a master's-level degree that includes theories of pedagogy and is research based. The expectation is that teachers learn not just to teach but to learn—and innovate and share what they find out—for the remainder of their careers. Teaching in Finland is a highly respected professional career, akin to being a medical doctor, lawyer, or architect (one poll even ranked teaching ahead of these three as being a "dream profession").[29]

It's not just that having good teachers enables policymakers to trust teachers without testing their students to death; not having the tests is what attracts and keeps the best teachers in the first place. It's a "culture of mutual trust," explains Sahlberg.[30] "Although the pursuit of transparency and accountability provides parents and politicians with more information, it also builds suspicion, low morale, and professional cynicism."[31] By the time they enter upper-secondary school, Finnish students will have *no* experience of taking high-stakes tests, progress instead being judged differentially by their teachers against students' respective characteristics and abilities.

So what happens when you let highly trained and respected teachers on the loose with no standardized tests to hold them accountable? You get a fantastic education system. Though most Finnish educators think PISA exams measure only a narrow band of what's important (one of the reasons they prefer no standardized testing is that it allows more time to be spent on 'noncore' subjects like art and music), the country scores exceedingly well on them, often placing first or second among other countries in math, science, and reading since the early 2000s. Yet Finnish fifteen-year-olds spend less time on homework (about thirty minutes per day) and in class than peers anywhere else.[32] And teachers spend almost five hundred fewer hours in the classroom per year than their American counterparts.[33] They understand that if quality is high and circumstances right, *less* teaching can mean *more* learning, as most students can only absorb so much in a passive lecture format anyway. They have to be out exploring, investigating, and arguing with their peers.

IN MANY FIELDS it's taken for granted that only the best can join. Teaching should be one of them. We need to elevate its position in our society. We should pay teachers more, hold them in high regard, and then hold them to the high standards they deserve. We need to trust them, treat them like professionals. As we'll see in the next chapter, doctors and nurses are distracted from caring for their patients when bureaucracy becomes too burdensome. The same is true for teachers who are subject to a huge number of regulatory and reporting requirements. If we respect our teachers, then instead of being recalcitrant labor unions, our teachers' associations could be an arbiter of professional quality like their counterparts in medicine, law, and engineering. As leading British educational reformer Sir Anthony Seldon puts it, "If teachers are to have the status of [these] other professions, they need to have a serious professional body at their head."[34]

Teacher unions certainly have their merits. In many places teachers face hostile work environments and are capriciously fired for teaching correct but unpopular views. Equally important, teachers are consistently underpaid in the United States, and unions have helped to secure better pay and benefits for their members. But there is an unavoidably insidious side to teacher unions: as much as they purport to represent students, they must always answer to their members' interests first. And the interests of teachers don't always coincide with the interests of their students.

Take teacher tenure, an issue that is the subject of several high-profile court cases. Of course no one should be fired arbitrarily or punished without due process. But tenure shouldn't protect bad teachers by giving them a free pass for life or make it unduly difficult to be fired if they're no good. As they do in private and charter schools, principals should be able to get rid of ineffective teachers. This issue was at the center of the *Vergara v. California* case decided in June 2014 and currently working its way through the appeals process. In *Vergara* nine public school students filed suit contending that by assigning them to ineffective teachers, the school districts were violating their civil rights. Unsurprisingly the court found in favor of the students. The disparities resulting from the "significant number of grossly ineffective teachers currently active in California classrooms . . . shock[s] the conscience," the judges wrote. Citing the plaintiff's evidence that to fire a bad teacher might take from two to ten years and cost anywhere from $50,000 to $450,000, the court found that tenure amounts to "*uber* due process [original emphasis]" that fails to equally protect the rights of students. Finally, the court found the "logic" of the "last in first out" provision "unfathomable," declaring it unconstitutional.[35]

I agree with teacher unions that good teachers ought to be protected and paid well. They should be afforded due process, allowed to teach important but controversial topics like sex ed and evolution in the face of parental opposition, and certainly shouldn't be judged on the basis of test scores. But it would be better if educators were treated like the professionals they are and on the same basis as those in other sectors. There has always been an implicit deal: teachers trade less pay for job security through tenure. Well, let's phase out tenure but pay them more (as Finland does), and let's pay them on their performance. Yes, this would penalize some teachers, but only the bad ones. And yes, it would jolt the system because America, unlike Finland, is not the land of universally good teachers. But as long as the current system stays in place, it never will be.

We could also trust students more. Instead of complicated, top-down systems for measuring teacher effectiveness—that aren't that useful anyway—why don't we just ask the students what's going on? One study found that asking students how much they agree or disagree with specific statements such as "In this class, we learn to correct our mistakes" or "My teacher wants us to share our thoughts" can tell you quite a lot. These questions allow for nuance; they are intentionally vague, making them both harder to game but also, more importantly, leveling the playing field between subjects that are easily quantified (math) and those that aren't (teamwork).[36]

A more human way of evaluating teachers is ever-more vital as we see a new threat of standardization and centralization coming over the horizon. Media companies like Pearson, Disney, McGraw-Hill, and Houghton-Mifflin Harcourt, some of which already own school textbook publishers, are also pushing into the classroom, leveraging education technology as a new sales and marketing strategy to get as many eyeballs as possible on their products.[37] Instead of repudiating the old factory model of standardized tests and all the depressing bureaucracy that surrounds them, these so-called reformers want more. In a Pearson report ominously titled "Preparing for a Renaissance in Assessment,"

authors Peter Hill and Michael Barber, in a shockingly blunt embrace
of the worst aspects of the factory-schools model, argue against teacher
autonomy and in favor of top-down testing to put them in their place:
"Without such a systematic, data-driven approach to instruction, teaching remains an imprecise and somewhat idiosyncratic process that is
too dependent on the personal intuition and competence of individual
teachers."[38] This desire—mania, really—to produce endless data, fed by
tests, is pure centralization. Uber-centralization, where teachers are the
problem and tests are the answer, where testing is a "solution" not to the
pedagogic challenge of educating children but to the management challenge of running a school.

If we end standardized testing, empower teachers, and close the factory schools, what should rise in their stead? Can we really have an education system designed to meet the modern world's dynamism and in-
terconnectivity? Rather than a lumpen, monolithic travesty designed for
the needs of the 'average' child, is it possible, on a mass scale, to teach all
our children in a way that puts each of them first, as humans?

DECENTRALIZING EDUCATION

New York City's education system used to be characterized by huge public schools with a capacity of up to three thousand each. They were disproportionately attended by poor and minority students, who had grad-
uation rates as low as 40 percent.[39] When Mayor Michael Bloomberg
came into office he set out to close these 'dropout factories.' He closed
many large failing high schools and replaced them with small specialized
ones. Called Small Schools of Choice (SSCs), they follow a localized,
competitive model: they were created independently by community
organizations featuring year groups no larger than a hundred students,
built around different themes, with personalized learning. These new
small schools are holistic; given that most of the students are at risk of
dropping out, they also offer community and social-service support. In
these new small schools 71.6 percent of students graduate, as opposed
to 62.2 percent in normal schools; among black male students, an especially vulnerable demographic, 42.3 percent enroll in college, compared
to 31 percent at conventional schools.[40] All this at a lower cost per student, because fewer students now need an extra year to finish. New York
is showing that moving to smaller, locally controlled schools—just like in
Finland—can make a big difference.

These examples and others, like Khan Lab School, Acton Academy, and many more, show us that there are now real alternatives to the century-old, one-size-fits-all school. These modern alternatives offer new and effective ways of educating our children, but the dominance of factory schools remains a structural barrier to a more human education system. Until, like Mayor Bloomberg, we actively close them down, the vision of educating most children in fresh, innovative, and more human ways will remain just that.

Some point to charter schools as the answer to removing this structural barrier. Charters are independent schools within the local state system. They're not private or fee paying, but they can avoid the rules and curricula forced on mainstream schools. They have a long heritage, first proposed as alternatives to conventional schools in the 1970s. Minnesota passed the first law permitting them in 1991, followed by California the following year. Presidential candidate Jeb Bush led the drive to legalize charter schools in Florida, overseeing as governor their proliferation across the state. He also made Florida the first state in the country to implement vouchers, allowing parents to choose where to send their children to school. Now charter schools are present in almost every state. Incredibly diverse, they take many forms—including small schools, large schools, schools operated by corporations, and schools that emphasize a variety of different themes and skill sets. All in all, charter schools have had some great successes.

But there's a problem. The charter school movement—major advance though it is—still doesn't address the underlying structural issue: that there are simply not enough fresh, innovative, and more human schools on offer. There are just under one hundred thousand public schools in the United States, and only six thousand of them are charters. But charters enroll far fewer students overall, under 4 percent of those in public education.[41] They're a sideshow to the current factory school model. And although many charter schools are small and autonomous, large corporate charter school chains—that are no less factory schools than many traditional public schools—are increasingly common.

CHANGING THE STRUCTURE OF THE SYSTEM

To provide more human schools for every child, we need to go deeper— to the very structure of the system. *Factory schools* is not some pejorative term plucked out of thin air. Our education system today is rooted

in the Industrial Revolution. Charles Dickens captured the essence of
the industrialized-education mindset in the form of Thomas Gradgrind,
the headmaster in his novel *Hard Times*. Gradgrind is determined to
suppress his students' imagination with facts, seeing children's transformation into machines as the ultimate educational virtue. William T.
Harris, the US commissioner of education at the end of the nineteenth
century, praised the direction schools were taking at the time. That a
"modern" school had the "appearance of a machine" was the very quality
that proved its worth. Machine schools, he found, fostered "punctuality,
silence, and conformity to order."[42] Perhaps Harris is excused by the context of his times: obedient factory workers were needed in abundance, as
those with "semi-mechanical virtues"—his words—were both more productive and less accident prone. Though it's hard to say which came first,
factory schools are perfectly intertwined with the government bureau-
cratization and centralization we discussed in the last chapter. Centralization, after all, is an industrial factory's distinguishing feature. Mass
manufacturing extended to the people who made the products: a standardized workforce required schools to work in concert, each producing
the same type of student. In a world where state legislatures control the
structure and delivery of our children's education from distant state capitals, a diverse schooling system would be complete anathema.

But because outputting uniform workers is no longer society's goal,
we need to move on. The centralization of our school system distorts and
deforms, giving power to those in charge but conferring almost no advantage on those who should come first—our children. Schooling, by its nature, should be a local, intimate process. We're so used to the status quo
that most of us never stop to acknowledge the fact that parents and teachers don't need the bureaucracy of the school system at all—the school
boards, education departments, and endless government officials getting
involved. In fact, you could argue that the whole regime of standardized
tests exposes this reality. Parents and teachers don't need standardized
tests to know which children are performing well and which need more
attention. We accept tests as the best way to monitor our students' learning, when really they're just the only tool distant administrators have at
their disposal. We 'need' the tests, because *they* need the tests. But the
deeper truth is, we don't actually need the administrators. In many ways
getting rid of them is even more important than getting rid of the tests.

Of course, we need a centralized education authority for a few specific things: the fair distribution of funding across regions and towns, an
accreditation process to ensure that not just anyone can claim to run a
proper school, some basic common standards to ensure that children are

taught what they're supposed to be taught—history that celebrates America's achievements without ignoring its abuses, for instance, or science that doesn't teach creationism as scientific theory. But that's about it.

In today's debate the discussion around the role of a centralized education authority focuses on the vexed issue of Common Core. Common Core is the most recent iteration of a concerted effort to give students across the country the same baseline. Working with governors, a team of education experts identified the skills and knowledge that, in their view, students ought to have. Proponents like former New York City Schools chancellor Joel Klein argue that Common Core is a necessary establishment of common standards. Identify the essential skills and knowledge that students should have at different points in their education, the thinking goes, without mandating *how* those skills are taught. For instance, one standard might be that at a certain grade level students can read the hour hand of the clock. This gives teachers space to determine *how* to teach that skill. Others argue that Common Core is a usurpation of local control of education, an unwarranted centralization of education that takes power away from the states who have traditionally had it.

This politicization and polarization of the debate into big government vs. states' rights isn't just overly simplistic; it isn't useful. Although I would be the first to argue that centralization of education has been a damaging and dehumanizing trend, Common Core is not the Frankenstein's monster of centralization it's been held out to be; indeed, its creators arduously consulted with states when they created it. When states opt out and make their own standards, they resemble Common Core.[43]

But the entire argument misses the point. The crux of the problem is the structure of the school system and the fact that public schools are run by bureaucracies rather than teachers accountable directly to parents. Frankly, whether the bureaucracy in question is the federal government, the state, or even the local district, it's still the wrong way of organizing education. We don't need any of them, and they all need to go. It should be about individual parents, individual teachers, and individual schools. We need a radical—indeed total—decentralization of the system.

REAL SCHOOL CHOICE

To do that, we must dispense once and for all with the idea that the right way to run education is for government to provide 'a good local school' in every neighborhood. The lazy philosophy of 'one school per neighborhood' is exactly what has led to the outdated factory school model we need to get away from. Even if government authorities give 'autonomy' to a local school, even if the local school is run as a charter or independent of formal bureaucratic control, the problem is that there is one local school—a monopoly. As in other areas of life, it's the fact of the monopoly that does the damage, that enables—indeed requires—standardization and a factory approach.

Yes, you can point to individual examples—wonderful, creative, innovative public schools within the current local monopoly structure. Lucky you if you happen to live near one. But these are the exceptions. Why shouldn't every child, everywhere, have the right to an exceptional education? That will only happen if we end the local school monopoly. Progress comes from innovation, innovation comes from competition, and competition comes from choice.

Of course 'school choice' has been a political slogan for decades. But the kind of choice that proponents of this idea usually argue for is barely choice at all. It's the illusion of choice—between one dominant school in an area and one alternative, or maybe, in larger towns and cities, between the closest big school and four or five others within a reasonable distance. It's no surprise that critics of school choice have found a receptive audience for their argument that this "isn't parents choosing schools, but schools choosing parents." I agree.

To get to a more human education system, one that gives every child the chance to go to a school that is perfect for them—whether that's something like the extreme entrepreneurial innovation of Acton Academy or the more mainstream version in Finland, whether it's a traditional school or a progressive one, an academic curriculum or one focused on character—whatever it is, whatever is perfect for every child (knowing that no two children are the same), the only way to achieve this is something wildly, fantastically more radical than anything we've seen or talked about up until now. Not just the odd boutique school here and there, not just two or three, or four or five, or even eight or ten schools in every area. I mean twenty, thirty local public schools for parents to choose from, schools that are smaller (a reasonable aim for a human-scale school would be, perhaps, 150 to 300 students) and schools that offer whatever approaches they think might attract parents and children in that neighborhood. Each child is unique, as is each teacher. In order to thrive they need to be able to find the school that fits them, that fits their uniqueness. This is what a more human education means.

We need a completely open, local marketplace for schools. Teachers, educational entrepreneurs, and groups of parents must be permitted to set up schools, free of bureaucratic restrictions and hassle. Parents should have a free choice of where to send their children, and a voucher should follow that choice. Government's role in the public school system would focus on fair funding and licensing, making sure that all children have equal access to a school and that only fit and proper individuals and organizations are permitted to establish and run them. School boards as we know them would become a thing of the past—along, it is to be hoped, with the factory schools that are their raison d'être.

To make sure that the local schools marketplace is truly fair and egalitarian, we must not discriminate against different types of schools run along different lines. Government-owned schools, charter schools, nonprofit social enterprises, for-profit schools . . . as long as they are all funded on a fair basis and are free rather than tuition-paying, true educational diversity means all of these being given an equal chance to offer children a great education in the public school system. It's particularly important that we should allow organizations that make a profit to run schools. The current discrimination against "profit-making schools" is random and bizarre, given that huge chunks of public school operations—the technology, the textbooks, the buildings, the testing(!)[44]—are provided by for-profit companies. I'm not quite clear why the idea of making profits is okay for all those activities but not for running schools. In fact, one of the most inspiring examples of social justice, emancipation of the poorest, and the transformative power of education that I've ever seen was a visit to a profit-making school. It happened to be in one of the world's worst slums, in Lagos, Nigeria.

JAMES TOOLEY, A PROFESSOR of education at Newcastle University, has helped establish and champion private, for-profit schools in some of the poorest parts of the world. These schools are transformationally better than the failing state-run schools so depressingly propped up by corrupt local bureaucrats, the United Nations, international aid, and the whole panoply of sanctimonious, ignorant, hypocritical hand-wringers who argue that the evil "profit motive" mustn't violate the noble innocence of education. (Oh, wait, apart from the private schools and private tutors used by the policymakers and pundits who peddle those views.)

When we were accompanying the prime minister on a 2011 visit to Africa, Rohan and I asked to see one of James Tooley's schools in one of the worst slums in Lagos, Nigeria. Whereas the UK-government-backed, state-run school was a disaster, the Tooley-backed for-profit school was a sensation: eager children in pristine uniforms learning literacy, math, science—with the help of a solar-powered computer. This is in the middle of a slum. Literally. To get there, Rohan and I had to pick our way through stinking, festering garbage, open sewers, ramshackle structures that could and would be washed away by the next rains. To arrive at that school, peep over the makeshift wall, and see rows and rows of eager pupils happily studying in the midst of utter chaos and squalor was completely astonishing, incomparably inspiring.

Let me repeat: this is a for-profit school. The parents—all of whom live in the slum, the poorest people in the world, part of that economic category lightly bandied around as 'living on less than a dollar a day'— these parents, who earn less money in a year than a liberal commentator who rails against 'profits in schools' would spend on a good lunch, choose the for-profit school over the free, state-run alternative. Why? Because it's better. And surely that's all we should care about—the quality of the education, not the organizational form, right?

SOME MIGHT SAY that the argument I've set out here is crazy: there's no way that in America we can abolish the state education authorities; get rid of monopoly state, city, county provision of public schools; close down local school boards; and create a completely open local schools marketplace. There's no way we can bring the kinds of educational approaches I've described in this chapter into the mainstream—they go way too far for most people. There's no way parents have either the time or the inclination to evaluate schools and choose between them in a local marketplace. In the innocuous but devastatingly destructive cliché, 'parents just want a good local school.'

Think of the parents in Nigeria, who actively sought out James Tooley's school. They live in one of the world's poorest slums and fight every day for access to clean water, shelter, and enough food to eat. Yet they take the initiative to find the best education for their children. If they, with everything stacked against them, can take an active role in education and choose a better local alternative, of course parents in America can too. Yes, there are some dysfunctional families who would struggle to do the best for their children in an open schools marketplace. But why should everyone else be denied the choice of a more human education just because of a problem few?

Critics of decentralization and choice ask how parents can decide on schools without a metric, some standardized measure to compare one school with another, based on a test of some kind. But the premise of the question is intrinsically flawed: tests can tell you something but not the most important things: the human things. Parents and students know what a good school is without looking at statistics. They just need to visit the school. They get a feel for the principal, the teachers, the building, the environment, the culture. I wrote earlier about the importance of trusting teachers and students. If we trust students and their parents, we can empower them to fuel a revolution in education.

Critics might also point to Khan Lab School or Acton Academy and say they're elite because they are private and tuition paying. Yes, they are. But why shouldn't we make the best, most innovative education available to everyone? Universities, secondary schools, even teaching basic literacy were once elite activities until we decided they were for everyone. The same applies here: Why should the best in education be a luxury for the few?

And this brings us to the final big change we need to make. In order to make a radically *decentralized* school structure work for the benefit of all, we need to go in the completely opposite direction in one crucial area: funding.

Making sure our children have an equitable start is one of the most important tasks of society, and schools are one of the most important institutions in a child's life. We should be troubled by the fact that different children in different places have vastly divergent and unequal experiences. The current school funding system, based on property and local taxes, is unfair and damaging. Wealthy communities enrich their public schools, whereas poor communities cannot, and the schools consequently lag behind. To make a local school marketplace work, funding needs to be centrally determined and distributed on an equitable basis. That's right: education should be funded on a per pupil basis across America. With the exception of variations based on objectively assessed regional cost differences, every child should have the same pot of money attached to their education—the value of the local school voucher.

This also means clamping down on another way in which inequity creeps into the system: private donations to schools. As Stanford professor Rob Reich argues, "Wanting to support your own children's education is understandable, but it also has unintended, pernicious effects," he writes. "When donors give to their own child's school or district, they are making a charitable contribution that the federal government treats in the same way as a donation to a food bank or disaster relief." Except this donation is essentially a tax-deductible form of private consumption for the children of the wealthy, no different from purchasing a piano or tak-ing a vacation. "Private giving to public schools widens the gap between rich and poor."[45]

So we need to discourage donations to individual schools. The mil-itary doesn't depend on bake sales and fundraising drives for fair and equitable funding to defend all of the country, so why should schools do so to educate all of our children? Government has the responsibility to fully and fairly fund schools, period. If parents and philanthropists wish to help fund schools, great. Let them contribute to a fund for a wide area so that its proceeds might be fairly and equitably shared. For too long Americans have used tax write-offs and real estate wealth to entrench educational advantages for their children at the expense of others'. That is not just inhuman; it is un-American.

THESE SOLUTIONS MIGHT seem extreme, but at their heart they are human. They simply involve trusting parents, teachers, and students. We need to shake up a system that has failed so many of our children. Piecemeal re-form has only made a small difference for a few. It's not enough: we need to fundamentally change our mindset toward learning, a mindset stuck for over 150 years. As long as education is centralized and run by govern-ment—whether federal, state, or local—as long as schools are factories, our children will suffer. They will continue to be treated like outputs, like commodities, like cogs in a machine. But children are not products. They are our future, and they deserve to be treated like individuals. It isn't about ideology; it's about the values of our society. Surely we want to live in a world that prizes creativity, rewards ingenuity, and fosters bril-liance? Our school system today is designed to crush these things. Let's create a system that encourages and inspires all of our children. Let's close the factory schools and make our schools more human.

chapter four

HEALTH

THE MEDICAL ADVANCES of the last century—even just the last decade—are nothing short of astonishing. We're living longer and fuller lives than at any prior point in human history. The things doctors can now do to improve the quality of our lives can often seem miraculous. And with the application of data science and gene technology to medical problems, we can expect this progress to accelerate, perhaps exponentially. For a good part of the last century there's no doubt that large-scale factory health care enabled health outcomes never before experienced. But we're in a new century now; science and technology have evolved to make this model out of date. With no more excuses to prop up the big, bureaucratized health system, it's time we moved on—because ignoring the human side of health care really misses the point.

As Dr. Elaine Goodman will testify.

SOME OF DR. GOODMAN'S most profound lessons in taking care of patients came not from her formal training but from the bedside of her sixty-three-year-old mother, where she sat many days after just having finished the first year of medical school. Though her mom was in the hospital to battle breast cancer, it seemed as if most of the time she was actually fighting the hospital, a nationally ranked facility near Seattle.

"My mom was on a seizure medication that needed the dose adjusted according to her nutritional status," Goodman recalls. "The physicians probably knew this, but with all the handoffs, a new doctor would come in, see the drug level was low in her blood—without carefully observing her nutrition—and then up the dose." As a result of these overdoses, Goodman's mom would sleep for days. "As somebody who has a life expectancy in the order of months, those days were very important to us."

But it got worse. Dr. Goodman's mom was being treated with a chemotherapy drug. Normally her oncologist would administer it on the weekend, and the therapy would last the rest of the week. But one weekend when the oncologist wasn't on duty, the covering physician not only gave her the wrong chemotherapy drug but administered it on the wrong day, a potentially life-threatening mistake: "My mom had effectively gone for a week without getting any treatment," recounts Goodman. "For her this probably didn't change her life expectancy drastically. . . . But this event itself was really terrifying. It had the potential to make a huge difference in the life expectancy of other patients." Goodman is sure that how her mother was treated in the hospital hastened her decline.[1]

This kind of story is all too typical in our healthcare system today: patient volume is high, physicians and staff are overbooked and forced to multitask, and distraction and fatigue are endemic. According to a recent study in the *Journal of Patient Safety*, approaching half a million patients suffer from some type of preventable harm that contributes to their unnecessary death each year in the United States. The figure—much higher than was previously believed—makes medical error now the third-leading cause of death in this country, behind only heart disease and cancer.[2]

It's easy to think of patients' poor treatment as an isolated issue or simply to blame doctors and nurses. But it's much worse than that. These incidents reflect a deeper, structural problem in how we think about health care, a problem that is at least as—if not more—important than our all-consuming debates about its funding. 'Obamacare,' 'single-payer,' 'choice of plan'—we never stop talking about how health care is paid for. It's time we also focused on how it's provided.

America's healthcare system is increasingly dominated by vast, bureaucratic, behemoth institutions that are losing touch with the human aspects of health care. By consolidating medical operations in gigantic centralized hospitals, we have created a clinical environment that actively fights intimacy and personalized care. The vast American hospital-insurance-pharmaceutical complex—now roughly the size of France's economy—that we have allowed to bloat, unchecked, has taken something that should be the epitome of humanity—what could be more human than to care for others?—and sent it down a path of industrialization, mechanization, and dehumanization. It's not the fault of the doctors, nurses, and support staff; as in so many other areas of life, it's the structure of the system that's to blame.

FACTORY HOSPITALS

It's hard to care in a factory hospital. Go to a hospital today, and it can be an ordeal: navigating the large parking lot, walking what feels like miles through corridors, traveling in giant elevators before finally reaching a soulless waiting room where you have to sit endlessly to be called. Need a test? Walk through another mile of corridors to another soulless room. Then wait hours or days for the results. This only describes the experience of people who are outpatients. For those who are admitted, it gets worse. Patients eat factory food—how else to serve it in such an institution? But the worst part is that they are seen as outputs: treatments are commodified, tests done without doctors ever entering the room, medicine performed on and around the patient but seldom *with* the patient.

Behind the treatment is a vast and costly bureaucracy. A nationally representative survey of 4,720 physicians found that each spent on average 8.7 hours per week on non-patient-related paperwork—at a total cost of physician time of $102 billion per year.[3] Moreover, greater time spent on administrative work correlated with lower career satisfaction. "Our crazy health financing system is demoralizing doctors and wasting vast resources," Dr. David Himmelstein, one of the study's authors, noted.[4]

Meanwhile nurses and medical assistants spend on average 20.6 hours per week interacting specifically with health plans—that is, with insurers and government payers. This compares to just 2.5 hours in Ontario, where nurses need only interact with Canada's single-payer agency. Reducing our red tape to match Ontario's would save us $27.6 billion per year.[5]

According to a study in the journal *Health Affairs*, hospital administrative spending is also outsized compared to advanced-country peers. In the United States it works out at $667 per person across the entire population. In the Netherlands it's only $323, $225 in England, and $211 in Wales. In Canada it's only $158. One reason? Billing in the US system is extraordinarily complex: each insurer has different payment rates, rules, and documentation requirements that only add to the burden.[6]

And as Big Health gets bigger, the bureaucracy is getting worse. With providers merging and consolidating, the bureaucracy increases, driving costs up further. Doctors who practice in groups of one hundred or more spend more time (19.7 percent) on administration than their counterparts in smaller groups (16.3 percent).[7] "Seldom does consolidation result in reduced costs for consumers," wrote the American Academy of Family Physicians in a letter to the Federal Trade Commission.[8] In a study published in the journal *Health Management, Policy and Innovation*, economists found that the 2007 merger of UnitedHealth Group and Sierra Health Services in Nevada was unequivocally bad: "If there were

any benefits to consumers realized from the merger, we could not observe them," the authors wrote. Meanwhile the merger caused premiums
to go up by 13.7 percent.[9]

But insurers and providers don't just grow larger to compete against
each other; becoming dominant buys political power, which leads to
rules and regulations in their favor. The Affordable Care Act was only
made possible by a series of backroom deals, facilitated by the $273 mil-
lion spent on lobbying by the healthcare industry in 2009,[10] in which
cost savings, such as the government reducing Medicare payments on
hospital care or prescription drugs, had to be carefully 'negotiated'—lest
the Obama administration face a nationwide barrage of antireform advertisements from the industry.[11] At one point during negotiations in
2009 the five largest insurance companies collectively contributed $86
million to a political action committee to be used for negative ads just in
case it became necessary.[12]

Obamacare is not the focus of this chapter. The Affordable Care Act
was not trivial—indeed, just the opposite. But too much of the debate
around health care focuses on the economics: How do we cut costs, increase coverage, set up the right incentives? It misses some fundamental
points about the kind of care we get. Of course we must debate payment
models, funding sources, and coverage limits—these things *are* vital. But
they're just one part of a much bigger picture. The debate neglects the
larger system of which it's all a part, and in overlooking the system and
its foundational structure, we overlook the actual impact it has on the
actual care at the point of the actual patient. This *human* part of health
care is rarely discussed.

iPATIENT, OR REAL PATIENT?
The argument for the status quo is that our standardized, bureaucratized, factory hospitals, healthcare providers, and insurers are 'efficient': they bring together the expertise, technology, and facilities
needed for specialist procedures, operations, and complex treatments.
Efficiency, of course, is the argument for many things, especially the
role of technology in health care. Used well, technology can be posi-
tively transformative in health care just as in other fields. But it can also
hinder care by putting efficiency ahead of the patient. Stanford medical
professor Dr. Abraham Verghese is an evangelist for the physical examination for this very reason. "I joke, but I only half-joke, that if you
come to one of our hospitals missing a limb, no one will believe you till
they get a CAT scan, MRI or orthopedic consult." Technological tests

can be invaluable, but not when doctors rely on them too much or even forsake actually examining the patient. "I've gotten into some trouble in Silicon Valley," Verghese says, "for saying that the patient in the bed has almost become an icon for the real patient who's in the computer. I've actually coined a term for that entity. . . . I call it the iPatient. The iPatient is getting wonderful care all across America. The real patient often wonders, where is everyone? When are they going to come by and explain things to me?"[13]

If technology replaces human contact when healing is what's called for, it makes health care less human. But interestingly, when it replaces the *bureaucracy* of health care, technology can make it more human. Used right, technological advances can create more space for doctors to interact with their patients. As technology gets cheaper and smaller, going to a big factory hospital will be less and less necessary; instead, local doctors will be able to use devices like GE's Vscan. Vscan is a hand-held ultrasound machine that replaces the huge ones otherwise used. Doctors can thus administer ultrasounds personally, even in a patient's home, and get instant results. The patient need never go into the cold, dark, testing room again.[14]

Telemedicine, once a pipe dream, is increasingly a reality that frees patients from the burden of cumbersome tests and lengthy hospital visits. In Estonia, digital monitoring is such that doctors often have no need to see their patients for routine tests. Like other European countries, Estonia faces a demographic pyramid, with the population of senior citizens expected to increase greatly. The key then to providing care to the aging and elderly, according to President Toomas Ilves, is to prevent them from getting sick in the first place. That's why Estonia is looking into telemedicine to monitor people who are especially at risk, like the elderly.[15] President Ilves predicts that "in the future, we'll be monitoring people constantly, certainly older people, so that before you get really sick you go see a doctor."[16]

Estonia has already revolutionized health information through its Electronic Health Record (EHR). Started in 2008, the EHR does not centralize medical records but rather integrates them into a standard format readily available for both the patients and their doctors. Estonians, through their national ID system, have digital access to their records and those of their children and can control which doctors can see which parts of their records. And although the government can compile statistical data or track disease outbreaks, that data is anonymized and is never outside a patient's control.

Electronic medicine needn't just be a question of digitizing records. Ali Parsa, the founder of a British health startup called Babylon, sees his virtual health service as the solution to several problems that have long plagued the medical system. First is the simple fact that most people in the world have little or no access to health care—and technology can get it to them. But like the Estonians, he also sees a future where medicine becomes preventive instead of reactive.[17]

Babylon doesn't preempt the traditional doctor yet—there is still a need for in-person procedures and examinations. Increasingly, though, much of medicine can be performed remotely. And that, Parsa, believes, is actually more human. His patients prefer to have a video conference on a phone or tablet rather than visiting the doctor's office or the hospital. "Patients appreciate not leaving the comforts of their own home to spend, on average, three hours to get to a doctor's surgery. My mother, for instance—every time she gets her blood pressure taken at her doctor's [office], it's high, while every time she has it done at home, it's not. We all know it's because of the stress of getting to the surgery at her age and meeting the doctor too." With telemedicine "patients use the same medium to talk to their doctor that they use to talk to their friends and family. It's a much friendlier experience." Increasingly, too, medicine can be brought to the patient. Parsa concedes that sometimes you need to go in for a test, but why bother if it's something that can be done at home? If a patient needs a run-of-the-mill blood test, Babylon sends a courier to deliver a simple prick-your-finger test that the patient can do at home and then send back by courier to get the results within the day.

It's not just with Babylon that we get a glimpse of what the future of medicine could be. Technology can be harnessed to put health care in the hands of the patient through medical apps and social networks. Health-Tap, an American startup, allows users to post questions to be answered by one of more than sixty thousand doctors in its "expert network." For a monthly subscription, users can connect via video to a doctor, who can write prescriptions, within minutes—twenty-four hours a day, seven days a week. For those with chronic conditions, parents with young children, or caregivers, such a service could be a lifesaver—or at least less of a hassle than multiple doctors' office trips a month.

Mango Health, a mobile app, ingeniously combines human behavior and technology to help patients better manage their medications and other treatments. Jason Oberfest, the company's founder and CEO, used to work in gaming and realized that "everything we've learned in behavioral design and user interface to keep people engaged in games could be applied to health care."[18] Oberfest and his team designed Mango Health like a game: users enter their medications and other treatments—for instance, specific exercises or reminders to drink water—into the app, as well as when and how to do it. The app will then remind them when it is time to do a treatment or take a pill. But just as a game has incremental rewards, Mango Health gives patients points every time a reminder is complied with. By partnering with third parties, Mango can offer rewards at certain levels of point accumulation.

Mango Health is also an example of how an app can help other areas of medical management. It has a database of every medication approved by the Food and Drug Administration, including negative interactions, so that if a patient enters a new medication that clashes with an existing one, the app will warn the patient of the conflict. It will also, if the patient allows it to, communicate with doctors, sending them real-time data about how their patients are complying with their treatment. The app prompts patients to record how they are feeling (with a few simple options like 'good' or 'so-so'), so instead of retrospectively asking a patient how they've been doing, doctors can actually know in real time, to correspond with the introduction of new treatments or failure to follow them.

Social networks are another way that technology is helping to make health care more human. Jamie Heywood's brother Stephen was diagnosed with ALS, or Lou Gehrig's Disease, in 2006. ALS is an orphan disease—one not prevalent enough to attract the attention of drug company research toward a cure. In addition to designing solutions to the daily physical obstacles Stephen faced, Jamie, an MIT engineer, set about developing a treatment for the disease itself, founding a research institute with Stephen's wife. Then he created PatientsLikeMe, a social network that connects patients suffering from the same diseases with each other and their doctors, creating 'feedback loops' whereby healthcare providers can quickly learn how patients respond to their treatments. "The faster the feedback loop, the more responsive it is to humans." So Patients LikeMe harnesses human connectivity to increase responsiveness.[19]

PatientsLikeMe has designed its system "to discover if interventions have impact in the real world" but goes a step further by actually empowering patients to make that determination. PatientsLikeMe aims to discover the overall efficacy of different approaches to treatment; it is designed to work globally: "Great systems learn across boundaries," Heywood says, and he is exactly right. If medicine is to get better, its practitioners and their results can't be walled off from one another. That's why PatientsLikeMe is so revolutionary: it is "inherently democratic." And it is intrinsically human. Patients log on and document their outcomes and experiences, giving doctors, drug companies, and everyone concerned a real-time social network to understand their practices better while, for the first time, giving patients a role as true partners, able to learn from and bolster each other in bad times. "Patients contribute research ideas, they are involved in the design of trials and experiments, and they keep doctors honest. They interact around the data themselves, so if there's something not quite right, they will dive right into that." Ultimately Heywood hopes to reinvent the healthcare system: "imagine a world where everyone else's experience can help improve your own."

HEALTH CARE THAT MAKES YOU SICK

Factory medical systems deliver one type of health care, typically in the form of a procedure or pill of some sort. But in the face of some conditions or diseases, certain behaviors and exercises or nutritional and lifestyle adjustments might be more effective. The factory health system is not designed to prescribe something nonmedical or innovative—or if it does, it's only after a battery of tests and exams to confirm that a more complicated procedure didn't work.

Obviously there are many conditions and diseases that are best treated by medical procedures or drugs. But health is not just a function of medicine. More than just optimizing the effectiveness of a particular procedure, a more human healthcare system would optimize individual health and well-being. As Jamie Heywood saw, today's medical system is based on how well a particular action was executed—"Was the hip successfully replaced? All right then, success!"—rather than its actual, ultimate effect on the patient: "Can you walk without pain since the procedure we did last year, Mrs. Smith?" As a result, the system needlessly precludes nonmedical interventions, not to mention the path almost never taken— nonintervention—from its repertoire of solutions.

Having feedback systems in place based on ultimate health outcomes would also help us see where treatments—even administered with the best of intentions—make us worse. Nassim Taleb talks at length about the danger of this phenomenon, *iatrogenesis*, the harm caused by treatment, that results from our deeply rooted desire to intervene or, as he puts it, "this need to do *something*."[20] The problem with this approach is that interventions aren't costless. There is no drug in the world without an adverse side effect. There is no surgery without risk of greater injury.

There are certainly many conditions for which we absolutely need the medical system. Steve Jobs famously tried to treat his pancreatic cancer with fasting and juice diets, later regretting his decision to forsake conventional treatment.[21] But without understanding the full, long-term costs and benefits of any one regimen, including less invasive treatment or nonintervention altogether—knowledge that a rigorous feedback system would give us—we take tremendous risks prescribing otherwise healthy people with powerful treatments.

Our bodies are exceptionally complex, and attempts to oversimplify the interactions that happen within them in order to mechanize them courts unintended consequences. Doctors almost automatically prescribe proton pump inhibitors (e.g., Prilosec, Nexium, Prevacid) to people experiencing heartburn or stress (over 100 million times in the United States per year), but around 60 percent of prescriptions are inappropriate according to the *Archives of Internal Medicine*.[22] The drug works by reducing acid levels in the stomach. This certainly eliminates heartburn, but it increases the risk of infection (acid kills germs in the things we eat) as well as vitamin deficiency (acid is also necessary to break our food down) and even heart attack.[23] Considering that for many people simple changes in diet or behavior, like eating an evening meal earlier, can eliminate acid reflux disease altogether, altering the chemistry of our bodies so casually for so many people seems haphazard at best.

Now, Nassim Taleb explains, pharmaceutical companies find themselves "scraping the bottom of the barrel, looking for disease among healthier and healthier people, lobbying for reclassification of conditions."[24] Perhaps restless leg syndrome (RLS) really is a medical condition, and for those it seriously afflicts, a treatment is a godsend. But did it require GlaxoSmithKline to run an aggressive marketing campaign promoting prescriptions of ropinirole, usually used to treat those with Parkinson's? They also lobbied doctors directly to 'educate' them about the disease.[25] Doctors in the journal *PLoS Medicine* accuse the company of "disease mongering."[26]

Restless leg syndrome isn't the only disorder with a 'modern cure.' The United States spent an incredible $2.3 billion to treat ADHD in children ages five to seventeen in 2007 (the latest year such data were compiled).[27] In 2014 we spent $10.1 billion on ADHD treatment overall, a 51 percent increase over the previous five years.[28] Dr. Michael Anderson, a pediatrician near Atlanta, Georgia, and an outspoken critic of the overtreatment of ADHD, still finds himself prescribing pills to the low-income elementary-aged patients he treats who are having trouble in school. "I don't have a whole lot of choice," he says. "We've decided as a society that it's too expensive to modify the kid's environment. So we have to modify the kid."[29] Our factory health system puts the needs of the children's factory-school system over the needs of children themselves. We're taking children with very normal child behavior—being energetic—and categorizing them as ill and in need of treatment for the convenience of the adult world that serves them. It's a completely inhuman "chemical straitjacket," says Dr. Nancy Rappaport, a child psychiatrist who works with low-income children.[30]

Such 'straitjackets' aren't costless. One family with four of its children in Dr. Anderson's care has a shelf lined up in the kitchen with all their medications: Adderall for the twelve- and nine-year-olds, Risperdal (an antipsychotic mood stabilizer) for the two eleven-year-olds, and—to top it all off—Clonidine, a sleep aid for all four of them to counteract the other drugs. When one of the children started to go through puberty, the Adderall he was on caused him to begin hearing voices and imagining people around him, a recognized side effect of the drug. Having become suicidal at one point, he even spent a week in a psychiatric hospital and was consequently switched to Risperdal.[31] This is surely madness, cruel madness.

"LESS MEDICINE, MORE HEALTH"

Dehumanized, factory health care is not just limited to pharmaceuticals. Americans undergo some 80 million CT scans each year, about a third of which are completely unnecessary (incidentally, according to a study in the *Archives of Internal Medicine*, around 14,500 cancer deaths each year are attributable to radiation exposure from CT scans alone).[32] But patients, shielded from the costs of any particular procedure, want answers, and doctors live in constant fear of malpractice litigation, so they err on the side of 'caution.' Of course, in a model where doctors and hospitals are paid for every service they provide, more tests mean more treatment, which means more money.

"Often, these are fishing expeditions, and since no one is perfectly normal," one doctor writes in the *New Yorker*, "you tend to find a lot of fish."[33]

And although this drives up financial costs, we pay the price in our health as well: we're *correctly* diagnosing conditions that will never actually bother us and then spending billions to 'fix' them, but without the attendant improvements in how many more years patients live or in their quality of life. "When it comes to human health," according to H. Gilbert Welch, an academic physician and professor at Dartmouth Medical School, "the idea of possibility, chance, or probability typically gets lost and a risk becomes a threat—a threat that must be dealt with by medical care."[34]

Screening for screening's sake is dangerous. According to Welch, "since the mid-1990s the incidence of thyroid cancer detection in the United States has increased threefold, while the death rate has remained stable. That doesn't sound like an epidemic of real disease; that sounds like an epidemic of diagnosis." In his book *Less Medicine, More Health*, Welch writes of a family friend who, having been found to have a small papillary thyroid cancer, was operated on. During surgery to correct the cancer 'problem,' his friend had a minor stroke and now has lost sensation and function of his lower arm and lower leg. He has difficulties enunciating words too. "Intraoperative stroke is rare," Welch points out, "but it is undoubtedly more common than anything bad happening had he left the small papillary thyroid cancer alone and waited to see if it became a problem."[35]

ALL THIS IS the entirely predictable product of Big Health, the factory healthcare system we have built: big hospitals operated by big bureaucracies working with big pharmaceutical and insurance companies. Patients—people—take a backseat to the imperatives of the system itself. One way to constrain this baleful trend is to switch from the current, dominant 'fee-for-service' medical payments model to some variant of a 'fee-for-outcome' model. 'Fee-for-service' means, simply, getting paid for what you do. In such a system the incentive is quite obviously to do more. The more treatments, the more procedures, the more you get paid. 'Fee-for-outcome,' however, pays for the end result, not the process. Because this encourages only those tests and procedures that effectively improve patients' health, cost savings, conditioned on meeting some standard of care, are split between the provider and the payer.

This is not a new idea. In 1984 the Texas Heart Institute developed 'packaged pricing' for cardiovascular surgery, an arrangement in which the cost of surgery as well as all associated physician and hospital charges were included in one 'bundled' rate.[36] In 1987 an orthopedic surgeon in Michigan offered a similar flat rate for various shoulder and knee surgeries. A two-year warranty for services following the procedure was even included in the price to cover the costs of abnormally long recovery, complications, or readmission, if necessary. Such 'episode-of-care' payment arrangements have been subsequently tried and tested across the country for various orthopedic surgeries, cataract and heart bypass procedures, and even prenatal care. Numerous studies have shown the model to almost invariably lower costs and improve outcomes.[37] It's not hard to see why: with one flat rate, physicians and hospitals are incentivized both to do a good job (so that the patient doesn't require as much follow-up care) as well as look for ways to reduce waste and unnecessary treatment (as any savings are kept and shared).[38] Yet uptake has been slow because establishing the benchmarks that determine what an appropriate payment should be—as well as what level of results indicate success—is tremendously fraught. Moreover, many medical providers still prefer a fee-for-service model because the chance of realizing some savings with a flat fee is a much less powerful incentive than running the risk that costs will go over.

The Obama administration to its credit continues to work with Medicare and Medicaid providers to adopt more outcome-oriented pay schemes. But even if 'episode-of-care' payments were adopted everywhere, they still fall short. Because even the highest quality, most cost-efficient knee replacement or heart bypass is far worse than avoiding either in the first place. Our healthcare system should be designed so that payers and providers actively try to help us avoid medical care altogether. Imagine if physicians and hospitals were paid . . . when we *don't* show up. To do that is to imagine a system that looks at health as something that goes far beyond the repertoire available at the doctor's office, emergency room, or operating room.

SLOW MEDICINE

The Slow Food movement, developed as a direct response to 'fast food,' (see Chapter 5), has inspired doctors as well. Proponents of 'slow medicine' argue that in making medicine 'reductive' and 'mechanical,' we forget that human bodies are complex organisms that can often heal themselves.

Dr. Victoria Sweet, who was a doctor at Laguna Honda Hospital in San Francisco, America's last almshouse (which has since closed), is one of those proponents. Laguna Honda Hospital was unique. "It looked like a medieval monastery," Sweet recalls. "It had cream-colored walls and a red-tiled roof and a bell tower and turrets. The hospital was huge, on 62 acres of land in the middle of San Francisco and it had 1,178 patients. [There was] the chapel, which looked more like a small church with polished wooden pews and real stained glass, and then we went outside and [there was the] greenhouse, the aviary, and the barnyard."[39]

Sweet was both a doctor and a historian of medicine. Her subject was the medieval abbess Hildegard of Bingen, who among her many talents as a composer, writer, and polymath also wrote on medicine. Hildegard believed that the human body was like a plant and, accordingly, "took a gardener's approach to the body. She did not focus down on the cellular level of the body; instead she stood back from her patient and looked around," describes Sweet. "She followed the patient's body; she did not lead."[40] Hildegard believed in the body's *viriditas*, or vitality, and that, given the right conditions, it was perfectly able to heal itself.

Sweet didn't really understand this concept until she treated her patient Terry Becker, who was homeless and an addict. Becker, Sweet recalls, had woken up one day paralyzed from the neck down. She was diagnosed with a very rare viral disease, but because it has no treatment and tends to get better with time, she was admitted to Laguna Honda. Medically Terry's biggest problem was that by sitting in a wheelchair, she had acquired an enormous bedsore. Doctors had tried skin grafts three times, but the bedsore had become too large to operate on.

"When I saw that bedsore for the first time, I was absolutely shocked," Sweet recalls. "It went from the middle of Terry's back to her tailbone. It was so deep that I could see the bone at the base of Terry's spine. It was filled with all this decayed tissue from the failed grafts. It would have to heal on its own. I couldn't imagine how Terry would survive all the infections she would get."[41]

Despairing over what to do, thinking that this bedsore was "probably the end of Terry Becker," Sweet asked herself: What would Hildegard do? "Maybe Hildegard would just remove what was in the way of Terry healing. So what was in the way? All the dead tissue was in the way and had to be moved. Anything that was uncomfortable, like wrinkled bed clothes or a hard mattress or any medication that she didn't absolutely need. . . . Then I thought, Hildegard would fortify Terry's *viriditas* with the basics: good food, fresh air, deep sleep, sunlight. So that's what I did. And it was amazing to see how fast Hildegard's prescription began to work."

At Laguna Honda, patients weren't treated mechanically but organically . . . humanly. "Medicine is personal, face to face. And when it's personal, it works," Sweet says. In our rush to offer an immediate prescription, a mechanical 'fix,' we often forget that time and care can be the most natural—and effective—treatments of all. This is what she calls "the efficiency of inefficiency." She is fond of a quote from Dr. Francis Peabody, a noted professor at Harvard Medical School in the early twentieth century: "The secret of the care of the patient is caring for the patient."[42] Often what would otherwise be seen as inefficient is actually most efficient. When we put bureaucracy ahead of patients, "in the interest of efficiency, we became less efficient," she says.[43]

A PIE IS in the oven, vintage tracks are playing, and half a dozen women are gathered around the kitchen counter at Pathstone Living, a nursing home in Minnesota tailored for those suffering from memory impairment. It's a typical afternoon there, with staff offering a wide range of activities for the senior citizens in their care. Staying busy, it turns out, can relieve the agitation that's common among those suffering from Alzheimer's or dementia. At another nursing home such agitation would be managed with antipsychotic medicines, which are approved to treat serious illness, like bipolar disease and schizophrenia: over three hundred thousand nursing-home residents are prescribed them annually in the United States. But antipsychotics increase the risk of death for those with dementia.[44]

Beatrice DeLeon experienced overmedication firsthand. An Alzheimer's patient, DeLeon was sent to a care facility not for her memory but because she had had multiple falls. Even though overprescription of antipsychotics—a 'chemical restraint'—is banned by law, "they just kept giving her more and more," says DeLeon's husband, Manuel. "And I noticed when I used to go see her, she'd just kind of mumble, like she was lost." Beatrice was administered two very strong drugs that effectively made her a mumbling pile of flesh, writes Ina Jaffe, the NPR reporter who visited her. Doctors prescribe these drugs like sweets; a 2011 US government study found that 88 percent of Medicare[45] claims for antipsychotics were for dementia or other conditions for which these drugs were not intended.[46]

Although enforcement against nursing homes that overprescribe antipsychotics is weak,[47] Dr. Tracy Tomac hopes Pathstone Living provides an alternative. Pathstone's new "anti-antipsychotic" approach came after Tomac, a psychiatrist and medical consultant there, decided with a colleague to see whether they could reduce the drug's use. They tried it at one of the smaller nursing homes run by the same charity, Ecumen. By six months in, they were successful—everyone was off antipsychotics. So

Ecumen decided to scale the approach to all of its nursing homes across the state, about a dozen in total. Their initial goal? Reduce their use by 20 percent. After the first year? Down 97 percent. Now at Pathstone, only 5 to 7 percent of patients are prescribed antipsychotics at all. Shelley Matthes, who's in charge of quality assurance for Ecumen, says that the numbers were not the only thing that changed: "They started interacting . . . people who hadn't been speaking were speaking. They came alive and awakened."

The program, which came to be known as "Awakenings," derives much of its success from training staff simply to pay attention to people. Although individualized dementia care is not an original concept—the nursing staff borrowed from techniques demonstrated elsewhere—attending closely to patients in a human way eliminates the need to medicate them for the behavioral problems dementia can create.[48]

DEATH AND DIGNITY

If there's one aspect of health care most guilty of an inhuman approach, it's how we care for those at the ends of their lives.

Sheila Marsh was dying. Stricken with cancer, the seventy-seven-year-old had one wish: to say good-bye to her favorite horse, Bronwen, for whom she had cared for twenty-five years at the stables near her home in Northwest England. So the staff at the hospital where Sheila stayed arranged for Bronwen and another of Sheila's horses to come and visit, wheeling her outside to greet and be nuzzled by them. Though unable to speak due to the ravages of her disease, she "gently called to Bronwen and the horse bent down tenderly and kissed her on the cheek as they said their last goodbyes," according to Gail Taylor, one of the nurses. Sheila died soon afterward, but her medical staff had helped end her life in quiet dignity, fulfilling her final wishes to bid farewell to the horses that had meant so much to her.[49]

That Sheila had such a dignified death in a hospital is extraordinary, really. Because death in much of the developed world is a horrendous experience. Most people, of course, want to die a quiet death at home surrounded by their loved ones. But instead, many die in a hospital, hooked up to ventilators and IV drips, surrounded by beeping monitors, lying in a sterile room, clinging to life but drained of soul.

We suffer tremendous indignity in the last years of our lives. Our bodies fail us, but doctors, obliged to preserve life at just about any cost, work to prop up our dying organs, our weakening limbs, our tenuous grip on reality. And we make things worse by letting people die exactly where they don't want to end their lives: 70 percent of Americans say they would prefer to die at home, and yet only 24 percent who are over the age of sixty-five do—35 percent die in hospitals, 28 percent in nursing homes.[50] The sad part is that of those who die in hospitals, many have no medical reason for being there—in Britain the figure is 40 percent.[51]

It is deeply inhuman that most people's final moments are not as they'd like them to be. And factory hospitals are inappropriate places for the elderly, as geriatrician Dennis McCullough points out: "Large 'industrial-scale' environments like hospitals focus on disease and tend to lose sight of the complexity of an older person. Speed is at a premium and slower-moving, slower-responding elders don't fit well with the pressured environment of fast medical care."[52] But hospitalizing elders is also, from a public policy perspective, a bad idea for the rest of us. Caring for patients in their final six months of life costs Medicare $170 billion—over a quarter of its annual budget.[53] What's more, approximately one-third of expenditures for the last year of life are incurred in the final month.[54] Much of these costs are incurred by unnecessarily aggressive treatment administered in hospitals, often in intensive-care units (one investigation found that acute care accounted for 78 percent of costs incurred in the final thirty days of life).[55] So if no one wants to die in hospital and it is so costly to the system for people to do so, why do they? And how can we give people a more dignified and more human end-of-life experience?

One of the great tragedies of end-of-life care is that we simply don't know what most people want. Erring on the side of the medical principle 'to do no harm,' doctors continue to intervene to prolong life, even when we might not want them to. That's where living wills, also called 'advance directives,' come in. Living wills help relatives and loved ones know what to do in case of medical dilemmas in which patients are incapacitated and can't make decisions for themselves. Most people don't have them—only 30 percent in the United States[56]—but having an end-of-life discussion not only ensures patients' desires are carried out, it also lowers costs.

Communities like the town of La Crosse, Wisconsin, are leading the way. Bud Hammes is a medical ethicist at Gundersen Health System, a local hospital in La Crosse. He found that without living wills, most of his patients' families had no idea what to do when patients were in a coma or on life-support machines. Despite years of illness, no one had thought to have the conversation. Consequently "the moral distress that these families were suffering was palpable. You could feel it in the room," he says. Hammes resolved to help families solve the problem in advance and started a program to train nurses to ask people if they wanted to fill out an advance directive. The idea caught on, and now it is the norm in La Crosse to have a living will; in fact, 96 percent of those who die in the town have documentation for their end-of-life wishes, and it is normal for neighbors to gossip about who doesn't have one. And although this wasn't the goal, medical costs at Gundersen Health System have declined as patients make clear they don't want to be kept on dehumanizing— and expensive—life support.[57] (One study found that for those patients with advanced cancer who had end-of-life conversations with their physicians, their overall cost of care was 35.7 percent lower than those who never discussed their preferences. And in case you think that lower costs mean lower quality of death, the study found just the opposite: it was those who incurred higher costs that tended to suffer more.)[58] By helping patients make their wishes known, Hammes has made death in La Crosse more dignified.

HENNEPIN HEALTH: GETTING CREATIVE ABOUT HEALTH CARE

February 25, 2013. It was a few minutes before 9 p.m. 'Ron' was getting ready for bed, and his phone started ringing. He was about to receive some very urgent news.

For four months Ron hadn't felt his usual self. At fifty-five, he was used to not feeling quite right, having spent his life working hard, physical jobs. But even a hardened construction worker can only take so much. Finally Ron scheduled a visit at a local clinic, and after describing his symptoms, the doctor there decided they should do some lab work. Later, just as he was getting ready for bed, came that phone call: it was the doctor he had seen earlier that day. Ron's blood sugar was high, so high that he had to go to the emergency room right away. If he went to sleep, she told him, there would be a good chance he would never wake up. Ron, he was told, had a kind of type 1 diabetes that is particularly slow to manifest and progress, and his was acute: his blood sugar would oscillate between tremendous extremes in a single day (one day between 36 milligrams of blood glucose per deciliter of blood to 586; to put this in context, most people's levels don't exceed 180). Such extremes complicated Ron's life beyond just the physical consequences of his condition. He soon lost his job of almost ten years because the now-frequent trembling he experienced made him unsafe (his boss saw him shaking as he descended a ladder). And though he found work elsewhere, because his diabetes could incapacitate him without any prior warning, it was challenging for him to keep even the jobs for which he was qualified, as employers wanted advance commitment to a full day's work. Finally, after falling into a diabetic coma that summer, Ron used up the last of his unemployment benefits. By September 15 he was homeless.

It's easy to think of Ron's case as one of a health problem leading to a social problem. But it was just as much a social problem exacerbating a health problem—a vicious cycle. Being homeless and diabetic is a deadly combination. Kim Evers, a diabetes expert who worked with Ron from his initial diagnosis, witnessed his health deteriorate further after he became homeless. Proper nutrition is paramount for managing diabetes, especially when it's as acute as Ron's. But whatever nutrition instructions Evers gave would be almost impossible for him to manage while he remained homeless: meals were irregular and, when available, often highly processed and sugar laden. Not having access to a refrigerator made storing insulin, which requires cold storage to prevent spoiling, almost impossible. Diabetics need somewhere to rest when tired, which happens easily and often, but shelters tend to close during the day. All in all, being homeless and diabetic can be a death sentence.

Thankfully Ron lives in Minneapolis, where he's part of an incredible healthcare experiment: Hennepin Health. Local leaders created it to serve people exactly like him.

With just over 1.1 million people, Hennepin County isn't huge, but with Minneapolis at its center (and over one in five Minnesotans), any experiment in healthcare delivery there would be ambitious, especially as this one was aimed at some of the most complicated and expensive users of the healthcare system. The project got its start after the state legislature moved to expand its Medicaid coverage to an additional eighty-four thousand people across Minnesota, as allowed under the 2010 Affordable Care Act, and passed a bill to allow the county to test new ways of serving these new patients. County officials' response led to one of the most unique healthcare organizations in the country.[59] Launched in 2012, Hennepin Health is a four-way partnership between departments or affiliates of the Hennepin County government, bringing together traditional health providers with social services. This hybrid organization receives a predetermined per-member-per-month payment from the state to cover the entire health costs of its beneficiaries. Such 'capitation payments' are actuarially determined for each person in the system, and any savings are kept as long as standard of care is maintained. This means that in Hennepin, the four partners, who were accustomed to operating independently, would now jointly share one budget so both cost savings and overruns would be spread equally across them.

Thanks to this incentive structure, the four partner agencies coordinate on nonmedical work as well as traditional health services. For example, although the county's main social services agency—one of the four—is funded separately from the Medicaid capitation payments, it now makes sure its programs are integrated with the medical services Hennepin Health provides because it receives a portion of any medical savings. The result is practical care aimed at the root causes of patients' poor health, regardless of how far outside the 'traditional' health sphere they fall.

Back to Ron, homeless and suffering from diabetes. In the eyes of his healthcare workers at Hennepin (like Kim Evers), finding Ron safe and stable public housing became a medical necessity. His homelessness was *their* business. So Evers 'prescribed' a team of social service workers trained in exactly this task to find Ron an affordable place to live. Now Ron has a place to rest when his blood sugar spikes or drops (sometimes causing blindness), to cook his own nutritious meals, and to refrigerate his insulin. He's still far from healthy; the road ahead is long and uncertain. But Ron now has a better shot at staying healthy than he ever would have. For him the best medicine wasn't in the refrigerator; it *was* the refrigerator.[60]

Hennepin is not the first to try a capitation payment model. Kaiser Permanente—a private provider—has shown that its fixed-fee-per-patient business model can improve outcomes and patient satisfaction. But the lesson from Hennepin—for all providers, private or government-run—goes much deeper: In every community, for every population type no matter how well off, there are a variety of components that form the fabric that is a person's health—all of which must be tended to.

Hennepin provides instructive lessons for all providers. In every community, for every population type, no matter how well off, there are a variety of components that form the fabric that is a person's health. This is precisely why traditional house calls—virtually killed off by modern medicine because they are 'inefficient'—are actually vital. Dr. Sandeep Jauhar passionately advocates house calls for some patients, because they can help doctors understand the real impediments to a patient's recovery. "One patient of mine had severe heart failure that rendered him too weak to come see me," Jauhar writes. "He lived only a mile from the hospital, so I went to visit him. In his kitchen sink was a mess of dirty dishes. I looked in the fridge; it was nearly empty. There were canned soups on the counter, all loaded with sodium, precisely what he should not have been consuming. . . . It didn't matter which medications I ordered at the pharmacy; he had no way to get them."[61]

Our health system and the providers within it should study the communities they serve to find ways to help enhance their members' health way beyond providing pharmaceuticals and medical procedures. Some of it is terrifically unoriginal: investing in parks and bike paths and sponsoring farmers' markets or school nutrition programs. But why stop there? Imagine health providers partnering with cooking schools, investing in adult sports leagues, building gyms and community centers—all of which not only keep people active but, perhaps even more importantly, foster the social relationships that maintain health into old age.[62] And given the health benefits of stable families (for more, see Chapters 8 and 9), perhaps one day our health providers will see their role as including parenting and relationship support too. That's what a more human healthcare system looks like—not just dishing out drugs and carrying out operations.

One nonprofit organization is already working with communities across the United States to do just this. Author and *National Geographic* explorer Dan Buettner set out in 2004 to document the lifestyles of people around the world who had lived past the age of one hundred. After he and the scientists he worked with interviewed hundreds of these centenarians, they identified five communities—Ikaria, Greece; Okinawa, Japan; Ogliastra Region, Sardinia; Loma Linda, California; and Nicoya Peninsula, Costa Rica—with an abnormally high number. Buettner designated them 'blue zones,' and founded a nonprofit, the Blue Zone Project, to spread the lessons. The Blue Zone Project now works with towns in Iowa, California, and Minnesota to identify and invest in projects that have been shown to increase longevity, like additional drinking fountains throughout town, color-coded parking places that add two hundred steps to get to the store, community gardens, community walking clubs, and volunteer programs for local business people to walk kids to and from school.[63]

Whether these ideas are exactly right is not the point; they represent the right type of thinking about the very human causes of and impediments to good health. We can no longer afford for our doctors, nurses, and carers to be cogs in the machinery of industrialized medicine. They must be stewards of health.

DECENTRALIZING HEALTH CARE

America's healthcare system needs a transformative reboot to undo the cumbersome factory health apparatus that, although built in the name of efficiency, now serves as a barrier to better—and less expensive—care. The essence of that reboot needs to be decentralization. To bring the human touch back to medicine, we need a system where care is devolved to the smallest practical unit. Of course it's true that there aren't enough—and there isn't enough demand for—specialist doctors to be spread around every community. But equally, there is no need to warehouse them in huge buildings—giant, Kafkaesque labyrinths that impose themselves on sick, frightened, and vulnerable people.

In practical terms this means a radical breakup of Big Health and a radical dispersal of healthcare provision from centralized to community-based locations. If we can make hospitals more human, we can take the first step toward setting a tone that puts people first. By working not in large hospitals or medical centers but small, local ones, doctors can establish a more personal relationship with their patients. For the vast majority of our health needs, a highly localized system is ideal—localized even to the point of your mobile device. We need a system built around people, their needs, and what really works for them—not the medical establishment. We need the direct opposite of the mergers and corporate consolidation creating the giant Big Health Frankensteins we're seeing more and more of today.

Decentralization would save money too. As of 2013 we spent $2.9 trillion on our health care—17.4 percent of the entire economy.[64] In general you could argue there's nothing wrong with a free society deciding to spend a big chunk of its income on whatever it wants. But the real issue is what outcomes these enormous sums are buying us. And the truth is that American health outcomes are no better than those in other countries that spend far less. The 17.4 percent of GDP we spent on health care is a full 8 percent above the average for developed nations, and 5 percent above the Netherlands, the country with the next highest share of spending. Yet life expectancy in the United States (78.7 years) is 1.5 years less than the developed country average,[65] whereas five-year survival rates for cancer are about the same as our best peers (who, of course, spend much less). And although it's true that we might treat certain highly specialized conditions better and that waiting times in the US system are far lower than in any other country—to what end? For some common conditions, like asthma, mortality rates are actually a lot worse.[66]

Rather than buying us more health, in the form of longer, healthier lives, our unusually elevated health spending simply buys us more healthcare activity—for example, twice as many MRI scans and 18 percent more C-section births per person than the average developed country.[67] But with the right reforms, driven by the right values, I believe it's possible for the costs—and cost-effectiveness—of the US healthcare system to fall in line with other advanced countries around the world.

A system dominated by a handful of large insurance, hospital, and pharmaceutical corporations, fortified by well-paid lobbyists and politicians, is obviously not going to get us there. We need change, and it needs to be much more fundamental than anything we've seen up to now.

TOWARD MORE HUMAN HEALTH CARE

Health care is a human right. It is essential for human dignity and necessary for society to function, making its common provision both a public good and good public policy. In the UK the National Health Service (NHS) is politically inviolable, a settled part of British society. We Brits are rightly proud of the idea of the NHS. Donald Trump once said that his policy on Obamacare was to replace it with "something terrific"; I think it's pretty terrific that in Britain everyone can receive health care as a right, based on their medical need and not their ability to pay.

As most readers will know, no one has to pay out of pocket for health care in the UK. There's no insurance bureaucracy for the patient, no applying for coverage. You don't have to think about it, don't have to worry about whether you're 'covered' for this that or the other. You don't have to consider questions of health coverage when you apply for a job or move to a different place . . . the very concept of 'health insurance' is alien to most British people. If you or a member of your family is ill, you go to the doctor. That's it.

Is the British system perfect? Of course not. Is it even, in a narrower sense, more human? Well, partly yes. I do think that the absence of the sheer hassle and anxiety caused by the bureaucracy of America's health insurance system does make the NHS, in that particular respect, more human. I am continually astonished by the passive acceptance on the part of so many US citizens of the waste of time and energy involved in interacting with healthcare red tape. It is an epic burden on people's lives, practically Soviet in its style and scope.

But when it comes to the delivery of health care to the patient in the UK, there are severe and well-documented problems. The NHS is tremendously centralized and bureaucratic. Some NHS hospitals have been described as 'conveyor belts' that 'churn' out their patients, who are treated like 'parcels.'[68] The burden of internal paperwork and an obsessive focus on 'efficiency' have led to demonstrably poorer outcomes. In one extreme case, Stafford Hospital, bureaucratic diktats were a contributing factor in the unnecessary deaths of between four hundred and twelve hundred patients over a four-year period. The human neglect in that hospital, despite it being a state-of-the-art facility, was unfathomable. One patient died after being left in her own feces and contracting an infection from three superbugs. Another died after lapsing into a diabetic coma when her nurses failed to provide her with her routine insulin.[69]

In fact, cases of poor patient care pervade the entire NHS system: long waiting times for routine operations; unpleasant, outdated, often dirty facilities; offhand or downright rude treatment by overworked, underpaid, and poorly motivated staff. Factory hospitals and a factory approach to health care are alive and well in the vast, unaccountable bureaucracy of the NHS, the fourth-largest employer in the world after the US military, the Chinese army, and Walmart.[70]

There's no surprise, then, that in discussions of healthcare reform in the United States, the inferior consumer experience associated with a 'single-payer' system like Britain's is often cited as the principal reason to avoid such a structure. American citizens prize the choice they have over their doctor, their coverage, their treatment. Yes, the defects of the US system are pretty widely understood here. But in the eyes of most Americans, it's still seen as preferable to a top-down, 'take-what-you're-given,' 'socialized' system. There are some who advocate a health system that is "Medicare for all." Yes, Medicare is technically a single-payer system. But Medicare is restrictive and bureaucratic, and for many patients it still requires supplemental private insurance. We shouldn't think, however, that the UK's NHS as it currently stands (or "Medicare for all") is the only possible version of single-payer health care.

The former Labour Party Health Secretary in Tony Blair's government, Alan Milburn, once said that the NHS should be "an idea, not an institution." The central idea of the NHS—universally available health care that is free at the point of use—is a great idea, worth cherishing. But just because such a system is funded by government doesn't mean it has to be provided by government in the form of a massive bureaucratic institution. I think this points the way toward the kind of reform we need in America.

To achieve true reform that improves lives and reduces costs, we need to create an outcome-oriented single-payer system with full consumer sovereignty. Make the funding of health care more socialized, but make the delivery of health care more consumerized. This combination would not only drive innovation, but drive it in the direction of patient satisfaction and lowered costs—a huge departure from any system today.

A bumper-sticker version would be this: 'single-payer, market provider.' We should aim for the best of both worlds: the security of guaranteed health care for all, free at the point of use, combined with the dynamism and choice of market provision. 'Single-payer, market provider.'

Let's look at each element in turn. I know that many Americans might chafe at being part of one single national healthcare network. But they don't realize they already are. Like it or not, every American is a member of the broader healthcare 'pool.' Whether they pay into an insurance plan or they are uninsured, a hospital won't refuse them treatment if they are in dire condition. As a result, uninsured patients' primary healthcare provider is not a family doctor but an emergency room in a public hospital, paid—much more expensively—by the taxpayer. The government, in effect, operates a backstop insurance policy that covers those left out of the current system but fails to deliver them anything but the most urgent emergency care. The public already guarantees some form of health care for all.

Second: 'market provider.' A more human healthcare system would feature a true market for healthcare services, where many different providers—from small to large, traditional to innovative—compete for patients on a level playing field. Why? Because when patients choose, we're more likely to have innovation and a focus on quality care. We're more likely to have a system where the incentives are designed to put people first: to satisfy patients rather than bureaucrats at Big Health insurance and medical companies. But at the moment, in America's allegedly more market-based system, patients don't choose—insurance companies do.

Of course, completely free markets don't really work for health care. For markets to work properly, you need good information available to all participants. In truth, even in the age of Googling your symptoms, patients will not have enough information to make really well-informed medical decisions. They certainly won't be able to anticipate the kind of care they'll need in the future, to be able to choose the best provider for themselves today. Even in the moment when care is needed, patients don't know whether they really need a treatment or not, relying on doctors—and an insurer or hospital company to tell the doctor what they should prescribe. In these ways health is different from education. In health you will always need some sort of provisioning authority to determine the appropriate standard of care for any given diagnosis. And to a certain extent you will always need some sort of rationing of care across the system. In the NHS it is commissioning bodies who decide what level of care is needed. In the United States, Americans experience this when they're told certain procedures or tests are covered or not under their insurance plans. It's the insurance companies that act as the government.

These characteristics of health care make it difficult to introduce supply-side choice. But just because a normal market wouldn't work for healthcare provision doesn't mean we should write off the use of market features entirely. You can have a single-payer system with a provisioning authority that determines the appropriate levels of care for any circumstance—all while letting a myriad of different organizations compete for the actual provision of care itself. This is a long way from the current model in the United States, which is not really a competitive market at all; it's a system that is increasingly stitched up by a small number of massive companies.

Wouldn't it be better if Americans could choose their doctors and other health providers directly instead of having their choice constrained by this cartel of insurance companies? A 'single-payer, market-provider' system would move us closer to that.

One clear way to make US health care more like a market would be to eliminate the extremely odd tradition we have of providing health coverage through employers. This makes no sense today. First, of course, not everyone is employed. Second, employer-sponsored health plans unnecessarily restrict personal freedom. If you don't like what plans are on offer, you're generally out of luck because it's almost always far less expensive to buy health care from your employer. And having the 'perfect' health plan—if there is such a thing—isn't just a question of how many checkups are covered per year. For some, it's deeply—and morally—personal. In 2014 the Supreme Court decided that an employer could deny its employees access to contraception and abortion coverage by not sponsoring plans that included them, based on the business owner's religious beliefs. Whether you agree with the decision or not, it would never have been an issue if health care wasn't provided—and determined—by our employers. But say you did have a health plan sponsored by your current employer, one, moreover, that is perfect for you. Now, if you can't find as good a plan or better from another employer, you're much more reluctant to leave your job. This is a completely artificial constraint on labor mobility—and the ACA exacerbates this problem further, forcing more employers to offer health care to more workers.

This employer dimension to health care is a massive burden on business. And in any event, why should an employer determine what kind of heath care its workers should have? Moving away from employer-sponsored health care is just one component of the larger, structural reforms that are needed for a more human system—and even that would represent an enormous upheaval. But really, the financial and bureaucratic burden the current system places on individuals—and, shockingly, in the so-called land of free enterprise, on businesses—is alarming and unsustainable.

THE HEALTHCARE DEBATE in America is almost completely stuck. Everyone knows the system is incredibly, unsustainably expensive; everyone can see that it's indescribably bureaucratic; everyone knows what they don't like about it. A system based on the broad principle of 'single-payer, market provider' could move us in a more human direction, breaking the bureaucratic, extortionate stranglehold of Big Health; opening things up to the kind of fresh, innovative approaches we've seen in this chapter; and putting power over health care in everyone's hands.

By combining the best of both worlds, a 'single-payer market-provider' system—with real consumer sovereignty built in—could help break the political logjam around health care in the country. For the left, it would guarantee health care as a right for all. But for opponents of big government, it would massively increase consumer choice over doctors and medical procedures, while driving a stake through the heart of the crony capitalism that so disfigures our health care system today. The right would also surely celebrate the enormous reduction in burdens on business that a 'single-payer, market-provider' system would entail.

Health care should not just be more human—it should be one of the *most* human things we do. This is a way to get there that everyone ought to be able to support.

chapter five

FOOD

WHAT HAS HAPPENED to us that we think it's all right to throw live chicks into a mincing machine just because they're male, that piglets' tails are chopped off and their front teeth broken to prevent 'stress-induced cannibalism' and chunks of their ears cut out for identification, all without painkillers; and that cows are milked to the breaking point so they live out just a third of their natural lives? This is how you get your food. This is how I get my food. This is where pretty much all of us get our food because what we typically eat today has been farmed in factories and manufactured in factories.

It's the 'farmed' part that's truly indefensible. The fake food concocted from artificial ingredients by vast industrial machines, food production that's just another branch of chemistry—well, it may be disgusting and make you unhealthy, but in the end it's a question of taste. (Although, as we'll see, it's not quite as simple as a question of consumer choice.) The way we treat animals, though? That's a question of ethics. Farmer and poet Wendell Berry describes eating as 'farming by proxy.' In the case of eating factory-farmed animals, it's cruelty by proxy. If we don't care about the sickening things I've just described, we've lost one of the qualities that is essential to human beings: the capacity to be empathetic. More animal cruelty = less human.

Of course none of us is deliberately choosing to torture a pig when we buy a hot dog. But as we've seen in other contexts, people are often made to behave in inhuman ways by the systems and structures around them. When it comes to factory food and cruelty to animals, our shopping and eating habits make us complicit in horrific acts. But it's simplistic just to blame consumers. That allows the real culprits off the hook: the politicians, regulators, and business executives of the culinary-industrial complex, whose grotesque practices are encouraged through subsidy and permitted through inadequate regulation. The resulting pervasiveness of factory food in our society makes it hard for even the most conscientious consumer to avoid propping up this rotten, inhuman system. It is a structural problem. That's why, if we're going to do anything about it, we need to go deeper than participating in campaigns to shop differently or supporting animal-welfare charities. We need to dismantle and reconstruct the entire food industry.

FACTORY FARMS

Most summers when I was young we would visit my family in Hungary. My grandmother grew most of her fruit and vegetables in the garden, and there were chickens running around the place. On the other side of town, with the other side of the family, it was pigs: my family owned a small salami factory. My cousin and I would help out, and that included killing pigs. And I mean really killing them—by hand. Lots of blood. But I was pretty young then, and anyway, over there they were . . . you know, Communist. A bit backward. Actually, as I now know, the way we treated and killed pigs in our small local meat-processing business was much more humane than the horrors taking place in the big, industrialized plants in the more 'advanced' UK where we lived.

For most of my life I—like most people, I suspect—never gave much thought to the origins of my food. I began to develop a greater understanding while working on these issues with some of our clients during my time running Good Business, the corporate-responsibility firm I started with Giles Gibbons in 1997. But then, in 2013, at Rohan's suggestion, I read Jonathan Safran Foer's *Eating Animals*. I know there are other books like it, but that's the book I read, and it influenced me hugely, opening my eyes to the sickening world of filth, pollution, and abuse that is responsible for the food we consume.

Factory farms are disgusting places. A quick YouTube search for one of the many undercover activist videos shot at chicken, egg, beef, milk, veal, or pork factories will suppress even the most robust appetite. But the point is this: it took reading a book for me to understand the unconscionable origins of much of the food I ate and prepared for family and friends. Reading a food label in the supermarket would have been useless. When I buy a burger for my children at the zoo café or eat in a restaurant, there isn't a label, not even a company website I can check. The vast majority of fast-food places have neither a brand to protect nor an incentive to respond to animal-welfare concerns. I'd love to know how many of the 'conservationists' at the San Diego Zoo, for example, who prattle on with tediously gushing self-righteousness about 'Asiatic lions' or 'Phillippine seahorses' or whatever, have the first idea about the lives of the chickens, pigs, and cows they serve up for lunch?

No one has the first idea, not the people at the zoo, not the shelf stacker at your supermarket, not the waiter in your restaurant. Of course, that's just how the Big Food industry likes it, going to aggressive lengths to stop activists from documenting what happens in factory farms. Keeping us in the dark makes the ethical issues abstract, not something that busy practical people trying to live their lives can spend time or energy on. There's no individual animal for us to picture in our mind's eye, looking back at us, suffering. Over the last two decades the factory farming industry in the United States has worked tirelessly in American state legislatures to make the documentation of factory farms unlawful. In some states such 'ag-gag' laws literally prohibit taking pictures or video of where the meat we feed ourselves and our children comes from. Laws in Kansas (on the books since 1990) and Montana (since 1991) make it illegal to enter any farm facility to take pictures.[1] In March 2015 Wyoming governor Matt Mead signed into law legislation making it illegal to gather any information on private property without permission.[2] Missouri exempts activists from prosecution . . . but only if they turn over any evidence they collect within twenty-four hours, thereby making it impossible to build a solid case of systematic abuse without alerting abusers to the investigation.[3] A bill passed last June in North Carolina—over the governor's veto, no less—doesn't make it illegal for employees to take photos or video, but they can be held liable for damages to the business that any whistleblowing incurs, including punitive damages of up to $5,000 for each day information was collected.[4]

Thanks to the work of some exceptionally brave campaigners, who pose undercover, sneak around at night, and risk harsh penalties, we know the abuse that goes on. Do not be in any doubt: the meat we eat relies on systematic cruelty that is documented, widespread, and beyond the most sadistic thoughts you can imagine. It's not a question of whether animals are being tortured for our food; it's a question of whether we care enough to stop it.

FOR ME, THIS is very personal. I love food. I love cooking. When we moved to California, Rachel and I decided to raise chickens with our sons, Ben and Sonny. It is one of the most pleasing things you can imagine—seeing your children run outside in the morning to let the chickens out of their coop, fascinated as the birds peck around, excited to collect the eggs. Of course, I see that this is the stuff of parody, that the first thing defenders of our inhuman, industrial food system will say is that objecting to it is all very well, but all very elitist. Big Food is cheap food, and most normal people can't keep chickens, can't afford your free-range, hand-reared, artisanal, grass-fed whatnots. Big Food and its lobbyists claim that intensive, 'efficient' production of food is the only way to feed the world's growing population affordably. This is false, as we shall see, but those who want to see food produced through more human, less barbaric means are often dismissed as being out of touch. You know: 'Let them eat seasonal, organic, locally sourced, fair-trade cake.'

This caricature of 'bad but cheap' versus 'good but expensive' misses the fundamental point: Why do you think factory food is cheap? It's not because it's inherently cheaper or more 'efficient' to farm animals and process them in a highly mechanized way. We've chosen to make it cheaper as a deliberate act of policy, through direct and indirect corporate subsidies, regulations, and laws designed to protect Big Food and crush any challenge to it from those who want to do things differently. "Most people have little idea just how much they are paying for food in hidden ways," says Patrick Holden, founding director of the UK-based Sustainable Food Trust and one of the world's most thoughtful food activists. "The failure to introduce true cost accounting into food and agricultural policy is the biggest single impediment to the wider uptake of more sustainable farming."[5] Humane food appears to be more expensive because all its costs are included in the price. With factory food, we pay its costs in other ways.

THERE IS A growing cost to our health. Our ability to treat infection is slowly coming under attack as a result of the excessive antibiotic use on factory farms. Most antibiotics in the United States—up to 80 percent—are used on farm animals, not people.[6] This is considered necessary not only to keep animals from dying—because their quarters are so squalid, overcrowded, and diseased—but also to promote quick growth. Thanks to a combination of aggressive breeding and antibiotics, chickens that would otherwise take fourteen weeks to mature require only six in a factory (according to poultry scientists in a 2013 article, if "humans grew at a similar rate, a 6.6 lb newborn baby would weigh 660 lbs after two months"[7]). In the last five years doctors have observed an alarming rise in urinary tract infections as well as sepsis, particularly from antibiotic-resistant strains of E. coli. This is part of a larger trend: already at least

2 million people annually in the United States acquire serious infections from bacteria that are resistant to the antibiotics designed to treat them; twenty-three thousand people die.[8]

Factory farming isn't responsible for all resistance to antibiotics; we use them on ourselves and even our pets at levels far higher than we should. But the genes in an increasing number of resistant cases have been found to match bacteria found on 'conventionally'—that is, industrially—raised meat, specifically those given antibiotics.[9] Antibiotics used to promote quick growth in livestock are now doing the same thing to people. According to studies by public-health researchers, 'chronic mass exposure' to antibiotic 'residue' is now believed to contribute directly to our growth, increasing our propensity to gain weight above and beyond food's 'nutrition facts.'[10] The World Health Organization and US Centers for Disease Control and Prevention have both sounded the alarm, yet the reaction from the factory food industry as well as most agricultural regulators has been slow to nonexistent.[11]

Although antibiotic resistance threatens everyone, including vegetarians and free-range enthusiasts, those of us who eat factory meat—and even crops from nearby fields—are much likelier to get ill directly from it.[12] Just as urban slums do among humans, the high density of animal confinement increases the chance of disease. These breeding grounds give us contaminated food: in the United States 69 percent of store-bought pork and beef and 92 percent of poultry are contaminated with E. coli bacteria, more than 85 percent of which is already resistant to antibiotics.[13] A salmonella outbreak at Foster Farms that ended in July 2014 spanned seventeen months, twenty-nine states, and 634 illnesses, including over 240 hospitalizations. That one came on the heels of a 'smaller' outbreak for which Foster Farms was responsible from 2012 to 2013 that sickened over a hundred people.[14] It's not just Foster Farms: Barber Foods recalled over 1.7 million pounds of chicken, fearing it could be contaminated with salmonella in July 2015.[15] Indeed, the FDA reports that salmonella contaminates one-fifth of all retail chicken.[16]

Factory farms operate out of proportion to nature. Consequently the only thing to do with the excess animal wastewater, feces, feathers, guts, blood, and other detritus is to dump it. According to the US Department of Agriculture, confined animals produce over 330 million tons of waste per year—forty times what's produced by humans.[17] Unlike cities, which have complex systems for the collection and treatment of human waste, animal waste is just dumped into "massive open-air cesspits" that, according to public health expert Dr. Michael Greger, "can leak and contaminate water used to irrigate our crops. That's how a deadly fecal pathogen like E. coli O157:H7 can end up contaminating our spinach."[18]

It's not just about animal confinement. The problem with our factory system is that food—all of it, not just meat—is combined, mixed, and re-distributed so widely that a single sick cow or contaminated batch of vegetables can infect the food supply across the country almost overnight. Consider that tainted beef from just one producer in California, Rancho Feeding Corp., spread to over thirty-five states and one US territory, leading to a 2014 recall of nearly 9 million pounds of meat across thousands of retailers.[19] Almost as if to ensure cross-contamination, poultry producers insist on chilling their birds not by air in large refrigerators but by water, which Tom Devine, the legal director of the Government Accountability Project, says "has been aptly named 'fecal soup' for all the filth and bacteria floating around."[20] Why would producers do this? "Air chilling," according to Jonathan Safran, "reduces the weight of a bird's carcass, but water-chilling causes a dead bird to soak up water (the same water known as 'fecal soup')." In other words, the industry converts wastewater into millions of dollars' worth of excess poundage—up to an allowable 12 percent to be precise.[21]

This industrialization of food might look 'efficient,' but it creates massive risks that make the whole system inherently vulnerable to devastating and costly outbreaks. This isn't to say that small-scale farmers aren't susceptible to animal infections, but at least in those cases meat can be more easily isolated and contained. With a national—international—system of collecting, mixing, and spreading food, one 'rotten apple' can cause problems on a vast scale.

"THIS FOOD IS KILLING US"

Factory food goes way beyond meat. Michael Moss, a Pulitzer Prize–winning journalist at the *New York Times*, spent over four years researching and reporting on the science behind processed food, talking to hundreds of people in or formerly employed by the food industry as well as combing through thousands of internal documents. In his revealing book, *Salt Sugar Fat*, he explains how factory food is engineered to be addictive.

Moss tells the story of Howard Moskowitz, one of the food industry's go-to consultants for fine-tuning its products. A mathematician with a PhD in experimental psychology from Harvard, he got his start in the unlikeliest of places: the US Army, which had called on him to help solve the problem of getting soldiers on the battlefield to eat the food rationed to them. (After a while, soldiers would find their ready-to-eat meals boring and not finish them, creating waste and possible energy deficits.) What *would* soldiers eat ad infinitum? White bread. Though it would never get them excited, Moskowitz explains, "They could eat lots and lots of it without feeling they'd had enough."[22]

This is called 'sensory-specific satiety.' According to Moss, "It is the tendency for big, distinct flavors to overwhelm the brain, which responds by depressing your desire to have more." Eating bland food (like white bread) might fill you up, but you don't feel like stopping. This insight would launch Moskowitz's long career helping food companies make their products more addictive. For over three decades he's been a paid 'optimization' consultant for Big Food companies like General Foods, Campbell Soup, Kraft, and PepsiCo. "I've optimized soups," he says. "I've optimized pizzas. I've optimized salad dressings and pickles."

To achieve this, consumers are paid to sit for hours in focus groups, giving their input on every sensory detail you can imagine—taste, touch, the rather creepy-sounding 'mouth feel,' packaging, smell, and so forth. The data is then processed using a complex statistical method called conjoint analysis. Moss explains, "It's not simply a matter of comparing Color 23 with Color 24. In the most complicated projects, Color 23 must be combined with Syrup 11 and Packing 6, and on and on, in seemingly infinite combinations." The goal: to find consumers' 'bliss point.'

How do you attain bliss? In case the title of Moss's book wasn't too much of a giveaway, it's with salt, sugar, and fat. Not necessarily more of all of them—there's a 'Goldilocks' point for each—but certainly nowhere close to moderation. The simple truth is that salt is addictive. Sugar is addictive. Fat is addictive. Who cares if eating too much of them makes people unhealthy? Certainly not Big Food. If you're running a factory-food company, the whole point is to get people to eat more and more of your product.

Let's look at sugar in particular. It's everywhere, and in excess. A typical Yoplait yogurt has more sugar (18 grams) per single-serving container than a Reese's Peanut Butter Cup.[23] A twelve-ounce can of Coca-Cola contains 39 grams of sugar—that's nearly ten teaspoons.[24] Meanwhile a grande Starbucks Caramel Frappuccino has 64 grams of sugar—sixteen teaspoons. Yes, sixteen teaspoons.[25] Disgusting if you actually imagine scooping each one in, but we don't because they're easily dissolved (i.e., camouflaged) directly into the food or drink.[26] You'll also find added sugar in your deli meats, bread—even the whole grain ones—frozen dinners, soups, chips . . . the list goes on. Subway's Meatball Marinara six-inch sub has 12 grams of sugar (three teaspoons).[27] Sugar is hidden in just about every processed food, mainly because it is addictive. Even one tablespoon of Heinz ketchup is 1 teaspoon of sugar (leaving just enough room for the actual tomatoes, of course).[28]

Making consumers physically addicted to their products is a carefully calibrated science into which the Big Food companies put huge effort. According to Moss, five hundred chemists, psychologists, and technicians were put to work at the Frito-Lay (maker of Lay's chips and other snack foods) research center in Dallas, measuring and optimizing every variable they could. My favorite tool described by him is the company's $40,000 chewing simulator. They used it to answer questions like how brittle the perfect chip ought to be: "People like a chip that snaps with about four pounds of pressure per square inch." Consider Cheetos. With annual worldwide sales of over $4 billion, it's a big business.[29] Its most important feature, according to food scientist Steve Witherly, is "vanishing caloric density"—the cheese puffs' ability to dissolve instantly on your tongue. "If something melts down quickly, your brain thinks that there's no calories in it . . . you can just keep eating it forever."[30]

As you might expect, this food is killing us. The rapid rise of heart disease and diabetes in Western society is directly linked to our diet. Obesity and overweight—these conditions' frequent precursor—account for 21 percent of American healthcare expenditures: $190 billion in 2005.[31] That's over $600 on average that each person pays per year in additional taxes and insurance premiums to subsidize the treatment of diet-related disease. By 2030 economists project these annual costs will have increased by between $48 and $66 billion.[32] Meanwhile, according to Columbia University's Mailman School of Public Health, workplace absenteeism from obesity-related diseases (diabetes, heart disease, among others) costs the American economy another $8.65 billion per year.[33]

The bottom line: factory food is toxic, and the only way to understand how it has become so pervasive is to understand the business of factory farming. Not just factory farms for animals but also the farms growing the crops on which this whole inhuman, industrialized monstrosity is built.

"NO FUTURE IN FARMING"

Matt Rothe always wanted to be a farmer. Raised on a large family farm in Colorado, perhaps the most exciting day in his childhood was the day his father showed him how to use the tractor . . . and let him drive it. "It's corn as far as you can see in any direction," Matt explains. "And despite the fact that you're only going three miles per hour, you're always making a little progress toward the end of the field, and there's such a sense of satisfaction when you get to that final row, and you turn around, and the whole thing is done." By his senior year in college in 1994 Rothe had been doing a lot of thinking about his future. In April he called his father and told him what he'd decided: he wanted to "come home and farm." He thought his father would be thrilled; instead, his father told him no, there's just no future in it. What he meant was, no future in farming the way they farmed. No future in a family farm. "It was hard for both of us," Rothe says. "I can't imagine being a father and listening to my son and telling him he couldn't come back and run the business—the business that had been in the family for twelve generations."

Rothe moved out to California and got a job running one of the best-known suppliers of humanely produced meat in the state.[34] After that he went to business school. Just as he was finishing his degree, he found out his dad had been diagnosed with pancreatic cancer—a year-long death sentence. Rothe started spending much more time at home, being with his father, helping him manage the farm's affairs, and getting a glimpse into what the business was really like. "I started taking a look at all the spreadsheets," he says, "all of the profit-and-loss statements, the balance sheet." It turned out the farm was close to bankruptcy. After his father passed away, Rothe and his mother had no choice but to sell. "There was this feeling of helplessness, of seeing the farm disappear for good in our family. My dad was the twelfth documented generation of family farmers in our family. And there wasn't going to be another one."

Several months before his father died the two had been sitting at the kitchen table, and Rothe's dad started to tell his son a story, the same story that, many years before, his own father had told him. It was the story of how the tractor ruined farming.

"It used to be that we had horses, and they did all of our work," he began. "The cycle of the day was that you'd get up in the morning, feed the horses, feed yourself, go out in the barn, saddle all the horses, get them all connected, and you'd go out and work in the field until noon. Then you'd come back, get the horses some water, a little food. You would eat. And you'd take the horses back out in the afternoon to work either until they couldn't work anymore or you couldn't work anymore. And at the end of the day you'd put the horses back in the stable. Everyone would go to sleep, and you'd get up the next morning and do it again. Then one day they invented the tractor. And this tractor was going to be the savior for farming. This was going to make farming easier; it was going to make it more profitable. We were all going to get rich: 'Go buy a tractor!' Think about it . . . you went from a horse, which is one horsepower, to a tractor, which is scores of horsepower. It was a giant leap forward in terms of technology on the farm."

But tractors were expensive. Farmers didn't have a lot of money, so they took out loans to buy them. That wasn't really a problem—after all, the tractor was going to make them exponentially more productive—but then the tractors broke down a lot and needed lots of fuel, so they had to take out loans to run them, and then they realized that the tractor was so productive, they were no longer limited by hours in the day but by how many acres they had. Except that without enough acres, they couldn't actually pay off the tractor. So they took out more loans, bought more land, and farmed it like never before.

"Everybody is getting a tractor," his dad continued. "All the neighbors now have tractors. Everybody is more productive, everybody is buying more land, everybody is producing more food. And because there's more of it in the market, the prices are declining. The reality is that we're not really any better off financially because prices have come down as a result of our productivity. And we have all this debt that we have to service. At least with the horse we had the promise of only working a twelve-hour day because that's all the horse could work. Now we're working all day every day just to service this tractor."

At that moment, sitting at the kitchen table, listening to his dad in his bathrobe talking about tractors, it all clicked for Rothe. "My grandfather's story of the tractor is basically an allegory for every technology that's been developed since. That includes artificial pesticides, fertilizers, genetically modified organisms. It includes the specialization of farming equipment and technology. It's all the same story."[35] These technologies we've developed—which on the surface have led to highly 'efficient' farming of the same crop in huge fields (much easier for the tractor to plow through)—actually mask the decline of productive capacity in our soils. We produce more calories now than we ever have, but it's an illusion. In reality the underlying asset, the soil, is declining—and not just its fertility: overworked farms leave soil overexposed to wind and water erosion. As Rothe explains, there's no question that this is a far 'cheaper' way to produce food. But that's only because its costs are borne by future generations of consumers and farmers for whom one day this system of monocultures, fossil-fuel-based fertilizers, and soil depletion will collapse.

Consider: as soil health declines, farmers must compensate with more and more nitrogen fertilizer. But not all of it gets taken up by crops; rather, it ends up in the air (fueling climate change as nitrous oxide), in our rivers and oceans (killing off entire marine ecosystems), and in our drinking water. And soil is relatively finite, taking five hundred years to produce just two centimeters.[36] There are also the pesticides we have to filter from our water, the flooding precipitated by eroded fields, the loss of habitats for critical species, let alone the species themselves . . . the list goes on. A 2004 Cornell University study estimated the societal costs of pesticides alone to be over $8 billion per year.[37] A 2015 study by scientists at the Environmental Protection Agency (EPA) calculates the nitrogen damage to the environment inflicted annually by agriculture to be in excess of $157 billion.[38]

FARMING NEVER USED to be a depletive act. It was the ultimate symbiotic relationship between man and nature. Though each crop would take something from the soil—how else would it grow?—it would give something back too. Legumes, like clover, would be planted during off-cycles to fix nitrogen in the soil, nitrogen that other crops like vegetables, fruits, and grains need to grow well. This is why for generations farmers would rotate the crops they grew within their fields each season. Meanwhile grazing livestock would create fertilizer—for free—greatly reducing if not eliminating the need to buy artificial inputs as well as making waste management a far easier task. Nitrogen fixation, a natural process, converts nitrogen in the air into ammonium in the soil, which can then be picked up by all other plant types and converted to plant protein. Simplistically: no nitrogen, no crops, no food.

The availability of food is obviously a basic requirement for humans, and until the mid-nineteenth century, population growth in Europe was largely constrained by the amount of reactive nitrogen in the food supply. To keep up with demand, reactive nitrogen was mined directly from coal, saltpeter, and guano. But then, at the start of the twentieth century, Fritz Haber, a German chemist, worked out how to convert natural gas into nitrogen fertilizer. It was considered nothing short of alchemy. Managing multiple crops on a farm, rotating them so that soil nutrients can be properly restored, isn't conducive to industrial techniques. But the availability of industrial fertilizer made possible the introduction of vast, tractor-able expanses of single crops like corn, wheat, soy, and sugar that can be farmed in massive volumes. Now these are the basic ingredients of the factory food—junk food—that has come to dominate our diet.

As technology like fertilizers, engineered seeds, and machinery made industrial farming possible, traditional family farms have been swallowed up into the giant factory farming corporations that dominate our food supply today. Industrialized feed production led to industrialized animal production, and the factory farm was born. As big companies tend to do, these giant agri-businesses—companies like Archer Daniels Midland, Cargill, Monsanto, Tyson, and Smithfield—have turned their market power into political power, successfully lobbying for the things that would make their life easier and the life of the ever-shrinking number of family farms harder.

NOWHERE IS THIS more egregious than in chicken farming, an industry that, for all intents and purposes, is nothing short of modern-day indentured servitude. Tyson, the nation's largest chicken producer, doesn't "produce" many chickens itself; rather, it uses its market power to insist farmers raise its chickens according to strict "take it or leave it" contracts.

Under such arrangements Tyson hatches chickens, which are then sent to contract farmers to raise. While there, they are fed with Tyson feed and monitored by Tyson technicians before being collected, six weeks later, by Tyson trucks. Farmers are then paid according to how well the chickens have grown—not according to a fair and competitive market but as compared to other farmers in the area, in a so-called tournament system. This means that no matter how well the group does, half the farmers by definition fall below average and are accordingly paid a lower price per bird (not that all the chickens won't be sold at high profit anyway).[39] Meanwhile, if the Tyson hatcher provides a bad batch of chickens or poorer quality feed, it's the farmer's loss. Tyson controls the whole process except the risky part, which it outsources to its farmers, many of whom are already impoverished.

Tyson has responded to criticism of its business model: "We want and need each of [our contract farmers] to succeed. We depend on them to supply livestock and raise our chickens. . . . [T]here are contract farmers who have successfully raised chickens for us for decades."[40] But according to journalist Christopher Leonard, who painstakingly investigated the meat industry in his book *The Meat Racket,* those farmers who fall behind in the tournament might find their contracts terminated. Tyson might offer them another chance if they take on loans to upgrade their facilities. Many farmers do. But as other farmers with newer and more modern facilities enter the system, the cycle inevitably starts again. Once more the choice is clear: take on more debt to keep up or declare bankruptcy. Many choose the former.[41]

You might ask: Why sign the contract in the first place? With no other buyers to turn to, there really is no choice. Aided and abetted by subsidies, legal loopholes, and a lack of proper antitrust enforcement (for more on this, see Chapter 6), Tyson and its peers use their oligopoly power to make the entire market extraordinarily uncompetitive. Their use of contracts has all but destroyed the open market.

The same practices have spread to the beef and pork industries. Until the 1990s all were traded on the market as commodities, with prices rising and falling as demand and supply fluctuated. It was far from a perfect system, but it was fair, and farmers could maintain their independence. But as mergers and consolidation proliferated, large meatpackers eventually gained enough market power to create whatever market worked best for them, regardless of the harm it did to others. Consider beef: "In the face of increasingly volatile prices and depressed profits, most cattle producers have opted to abandon the free market altogether," Leonard explains. Instead, like so many chicken farmers, they sell under exclusive contract to one producer, locking in a low but guaranteed price. "The remaining minority of cattle producers who sell their animals on the open market find that they must often take the price that is dictated to them by Tyson, Cargill, or JBS," who, along with National Beef, control 76 percent of beef in the United States.[42] After all, Leonard says, "It's hard to get a better price when the buyers refuse to bid against one another."[43]

WHEN PEOPLE SAY it's elitist to want a more human food system because factory food at least delivers cheap food for hard-pressed families, tell them about the subsidies. Factory food is 'cheap' because it's subsidized in multiple ways. Through a variety of programs, American growers of commodities crops—namely corn and soy, which are the primary ingredients for both factory livestock feed as well as processed junk foods—will receive $134.3 billion of federal government support from 2014 to 2023.[44] Meanwhile on specialty crops—like vegetables, fruits, and nuts—through a variety of small programs, research grants, export enhancements, and other provisions, the government will spend just $4 billion.[45]

As eye-watering as those figures are, it's not simply a question of money. Tamar Haspel, a farmer and *Washington Post* journalist explains,

What's important about how we subsidize farms isn't necessarily the overall dollar amount—it comes to 5 percent to 10 percent of the market price of most of the subsidized crops—it's that it takes some of the risk out of farming grains and oil seeds, but not fruits and vegetables. . . . For farmers, crops that are given guaranteed protection from both losses and price drops are lower-risk propositions. . . . That's one of the reasons that, of the 300-million-plus acres planted with food (other than grass, hay and forage for animals) in this country, half are corn and soy. Another 50 million are wheat. Only 14 million are devoted to fruits and vegetables, from peas (1.2 million acres) to mangosteens (1 acre, which I'd dearly love to visit).[46]

In many ways the subsidies that really matter are implicit: the indirect subsidies that are multiple orders of magnitude bigger: we pay the financial costs of the health and environmental damage that the Big Food companies cause—costs that they avoid. This means we first pay for factory food when we buy it, then we pay taxes and higher insurance premiums to counter its negative impact on our health and environment, and then again we pay through our taxes that subsidize the Big Food companies. Taxes are supposed to pay for things that are good for society but wouldn't happen otherwise. And yet here we are, subsidizing commercial activity that harms the public. It's nuts.

We can change this. We can design a food system that's better for our health, better for the environment, better for animals. We can design a food system that is more human.

THE NIMAN RANCH PORK COMPANY

When I worked in the British government we tried to reduce the harm done by Big Food through voluntary agreements—what we called "Responsibility Deals"—through which the companies would make their food less toxic. The idea was that this would actually be a quicker way to achieve concrete outcomes like reductions in salt, fat, and sugar than going through a process of regulation. These efforts were ultimately superficial because they didn't address the deep structural forces at play. The key to making food more human on a mass scale lies in new business models that can produce better, healthier food *systematically*. In this respect entrepreneurs—big and small—are leading the way.

In 2015, Chipotle, the US-based seventeen-hundred-branch chain (with locations now in Europe and Canada) serving custom-built tacos and burritos made from freshly prepared, recognizable ingredients, was hit by a series of food-related sickness outbreaks that called into question the chain's food safety practices, which are still under investigation at the time of this writing. Any flaws in Chipotle's food safety standards, however, do not detract from its leadership on animal welfare, where it still ranks among the best in the industry. Case in point: when one supplier failed animal welfare inspections, Chipotle temporarily stopped serving pork at over a third of its restaurants rather than continue buying and selling the inhumanely raised meat.[47] Chipotle's commitment to food that's produced in a more human way is a key part of its brand. They're proving that fast food can be made at scale using humane, sustainable meat. What's less well known is that much of Chipotle's ability to buy humane pork at the scale it does rests on the ingenuity of one man determined to prove it is possible.

A little over a decade ago Steve Ells, Chipotle's founder, read an article called "The Lost Taste of Pork" in an obscure food magazine called the *Art of Eating*. In it writer Edward Behr describes the "best pork" he had ever eaten and details the old-fashioned practices of the farm it came from, run by a man named Paul Willis. After ordering some to try for himself, Ells was hooked. He was determined to make his burritos with meat from farms like Willis's.[48] But how could one small farm supply thousands of restaurants around the world?

A down-to-earth, fourth-generation farmer from Iowa, Willis has been raising pigs—all free-range—since the mid-1970s. "I learned to do this when I grew up, and it was common," he explains. "I liked the idea of the animals being out on the pasture. Pigs were part of your crop rotation—we were growing corn, soybeans, oats, and hay—and one of the things you had were pigs." Over time Willis was able to grow the farm to over a thousand pigs. Like many other pig farmers around the country, he had built a sustainable, profitable livelihood for himself, one that respected the land, the animals, and the community.

Then at some point in the 1980s Willis started to notice confinement buildings popping up, buildings designed to house tens of thousands of livestock packed together as closely as possible. They started out small—individual buildings on farmers' land—but by the 1990s, when factory farms had infiltrated the pig industry, buyers no longer wanted to deal with small farms like his. "They started to squeeze us out of the marketplace. They would bid us a lesser price or rate our meat poorer quality, since it yielded less." (Pigs raised outdoors have bigger lungs and hearts because they use them running around and doing what pigs naturally do.) But Willis refused to change. "Going in one of those buildings convinced me that I just never wanted to raise animals like that." The sound, the crowded conditions, the concrete, the palpable misery—all have an overwhelming effect on anyone who sets foot in a modern factory farm.

"I think the thing that really knocks me over is the odor—the hydrogen sulfide and ammonia. You can't take enough showers to get rid of it, even if you're in there only a minute. I lived on a farm, grew up with farms— my grandparents, my parents and so forth. And this was a brand-new smell, something we had never experienced before."

Willis makes sure his "pigs can be pigs." Recognizing that they, like humans, require companionship, he never introduces one animal into a social group that's already established. He'll also make "retreat areas" with straw bales to give timid animals a place to get away from their aggressive peers. (Contrast this with the 80 percent of pregnant sows in factory farms, churning out piglets with little respite their entire lives, raised in steel-and-concrete pens that prohibit them from turning around, a practice defended on the grounds that it prevents the cruelly stressed pigs from injuring each other.[49])

As farms consolidated around him, Willis looked for a way to keep farming the way he knew was right. His answer was also consolidation— but on farmers' terms, not industry's. He started reaching out to other local-farmer networks, finding people who raised pigs in a similar way and paying them a premium price. Little by little, welfare standards were established, and with fellow humane livestock pioneer Bill Niman as a partner, the Niman Ranch Pork Company was established. Today it comprises five hundred farmers and can't increase supply fast enough.[50]

In addition to a price premium, the pork company members receive a guaranteed price floor, to protect against unexpected drops in the market, and are able to use their scale to economize on processing, distribution, and marketing. Willis and Niman created a business model that would allow farmers to confidently stick to a more human approach even in the face of their industrialized, mechanized competitors. Now, thanks to Paul Willis, you can buy humane pork not just at high-end restaurants and grocery stores but also in the mass marketplace.

A different but equally promising challenge to the industrialized food system is being pioneered by Belcampo Meat Company, based in Oakland. Its business model focuses on just one ranch, owning some twenty thousand acres in northern California as well as the entire supply chain needed to support it. For its two thousand cattle and thirteen thousand other animals such as quail, sheep, goats, rabbits, and chickens, that means one slaughterhouse and a handful of retail butcher shops (there are seven already in California). The farm, the processing, the retail— all in one business. According to founder Anya Fernald, bringing it all together isn't only more profitable; it also assures that standards are upheld. Raising the animals is really only half the battle, after all. You could be the most caring, humane rancher in the world but still have to use a third-party slaughterhouse who doesn't share your values. This leaves far too many questions unanswered. Fernald wants to know: "How was it actually killed? How was the handling leading up to the kill? How long was it sitting on the truck?[51] She designed Belcampo to make sure there were no missing links in the supply chain.

The key for Belcampo is bringing everyone together, from the rancher and slaughterhouse cutter to the butcher and customer, such that where your food comes from is no longer some black box—in fact, every single piece of meat is completely traceable, as the system is so straightforward and transparent. It's human scaled. Fernald acknowledges that Belcampo can't sustainably grow beyond eight or nine stores, but this doesn't mean the model can't. She envisages a multiplicity of Belcampos, each with its own management team, butcher shops, slaughterhouse, and ranch. "When businesses that are producing food get to a large scale, quality takes a nosedive and communication breaks down." For a meat model that's focused on health and husbandry to work profitably, she insists, the supporting business structure must be large enough to turn a profit but not so large that it becomes out of touch.

JAMIE AND THE FOOD REVOLUTION

So yes, a more human approach to food is emerging. How can we encourage it? Some have argued that consumer information and education—changing our food culture—holds the key. Ending bad food starts with an appreciation of good food—not just how to eat it but knowing where it comes from and how to cook it. A good place to start? Our children. If you think food marketing to adults is deceptive, what the food industry does to children is far worse, with a combination of cartoon characters, prizes, online games, and social pressure used to full effect (more on this in Chapter 7). But even if parents guard against the insidious influence of food media, schools can often let them down.

No one has done more to shine a spotlight on this over the years than the heroic Jamie Oliver. *Jamie Oliver's Food Revolution*, a TV show he produced with Ryan Seacrest in 2010 and 2011 revealed not only the lack of food education for children in some of America's most overweight communities (a group of whom had trouble identifying fruits and vegetables in one now-famous clip) but also on school board officials' attempts in places like Los Angeles to obscure the heavily processed junk food they serve their students several times each day. Most notably, his efforts to show how 'pink slime,' a beef byproduct made by combining inedible parts of the cow carcass with ammonium hydroxide or citric acid and often found in school and fast-food burgers, prompted a national consumer revolt. His success was bittersweet though: pink slime is still served up across the country—including in schools—and as drought drives beef prices up, producers are turning back to pink slime to keep prices down. But without any mandatory labeling (pink slime can legally make up 15 percent of a burger's content while still being called 100 percent 'ground beef'), how can parents—or anyone—know?[52]

A wonderful counterpoint to the world of pink slime is provided by Alice Waters, the visionary pioneer from Berkeley, California, whose Chez Panisse restaurant helped bring healthy, sustainable food to the height of global popularity (at least among elites and hipsters) that it now enjoys. Waters's mission is to take her food revolution mainstream. After she started a garden and teaching kitchen at a nearby middle school some twenty years ago, her Edible Schoolyard project has grown into a fully fledged educational resource center. Its in-person seminars and online network provide curricula and practical resources for educators who not only see the vital connection between well-nourished children and their educational outcomes but also understand the need to teach students about the food they eat and where it comes from.

But as Jamie Oliver and others have found, the culinary-industrial complex doesn't want you to know about the food you eat and where it comes from.

Upset by a planned McDonald's restaurant near the Spanish Steps in Rome, Carlo Petrini, an Italian journalist from Piedmont, founded an organization called Slow Food. Since its founding in 1986, Slow Food has become a global movement, coming to represent much more than an opposition to fast food. Its motto, "Good, clean and fair," captures precisely the opposite of what our food system has become. Its conference in Turin every two years brings together thousands of farmers, fishers, ranchers, food artisans—and, of course, eaters—from every corner of the earth to share each other's cultures and, most importantly, put a face—a story—behind what's being enjoyed. One of Slow Food's most compelling proposals is a "narrative label" for foods, with details like animal breeds, types of feed, pasture type and location, and animal welfare all clearly spelled out.

Why focus on the narrative? What about all those certification schemes you see everywhere? Standards, labels, different terms approved by governments and regulators—isn't that the way to inform consumers and thereby change behavior? The problem is, these bureaucratic schemes are just another black box that consumers don't really understand and can't see into; they're not human, just like PISA scores in education. With a few exceptions, they can be easily gamed, obscuring the truth so that a carefully crafted facade can be more easily believed.

THERE'S A TV AD (for Geico insurance, as it happens) about a chicken traveling across the country. Wherever it goes—along train tracks, into a diner—it sends selfies back to the farmers who raised it. As the camera pans out from the farmers sitting on their veranda, we see hundreds of chickens roaming freely across the countryside to the narrator's message: "If you're a free-range chicken, you roam free. It's what you do."[53] This is what you might imagine when you see 'free range' on meat you buy in the supermarket. It's what you're supposed to imagine. It's what the words 'free range' literally mean: freedom. Rolling outdoor pastures, animals able to behave naturally, roaming about, eating grass, little bugs, whatever they want.

Well, roaming free may be what you do if you're a chicken in an insurance ad, but it's highly unlikely to be what you do if you're an actual free-range chicken in the real world. It is perfectly permissible, within the relevant USDA labeling rules, for "free-range" chickens to spend most of their lives cramped inside huge indoor barns. What about "cage free"? Sounds good, no? Although cage-free chickens are literally not housed in cages, farmers can get away with providing them as little space as they want (the industry "cage-free" average is about one square foot per bird, with no outdoor access).[54] And within both free-range and cage-free labeling schemes, it is perfectly acceptable to treat animals with antibiotics and to carry out cruel and disgusting practices like throwing live chicks into mincing machines.

The truly depressing fact is that this is what passes for good in our current system. Most of these 'humane' free-range and cage-free producers are slightly better than the vast majority of meat and dairy products with no animal welfare claims at all. (Caged hens, which lay more than 95 percent of eggs sold in the United States, are typically confined to less space than a sheet of letter-sized paper.[55]) But nothing is worse than

the use of humane-sounding terms that have no specific standards associated with them at all, terms like '100% natural,' 'farm fresh,' 'high
animal welfare,' 'corn fed,' or 'no added hormones.' (These last two are
particularly egregious, as you will often see them on the menus of smart
restaurants trying to give themselves an aura of quality. All chickens are
'corn fed,' and it is illegal to inject any poultry with hormones; saying so
doesn't tell you anything about whether or not they were raised in horrific conditions.) The use of these terms amounts to deliberate lying by
the culinary-industrial complex to cover up factory farming's grotesque
cruelty to animals. It is a scandal.

This kind of jaw-dropping hypocrisy is everywhere in the food industry. Here's Jim Perdue, chairman of Perdue Chicken, one of the world's
largest producers, in a 2011 promotional video: "Doing the right thing
is things like treating your chickens humanely."[56] To prove it, the company prints "raised cage free" on its packages. Until late 2014 it even
claimed its chickens were "humanely raised." Craig Watts, a Perdue producer, disagrees. He has produced 720,000 birds per year for the company since 1992. "It couldn't get any further from the truth," he says.
Watts, whose family has owned their farm since the 1700s, has followed
Perdue's guidelines to the letter. His chickens are anything but humanely
raised. When he invited Compassion in World Farming to look at his four
barns, they videoed oversized chickens scraping by, with bellies rubbed
free of feathers—red and raw. Cage free? Certainly, though this is totally misleading, as chickens grown for meat have never been raised in
cages. "Humanely raised"? Absolutely not.[57] And although they admitted
no wrongdoing, Perdue settled in 2014 with the Humane Society of the
United States, who sued for its use of the phrase. The company has now
agreed to remove it from some of its packaging.[58]

Information is a vital part of making markets work properly, but in
the food market today the information that's supposed to efficiently connect buyers and sellers is not information at all. Despite all the controls
and specifications that govern food labeling and advertising, consumers
are misled and lied to on a daily basis. Why is it acceptable for my milk
carton to feature images of cows strolling around on grassy hills when
they're actually confined inside and fed unhealthy diets of corn and soy,
not the grass their digestive systems were designed to eat? Why is it acceptable for chickens to be called "free range" when they're captive in-
doors for half their lives? Why don't I have a right to know what kinds
of antibiotics were pumped into the bacon I'm about to serve my family
at breakfast? What about the TV ad for pasta sauce that suggests it was

cooked in some home-style kitchen? How can the Big Food company responsible give that impression when it was actually made in some giant gray industrial vat with a whole slew of chemicals that wouldn't be out of place in a science lab?

As we are misled on animal welfare, so too are we misled about our food's nutritional value. The latest marketing gimmick from Big Food is to trumpet the vitamins their food contains. But this is a con. In order to cut costs and increase shelf life, natural nutrients are removed during processing. Then, to be able to tout their products' nutritional benefits, factory food companies add artificial nutrients back to replace what their own machines have stripped bare. The result is a total deception; food brands advertise the vitamins they've added, signaling to the consumer that no matter how much salt, fat, or sugar is present, it has nutritional value and is 'healthy.' Even commercial "whole wheat" is often just white flour to which bran and germ are added back in.[59] Meanwhile we lose the benefits of nutrients that work better in their natural forms. In addition, although the advertised vitamins and nutrients might be good for us, they don't help with diet-related diseases like heart disease and obesity. Processed 'health' food is healthy in all the wrong ways. Westerners are really not at risk from vitamin deficiency (compared to the 2 billion in poor countries who are), and yet we eat this 'healthy' processed food that actually makes us obese and diabetic.[60]

It's not just that loosely regulated claims, certification schemes, packaging, and advertising misrepresent what's gone into the food we buy. In many cases it really is outright lying. One study in Leicester, England, found that over 40 percent of meat products collected from butchers, retailers, wholesalers, manufacturers, fast-food outlets, and caterers contained other species of meat than those that appeared on the labels. In 17 percent of samples meat of the undeclared species was the primary ingredient.[61] Fish in the United States are so regularly mislabeled that the government actually has a task force devoted to fighting "seafood fraud."[62] Whereas 74 percent of sushi bars were found to mislabel their seafood, 94 percent of random samples of red snapper taken from retailers across the United States were found to not actually be red snapper.[63]

Carlo Petrini's idea of narrative labeling takes us toward a more human—and more effective—answer: just let people see what's going on. In 1906 journalist Upton Sinclair published *The Jungle,* which exposed the dreadful conditions in the American meatpacking industry. The public uproar that ensued led to one of the most significant consumer protection laws ever passed: the Pure Food and Drug Act. I think it's time for another uproar.

There's a simple rule we should introduce that would start to address Big Food's lying and misrepresentation. Any food product must have a reasonable proportion of its packaging and any promotional materials, such as TV ads, devoted to showing the precise conditions it was made in. A pack of frozen chicken nuggets would have a photo of the actual farm the chicken came from. A TV ad for hot dogs . . . a video of the pig pen. That 'homemade' pasta sauce? Let's see a picture of the factory, steel vats and all, not some fake pastiche Italian country kitchen constructed in a studio. Look, I'm not saying all of the packaging and promotion of food products should be truthful, just a reasonable amount—say, 20 percent. That still leaves 80 percent for lies and deception. To make sure it's all real and above board, there should be a requirement that every part of every facility of every factory farm and every food factory be live-streamed on the Internet so people can see exactly what's going on and track their food if they want to. In a world of cameras in every smartphone, the cost for producers would be negligible—and radical transparency of this kind would be more effective than any number of regulations and certifications. Who could object to it?

Well, people who get cross about 'the nanny state,' I guess. Hmm. "It's curious that we're open to social engineering when it's being done by corporations," says the food writer and activist Michael Pollan. "You're socially engineered every time you walk through the cereal aisle in the supermarket. The healthy stuff is down at your feet and the stuff with the most sugar and chocolate is at your eye level—or your child's eye level. That doesn't seem to bother us. But as soon as it's done by elected officials on our behalf, it's anathema."[64] Kelly Brownell, a professor of psychology and public health at Yale University, argues, "As a culture, we've become upset by the tobacco companies advertising to children, but we sit idly by while the food companies do the very same thing. And we could make a claim that the toll taken on the public health by a poor diet rivals that taken by tobacco."[65] Perhaps the best advice is in fact Michael Pollan's: never eat food that has been advertised.

BEATING BIG FOOD

But in the end, changing our food culture, consumer pressure, more transparency . . . it's not enough. Despite all the campaigns and heightened awareness, the problem is getting worse, not better. As chef and author Dan Barber wrote in 2014:

> Big Food is getting bigger, not smaller. In the last five years, we've lost nearly 100,000 farms (mostly midsize ones). Today, 1.1 percent of farms in the United States account for nearly 45 percent of farm revenues. Despite being farm-to-table's favorite targets, corn and soy account for more than 50 percent of our harvested acres for the first time ever. Between 2006 and 2011, over a million acres of native prairie were plowed up in the so-called Western Corn Belt to make way for these two crops, the most rapid loss of grasslands since we started using tractors to bust sod on the Great Plains in the 1920s.[66]

In any case it's not fair to put the burden for change on consumers when the Big Food producers have all their structural advantages: the subsidies, the lax regulation. To say that people should care more, that they really should shop differently, misses the point. They already care. But it's such an effort to shop differently. Hardly anyone has the time or inclination to investigate their poultry producer or get up early on Sunday morning for the local farmers' market. People are busy trying to earn a living, raise children, take care of their families. Food may be of great concern to some—as a hobby, as a way of life. But for those whose interests lie elsewhere, for whom grocery shopping happens online between paying the bills and replying to e-mails, for whom dinner is squeezed between two part-time shifts—why should good food be an out-of-reach privilege? How civilized can a society really call itself if humane, healthy, wholesome food is a luxury for those with the time and money to look for it? We need to make food that is produced in a more human way the norm. That will take much more aggressive action than fiddling around with labels or even TV ads, welcome as that would be.

STEP ONE: WE MUST account for the true cost of our factory food and adjust our tax, subsidy, and regulatory regimes accordingly. Just as we have applied the 'polluter pays' principle to companies that damage the environment, we should require food companies to pay for their negative impact on the environment and public health. We already do this for ships responsible for oil spills off the coast. Extending a similar 'price correcting' penalty mechanism to food would finally set the true costs of factory food straight. These penalties would apply at several levels. For, say, livestock waste dumped from animal factories or soil erosion from vast, homogenous fields of corn, it would be applied to the whole operation or farm. But many of these penalties could be much more precise. For example, we should introduce a Nitrogen Tax to discourage the use of depletive artificial fertilizers and to encourage positive alternatives like crop rotation. This would make it feasible to introduce an outright ban on the most dangerous synthetic pesticides, since a more natural system of land husbandry would require less of their use. We also need to challenge the relentless march of genetic modification in our agriculture. This is not progress as some assert but a reckless interference with nature's finely balanced ecosystems, and it's time to call a halt.

True-cost accounting also means looking at harm that happens off the farm. For example, we know that added sugar in processed food creates extra health costs. Just as we apply taxes to cigarettes and alcohol, we could (and should) do the same to sugar. But a Sugar Tax should not just apply to sodas and artificially sweetened beverages alone (as advocated by Mike Bloomberg and Jamie Oliver); it should apply across the board, to sugary candies, cereals, and even that Subway Meatball Marinara sandwich. This was the recommendation the federal Dietary Guidelines Advisory Committee made to the USDA and Department of Health and Human Services last year.[67] In such a system, industrial agriculture businesses would be free to exist, but they would have to pay for the costs of the harm they inflict. Any profits, then, would come from the *real* value they offer consumers and producers, not from the exploitation of animals, farmers, taxpayers, or the environment.

But a true-cost system can't work if enforcement authorities like the USDA and EPA are incapable of supervising even existing laws and regulations. We've seen how hamstrung the USDA is in enforcing food safety (the USDA wasn't just unable to legally force Foster Farms to recall its contaminated poultry; its methods of inspection were so inadequate that it wasn't until people were getting sick that it acknowledged a salmonella outbreak had even occurred).[68] We have to fix this—with better funding (paid for by Big Food itself), tighter supervision, and less of a revolving door with industry (for more on this, see Chapter 6).

WE CAN'T JUST focus on the bad, though. We have to support the good. So we should redirect taxpayer subsidies to farmers and producers who are doing the right thing. By 'redirect,' I mean, of course, taking them away from Big Food.

Now, if government tried to end the factory-food companies' subsidies and make them pay the true costs of their operations, here's what would happen. The bosses of the big food corporations would take to the airwaves and say the price of food would go up. Politicians, terrified of doing anything that raises "the cost of living," would back off. But the "cost of living" as measured by food prices doesn't include the cost of *dying*—the cost of us dying of heart disease and diabetes, of local habitats dying around us, of animals dying in disgusting circumstances that spread disease. None of that—nor other associated costs—is included in the price of factory food, in the cost-of-living figures. That's why nothing gets done.

If we redirect the subsidies while holding Big Food corporations financially responsible for the pollution (of all kinds) they get away with, the price of bad food will go up, but the price of good food—more human food—will go down. If we stopped subsidizing industrial food—instead letting a fair, competitive, and properly priced and regulated market take its place—and chose to lower the costs of fresh fruits and vegetables and humanely raised meat, we would save money for the taxpayer *and* lead happier, healthier, longer lives. (By the way, there is no excuse for good food to be expensive: farms and retailers throw away 12 percent of fresh produce; overall, we discard 29 percent of food unnecessarily—worth well over $165 billion per year.[69])

IT HAS TO be said, though, that there is little chance of seeing the kind of political leadership we need in order to impose these measures. So here's option two: beat Big Food at its own game. There is an exciting approach being pioneered by the prominent London-based investor Jeremy Coller. He argues that factory farms pose an increasing threat to companies'—and their investors'—financial returns, that they create risks for the industry as a whole but that the markets ignore these risks.[70] So Coller and his foundation argue that the directors of any company in the food industry should assess and report these risks so their share prices accurately reflect the financial implications of the factory model. This would have the indirect effect of incentivizing a more human, more sustainable model. But as an investor himself, Coller takes a more active stance and promotes the same to his peers. Coller Capital insists that all its own investments take animal welfare into account. This not only allows Coller to avoid companies that refuse to improve their abusive business model but also to argue directly for change in the practices of companies they're already invested in.

A MORAL IMPERATIVE

I think we should go much further, though. I believe that animal cruelty is an absolute moral outrage: there really is no incremental improvement, no optimal compromise to be had. So I think it's reasonable to take an absolutist policy position, as we do in defense of other moral principles. We don't tolerate a moderate view on rape or torture, nor should we. Over time our progress as a civilized species has been defined by what is added to this list of 'moral universalisms.' One of the most profound was on the subject of slavery, which used to be ubiquitous. Now, of course, it is accepted that slavery is morally wrong. Our norms, along with our economy (as profoundly tied to slavery as it was), adjusted, and we adapted. I think it's time we consider factory farms the same way.

In the introduction to this book I spoke of the empathy evolution: we have increasingly expanded our moral consciousness to include others less like us. Our ability to empathize is fundamental, its expression recognized in infants as young as one day old.[71] Every time we extend empathy, society moves forward. The philosopher Jeremy Bentham argued that if slavery is tyranny and people shouldn't be treated differently by race, why should animals be mistreated simply because they have a different number of legs or the inability to converse? In his mind difference created a slippery slope that allowed the cruel and tyrannical domination of one group over another. Who—or what—made up that 'other' group was immaterial: "The question," he wrote, "is not, *Can they reason?* or *Can they talk?* but *Can they suffer?*"[72]

As proud as we are of our history, we also reflect with shame on atrocities committed by our great-grandfathers—and gratitude that we've come as far as we have in our moral evolution. When our great-grandchildren look back on today, they'll shake their heads at our gross abuse of animals. So the right policy response to factory farms is clear. We shouldn't just 'not subsidize' them. We shouldn't just regulate them better or make them more transparent. We should ban them.

To decide how a ban would be applied, we should look to existing definitions, like the practices itemized in the Business Benchmark on Farm Animal Welfare: close confinement, nontherapeutic use of antibiotics and other growth-promoting drugs, routine mutilation (like tail docking and breaking beaks), partially conscious slaughter, and long-distance transport.[73] Compassion in World Farming argues that animals ought to be free from thirst and hunger, discomfort, pain and disease, fear and distress and should be able to behave in a natural way.[74] Their goal is to eliminate factory farming by 2050.[75] And, of course, in our open, inter-connected global economy, it must happen around the world, not just in one country. But someone has to take the lead, just as Britain did in banning slavery.

When he saw the subtitle of this book ("Designing a World Where People Come First"), my then seven-year-old son Ben said, "for the next version, Dad, I think you should change it to make animals come first, and that's fair to everyone because humans are animals too." Banning factory farms won't just be better for animals; it will make us better humans. In *Eating Animals* Jonathan Safran Foer notes, "Factory Farm—This is a term sure to fall out of use in the next generation or so, either because there will be no more factory farms, or because there will be no more family farms to compare them to."[76] It's up to us.

chapter six

CAPITALISM

"OUT OF THE blue one day, we were told to build a thirty-foot stage."

So begins the most powerful political ad of the 2012 presidential election. To foreboding music and a montage of black-and-white photographs, Mike Earnest tells his story, and that of his colleagues, at a paper plant in Marion, Indiana. Building a stage was an unusual task for mill workers, but they did it, quickly and without question. A few hours later they were summoned back to the warehouse where earlier they had set up the stage, and a group of people walked out—the plant management. The stage was for them. Assembled in front of the management, the workers were then told that all of them, all three shifts, were fired. Even though the factory was profitable, it wasn't profitable enough; the plant would have to close. And just like that, after years—for some, decades—of employment, they no longer had a job. "Turns out that when we built that stage, it was like building my own coffin."[1]

Who was allegedly behind this inhuman treatment of the loyal workers in that plant? The company that bought it and then sold it, Bain Capital, who the ad tells us made $100 million by firing all those workers. And who was behind Bain Capital? The 2012 Republican presidential nominee, Mitt Romney. Critics of the ad, including Democratic rising star and now senator Cory Booker of New Jersey, protested that it unfairly distorted Romney's business career and was profoundly anticapitalist. But to no avail.

Mitt Romney assumed that his exemplary—stellar—track record in business would help propel him to the most powerful job on earth. At a time of economic difficulty, surely the American people would choose an experienced business leader, who has turned around company after company, to turn around America's stagnating economy? It didn't work out that way. In fact, the opposite was the case. It was precisely Mitt Romney's business background that was used by the Obama campaign to destroy him. Week after week Romney was pummeled with ads attacking him for being . . . a capitalist. "The Stage" was simply the most effective of many such spots. More recently the front-runner for the 2016 Democratic presidential nomination, Hillary Clinton, said in a speech in 2014: "Don't let anybody tell you that, you know, it's corporations and businesses that create jobs."[2]

It's not just the Occupy protesters, it seems. Anticapitalist sentiment has gone mainstream—even here in America, one of the most pro-business countries in the world.

In many ways it's understandable. But it's also dangerous. Our progress as a society and our well-being as individuals depend on capitalism and on businesses being successful. In this chapter we'll get to the heart of what's gone wrong and show how we can change things for the better, how we can help build a more human economy. But first we need to remind ourselves of some basic truths that often get lost in the shouting matches of day-to-day debate.

"A SCRIPT OF HOPE"

Consider why capitalism exists in the first place. It's for the simple reason that individuals, acting together through a private organization and backed with outside investment, by pooling resources, skills, and labor, can produce more than the sum of their parts—not just 'profits' for 'capitalists' but also the goods and services we use every day and the innovations that have added years to our lives. Without capitalism, government could not provide social safety nets, pensions, free education, and health care. Of course, that means businesses have to make profits; if they didn't, they would not attract investment, they would go out of business, people would lose their jobs, and governments wouldn't get their tax revenue. Nor would we get the goods and services and innovation that make our lives better. This positive circle is the mechanism that has helped billions of humans escape poverty and provided them with a quality of life that was unimaginable decades ago. When you boil it all down, the mechanism is really quite simple: it's just producing, selling, and buying goods and services. It's also, as former British chief rabbi Jonathan Sacks observes, really quite human:

In the market economy throughout all of history, differences between cultures and nations have led to one of two possible consequences. When different nations meet, they either make war or they trade. The difference is that from war at the very least one side loses, and in the long run, both sides lose. From trade, both sides gain. When we value difference the way the market values difference . . . we turn the narrative of tragedy, of war, into a script of hope.[3]

The vast majority of companies profit from providing something people want, without doing harm to others. Making a profit and not polluting, or making a profit and paying a living wage—these are not mutually exclusive. It's self-defeating for anyone who cares about society or the environment to be 'anti-capitalist' or 'anti-profit.' It's all about how: How is capitalism carried out? How are profits made? That's what we should focus on, not a generalized condemnation of the whole enterprise.

And that word, enterprise, is important too. Trace any business back to its origins, and you will generally find an entrepreneur: an individual or group of individuals who had an idea, a dream, a mission, to make that better cart, to build that better car, to design that better cargo ship, and, now in the twenty-first century, to send that better rocket out into space—and back. The very notion of enterprise, the calling of the entrepreneur, is profoundly human. To believe in something, to believe you can do better than what's out there at the moment, to believe you can persuade other people to buy it from you, to believe it's worth taking a risk with your life, your reputation, your money or other people's money in order to start a business, that is a uniquely human thing to do. This is what we should remember. In our system of capitalism businesses— real businesses—are human. They're about bringing people together in a structured way to benefit each other and society.

Hewlett-Packard cofounder David Packard put it well in a speech to employees in 1960. This quote appears in my earlier book *Good Business*, and I'd like to include it here too:

Why are we here? I think many people assume, wrongly, that a company exists simply to make money. While this is an important result of a company's existence, we have to go deeper and find the real reasons for our being. As we investigate this, we inevitably come to the conclusion that a group of people get together and exist as an institution that we call a company so they are able to accomplish something collectively that they could not accomplish separately—they make a contribution to society, a phrase which sounds trite but is fundamental.[4]

That social contribution of capitalism is achieved through trade. Trade is unique to us as a species and is essential for human progress. We've farmed for around ten thousand years, but we've traded for a hundred thousand.[5] Trade was inextricably linked to and financed the energy and communication revolutions that were instrumental in connecting disparate cultures from across the globe. Trade isn't just human; it gave rise to the society we know today. Science writer Matt Ridley explains that "through exchange and specialisation, we've created the ability to do things we don't even understand."[6] No individual knows how to do everything; we are a symbiotic community in which individuals need to work with others who have different talents. In place of destruction, peaceful economic cooperation ensures progress.

Trade rests on a simple premise, however, an implicit promise that if what you do is worthwhile, others will recognize you for it. This basic principle has throughout history empowered people to do great things with their knowledge and skills, to improve some little part of the world, putting food on the table, a roof over heads, and earning a sense of accomplishment, of contribution. Cumulatively these capitalist basics add up to human progress and a better society.

YET THERE IS a deep sense of hostility toward capitalism today—the kind that has given rise to populists on both left and right. You could say: Who cares if there is such strong antibusiness sentiment today? Why does it matter if business, trade, and capitalism are becoming more unpopular? It matters because rhetoric and attitudes have a real effect: if politicians see the public turn against capitalism, they are far more likely to enact policies and regulations that channel public anger and attack business. And that is self-defeating. If we undermine the climate for business overall, instead of addressing specific justifiable grievances, that will lead to less innovation, fewer jobs, fewer goods and services that make our lives better, and less money for government to spend on social problems and all the things we say we want from it. There's another real-world problem caused by anticapitalist sentiment: if people get the idea that business is basically bad, they won't want to go into it. The whole positive circle of business, trade, and capitalism depends on entrepreneurs feeling supported as they dream and plan and build. We shouldn't be putting them off; we should be encouraging them.

BUSINESS GONE AWRY

What all this requires is a much more forensic approach than anything we've seen up until now. Although it is self-defeating to be simplistically 'anti-capitalism,' it's equally wrong for its supporters to airily dismiss the public's concerns. The truth is, the Occupy movement made some very good points. And even though most people wouldn't dream of actually joining an Occupy protest, they share many of its sentiments, especially about that great demon of our times: Big Business. Yes, when it comes to Big Business, people are really angry.

We are angry with big businesses for paying obscenely high salaries to their bosses and exceedingly low ones to their workers. We are angry that the leaders of the businesses that caused the economic crisis are doing better than before. We're angry—we're driven mad by—terrible, inhuman, unresponsive, bureaucratic service; the stupid rules and fine print; the relentless sales tricks; the systems designed to suit the company rather than the customer; the infuriating phone menus; the impossibility of speaking to a human being; the inability of a human being, if we ever do get hold of one, to actually understand what we want, to empathize, to take responsibility, to help. We are angry about the homogenization of our communities by chain stores. We're angry about pollution of the air, land, sea—and mind—caused by irresponsible manufacturing and marketing practices. And we are angry that these problems never seem to improve; in fact, they just seem to get worse. Business is big and getting bigger. Executive pay is high and getting higher. Homogenized malls are bland and getting blander. Social and environmental problems are grave and getting graver. Customer service is worse and getting . . . well, you get the point.

On issues that are blatant, corporate culture seems hopelessly tone deaf. Take executive pay. In over thirty years between 1979 and 2013, real hourly wages for median workers increased just 6 percent; for low-wage workers, they actually fell by 5 percent. This represents a real wedge between productivity—which grew by over 60 percent in that time—and pay. It didn't used to be this way: in the thirty years prior, productivity rose by 93 percent while average compensation kept up, increasing by 108 percent. So where have the productivity gains since the 1980s actually gone? The top. Between 1979 and 2013 wages of those in the top 5 percent of income earners increased 41 percent.[7] And wages of the top 1 percent of earners grew by 138 percent.[8]

The past few years have been the worst. Since 2009, while median income has continued to stay flat, the median pay of CEOs is up 54 percent; since 1978 an astronomical 997.2 percent.[9] Apple paid Tim Cook over $100 million in 2014.[10] Does anyone seriously believe that Tim Cook, who strikes me as being an incredibly decent, modest man, highly devoted to his company, would leave or work less hard unless he continues to get paid $100 million a year? At least his company is performing well under his leadership. Martin Sullivan was paid $47 million when he left AIG—despite a share decline in excess of 50 percent on his watch and a $182 billion bailout from the US government.[11] In 1965 the average CEO at the 350 largest public US firms earned twenty times the bottom-level employee; now that ratio is 296-to-1.[12]

This grand canyon of a pay gap isn't just bad for employees; it's bad for business. Between 2001 and 2013 the value of the top one hundred companies traded on the London Stock Exchange increased 31 percent; profits, 47 percent. Director pay? 315 percent.[13] Executives are taking an increasingly large portion of the pie.

We are—finally—seeing some tangible policies to address this. The SEC recently adopted a rule that requires public companies to publish the ratio of pay between their CEO and median-earning employee.[14] Of course, transparency on pay is a good thing, and I argued for this in government in the UK. But it's just a small step in the right direction. Other efforts try to shift incentives: a bill introduced in the California legislature in 2014, for example, proposed pegging corporate tax rates to CEO pay ratios.[15]

Because the most egregious examples of personal and corporate greed—and other vivid illustrations of capitalism going awry—tend to occur in large companies, many hold a powerful impulse that big business is bad and small business is good. I understand that impulse. It's emotional, and I sometimes feel it too. But it's simplistic and doesn't take you very far: some big businesses do bad things, but small businesses do too. Many big businesses do good things, and we should want them to continue. For example, size can enable innovation to be incubated and deployed in a way that benefits real people in the real world on a scale that's not possible in a small business. General Electric, Samsung, and Honda exemplify this in industry; Google, Apple, and Amazon in technology. It goes wrong when companies use their size or market position to get away with practices that hurt consumers, employees, suppliers, the marketplace, or society at large. The problem is not capitalism itself; it's not even big business. It's something else, and to discover what that is, we need to look at some specific examples.

BANKS

Banks are the dominant example of what's wrong with capitalism and what needs to be fixed. When large banks—having long ago lost touch with any sense of human scale—screw up, they cause systemic problems. One of the people who understands this better than anyone is Nassim Taleb. As an insider, he has been highly critical of 'too big to fail' financial institutions. Nature, Taleb argues, never made anything larger than an elephant or whale for a reason: size breeds complexity, which in turns brings risk. As he argues in *The Black Swan*, much of that risk is hidden and is not always where we think it will be. When large institutions—like banks—get too big, the risk of a catastrophic failure multiples:

> Financial Institutions have been merging into a smaller number of very large banks. Almost all banks are interrelated. So the financial ecology is swelling into gigantic, incestuous, bureaucratic banks—when one fails, they all fall. The increased concentration among banks seems to have the effect of making financial crisis less likely, but when they happen they are more global in scale and hit us very hard. We have moved from a diversified ecology of small banks, with varied lending policies, to a more homogeneous framework of firms that all resemble one another. True, we now have fewer failures, but when they occur . . . I shiver at the thought.[16]

He said this in 2007. If only he knew just how soon he would be proven right. Think about the big banks. Their lesson from the 2008 crisis: if they are enormous and unwieldy enough to be 'too big to fail,' governments will have no choice but to rescue them. When Lehman Brothers was allowed to fail, the results proved that the contagion was too great; any more comparable failures would be catastrophic for the economy. Eric Holder, former US attorney general, has admitted government's impotence: "I am concerned that the size of some of these institutions becomes so large that it does become difficult for us to prosecute them when we are hit with indications that if you do prosecute, if you do bring a criminal charge, it will have a negative impact on the national economy, perhaps even the world economy."[17]

The banks' concentration of economic power equates to political power. Big banks get in the door of government and have disproportionate say once they do. What do they want? Rules that benefit them. They want to know they'll be fine, regardless of any mistakes they make. Their brand of capitalism is lobbying—and it works. In December 2014

Republicans slipped into a $1.1 trillion Budget Bill a measure that al-
lows traditional banks, whose deposits are federally insured, to invest in
a wider array of financial derivatives—the same type of risky investments
that contributed to the 2008 financial crisis (and had been banned since
the Dodd-Frank financial reform legislation was passed in 2010).[18] As
bad as the measure is, how it got in the bill is even worse. Inserted by
Kansas Republican congressman Kevin Yoder, who personally receives
more money from the financial industry than any other in campaign contributions,[19] it was actually written by Citigroup in 2013 as part of legislation proposed then. A *New York Times* analysis concluded that seventy
lines of the eighty-five-line section can be traced directly to the bank.[20]
The move was so blatant that one satirical headline in the *New Yorker*
read, "Citigroup to Move Headquarters to US Capitol Building."[21] According to the *Washington Post*, Jamie Dimon, CEO of JPMorgan Chase,
actually called individual lawmakers personally to urge their support.[22]
Rather than take entrepreneurial risks like a real businessman, Dimon
holds government to ransom to protect his company from risk through
special favors.

To use the academic term, Dimon, JPMorgan Chase, and the other
big banks engage in 'rent seeking' behavior. Rent seeking is a technical
way of saying that instead of profiting through the proper use of markets,
the 'rentier' unfairly uses its power—or the industry's—to gain profits
that exceed the benefits they are providing to society; that is, they make
money by grabbing more of the pie rather than making it larger. Banks
are unquestionably beneficial and necessary for all the good things about
capitalism to exist—after all, they literally provide the capital—but by
making themselves individually indispensable, they've given themselves
the ultimate taxpayer-backed guarantee, off of which they then profit.

Legislating the banking sector is difficult, perhaps, because banks and
lawmakers are so intertwined. So many US House members want to be
on the Financial Services Committee, which regulates the American
banking industry, that four rows of seats have been added since 1980
to accommodate the demand. But members aren't joining out of their
zeal for preventing another banking crisis or their passion for economic
policy; instead, it's about personal, political finance. The "cash committee," as it is known on Capitol Hill, guarantees fundraising success, a
necessity for any member of Congress but especially for new members
who need to consolidate their position in their districts: remember that
members of the House of Representatives face election every two years.
The *New York Times* reported that Congressman Andy Barr, a freshman

Republican, raised almost as much money in the first two quarters of
2013 from the financial industry as former House Speaker John Boehner.
The committee chair, Republican congressman Jeb Hensarling, is one of
the leading recipients of campaign money from the financial industry.
What does it say when the man in charge of regulating big banks receives
such a significant proportion of his campaign cash from them?[23] Neither
Barr nor Hensarling are necessarily corrupt in the personal sense—although as the case of former Virginia Governor Bob McDonnell showed,
there's plenty of that too—but it's hard to believe that money doesn't buy
some kind of influence. Is it a surprise that regulations aimed at con-
straining special interests end up benefiting them?

Of course, it's also easier for banks to obtain the political outcomes
they want when so many bankers serve in government and so many politicians and regulators work in banks. The revolving door whirs away
at the heart of the incestuous relationship between them. Current US
treasury secretary Jack Lew was once COO at Citigroup.[24] In 2008 Larry
Summers, treasury secretary under President Clinton, received $2.7 mil-
lion from banks, including JPMorgan Chase, Citigroup, Goldman Sachs,
Lehman Brothers, and Merrill Lynch as well as over $5 million to advise
hedge fund D. E. Shaw, before President Obama appointed him chairman of his Council of Economic Advisors later that year.[25] Tim Geithner,
chair of the New York Federal Reserve Bank during the financial crisis
and then Obama's first treasury secretary, now runs the private equity
firm Warburg Pincus. George W. Bush's treasury secretary, Hank Paul-
son, who oversaw the 2007 financial bailout, had previously been the
chairman and CEO of Goldman Sachs. Before he held the same post
under President Clinton, Robert Rubin was an executive at Goldman
Sachs; afterward he became chairman of Citigroup. Even Federal Reserve Chairman Alan Greenspan became an adviser to Deutsche Bank
in 2007 after leaving office.[26] Incidentally Greenspan, Rubin, and Summers were instrumental in the deregulatory fervor in the 1990s to which
many attribute the 2008 crash.

It all stinks. The systemic corruption is truly shocking. While they're
in the banks, they know they can one day end up supervising them in
government. While they're in government, they know they can one day
end up in senior positions in the banks. Who doesn't think for one second that these men—yes, they are mostly men—put the interests of the
banks and the untouchable 'financial services industry' before the interests of the people? What is so laughable is that these same grand figures
of the Establishment look down their snooty noses at the kleptocracy of

Putin's Russia or the rampant corruption in places like China, and seem to think they're better than all that. They're worse. At least in Russia the corrupt elites aren't hypocrites too.

TELECOMS

Although banking is perhaps the most egregious example, other indus-tries aren't immune to oligopoly, where a small group of big companies holds all the power. Like the banks, the telecommunications companies that provide cable and Internet access are more of a racket than a le-gitimate capitalist industry. "Three-quarters of American homes have no competitive choice for the essential infrastructure for 21st-century economics and democracy," FCC chairman Tom Wheeler said in a 2014 speech, referring to high-speed Internet access.[27] At least he took his own findings to heart; in February 2015 the FCC halted the potential merger between AOL-Time Warner and Comcast, a stitch-up that would have resulted in a monstrous new entity that controlled 57 percent of the fixed broadband market nationwide.[28] But although that prevented further catastrophe for consumers, the FCC still has lots of work to do. "The average market has one or two serious Internet providers, and they set their prices at monopoly or duopoly pricing," says Tim Wu, a Columbia University professor who studies competition.[29] (A merger between Time Warner and Charter Communications currently under review would create the second-largest cable company in the United States.) As a result, the United States still lags behind Europe and Asia in broadband speeds. In Seoul, Hong Kong, and Tokyo, broadband speeds of 1,000 megabytes per second can be had for a cost of between $30 and $40 a month. In Los Angeles, New York, and Washington, DC, the fastest broadband provider is Verizon, which charges $275 per month for 500 megabytes per second—in other words, nearly ten times the price for half the speed. When cable and Internet providers lack competition, they have no incentive to improve service, resulting in such disparities. Even in Silicon Valley, Internet speeds are a joke: in San Francisco the fastest broadband is Webpass. It almost matches Seoul and Hong Kong at $46 per month, but only for between 200 to 300 MBS, or about a fifth of Seoul's speed—and it's limited to certain specific buildings.[30] With current trends in both countries, South Korean Internet speeds will be 1,000 times faster in 2020, sixty times what the FCC hopes the average US household will have access to by then.[31]

UNFRIENDLY SKIES

When man took to the air, it was miraculous—"revolutionary," as one historian describes it.[32] And yet the 'friendly' skies are anything but. Up there, airlines have merged their competition away. Since 2008 eight major US carriers became four, between them controlling 82 percent of the domestic US airline market.[33] When United and Continental Airlines merged in 2010 to create the world's largest airline, they promised their customers it would result in lower prices and better customer service. The opposite transpired: higher change and baggage fees[34] and the elimination of early boarding for families.And unbelievably, as service declines, prices go up, not down. For instance, United, with a hub in Chicago, and Continental, with a hub in Houston, used to compete over the route between the two cities. The combined airline now controls 79 percent of flights on that route, and the fare increased by 57 percent (compared to a 16 percent per-mile price rise on average for domestic flights).[35] As airlines consolidate, researchers at MIT conclude, the more they restrict flight capacity and the more fares go up.[36]

There was briefly hope that the Justice Department had seen the error of its facilitation of airline oligopoly, conceding that the trend of "increasing consolidation among large airlines has hurt passengers" and that the United-Continental merger "reduced capacity at nearly all its major hubs" and "at many other airports where the two airlines previously competed."[37] But it seems the Justice Department didn't listen to its own advice: the American Airlines and US Airways merger successfully went through in 2013. In July 2015 the Justice Department finally launched an investigation of American, United, Delta, and Southwest for possible collusion to reduce seat supply to artificially inflate fare prices.[38]

As airlines continue to follow each other in consolidation, they also demonstrate a more insidious effect of their market power: instead of competing in the best interests of their customers or employees, they copy each other to lower standards and raise prices. It is a sort of unofficial collusion; when an airline introduces a new surcharge or takes away an amenity, sure enough, it becomes industry standard a few months later. With fewer airlines, consumers can't just choose a different alternative; instead, they have to pick between bad and terrible. And when an upstart airline comes on the scene incumbents viciously fight it. When Sir Richard Branson started Virgin America in 2005 it took two years of legal fights and the sacrifice of the airline's first CEO before the other US airlines stopped their legal challenges to its very existence.

CABLE AND AIRLINE industry consolidation are part of a larger trend. In health care, insurance, and pharmaceuticals, as we saw in Chapter 4; food and agriculture, as we saw in Chapter 5; and in a host of other sectors too. A proposed merger between brewers Anheuser-Busch InBev NV and SABMiller PLC, already the product of prior megamergers, would command almost 30 percent of the global beer market. In the appliance sector there are two-thirds fewer manufacturers than there were in 1996. The four largest American grocers have increased their market share by half from 1997. According to analysis by USC researchers, most publicly traded companies are now in more concentrated industries than they were in 1996.[39] And yet, according to the *Wall Street Journal*, these mergers are going by with little contestation from antitrust authorities.[40]

In so many industries the concentration of economic—and thus political—power in the hands of a small number of big corporations is incontrovertible. Regulatory regimes have failed to achieve the kind of real capitalist competition we should want to see. Politicians, of course, instead of challenging these destructive, inhuman leviathans, laud their bosses and put them on panels to advise them on 'business.' By what stretch of the imagination are these businesses? Why can't we just be honest about it and admit that when it comes to many of the most important industries that affect our daily lives, the United States is not actually a proper capitalist economy with real businesses competing in open markets but rather a corrupt, cozy cartel. But it's not the idea of capitalism that's at fault; it's the structure we've allowed it to assume.

LOBBYING

Rather than fairly competing in the marketplace like real businesses, big businesses in all industries—not just the uncompetitive ones—consistently seek to capture the levers of power to serve their commercial ends. No practice exemplifies this better than lobbying, an industry itself these days, especially in places where regulatory power is concentrated, like Washington, DC. Politicians and aides go through a revolving door of public- and private-sector positions. The foxes don't just guard the henhouse; they build it—with a hidden backdoor. In DC some 50 percent of senators and 42 percent of congressmen become lobbyists after they retire—up from just 3 percent in 1974.[41] And now staffers don't even have to retire before becoming lobbyists; many top political advisers to senior congressional Democrats and Republicans run their Super PACs while working for clients at lobbying firms.[42] As government has grown, the possibilities for lobbying have grown too. New agencies and more rulemaking make for more—and easier—targets. These lobbyists officially spent $2.4 billion in 2014 (although estimates of that plus unofficial spending are $9 billion a year).[43] And their reach is impressive: Senator Elizabeth Warren points out that while each round of federal budget cuts hits programs for the working poor and middle-income earners, subsidies and tax breaks for businesses that make billions in profit remain funded at full level.[44]

But it's instructive to look beyond just the federal government. In Chapter 2 we saw the great promise of decentralized power and how the American states, as 'laboratories of democracy,' show the best aspects of decentralized power. They are indeed a great model—unless they've been captured by corporate lobbying as well.

The American Legislative Exchange Council (ALEC) is the country's premier forum for legislators, think tanks, and corporations to meet to discuss issues. Unsurprisingly for a group run by corporate interests, ALEC pushes for bills that suit corporations. But delegates at ALEC meetings do more than just talk; they actually write legislation in committee. At these meetings legislators, whose trips to ALEC meetings are often paid for through a corporate 'scholarship fund,' are joined by policy analysts and representatives from ALEC's corporate members, who pay between $3,000 and $25,000 to participate. Together they write bills that can be adapted across multiple states, often as a backdoor to legislative outcomes that are difficult to achieve at the federal level or as attempts to undermine federal rules outright. The committee then votes on a proposed bill. If a majority of both the legislators and corporate representatives on the committee approve it, it becomes "model legislation" and is posted on ALEC's website for legislators across the country to use in their own states.[45] Indeed, broad applicability is the aim; they feature "insert state here" placeholders so all legislators have to do is remember where they live.[46] One set of identical ALEC-backed energy bills was introduced in Oregon, New Mexico, and New Hampshire; the bills, which benefited companies like ExxonMobil and Koch Industries, were, naturally, written at ALEC meetings in which representatives of those companies participated.[47] Remember the ag-gag laws Big Food uses to silence critics of its abusive practices? ALEC's Animal & Ecological Terrorism in America Act was the model for many of them.[48] In total, more than one thousand ALEC bills are introduced a year, with over two hundred passed into law.[49]

I'm no constitutional expert, but I doubt that corporations paying to write 'model legislation' that is implemented across the nation was what the framers had in mind for American democracy.

Some would argue that businesses writing legislation is not quite as bad as it sounds: at least they understand the issues, and so the legislation is less likely to have the errors and unintended consequences that often arise from a bureaucrat's lack of specific knowledge. That is undoubtedly true: the model legislation written by these companies will, I'm sure, accurately address the relevant issues. But accuracy isn't really the point. The point is accountability: How can people have confidence in their democracy when companies can literally purchase the right to draft legislation? What has this got to do with capitalism? With real business? With enterprise? With markets?

ALEC might be one of the worst culprits, but the instances of businesses distorting what capitalism is supposed to be about are nearly endless. If state legislatures are seemingly up for grabs, so too are state attorneys general. In America state attorneys general pursue cases in the public interest, cases that—predictably—often address corporate wrongdoing. In a groundbreaking series of articles, *New York Times* reporter Eric Lipton showed how despite their public mission, attorneys general, as elected officeholders, fall under corporate sway. Lipton reports that like ALEC-affiliated legislators, attorneys general often use language in legal filings written by private lawyers. Sometimes, in cases that are complex and expensive to investigate, corporate lawyers on secondment will work with attorneys general directly, providing legal backup in exchange for parts of settlements.[50]

In the same way that corporations use ALEC and its affiliated legislators to beat back federal legislation state by state, corporate lawyers have explicitly allied with attorneys general to unravel federal policies they don't like in the legal arena. Oklahoma attorney general Scott Pruitt, for example, wrote a letter to the Environmental Protection Agency in 2011 accusing it of heavy-handed rules on fracking that overestimated its effect on air pollution. Apart from a few edits and the addition of the state's seal, the letter was written by lawyers for Devon Energy and given to Pruitt directly by the company's government relations executive. "Outstanding," wrote executive William F. Whitsitt in a note to Pruitt's office. "Please pass along Devon's thanks to Attorney General Pruitt."[51] Outstanding indeed.

How does this happen? Political donations. Each major party's association of attorneys general can receive unlimited campaign funding, which
it then distributes to its state candidates. Many corporate interests with
business before state legal offices donate to these organizations, including Devon Energy, Reynolds America (a cigarette manufacturer seeking
to influence new rules on e-cigarettes and settlements of past tobacco
suits), Sheldon Adelson (the casino tycoon who wants support to ban
online poker), and 5-Hour Energy (an energy drink firm accused of false
advertising claims).[52] Attorneys for the latter, Lipton reports, showed
up at a fundraiser for the Democratic Attorneys General Association,
singling out Chris Koster, Missouri's attorney general, whose office was
investigating it. Koster called his office; by the end of the weekend the
investigation had been pulled.[53]

If corporate interests can't afford to buy an attorney general, they can
do the more economical thing and buy a judge. Thirty-eight American
states hold elections for judges,[54] which means that some 90 percent
of state judges will face votes at some point in their careers.[55] Much of
American law is made and adjudicated in state courts, before which many
corporations have business that directly affects their operations and profits. Millions might be spent on judicial elections, but it often pays off.[56]
In one 2004 case in West Virginia, Don Blankenship, the CEO of coal
company Massey Energy, spent $3 million backing a state supreme court
candidate who later cast the deciding vote in Massey's favor in a decision
over whether or not to overturn a $50 million judgment against the com-
pany. It was a 1,600 percent return on Blankenship's investment.[57]

These gains are common and widespread. A 2009 study found that a
1 percent increase in lobbying expenditure is expected to reduce a corporation's next-year tax rate between 0.5 percentage points and 1.6 percentage points.[58] In forty-eight different states a $1 corporate campaign
contribution is worth $6.65 in lower state corporate taxes.[59] Strate-
gas Research Partners, a financial analysis firm, estimates that firms
that lobby have outperformed the stock market for fifteen consecutive
years.[60] Christopher Witko, a political scientist from the University of
Saint Louis, analyzed campaign contributions and government contract
tenders from 1976 to 2006 and found that the more a firm contributes to
federal election campaigns, the more likely it is to be awarded a federal
contract.[61] Increasingly, companies facing commercial challenges from
new, innovative competitors are resorting to extremely noncommercial
tactics to win. Car dealers in New Jersey spent $155,000 in campaign
contributions in 2013 so that local laws ensured that cars can be sold only

through dealerships rather than directly through manufacturers, as new electric car maker Tesla wants to do.[62]

State and municipal lobbying is certainly not an indictment against the localism we should want to see. But it does call for more concerted action to pry corporate fingers from the levers of local power too.

In his recent book, *The Business of America Is Lobbying*, political scientist Lee Drutman points out that business lobbying now dwarfs that of all other interest groups. Business spent $56 for every dollar unions spent lobbying in 2012, and $86 for every dollar nonbusiness, nonunion groups spent. These ratios have steadily grown wider over the last two decades.[63] Business lobbying has also grown in absolute terms, having increased 62 percent in the same period. And with lobbying, scale really matters. Drutman explains how companies with large lobbying functions exploit under-resourced policymakers and regulators:

> While the relationship between inputs and outputs may be far from predictable, the conditions under which lobbying now takes place are more favorable than ever to the corporations who can afford to build multimillion-dollar lobbying operations that allow them to invest their resources everywhere and anywhere. In a competitive policy environment, the price of entry is high. In a policymaking process marked by increasing complexity and big bills, it is easier to insert a provision here and there with limited scrutiny, and to become the go-to source for policy expertise for stretched-too-thin congressional staffers and even agency rule makers. Collectively, these changes give businesses a more central role in the policymaking process, since businesses are best-positioned to take advantage given their ability to marshal significant financial resources to politics.[64]

Drutman's argument reflects a key point: lobbying is not just about politicians like the congressmen on the "cash committee" or the revolving door brigade. Targeting the government civil servants who write and implement the rules and regulations is often much more consequential for a company's commercial outcomes and, especially as the spotlight inevitably falls on politicians instead, is much easier.

Big business has a final advantage in the public sphere, one that is more subtle but just as powerful. When policy decisions affecting industries are made, big businesses, regardless of whether they or their representatives are physically present, are often the loudest voices in the room. This is because they have a powerful arm lock on politicians who are terrified of being branded 'antibusiness.' They are culturally cowed into writing rules that benefit the dominant existing players and work to keep smaller, innovative challengers out.

Small businesses are having an increasingly difficult time, and it's no wonder: their big competitors have used their power unfairly to bully, cajole, and manipulate in order to muscle their way into maintaining market share. Sometimes this even extends beyond politics. Look how the pharmaceutical industry pays off doctors in order to sell drugs. Rather than spend this money on research and innovation to benefit patients, these companies invest in more creative ways to squeeze profits from their vulnerable clients. According to a US government database, in 2014 drug and medical device makers made almost 11 million payments to healthcare professionals, totaling $6.5 billion (fewer than half of which were 'research grants,' with the rest composed of gifts, speaking and 'consulting' fees, royalties, and investment interest).[65] City of Hope, a cancer hospital in California, received $213 million in royalties from Genentech for its sale of several products, including drugs Herceptin, Rituxan, and Avastin.[66] One Manhattan-based orthopedic surgeon earned nearly $1.3 million from an orthopedic unit of Johnson & Johnson.[67] Pharmaceutical companies also pay generic drug makers to delay production of cheaper, off-label substitutes of their name-brand products, effectively extending the life of their patents. This costs consumers considerably: a $300 medication could cost as little as $30 when its production is opened up to generic competition. Such "pay for delay" agreements cost consumers an estimated $3.5 billion annually.[68]

It's worth noting that the immense lobbying power of business is matched in many cases by the immense lobbying power of public sector unions, especially at the state and local levels where they use the same techniques as big business to capture many of the same levers of power. Through campaign contributions, lobbying, and the choreographed deployment of their millions of members, these unions have managed to scare generations of politicians into giving them increasingly better deals at the expense of citizens and taxpayers. While sometimes unfairly maligned, more often they have been a drain on the public purse, standing in the way of meaningful reforms and infrastructure investment. In California, for example, as spending has stagnated or even declined in higher education, courts, infrastructure, and social care despite rising tax rates and revenue, spending on public employee retirement benefits has more than doubled in the last decade and unfunded retirement liabilities now exceed $200 billion (one academic estimate puts the statewide figure near $1 trillion),[69] nearly three times the outstanding bonds approved by voters for infrastructure and other purposes.[70] Even as Governor Jerry

Brown brought the state back to short-term fiscal solvency, he has battled with unions and their enablers in both the Republican Party (which
is heavily influenced by public safety unions, like the prison guards), as
well as his own Democratic Party, that refuse to allow reforms that would
benefit the taxpayer. Governor Brown's budget success has been in spite
of the public sector unions, not because of them.

I point them out here because unions, especially those in the public
sector, are beset by the same 'bureaucratic' imperatives as companies:
to continue expanding their revenue, ranks, and relative influence at all
costs. To the extent that they truly advocate for their members against
adversity and unfair attack, they do an important job. But many simply
exist to perpetuate the status quo that entrenches them in power, even
when that leads to worse outcomes for the consumers of the public services union members provide.

Capitalism should not crush small businesses; it should enable upstarts to thrive and grow. Politicians who unquestioningly back business
make a terrible error. They confuse big business with all business, and
they confuse stitched-up oligopolies with competitive markets. The correct posture on capitalism, the one that fairly benefits business and society alike, is to be pro-market, pro-competition, pro-enterprise. That does
not equate to doing the bidding of our biggest companies.

BUSINESS OR BUREAUCRACY?

Big market power is bad for the economy, distorts our political system,
and is bad for society. But what is it that lies behind the key players
in capitalism becoming so distant from and dismissive of human concerns? We could just blame the people in charge, writing it off to the fact
that they're simply the 'greedy capitalists' of caricature. That is simple-
minded. It's not the people, any more than it was in our opening story involving JetBlue. It's a *structural* problem with our economy, and it needs
a structural solution. What we are experiencing today is a landscape of
capitalism dominated by institutions that have become large, sclerotic,
and driven by their own organizational interests rather than those of the
people they touch, capitalism that is far removed from human scale.

The banks, the insurance companies, the telecom corporations, the
other inhuman institutions that behave in these ways: they have nothing
of the entrepreneur, the risk taker, the real capitalist about them. They
don't want to win by creating better products; they want to win by getting the government to rig the market so they won't be challenged. They

are not real capitalist businesses at all; they are private-sector bureaucracies. Real capitalist businesses are different. They do not depend on
regulatory capture for their commercial success. Real businesses want
to do great things—for themselves, obviously, but also for their employees, their customers, their suppliers, their communities, and the wider
world. Great entrepreneurs don't rely on loopholes to make profits. Of
course they want to win, but they want to win by having the best products and services—not the best lobbyists and lawyers.

Over the past few decades, as globalization has gathered pace and
business has become more bureaucratic and less human, successive
campaigns—be they Nader's Raiders, the young activists inspired by
Ralph Nader's consumer advocacy in the 1960s and 1970s; the anti-
globalizers of the 1980s and 1990s; or more recently the 'Occupiers'—
have fought for social and environmental justice, stood up for the 'little
guy' against the big corporations, raised awareness, and gained a great
deal of public support. But nothing has really changed, for a simple reason. The 'anticapitalist' movement, in all its various forms, with all its
valid points, has been aiming at the wrong target.

They've been aiming at the symptoms, not the cause. The cause of
the discontent that people feel with business today is not capitalism itself but the concentration of economic power in fewer and fewer hands.
It's the transformation of businesses into bureaucracies, practically part
of the government, writing their own laws, writing their own rules.
And it's not just the activists and the campaigners. Policymakers got it
wrong too. The policy and regulatory response to the social and environmental problems caused by capitalism-as-bureaucracy has been yet
more bureaucracy—more rules, more regulations. But as we've seen, the
business bureaucracies that cause the problems in the first place know
exactly how to get around rules, avoid regulations, and go their own way.

As the real target comes into view, so too does the solution. It's not
to pass still more fiddly regulations attempting to deal with this or that
manifestation of what's gone wrong with capitalism. We've tried that,
and it doesn't work. The real solution is one that we can find deep within
ourselves, in a very human instinct.

FAIR COMPETITION

Just as to trade is human, to compete is human too. If you watch two children at play, boys or girls, somehow or another they find a way to make

whatever game they are playing into a competition. Sure, they have fun. But half the fun is that they are aiming for some sort of purpose, a victory, however small. Competition is built into us, even at an early age. And it has helped build the world we live in today.

But it has to be fair. It's not just competition that's hardwired. It's fair competition. Behavioral experiments have shown that to a surprisingly high threshold, we innately care more about fairness than rewards.[71] But you don't need a social scientist to tell you this. Just think about how we feel about cheating in our everyday lives. We love fair competition (Olympic underdogs!), but nothing grates on us more than cheaters (Olympic dopers!) When a number of beloved Major League Baseball players were discovered to be using steroids, the outcry led all the way to congressional investigations. This disgust at unfairness is strong and instinctive.

Trade and fair competition—so brilliantly blended by free markets—are naturally and distinctly human, both by themselves and together. And they represent the correct response to the very evident problems with the way capitalism is working today.

This is far from the current political debate. Some say we need more rules and intervention to constrain and control capitalism. Hillary Clinton wants government to tell businesses how to operate; Bernie Sanders focuses on redistributing wealth and restricting trade, and that arch-capitalist Donald Trump is himself not so far away from this kind of economic populism. Most other GOP presidential candidates say the problem with capitalism is that it's already too constrained and controlled by government. They want more laissez-faire economics.

I'm afraid they're all wrong—on both sides.

Capitalism, left to its own devices, quickly becomes concentrated and ossified—into bureaucracies that are neither fair nor competitive. So when 'pro-business' politicians say they want to leave business alone, what they're really saying is that they want to maintain the unfair, often uncompetitive status quo. They want a free market only after it has been structured to unfairly privilege their donors. Those on the Left also want to privilege *their* special interests (often labor unions) and broader ideological aims. But like those 'pro-business' politicians, they also ignore the underlying structure of capitalism, preferring to tinker all over the place to create the ideal economy they envision. They want a fair economy, but not a market one. This doesn't work either.

So what we need now—the practical, positive, constructive response to 'anticapitalist' sentiment—is a massive shake-up in our economic structures, to make them more fair *and* more competitive. In a 2015 paper examining the world's billionaires, economists Sutirtha Bagchi of Villanova University and Jan Svejnar of Columbia University found that only when billionaires amassed their fortunes through political connections did the ensuing wealth inequality drag on economic growth. When billionaires earn their wealth through entrepreneurship, there's no negative effect.[72] Government has a role to play to ensure that the structure of capitalism—fair competition—is in proper working order, making and enforcing the rules that facilitate a healthy, fair, competitive market economy. What we have now is not real capitalism with fair competition; it is not a market economy. It is an economy of bureaucracies, by bureaucracies, for bureaucracies. Except they have the nerve to call themselves businesses.

Competition regulation needs to become much more aggressive. Fines should mean something and not just be part of the 'cost of doing business.' Scholars John Connor and Robert Lande found that collusion is too often a "rational business strategy" and that participating in a cartel "is a crime that, on average, pays."[73] Regulation of capitalism is necessary, but that doesn't necessarily mean more rules; it means fewer, better rules, rules about the structure of markets more than the behavior of individual companies—and better enforcement of those structural rules.

For guidance, we might look back to the reformers of the last Gilded Age. America may have been the place where laissez-faire capitalism first truly flourished, but it was also where leaders recognized the harms that a completely unfettered free market could have. Andrew Carnegie, John D. Rockefeller, J. P. Morgan, Leland Stanford—all were brilliant and innovative businessmen who truly helped to build the modern American economy and left lasting philanthropic legacies like Stanford University.[74] But they were guilty of enormous excess in their business careers, creating monopolies that limited the flow of American wealth to a small elite, to the detriment not just of their competitors but of the broader American economy that correspondingly lost out. Reacting to this excess, leaders like Senator John Sherman and President Theodore Roosevelt launched reform efforts. "If we will not endure a king as a political power, we should not endure a king over the production, transportation and sale" of the fruits of America's economy, decried Sherman. He would go on to sponsor the Sherman Antitrust Act in 1890. His work laid the groundwork for Roosevelt's "Square Deal," which provides a useful example of how government can help guide the free market to a fair balance. He recognized that the status quo was untenable, and he led the fight against predatory big businesses, the "trusts," as they were called. With his mantra that every man deserved a "square deal," he became known for taking on big corporate power. Among the many accomplishments of his so-called trust-busting, he struck an accord with J. P. Morgan to win concessions for striking coal miners, passed the Meat Inspection Act and Pure Food and Drug Act to ensure safe and relatively transparent food and drug supplies, and broke up dozens of monopolies, including the railroad giants and the largest oil firm in the country, Rockefeller's Standard Oil.

Despite this storied history, America's—and Britain's and Europe's—competition authorities have lost sight of the proud heritage that precedes them. They follow the mandates set for them by politicians, mandates that are lackluster at best and far from their original intent. "Economic and political power can't be separated because dominant corporations gain political influence over how markets are maintained and enforced, which enlarges their economic power further," writes economist and former Secretary of Labor Robert Reich. "One of the original goals of antitrust law was to prevent this."[75] So whereas current laws might stop a business from literally becoming a monopoly, they don't prevent the harmful practices of dominant players and certainly don't meet the standard Sherman or Roosevelt would have intended for them.

The definition of a competitive market should be radically strengthened. The crucial question should be: What are the 'barriers to entry'—how easily can a new firm establish itself and compete in the marketplace? The rate of new-company creation has steadily declined since the 1970s, and although there are many reasons for that, uncompetitive barriers are certainly a part of the story.[76] This doesn't necessarily mean regulating the size of incumbents, although that's often a crucial component, but whether they are able to use their power—be it size, political connections, ownership of assets and infrastructure, partnerships and contracts, and even cash—to unfairly stack the deck in their favor and keep new competitors out.

This is what the competition authorities should enforce. At the same time, the interpretation of the harm done by anticompetitive practices should be broadened. Today the competition rules are focused on one thing: 'customer welfare.' In other words, as long as authorities think service is good enough, quality is high enough, and price is low enough—regardless of the harm that's done to achieve those things—then all is well. This obviously neglects harms to society like putting small firms, whether competitors or suppliers, out of business or driving wages and working conditions down by unfairly using the advantages of scale and incumbency. We need to change that.

We need competition not just for our economy to succeed but also for our society to flourish. Capitalism is the most efficient and effective way we have for distributing resources, spurring innovation, and spreading prosperity. When businesses are fair with their customers, their employees, their suppliers, their communities, and themselves, capitalism is truly a beautiful and successful system. But uncompetitive capitalism, despite the short-term gains possible with it, ultimately collapses upon itself like a deck of cards. Monopoly can only last so long before it stagnates or overreaches. That's why we should privilege the sanctity of proper markets.

REAL CAPITALISM: CHALLENGING INCUMBENTS

Today the sector I know best, technology, provides the most apt examples of what that looks like in the twenty-first century. Technology companies have been criticized for concentrating gains in the hands of a small number of people; indeed, many accuse the largest tech giants of being outright anticompetitive. But this debate is fraught with misunderstanding. Because technology companies have the ability to create wealth in a timeframe and on a scale implausible in almost any other industry, their gains seem inherently suspect. Surely, many argue, when so much wealth goes to so few so quickly, something is going wrong. But this misunderstands the sector. In tech, size, scale, or even market share, on their face, do not automatically translate to structural dominance. The costs of building and scaling a software company are low and falling. Just as a giant company can rise rapidly, another can easily replace it. That's why the technology sector is a good example of a competitive market, and the kind of competitive pressure the leaders of tech companies feel is exactly the kind of pressure we should want to see applied to all companies in every sector of the economy.

I'm the first to criticize the often absurd, arrogant, and frankly quite creepy techno-salvationism of many in Silicon Valley, successfully satirized by the TV show of the same name. But by looking at entrepreneurialism there, we can get a sense of what markets with high levels of entrepreneurialism, innovation, and, above all, competition, might look like elsewhere in the capitalist world.

Take Red Dress Boutique. Its founder, Diana Harbour, was bored with her "secure but soul-sucking" office job, but she loved fashion. As an aspiring designer, she decided to build a boutique, curating fashionable but affordable outfits. So she started on eBay, selling outfits from her basement. Realizing she needed to expand, she and her husband Josh dug into their savings and opened a shop in Athens, Georgia. After some initial success they moved online in 2010, at which point the business skyrocketed: $63,000 in sales in 2010 transformed to $7 million in 2013 and then to over $12 million in 2014, with a net profit of $2 million. Diana had something of value to offer the world, and the Internet enabled her to share it.[77]

Another Internet marketplace, Etsy, unleashes the wares of small designers using a platform that helps them compete with big retailers and global brands. By giving consumers the chance to buy unique items directly from artisans who make them—and to communicate with them as well—Etsy doesn't just support those whose local markets would be too small to survive; it also forges a human connection between maker and consumer. And it helps bring to market items that might never have been economical to manufacture on any scale or to stock in a store.

A more human economy is one in which people control both their own labor and their own assets. Technology is helping here, linking us in the emerging 'sharing economy.' By enabling people to provide services directly to others without substantial corporate infrastructure or intermediation, the sharing economy builds community in ways that typical corporate-consumer relationships do not. The essence of the sharing economy is that customers receive services not from professionals but from people like themselves. By definition, it's more human.

Airbnb epitomizes the sharing economy. It's now a big company that competes with hotels (its latest valuation surpasses Hyatt),[78] but more importantly it is a platform for the actual sharing of assets. Airbnb is transforming the way people travel. It gives everyday people extra income by renting out spare rooms, and they get to meet others. Airbnb hosts are completely autonomous; they set their own policies, their own prices, their own schedules. Guests get to connect with real people offering rooms, apartments, and houses. Rather than staying in a sterile hotel room, Airbnb connects travelers with a real Londoner, Chicagoan, or Hong Konger. Often Airbnb guests socialize with their hosts and even develop friendships over repeated or reciprocal visits. It's a great example of the argument that in business 'big' is not necessarily bad; 'big' can be human—as long as it is a real business competing fairly in a real market.

Competition is always snapping at the heels of tech companies—even the biggest. Just as Amazon emerged to challenge the traditional retail industry, in an exhilarating turn of the circle, we're now seeing more human competitors challenging Amazon. Postmates is a firm that would have been physically impossible to run, let alone conceive, without the latest technology. Postmates resembles Amazon in many ways: it sells a multitude of products in its online store, is based on mobile technology, and delivers products directly to consumers using a network of couriers, not unlike those seen in ride-sharing or meal-delivery services. But there's one big caveat.

"Everything that we're doing is anti-Amazon," says Bastian Lehmann, the startup's cofounder. Instead of sourcing and sorting products itself, Postmates sells the products of a network of local bricks-and-mortar retailers. Why bother with the logistics of a warehouse operation when there are stores already fulfilling that function? Instacart, another shopping delivery startup, takes the same philosophy, delivering from both chain stores and local independent shops. "We want to use the city as our warehouse instead of building a warehouse outside the city," says Lehmann of Postmates. "We want to be part of a city versus saying: 'Here's a way that you can save $2 on an item, but nobody in your city earns a dime, but now you have a cheap DVD player—congratulations!'"[79] As innovative as Amazon is, it's already being disrupted. That is real, competitive capitalism, not bureaucracy. The fact that Amazon's challengers are trying to travel a more human road simply offers more evidence of business's power for good. Competition doesn't just force companies to offer better prices or better products; it can force them to think about how best to serve the whole human community.

Here's another example of the great, dynamic, positive circle that real, competitive capitalism represents. One of the challenges for participants in the sharing economy is the lack of predictability and stability. Working for a large corporation might often seem like soulless drudgery, but at least it's mostly stable: regular hours and a pension. Of course, even the grandest of corporations can go belly-up overnight, and there is nothing to prevent you from being laid off without much notice. But workers in the sharing economy experience hourly volatility, often not knowing how much money they'll make in a given day, let alone week or month.

Now entrepreneurs—once again, with technology—are tackling those challenges. Peers, a San Francisco-based organization with 250,000 members, offers products and services to support so-called gig workers. Take its Keep Driving program. For $20 a month it gives drivers for car-sharing services like Lyft access to a temporary car in the event that their own is damaged or stolen. For drivers like San Franciscan Michael Bendorf, whose hybrid Volkswagen was rear-ended in a four-car collision, this service prevented him from losing the $5,000 to $7,000 per month he normally would have earned during the time his car was being repaired. Peers is also filling other gaps that often pop up in the sharing economy, like insurance (many car and property insurers will cancel your policy if you lend or charge to share your car or home). Peers now offers a $1 million liability policy, in one-month increments (with no minimum), for those who make their space available to travelers via Airbnb, HomeAway, FlipKey, or even Craigslist. "What we're trying to do here is recognize the needs of a new class of worker," says Shelby Clark, the company's executive director. "There are hundreds of thousands of people across the country earning money in new ways. While they love the flexibility and that they can start earning right away, at the same time they're encountering new challenges, like making sure they have stable income."[80]

One of the advantages that established firms have traditionally had over startups and 'gig workers' is that their scale has enabled bulk-buying discounts on things like administration, workspace, and insurance. But the Internet is increasingly making this a moot point. Whereas firms like Etsy enable makers to sell their wares online, new payment services like Square allow small shop and restaurant owners to use nothing more than an iPad and a small plastic card reader to process card payments in person. Gone are the days when small entrepreneurs had to choose between 'cash only' or big, bulky, and expensive IBM cash registers.

With dreary predictability, however, obviously beneficial products and services like these are being confronted by bureaucratic government resistance. With its breakthrough battery technology, Tesla is doing more than almost anyone to make electric cars economical on a large scale. But Tesla's innovations aren't limited to technology—and therein lies the problem. Rather than sell through dealer middlemen, Tesla sells its vehicles directly to the public through its own stores, where customers can explore one or two model vehicles and an example of the battery packs, then use touch-screen terminals to customize their order. This, however, disrupts the entire way dealerships operate. Across America Tesla has had to contend with lawsuits and legislative battles just for the right to sell its cars.[81] In some states it is only allowed to have 'galleries,' where visitors can see cars but employees are prohibited from discussing prices or how to buy a car. And even those limitations aren't enough in some other states. In October 2014, for example, Michigan—home of Ford,

GM, and Chrysler—passed a law that bans even galleries.[82] It's a perfect example of government bureaucrats siding with private-sector bureaucrats, using outdated protectionist regulations to keep challengers out.

The Internet, argues leading Silicon Valley entrepreneur and investor Peter Thiel, makes it easy for customers to switch to the best products in a heartbeat. Although this ease is what enables the really great businesses to balloon in size overnight, it's what also makes even the most successful, established tech firms so inherently 'disruptable.' The companies I've highlighted aren't necessarily 'good' companies in the sense of their overall social impact, but they're proof of what insurgents can do when barriers are low. Unlike old industries in which control of one bit of infrastructure, like oil wells or pipelines or steel mills or railroads, enabled firms to lock challengers out and charge consumers whatever price they wanted, with the Internet, tiny upstarts can topple giants. Facebook was born in a dorm room and upended the seemingly formidable Myspace. Google became more popular than Microsoft, but Microsoft had put IBM in its place before that. Look at the success of Instagram, WhatsApp, Snapchat, Slack, and Stripe. From nowhere risk takers who had a vision built these companies, and they were rewarded because the market posed minimal barriers to entry. Facebook's acquisition of the first two (and attempt to buy the third) not only demonstrates the value these entrepreneurs created but also how susceptible it is to competitive pressure, despite its dominance and market size. And such acquisitions only encourage more innovation.

CAPITALISM IS A force for good, but its distortion into private-sector bureaucracy, with uncompetitive markets dominated by entrenched corporations, is a fundamental malaise. There's nothing wrong with dominant companies, and there's nothing wrong with dominant companies that continue to dominate. But they must do so on their merits and not by entrenching their advantages through political power. The central answer is conceptually simple but will require immensely strong leadership to implement: take on the wealthy, powerful, endemically corrupt business elites and make them compete in the marketplace on fair terms. That's what capitalism ought to be; closer to what's happening in the technology sector today. Only that kind of deep, structural reform will succeed in making capitalism more human.

chapter seven

BUSINESS

IN SAVAR, BANGLADESH, next to the Genda Government Primary School, there's a river full of toxins from nearby textile factories. The 'suffocating' odor in the air makes students and teachers feel dizzy, vomit, and lose focus. Debilitating headaches for students and teachers aren't uncommon; occasionally students faint. Ironically, the children of Savar are entirely dependent on these factories, which make the clothes we buy in the West. The income their parents earn allows them to go to school. But those factories are also the worst fixture in their lives.

They do protest the pollution. But the industrial interests always win out. According to the school's headmaster, Mohammed Abdul Ali, "We've never seen the owners take our appeals seriously . . . everything is going on as usual. They have a good relationship with the politicians. That is why they don't care." Every now and again a reforming minister or regulator comes to power and attempts to do something but is inevitably stifled. For a short period Munir Chowdhury, an environmental official, held textile factories accountable, conducting raids and imposing fines. He didn't last; he was transferred to another department. More often than not, ministers are part of the problem. "These people who are setting up industries and factories here are much more powerful than me," says Mohammed Abdul Kader, the mayor of Savar. "When a government minister calls me and tells me to give permission to someone to set up a factory in Savar, I can't refuse."[1]

I ARGUED IN the previous chapter that business is the most powerful force for progress the world has ever seen. One way or another, we all depend on trade, capitalism, and the profit motive for the big positive changes we want to see in the world, from creating opportunity and tackling inequality, to providing the products and services that help make our lives richer and more pleasurable, to the innovations that help fight poverty, hunger, and disease. There is no government in the world, no part of the public sector anywhere that does not rely on successful, profitable businesses for its very existence. To combine businesses with markets is evidence of our ability to create institutions that, broadly speaking, deliver human progress and make the world a better—and more human—place.

But too often business fails us. In the last chapter we saw how the structure of modern capitalism has helped create massive, often global corporations that manipulate laws, purchase political power, and use their economic might and incumbent advantages to suppress competition. These businesses objectively make a mockery of capitalism. There are plenty of others, however, that fail on a different count. They may operate in competitive markets; they might not lobby or litigate their way to the top, but they nonetheless do harm, not through their dominance of anticompetitive practices but simply by the way they behave.

SUPPLY CHAIN

In our globalized economy, to save themselves—and us, as consumers—money, many companies base their supply chains in places like Savar, where the rule of law is weak and the potential for corruption high. Too often they take advantage of holes and blind spots in the system that allow them to pass on all of the costs of their operations to exceedingly vulnerable populations.

Take the ubiquitous pair of denim jeans. Their blue color might be their most inhuman feature. In countries like China, India, and Bangladesh, wastewater that is used to dye and process textiles is routinely dumped untreated, saturating rivers and streams with carcinogens like chromium, lead, cadmium, arsenic, and mercury. This not only poisons the factory workers and their families who live nearby; it kills off fields and local fish supplies as well. In the Pearl River Delta in China's Guangdong Province the water literally runs blue from the synthetic pigments used to process 200 million pairs of jeans dyed there every year.[2] According to Green Cross Switzerland, 9 trillion gallons of water are used annually in textile production around the world. Most of it is dumped untreated.[3]

Sometimes our quest for low prices even kills: in 2013 garment makers in the Rana Plaza building in Dhaka, Bangladesh, were ordered back to work the day after cracks appeared in its structure. It collapsed soon after, killing 1,129 people.[4]

Over the past decade the Internet has done a great deal to help concerned consumers choose alternative, ethically produced goods. "We sell online and through our store directly and skip middlemen," explains Mark Spera, cofounder of BeGood Clothing, a San Francisco startup. "That's how we've been able to offer a disruptively low $15 price point on our T-shirts."[5] The entire clothing line is made in Los Angeles and San Francisco in good conditions, by workers paid fair wages. And all from materials that are organically harvested and processed sustainably, without the use of harsh chemicals. The Internet has also allowed BeGood to be maximally transparent about how suppliers are treated. At their store and online each item carries an explanation of the materials and processes involved as well as the people and places along its supply chain. More information means better, more conscious choices.

The problem is that the jeans produced in Guangdong or the shirts made at Rana Plaza are cheap; the shirts sold at BeGood in San Francisco are, although relatively inexpensive, still not competitive with what's sold to the average Western consumer. But the only reason sweatshop textiles are cheap is because the businesses that produce them choose not to treat people decently. Taxpayers, not the businesses, then foot the bill for the harm they cause—assuming local officials or international governments do anything at all. So rather than perpetuating the fiction that social and environmental responsibility is an indulgence for the rich, we should be asking why we continue to subsidize companies that offload the true costs of their operations onto taxpayers.

Even supply chains that don't explicitly pollute incur costs we don't see. I live in California, where an epochal drought has led to severe water restrictions, replete with parched lawns, untilled acres, and unflushed toilets. And yet while we worry about leaving the faucet running, many of the products we use and consume require far more water to produce and to bring to us than we ever could consume through our taps. The almond has famously gotten a bad rap (each one needs about a gallon of water to grow), but other foods are just as bad: two ounces of rice take 15.1 gallons; a strawberry takes a quart. Animal products are even worse: four glasses of milk require 143 gallons of water, whereas just 1.75 ounces of beef require 86 gallons.[6] Meanwhile the average American uses thirty-five pounds of cotton per year, equal to 3,500 gallons, and a one-way cross-country flight uses as much water as 1,700 toilet flushes.[7] But again, because these processes are obscured, we don't understand them.

WORKPLACE

Although the Internet might help concerned shoppers find BeGood's T-shirts (or indeed, save water), it can also do just as much to obscure abuse and harm. We make a fuss about corporations like Walmart because we can identify their employees—we see them in the aisles and at the registers. But online retailers like Amazon, however innovative and cost saving for consumers, can hide how they treat their people behind the clean facade the Internet allows them to put up. Amazon's workers are out of sight and, as a result, easily out of mind. Undercover investigations have revealed employees toiling in warehouses for low wages in slave-like conditions. One investigative report describes life for a temporary worker in his fifties at an Amazon warehouse in Allentown, Pennsylvania:

> [He] . . . worked ten hours a day as a picker, taking items from bins and delivering them to the shelves. He would walk thirteen to fifteen miles daily. He was told he had to pick 1,200 items in a ten-hour shift, or 1 item every thirty seconds. He had to get down on his hands and knees 250 to 300 times a day to do this. He got written up for not working fast enough, and when he was fired only three of the one hundred temporary workers hired with him had survived.[8]

At an Amazon facility in Wales, employees work fifty-plus-hour weeks at minimum wage. They'll be fired if they take more than three sick days in a three-month period (or get sick twice and show up late by a minute twice, or get sick once and are late four times, and so on). According to one undercover journalist who visited in 2013, strict fifteen-minute breaks start wherever the worker happens to be in the warehouse at the time, which could be a long walk away from a place to sit down. And that's after passing through airport-like security to be patted down (to prevent theft).[9] At the Pennsylvania warehouse employees are actually tagged with their own personal GPS so managers can govern their movements 'scientifically.' If employees don't go to the toilet nearest them, they are asked why.[10] Treating people like this is humiliating and undignified.

It's not just warehouse workers. A recent report in the *New York Times* highlighted the intense pressure on Amazon's white-collar employees, those working on software, product development, and marketing.

Employees faced "annual cullings," often based on anonymous feedback from colleagues, who were all competing against each other; they openly wept in the office under the pressure; facing a boss described as an "insatiable taskmaster," some employees worked for days without sleeping. Perhaps most troubling were the reports of employees in deep personal distress, facing family crises or even cancer diagnoses, who were given little to no flexibility and faced serious repercussions for their corresponding shortcomings.[11] This lack of compassion, this treatment of employees as mere cogs in a well-oiled machine, is certainly within the legal rights of an employer to do. But it's not human. Yes, Amazon workers might be marginally more productive, but at what cost? Surely there is a better way to run a business.

In fairness, although Amazon did not dispute the accuracy of the allegations, Jeff Bezos, the company's visionary founder and CEO, has said these reports don't depict what he believes he's building. "The article doesn't describe the Amazon I know or the caring Amazonians I work with every day," he wrote, acknowledging that he would leave such a company himself if he thought the article painted a full and complete picture. Indeed, he said that any employee facing circumstances as described by the *Times* should immediately escalate the issue to Amazon's human resources department.[12]

In response to the earlier warehouse exposé, Amazon said, "We're working hard to make sure that we are better tomorrow than we are today." No doubt they are. But warehouse employees, many paid just a few dollars above minimum wage, are still often required to sign heavily restrictive noncompete contracts, thereby limiting their ability to change jobs, even if they're just working seasonally. When one warehouse in Coffeyville, Kansas, was shut down, laid-off employees were admonished in their severance agreement to "fully comply" with the noncompetition agreement as they struggled to find new jobs.[13]

At Amazon, as at many big companies, it's the subordination of human values that allows harm to take place. Bureaucratic, tech-enabled systems eliminate basic humanity and the personal connection, kindness, and empathy natural to nearly all of us. I don't know him, so I can't be sure, but I sincerely doubt that Bezos would, if he found himself in one of his warehouses with an employee betrayed by the personal GPS as having gone to the 'wrong' toilet, actually ask that employee why. The system, the process, the bureaucracy—these are things that distance people from each other.[14]

A CULTURE OF FAIR PAY

Amazon is not alone. Companies everywhere proclaim that "people are our greatest resource," yet too many treat their employees as nothing more than units of production, paying them as little as they can get away with, putting them on zero-hours contracts, imposing incredibly stingy—and counterproductive—sick, holiday, and leave policies. But others choose to do things differently.

As we'll see in the following chapter, Costco pays its employees well above the living wage, and it is one of the most successful companies in the world—in a cut-throat, slim-margins industry. For them, paying a decent wage increases productivity, makes recruiting easier, and lowers turnover. Whole Foods publishes the pay of every employee, from top to bottom. This might seem extreme, but it engenders social solidarity. When top executives make hundreds of times more than those at the bottom (they don't at Whole Foods), it's demoralizing. J. P. Morgan purportedly said that he would never lend money to a company whose best employees were paid more than twenty times anyone else because it would be unstable. (In 2014 Jamie Dimon, JPMorgan Chase's CEO, made about 160 times his average employee's salary.[15])

This is not some immutable law of business. Ethan Berman was the founder and CEO of RiskMetrics, a financial services company that was, ironically, spun out of JPMorgan Chase in 1998. He insisted in a letter to his board that he be paid *less*. He wrote, "Last year I was disappointed in the way I was compensated and I have therefore taken to writing this note in the hope that it does not happen again in 2005." He continues, "As I told the committee before last year's meeting, there is no amount of stock options, restricted stock or any other stock-based compensation that would make me feel more of an owner, or increase my commitment to the company," he advised. "Instead, I ask the committee in looking at the list to broaden its definition of 'leaders' beyond employees with significant managerial or financial responsibilities to those who display time and time again the values that we as a company believe in and therefore 'lead' others by example not by mandate. That, as much as any other attribute, will create value in the long run."[16]

Berman was right: In 2008 RiskMetrics went public at a valuation of just over $1 billion. In 2010 it was acquired by MSCI for $1.55 billion—a 48 percent increase in just twenty-four months.[17]

TIME SOVEREIGNTY

Treating people as human beings in the workplace means more than just paying them fairly, though. Businesses are in control of a broad range of conditions for their workers, including how much of their time they demand. Work is just one part of people's lives, and although employees have obligations to their employers, employers should respect employees' obligations to their friends, parents, children, or relatives and afford them as much flexibility as possible. Often totally unnecessarily from a business point of view, workplace culture too often enforces norms of working twelve hour or more days. When new employees think the only way to be promoted is to work excessive hours, then the cycle simply continues. As one psychologist put it, "Long hours has become a proxy for good performance."[18]

Sir Richard Branson, founder of the Virgin Group, is one boss who decided enough was enough. After an encouraging note from his daughter and reading that the 'take as much holiday as you want' policy at Netflix increased morale, creativity, and productivity, he decided to do the same for salaried employees across Virgin. He wrote, "It is left to the employee alone to decide if and when he or she feels like taking a few hours, a day, a week or a month off, the assumption being that they are only going to do it when they feel a hundred percent comfortable that they and their team are up to date on every project and that their absence will not in any way damage the business—or, for that matter, their careers!"[19] Of course, this model has its pitfalls: social pressure may lead employees to take *less* vacation. But it should be admired for its innovative spirit. Americans especially need to take more time off (they take an average of fourteen days a year to the Europeans' twenty-eight), and any serious idea to encourage that should be welcomed.[20]

Time-off policies are critical to get right because they can have enormous impacts on family life. Becoming a parent should be a joyous milestone, not an occasion to lose a chance at a career or be laid off, as it is for many who work. Mothers in particular face brutal challenges upon having children, with workplace policies and cultures that make it difficult if not impossible to resume their careers. Couples should be able to get pregnant whenever it is right for *them*, and there should be comprehensive job protection for mothers who are. Until such formal protections are in place—and corporate culture to match—I'm afraid Princeton political scientist, think tank executive, and former State

Department official Anne-Marie Slaughter is right: "Women still can't have it all."[21]

It isn't just about maternity or paternity leave, though. It's also about allowing parents to take care of their children, and sons and daughters to take care of their aging parents. Many businesses impose negative consequences on workers who have to take time off due to a family emergency. Again, though this is a problem that affects all types of workers, it is felt acutely by low-wage earners. As with holiday time, whereas 90 percent of high-wage workers have the flexibility to take paid time off or move their schedule around during a family crisis, less than half of low-paid workers have these same benefits.[22]

This is inherently inhuman. Family is central to human nature and the most important institution in society: being a parent is one of the most human acts possible, giving birth to a child even more so. But by becoming mothers, women end up bearing a steep cost for this indispensable duty. They suffer the indignity of losing out on career advancement, of being forced to choose between meaningful work and spending time with their children, and of every choice they make being wrapped in terrible guilt thanks to the failure of business culture to adapt to a world of gender equality.

Helping parents be better workers *and* better mothers and fathers at the same time is central to treating employees like people and making business more human. Better family leave policy especially matters to low-wage employees. Predictable hours, workplace flexibility, paid leave, days off—these are all part of the same theme: respecting workers by treating them well, treating them in a way that is more human.

DISCRETION AND AUTONOMY

You see the trend toward inhuman treatment of workers in other ways too, and again, technology can exacerbate but also help. Bosses are often incentivized by systems created by management consultants or software programs bought in order to help improve 'efficiency.' The result: employees are inhibited from exercising their abilities to the fullest and not trusted to use their judgment, work autonomously, or make decisions outside of specific frameworks.

Much of this comes from the drive to quantify performance. You can understand the impulse that led to Amazon forcing its warehouse employees to track themselves with countdown-beeping GPS devices, but how can that justifiable impulse be channeled into a more human approach?

Consider the annual performance review. Studies have shown that they are demotivating and serve little purpose, as bosses score most of their employees in the middle to avoid awkwardness.[23] The more human alternative is also the one that, more simply, improves performance: frequent, informal meetings. Most employees want to learn and improve anyway. Telling workers what's wrong or what could be improved ahead of time gives everyone a chance to take action: "The boss's job is to fill in the gaps and accomplish results," UCLA business professor Sam Culbert argues. "It's not to give report cards."[24]

Generally workers at every level want to take action to excel at their jobs. But for that they need sovereignty over how to go about doing them. It's easy to see how managers' impulse for 'quality control' leads to structures that drastically curtail discretion, but by treating workers like robots, they send a tacit message that they simply aren't smart, observant, or creative enough to know how to accomplish the task at hand. This is inhuman. And it causes them to be inhuman toward others.

Some businesses are choosing to behave differently. MetroBank in the UK was founded only six years ago and determined to break the mold of its competitors (which universally rank badly for customer service). Its staff are incentivized with bonuses based not only on profit but also on customer service results. Branches are open 361 days a year, from 8 a.m. to 8 p.m. on weekdays, and calls must be answered by the third ring, twenty-four hours a day, seven days a week. Most impressively, customer-facing employees are to say "yes" to customer requests as much as possible. They can say "no," but only after seeking a second opinion from a colleague first.[25]

Zappos, the online retailer (now owned by Amazon), has built a brand on customer—and employee—happiness. In 2010 it even ran an advertising campaign featuring real-life recordings of calls its employees had with customers. The fact that employees are encouraged (and trusted—there are no phone scripts) to go out of their way to make customers happy is part of its business model and one of the reasons customers come back. In 2011 a Zappos employee sent a large bouquet of flowers to a woman she had spoken to on the phone after she was having trouble finding shoes that were comfortable enough for her sensitive feet that had been damaged by medical treatments.[26] Another time a customer service agent went in person to another store to buy a pair of shoes that were out of stock and deliver them to a customer who happened to be staying nearby the company's headquarters in Las Vegas . . . for free.[27]

IN HIS INFLUENTIAL business book, *The Outsiders*, investor William Thorndike Jr. profiles eight CEOs whom he found, over the course of almost a decade's worth of research, to be exceptionally successful. Though he didn't originally set out to write a book, his interest was piqued after discovering that many of his subjects managed their companies in the same way.[28] For example, "there are two basic types of resources that any CEO needs to allocate," Thorndike writes, "financial and human."[29] In addition to being frugal and humble, the best CEOs, he found, were expert at managing both. When it came to allocating capital, they were obsessive and hands-on. But when it came to managing people, Thorndike found that the best CEOs were master delegators, "running highly decentralized organizations and pushing operating decisions down to the lowest, most local levels in their organizations."[30]

At the time CEO William Anders took the helm of defense contractor General Dynamics in 1990, the military-industrial complex, propped up for decades by the Cold War, was collapsing around him. General Dynamics was in no better position: straddled with $600 million of debt and negative cash flow, it was not clear the firm would survive.

Coming from the military, most defense executives had brought with them the same highly centralized, bureaucratic style of management they were used to. Things would be different under Anders, though. After he sold off many of the company's units to focus on a few specific markets, Anders (and later his successors, James Mellor and Nicholas Chabraja) made it General Dynamic's top priority to spend capital efficiently and radically decentralize, with responsibility pushed as far down as possible into the organization. Management from then on was to involve itself minimally in each division, holding subordinate managers "severely accountable" (in the words of Chabraja) but left alone if they were performing well. "By the end of Chabraja's tenure," according to Thorndike, "the company would have more employees than when Anders arrived but only a quarter as many people at corporate headquarters."[31] Today General Dynamics is thriving: with over $2.5 billion in profits, the company is now worth over four times what it was when Anders took over. "There is a fundamental humility to decentralization," Thorndike observes, "an admission that headquarters does not have all the answers and that much of the real value is created by local managers in the field."[32]

More human businesses give discretion to their employees. It's not a free-for-all, of course, but companies with even a somewhat decentralized culture are organizations filled with empowered problem solvers who understand their limits, know when to ask others for help (or refer upward when need be), and use the creativity each of us has to make the little part of the company they're responsible for better. At Johnson & Johnson decentralization is not only key to its business strategy but also how it supports employees. "It gives you a tremendous opportunity to develop people," according to William Weldon, the company's CEO. "You give them a lot of opportunity to work in different areas, to work in smaller companies, to make mistakes and to ultimately move to larger companies." Centralization, however, is a tremendous risk: "If one person makes one mistake, it can cripple the whole organization."[33]

MARKETING

Regardless of their structure, there are certain behaviors that should be beyond the pale for every business, and one of the most widespread abuses today is targeted marketing to children. Children are exactly that—children—and it is simply not human for businesses to treat them as consumers. Yet the food and beverage industry, for example, spends $10 billion each year advertising food—mostly junk—to children and adolescents.[34] As a result, children between two and eleven view over four thousand ads for food and beverages per year, adolescents twelve to seventeen almost six thousand.[35] For every advertisement promoting fruits or vegetables, children in 2014 saw fourteen for candy and thirty-one for fast food.

And it works. According to the Institute of Medicine, food advertising directly affects food choices and purchase requests, in turn shaping diet and health.[36] Moreover, food marketed with cartoon characters, such as Dora the Explorer, Scooby Doo, and Shrek tastes better to children. In one study 85 percent of children chose graham crackers with cartoon-decorated labels over the plainly wrapped alternatives; 55 percent of them said the (identical) crackers from the cartoon package tasted better. For gummy candies, the bias was the same.[37]

Which is why it's even more insidious that factory-food marketers target children in low-income areas. According to Yale University's Rudd Center, low-income Latino neighborhoods have up to nine times the density of outdoor advertising for fast food and sugary drinks than more affluent, predominantly white areas. Two-thirds of food ads seen by children on Spanish language TV are for fast food, candy, sugary drinks, and snacks. Advertising for dairy, 100 percent juice, plain water, fruits, and vegetables—combined—comprises just 3 percent.[38]

It's not just on TV. Advertising is in even more places today, pervading mobile apps and games, social media, and online banners. A 2012 study found that advertisements support 87 percent of the most popular children's websites.[39] At least these ads are identifiable. The boundary between marketing and content, especially for children, is increasingly blurred. Food manufacturers now create websites with videos, original content, and games, and 81 percent of websites for foods that had been marketed on children's TV networks have games designed for children.[40] Product placement in TV shows and even in video games blurs the lines further. One study calculated that children view ten times as many Coke brand appearances through such embedded advertising than they do through traditional commercials.[41]

On top of the actual direct harm they do, these inhuman practices also give rise to the worst kind of corporate cynicism and spin. All the big offenders happily participate in studies and conferences about responsible marketing. I remember when running Good Business, I would be completely dumbfounded by some of the things clients of ours would say. Coca-Cola flat-out denied they ever marketed to children, despite their massive sponsorship of sports like soccer or their annual TV ad featuring "Santa Claus coming to town." Ho-ho-ho, Atlanta. McDonald's used to say, hilariously, "We don't market to children. We market to families, and families have children in them." Well, that's all right then.

But companies can choose to use their brand and product marketing for good. The makers of the popular children's television show *Sesame Street* signed a deal in 2013 with the Produce Marketing Association, which promotes fruits and vegetables, to license its characters for free.[42] After becoming aware of company research that showed only 4 percent of women consider themselves beautiful, Unilever launched the Dove Campaign for Real Beauty in 2005 and has been running it ever since. Its 2006 "Evolution" video, which shows in time lapse how makeup and digital editing can transform an average woman to looking like a supermodel, has over 18 million views on YouTube. It not only was shown to have a tangible—albeit short-term—effect on the self-esteem of girls who viewed the ad[43] but also sparked a global outcry calling for unmanipulated images in ads and media spreads; *Jezebel*, an online feminist news site founded the following year launched with an offer of $10,000 for the best example of a magazine cover photo being retouched.[44] Dove's choice to sell products that not only avoid distortive views of female beauty but actually challenge stereotypes serves in stark contrast to the rest of the industry, which unfortunately has failed to catch up.

Although young children aren't necessarily buying the clothing and beauty products, the effects of advertisements promoting them have serious consequences. According to Common Sense Media, a San Francisco–based nonprofit, "Almost as soon as preschoolers complete the developmental task of mastering a concept of their bodies, they begin to express concerns about their bodies."[45] Nearly a third of five- and six-year olds think their ideal body size is thinner than what they perceive to be their own.[46] Remember: this is not kindergartners with a healthy awareness of their own obesity risks, this is mental illness in the form of body dysmorphia. According to research conducted by the Girl Scouts, 48 percent of girls aged thirteen to seventeen "wish they were as skinny as fashion magazine models."[47]

SUSTAINABILITY

No one should underestimate the value—and difficulty!—of delivering the business basics: as any entrepreneur or CEO will tell you, it's really hard to make a good product, provide a good service, and earn a profit on it. But when companies like Dove use their incredible power to simultaneously mix profit with positive social impact, we see the truly amazing potential of business. And one of the most encouraging business trends over the past several decades is business leaders' realization that companies can take serious steps to minimize their negative environmental impact and still be profitable.

Ray Anderson founded his Georgia-based carpet business, what would become Interface, Inc., in 1973 after seeing modular carpet for the first time in England. With each tile easily installed and removed, it was the perfect flooring to accommodate the rise of cubicles (and proliferation of wires and cords) across corporate America. Plus, damaged tiles could be easily removed and replaced, drastically cutting the cost of maintenance. "I fell in love with the idea," he said in an interview before he died. "It just made so much sense."[48] Customers agreed: within a decade the company had gone public. Over the next ten years Anderson would expand his empire to Europe and the Middle East, later expanding to Asia as well and, over time, acquiring more than fifty other companies.

Today Interface has grown to become one of the world's largest carpet manufacturers, with over $1 billion dollars in annual revenue.[49]

Carpets, however, are made primarily from petroleum; their manufacture requires an enormous amount of it—not to mention water and energy—and it produces a huge amount of unrecyclable waste. By the early 1990s people were starting to take notice. "We'd begun to hear this question from customers that we'd never heard before—in so many words—'What's your company doing for the environment?'" Anderson recalls, "We had no answers. . . . It was very embarrassing. It was awkward for our sales people. It was awkward for our manufacturing people. For our research people." So in 1994 the company assembled a task force to look into sustainability. Right before they launched their initiative the team asked Anderson—a prolific speechmaker—to say some words. Though he supported the task force's goals, he didn't really have anything to say—that is, until someone gave him a copy of environmentalist Paul Hawken's book *The Ecology of Commerce*.

"I had never given a thought to what we had taken from the earth or were doing to the earth to make our products—except to always be sure that there's enough of that stuff running through the pipeline to keep our factories running. It was a spear in the chest experience," Anderson said. "I read it and wept. It laid out so clearly the problems of the industrial system. The system of which my company, my creation—this third child of mine—was an integral part."

Now his personal mission, Anderson pushed Interface researchers to look into every aspect of the enterprise that could be made more sustainable. They switched to renewable energy, eliminated as much waste as possible from their manufacturing plants, and made concerted efforts to 'close the loop' on their products so that they could be fully recycled at the end of their useful lives and turned into new products once again. Anderson's vision—what became known as Mission Zero—was for Interface to have no negative environmental impact by 2020. Ray Anderson died of cancer in 2011. He didn't live long enough to see Mission Zero accomplished. But company executives say that in the seventeen years leading up to his death, their environmental initiatives have reduced greenhouse gas emissions by 24 percent, fossil fuel consumption by 60 percent, landfill waste by 82 percent, and water use by 82 percent—all while avoiding over $450 million in costs.[50]

Around the same time Anderson had his epiphany, Bill Whiting, the marketing director (and, later, CEO) of B&Q, the British equivalent to Home Depot, had a similar experience. When a journalist asked him at a press conference how much tropical hardwood, much of which comes from precious rainforest, B&Q stocked, he confessed he didn't know. "Well, if you don't know, you don't care," the journalist replied. Stung, and now determined to know the answer, he hired a scientist, Dr. Alan Knight, to come work for B&Q as an environmental specialist. Knight dove right in, investigating the social and environmental problems associated with the timber B&Q sourced. He discovered that much of the company's timber was harvested using clear-cutting techniques, whereby entire forests are practically mowed down, devastating both natural ecosystems and local communities. So in 1991 B&Q announced that within five years it would only source timber from 'well-managed forests'—that is, forests where such destructive processes were not allowed.

But in 1991 there was little expertise on how to 'manage forests well,' especially to meet the business needs of a large multinational firm with a complex supply chain like B&Q's. So Knight oversaw a forest laboratory in Papua New Guinea, where destructive logging techniques were commonplace. He and his team were interested in developing techniques to train local communities to manage their own forest resources in an environmentally responsible way (e.g., using portable sawmills allowed them to harvest only high-value timber, minimizing damage and ensuring future yields). The project also developed systems for independent verification of well-managed forests so that timber buyers other than B&Q knew where their product came from and how it was harvested.

With this expertise B&Q was able to help create the Forest Stewardship Council in 1992, an independent NGO to set forest-management standards and oversee sustainable timber certification at a global level. As a result, countless forests—and the communities they support—have thrived. And B&Q—hardly a niche, 'ethical' brand on the fringes of the marketplace—was able to not only meet its target but also to apply the techniques it had learned to other products throughout its supply chain, setting the company off on an ongoing quest to better steward the people and nature it touched.[51]

TECHNOLOGY'S PROMISE

Although, as we have seen, technology can have a baleful impact on the human side of business, it can also work the other way, especially by improving information. The Internet enables consumers to discriminate on the basis of more than just quality and price: they can increasingly take human and environmental impact into account too. As companies like BeGood raise the bar about how much information is provided about consumer products, social impact becomes a consumer feature just like any other. This has been a winning strategy for firms like Patagonia, the environmentally sensitive—and enormously successful—maker of outdoor clothing. It has used its websites to show where and how its products are made, recently announcing the completion of a seven-year process to make sure all the down feathers used in jackets and sweaters are 100 percent traceable and cruelty-free. One section of their website, the Footprint Chronicles, traces the journey of some of their products around a global map, showing images, videos, and descriptions of each step along the way.

Or browse the website of Everlane, a much younger clothing maker. On the top of its homepage are links to its main sections: "Men's," "Women's," then "Factories." When you click on the page, up pops a map pinpointing each part of its supply chain, from leather shops to distribution centers to mills and factories. Each of them has a dedicated page showing basic data, like the number of employees, the date it was established, even current time and weather. Further down is a description of which products are made there, how Everlane found this particular factory, details on the materials it sources, and information about the factory's owner. If you scroll down, you can look at high-resolution images taken by Everlane's staff. Back on the individual product pages, which all link to their relevant factory-profile pages, Everlane takes transparency a step further, breaking down where every penny of the purchase price goes—from materials and labor to transport and profit.

PCH breaks down the supply chain even further. Founded by the Irish entrepreneur Liam Casey, PCH is one of the world's largest technology hardware manufacturing companies; it also makes most of its products in China. But that doesn't mean consumers can't see exactly how their products are made. PCH customers can go to the company's website, click on a product, and see where it is made. But more than that, they can see the individual workers who worked on it; they can literally see their names and the times they clocked in and out of the factory. "You see photos of production workers all the time. We actually name the workers," says Casey. Rather than keep them anonymous, Casey feels it's important that his workers, wherever they are in the world, are credited for their contribution. "It's natural," he says, to highlight them. "When you spend nineteen years building a company and these people work with you, they're a part of that story, so it's only right that you share the success with them and that they understand all the products they're working on and where they go."

"Transparency is about a lot more than worker relations. It's also about engaging with consumers. . . . You can track a product right through all the workers involved in a product, the factories. Shipping time." Casey believes that educating the consumer so completely allows them to not just buy a better product but also to make a purchasing decision that has wider benefits. "If you give consumers the choice—here's information that shows a well-managed supply chain vs. one that's a black box—if you can share that information, they will make a decision that is a better decision."[52]

It's not the Internet alone that's having a huge effect on businesses' social and environmental impact. Ubiquitous mobile technology can enable a hyper-transparent supply chain we could never have imagined twenty years ago. In previous decades 'corporate responsibility' meant the occasional, unannounced inspection, with the results being filed away or scanned into big PDFs hidden on investor-relations websites. But now, with mobile technology nearly everywhere, we can fundamentally change how we evaluate a company's working conditions, not to mention its overall impact on vulnerable communities.

"The current tool is an audit and certificate," says David Bonbright, head of Covox, an innovative human-rights monitoring firm. "It doesn't tell you how to solve any problems that might arise, just that there are problems." So Covox takes a more human, twenty-first-century approach based on the fact that nearly every worker in the developing world—even the poorest—has a mobile phone. Workers are asked directly about their own conditions, questions like: "Does your employer treat you fairly?" "Are working conditions healthy and safe?" and "Does the company respect your community's rights and behave like a good neighbor?" Every day a question like this is posed to a different representative sample of workers via text message to their mobiles; this way everyone's voice is heard. The results are immediately reported, collated, and delivered. Now, rather than a twelve- to twenty-four-month lag in discovering that something is wrong on the ground, issues can be discovered and diagnosed continuously. And with basic (anonymized) user data such as gender and age, Covox can gain even further insight into particular issues and how they're affecting workers and their community. It's more than mere compliance, Bonbright explains. "It's about capturing the voice of marginalized people who are part of the supply chain."[53]

Tools like Covox aren't in the hands of every consumer yet. But they could be. And even if consumers are unable or unwilling to pressure for change, companies' embrace of such technology can improve local communities' ability to hold their own legal and regulatory bodies accountable. Indeed, it may be the key—or at least play a significant role—in building and sustaining legitimate local governance in some of the most corrupt and oppressive corners of the world. This is where technology proves itself, when wielded correctly, as an enabler of good business— and good govenment—empowering society to make sure corporations put people first.

EMBRACING COMPETITION

Most technology companies seek patents so they can jealously guard their tech from their competitors. Tesla, the electric car company based in Palo Alto, has instead done the opposite, opening up all of its proprietary technology to the public in the spirit of moving the electric car industry forward. Originally, writes Tesla founder and CEO Elon Musk, "We felt compelled to create patents out of concern that the big car companies would copy our technology and then use their massive manufacturing, sales and marketing power to overwhelm Tesla. We couldn't have been more wrong. The unfortunate reality is the opposite: electric car programs (or programs for any vehicle that doesn't burn hydrocarbons) at the major manufacturers are small to non-existent." Musk's goal is a future of environmentally sustainable cars; he hopes to profit, of course, through Tesla, but he also realizes that Tesla doesn't have the capacity to rapidly supply the world with electric cars. If the world is to wean itself from fossil fuels, he reasons, Tesla can't be the only electric car.

Musk's philosophy is admirably civic minded, but it also reveals the frustration many entrepreneurs have with the way our legal system seems to serve entrenched interests (as we saw in the previous chapter) rather than true innovators. "Too often these days [patents] serve merely to stifle progress, entrench the positions of giant corporations and enrich those in the legal profession, rather than the actual inventors," he goes on to say in his letter announcing Tesla's decision to make public its technology. "After Zip2 [his first company], when I realized that receiving a patent really just meant that you bought a lottery ticket to a lawsuit, I avoided them whenever possible."[54] Innovation is really hard, but when companies approach it in the right way, collaborative competition rather than zealous rivalry can help move society forward.

SOMETIMES, THOUGH, LARGE corporations aren't well placed to push innovation forward. Although they might be good at producing certain core goods and services efficiently and effectively, they just aren't the best at new thinking. Businesses that find themselves in this situation can react in one of two ways: they can either invest in erecting barriers to entry so that new, more innovative competitors can't get off the ground (see Chapter 6), or they can work with new entrants and form mutually beneficial relationships that produce more value for society than what either can offer on their own.

Executives at Santander UK, the British division of the global banking giant, decided several years ago that they weren't in the best position to lend to small businesses. So it now works with Funding Circle, a peer-to-peer financing platform, to direct customers there when it makes sense. "SMEs need access to multiple sources of finance, and Santander's partnership with Funding Circle is a good example of how traditional and alternative finance can work together to help the nation's SMEs prosper," Santander's CEO Ana Botín said when the partnership was announced in June 2014.[55] It's also a good way for Santander to stay relevant—and survive—in the new banking economy. Since then, other banks have struck similar deals, either with Funding Circle or its competitors.[56]

Santander has also set up its own venture fund to find and invest in promising upstarts in the banking sector, upstarts that may very well disrupt itself. Santander is not alone. Investing in accelerators, incubators, and venture funds is a growing trend among some large companies—from SAP to Walmart, Deutsche Telekom to Nike—who might otherwise try to lobby government to regulate and close down insurgents. Of course, many of these companies still do engage in the type of antimarket, anticompetitive behavior we saw in the last chapter (Comcast has a venture investment division too), but that doesn't diminish the promise of more corporate engagement with innovators.

MISSION

My favorite businesses, though, are not just those that provide value to the marketplace without doing harm but those whose profits are intrinsically linked to solving social or environmental problems. In the past five years thirty-one states have passed benefit corporation legislation, allowing for-profit companies to legally pursue social and environmental impact in addition to profit.[57] The proliferation of 'B-corps,' including the now publicly traded Etsy, shows that multiple bottom lines are not mutually exclusive.

Consider Revolution Foods: started in 2006 by two mothers who met in business school, the company has figured out how to inexpensively make and distribute wholesome, additive-free lunches to children eligible for government-subsidized meals at their schools. To make food kids will actually eat, chefs visit schools to conduct taste tests—cofounder Kristin Groos Richmond describes their meals as 'kid-designed'—and regional specialties, like jambalaya in Louisiana, are included on the menu.[58] The company feeds hundreds of thousands of students in a thousand schools in twenty-six cities, delivering over a million meals a week and generating close to $100 million in revenue. Most importantly, 80 percent of their meals go to underserved communities. It's a business model that embodies the intersection of good public policy, human-centered design, and real entrepreneurial spirit.[59]

Here's another wonderful, mission-driven company. In the tech industry, despite high rates of pay and high levels of unemployed workers across the United States, there is a dire shortage of qualified software engineers. Meanwhile millions in Africa can't find work. So Andela, a human resources firm, finds and trains top recruits in Africa to then work remotely for top tech companies, far more affordably than recruiting engineers at home. Each candidate is trained for at least one thousand hours.[60] And rather than pay tuition, Andela pays them—at a combined cost of about $10,000 per fellow, as they're called, for four months of training. Fellows then make a four-year commitment to the tech firms for which they'll work, which include Microsoft and Udacity (which we'll hear some more about in Chapter 9), and they can continue taking professional development courses throughout their tenure. Andela's founder, Jeremy Johnson, was inspired to start the company after a trip to Nairobi several years ago: "I just became kind of blown away by the incredible under-utilized human capital that I saw everywhere," he says.[61] The company has already had more than fifteen thousand applicants. Though they've only been able to accept less than 1 percent of them, Johnson's goal is to train one hundred thousand developers across Africa over the next decade. "Our hope and expectation is that the Andela fellows, as they go through the program and graduate, play a key role in the continued growth of the continent."[62]

BUSINESSES ARE NOT governments. They can neither lock us up nor take our property. But they are tremendous organizations that accomplish tremendous things. Human progress owes an immeasurable debt to the ingenuity of the entrepreneurs, inventors, and innovators who have used the vehicle of business to benefit us all. Business isn't without its faults, though. In this chapter we have seen examples of the good and the bad, and it's obvious that if we want to make business more human, we need to encourage the former and discourage the latter. Some of that, as we saw in the previous chapter (and the one before that, Food) can be achieved by reforming the structure of certain industries—to make them fully competitive or to eliminate subsidies that harm society. Other aspects of inhuman business that cause concern can and should be tackled by government through specific legislation and regulation—for example, to mandate more human family leave policies in the workplace.

But it can't all be done by government. In the end the many millions of businesses that exist in the world—most of them small—are run by people. We need those people to make more human choices about how they and their businesses behave. Just because new techniques, increased public consciousness, or smart technology make running a *good* business more and more feasible—and at a profit too—does not mean it's inevitable. Businesses must *choose* to be good. And we must encourage them. Just as government should set the rules for fair markets, we should also demand it as investors, consumers, and suppliers, and—wherever possible—from within, as managers and employees. If demanding is too aggressive, then we at least need to be more curious. In our daily lives, we should all be asking, "Where does this come from?" "How were the people who made it treated?" "What are the effects on the environment?" Of course, for us to have these conversations, we need to know more. That's why moving toward a norm of openness, transparency, and accountability—through a combination of technology, regulation, and public pressure—is such a big part of the answer, a way to make all businesses more human businesses.

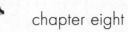

chapter eight

POVERTY

THIS IS HOW we deal with poverty today: there is a boy—let's call him Chris—from a poor family in East London. Like so many others in similar circumstances—in London, in America, in rich countries everywhere—Chris has all sorts of problems: mental health issues, acting out in school, getting in trouble with the police. Chris also has many well-meaning people from government trying to help him: social workers, probation officers, counselors. One day the adults responsible for all the different aspects of his life planned a conference to discuss his situation. There were going to be eleven professionals present. Chris's mother went to see David Robinson, founder of Community Links, a remarkable organization that for over twenty-five years has been fighting poverty in some of Britain's poorest neighborhoods. She asked him to come too. "Why?" he asked. There were, after all, already going to be nearly a dozen people there. She pleaded, "I need someone on my side."

How heartbreaking. She saw the social workers, the court officers—all of them—as her son's enemies.As David Robinson says, the well-meaning but ineffectual government assistance was so overwhelming that the mother practically needed an assistant to keep up.[1] They were all working on her son's problems piecemeal, with a different caseworker (or more) for each of his problems, pursuing the priorities and processes set by their part of the bureaucracy.

Yes, this is how we deal with poverty today—in a way that is inhuman. Chris and his mother's personal experience illustrate a broader disease. Today's vast, complex welfare system is clearly not working: How have we had a 'war on poverty' since 1964 and still have so many poor people? With generation after generation in poverty, we're obviously not dealing with its root causes. But the truly remarkable thing, given how much money we spend on it, is that we're not even dealing properly with its symptoms.

THE SYMPTOMS OF POVERTY

Every year HSBC, the international bank based in London, recently under fire for its sterling work helping the super-rich—including its own senior executives—avoid taxes, holds its annual general meeting where shareholders gather to discuss financial results, hear executives speak, and make decisions about the company's governance. These meetings tend to be pretty boring, almost entirely predictable. But in 2003 the meeting was quite different. Sir John Bond, the company's chairman, had just finished his address. There was a celebratory mood in the air; much of the assembly had centered around HSBC's planned acquisition of Household International, an American loan company, and William Aldinger, its head, had been persuaded to join HSBC's management. As is customary, Sir John opened the floor to questions.

Up stood perhaps the last person he would have expected to see. The proud owner of just enough donated shares to earn him a spot at the meeting, the man standing to ask Sir John a question was the man who cleaned his office every night. He said,

> Sir John Bond, distinguished ladies and gentlemen, my name is Abdul Durrant, I work in the same office as the board members, the only difference is I don't operate computers. My function is to operate a mop and bucket. Yes, I am one of the invisible night cleaners. You may be wondering what the hell is a night cleaner doing here: we're supposed to be invisible. Well, I am here on behalf of all the contract staff at HSBC and the families of East London. We receive £5 per hour—a whole £5 per hour![2]—no pension, and a measly sick-pay scheme. In our struggles our children go to school without adequate lunch. We are unable to provide necessary books for their education. School outings in particular they miss out on. In the end, many of our children prefer a life of crime to being a cleaner. . . . Sir John, we have met before. Will you consider your previous decision not to review the cleaning contract with OCS, so that I and my colleagues receive a living wage?[3]

THE WORKING POOR

Abdul's story touched everyone in the room, particularly Sir John. It wasn't just that the story was moving or that people were impressed by Abdul's eloquence despite the fact that he was so completely out of place. His story was especially poignant because the board had just discussed the pay package for Mr. Aldinger, who was now joining HSBC's management. His salary? £23 million (in excess of $35 million at the time) over the next three years. It was a contrast too stark for even the most avowed capitalists in the room. Abdul had made his point.

His situation was not—is not—unusual. He is among the 1.4 million or so British workers—about one in twenty—who earn the legal minimum wage.[4] In America the Pew Research Center estimates that there are some 20.6 million "near-minimum-wage" earners, constituting 30 percent of all hourly, non-self-employed workers eighteen and older.[5] These are the working poor. And for them life is terrible. Their struggles are not just about money but also dignity. Financial poverty leads to deprivations and challenges that are inconceivable for the rest of us. According to behavioral economist Sendhil Mullainathan, "There's money poverty, there's time poverty, and there's bandwidth poverty. . . . One of the things the poor lack most is bandwidth. The very struggle of making ends meet leaves them with less of this vital resource"—a resource essential to performing simple tasks and getting through life.[6] The poor are worse parents, they forget to take medications, they make bad decisions. But it is not about lack of love or skills; it's simply the inability to cope with so many things at once.[7] The rich can buy bandwidth in ways the poor cannot—they hire housekeepers, gardeners, assistants, accountants, and nannies. They can go 'away for the weekend'; they take vacations. They can afford to take their time when making financial decisions. They can buy a shorter commute by choosing to live near where they work.

When poor people are constantly worrying about money, they neglect other areas of their lives. Scarcity of money affects scarcity of time, which in turn affects scarcity of mental bandwidth. All of these things feed on themselves, leading to worse and worse decision making. And although most of us might take a break when life feels overwhelming, the poor cannot. "Poor people can't say, 'I'll take a vacation from being poor,'" Mullainathan explains.[8]

Unsurprisingly given the psychological stress of poverty, "there's a strong association between poverty and low mental health," says Princeton psychologist Johannes Haushofer.[9] This has broader health implications. When the poor neglect daily tasks, they also neglect to take care of themselves. "I estimate 12 million Americans living in poverty suffer from at least one neglected parasitic or tropical disease," says Dr. Peter Hotez.[10]

We should remember that the working poor are not some 'underclass,' bent on cheating the system. Or even teenagers earning a little extra cash in summertime.[11] In 2014 over 60 million Americans—including 15 million children—lived in low-wage families.[12] They're not poor for want of trying.[13] Low pay is often bandied about in political debates as a talking point. But just think about it for a minute. Think about it on an individual, human level.

Imagine if it were you. Imagine you got up every day, worked to the point where you were so exhausted you couldn't move, worked so hard you felt permanently, achingly guilty that you weren't spending enough time with your children and were missing moments with them that would literally never come again; imagine you worked like that, but your wages were so low that you still didn't have enough to live on. You'd then have a choice: you might take on an additional job, spend even less time at home, burden your body even more. Or you could take the physically easier but emotionally more difficult choice of giving up even more of your humanity: on top of all the other indignities you could go to the government, give up your independence, and ask for a welfare payment—a handout, even though you were working as hard as you possibly could. Imagine how that would make you feel. This is a scandal.

We ended slavery because it was inhuman and wrong. As we saw in Chapter 5, it is time to end animal cruelty, because it's inhuman and wrong. And now I want to show you how we can end the moral scourge represented by the very notion of the 'working poor.' I'm not arguing this on the basis of 'efficiency' or 'growth' or any other financial or economic objective. I'm arguing this because I think it's morally unacceptable that anyone who works should not be able to live off what they earn.

The policy intervention most obviously aimed at helping to end poverty pay is the government-established 'minimum wage,' based on the principle that no one should work without fair compensation. The idea got its start in 1896 when Australians, having just seen the abolition of slavery, resolved to treat all workers with dignity. They believed it was morally necessary to recognize workers as human beings, rather than costs of production, which is what many, as slaves, had literally been considered just a short time before. "It would demean us all," argued Alfred Deakin in 1896, an Australian legislator and later prime minister, "if those who made our food and clothing or tended to our comforts and well-being were treated as inferior beings."[14] By 1907 Australia's minimum wage had become a symbol of pride—and a beacon for reformers worldwide.

Britain owes the roots of its minimum wage to Sir Winston Churchill, a champion of free markets, who backed the country's first minimum-wage legislation in 1909. Arguing for it in Parliament, Churchill put it as well as anyone: "It is a serious national evil that any class of His Majesty's subjects should receive less than a living wage in return for their utmost exertions."[15]

In America the first minimum wage came with the Fair Labor Standards Act of 1938. Enacted by President Franklin Roosevelt, it was part of a broader fight to improve working conditions in Depression-era America. As it is today, the minimum wage was a controversial issue and inspired court challenges and prolonged political fights before it was passed and signed.[16] Since then, although a federal minimum wage has been the floor, different jurisdictions like states, counties, and municipalities have opted to raise it higher to account for local conditions and priorities.

The actual introduction of the minimum wage comprehensively defeated the arguments of those who had opposed it: it seemed to have no negative impact on employment or the economy more generally, and today at least the idea has bipartisan support.[17] But $7.25 an hour isn't enough. Some 21 million American workers make less than $10.10 an hour, the minimum wage President Obama declared as a national aim (about $21,000 a year).[18] Some 42 percent of American workers make less than $15 an hour (just over $31,000 a year), the wage many worker advocates want the minimum wage raised to.[19]

Earning your own living is essential to human dignity, and psychologists have shown that autonomy and independence are vital for well-being. Yet millions of people work full time while being paid by their employers at a level they can't live on. Although it's impossible to know exactly how many work full time or part time, some 27 million families and individuals qualified for the Earned Income Tax Credit (just one of many forms of public assistance designed to benefit low pay workers) in 2013, including 11 million children. Of those, the EITC lifted 6.2 million people—3.2 million children—out of poverty.[20] These families worked—some perhaps even made above minimum wage—but they were forced to rely on welfare handouts from the government. How can the minimum wage be an antidote to poverty when it doesn't provide enough to live on?

None of us should feel comfortable living in such a society. That many should have to work multiple jobs—tough, physical, and sometimes demeaning jobs—in order to make ends meet is surely unacceptable. Of course, there's a distinction between part time and full time: if you work twenty hours a week, you shouldn't expect to make the same as someone who works forty hours. But if you work full time, you should be paid enough to live on. End of story. There will, of course, always be people on benefits out of necessity, like the elderly or disabled, but society, quite rightly, does not expect them to work for a living. Everyone else should. There should be no such thing as the working poor.

A 'LIVING WAGE' is the amount that's enough to live on if you work full time, based on the costs of food, housing, energy, transport, basic leisure, and so on. There are various definitions, and the rate is different in different places (the MIT Living Wage Calculator breaks down the living wage by county and by household type).[21] In Australia—way back in 1907—the minimum wage was a living wage: that's how it was defined.[22] It's what Churchill meant too when he equated a minimum wage with a living wage. But today the minimum wage is obviously not enough to live on. If it were, we wouldn't need to top it off with welfare payments. Wouldn't it be better—more human—if we dealt with this by paying a living wage in the first place? After many years of campaigns and advocacy by a wide range of individuals and organizations (including by me in the UK version of this book), Conservative chancellor of the Exchequer George Osborne introduced Britain's first National Living Wage in his 2015 budget. It's not perfect: it will take until 2020 to come fully into effect and ought to be higher to take into account proposed cuts in the welfare budget, but it does make Britain the only country in the world to uphold the value of work by mandating a living wage.

In the United States the issue is much more contentious. There is no political consensus around raising the minimum wage, let alone raising it to the level of a living wage. But what is impossible to ignore, what is in fact a moral failure, is that so many millions of 'hard-working Americans,' so beloved of the politicians' slogans, are forced to live in the most inhuman way, for no real reason, trapped there by political inertia and pointless bureaucracy.

DO THE RIGHT THING—IT PAYS

There is an assumption that requiring employers to pay a living wage will cost jobs on a massive scale. As the original opponents of a minimum wage argued, higher wages mean higher costs for employers. But we don't need to speculate about this. We can look at some of the companies that have implemented a living wage. Like Costco.

Costco isn't just big in the United States; it's the second-largest retailer in the world.[23] Its business model is simple: huge warehouses, cheap products, stacked high. And yet Costco pays its workers way over the living wage. Repeat: way over the living wage. In the United States employees earn, on average, $20.89 per hour, not including overtime. And 88 percent of employees have employer-sponsored health insurance.[24] For Costco a living wage is good business. Writing to Congress in support of a higher minimum wage, CEO Craig Jelinek wrote, "We know it's a lot more profitable in the long term to minimize employee turnover and maximize employee productivity, commitment and loyalty." Consider that 70 percent of Costco's warehouse managers got their start on the floor, stacking boxes and collecting carts. Turnover is 5 percent for those who have been there over a year. It's easy to understand where the loyalty comes from: management has increased wages every three years. During the 2009 downturn, when retail shops were laying employees off and cutting pay and benefits, founder and then CEO Jim Sinegal decided to do exactly the opposite: he gave workers a raise of $1.50 an hour. According to CFO Richard Galanti, "The first thing out of Jim's mouth was, 'This economy is bad. We should be figuring out how to give them more, not less.'"

How much do these 'generous' policies cost? Admittedly, lower profits in the short term. But in the long term this ethos has paid off. Last year Costco made over $2 billion in profits.[25] Its share price has more than doubled since its prerecession peak. And it's not as if Costco is passing on these costs to customers. It has a general policy to mark items up at no more than 15 percent. For Costco, paying employees well makes financial sense. Of course, every company is different. But Costco demonstrates a fundamental principle: a living wage is not necessarily bad for business or jobs, even in a sector with as slim margins as grocery and discount retailing.

THINK ABOUT THE money a company makes as a surplus: it can choose to distribute that in various ways. Simplistically a company can choose to invest its profits in new technology or innovative processes, it can give that money to its customers in the form of lower prices or higher value products for the same prices, it can give the money to its shareholders, or it can give the money to its workers in the form of higher pay and benefits. Obviously most well-run companies do a combination of these

things. But what is the balance? At Costco it's tilted more toward workers. But elsewhere across the economy, instead of sharing more of their
surplus with workers, companies have been choosing to give it to shareholders. Could that be because senior executives' pay and compensation
are now so closely tied to their company's short-term share price? Whatever the motivation, the end result is that over the last ten years companies on the S&P 500 have spent almost 90 percent of their profits on
shareholder dividends and stock buybacks.[26]

The most frustrating part is that, as Costco has found, treating your
workers fairly and paying them a living wage can actually help your business and, in the long term, boost share price. It is a lazy assumption,
contradicted by the evidence, that putting shareholders first is the best
way to succeed. It's especially ironic given the example set by one of
America's great heroes of capitalism, Henry Ford. Ford doubled the daily
wages of his employees amidst a deep recession in 1914, declaring, "If an
employer does not share prosperity with those who make him prosperous, then pretty soon there will be no prosperity to share. That is why we
think it good business always to raise wages and never to lower them.
We like to have plenty of customers."[27] He's not alone. Jack Welch, the
former chief of General Electric, recently said that maximizing shareholder value "is the dumbest idea in the world."[28] Paul Polman, CEO of
Unilever, has called it a "cult."[29]

Better-paid employees work harder, are more open to changing job
roles to suit their company's needs, and call in sick far less—one business that adopted the living wage reported a drop in absenteeism by as
much as 25 percent.[30] Living wage employers see higher morale (among
all employees, not just the low-paid ones), an improved reputation, and
lower staff turnover.[31]

One objection you hear to the idea of a universal living wage is that
although it may be possible for large or even medium-sized businesses, it
would be devastating for small businesses. And that matters a lot when
so many of the working poor are in the retail and hospitality sectors,
where small firms dominate. It turns out that here, too, there's no iron
rule—it's a question of choice. If you build higher wages into your business plan, you can make it work: a restaurant in Philadelphia, William
Street Common, attracted national attention when it banned tipping
in favor of a flat-rate 20 percent service charge and chose to pay all its
employees at least $15 an hour. The trend is spreading: now Joe's Crab
Shack, a popular seafood chain, is testing the model out in 18 of its 130
restaurants across the country.[32]

Still, no matter how much evidence you provide or how many case studies you cite, people will ask, "How can we afford it?" If we really want to make this happen, we need to make it easier for businesses. We need a 'business-friendly living wage.' Here's how it can be done.

The debate over low pay and the working poor captures only half the argument. It's not just about wages; it's also about taxes—business taxes. Think about what an inadequate minimum wage actually is. It allows a company to pay workers less than they need to live because the government will make up the difference through welfare. A minimum wage that's too low for people to live on is a subsidy to business. In policy circles the fashionable vehicle for these subsidies is the concept of the 'tax credit' paid to low-wage workers; here in America, the Earned Income Tax Credit (EITC) is the leading example. The EITC gives unemployed people incentives to get into work, even if it's low paid. It has partly achieved that aim and done some good in lifting people from poverty,[33] but research shows that although wage subsidies like this increase employment, they also depress wages by allowing employers to pay less: one study found that for every dollar spent on the EITC, only 28 cents were a net benefit to the recipient; 72 cents were captured by the employer in the form of lower wages paid.[34]

In the end it's still welfare, with the government topping up low pay—a subsidy to the employer and an insult to the worker. It's especially shocking that free marketers and conservatives seem to support these subsidies to businesses, presumably because they are branded 'tax credits.' What a triumph of spin. The really mad part is that at the same time as receiving wage subsidies *from* the government, companies are paying corporate and payroll taxes *to* the government. This is an insane merry-go-round of money: a company pays low wages to its workers; it pays tax to the government; the government then takes the tax and gives it back to the workers.

Walmart, a leading low-wage employer, has figured out how to milk the taxpayer even more.[35] It benefits from what I'll call 'Walmart Welfare.' A significant percentage of Walmart employees—as many as 15 percent in one state—don't make enough to afford their own groceries.[36] They are forced to rely on food stamps to feed their families, which they use to buy food at Walmart at the end of their shift. America's taxpayers are helping to cut Walmart's labor costs while directly contributing to its sales. Walmart, the country's largest private employer and chief recipient of food stamp monies, is also likely the country's largest employer with employees on food stamps.[37] In 2013 the store made an estimated $13.2

billion from taxpayer-funded food stamp revenue—18 percent of all US food stamp receipts and 4 percent of its annual sales.[38] For Walmart it's a virtuous cycle; for its employees, it's just vicious. A report by Americans for Tax Fairness calculated that Walmart employees require $6 billion in welfare annually.[39]

Economically, low pay is an unfair subsidy to big business. Politically it contributes to the need for a vast bureaucracy to slush money around the system. Socially it perpetuates cycles of welfare and a loss of human independence and dignity. Morally it dishonors the work of millions of people on whose labor society depends.

Here's a simple way to end it: let's introduce a federal *living* wage in America and cut employers' taxes by the same amount they're paying in higher wages. Of course, the exact level would have to vary from place to place. But a federal mandate would require local authorities to set the minimum wage in their area at a level that every full-time worker could live on, without government or other handouts. The crucial element of this change, however, would be the compensating reduction in business taxes—aiming for a revenue-neutral impact on employers. The business tax cut would pay for itself in two ways: less spending on public assistance programs and higher income tax receipts from workers' raised salaries.[40]

THE CAUSES OF POVERTY

A business-friendly federal living wage would, by definition, end in-work poverty. But that isn't nearly enough; we need to tackle the causes of poverty too. In far too many cases poverty is generational, handed down like some perverse inheritance within a family. To end poverty we must break that cycle. Although economic policies can help fight the symptoms of poverty, it is social policy that will help us fight the causes. That has to start with children—like Sasha.

Sasha lives in the Bayview, one of San Francisco's poorest communities. Violence is rampant not only in her neighborhood (she knew three people who were murdered) but also in her home: when her father drinks, he's physically abusive. He's in prison, but although he's not there to abuse her, his absence causes other problems. Sasha's mother had to work evenings to make ends meet, but because she couldn't find a babysitter for Sasha, she lost her job and, with it, the income to pay the rent. Now they live in subsidized housing, but not before a bout of homelessness. Meanwhile Sasha—ashamed of herself and her family—is almost always tense with her mother, who is depressed but, because she is uninsured, is unable to get effective mental health treatment. Sasha has a hard time focusing in class, so she misbehaves: she is jumpy and often overreacts to provocation. She was recently suspended for kicking another girl. Her action wasn't justified, but she thought she was being threatened. After a life in her shoes, it was the only way she really knew how to respond. Sasha is eleven years old.[41]

She is also a patient of Dr. Nadine Burke Harris, a local pediatrician. Her medical training took her to some of America's best universities: Stanford, Harvard, Berkeley. Yet when she chose where to locate her medical practice, she came to one of the country's most difficult neighborhoods.[42] Soon after setting up her pediatric clinic in the Bayview, Burke Harris grew uneasy. She knew, as we all instinctively do, that being poor is not good for anyone's health. It's difficult to eat right; sleep is often disrupted; getting exercise is hard. But even these basic realities couldn't explain the common health problems she was seeing across her patients—conditions like asthma, learning disabilities, behavioral issues—far in excess of what was normal for children at their age. She began to wonder whether these conditions were somehow connected to the children's challenging circumstances. What if her patients' health problems were actually symptoms of something deeper, something more structural in their lives?

TOXIC STRESS

In 1985 Dr. Vincent Felitti was running an obesity clinic in San Diego, California. And he was stumped. Around half the patients who were participating in the program, designed for those who were massively overweight, were dropping out, even when they were losing weight. He wanted to know why. He brought a couple of hundred of them into his clinic and asked them a standard set of questions, like, "How much did you weigh when you started first grade?" "How much did you weigh when you started high school?" "How old were you when you married?" For a while nothing unusual surfaced. Then he made a mistake.

"I misspoke," he remembers. "Instead of asking, 'How old were you when you were first sexually active?' I asked: 'How much did you *weigh* when you were first sexually active?' The patient, a woman, answered: 'Forty pounds.'" Not quite understanding her, he asked the same question again. Her first sexual experience, it turned out, was with her father when she was four years old. Felitti was dumbfounded. "I remembered

thinking: 'This is only the second incest case I've had in 23 years of practice.'" So he continued the line of questioning with others. "About 10 days
later, I ran into the same thing. It was very disturbing. Every other person was providing information about childhood sexual abuse. I thought:
'This can't be true. Someone would have told me in medical school.'"

Still not convinced he wasn't somehow biasing his patients, he asked
other doctors at the clinic to ask the same thing. Sure enough, of the 286
people interviewed, most of them had been the victims of sexual abuse.
For some, eating was a coping mechanism, a 'drug' that made them feel
better, soothing depression, anger, fear. For others, being overweight
provided a form of protection: in the case of one man, it had prevented
other kids from beating him up in the school yard. For one woman, being
fat made her an undesirable rape victim (when she was seven, her father
told her the only reason he wasn't abusing her sister was that she was
fat).

Despite many doctors' skepticism, Felitti found allies in Dr. David Williamson and Dr. Robert Anda, epidemiologists at the US Centers for Disease Control and Prevention. After years researching childhood trauma,
determining which questions they would ask, and setting up the ques-
tionnaires, they began a trial in 1995. By 1997 they had asked over seventeen thousand patients passing through a San Diego clinic about ten
types of childhood trauma, including sexual, verbal, and physical abuse,
family dysfunction, and emotional and physical neglect. They then were
able to draw correlations between childhood circumstances and health
conditions.[43]

The home environment, they discovered, played a crucial role in the
health of the people they interviewed, particularly the children. Of the
ten specific adverse childhood experiences (ACEs, as they dubbed them)
they asked about, some two-thirds of the study participants had had at
least one.[44] The doctors created a simple scoring system: one point for
the presence of each type of ACE in a child's life. For example, if your
parents had divorced during your childhood, you had a score of 1. If you
were abused and had divorced parents, you had a score of 2. And so on.
As traumatic experiences added up—as the ACE score increased—the
worse the health outcomes. In the 1998 article where they published
their results, they wrote that compared to someone with no ACEs, someone with an ACE score of 4 was 3.9 times more likely to have emphysema
or chronic bronchitis, 2.4 times more likely to have hepatitis or jaundice,
and 1.6 times likelier to have had skeletal fractures. They also found a
significant relationship between ACE scores and risk factors for heart

disease, liver disease, and cancer. Those with an ACE score of 4 or higher were 2.2 times likelier to smoke, 1.6 times likelier to be obese, 4.6 times likelier to have been depressed in the past year, and over 12.2 times likelier to have ever attempted suicide.[45]

NADINE BURKE HARRIS'S own experiences in her Bayview clinic—and her hunch that something deeper was going on with her patients than just the symptoms of poverty—led her to Felitti and Anda's research. She realized she was witnessing ACEs taking place . . . in real time. Her patients' problems had little to do with health per se; they had everything to do with their family environments. Sasha's domestic problems—the alcoholic father who physically abused her and her mother, the violence and murder all around her—these were not just unfortunate coincidences alongside her health problems. They were their cause. And the connection? A phenomenon called toxic stress.

Not all stress is bad. Positive stress is a mild response to a challenge or exciting event, like an exam, a big sports game, or a public performance. Although it might not feel great in the short term, experiencing positive stress as a child can help build strength and grit. Tolerable stress is severe and negative but is usually in response to a one-off event, like a death in the family. If managed with the help of a caring adult, a child can overcome tolerable stress. But toxic stress is different. It *is* toxic— literally poison. Medically defined as the "extreme, frequent or extended activation of [the body's] stress response without the buffering presence of a supportive adult,"[46] toxic stress is exactly what you would imagine is created by those ACEs. In the absence of enough compensating warmth, love, and affection from at least one parent or primary caregiver, it creates physical, molecular changes in the brain.

When the body senses stress or anxiety, it activates defenses that cause chemical and physical reactions. As it is temporary, positive or tolerable stress doesn't pose a problem. But repeated stress disables the ability to respond correctly. "If you are growing up in an environment where there are constant threats, the brain adapts in a way that reacts to those threats," explains Burke Harris. Children exhibit relatively minor symptoms like the inability to sit still. But as adults they become unable to cope and wind up behaving destructively. "When we were evolving, the threats were saber-toothed tigers and lions and bears, and this made a ton of sense," says Burke Harris. "Whatever it is, you'd have to jump on it and beat the crap out of it in order to survive. Nowadays when you do that, you end up incarcerated or, if you're trying to sit still in a classroom and the kid next to you hits you or pokes you, then you end up getting kicked out of class. What we see in children who are experiencing toxic stress is tremendous difficulty in self-regulation."[47]

Children with toxic stress have higher levels of the long-term stress hormone, cortisol, in their brains. This is particularly problematic for younger children because of neuroplasticity, the way our brains physically change and evolve. Neuroplasticity isn't unique to stressed children— everyone's brain architecture and chemistry are affected by experiences. But children younger than five years old are especially vulnerable to environmental stressors. This is because there are two types of neuroplasticity. One is synaptic plasticity (the strength of connections between brain cells), which occurs throughout our lifetimes. The other is cellular plasticity (the number of those connections), which occurs primarily in the first five years of a child's life. The elevated levels of cortisol from toxic stress disrupt that development and can cause long-term damage. For children, failure to inhibit the stress hormones in their brain inhibits their own maturation. This permanent, toxic stress leads not just to bad health outcomes for children but bad life outcomes that are at the heart of the fight against poverty.

THE COSTS OF POVERTY

Welfare in America costs $212 billion per year.[48] Alcohol addiction: $223.5 billion.[49] Illicit drugs: $193 billion.[50] Child poverty: $500 billion.[51] Crime: $194 billion.[52] Each cohort of high school dropouts costs the economy around $150 billion.[53] These social problems, almost by definition, are overwhelmingly concentrated among the poor. As the saying goes, some of this "will always be with us." But so many of these costs would be reducible, avoidable, if we took more interest in their deep, structural causes rather than just (expensively) addressing the symptoms. This would mean addressing poverty on a more human level, concentrating on the individual person from their very earliest days and how they end up part of a 'social problem.' All those big numbers—the costs of welfare, crime, addiction—are composed of individual people with their own stories and circumstances. And one thing we can now say with confidence is that for a vast majority of them, adverse childhood experiences—and the toxic stress that goes with them—are part of their story and circumstances.

We typically attempt to intervene after kids commit crime or drop out of school, but we fail to prevent these problems in the first place. By the time the 'system' even realizes someone like Sasha exists, she is already deeply in crisis and needs lots of costly help to get out. But if we look at where ACEs mostly arise, it's at home, in the family context. That's not surprising: the family is the core unit of life. Families care for each other, teach each other, play together, eat together, love together. Most importantly families raise children. Generally, happy and successful children tend to come from stable, loving families; troubled children tend to come from troubled homes.

There are caveats, of course. Some people who are extremely successful—and sometimes even happy—grew up in homes that were far from being stable and loving. There's a theory that overcoming early adversity was for many of the world's most successful people a direct spur to their accomplishments. But what we don't know—and will never know—is: What if the adversity wasn't a spur but a harness, that they achieved amazing things despite the difficulties they experienced at an early age? Imagine how much more might have been possible. And remember, it's not just about avoiding social costs; it's about the benefits too, the benefits to all of us if children develop in the right way from an early age.

FAMILY FIRST

Here's the big idea. The easiest, most effective, most cost-effective way to end poverty, reduce inequality, promote better health and well-being, cut crime and antisocial behavior, spur entrepreneurship and innovation; the best way to achieve the outcomes we all want for our society and economy; the single-most valuable thing we can do in government and outside of it to make the world a better place for all . . . is to invest in the infrastructure that matters most: the human infrastructure of the family.

Most families work well. In their own ways they do a good job of preparing their children to succeed as adults. All we need to do is help the minority of families where that's not happening to get their act together—to become at least as good as average. That single change would do more to end poverty and improve our society and economy than anything else. And it is possible. We have done much harder things than this. We have mobilized resources on a much bigger scale, more quickly, than would be needed for this. We have invaded countries. We have put a man on the moon. Now we can end poverty—the human way.

We are getting this so wrong at the moment. We leave it far too late to pay attention to the things that matter. A child's path is a little like steering a large ship. Shifting 1 degree at the start is much easier than making a 90-degree course correction later on, hundreds of miles away from harbor. For children, acting early to make sure they're on track means fewer kids will get into trouble as teenagers or young adults. It's a lot harder to help a delinquent youth or a dropout than it is to help a toddler. Social problems begin early and then multiply. Stress, as other recent studies have found, is contagious, adding to cycles of toxic stress in struggling families.[54] And one of the biggest sources of stress is family structure itself, specifically in the form of children raised without their father, or a consistent father figure, in the home. Men who don't stay around to raise their children are one of the primary causes of social breakdown. Families break at different points, but many do so in part because of the stress of having children. And the experience of family breakdown, combined with the circumstances of poverty, leaves an often-indelible imprint on the children affected.

Recall David Robinson of Community Links in East London and the boy with eleven caseworkers. That story doesn't just make the case for streamlining social services for families; it also points to a broader issue. Even when government tries to help people living in poverty, it often does so haphazardly. The problems of poverty don't neatly stack into whatever program we've created to tackle them.

We've seen throughout this book that in many policy areas we try to compensate for their complexity by putting them into neat boxes—'silos' in policy-speak—thinking that by simplifying or neatly packaging and assigning them to a particular agency, law, or program, everything will be made easier. This is inherently not human; the human world is a messy place, and most things are interconnected. Many chapters in this book overlap with each other, and that's not a coincidence. After all, you can't solve unemployment without thinking about education; you can't think about health without thinking about food. And no social issue can be solved without thinking about our most fundamental social unit, the family.

Instead of helping the East London boy piecemeal—in school, through his probation officer, or in his after-school program—those efforts should have been put into a broader context: What is his family situation? What is his home physically like? What were his ACEs? Is he suffering from toxic stress? To turn around the lives of troubled children and help them escape poverty for good, we don't just need to streamline the help we

give them; we need to provide the right infrastructure for them to succeed. We need to help their entire family.

If we fail to take a broad view of a family and its problems, solutions will
only be patches that treat symptoms rather than the underlying cause.
Poverty stems from multiple things going wrong: perhaps the stress of a
difficult relationship or a breakup leads to substance abuse and the loss
of a job; perhaps someone who has received government assistance and
training can't get a job because she can't afford childcare or transport to
work. These problems are all related, and those who suffer them are often least equipped to handle them. If you have a stable income or a good
social-support network, a breakup or substance abuse can be overcome.
But if several of these things happen at once, that missing support network exacerbates the severity of each problem. For children born into
families living under these circumstances, they're swimming against the
tide from before they're even born.

All this is made much worse, of course, by the scale and distance of
government. The parts of government that typically provide services for
families are responsible for many hundreds of thousands of people. It's
no surprise that these large bureaucracies end up putting their own systems and procedures first—often in the name of 'efficiency'—and the
individual circumstances of real people a distant second.

That's why we need organizations like Single Stop USA. With over
one hundred locations, it has helped over 1 million households since
2007 gain access to benefits and services. Staff educate clients about programs that might be helpful for them and help determine their eligibility.
They also help them navigate the bureaucracy that life throws at them.
Founder Michael Weinstein recalls a client who was having trouble with
his landlord. Weinstein helped the client find a legal advocate but also
helped him set up a bank account to handle financial transactions like
rent. "The landlord was paid. The problem disappeared. Single Stop is a
problem-solving device."[55]

Promise Neighborhoods is another such program present in dozens
of communities across the country. Based on Harlem Children's Zone
(HCZ), a now deservedly well-known program in New York that aims to
provide cradle-to-college services in a comprehensive fashion, Promise
aims to bridge service providers. Rohan and I visited HCZ and met its
inspiring, charismatic leader, Geoffrey Canada, while we were researching policy ideas in 2010. The HCZ model focuses programs not only on
children—its centerpiece is a series of charter schools—but also on the
environment around them. Among the many programs are parenting

classes, coaches for teachers, healthy eating initiatives, tax preparation clinics, test-prep classes, and more. HCZ recognizes the importance of early childhood, so it targets expectant parents and works with them and their children until college. Its Baby College gives parents tools and advice, whereas its Three-Year Journey program works as a weekly support network to which parents bring their children. As the parents meet and take part in workshops, their children play together in a structured environment.

As children grow up, they and their families get age-appropriate support, from a recreation center to an employment and technology center, where, in addition to getting access to technology, youths can get tutoring and academic counseling. Tying all these programs together is communication: rather than have dozens of agencies independently handling these tasks, a child or family works within a single network.[56] The result is an elimination of red tape as well as continuity and stability.

The goal of Promise Neighborhoods is to spread the HCZ model across the United States with grants from the Obama administration to existing local organizations in poor communities. The Promise Neighborhood Institute (PNI), meanwhile, provides training, tools for continuous feedback, and lessons from best practices across the country. In a way PNI exemplifies the localism I discussed in Chapter 2: local service delivery that helps communities solve their own problems, buttressed by a central infrastructure that provides support that can only be organized at scale.[57] These efforts show promise, but they are only in the nascent stages of development. We need to encourage these essential experiments.

But in the end, however it's organized or delivered, it comes down to the individual, human level: one person working with one family to help its members get their lives back on track. These services flourish on the basis of simplicity: having one counselor, adviser, or advocate is better than ten. That simple idea was the starting point for one program I'm especially proud of having helped start in government in the UK.

WE KNEW INTUITIVELY–AND then once we took office had the detailed research to back it up—that a relatively small group of completely broken families suffers and creates the most problems in British society. These families, around 120,000 of them, cost taxpayers some £9 billion ($14 billion) annually (£75,000, or $117,000, per family on average).[58] Their interconnected problems—unemployment, debt, substance abuse, violence, educational failure—read like a template for the adverse child-hood experiences Nadine Burke Harris sees in San Francisco. For decades government at all levels had failed to get a grip on these deep problems, and I was determined that we would be different. I also knew that a traditional bureaucratic approach would never work. We needed something more human, and I knew exactly the person for the job.

If you want to meet the personification of a 'human' civil servant, meet Louise Casey. A former deputy director of the British homeless charity Shelter, she came to prominence when Tony Blair appointed her head of the Rough Sleepers Unit in 1999 to solve the decades-old problem of homeless people sleeping out on the streets of London. She succeeded—and then went on to take a number of high-profile positions in government. Her Wikipedia entry describes her as "known for being outspoken." You can say that again.

In 2011 we asked Louise to lead a new Troubled Families Unit with a dedicated budget and very clear brief: £448 million in funding over three years to turn around the lives of those 120,000 most chaotic, dysfunctional families by the end of the Parliament in 2015.[59] The crucial difference was the approach: a more human one, focusing a family worker on each of these families. The family workers would be given the training and discretion to respond creatively to the very different, human needs of the people they were trying to help. "On the whole most politicians think there are two ways to get something done in government. One is to pass laws through Parliament. Of course, you can get some change through passing laws," Louise explains, "but it's a blunt instrument. The other way is through fiscal change. When it comes to poverty or families, either they think they need to change the laws, that is, introduce a measure to tackle antisocial behavior, or they think the thing to do is tax credits."[60]

"Large institutions," she says, "operate around numbers and targets; they don't operate around people, behavior, and change." But that institutional setting is especially problematic for troubled families and their plethora of problems. "My families have an average of nine very significant problems and multiple agencies around them, each operating within their own systems. It's no shock to me that you can often find over fourteen different agencies running around them." The approach Louise's team takes is to try to work with families to get to the root of their problems. They recognize that these problems are not based in government, so neither are the solutions; instead, they try to understand the exact context of a family's situation, in all its complexity. They work on the family's terms, not the government's. For instance, in many cases a family might be receiving state services that are either unhelpful or counterproductive, so the Troubled Families Unit will stop them. In other cases they work with local councils, police, health, voluntary, and community sectors to ensure coordinated, unduplicated services for families. As with Single Stop, Harlem Children's Zone, and Promise Neighborhoods, taking complexity out of people's lives is one of the best antidotes to their problems.

Perhaps most importantly, instead of being reactive, the unit tries to be proactive, asking how it can prevent a family from falling into further crisis. "I met this girl who lived a life of abuse, handing it on to her three children. [Because she was a drug abuser, the social workers] said 'prevention' and prescribed her methadone so she doesn't go out and shoplift anymore. That's not prevention!" Louise exclaims. "That is too late and not enough done. The problem is no one wants to go about it directly. People think that's judging families: some on the Left don't like it because they think it's judging the poor; some on the Right don't like it because they can't accept that these people need help getting back on their feet and it's not just about getting a job."

This is the whole point: we need to get out of an ideological mindset and think about these people as they are, not as our grand political theories paint them. "I profoundly think that when you're dealing with people like my families, they need an inspirational, sometimes judgmental mentor," Louise says. "You need a human being to enter their lives skillfully, lovingly, and to create a connection with them where everyone else has otherwise failed to connect."

Sometimes the best person can be found within the family itself. Louise's most profound insight into how best to help troubled families is simple: most parents—even abusive ones—love their children and are their best hope for a successful childhood. "I can predict the families that have histories of abuse; they have a lack of boundaries: no sense of what's right and wrong, no sense of how to create relationships with people, how to love well. People beat people even though they love them." Although there is a line to be drawn and children should be protected from abusive parents, the default reaction shouldn't be for government to swoop in and alienate them. Children's relationship with their parents is the most important relationship in their life, and to sever it without working to repair it first is dangerous and short-sighted. That's why we need a different model that works as much as possible within the communities in which children live, a model that avoids making ideological and presumptuous pronouncements. That is the point of the Troubled Families Unit and its shift to a more human policy approach. It is already showing results: by February 2015 almost 90 percent of families it has worked with have turned their lives around.[61]

THERE ARE MANY more families where children are growing up in intergenerational poverty than the truly chaotic and dysfunctional families who are the focus of Louise's work. Without action, we can be pretty sure that the children in those families will be the ones who end up on welfare, in the criminal justice system, or, at the very least, lacking the opportunities most of us take for granted. As my former colleague in the UK government, policy adviser Richard Reeves, puts it, "The bigger challenge is to help the millions of parents who are not directly threatening their children, but are nonetheless damaging their long-term life chances by raising them poorly. Targeted interventions often seem to make the most sense in terms of making the best use of limited resources. But precisely because they are targeted, they run the risk of creating a stigma."[62] When I was thinking about our family policies and how to help this wider group without stigmatizing them, an answer came to me in the most personal possible way, in the form of one of the great British inventions, an innovation we can trace all the way back to England over 150 years ago.

THE HUMAN FACE OF SOCIAL POLICY

In 1862 the first health visitors were employed by the English municipality of Salford, known in those days as 'sanitary visitors,' and introduced in response to the high levels of infant mortality and poor living conditions in nineteenth-century working-class areas. The idea was for trained workers to come into people's homes and develop a trusting relationship with families over time, proffering advice on nutrition, health, looking after young children—whatever a family needed. In 1929 health visiting was made a universal statutory service, and it has evolved considerably over time, including its incorporation into the world of professional nursing in 1945 and then fully into the National Health Service in 1974. But it was my personal, human experience of health visiting at the time of the birth of my first son that convinced me that Britain's long tradition of health visitors could be the centerpiece of a modern revitalization of family policy.

The key, as with so many of the most successful policy interventions, is the human touch. Health visitors, who first come into your home at a time of great stress and anxiety—the birth of a child—have the potential to become the single-best way to help families with problems, way beyond the immediate pressures of caring for a newborn. Home visiting can be much more than an early-warning system; it can be a central component of a more human family policy—and not just in the UK. I think we need this—urgently—in America too.

Home visitors could offer a lot more than just checking that a baby is well fed and looked after; they should be trained for the fully fledged family work that the best of them already perform. They can identify relationship problems, parenting problems, substance-abuse problems, mental health issues—and then direct families to locally available help and support. It's natural for home visitors to be the primary connection between the state and families. They are already in the home, and not because anything's gone wrong. And unlike other agents of government, they are trusted: the bonds they've forged with parents and children can be built upon. They are the human face of social policy.

We know this approach really works. From its origins in Victorian Britain, home-visiting services have been emulated in many other countries, including the United States. One of the world's most evaluated social policy interventions is the Nurse-Family Partnership (NFP) service first developed by David Olds, professor of pediatrics, psychiatry, and preventive medicine at the University of Colorado in Denver. It is very similar in intent to the concept of health visiting in Britain, although in the United States it has been focused on low-income families since its conception in the early 1970s. Studies show that it works: one by the RAND Corporation showed that children in the program end up being arrested less, while their mothers have fewer children and spend less time on welfare. For high-risk mothers each dollar invested in NFP produced $5.70 in value.[63]

As part of the Affordable Care Act, the Obama administration started the Maternal, Infant, and Early Childhood Home Visiting Program, which, as of 2015, had funded NFP and other similar programs like Child First with $1.5 billion.[64] Although it's still too early to know the end results, early indications are that the program, which has drawn bipartisan support, is working. Children in NFP or similar programs perform better academically and are less likely to live in a home with safety hazards—and thus require fewer emergency treatments for injuries. Later on they are less likely to abuse drugs or alcohol or break the law. Meanwhile parents are less likely to have more children, fathers are more involved in childrearing, and families use less welfare.[65]

We've seen that families living in poverty are already overburdened with too many social workers and state agents. A home visitor can be a coordinator of care—when operating properly, a guide to the best that the state, voluntary, and private sectors have to offer and the definition of a more human public sector. That's why, in government in the UK, we chose to overhaul the health-visitor service by investing in recruitment, training, and organization. If we created a similar program right here in America, we could revolutionize the practical help families get, creating a practical, effective—and cost-effective—ladder out of poverty.

So let's do it: a Universal Home Visiting Service across America for every child in every home. A home visitor would be a registered nurse with additional training in broader nonmedical family issues, such as those that have dominated this chapter. Home visitors would have deep knowledge not only about which solutions work across the many situations that face families but also in the local resources and support services that could help each family. We now know from the evidence that what happens before a child gets to elementary school is actually more important in determining their life chances than what happens once they're in school. So let's think of home visiting just like elementary school: mandated across the United States but implemented locally, in the context of the neighborhood.

To ensure it remains the truly life-changing—and long-term cost-saving—program it should be, caseloads for each home visitor *must* be capped, allowing for a proper amount of time to be dedicated to each child and family. And when I say "proper time," I mean it: daily visits for the first two weeks of a child's birth, weekly for the first three months, monthly for the rest of the year, and then quarterly until enrollment in preschool or kindergarten. This is the level of investment required. Anything short of that will almost certainly degenerate into an expensive waste—and a missed opportunity to end poverty in America while transforming the opportunities for all children, not just the poorest.

Of course, there are many details to work out—specific visiting schedules; training; connecting with local services; overall funding, management, and accountability; and how home visitors' safety will be guaranteed in tough neighborhoods where families often need them the most. But if we're serious about giving every American child an equal shot, this is what we have to do—and I'm going to make it my life's work to make it happen.

I WROTE IN Chapter 2 about the terrible waste caused by government's short-term approach. Our children are not line items on budgets; their childhoods are not measurable in quarterly increments. The early interventions I've described in this chapter are the most effective—and, for those who count money, cheapest—way to solve big social problems. But they don't mesh well with the political calendar. Poverty is a complex, difficult issue that takes time, effort, and resources to solve. The old bureaucratic approach has made little headway—except to expand the bureaucracy. A more human way is better: in the short term, a business-friendly living wage to make sure no one who works full time is poor. For the long term, fighting the causes of poverty with one-to-one help for the families for whom poverty is a cycle that needs to be broken.

Central to fighting poverty is avoiding the glib and patronizing assumption that if only the poor acted like the rich, they would be better off. Yes, wealthier parents often practice better habits, but it's not because they are more loving or better parents. They're certainly not 'better' in any moral sense. It's because they have built-in advantages, both economic and social resources, often inherited and entrenched for generations. Poor parents, however, as we've often seen, have to struggle against impossibly difficult, seemingly immutable circumstances that they themselves might have been born into. Those circumstances are frequently rooted in broader social ills, from institutional racism to the failures of past antipoverty programs. It's not just a matter of telling them they should try harder. Thus, society has dual responsibilities: first, to extend a hand to help people overcome the obstacles they face, and then to work to fix those structural obstacles in the long run. "When the evidence is overwhelming that we fail kids before they fail us, when certain programs would actually save public money while elevating personal responsibility," writes Nicholas Kristof, "isn't it also time to stop making excuses for our own self-destructive behaviors as a society?"[66]

Building the right support for families is like the construction of great physical infrastructure: you won't see results immediately, but in the end it will be hugely effective and worthwhile. That's how we will end poverty for good.

chapter nine

INEQUALITY

IN MANY WAYS Sebastian Thrun personifies Silicon Valley. A German computer scientist, his career spans success in academia as a Stanford professor, industry as an engineer at Google and founder of its Google X lab, and now in startups as the founder of Udacity, a business aiming to revolutionize how we learn. He is responsible for technology—from self-driving cars to wearable computing—that represents the future. Sebastian is among the world's foremost authorities on artificial intelligence and automation, and he's worried. On the one hand, technology will make us so productive that the cost of goods, Sebastian speculates, could approach free. We have the potential to reach new heights of human creativity as a result. On the other hand, there will be a significant cost: "The thing I can't wrap my head around with artificial intelligence is its effect of doing away with the value you bring to the table in terms of labor. The ability to contribute is diminishing. There are fewer and fewer jobs where people can go home satisfied in the evening and say I did something amazing today." That, he thinks, is "eating into the middle class, eating into employment," and will have serious social, economic, and political ramifications. "The world where people can contribute productively is limited to a small number."[1]

Sebastian's uncertainty reflects the central economic question of our time: What can we do about stalled social mobility and our increasingly unequal society?

THE SYMPTOMS OF INEQUALITY

I believe in the positive power of business and the market economy. But something has gone wrong. Capitalism doesn't seem to be working at the human level, even though statistics can tell a positive story. Economic growth no longer lifts household incomes the way it used to.

Until the late 1970s the incomes of everyone broadly grew at the same rate—a period of 'shared prosperity.'[2] But since 1979 the path of the wealthy has diverged from those in the middle. Whereas incomes of the middle 60 percent have increased by 40 percent, incomes of the top 1 percent have increased by 200 percent.[3] From 1993 to 2013 59 percent of all the income gains went to the top 1 percent. Whereas the share of pretax income going to the top 10 percent used to hold steady between 30 and 35 percent, by 2013 it was hovering around 50 percent. Since the Great Recession middle-class incomes have stagnated, while the incomes of the richest have soared: 99 percent of all new income is going to the top 1 percent.[4]

Those income figures are, of course, for people who have pay. Overall labor-force participation, which includes those in work and those actively searching for a job, is at its lowest since the 1970s.[5] Underemployment among recent college graduates is still higher than it was before the recession.[6] Despite small improvements, long-term unemployment is at its highest rate since the Great Depression.[7] Even as official unemployment rates fall, relatively fewer people are working; many have just given up, removing themselves from the workforce entirely. The "key statistic," according to economist Tyler Cowen, is that the share of twenty-five- to fifty-four-year-olds—the key working-age demographic—not working has doubled since the 1970s, and that one in six prime working-aged men are out of the labor force entirely.[8] And those who do work are getting less of its gains: workers' share of income is trending downward[9] as it declines in favor of returns to those who own capital.[10]

It's not just income; inequality of wealth is worsening as well. The middle class grew its wealth along with the rich in the postwar years. But now there is a divergence. According to economists Emmanuel Saez and Gabriel Zucman, the share of household wealth controlled by the top 0.1 percent grew from 7 percent in the 1970s to 22 percent in 2012, a figure that nears inequality levels at the peak of the Gilded Age. Since the financial crisis, as the rich have largely recovered their wealth, the wealth of the bottom 90 percent has stagnated at mid-1990s levels. And according to Saez and Zucman, the trend in income inequality fuels the trend in wealth inequality. As real wages for the top 1 percent have grown, the rich have been able to save more of their income and convert it to wealth. But as wages for the rest have stagnated, the middle class and poor have not been able to save. "Today, the top 1 percent families save about 35 percent of their income," they write, "while [the] bottom 90 percent families save about zero."[11] Overall the top one-tenth of the richest 1 percent own almost as much wealth as the bottom 90 percent.[12]

Fifty years ago the low-skilled and undereducated shifted from stable, decent-paying jobs in the fields to stable, slightly better-paying jobs in factories, right out of school. The labor market was "more flexible," according to Tyler Cowen, "because the technologies of those times often relied on accompanying manual labor."[13] Few new jobs today are like that. In studying the long-term unemployed, Princeton economists Alan Krueger, Judd Cramer, and David Cho describe them as a new permanent class for whom the main economic policy levers—like tax cuts or interest rate changes—simply don't work because they lack the skills to do the jobs available.[14] Meanwhile higher education isn't guaranteeing success either. According to one report, as many as a third of university graduates are working jobs that don't require the degree they have.[15]

This shift in the type and number of jobs available—and, by extension, inequality—is going to get worse. The twin forces of globalization and technology have already wiped out jobs in manufacturing. That will soon be matched in the clerical, administrative, and professional classes—doctors and lawyers too. (Despite the training and specialization that goes into them, many of these careers will be made obsolete by off-shoring, replacement by robots or an algorithm, or both). A report by Oxford economists Carl Frey and Michael Osborne estimates that some 47 percent of America's jobs will eventually be lost to automation over the next decade or two.[16] And of the jobs that remain, many, according to LSE anthropologist David Graeber, will be "bullshit jobs." They will be

> the kind of jobs that even those who work them feel do not really need to exist. A lot of them are made-up middle management, you know, I'm the "East Coast strategic vision coordinator" for some big firm, which basically means you spend all your time at meetings or forming teams that then send reports to one another. . . . And then think about the ancillary workers that support people doing the bullshit jobs: here's an office where people basically translate German formatted paperwork into British formatted paperwork or some such, and there has to be a whole infrastructure of receptionists, janitors, security guards, computer maintenance people, which are kind of second-order bullshit jobs, they're actually doing something, but they're doing it to support people who are doing nothing.[17]

Another factor is the way businesses account for investment. In the same way government invests myopically, as we saw in Chapter 2, business does as well, according to the world's leading management guru Clay

Christensen, and this myopia is central to the link between business innovation and jobs. He describes three types of innovations. *Empowering
innovations* create new sectors of the economy, bringing products and
services to the masses, leading to many new jobs. Think Ford's Model T
or Intel's chips. A *sustaining innovation* is neutral; it improves the empowering innovation but creates few new jobs because it basically replaces
it. "Whenever Toyota sells a Prius," Christensen says, "they don't sell a
Camry." The third type, *efficiency innovations*, are what he believes are at
the heart of our problems. Efficiency innovations allow firms to make
the same product for the same customer, but more cheaply. Although
Walmart, according to Christensen, lowers costs by about 15 percent, it
also lowers retail employment in the areas it enters by around the same
amount. This is good for consumers but harms the overall economy.

In the 1980s the spreadsheet was introduced into the daily life of businesses. For the first time, management consultants could pinpoint the
different ways to profit: invest in innovations that profit over time or
those that profit quickly. Empowering innovations take years to develop;
efficiency innovations might return capital in a year or two. Unsurprisingly executives—with their pay linked to short-term share-price gains—
chose the latter. More profits, but fewer jobs and long-term investments.
Banks are 'awash with capital,' but small businesses can't get funded to
expand their enterprises, and our economic recoveries generate fewer
jobs each time. According to Christensen, it's the accounting software
that has misdirected investment in this way. Higher rewards for shareholders, lower rewards for workers, fewer jobs created.[18] So if you want
someone to blame for inequality, blame Dan Bricklin, the inventor of the
spreadsheet. A bit, anyway.

These problems of economic inequality are exacerbated by something
else: structural inequality. In recent decades we saw the emergence of
something close to a meritocracy in which the best could rise to the top
and anyone who worked hard could have a stable, middle-class life. But
that security has gone. And now those who succeed in this new world
are piling on their advantages and cementing them for their children
through marriage, parenting, and education choices. Those who have
'made it' are inadvertently shutting down opportunity for the rest of society. We need solutions to this structural, family-based inequality too.

THE BIG TRENDS

So we know the problems. We see these giant, overwhelming forces that
seem to be way beyond the control of any country or government, and

we wonder whether anything can be done, whether we just have to accept our fate and do what we can to help people cope with the worst
effects. We get angry. Over the last few years, as I've seen some of the
terrible failings and destructive consequences of global capitalism, I too
have been tempted by the arguments of the anticapitalist, antiglobaliza-
tion movement. On many occasions I have felt emotionally on their side.
So are they right?

Let's see. Paradoxically, inequality has risen dramatically in the West,
global inequality is at its lowest rates ever; the number of people in poverty worldwide has been halved in twenty-five years.[19] So to 'stop' or even
'slow down' globalization—whatever that means—because we fear its
impact on ourselves would be selfish and short-sighted. Remember how
deep a human instinct it is to trade: we would hurt ourselves not just economically but also in our evolution as humans, reversing centuries-long
progress as economic cooperation brought humanity closer. Inhibiting
globalization would mean closing ourselves off and moving backward:
less connected, less empathetic, less human. I sometimes feel like lashing
out at the faceless money-shuffling global corporations and going back to
some blissful prelapsarian state. But it's really not the answer. It's not rational. Even if it were possible, it would do more harm than good: people
would be hurt, mostly poorer people in other countries who are desperate to participate in the global economy that we so lightly disparage.

Does the answer to inequality lie in stopping technology, then, or at
least checking its remorseless advance? This is also an easy conclusion
to reach, especially for me, someone who refuses to have a cell phone
(much to the irritation of those close to me)[20] and who is prone to emotionally charged rants about how technology is 'ruining our lives.' Trying
to tame technology may also seem the obvious conclusion from the very
idea of this book; after all, if we want things to be 'more human,' if we're
'designing a world where people come first,' surely we should put human
beings and the decent, well-paid jobs they need ahead of the latest 'inhuman' technology? Right?

Wrong. Again, it's important not to let emotions lead us down a self-
defeating path. We need to take a step back from whatever contemporary concerns we may have about technology and look at the big picture.
We need to remember our history. The moment when I really understood the impact of technology on humanity was when I read the first
volume of Robert Caro's biography of Lyndon Johnson, *The Path to Power*;
specifically, chapter 27. There you will find a description of life in the
Hill Country of Texas in the 1920s, where the future president grew up,

before electricity. It is a vivid portrayal of life's 'drudgery,' especially for women—before technology intervened:

> Without electricity, even boiling water was work. . . . If the source was a stream, water had to be carried from it to the house, and since, in a country subject to constant flooding, houses were built well away from the streams, it had to be carried a long way. If the source was a well it had to be lifted to the surface—a bucket at a time. It had to be lifted quite a long way: in the hills it was a hundred feet or more. And so much water was needed! . . . the average family farm used 200 gallons, or four-fifths of a ton, of water each day—73,000 gallons, or almost 300 tons, in a year. . . . On the average, the well was located 253 feet from the house—[so] to pump by hand and carry to the house 73,000 gallons of water a year would require someone to put in during that year 63 eight-hours days, and walk 1,750 miles.[21]

Worse, without electric heaters, they also had to haul wood to fuel their stoves. Then there was laundry day: laundry was done outside by hand in a tub. Imagine physically scrubbing clothes, 'agitating' them like an electric washer, carrying them in heavy wet tubs (three tubs of water per load—and remember how hard it is to get water), then wringing them out, then "punching" the clothes. This was hard, physical, onerous, labor. "Living—just *living*—was a problem," Caro quotes one person who endured it. "That was farm life for us. God, city people think there was something fine about it. If they only knew."[22]

Any time you think technology is a bad thing for humanity, just read those passages and be thankful that you are alive now. Technological progress can free us to spend time on things that are more pleasurable and creative than domestic and professional drudgery. Think about the incredible impact even basic technology, like the washing machine, had on the lives—and life chances—of women. The early- and mid-twentieth century's wave of household innovation meant more time to be human. There is no reason to believe that the technology of today and tomorrow will be different.

HUMAN PRODUCTIVITY

So despite sometimes being emotionally drawn to the notion that the answer to rising inequality is to stop, slow down, or reverse the powerful forces (globalization and technology) that have contributed to it, it's not what I think. On balance, they are positive for humanity. So what *is* the answer?

Over the last few years the debate has focused on education and skills—increasing the individual productivity of workers, and the overall productive capacity of the economy. We have a dearth of skilled workers for the jobs at the top, and too many underskilled—but, more often than might be expected, over-educated—people fighting for positions at the bottom. This results in a paradox of not enough competition for the most highly paid jobs (driving high wages for the few even higher) and tremendous oversupply of low and unskilled workers at the bottom (driving low wages for the many even lower). Our inability to match skills to economic needs is one of the biggest factors driving income inequality.

None of this is news. For as long as I can remember politicians on all sides have been reciting the mantra that we need to equip people with the skills to do well in the economy of the future. Well, yes. Policies have come and gone, funded and organized by governments, by the private sector, in partnerships between them. The trouble is, none of it seems to have made any difference.

The person who has the clearest insights on this is Rohan. In a documentary for the BBC's Panorama[23] series he argues that a big part of the answer to inequality is something that is very much a poor relation in our politics, a subject that rarely gets debated in our election campaigns, Washington salons, or the editorial pages of our newspapers, that never leads the agenda on news programs, something much less vivid a concept than 'inequality': training. His view is that we need to think about training completely differently, in a more human way. Not as a policy but as a way of life—everyone's life. We need an infrastructure that makes it possible for every adult to benefit from repeated bursts of training. More importantly, we need to understand that the barriers are often in the mind, in people's attitude to training. So we need a total change of culture; a shift in which self-improvement isn't just for TV reality shows but rather a constant process for everyone; we have to normalize readjustment and reinvention throughout life.

As I write this, I am in the midst of my own career shift, from policy implementation at 10 Downing Street to teaching at Stanford University and creating a technology business in Silicon Valley. My experience shows how the idea that still dominates education today—that we get trained for our careers in our late teens and early twenties and then are done—is preposterously antiquated. I could never have predicted where

I'd be today when I was at university. We are ill served by a system and a culture that assumes we've filled our brains once we're finished with secondary or higher education. Changing this should not be a burden: to learn is one of the most human qualities there is. Game designers worked this out a long time ago—video games are addictive precisely because they constantly challenge players to improve and reward them when they do. Once you've mastered a new level—usually having failed a couple of times first—it's that sense of accomplishment, being recognized for a newly improved ability, that keeps players going, not to mention a temporary high when the chemical dopamine is released in the brain.[24] Achieving competency is an innate psychological need, directly related to well-being.[25] This is learning in action. And it's one of the most distinguishing characteristics between humans and other animals.

A serious assault on inequality means drastically changing the way training is provided, to make it as malleable and dynamic as the world of work now is. That won't happen unless we design training with people's real lives in mind. In further education the debate is always about fees and funding. But for those who drop out or don't even start, the real barriers are more complex: things like difficulty getting to class, family obligations, health problems, pregnancy, even the burdens of a current, unfulfilling job. And the intriguing possibility is that many of these barriers can now be overcome by the very thing that automates jobs away: technology.

"NANODEGREES"

Back to Sebastian Thrun. He was an early pioneer of what we now know as MOOCs—massive, open, online courses. In 2012 he decided to put his Stanford Artificial Intelligence course online and was astonished to see 160,000 participants within days. It gave him the idea for his next venture. "A lot of people in life are stranded because of the lack of life-long learning," Sebastian says. In his view, though, learning is only one piece of the puzzle. Accreditation is just as important. Imagine, he says, a teacher who also has computer science skills and wants to leave education to work at a tech company. "You might be a really great software engineer, but you will never get a job at a company like Facebook because your CV will say 'high school, high school, high school.' So the model today buckets people in life, with the choices they make early on restricting choices they make later, leading to social immobility." That's why training is such a vital weapon in the fight against inequality. We just have to rethink how it is designed and delivered.

Sebastian's solution: Udacity's 'nanodegrees.' Nanodegrees are for those who have neither the time nor the inclination to pursue a conventional degree program. They are short, online courses for people who want to learn or improve on a specific skill. Many are created in partnership with employers—so nanocourse users know that the skills they learn will improve their employability. Nanocourses are structured with the utmost flexibility: you go at your own pace, on your own devices, and can repeat sections as often as you want. "Learning for a dedicated period of time in a dedicated physical location is something we can only really afford in our youth when we have no obligations: no family, no kids, no mortgage," Sebastian says. Nanocourses benefit from technology that allows learners to overcome distance—the first hurdle—but, more than that, overcome the pace of the traditional classroom, which forces students to go through a course at the same time as everyone else. "Ideally," Thrun says, "you have a teacher-student ratio of one to one, but in any setting right now that's uneconomic." But with so many users on each course, Udacity can make the best professors available to everyone.

Such flexibility enables incremental learning anytime and anywhere. Thrun likens it to "toothbrush technology," borrowing a term from Google cofounder Larry Page: something you do for a short time at least twice a day, anywhere—"on the toilet even!" he says.[26] Here is an instance where technology could help create a new social norm: like going to the gym, gaining skills and knowledge should be one of those things you just do throughout your life as part of a regular routine, a practical step toward a more mobile society and less unequal economy.

Just as the skills we use will change with ever-greater frequency, so too will our careers. Rather than bemoan this fact, we should design policies that help. Danish policymakers get this, aiming not for job security but employment security. Labor law makes it intentionally easy to hire and fire employees; it's a two-way street. Though this results in a large number of dismissals during downturns, it allows firms to adapt to changing circumstances and workers to end up where they can add the most value. A quarter of Danish private-sector workers change jobs each year, but to smooth these transitions the unemployed are guaranteed a relatively generous benefit (up to 90 percent of a normal salary for the lowest-paid workers[27]) as well as education, skills training, or subsidized work placement, if not placement in a new job.[28] To prevent firms from underinvesting in skills development, one downside of high employee turnover, 'continuing vocational training,' a hallmark of the Danish Flex-icurity system, is generously funded by the state. Individuals can work toward part-time degrees or certificates at universities or training cen-ters.[29] No wonder Denmark has one of the lowest rates of inequality in the world.[30]

By allowing people flexible jobs and the ability to make money from assets they aren't using, many have trumpeted the 'sharing economy' as a modern answer to wealth inequality and social mobility. Assuming reg-ulators update employment rules to make it as easy for 'gig' employees to access some of the benefits full-time employees are used to—such as affordable insurance and workers' compensation in the event of in-work disability—this could indeed be the case for some. But there are compa-nies frequently described as being part of the sharing economy in which people are 'sharing' not an unused asset but simply their labor: compa-nies like DoorDash, which brings food from restaurants, and TaskRabbit, which lets people outsource errands and small tasks. Although this may be convenient for users of the services, let's not fool ourselves into think-ing that this is going to help in the fight against inequality—it may in fact make it worse. As journalist Leo Mirani deftly explains, this part of the "gig economy" is the latest incarnation of an old-fashioned service relationship in places with a large-enough concentration of rich people who are willing to pay for mobile convenience:

> Of the many attractions offered by my hometown, a west coast penin-sula famed for its deep natural harbor, perhaps the most striking is that you never have to leave the house. With nothing more technologically ad-vanced than a phone, you can arrange to have delivered to your doorstep, often in less than an hour, takeaway food, your weekly groceries, alco-hol, cigarettes, drugs (over-the-counter, prescription, proscribed), books, newspapers, a dozen eggs, half a dozen eggs, a single egg. I once had a single bottle of Coke sent to my home at the same price I would have paid had I gone to a shop myself.
>
> The same goes for services. When I lived there, a man came around ev-ery morning to collect my clothes and bring them back crisply ironed the next day; he would have washed them, too, but I had a washing machine.
>
> These luxuries are not new. I took advantage of them long before Uber became a verb, before the world saw the first iPhone in 2007, even before the first submarine fibre-optic cable landed on our shores in 1997. In my hometown of Mumbai, we have had many of these conveniences for at least as long as we have had landlines—and some even earlier than that.

It did not take technology to spur the on-demand economy. It took masses of poor people.[31]

San Francisco, where many of these services originate and are now based, Mirani points out, has more severe income inequality than Mumbai. So let's not kid ourselves: much of the sharing economy is simply a modern version of the service economy. Although parts of it can indeed give people a stake in the economy, it will only ever be a part of the solution.

Training, lifelong learning—even parts of the sharing economy—might alleviate some of the problems associated with rising inequality. But our digital, globalized fate is inevitable, and the increasing precariousness of employment may require us—yes, even in America—to consider a new kind of safety net, like Danish-style Flexicurity, which combines the best of a vigorous, 'employment-at-will' US approach with a more European emphasis on social stability. Either way, we will need to ensure that American workers are given the skills, tools, and training that will allow them to adjust to whatever comes next.

THE THIRD CAUSE OF INEQUALITY

Like poverty, inequality has symptoms and causes. An economy-wide skills mismatch is a symptom whose solution is more and better training, but its causes are much deeper, and we've already discussed two of them: technology and globalization. There is a third cause of inequality, though, potentially more pervasive than the other two combined. It is structural, often family based, and warrants vigorous attack.

Today's debate around inequality often focuses on 'the 1 percent,' the bankers and CEOs making millions or billions of dollars for often no justifiable reason. Although they certainly contribute to inequality overall, they represent just a small part of the problem. The wider affluent classes—the lawyers, doctors, engineers, and middle-tier executives—also contribute to inequality, but their contribution is less financial than cultural and behavioral. They are entrenching privilege for their children. With all their environmental advantages—from safe neighborhoods to good nutrition to access to tutors, music lessons, extracurricular activities, and travel—the children of the rich are lapping their poorer peers, even when the latter are naturally brighter. As the British economist Leon Feinstein has shown, although students from privileged backgrounds with innate ability maintain their trajectory, similar students from less privileged backgrounds don't just regress over time; they are eventually overtaken by initially low-achieving but richer peers.[32] Affluent children are not succeeding just because of nepotism—although there's plenty of that around—but their success is undeniably a function of the family and social infrastructure into which they are born, an infrastructure that enables them to be exceptionally well prepared for the challenges of the modern economy. The world remains merit based, but it's a meritocracy in only a partial sense of the word. Yes, the winners are qualified for their positions, but too many losers fall short not for lack of effort or intellect but because they start so far back that they're never even competing.

Some of this 'affluent glass ceiling' is explicit. Consider professional licenses. Although a doctor or lawyer should obviously be licensed, it is increasingly common for even moderately skilled jobs like childcare or teeth whitening to require a license. In the 1950s only one in twenty workers needed a license in America; now three in ten do.[33] Why might this be? Well, as author and commentator Reihan Salam argues, professionals don't want the competition; dentists want to maintain the exclusive right to clean teeth, so they have erected an artificial barrier to those who wish to do it. As a result, those who might enter slightly higher-skilled fields for better opportunities find themselves facing expensive credential schemes and onerous requirements.[34] This has made mobility more difficult while entrenching the privileges of those already occupying these higher-status professions.

Inequality is further ingrained when the affluent marry each other. Their "assortative mating," as it has been called, results not only in high-earning, two-income families but also in brighter offspring who, by inheriting brainy genes from brainy parents, inevitably do well in the educational rat race themselves (test scores, remember, near perfectly correlate with income).[35]

As a result, those who are on the winning side of technology and globalization enjoy those benefits now and pass them along to their children, creating what *The Economist* calls a "hereditary meritocracy."[36] For those displaced in today's economy, the outlook is grim: where your economic station is inherited, the consequences of being adversely affected by technology and globalization don't just damn you; they damn your children and grandchildren. As with poverty, inequality has the regrettable feature of worsening itself. So in the same way, we need to come back to the real source of the inequality: what goes on at home, in the family. For too many, "America is stuck," as Brookings scholar Richard Reeves writes.[37] Children not born into affluence need better schools and, eventually, better training. But even more, they need better support from the start. If we're going to fight inequality, chucking bricks at the "1 percent" will be largely futile; we have to narrow the gap by raising up those being left behind.

FAMILY, AGAIN

What do the inequities look like in practice? They're small things, really, but they start early and can quickly add up to a profound impact before children even get to primary school. For instance, research shows that hearing lots of words—both in quantity and variety—is important for a child's development. More affluent and educated families speak to their children significantly more often and with a larger vocabulary than their poorer and less educated counterparts. By the age of three, rich kids have heard some 30 million more words than their poorer peers, creating a 'word gap' that leaves poor children academically and developmentally behind.[38]

Early interactions, developmental psychologists tell us, can make a huge difference to a child's well-being. According to developmental psychologist Ann Bigelow, something as simple as skin-to-skin contact between a baby and its mother is incredibly valuable: "It helps calm babies: they cry less and it helps them sleep better. There are some studies that show their brain development is facilitated—probably because they are calmer and sleep better." And it helps the mothers (and fathers) too: they are less depressed, more sensitive to their babies' cues, and gain better responsiveness from the babies. Another important interaction: simply by responding to infants, usually by repeating motions back to them, parents show their children that they are causal agents and have an interactive role to play in the world. According to Bigelow: "Seeing [their behavior] reflected back helps [babies] understand themselves. . . . The more experience babies have with someone who is going to be emotionally engaged with them, the better off they're going to be."[39] Even watching the children's television show *Sesame Street*, says economists Melissa Kearney and Phillip Levine—one of the largest ever early interventions, which they describe as the "first MOOC"—can improve school readiness, especially for disadvantaged minority children.[40]

It's easy to airily assume that all this is known by and comes naturally to every parent. Not at all. Educating, encouraging, and helping parents to interact with their children in constructive ways is step one on the road to a more equal society. We know now that the quality and style of

parenting received by a child is a better predictor of success than anything else, including the economic circumstances of the family.

There is not—nor should there be—one 'ideal' family or parenting
approach. But there are some circumstances that are more ideal than
others. Of course, it's about making sure children grow up in a loving
home, but a word that comes up over and over again in any discussion
of child development and family policy is 'stable.' Stability is what gives
children the structure within which to grow and develop and thrive; it is
one of the best things we can give children, both for their own happiness
and flourishing and for that of our society and economy too.

That's why marriage is so important and central to the argument on
inequality. Studies have consistently shown that children whose parents
are married or who live together and marry later do better in behavioral,
cognitive, and health outcomes than those who just live together.[41] Both
groups do better, though, than children whose parents divorce or who
never marry at all. Children born into families with delinquent dads fare
the worst.[42] And yet stability increasingly eludes us as today's adults often
put their needs before those of their children. Family breakdown in the
United States has risen dramatically: according to Pew Research analysis
of US Census data, the divorce rate has increased by tenfold since 1940.
And as we're divorcing more, we're marrying less: since 1970 the marriage rate has fallen from a high of 72.2 percent in 1960 to 50.5 percent
in 2012.[43] These trends have affected how families are structured. From
1929 to 2010 the percentage of children born to married parents plunged
from above 95 percent to 59.2 percent.[44] More than half of young adults,
aged twenty-six to thirty-one, who've had a child had had at least one outside of marriage.[45] Parents—mostly mothers—are increasingly comfortable bringing up children not only outside marriage but also on their own.

Disastrously for inequality, marriage is increasingly the preserve of
the university educated and well off.[46] Working-class and non-university-
educated women who still want children are now more willing to have
them without a father in the home. Although many judge women for
bringing children into the world in less-than-ideal circumstances, think
about their situation—especially when compared to their university-
educated peers—before judging: "College-educated young adults can
see a good future, where they're likely to find a good partner, pool two
incomes, and they're willing to wait to have kids till they can do that,"
says Andrew Cherlin, a sociologist who's studied long-term family and
social trends. Less-educated women, however, "don't see the possibility of finding partners with good incomes. And many are unwilling to

give up the opportunity to have a child by waiting."[47] For some of those without a university or even high school education and sparse hopes for career advancement, it doesn't matter: parenthood is the one marker of adulthood they can attain.

What this means is that affluent children, on average, start life with the benefit of a lot more emotional as well as financial stability. It's no wonder they leap ahead. For the vast majority of children lacking the in-built advantages of wealthy and educated parents, instability is especially acute. This is why anyone who cares about inequality needs to care about finding ways to help parents maintain their relationship in the first place so broken homes can be avoided. It all gets back to Louise Casey's point from the previous chapter: a child's parents are the best agents for good in that child's life, no matter how imperfect. And as simple a fact as that is, our culture today has tacitly approved separated families. Because the issues involved are so highly personal and intimate, we have hesitated to take a position or make a judgment. If two adults as a couple decide they can no longer live together, well, that's their business and no one else's, right? Wrong—not if they have young children. When the costs and benefits affect everyone, as they do, we can't just privatize this issue. It's a matter of social responsibility, not just personal choice. Of course, it's true that raising a family is immensely challenging. But it seems as if, increasingly, the socially acceptable position is to prioritize the experience of the parents. That's important, but it's the wrong priority. If you care about future opportunity and a more equal society, the interests of children should be the priority.

When the evidence shows that it's better for people—and society—when children grow up in stable, loving homes, then a more human way of tackling inequality means accepting that marriage is a vital issue of public policy. But this has often been misunderstood—or deliberately distorted—as a simplistic assertion that married couples make better parents than their unmarried counterparts. Of course that's not true. The argument is about family stability. Marriage is what social scientists call a commitment device. It creates inertia in the relationship, making it more likely that couples will stay together in the face of the inevitable stresses and pressures, providing a more stable set of relationships—and stable relationships lead to better life chances for children.

Of course, it's possible that married parents are more likely to stay together because they're likelier to have the characteristics of a more stable couple in the first place. But that still tells us something. Wealthier and better educated parents wait to have children until they are married and in a stable position. They don't rush into commitments—either relating to marriage or to children. For them, marriage is a mark of maturity in a relationship, a signal that they are ready to take on more responsibilities together. If we want to encourage all potential parents to think about their readiness for children—and we should—marriage is as good a tool as any.

The value of that commitment device is never tested more than during the unprecedented stress that arrives with children; child-rearing, studies tell us, directly contributes to making already unstable relationships even less stable.[48] "Children do seem to increase happiness [while] you're expecting them, but as soon as you have them, trouble sets in," Harvard psychologist Dan Gilbert explains. "People are extremely happy before they have children and then their happiness goes down, and it takes another big hit when kids reach adolescence. When does it come back to its original baseline? Oh, about the time the children grow up and go away."[49] Although having children strains all couples' relationships with each other, the commitment device of wedding vows helps keeps them together,[50] and this is overwhelmingly in the interests of children unless something terrible is going on. Although 37 percent of cohabiting couples split up by their child's fifth birthday, less than 6 percent of married couples do. And though marrying after the birth of a child helps, those couples still have a significant gap with couples who were already married before. Put differently, two in three children born to cohabitating couples will see their biological parents break up by age twelve, compared with only one in four in married-couple families.[51]

By the way, what we feel—and, increasingly, scientifically know—about child development in the context of family structure is one of the reasons we should support marriage equality. Encouraging marriage is not about promoting some traditional or moral view about what's right or wrong for adults; it's about what's best for children. And the evidence suggests that children are better off being raised by a married gay couple who provide a stable, loving home than by an unmarried—and unstable—straight couple.[52]

But even if you're not persuaded by the evidence in support of the collective, societal benefits of marriage, there's now a strong body of work highlighting the individual benefits. It turns out that marriage is just better for you than the alternative. According to Gilbert, married couples are on average happier, healthier, wealthier, live longer, and even have better sex.[53] (How does he know?) A 2014 paper showed that, even taking premarital happiness levels into account, "the married are still more satisfied" and that marriage helps people through midlife dips in unhappiness.[54] According to co-author Shawn Grover, "Marriage may be most important when there is that stress in life and when things are going wrong."[55] Spouses are friends, and that friendship helps get each other through difficult times. "The biggest benefits [of marriage] come in high-stress environments," says John Helliwell, the study's other co-author. "People who are married can handle midlife stress better than those who aren't because they have a shared load and shared friendship."[56]

Married couples are happier, happier couples are more stable, and homes that are more stable give children a better chance in life. That's why the growing marriage gap between the rich and the rest is so alarming.

It goes without saying that there are circumstances when single parenthood is the better option. A parent in an abusive relationship should get out of it, in the interests of both themselves and their child. But we need to work to avoid those drastic outcomes. Being in a relationship is hard; being a parent is harder and more stressful. Although children can bring out the best in us, they can also bring out the worst, especially when there are underlying tensions between a couple that bubble to the surface.

So if richer, better educated, more successful prospective parents are getting married, and the poorer, worse educated, less successful ones aren't, how do we get the latter to marry before having children—or at least to wait until they're in a stable relationship? The go-to policy response has typically been tax incentives. That may help in a symbolic sense, signaling the value society places on marriage, but from a practical perspective, past efforts have fallen flat.[57] Instead, we urgently need to enlist the help of behavioral science experts and practitioners of human-centered design. There aren't many areas where an effective 'nudge' would make more difference than this.

WHATEVER THE POLICY, society can help all parents by creating better circumstances in which families can raise children. Shared parenting is a crucial part of this picture. In poorer families welfare programs undermine fathers who aren't married to their child's mothers by excluding them: many means-tested programs only extend eligibility to one parent. Because courts tend to award custody to mothers, fathers, who might have several children in different homes to support as an added burden, are often ineligible for those benefits even though they are just as poor and responsible for an equal share of child support. The mothers, meanwhile, benefit from the father's contribution as well as their own income.

So although mothers get help, fathers don't, impoverishing and alienating them even more. Another fatal flaw: some programs disqualify families with more than one working family member. Ironically, one of the 'best' family setups possible under the logic of the welfare system is for a mother to live with a boyfriend who is not related to any of her children; he can bring in extra cash while the mother can gain from welfare payments. If she lived with the father of her child, his income would count against the means test, and then they might not get any government help at all. Although government programs struggle to keep up with evolving family structures, fathers suffer, as do their children.

The sad part is that by stigmatizing and treating fathers as 'unhelpful,' 'deadbeat,' or 'lay-about,' we drive them away from playing a productive role in their children's upbringing, a role we know their children will benefit from. If given the chance, fathers can and will play constructive roles. "The data does not indicate that during the first three years of the child's life, most low-income fathers are irresponsible," says Ronald Mincy of Columbia University. "Fathers are helping during the pregnancy, making financial contributions and visiting the child. But over time these informal contributions wane as the relationship between the couple deteriorates. The father becomes discouraged and the mother gets annoyed. The father's inability to make financial contributions seems part of that deterioration. Static will be introduced in the relationship that will serve to bar fathers from seeing their kids."[58] Although 'delinquent dads' certainly aren't blameless, it's not enough just to chastise them.

Around 24 million children in the United States—about one in three— live without their biological fathers,[59] and this leads to overwhelmingly worse life outcomes for those children. Boys with absent fathers are more likely to go to prison;[60] girls are more likely to become pregnant as teenagers.[61] Meanwhile children who grow up with contact with their fathers have better social and emotional health and perform better academically[62]; one study found that a father's involvement is associated with a higher likelihood of getting mostly As.[63] Clearly delinquent dads have different circumstances that require different solutions. And any reform of family policy needs to incorporate the criminal justice system too, given the devastating impact on American family life wrought by the mass incarceration of young men. The important point is that we need to focus on ways to forge productive relationships between all parents and their children, not just for the present generation but for future generations too. As the saying goes, when you bring up a child, you bring up a parent.

In some cases, courses specifically for fathers can work best. That's what one group in Baltimore, Maryland, is doing. Community worker Joseph Jones realized that because the vicious cycle of poverty, drugs, and crime robs many men of their fathers, they in turn have little experience of what being a good father actually looks like. So Jones created the Baltimore Responsible Fatherhood Project to give fathers the skills and tools to be responsible dads. The teachers, called fatherhood specialists, don't lecture but instead help lead discussions with groups of predominantly black fathers on how to overcome practical challenges in their lives. "This is my sanctuary," says forty-year-old LaKeeth Blackmon, "a place where I can be myself and meet good people and not get caught up with what's going on in the streets." Blackmon's experience is typical of the fathers who participate in the program: he has six kids with three different mothers, has served time in prison, and is facing trial for dealing marijuana. But he hopes his participation in the Fatherhood Project will help him be a better father and set a positive example for his own children. After all, says Jones, "How do you become a man if you've never seen somebody be a man, if the people in your life have abdicated their responsibilities and left you as a little person?"

IT'S NOT JUST about men, of course. Our social norms around family life have failed miserably to catch up with the progress women have made over the last few decades. This is the cause of much of the stress that undermines many marriages today. Women worry more about parenthood than men do and are more likely to change their career trajectories in anticipation of it.[64] As Anne-Marie Slaughter points out, whereas mothers feel obliged to put their families ahead of their work, men are often praised for their sacrifice of home life—and valuable time with their children—in service to their careers. "Why should we want leaders who fall short on personal responsibilities?" Slaughter asks. "Ultimately, it is society that must change, coming to value choices to put family ahead of work just as much as those to put work ahead of family."[65] This is exactly right: professional culture must value family life for both mothers and fathers. We have to make it easier both for mothers to be professional women and for professional men to be fathers.

Parental leave would be a good start. It's a national embarrassment that the United States is the only developed country in the world that does not guarantee paid leave for all working mothers at birth. But that's just the start. Generous *paternity* leave is also critical. The first few weeks and months after a child are born is when domestic duties are renegotiated; if the mother is at home and the father at work, by default the mother often ends up taking over more domestic duties. By sharing those duties with fathers, mothers get a fairer deal in the long run.[66] Paternity leave also helps mothers avoid the stigma of new motherhood in the workplace. Mothers often face brutal challenges upon having children, with workplace policies and cultures that make it difficult if not impossible to resume their careers. Those with access to paid maternity leave are likelier to return to their prior employer, and 97.6 percent of them make the same salary or more upon returning. However, 30.6 percent of women who have to change where they work experience a pay drop.[67]

But parental leave at birth isn't enough; we need to help parents spend time with their families throughout the years their children are growing up. If both parents—especially fathers—continue to make efforts to share parenting and household duties, it will make for a happier and more stable marriage, which, in turn, is good for their children.[68] This means better family leave and giving workers more control over their hours so they can choose what to prioritize. For example, although we know that a child's early years are crucial, we mustn't neglect other important stages. Parents with teenagers know that it's actually in those later years, when emotional and physical development can cause all sorts of problems as well as joys and opportunities, when children need their parents around just to talk to and spend time with. Inequality can be rooted in something as mundane as how often a family eats together.[69]

Employers tend to see paid family leave as harmful to business. But in a study of California's family leave law, the authors found that "the vast majority of employers reported that it has had a minimal impact"; indeed, some employers even reported cost savings.[70] So although maternity leave doesn't hurt business, the lack of paternity leave does harm women. Many are cast aside for promotion ahead of time because their bosses know they might soon be taking anywhere from a few months to a few years off.[71] If fathers took similar leave, such discrimination would obviously decline: if both parents took leave, there would be less reason to discriminate against mothers who biologically have to. Obviously mothers (and fathers) might choose to remain at home in the long run—that's a perfectly valid choice— but in an age when women are breaking down barriers in the workplace, shouldn't the norms around parenting change too? Although maternity and paternity leave don't seem like issues of inequality, they really are: they can help close the gaps between upper-income and lower-income families and between men and women in the workplace.

HELPING PARENTS

Precisely because being a parent is so hard, there is not one parent who would not benefit from better information and support. To be more direct: there's not one family, not one parent, who wouldn't benefit from parenting education.[72] But the stigma associated with anything that sounds like 'parenting classes' is massive. What a terrible shame, a silly prejudice that directly affects inequality. Octavius Black, founder of an excellent new parenting program in the UK, Parent Gym, observes that "challenging someone's parenting skills is one of the strongest challenges to their identity";[73] it smacks of government intervention and the nanny state. But so many lives would be improved if it were as normal to learn about being a better parent as it is to learn how to drive. It's already seen as completely normal to buy parenting guides, to read the books and magazines—there are even parenting apps. Many mothers complain that they receive no medical advice on crucial questions like breastfeeding and where their baby should sleep.[74] But there's something about parenting classes that is socially unacceptable, a fear of looking foolish in front of others, an admission of incompetence, or even a punishment.

I saw this firsthand when I was developing our family-policy agenda in the UK. As you'd expect, I spoke to experts in the theory of parenting education and worked with some fine civil servants with fantastic knowledge and commitment. But nothing was as striking for me as attending some classes in person. Even though I was there for the purposes of policy research, I took part myself (I could hardly just sit at the back taking notes!). And I learned, even in a few two-hour sessions (courses usually run eight to ten weeks), incredibly useful tips and techniques that have made a real, practical difference in my own family. The most amazing thing, though, was talking to the other parents afterward. Without exception they used the same phrase to describe the experience: "This has changed my life." Perhaps most interesting was the testimony of parents who had been sent to the classes by a court or local authority or some other arm of the state because their children were considered out of control. These parents were even more enthusiastic than those who had signed up voluntarily, but they all told me some version of the same story: "I had to be dragged kicking and screaming to come to this, but after the first one I could see it would change my life." That phrase again: "I wish someone had told me about this years ago—it would have changed everything." Another parent recounted through tears how her relationship with her seven-year-old son had completely transformed just over the course of the eight weeks she'd been going to the sessions. One reason seems to be a very human one: the fact that you're there with a small group of other parents. You can be honest about your anxieties and learn from each other. Everyone has trouble with parenting; there's great relief in realizing you're no worse at it than most people.

There are many, many providers of parenting classes and, as you'd expect, some are great, some are all right, and some are terrible. What we need to see is a massive opening up and 'mainstreaming' of this market, a little like the exercise and fitness market, perhaps. There was a time when there were practically no gyms anywhere except in universities and army barracks; now they're everywhere. There was a time when having a personal trainer meant you were a Hollywood celebrity or multimillionaire. Now it is mainstream, and my question is: If it's socially acceptable to learn how to exercise, don't you think we might take the same approach when it comes to looking after our children?

In government we took a small step in that direction with a pilot program in 2012. The idea was to help stimulate a market for parenting courses by giving people vouchers they could spend with approved providers in their area. To reduce the stigma and make the whole thing seem normal and not part of some welfare scheme, we worked with Boots (a popular British pharmacy chain), which helped give out the vouchers in their stores. The pilot was broadly successful, increasing both demand and supply for parenting courses, but perhaps more importantly, it did actually decrease their stigma.[75] Nonetheless, public awareness is still low, and we have much more work to do to create a culture more receptive to parenting support, as Prime Minister David Cameron argued in a 2016 speech setting out his expansive agenda for boosting every child's life chances. Here's the bottom line: we need to make parenting education aspirational. Instead of being seen as something done to you by the government because you're a bad parent, it needs to be something everyone chooses to do because it's part of being a good parent.

Parents can't be all things for all children, and as with any institution in which people are involved, we must recognize that all parents have their limitations. Many of the least well-off parents face difficulties that stem not from any personal fault but structural adversities in society, particularly institutional sexism and racism. It's incumbent upon us to fix those problems, but in the interim, society must do all it can to help those parents give their children better life chances.

In fact, if you look at the children and young people who succeed— especially those who overcome adverse circumstances—most of them have someone else looking out for them, be it a teacher, a coach, or a Big Brother or Sister. Remember the adults—some of them middle aged—taking the Starbucks college courses? Having a counselor, a cheerleader, an adviser was one of the most important aspects of their success. In the same way that those students succeeded, in the same way that parents need a bit of mentoring, it's only natural to mentor children as well. For children of privilege or family stability, such mentor figures are often commonplace. If they don't have a supportive parent or teacher, they have a music teacher, soccer coach, or tutor to provide support instead. Here, the worlds of education and technology collide to offer a potential solution. Technology could liberate teachers and coaches to focus on the interpersonal skills only a mentor can provide. Technology can't care, but people can.

Likewise, government can't raise children, but it can create the infrastructure necessary for them to flourish. Family stability, parental leave, parenting education—they're all about the same thing: giving children better chances by helping families of every circumstance do well. Combining such family interventions with a new approach to training would grow opportunity.

Failure to get this right will reinforce inequality, one of the most urgent questions of our times. Technology is making obsolete many tasks once done by people. And those who have the resources and education keep solidifying their advantages, while those who don't, fall behind.

The former is an inescapable fact. The latter is not.

RATHER THAN LAMENT change, we should embrace it as an opportunity to make work more human and opportunity more abundant. In the face of technology's onslaught "a better strategy," according to Geoff Colvin in his book *Humans Are Underrated*, is to ask: "What are the activities that we humans, driven by our deepest nature or by the realities of daily life, will simply insist be performed by other humans, even if computers could do them?" We once washed clothes using washboards; now we have washing machines. We once stoked furnaces by hand with coal; now we fuel furnaces through gas lines. Have we suffered for it? No. We've become only more prosperous. Let's forget those inhuman jobs and instead focus on the skills that are most human and create economies around *them.* "It used to be that you had to be good at being machine-like," notes Colvin. "Now, increasingly, you have to be good at being a person." This is wonderful news, he goes on to say: we're being asked "to become more

essentially human."[76] People are innovative, creative, caring, and nuanced. Let's create an economy that embraces these qualities. We should
be happy to rid ourselves of the automated, mind-crushingly boring, administrative, cubicle jobs and the back-breaking, dehydrating, physically
dangerous factory and agricultural ones. Wouldn't those workers be the
first to agree that they'd be better off if they did something that engaged
them as people, not workhorses? They would be better off in terms of
wealth, health, and general well-being. As would the rest of us.

The debate around inequality is often focused on outcomes: who's rich
and who's not. That's the wrong way to look at it. Instead, we should be
examining mobility: Who is falling behind because they aren't getting
a fair shot? Yes, this includes the workers who are dropping out of the
labor force because of lack of skills, but it also includes their children—
and those of the larger middle classes—who are losing out on the chance
to get ahead because of their home and family lives.

No one wants to see a society with a few people at the top doing incredibly well while everyone else is struggling, yet that really seems to
be where we're heading. As long as generational inequality persists, our
society will fail to live up to the standard it has set for itself: that everyone be given the chance to fairly compete on the same terms, a true
meritocracy.

We can go in a different direction, however, if we cast the inequality
debate in more human terms, making it normal for every individual to
train and gain skills all the way through life, strengthening marriage and
families, and giving better support to parents so we bridge the gaps between the worst- and best-off children. That is the basis of a more human
economy—a more human society—in which opportunity is more equal
and prosperity more widely shared.

chapter ten

CHILDHOOD

CHILDREN ARE VULNERABLE, so we protect them. Children need nurturing and guidance, so we put their needs first. These are basic, human instincts. But today we're getting childhood all wrong, simultaneously overprotecting and underprotecting.

It's human to fall in the playground and hurt yourself; it's human to be lost or bored. If we overprotect our children, we inhibit their development—mentally, physically, and emotionally—and risk them developing unhealthy fears and behaviors. But it's also human to be a child during childhood, and although we're overprotecting children's play with ridiculous, risk-averse safety measures, we are at the same time underprotecting them, allowing them to experience the adult world prematurely because we're too lazy to properly invigilate or too weak to say no. We think we're being kind, but we're doing real and lasting harm.

There is a particular problem with technology. Devices have brought children entertainment and education, but they've also erased the boundaries between the child and adult worlds. We need to better police the border between children and technology because unconstrained, unlimited access to the Internet prematurely exposes children to unhealthy sexual norms, inhibits their cognitive abilities, and disturbs normal social interactions. Perhaps worst of all, technology is resurrecting old ideas of misogyny, setting back one of our society's greatest recent achievements.

Let's not blame 'kids today' for these trends; it's our fault as adults for putting up senseless boundaries while failing to set up sensible ones. But it's not too late; we can turn things around. We need to—because children are humans too.

OVERPROTECTION

Berkeley, California, is famous for its world-class university, periodic outbursts of student radicalism, and—if you care about food and where it comes from—Alice Waters's pioneering restaurant Chez Panisse (see Chapter 5). But there's something else Berkeley ought to be famous for: the most extraordinary and wonderful children's playground you've ever seen. The Berkeley Adventure Playground is built by the people who use it, constructed of salvaged wood, old rubber tires, scraps of sails, all decorated with graffiti-like smears of paint. Enter with your young children, and you are handed a container of nails and a hammer. Walk around, and you'll see children as young as six and seven sawing pieces of wood. No safety equipment. No bossy rules. Just families having fun, being creative, and, above all, being human. It's a little bit terrifying, and it's hard to believe you're still in the United States—the land of the waiver, lawsuit, and helicopter parent.

The people who run the Berkeley Adventure Playground understand the true essence of children's play. But in recent years we've managed to dehumanize it. Whether as parents or policymakers, we have become so irrationally fearful of every risk that we've outlawed and restricted and regulated children's lives to the point at which things seem to be designed more for our peace of mind than our children's recreation and benefit.

This mindset has so conquered our collective psyche that those who want to give their children more leeway are ostracized, even penalized. Brooklyn mother Lenore Skenazy's nine-year-old son wanted to experience some independence, so she and her husband armed him with a MetroCard, some quarters for a phone, $20 in cash, and a map—and left him at a department store that sat directly above a station for their local subway line. Forty-five minutes later, exhilarated, he returned home. When she wrote up this positive experience, she was quickly dubbed "America's Worst Mom."[1]

Skenazy, a middle-class mother, was relatively lucky in that the only punishment she got was name calling. Consider the shocking experience of Debra Harrell, a single mother in Tennessee. Harrell is one of the millions of low-paid, overstressed workers we met in Chapter 8. She works hard to support herself and her daughter but can't afford childcare. Rather than having her nine-year-old daughter sit in the McDonald's where she works all day, Harrell gave her a cell phone and let her play in the local park down the street. Park-goers, suspicious of a child playing by herself, reported her to the authorities. Harrell was arrested, charged with unlawful neglect of a child, and subsequently fired. Because Harrell is a single parent, her daughter was then taken from her home and placed in the care of local social services. Following a public outcry,

Harrell thankfully got her daughter and job back. But imagine the ordeal she has had to go through. Imagine how much worse off her daughter is, living forever with the experience of having her mother imprisoned and spending time in public-sector care. All this because a mother trusted her daughter and let her play outside.

This overprotective attitude is harming children. Whether it's aggressive bureaucracy removing any remotely challenging play equipment from playgrounds or panicking over the idea that a child might encounter a single germ or piece of dirt, we are cutting away at the basic humanity of childhood experience. By trying to create a risk-free existence for our children, we are gradually shutting them off from the world. Neighborhoods friendlier to cars than kids, public space appropriated for shopping rather than playing, energy and investment going into superficially more captivating indoor alternatives, particularly involving technology. We ply our kids with electronics to keep them busy—and give us a breather—and we prevent them from playing outside because we fear what might happen to them. But we forget that an important part of many of our own childhoods involved engaging in the world, not being 'protected' from it.

Of course, to a certain extent, caution is natural and proper: our instincts and emotions guide us to protect our children, after all. But it's gone way too far. The dreary and soulless trend toward the avoidance of any risk reflects good instincts and good intentions that have been perverted by a culture of hysteria, lawsuits, and puffed-up bureaucracies.

'Playground safety,' for example, is mostly a solution in search of a problem, argues the play expert Tim Gill in his book, *No Fear*. Despite the occasional sensational headline, serious playground injuries are rare, deaths even more so. The facts show that a child has about a one-in-sixteen chance of being injured on a playground and only a one-in-two-hundred chance of receiving an injury requiring medical attention.[2] Nonetheless, when something does go wrong, it is amplified disproportionately in the media: tragic accidents are emotional, and emotion makes for better stories. But although the overdramatization of danger to children may generate more clicks, sell more newspapers, keep a few more viewers from turning off the local news, it also breeds fear of previously uncontemplated risks. The result is an illogical debate that leads to unnecessary rules, irrational insurance policies, and a whole new miserable, exhausting world of paranoid language, bureaucracy, and culture to enforce it all. Parents, terrified for their children, and insurers, terrified of lawsuits, have pushed for new guidelines and regulations on anything that touches children's lives. But because, as Gill writes, "there was little or no attempt to look systematically at accident data or to place playground accidents in a wider context," these trends merely "reinforced the idea that playgrounds should be free of risk," leading to policies that put the prevention of any injury whatsoever over the goal of having the best playgrounds for children.[3]

This is terribly wrong. We shouldn't ignore passionate parents, but we shouldn't make policy decisions to mollify them either, because rather than solving problems, parents' unjustified fears have created new ones. Go to any public playground today, and you'll see that the equipment is increasingly dull and uninspiring, making playtime less fun and less adventurous. This is not just a shame; it stunts crucial aspects of child development. Even worse, some safety rules have actually made children less safe. For example, it turns out that the cushioned safety surfacing often required to be in place to break children's falls is really only meant to prevent serious head injuries—an extremely rare occurrence—and in fact leads to more broken bones.[4]

What's more, safety surfacing is so expensive, it means that other more cost-effective ways of keeping children safe are ignored. A cost-benefit analysis done in the UK found that spending up to £250 million (almost $380 million) over five years on playground safety surfacing would have saved one child's life during that time. Of course, every child's life is incalculably precious. But imagine how much more agony could be spared if those resources were invested in ways of protecting children from genuine danger, such as road traffic, which typically kills well over two hundred children and injures around ten thousand per year in the United States.[5] If you want to be statistically brutal—but accurate—about it, making our children infinitesimally safer at playgrounds condemns them to die elsewhere at a much higher rate.

HARD AT PLAY? OR HARDLY PLAYING?

But play is being undermined and distorted in more places than playgrounds. Our society increasingly sees play as a neat and tidy occupation that should occur in prescribed ways. When children try to break out of these artificial shackles, they—especially boys—are deemed to be 'troublemaking' or 'antisocial' for perfectly innocent offenses like making noise, hitting things (and occasionally each other), and climbing trees. Of course, there are risks for our children—there always have been and there always will be. But we should focus on the real hazards, not imagined ones. Society has worked itself into a frenzy that the world is ever more dangerous. But it's not true. Consider child abduction: compared to forty years ago, we perceive a growing threat, although it's no more likely to happen than it was in the 1970s. The odds of a child being kid-napped and murdered by a stranger are one in 1.5 million.[6] We fear that our children might be assaulted by strangers, but they are far likelier to fall victim to an abusive relative or family friend.[7] Instead of working harder to protect children from domestic abuse, we teach them to avoid strangers—the vast majority of whom would be a source of help should they ever need it.

"Today's children," writes author Jay Griffiths, "are enclosed in school and home, enclosed in cars to shuttle between them, enclosed by fear, by surveillance and poverty and enclosed in rigid schedules of time. These enclosures compound each other and make children bitterly unhappy."[8] Our children are virtual prisoners of their parents and caregivers. In 1969 the National Personal Transportation Survey found that 40.7 percent of students walked or biked to school; by 2001 that figure had dropped to 12.9 percent. For a child living within a mile of school the figures are just as stark, dropping from 85.9 to 49.9 percent.[9] We instinctively distrust children, forgetting that they can handle themselves much earlier and far more effectively than we give them credit for. When parents do trust their children, society condemns them. It took six months for a Mary-land couple to be cleared of neglect charges for letting their children (ages six and ten) walk home together from a neighborhood park in late 2014.[10]

In our attempts to shield children from risk, we've not just made their play dull or wasted public money on largely pointless safety measures; we've also inadvertently hampered children's development. The life les-sons that come with play are some of the most essential. Among other things, high-quality, unencumbered, imaginative, and adventurous play teaches children resourcefulness, entrepreneurship, hand-eye coordina-tion, creativity, cooperation, and social skills. A sense of adventure is not only an integral part of being a child; it is essential for their biological, human development. When doctors want to inoculate a patient against a disease, they make a vaccine containing a bit of the disease so that the body can identify it and learn to overcome it; this is the only way vac-cines work. Fear works in much the same way. A Norwegian study by early-childhood education professor Ellen Sandseter found that safe play is actually detrimental to the process of child development. She found that children were exhilarated when exposed to stimuli they had pre-viously feared. As they gradually matured and mastered new skills and explored new environments, their natural—and perfectly healthy—in-hibitions, which protected them from any serious danger, correspond-ingly declined. In other words, the thrill helped them overcome their phobia. If they didn't experience risky play, their natural phobias became pathologized and unhealthy later on. Sandseter concluded that lack of risky play might lead to an increase in psychopathy and neuroticism as children grow up.[11]

Play is essential, but not just to any one child's development; it's es-sential for the development of humanity itself. This is obvious to those who observe it up close. What is play but tinkering, trying new things, new combinations, new rules, new roles, new ideas? Play is the essence of experimentation, of risk taking, of innovation. Play leads to progress.

"FREE-RANGE KIDS"

The good news is that we don't have to do anything too radical to make play more human. The Berkeley Adventure Playground isn't the only example of enlightened thinking; advocates of authentic play—and the fantastic playgrounds they support—exist all around the world, and the movement is growing. But it is nonetheless still under attack, and we need to support those who are fighting back. As communities remove swing sets and other 'unsafe' features from playgrounds or build dull new ones, we need to support those who campaign against such moves, advo-cating for playgrounds that engage children and facilitate play in fun and educational ways. This also means shedding light on both real and imag-ined dangers. For example, knowing that cars are a legitimate concern, towns like Seattle and New York have experimented with closing down streets for periods and setting up temporary play spaces, like a life-sized Monopoly board with each house on the street a different property.

So one solution is simply to create more permanent play spaces, both formal and informal. It just needs to be made more of a priority in the ur-ban planning and property-development process. It is a choice that could be made. Of course, there needn't be just one model for reforming play. Adventure playgrounds often discourage parental involvement, with the idea being that children better develop their independence away from the anxious eyes of overprotective mothers and fathers. For chil-dren without easy access to the outdoors, organized 'forest schools' have emerged whereby children regularly visit woodland sites, in all weather, not only to play in a way that provides healthy exposure to nature but also to learn skills in survival, ecology, craft, self-regulation, and team-work. Finding more ways for children to play outside is crucial. As Paul

Hocker, a British play advocate, says, "The more kids outside, the safer it is."[12]

But even if we make playtime more human and convince the powers-that-be—from parents to policymakers—that real play is fine and needs to be supported with more and better play spaces, perhaps the biggest threat to play is the new rat race that discourages it altogether in favor of hyperorganized and didactic leisure activities. Although for many over-scheduled children of overachieving and overanxious parents in places like San Francisco and New York, 'leisure' is hardly the word. You have to feel sorry for these kids. Their parents have bought into the anxiety that soccer and even piano lessons aren't enough, so we have to add Mandarin Chinese lessons, the violin, ballet, extra math—extra everything with expensive tutors. And all of these activities must be structured and supervised with benchmarks and rankings. But as crazy as this sounds, parents are under immense pressure; we have been led to believe that if our children aren't doing everything, they won't do well in preschool or elementary school or, later on, with their AP classes and standardized tests and, thus, will fail to get into a good university. And then their lives are basically over.

Ironically, whereas rich and middle-class parents have scheduled healthy play out of their children's lives, poor children end up without it for different reasons. Recognizing that poverty doesn't just contribute to stress (as we saw in Chapter 8) but that it also stops families from playing, especially in urban areas with limited space, we have to make sure a playful childhood is still accessible to all, even if that means fitting it amongst otherwise routine activities. KaBOOM!, a nonprofit that got started bringing communities together to build playgrounds for kids in need, has recently turned its focus to making sure play can happen throughout the day, especially in areas where 'trips to the playground' are few and far between. "Cities across the country are beginning to make great strides in creating communities that foster walkability and bikeability," KaBOOM! president James Siegal writes. "Now it is time for cities to put kids first and embrace Playability."[13] So yes, we need more parks, play fields, and playgrounds . . . but we need more bus stops with swings, crosswalks with hopscotch marks, and games in waiting rooms.

Lenore Skenazy, the New York mother who let her son take the subway on his own, has started the Free-Range Kids movement to advocate for a less structured and supervised approach to parenting. In her book and on her website Skenazy draws attention to the social norms we've embraced as parents without really thinking through their ramifications.

She points out that the idea of even having to define a 'free-range kid' is ridiculous: thirty, forty, fifty years ago being a kid and being a free-range kid were one and the same thing. But now parents are made to feel guilty about everything from not breastfeeding to not buying the right knee pad for playing outside. Meanwhile we need to listen less to the hype about dangers to children and focus on the things that really threaten them. For example, the idea of 'stranger danger' is an outdated and unhelpful one. We need to teach our children how to talk to strangers so they know who to turn to in case of real danger.

This is not to say that there aren't some children who need better support and supervision. Education writer Paul Tough points out that although risk is indeed elusive for the richest children, it is a daily occurrence for the poorest and most vulnerable kids. Whereas rich children can benefit from risk, poor children are overwhelmed, suffering adverse consequences like toxic stress. As one critic put it in a review of Tough's book, there are two childhood extremes: "For rich kids, a safety net drawn so tight it's a harness; for poor kids, almost nothing to break their fall." Helping children develop character by persevering through the challenges of childhood and adolescence is how we can help them succeed.[14]

We need to let children explore the world on their own terms. And we need to recognize that play is natural—naturally human. Rather than fight it, let's harness it productively. All of those involved with the upbringing of children—parents, policymakers, educators, coaches, neighbors—need to step back and think: Are we really protecting children, or are we allaying our own fears instead? Chances are, if you're a parent reading this, you had a carefree childhood. You survived. Your children will too.

UNDERPROTECTION

A carefree childhood doesn't mean total freedom. There is an important sense in which we are not protecting children enough. It is bizarre that at a time when adult life is being extended in dramatic ways upward—people are living longer, working longer, staying active longer—we also seem determined to extend adult life downward, forcing—or, at best, allowing—children to become consumers earlier, to become sexual earlier, and to take on board at an earlier and earlier age the very adult burdens of stress and anxiety. Why? What's the hurry? Our culture mocks notions of childhood innocence. We don't treat children like children anymore. We are, in fact, inhuman toward them because we treat them like something they're not: adults. This not only threatens the healthy development of an entire generation; it also stands to reverse one of society's most important advances of the last fifty years: women's emancipation.

LEANING OUT

At long last women are now taking up roles of power and influence, asserting equality at work, and claiming their place in areas previously the sole domain of men. We've seen the success of strong women who forged a path for others—pioneers like Virginia Woolf and Gloria Steinem, Germaine Greer and Betty Friedan—and those who have taken that path up, like Margaret Thatcher, Hillary Clinton, Christine Lagarde, Janet Yellen, Mary Barra. For the first time ever, in 2015 all the top jobs in an American city, Washington, DC—mayor, police chief, schools commissioner— were held by women. In Nordic countries gender equality has been the social norm and practical reality for decades. Obviously there's further to go. Pay inequality, offensive stereotypes, sexism, and gender gaps persist. The 2015 Congress was only 20 percent female. Just twenty-three women currently lead one of the companies listed in the S&P 500—that's 4.6 percent.[15] Despite all the barriers she's broken, even Hillary Clinton had to put up with Barack Obama commenting on her clothes in a televised debate during her 2008 presidential bid.

Thankfully we have great champions today. As secretary of state and now presidential candidate, Clinton has been a tireless advocate for women's emancipation, economic empowerment, and leadership. Pakistani teenager Malala Yousafzai continues her inspiring campaign for the rights of girls simply to go to school. One of the most prominent advocates for women can be found in Silicon Valley: with her book *Lean In*, Facebook executive Sheryl Sandberg calls on women to overcome the forces holding them back professionally. But there's some irony in the fact that the latest leader to carry the flag of gender equality is the chief operating officer of a technology giant. That's because one of the biggest threats to gender equality in the world today actually comes from technology, from something that is literally before our eyes, reversing feminism's hard-fought gains: the smartphone.

The fundamental battle on gender equality is in the mind. Gender equality is rooted in people's attitudes, whether it's women's attitudes about their role in life, society, and the economy; men's attitudes about theirs; or both about each other. In my generation that battle is being won. We are moving firmly away from obnoxious and anachronistic stereotypes of women as housewives, mothers, and nothing more, and as sex objects, subordinate to men, defined by appearance rather than brains or talent. Those attitudes are just not socially acceptable anymore.

But when we look at what's going on with young children and teenagers and ask whether progress is being made—let alone maintained—the answer is no. Young people are increasingly being exposed to depictions of and attitudes toward women that we thought we'd consigned to the history books: as sex objects defined by looks.[16] Children's clothing is ever more sexualized: one study found that almost 30 percent of preteen clothing had 'sexual' characteristics that highlighted breasts, buttocks, or slimness.[17] As cultural pressures like impossibly high standards in beauty, fashion, and grooming are communicated across all age groups, they have a significant effect on impressionable girls.[18] This has real-world consequences. Self-objectification is common in young girls and women and has been found to impair cognitive function (because young women are so distracted by worrying about their body image) and to cause emotional distress.[19] Shame, anxiety, and self-disgust regularly occur now in preteen girls.[20] And it is causing unnatural and frankly scary behavior. Driven by images and videos of models, pop-culture icons, and porn performers showing the perfect wax job, as well as the consequent expectations of boys, girls as young as eleven are starting to shave their pubic hair.[21]

The assault on gender equality is not happening in the political arena, where progress at the legislative and regulatory level—even the representative one—is steady, if slow. It's not happening in the workplace, where, despite the need for more change, as we saw in the previous chapter, women's equality is becoming gradually accepted. No, the assault on gender equality is most evident in the younger generation and its culture. And we can be even more precise than that. The potentially disastrous unwinding of progress toward equal treatment of men and women is happening in the place where young children spend more and more of their time: the online world. Specifically their gateway to that world: the smartphone and other mobile Internet-enabled devices (MIEDs). Nearly four decades after Susie Orbach published *Fat Is a Feminist Issue*, we can today identify the twenty-first-century update: phones are a feminist issue. For children, this is where we need more protection, not less.

SEXUALIZED CHILDHOOD

One-quarter of children under seven own tablets; by time they reach eleven years old, the proportion climbs to 43 percent.[22] A 2014 study found that 44 percent of elementary school students use smartphones regularly, up from just 35 percent the year before.[23] More comprehensive data collected by British regulators show that nearly half of three- to four-year-olds own some kind of device, whereas a majority of those aged eight to fifteen have three or more.[24] Let me repeat: more than half of these children have at least three media devices. In a survey of mostly low-income parents visiting a medical center in Philadelphia, three-quarters of children by age four had their own mobile device. (Tablets in particular were widely owned: 20 percent of one-year-olds, 38 percent of two-years-olds, and over half of three-year-olds had a tablet.) Astonishingly, 4 percent of under-ones owned a smartphone; 60 percent of parents reported letting their children use devices while they were out running errands.[25] So after that barrage of numbers, let's just agree the simple points: it is normal for young children to be inundated with technology, they're using smartphones and tablets to go online without supervision, and these trends are accelerating. True, many parents *say* they monitor their children on the Internet, ranging from asking them what they've been doing to actively checking their browser history or sitting beside them as they use it. But when the device in question is a mobile Internet-enabled device (MIED), then, of course, parents cannot always watch what their child is doing. Nor can they know what content their children are viewing on another child's MIED or when their child is not at home. Consider: a study commissioned by McAfee, an Internet security company, found that although many parents say they maintain some sort of vigilance, 61 percent of teens feel confident they can hide whatever they're doing online from their parents.[26] In another survey 49 percent of teens claim their parents do nothing to monitor their devices.[27]

The ubiquity of smartphones has enabled the ubiquity of pornography and other sexual or sexualized content (e.g., in music videos) not suitable for children. Over half of twelve- to fifteen-year-olds use the Internet to view sexually explicit material,[28] and a significant number of children are exposed to explicit content at ten or eleven years old.[29] This premature sexualization gives children incorrect notions of healthy sex and relationship dynamics. It inculcates in young, impressionable minds—starkly and brutally—the idea we have fought to banish from our culture: that women's primary role is as the object of sexual gratification for men.

For many children pornography is what they think real-life sex is or should be. As most online porn is created for men and is often aggressive if not violent, MIEDs are creating in this generation absolutely shocking, dark patterns of expectation and behavior when it comes to sex. Young girls think they have to look and behave like porn performers, shaving their bodies and taking part in sexual activity that is often painful and disturbing to them, like anal sex or sex with more than one boy at a time. (The silver lining in this very dark cloud is that the increased incidence of anal sex is leading to less teen pregnancy, according to anecdotal reports. But really, is this what we have become?) Boys, meanwhile, are freed from any moral or cultural restraint to treat girls with respect or affection. The shared understanding of what sex means today is the grim, inhuman, exploitative version that the porn industry has manufactured.

These concerns are real. Young people increasingly report that they learn about sex from pornography; some 45 percent of young men believe it is educational, and three-quarters of young women believe it puts pressure on girls to act and look 'a certain way.'[30] Consequently young men expect girls to conform to the fantasized version of sex they see in porn and are themselves, unsurprisingly, more likely to be sexist.[31] Men who watch porn are more likely to see women as sexual 'playthings.'[32] Worse, that education is one of violence: more than one-third of sex offenses committed against juveniles in the United States are by other children.[33] Child sex offenders in Britain, some as young as five, have been found to mimic behavior seen in porn.[34] "When you interview young women about their experiences of sex, you see an increased level of violence—rough, violent sex." That, according to Professor Gail Dines, a leading antiporn campaigner, "is directly because of porn, as young boys are getting their sexual cues from men in porn who are acting as if they're sexual psychopaths."[35] Men can be victims too: Irish and Canadian researchers have found that exposure to porn directly affects male perceptions of body image and self-esteem.[36] "Pornography," adds Dines, "is sexually traumatising an entire generation of boys."[37]

Yes, I know, porn has never exactly been good on this account. And yes, children have always happened across the proverbial copy of *Playboy* or *Hustler* or whatever in their father's drawer. But the scale and nature of it today is completely different from anything our society has ever seen before. At younger and younger ages, children are spending more and more time on smartphones. And it's on smartphones where porn today is being watched: 68 percent of traffic at Pornhub, one of the Internet's most trafficked porn sites, in the United States comes from a mobile device; 56 percent of Pornhub's international traffic—79 billion video views in total in 2014—comes from a mobile device.[38] Before Internet porn there was regulation, of sorts. The kind of material available at the local sex shop or on the top shelf of the bookstore or in the *Sports Illustrated* swimsuit issue might have degraded women, but it wasn't in the same league of depravity that any child can access today with a couple of clicks on their MIED.

We know that things are bad when it's the porn editors who say so. Martin Daubney is the former editor of *Loaded*, a British men's magazine that features plenty of sexual imagery of women. Accused of peddling pornography, he "agonised" that his "magazine may have switched a generation onto more explicit online porn." When he set out to investigate the effects of this culture on young people, it was worse than he imagined. "I used to be sceptical that porn was as damaging a force as the headlines and David Cameron—who recently said it was 'corroding childhood'—suggest . . . but what I saw . . . changed my opinion of pornography forever," he wrote in 2013.[39] He describes attending a panel of young teenagers assembled by sex-education consultant Jonny Hunt, who asked them to write A-to-Z lists of all the sexual terms they were familiar with. It turned out that it was the adults who had insufficient vocabulary.

"'Nugget, what's that?' asked Jonny," Daubney recalls. "'A nugget is a girl who has no arms or legs and has sex in a porno movie,' chortled one young, pimply boy, to an outburst of embarrassed laughter from some." More shocking were the mundane answers. "For example, the first word every single boy and girl in the group put on their list was 'anal.'" One teenage boy described a pornographic scene featuring bestiality (which is illegal in most places).

Porn, Daubney concludes, "is the most pernicious threat facing children today." Children are fed a steady diet of submissive and abused women as norms. Their idea of proper sexual behavior is that boys can get away with whatever they want and girls think they should allow it. And although in the well- known phrase, smartphones are the "sewer not the sewage," these devices have done as much as anything in recent years to turn back the clock on feminism, as girls' images of themselves and their potential are reversed.

But the most tragic part of the triangle of sex, MIEDs, and young people isn't even exposure to pornography, it's that they expose themselves.

Law-enforcement officers around the world have long battled child pornography, but they are increasingly wondering how to battle child pornography committed by the victims. Technically minors who possess nude images of even themselves run afoul of child-pornography laws, but as one columnist put it, charging them as pedophiles "makes as much sense as charging a kid who brings a squirt gun to school with possession of an unlicensed firearm."[40] And so police officers, school administrators, and parents are left in a gray area, desperate to communicate the severity of 'sexting,' as the perky euphemism goes, without ruining their children's futures.

An otherwise unassuming rural region in central Virginia, Louisa County, became the center of a firestorm in early 2014 when a sexting scandal erupted after a local high school girl saw her naked image on an online bulletin board and her mother reported it. Journalist Hanna Rosin of the *Atlantic* spent several weeks there to try to understand the ordeal that followed. Police started with the girls whose pictures were on the site and the boys who followed them on Instagram. Every interview yielded more names of high school students who had sent or received 'sexts'; the confiscated smartphones started to pile up. Donald Lowe, the police officer leading the investigation, said that his characterization of the girls evolved from "victims" to "I guess I'll call them victims" to "they just fell into this category where they victimized themselves."[41]

The problem with smartphones is that they amplify and escalate normal 'teenagers being teenagers' behavior into something much worse. As Rosin writes, technology has the power to turn an otherwise private experience into a public hell. Where once a girl might have flashed a boy she liked in an empty room and that was the end of it, now that 'flashing' has a permanent record. Kids who illicitly forward these pictures without permission are unquestionably committing sex crimes, and the majority who do so might know it's wrong, but they certainly don't think of themselves as criminals. Are these 'youthful indiscretions' any worse than anything that previous generations did? They may or may not be, but one thing is clear: because of the technology and its ubiquity, the consequences are far worse.

Today 52 percent of teenagers use Instagram to share photos (61 percent of girls), with an average of 150 followers; 41 percent use Snapchat (51 percent of girls).[42] The boys Lowe interviewed told him that sharing nude pictures was "nothing unusual. It happens all the time." When Rosin asked students how many of their peers they thought sexted, the answer was "everyone."[43] Boys now expect sexual pictures from girls, flattering and cajoling them until they cave in, but then immediately think of the girls as *thots*—best translated ("that ho over there") as 'slut' or 'whore'— when they send a picture. Last November over one hundred students at a Colorado high school were part of an elaborate 'sexting ring' in which participants gained points depending on which photos they collected.[44] A study of several high schools in Texas found that over half (57 percent) of students have been asked to send a naked photo; 28 percent have sent one, and almost a third have asked for sexts in return.[45] The ubiquity of phones and the Internet is bad enough when it exposes young people to porn and unhealthy and backward attitudes toward sex, violence, and the opposite sex. But by eliminating all but the smallest barriers to communicating explicit material of oneself or another far and wide, MIEDs haven't just spurred this behavior; they've often, as in sexting, created it.

"I'D LIKE TO LEARN HOW TO HAVE A CONVERSATION"

A common response to all this would be, "Well, yes, I know, it's terrible, but really, what can we do about it? The Internet and phones and technology—they bring all these good things, but they bring some bad things too, and we just have to accept it and do the best we can to deal with the worst parts of it. You can't turn the clock back."

"You can't turn the clock back." "You've got to take the rough with the smooth." "You can't put the genie back in the bottle." These are some of the clichés that are bandied about in any discussion of the impact of the Internet on society. Generally I would say they're probably true. Generally it's true that the Internet is like all new technology that becomes widely adopted: it has become widely adopted because we find it useful and good and accept its downsides as part of the price we pay for the far larger upsides. Generally I agree that you can't and shouldn't try to turn the clock back. Generally.

But the issue I'm talking about in this chapter is not general. It's specific. The issue is of children having unsupervised access to the Internet. Not children using technology or children using tablets or smartphones or going on the Internet or even children owning mobile phones. The issue is *unsupervised access to the Internet*. That's a pretty narrow, specific issue. And there is something we can do about it. More to the point, I believe there's something we must do about it because MIEDs are putting at risk one of the best and most important social changes in human history: the empowerment of women. It's great that Sheryl Sandberg's Lean In

Foundation created a partnership with Getty Images to create a new library of stock images showing women in traditionally male professional roles. Now let's see some action on smartphones too. As mobile phones became camera-phones and then smartphones connected to the Internet, it was like handing young people the keys to the liquor cabinet—it was only a matter of time before something went horribly wrong. Technology ran way ahead of our ability to handle it; for many young people, navigating the intersections of the Internet, mobile devices, and social media has been a baptism by fire. Just as with alcohol, we need to keep it away from our children unless we're there to supervise, not least because phones aren't just a feminist issue. They are a developmental issue too.

WE KNOW WHAT a good childhood looks like—and it turns out that modern brain science backs up what we knew by instinct all the time. The things that are generally associated with happy children who go on to be successful adults are human things, including time spent with people who love them, physical activity,[46] walking in and spending time in nature, and playing. Traditional toys, argues Brian Verdine, a postdoctoral fellow at the University of Delaware in Newark, are much better than "electronic toys and apps" at helping children learn spatial skills. "Skills, including early geometry and knowing the names of shapes, help kids learn the math skills they pick up in kindergarten," he says. "And if they already have those (before they begin school), they are ahead of the curve."[47] None of these things are provided by smartphones, tablets, and other MIEDs, and yet an increasing—and alarming—proportion of children's time is being diverted from the positive things we know are good for them. One recent study found that 'educational' toys that light up, play music, and talk back to children lead to 'decreased quantity and quality of language' compared to more human approaches.[48]

"Parents see that children will watch these screens and look like they understand, but they are not looking and perceiving in a way that is helping them learn," says Marsha Gerdes, a psychologist at the Children's Hospital of Pennsylvania. "Kids are not learning as much as when they are actually looking at their parent's face and listening to them sing a song when they are watching a pattern on a screen."[49] Research has shown that children who play with blocks do better in math later on,[50] and yet children are spending between two and four hours a day on screens.[51] It should alarm us that devices are now more popular than traditional toys.[52] As we saw earlier, the problem of overexposure to screens and

tech is pretty evenly spread across the income groups. But the difference is, middle- and upper-class families at least have the money and
the time to build positive physical—not screen-based—experiences into
their children's lives. Not so for poor families, where the device can be
a blessed relief from the stresses of parenting in difficult circumstances.
You can understand why, but it doesn't make it right.

Studies are starting to tell us that when we allow children to shut out
the world to focus on devices, we harm not just social relationships but
basic human abilities as well. Chief among them is the skill of conversation. Sherry Turkle, an MIT professor who studies the interaction between people and technology, recounts a recent conversation she had
had in the course of her research: "An 18-year-old boy who uses texting
for almost everything says to me wistfully: 'Someday, someday, but certainly not now, I'd like to learn how to have a conversation.'[53] Turkle
found that people increasingly eschew conversations because they can't
control what is said. In text messaging, e-mail, and social media, they
can. What's more, people can customize their communications, tuning
in and out without having to endure one second of content they don't
care about. But there are costs. As Turkle puts it, "You can end up hiding
from each other, even as we're all constantly connected to each other."
And they—our children—are suffering the consequences: ironically,
more connectivity dehumanizes.

In her book *Alone Together* Turkle writes about an encounter she had
with a teenager: "'There is a difference between someone laughing and
someone writing that they're laughing.' He says, 'My friends are so used
to giving their phones all the attention . . . they forget that people are
still there to give attention to.'"[54] This phenomenon is leading to slightly
tragic new rules of etiquette, like the number of people in a group who
can acceptably be looking down at their screen at any one time.[55] Neglected friendships are one thing, but what about parents neglecting
their children? When parents spend so much time on their devices, it
is, Turkle says, problematic for their children. "These kids are extremely
lonely. We are giving everybody the impression that we aren't really there
for them. It's toxic."[56] A detailed 2015 survey of teens' media habits by
Common Sense Kids Action revealed that American teenagers spend, on
average, a total of nine hours a day on screens—not including any screen
time at school.[57]

Although it's bad enough to be experimenting on ourselves with
screens and devices, we run great risks that the connectivity enabled by
technology will have outsized impact on impressionable children. As we

learned with the work of Nadine Burke Harris in Chapter 8, children are especially affected by neuroplasticity. Keeping that in mind, imagine how much it affects you, then imagine your children, who now have to grow up in this toxic environment, unable to access any space that's technology-free or without a device. We're experimenting with their very ability to think.

WE ARE NOT POWERLESS

MIEDs are incredible inventions and fantastic tools for all sorts of things. They facilitate learning through education programs and apps, allow parents to keep in touch with their children, save time and hassle, and enhance our daily lives. They can free us from drudgery to spend time on things of more value. Without question, children need to be comfortable with and adept at using the latest technology. But because there are undeniable adverse side effects, we should try to address them rather than assuming there's not really anything we can do about all this, that we have to "take the rough with the smooth," "can't turn the clock back," "can't put the genie back in the bottle," and so on.

That response is weak, feeble, pathetic. Of course it's possible to protect our children while enabling them to successfully navigate our technologically advanced, connected society. This is not a generalized, existential problem with technology or the Internet; it is a highly specific, narrow, solvable problem: How do we prevent the negative social consequences of unsupervised child access to the Internet?

There are lots of well-meaning efforts. You now see a steady stream of books and articles on 'digital detoxing' and similar self-denying ordinances as well as advice to parents on how to limit their children's screen time. Turkle recommends we establish 'sacred spaces' at home and at work away from our devices so we can reflect on our thoughts and connect with others. An app called TeenSafe lets parents monitor their children's mobile activity, which is fine, but it doesn't exactly get to the root of the problem. (Besides, what parent wants to so blatantly spy on their children?) More promising are 'digital detox' apps like RescueTime and Anti-Social. But although these can help solve some of the problems of adult over-reliance on tech, I don't think the 'self-denying ordinance' approach comes close to being the solution we need for children.

One serious way forward lies in the design of tech products themselves. Many of the biggest tech companies have put huge amounts of effort into building versions of their core products that prevent children from seeing adult content on the Internet. Examples include Apple's Family Sharing, Google's SafeSearch, and YouTube's Safety Mode (full disclosure: my wife, Rachel, was a leading advocate for child-protection efforts when she worked at Google). There are also apps like Net Nanny that claim to offer the same kinds of protections. Another version of this argument is that parents should not give children smartphones with data plans, thus limiting their use to phoning and texting.

These are all positive steps to address the problems we've seen in this chapter. But they don't go far enough. First, phones and tablets are increasingly sophisticated, and although parents may have options for more control, children are often two steps ahead. There are too many stories of children easily getting around various child-protection controls for anyone to have confidence in this approach. One so-called 'vault app' used by students in the Colorado sexting ring hides illicit photos behind what looks like a calculator (into which children can surreptitiously enter their passwords).[58] But there's an even more serious objection, and it's rooted in a very human concept we've seen a few times already in this book: social pressure. This problem of children seeing adult content and being able to use the Internet to harm themselves and others, this phenomenon of phones as a feminist issue, phones as a developmental issue, phones as an antisocial issue—it's not a product issue or a technical issue. It's a behavioral issue.

It's not just about whatever controls or restrictions you as a parent put on your child's use; it's about everyone else's children and their access to the Internet on whatever devices their parents have allowed them. However much some parents might not wish their children to have these devices outside the home or classroom, unsupervised, or whatever controls they successfully—or unsuccessfully—place on their own children's usage, they simply have no way of supervising their access to other children's devices. What do you do if you don't want your children to have a MIED? Should they be stigmatized or face peer pressure to get one?[59] I'm obviously alert to the risk that my own children might lose out because they aren't carrying the latest smartphone, tablet, or 'wearable.' As a parent, I will be forced to decide between what I believe to be good for my children's emotional and neurological development and what is best for them socially. That's a terrible choice, for me and for all parents.

That's why we need a fundamental rethink: this problem is not an individual problem; it's a collective one, like pollution, and that's how we need to deal with it. Unconstrained, unsupervised Internet use by children is mental pollution, and there is a simple solution for that kind of thing, one we know well and are used to applying.

Here's a way we could make life easier for parents, better for children, and retain the benefits of technology while making life more human. We need to create a social norm that children should never have access to the Internet without supervision. Because the principal method through which children access the Internet unsupervised is through smartphones or other MIEDs, that's where we have to take the fight. Just as we've banned smoking or drinking for under-sixteens because we think those things are bad for them, we should ban smartphones and other mobile Internet-enabled devices for children too—to protect under-sixteens from unsupervised content. They could still have so-called feature phones to call their parents in an emergency or send text messages, but they would not be able to view pornography and other illicit video and photo content or to take and post pictures of themselves whenever they wanted. Establishing this as a norm would license parents' enforcement of what would be an (inevitably) unpopular rule: 'It's not my fault. It's the law.'

Of course, children should have the benefits of the Internet when they're learning, exploring, and connecting with the world. As we saw in Chapter 3, technology can help students and teachers alike. But all of this can be achieved under supervision, in the home with parents and at school. If we allow uncontrolled use, devices will dominate our children's lives to the detriment of making friends, gaining tactile knowledge, and playing outside—in short, everything that makes childhood so wonderful, vital, human. That's why we need more protection. That's why we need a ban.

I realize this might sound extreme or fanciful, but you can't tell me it's impossible. It's not. My family is living proof of it. Our sons do not have phones or tablets, only use a computer at school, and at home have perhaps a half-hour or so of screen time three or four days a week, watching videos, not TV. I myself do not have a smartphone, and no, I don't say this from some cabin in the woods but a few miles from Stanford and as the CEO of a tech startup and husband of an Uber executive. I feel perfectly connected and perfectly happy not to be chained to screens.[60]

Some will say, "How can you justify something as draconian as banning kids from having smartphones or tablets?" I think it's reasonable to put the burden of justification on them: "Could you please explain why you want children to have unsupervised, unlimited access to the Internet?" For those who think my idea of a ban is unenforceable in a practical sense and who point to underage drinking and smoking despite similar bans, I'd say, of course, no ban ever achieves complete, 100 percent compliance. But they can be made to be effective in the vast majority of cases, and perhaps most importantly, a ban helps set a social norm. It draws a line and upholds society's standards and collective sense of right and wrong.

As society adapts to the digital age we need to push back a bit and make the digital age adapt to us. On the one hand, technology, especially in the form of mobile devices, has built a whole new world of progress. On the other hand, devices have unintended and serious negative side effects that we need to recognize and address if we are to maintain a healthy relationship with technology and retain our humanity. Ending children's unsupervised access to the Internet is a step in the right—and more human—direction.

BEING A PARENT has always been hard, and today seems ever harder. But as in so many other areas of life, we now have the evidence to know what our children need and what they don't. They need the freedom to play, to interact in the world, to discover themselves. They don't need the freedom to roam the Internet. We can't make childhood perfect, but we can set sensible rules and boundaries that best suit our children's very real limitations, needs, and aspirations. We should allow children to have a childhood that's more human.

chapter eleven

SPACES

WALK DOWN EAST LONDON'S famous Brick Lane, pulsing with life and energy at the intersection of the worlds of art and fashion and music and tech startups and waves of immigrants who have made this incredible place their home over the centuries, turn into Hanbury Street, and soon you'll come to a building as intriguing and important as any that have been created in the world these past few years.

The first things you'll see are trees—carefully selected to make sure one of them is flowering, whatever the season. Then you'll notice a strange, bubble-shaped orange wall emerging from the side of the building. Go in, and you'll be struck by the colors—amazing, bright colors. Poke around a bit. There's a café, desks, midcentury furniture, offices. But everywhere there are plants—not just stuck in pots, as you'll find in the beige-topia office buildings the world over, but plants that are actually growing up and along the walls and columns. Hydroponically, if you please. What is this place?

I'm so proud to say that it's the first Second Home, a business that Rohan started as an expression of his belief that our physical surroundings have a huge part to play in the quality of our lives—our personal lives and, as in the case of Second Home, our working lives. With his business partner Sam Aldenton and two thrillingly inventive Spanish architects, José Selgas and Lucía Cano, Rohan is showing in a practical way what we can achieve by aiming higher when it comes to designing our surroundings. (The *Architectural Review* asked rhetorically whether Second Home is "the best office in the world."[1]) According to Selgas and Cano, "Everything for us is related to how the brain works, whether that is a homespace or a workspace. The brain is more related to nature. If you are in an artificial rectangular space, your brain is restricted."[2] As a result, Second Home is full of nature, and to reflect the natural world, there are no right angles in the whole building. As Rohan says, "We didn't evolve with straight lines."[3]

But Rohan's vision is not simply about melding nature and people. In his original building in London as well as in future Second Homes planned in America and around the world, it's also about making people more comfortable in their environment. "Space is not just a commodity," he says; it's about "community and serendipity." It has to be "curated." People want to interact with one another, so Second Home works to ensure a diverse community where people and ideas can cross-pollinate. But Rohan and Sam also understand that people want time and space for themselves. They've designed Second Home for both, enabling members to regulate their own social interaction. For example, side entrances and exits allow you to avoid seeing others if you just want to slip in and out.

Second Home is a living, contemporary manifestation of a phrase that has come to capture the essence of why spaces matter. In 1943 Winston Churchill was asked to comment on the design of the new House of Commons building in Westminster. He explained his view that the physical characteristics of the building would have a major influence on how the politicians who used it would behave and, ultimately, on the policies that resulted. He quipped, "We shape our buildings, and afterward our buildings shape us."[4] Far too many architects and city planners have forgotten this essential truth—despite how obvious it seems. In Chapter 2 we looked at the idea of human-centered design in the context of government and public policy; in this chapter we're going to apply the same principle—human-centeredness—to the design of the physical space around us.

PARADOXICALLY, THE MORE sophisticated we've become, the more our physical interactions with the world have become thoughtless and unnatural. Look at the buildings and public spaces we use every day. Why are so many of them so terrible? Why is so much of the man-made world seemingly designed without any regard for us, the people who actually have to live in it? We have settled for industrially designed and manufactured homes and offices, suburbs that are 'good enough,' but our inhuman attitudes toward the built environment make many aspects of our lives, from education and health care to childhood play, much worse. We need places that work on a human scale and a human level.

In 1931 German psychologist Kurt Lewin proposed what would come to be known as Lewin's equation: $B = f(P, E)$—that is, human behavior is a function of a person and his or her environment. This was groundbreaking at the time: most psychologists assumed a person's habits and behaviors were a result simply of the type of person they were. Lewin thought otherwise. "Only by the concrete whole which comprises the object and the situation are the vectors which determine the dynamics of the event defined," he remarked when the theory was first proposed.[5] Several decades later psychologists would coin the term situationism to describe the overwhelming influence that external factors have on a person's behavior, as opposed to internal characteristics like mood, personality, and preferences. In the ensuing decades experiment after experiment in the lab as well as in the real world has proved this to be the case, lending even more weight to those wartime words of Winston Churchill. Our surroundings play such an important role in determining how happy, healthy, and productive we are. It's time we made them more human.

SPACE AND THE QUALITY OF EVERYDAY LIFE

Home might be where the heart is, but when it comes to the communities in which we live and work, many urban planners and architects seem to have followed only their heads. Obsessed with their own notions of how a perfectly rational society would look and function, they spent the twentieth century experimenting with our neighborhoods, often with awful results. There is no more iconic example of inhuman architecture than the work of Swiss architect Le Corbusier, who inspired many of France's urban housing projects in the mid-twentieth century— high-rises that have mostly served to isolate poor individuals from the rest of the community. The very term he used to describe his buildings is exactly what's wrong with them: "machines for living in." It's hard to imagine a less human approach. One of this architecture's best critiques was offered by Jane Jacobs, who had studied social housing as a reporter for *Architectural Forum* in the 1950s. As Canadian journalist Robert Fulford reports,

> On paper [the housing developments] looked fine, but when Jacobs visited them she discovered that the open spaces were empty of people. Planners had segregated residences, retail stores, business offices, and schools, an arrangement that was tidy but also inhuman and uninteresting. An environment created out of goodwill and careful thought had turned out to be boring, dangerous, and ultimately unliveable. The new developments had literally been planned to death: they left no room for happy accidents, and no room for life.[6]

If ever there were an advocate of human-centered design, it was Jacobs. In her classic—and now thankfully influential—book, *The Death
and Life of American Cities*, she lays out both her critique of and antidote to the 'visionary' planning that typified public projects in the mid-
twentieth century (and government programs more generally today).
Jacobs's legitimacy derived not from theory, which she ignored, or any
advanced degree, which she lacked, but from street-level observations
of people themselves and how buildings and streets influenced their interaction. She was only concerned about how cities worked 'in real life,'
as she put it, because that was the only way to understand how to plan,
rebuild, or develop a neighborhood for economic and social success.[7] For
'planners' to be captivated by their own visions of order and beauty was
to forget about how people actually lived. If you pick up her book, which
reads as much as a work of literature as an urban planning guide, you
might be surprised at the simplicity of many of her suggestions and the
length she devotes to each. There's an entire chapter discussing the need
for short street blocks (with many possible routes to any given destina-
tion, an area "opens up"), another on old buildings, and four chapters on
sidewalks. To many these are trivial features that merely enhance a city's
functions; to Jacobs they were central to its fundamental vitality. These
issues are brilliantly brought to life in that most iconic of cities, Paris. It
is a place that tells a powerful tale of contrasts, providing a juxtaposition
between a human, Jane Jacobs world and an inhuman, Le Corbusier one.

When he seized power as emperor in 1852, Napoleon III had an almost 'messianic' plan for Paris.[8] To build his vision, he appointed Baron
Georges-Eugène Haussmann, a Parisian native who had been prefect in
various other French cities, to be the new "Prefect of the Seine." Paris
had many ills. The medieval streets were difficult to navigate and often
impassable, paved with stones that "offered an uncertain footing for pedestrians and horses alike" and made of dirt that the "slightest rain . . .
turned into black mud."[9] Paris was, according to French writer Maxime
du Camp, "on the point of becoming uninhabitable. Its population [was]
suffocating in the tiny, narrow, putrid, and tangled streets in which it
had been dumped. As a result of this state of affairs, everything suffered:
hygiene, security, speed of communication and public morality."[10] Much
of this stemmed from lack of good plumbing and sanitation; sewers over-
flowed and emptied into the Seine, which was in turn a source of drinking water.

Napoleon and Haussmann were determined to modernize Paris. They
knew that a city, as a physical space, encompassed a complex ecosystem.

Accordingly, writes historian Colin Jones, they "saw themselves as physician-urbanists, whose task was to ensure Paris's nourishment, to regulate and to speed up circulation in its arteries (namely, its streets), to give it more powerful lungs so as to let it breathe (notably, through green spaces), and to ensure that its waste products were hygienically and effectively disposed of."[11] Haussmann channeled his patron's dictatorial powers by aggressively attacking the city in order to change it. In one sense his reforms were the epitome of inhumanity: instead of rebuilding piecemeal, he demolished whole neighborhoods to recreate Paris in a neater grid, building wide avenues on straight axes to ease movement in the city. The new apartments that lined them were uniform and modern, in the now-famous Haussmannian style. But they were in the service of human outcomes: Haussmann created wide avenues so pedestrians could have spacious promenades, he built new buildings to modernize living spaces and allow light to come to the streets, and he constructed several huge new parks to give all Parisians access to green space, "green lungs" for the overcrowded and polluted city.[12] He fulfilled some of Parisians' most basic human needs—creating a modern plumbing system that brought fresh water from outside the city while disposing of waste in a sanitary manner—but he also promoted their aspirational ones by building the Opéra Garnier as a monument to culture. There's no doubt today that Paris is a beautiful, modern city.

That is, at its center. When you contrast the center of Paris with its *banlieues*, or suburbs, full of housing projects (called *Habitation à Loyer Modéré*, or 'rent-controlled housing') inspired by Le Corbusier, you find a different, sadder story. These built-up 'utopias' are cruel traps: residents have sunlight and fresh air but are left in thrall to whichever gang controls the elevators. More fundamentally Le Corbusier forgot that as people move through life, they want different kinds of residences— urban apartments for young people, then space for raising a family, and then a pleasant retreat for retirement. "If you don't vary the housing units in a given neighborhood—if you fill entire quarters of the city with standard-issue monoliths—you condemn upwardly mobile people to constant movement," observes American journalist Christopher Caldwell, who has studied the banlieues in great depth. "The only people who develop any sense of place are those trapped in the poverty they started in."[13] At first glance Haussmann's Napoleon-era reforms and the construction of the Le Corbusier–inspired high-rises seem similar: both stemmed from the top-down visions of hubristic planners, but both, too, had 'more human' goals at their centers.

However, despite the inhuman process, Haussmann's vision in Paris worked. The banlieues did not. Central Paris is beautiful, with plentiful transport connecting mixed-use buildings everywhere. On almost every street the ground floor is a shop or business with offices and housing above. The banlieues, on the other hand, have become synonymous with disaster, most recently burdened by massive riots in 2005. The rioters, mostly first- and second-generation North Africans, had plenty of grievances: unemployment, racism, France's failure to integrate them into society. But their grievances were exacerbated by the inhuman architecture of the banlieues. By concentrating the city's poorest, most desperate, and most violent residents, French planners inadvertently created a powder keg that duly burst when three youths from a banlieue, thinking they were being chased by the police, hid in a power station and were electrocuted. Two died, a third was gravely injured, and an entire community of young people rose in rebellion against the society they felt was responsible. Neighborhood design did not cause the weeks of ensuing riot, but the daily indignities of inhuman architecture and planning certainly contributed to them.

The reason central Paris 'works' is because with different types of people using the same streets at all times of day, Haussmann inadvertently created a 'Jacobsian' city: there are always, in her famous phrase, "eyes on the street" to watch over it. The banlieues, with their isolated, single-use buildings dominated by gangs, are the precise, inhuman opposite.

ONE OF THE marks of a great, human neighborhood is that you can't really tell where it begins or ends—one area just flows into the next. Sooner or later you know you're somewhere special, but the precise moment never really announces itself.

For decades it was pretty easy to know when you had entered St. Lawrence, Toronto. Situated close to the bustling downtown, Toronto Harbor, and the Canadian national railways yard, the neighborhood had once been a busy port area, but by the 1960s it had grown blighted and vacant. But affordable housing was high on the agenda of 1970s mayor David Crombie, and despite its grittiness, St. Lawrence offered prime real estate in the heart of the city. The city-hall bureaucrats were nervous about any sort of large new development; prior years and decades had already been scarred by grand efforts at urban renewal in the style of Le Corbusier and like-minded city planners around the world. Toronto's leaders had fresh memories of their own: Regent Park, a 1950s 'tower in the park' housing project near downtown, had fallen into disrepair and crime after ten years, and the 1960s high-rise development of St. James Town just to the north is ridden with crime to this day.

But 1970s Toronto would be different. Jane Jacobs moved there from New York in 1968 and had already begun influencing its activists and politicians alike. Mayor Crombie and Michael Dennis, the city's housing commissioner, were eager pupils of her ideas and prepared to throw out the existing textbooks on urban planning in favor of a completely new approach. Their first move with St. Lawrence was to bring in an outside architect, Alan Littlewood, at Jacobs's recommendation (perhaps his appeal was precisely that he had no formal planning degree). From the start he saw the project as a process of "invisible mending"[14]; that is, rather than raze entire city blocks and rebuild a 'utopian' community, Littlewood kept as much of the neighborhood's original features—and historic brick character—as possible, tucking new housing in where he could among its existing roads and buildings as well as its treasured mid-nineteenth-century structures like the wedge-shaped Gooderham flatiron building, the Cathedral Church of St. James, St. Lawrence Hall, and St. Lawrence Market, which now houses what *National Geographic* magazine has called the world's best food market.[15]

St. Lawrence would come to typify the recommendations Jacobs had made in her seminal book a decade before. It would be more human. To prevent the banlieue problem à la Paris, the neighborhood was built to appeal to a broad spectrum of individuals and families, using a variety of dwelling types—apartments, condominiums, houses—to meet the needs of residents of all ages and incomes, as both market and social housing were intermixed. And unlike most new developments at the time, which kept traffic strictly separated from pedestrians with long and wide 'superblock' roads next to large parks and plazas, St. Lawrence preserved its nineteenth-century street grid of short, frequent blocks. This allows for the type of serendipitous "street ballet" adored by Jacobs. She writes,

> Under the seeming disorder of the old city, wherever the old city is working successfully, is a marvelous order for maintaining the safety of the streets and the freedom of the city. It is a complex order. Its essence is intricacy of sidewalk use, bringing with it a constant succession of eyes. This order is all composed of movement and change, and although it is life, not art, we may fancifully call it the art form of the city and liken it to the dance, . . . an intricate ballet in which the individual dancers and ensembles all have distinctive parts which miraculously reinforce each other and compose an orderly whole.[16]

St. Lawrence has been successful because the long-term realities of people were put before the—often short-sighted—needs of planners, developers, and bureaucrats. Unlike many ego-driven projects, the place is special precisely because it doesn't immediately appear to be anything special; it's the people who live there, flourishing, who take center stage.[17] Not a machine, but a neighborhood for living.[18]

Toronto isn't alone. The United States has its fair share of beautifully livable neighborhoods. Neighborhoods where architecture was clearly not just thought of as that 'step before engineering' but as the skill and practice necessary to give a place real character; that make their streets safe and usable for pedestrians and bicyclists, not just cars; that encourage local shops and restaurants; that integrate trees and green space into the hustle of daily life. Cities like Portland, Oregon, exemplify how thriving American urban areas can embrace more human urban design. Not only are its city blocks among the shortest in the country, but its myriad neighborhoods are all connected by plentiful public transit as well as 'bicycle boulevards,' which allow cyclists to avoid main arterial streets.

Of course, it's not feasible for most cities to rebuild themselves, but municipal leaders needn't make large changes to their civil infrastructure to make their neighborhoods more human; small improvements can have a transformative effect. Consider dense and bustling New York. Mayor Mike Bloomberg saw an opportunity to reduce traffic fatalities while improving the health and happiness of cyclists and pedestrians by adopting 'complete streets' through parts of Manhattan. Now not only do many streets have bike lanes, but parked cars have also been moved to their street side to serve as a barrier between auto and bike traffic.

Meanwhile his planning commissioner, Amanda Burden, approached the city with a new philosophy to "tap into [her] humanity," asking herself of public spaces: "Would you want to go there? Would you want to stay there?" Her answer was a series of unique projects throughout the city to make it more livable and connected, transforming an old elevated railway trestle into the High Line, a one-and-a-half-mile park through the heart of three neighborhoods in Manhattan's West Side, as well as over three hundred acres of dilapidated waterfront into dynamic new parks.[19] She worked with transport commissioner Janette Sadik-Khan, who took the lead in experimenting with the creation of pedestrian- and cyclist-friendly streets, even closing some to create car-free plazas. Her best tactic? Iterating with temporary materials, like paint, "so if it worked better for traffic, if it was better for mobility, if it was safer, better for business, we would keep it, and if it didn't work, no harm, no foul, we could put it back the way that it was," she says. There is "much less anxiety when you think that something can be put back. But the results were overwhelming."[20]

SPACE AND FUNCTION

The built environment is, in a very literal way, the infrastructure of our daily lives. If we get it wrong, the consequences extend beyond mere aesthetics. Just consider many cities' housing policies, whereby already-established residents often welcome new companies with the attendant jobs and higher salaries without allowing the necessary housing to be developed alongside. Nowhere is this more obvious than in San Francisco, my adopted home. It's outrageous that while city officials had little difficulty finding space (and tax breaks) to house Twitter and other large tech companies, most of the people who make the city tick—not just line cooks and janitors but teachers and police officers too—must live elsewhere . . . far elsewhere. And it's not for lack of space; it's for lack of courage among our political leaders to stand up to their property-owning residents. One particularly illustrative example comes from the late 1990s, when the construction of an affordable apartment building for teachers was proposed, and residents in the surrounding middle-class neighborhood opposed it—"not in my backyard" they collectively asserted; city officials predictably gave in.[21] Meanwhile current programs to help teachers afford to live in the city whose children they teach are drained of funds. At least teachers have a program—most workers have no support whatsoever.

UC Berkeley economist Enrico Moretti has calculated that each new tech job creates five local-services jobs.[22] But in San Francisco the figure is just slightly north of two. As journalist Kim-Mai Cutler points out, if we were to ease the city's burdensome permitting process and reform its zoning and height laws, "it would not only make living affordable for most people, it would allow a far larger portion of the population to find jobs and do things like save or spend money instead of moving somewhere distant and spending their money on driving, or even being unemployed."[23]

When a large portion of a region's workers have to commute hours each morning and evening, it isn't just a question of personal convenience—or even the well-documented environmental or health consequences of long commutes.[24] When these working parents spend their nonworking hours in gridlock traffic, they aren't at home with their children—eating dinner, doing homework, reading stories. Short-sighted housing policies keep families from spending time together—the time we know is critical to child development—and exacerbates inequality.

As with so many other areas of policy, as we've seen throughout this book, the real reason for San Francisco's housing crisis is structural: a land-use system that favors big developers and incumbent property owners. Much-trumpeted schemes from city leaders to boost housing supply are a drop in the bucket compared to what is needed. But until they are prepared to take on the special interests in the property market, nothing much, sadly, will change.

Today, even as our public spaces on the outside give the appearance of having evolved beyond Le Corbusier cubes, the facades of most buildings merely obscure the ugly truth within: that we are living and working in machines as much as—if not more than—ever before. Too much of our built environment, both public and private, is designed to maximize overall 'efficiency' and minimize cost rather than serve our most human needs. This is absolutely the wrong way to think about what our built environment is. Our inhuman approach to space contributes not just to public policy problems but also to poor workplace productivity. Marlon Nieuwenhuis, a psychologist at Cardiff University, found that adding plants to otherwise spartan offices increased productivity 15 percent.[25] (Second Home London has a thousand of them.) A study by Northwestern University and the University of Illinois at Urbana-Champaign found that office workers with window exposure to natural light slept longer and better, were more physically active, and enjoyed better overall quality of life than their counterparts without.[26] Of those spaces that aren't explicitly 'broken,' many just serve their minimal function—think of windowless classrooms, soulless offices, treeless streets—processing people through the day rather than providing the setting in which they can lead happier and more fulfilled lives. In a twist of irony, the spaces we live and work in are often designed to better serve other machines— cars, trucks, computers—than humans.

According to Carlo Ratti, a designer and architect who works on the nexus of technology and the physical world at MIT, technology could help change this. The original computers were so large that to use them, people had to work in large, dark, air-conditioned rooms, often squirreled away in basements. "The machine determined the physical condition of the space around it," he says. "It was 90 percent machine, 10 percent human." Now technology has literally untethered us. The advent of small, powerful, and mobile devices coupled with ubiquitous wireless Internet allows us to work anywhere—even outside. And this "ubiquitous computing" marks a profound shift in how we design spaces. There is a paradox, Carlo says, in that when technology is all around us, "we can focus much more on the architecture, on the human side of things, and design offices, homes, and buildings around people instead of around machines."[27] Indeed, the whole reason we can discuss open-plan offices or flexible homes is because technology is no longer the limiting factor in building spaces. We can focus on our environments in other ways, like helping us to be healthier, more productive, more creative—in short, more human. And we are getting better and better at it.

Around the world school administrators, factory owners, and office managers observe firsthand the difference that can be made by space designed with people in mind. It can even be a competitive advantage: Steve Jobs famously insisted that the bathrooms at Pixar Studios (creator of hits like *Toy Story* and *Finding Nemo*) be located in the center of the building so people from different departments would run into each other throughout the day, sparking spontaneous human interaction and creative collaboration.

If any company understands the importance of putting people at the center of the design process, it's furniture manufacturer Herman Miller, which makes some of the most ergonomic furniture in the world. For many years, though, the human-first principles they applied to their furniture making didn't extend to their workers. After a transformative factory redesign—infusing both the manufacturing and office areas with natural light; connecting different parts of the building by an indoor, bamboo-plant-lined "boulevard"; and adding and expanding operable windows throughout the plant—they saw employee happiness and sense of belonging skyrocket and productivity significantly improve.[28] The executives of SnowPeak, a Japanese camping-gear company, thought they would create better products if they could observe their customers using them. So the company adapted the concept of a factory store: they created a "factory camping ground." When they built their headquarters, they sacrificed large amounts of land around the building so loyal—and, perhaps, curious—customers could come and camp in view of the windows. As a result, product designers and makers can see exactly how their equipment is used and better understand what works and what doesn't. SnowPeak's commitment to transparency works both ways. There are no opaque walls or doors—all is glass. No space is off limits, so staff and customers can fully see what's going on and can give feedback. And although everyone can see in, all you need to do is turn toward an outside 'wall' to see the beautiful mountains beyond, a constant reminder of the company's mission to connect customers with nature.[29]

Although some aspects of space design are unequivocally 'better,' different spaces suit different needs, especially in the workplace. Companies that want internal groups to work together effectively and creatively will likely want an open plan; those that want to mix up employees from different departments might add flexible seating. But where individuals need to be productive on their own, companies might want to keep the traditional model, or at least a more enlightened variant of it.[30] That means considering employees' needs, not just the corporate view. Open-space offices might boost creativity, but they can also create anxiety, with employees paranoid that their bosses are watching what they're up to. Balancing open and private space is critical; employees need room for themselves, whether to think, work, or simply have a phone call without fear of eavesdroppers. In one recent survey 88 percent of the most satisfied workers were those who could work where they wanted.[31] The key, as Rohan is showing in Second Home, is to give workers a choice so they can adjust to their own preferences.

The power of space to enhance creativity, productivity, or employee health needn't be limited to the workplace, though. Thoughtful architects have shown that extending more human design to our schools can improve pupils' performance as well. In Finland, whose excellent schools we discussed in Chapter 3, it should come as no surprise that educators are equally thoughtful about school design. School architects in Helsinki consider questions such as whether the structure allows pupils and staff to break their routines and try new things; whether the environment fosters creativity, enabling observation and investigation of everyday phenomena; whether the building protects against violence and bullying; and even whether the school welcomes visiting parents.[32]

SPACE AS SOLUTION

Spaces, as we have seen, can have an immense impact on daily life and can help us be more human in our homes, workplaces, and play spaces. But they can also help solve social and environmental problems. In 1982 James Q. Wilson and George L. Kelling put forward their famous 'broken windows' theory—that visible, physical signs of disorder signal crime as an acceptable norm, perpetuating further crime. Small fixes to the physical environment, such as cleaning up graffiti and litter as well as repairing broken street furniture like park benches, can have more of an impact on crime than direct police intervention or increased social services.[33]

In Lowell, Massachusetts, authorities identified thirty-four crime 'hot spots' and proceeded to clean half of them up. They found that in the half where litter was collected and debris removed, there was a 20 percent drop in police calls.[34] At the University of Groningen in the Netherlands psychologists repeatedly left an envelope with a €5 note clearly inside half-sticking out of a postbox. When the street was orderly, 13 percent of passers-by took it (the rest pushed it back in); when litter surrounded the area, 25 percent took it; and when the postbox itself was covered in graffiti, the number increased to 27 percent. Disorder on the street doubled the propensity of passers-by to become thieves.*[35]

Street-level nudges can be remarkably effective for other problems as well. Sweden's Vision Zero program, which aims to eliminate road deaths, has given Sweden one of the best road-safety records in the world.[36] Since it started in 1997, annual road deaths have come down by four-fifths compared to 1965, despite a doubling of traffic.[37] Vision Zero has a simple but radically human-centered message: "In every situation a person might fail, the road system should not."[38] The Swedes have thus tried to design a road system nationwide that aims to maintain and increase mobility but never at the expense of people's lives. They understand that people make mistakes, but they believe that death should not be the consequence. This is not, the Swedes argue, any different from how we approach other systems: "If you take a nuclear power station, aviation, a rail system, all of them are based on the idea that they are operated by people who can make a mistake," says Claes Tingvall of the Swedish National Road Administration. With that in mind, roads are designed in Sweden so that although mistakes might cause an accident, there are no fatalities or serious injuries. "You have to take the human in

*Unfortunately, misinterpretation of the theory has been used to support other, only partially related policies. Critics use (far too-frequent) occasions of abusive police overreaction as an indictment of 'broken-windows' policing writ large. Such criticism is an inaccurate conflation of two completely different phenomena. Yes, broken-windows theory suggests it's important to police petty crime. But it also suggests that community policing—more human policing, whereby officers walk the beat and actively foster relationships—is the answer. A proper application of broken-windows policing is community engagement, not creating an authoritarian police state.

our behavior into account when you design the road transport system. It is understanding that we will never be perfect," says Tingvall. For example, knowing that drivers will try to overtake other cars on two-lane roads, Sweden has installed '2+1' roads, where each direction of traffic takes turns using a middle third lane to overtake. In its first decade that one improvement saved 145 lives.[39]

My favorite example of more human design for public space is from the Netherlands. Consider how Amsterdam became one of the most bike- and pedestrian-friendly cities in the world, with cars used for only 22 percent of all trips (the rest are by bike, public transport, or foot).[40] In the early 1970s Amsterdam was like most urban environments around the world: traffic clogged and dangerous. At rush hour streets resembled car parks, and the air was choked with exhaust fumes. Car accidents killed more than three thousand people annually across Holland in the early 1970s, including over five hundred children.[41] In 1972 one group of children living in central Amsterdam had had enough. The neighborhood called De Pijp ('the pipe') was about a hundred years old, five times denser than the rest of the city, and not built for the cars that the forty thousand inhabitants brought with them and filled the streets with.[42] Pupils at one of the local schools started a petition to make the streets less convenient for cars and safer for children like them, launching a campaign that quickly outgrew the tiny classroom from which it started. They even took matters into their own hands, temporarily closing a street to physically demonstrate the need for a safe place to play.

This was part of the birth of a larger movement, Stop de Kindermoord ('stop child murder'), that would transform streets in Amsterdam and greater Holland. It wasn't easy—there's a famous video of an irate driver picking up and throwing a roadblock children had erected to turn a small part of a street into a car-free zone. Despite the violent backlash against the anticar campaign, the children, supported by their teacher, stuck to their guns. All they wanted was a safe place to play. And through their action they started a worldwide urban-design movement that today has mainstreamed pedestrian zones, bike lanes, street furniture, tree planting, and so on. The children recognized that the space they lived in was not designed for their human needs—to play, to walk to school, and to socialize with their friends and families—and they did something about it. One group of children, in one school in Amsterdam. What a lovely, inspiring tale of more human social change.

In many cases making space more human is really just about recognizing how people actually behave in certain contexts—as opposed to how we assume they do—and designing our environments with this in mind. A Stanford University project that Jason (the Jason who, along with his brother Scott, helped me write this book) was involved in, designing a 'concept home' that would be net-zero-energy, shows how a human-centered approach can help solve environmental problems too. Jason first mapped all the places people interact with their homes in ways that consume energy—light switches, thermostats, and so on. His team's key insight was that few people actually want to waste resources; we just do so because there are small, seemingly insignificant barriers that, for reasons of forgetfulness, lack of attention, or even just laziness, get in our way. If the team could remove as many of these barriers as possible, people's intention to either save money, do good for the environment, or simply avoid waste would be less impeded.

Of the handful of innovative products his team developed and built in the house, my favorite was a 'room switch' that would make the people at Nest (producers of beautiful and practical home services like thermostats) blush. "We wanted to rethink the whole idea of the light switch," Jason says. There are all sorts of different electronic items plugged into the wall that draw energy, even when they're off—device chargers, televisions, kitchen appliances. Jason and his team wanted to design a 'light' switch that worked for the whole room, one that could turn everything off, not just the lights. "Simplicity was important—part of the reason people don't unplug things is because it's a pain." The solution, as is so often the case, lay right in front of them. Most of the team had Apple laptops, which have what are called 'trackpads.' Inspired, they built a similar control in place of where a light switch would normally be: instead of a toggle switch or even a screen, you touch an opaque surface. As Jason puts it, "You can achieve an incredible amount of functionality based on your gestures and how many fingers you use to draw them, all without automating away users' agency." Yet most importantly, with any 'room switch,' it just took one touch to turn off every electrical appliance in a room or even put the whole house 'to sleep.'

SPACES AND HUMAN IMPACT

"First life, then spaces, then buildings—the other way around never works." At seventy-nine years old, Danish architect Jan Gehl still has strong opinions about the way our cities are designed. He's spent the past fifty years developing the principles of what makes a city 'livable' and leading an unwavering campaign for "architecture that considers human scale and interaction."[43]

I was fortunate to be introduced to Gehl's work by Richard Rogers, who, along with the great British architect, Thomas Heatherwick, has taught me so much about architecture and urban design and is a fantastic champion for the future of cities. "Cities—like books—can be read, and Jan Gehl understands their language," he writes in the foreword to Gehl's book, *Cities for People*. "The street, the footpath, the square, and the park are the grammar of the city; they provide the structure that enables cities to come to life, and to encourage and accommodate diverse activities, from the quiet and contemplative to the noisy and busy. A humane city— with carefully designed streets, squares, and parks—creates pleasure for visitors and passers-by, as well as for those who live, work, and play there every day." Denser and more sustainable cities, Rogers adds, are the future, but only if we build them with space to walk, cycle, and breathe in, with "beautiful public spaces that are human in scale, sustainable, healthy, and lively."[44] Like the thinking of Jane Jacobs, Rogers's and Gehl's philosophies of cities resonate with me deeply.

It turns out that Gehl might not have learned the language of cities at all had love not intervened. It was 1960, and like all formally trained architects at the time, he was perfectly prepared to build exactly those types of 'modern cities' that Jane Jacobs would soon complain about, cities that, in his words, were full of "high rises and a lot of lawns and good open space—good windy spaces."[45] Had he not met Ingrid Mundt, a psychologist who would become his wife, his life might have turned out drastically different. As someone who studied "people rather than bricks" as Gehl puts it, Mundt inspired a host of conversations among their combined peers. Why weren't architects interested in people? Why weren't they paying attention to how architecture could "influence people's lives"? Why couldn't they work out how to make cities that would make people happier?

Gehl's philosophy was forever changed. "Brasilia, the capital of Brazil, is a great example," he said. "From the air it's very interesting. It's interesting for a bird or eagle. From the helicopter view, it has got wonderful districts with sharp and precise government buildings and residential buildings. However, nobody spent three minutes to think about what Brasilia would look like at the eye level. . . . Nobody was responsible for looking after the people."[46]

In 1965 they created the PSPL, a "public space/public life" survey in Siena, Italy. The initial goal was simple: keep track of the number of people in a public space and what they were using it for.[47] Such 'street-level' observations would inform recommendations for improvements to various neighborhoods. Fast-forward half a century, and Gehl has now surveyed cities around the world. His focus is almost entirely on considering the city, however large, at the human scale. To him that's the only way to understand the effect architecture ultimately has on people.

From São Paulo and Amman to Brighton and New York, Gehl and his team spend weeks surveying people at all times of day, watching how they interact with the urban space in question—where they walk, where they spend time, what they do. Just as in Siena, he and his firm can take this base knowledge and use it to advise clients on questions of urban design and master-planning. In all these years his goal remains the same: create 'cities for people.' Through this work Gehl has created a list of twelve criteria for any public space, based on what he and his colleagues believe are the things people need from their urban environments. They span three categories: *protection* (from traffic, crime, and pollution); *comfort* (to be able to walk, stand or sit, converse, and play without impediment), and *enjoyment* (of the weather—hot, cold, rain, or snow—and of aesthetic qualities). Their approach is meticulous, combining highly studious ethnography with traditional surveys to capture every on-the-ground detail. In one project aimed at improving London's walkability, surveyors counted thousands of pedestrians, measured precise distances between curbs and pavement obstacles, like trash cans and street poles, and keenly observed every sort of behavior they could catalog, from mothers enlisting passers-by to help carry a stroller down steps, to how many people cross against a red signal. They even compare measurements between weekdays and weekends, summer and winter. Though they don't provide a score per se, their reports are exhaustive, combining qualitative and quantitative elements, including photographs, charts, and annotated maps to give planners a sense of where they are strong and where they are deficient in each category.[48]

To do this for every space, from schools to offices, houses to neighborhoods, would be extreme. But Gehl is onto something. We don't need specific measurements or a points system to be able to assess whether a space fulfills human needs; acknowledging them during its design is half the battle. So here's a simple way for us to make our spaces more human. Today every building that's constructed has, at the very least, basic safety standards it has to pass as well as extra hurdles like environmental impact reports. On top of that, almost every type of space is subject to seemingly endless rules and regulations, standards, and requirements.

What I propose is far simpler: a report, nothing too long or onerous, let's call it a Human Impact Report. No specific regulations or requirements. Just a short, straightforward statement of how any development—home, office, city block, or neighborhood redevelopment—fulfills each of Gehl's twelve criteria. In the spirit of 'nudging' outlined in Chapter 2, the point here is not to create another layer of burdensome bureaucracy; rather, if architects, planners, designers, builders, and engineers are prompted to start thinking along these lines, that simple act will end up making a difference—because it will make people think. It will make people think about people. And when this becomes part of the planning vernacular, when buyers, tenants, residents, citizens, and everyone else who occupies a space is exposed to these questions—and how builders answer them—'human-ness' will become a real competitive advantage. Imagine that: a system in which developers and builders and architects and urban planners compete with each other to make the world around us more human.

That's a world I'd want to call home.

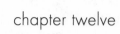

chapter twelve

NATURE

THERE'S A CLASSIC speech that park rangers deliver whenever they catch a child trying to make off with a 'natural' souvenir. "You are supposed to calmly kneel down and say, 'I saw you picking the flower. That is so pretty! Now think about what would happen if every child picked a flower,'" explains Matthew Browning, a former park ranger at North Carolina's Mount Mitchell State Park. "And then they are supposed to have this moment of guilt." One day in 2009 Browning saw a fellow ranger give the speech to a boy, about eight years old, in the park's restaurant. Instead of picking flowers, the boy had picked up a small handful of 'rocks.' In fact, it was gravel that the rangers had bought at the local supply store to spread over the road. Browning had an epiphany. "It made me sick. The boy was crestfallen. He was so excited about coming to the park that he wanted to take a little memento back with him. More than feeling empowered or excited to protect the natural world, now he is going to associate going to state parks with getting into trouble."[1]

But it's not just picking flowers and rocks that get you into trouble. Mount Mitchell—and most parks, for that matter—prohibit all sorts of things: going off the official footpath, climbing trees, shouting, playing with sticks, digging holes . . . you name it. Disillusioned, Browning left the park and enrolled in graduate school to study the recreational use of natural areas. Hearing about so-called nature play areas in Europe where children are allowed to play with abandon, he set off to Sweden to observe some firsthand. He ended up finding one near just about every primary school he visited (Sweden has a lot of forests). "They all had plenty of forest and plenty of kids playing in the woods." Browning didn't interact much with the children, preferring to observe rather than interrupt. But one day he met a twelve-year-old boy. "He was talking about how he would break branches and build forts and throw rocks," Browning said. "He had a knife with him. He said: 'I carve sticks into spears and stuff like that.'" So Browning asked him whether he would ever stick the knife into a tree. The boy was shocked: "'No! It would hurt the tree; it would hurt the tree just like it would hurt me.'"

This twelve-year-old's instinct highlights the human instinct of wanting to connect with nature. In 1984 the world's leading evolutionary biologist E. O. Wilson introduced the biophilia hypothesis: the human "urge to affiliate with other forms of life."[2] He uses it to explain the fact that for much of human history, we've surrounded ourselves with plants and animals, either domesticated in our homes, gardens and communities, or close by in adjacent parks. You even see it in zoos, where animals exhibit unnatural behavior when their pens don't mimic the natural environments from which they come.[3] It's an inborn desire we all share.

Indeed, study after study has substantiated the important beneficial effects of nature on human health and well-being. Views of nature and natural settings reduce stress and improve attention—walking in it even more so.[4] Though running reduces anxiety and depression wherever it is done, Swedish researchers have found the effects are amplified when it is done in nature.[5] In a Pennsylvania hospital patients with a view of trees had shorter stays, by almost a day on average, and required fewer pain medications than those in rooms facing a brick wall.[6]

UNNATURAL BEHAVIOR

Despite nature's great importance to us, for most of our history we've gone out of our way to conquer the natural world. We've tilled the land, hunted and then domesticated animals, cut down forests, dammed rivers, mined mountains, built cities. Now we're manipulating genetics with biotechnology and even toying with the idea of engineering the climate—to fix the damage we ourselves have inflicted. We have tried to bend nature to human will. We have tried to make nature . . . more human.

For generations this relationship worked because the scale and power of nature so exceeded that of human civilization. Our efforts to surmount nature enabled our survival and progress as a species without, it seemed, doing nature much harm. But that has changed as we have become more mechanized and industrialized. As humanity began to outpace its natural context, the costs of our way of doing things became apparent. We saw pollution, spoilt landscapes, and filthy cities. In 1952 London was hit by the Great Smog, a combination of cold weather and windless conditions that trapped air pollution, mostly from burning coal, for four days in and around the city, creating smog so thick that it is estimated to have prematurely killed at least four thousand people.[7] A similar event killed nineteen people in Donora, a small mill town in southwestern Pennsylvania, just four years before that. There, weather conditions led to toxic smoke from the town's steel and zinc mills blanketing the town for five days in a row.[8] The nation's consciousness was perhaps seared most after widespread media coverage in 1969 of the Santa Barbara oil spill and later that year of the Cuyahoga, a river that runs through Cleveland, literally on fire, fueled by the copious oil and debris it contained.[9]

We reacted, the pendulum swung a bit toward conservation, and we cleaned things up. A bit. Earlier progressives like John Muir and Theodore Roosevelt had championed the cause of nature, greatly expanding its protection through the National Park system.[10] But the inexorable march of industry went on throughout the twentieth century. A decade that saw a high-water mark of environmental awareness and activism in the 1960s and 1970s—Earth Day, the Environmental Protection Agency, the Clean Air and Water Acts, and, of course, the publication of Rachel Carson's *Silent Spring*—then receded into an era of cheap plastics, mass manufacturing, and ever-growing urban sprawl and fossil-fuel consumption. As quickly as we learned our lessons, it seems, we swiftly forgot them. So today we live with a tomorrow that has never been more at risk.

Humanity's hubris—our hubris—was thinking that we could endlessly extract from nature with little or no adverse consequences. Our fundamental mistake, according to the influential twentieth-century economist E. F. Schumacher, was to treat nature like an infinite bank account from which we could forever make withdrawals. But such an adversarial relationship is a fallacy: if man won his battle with nature, "he would find himself on the losing side."[11] Despite our best efforts, there's just no way to bend all of nature's vast, incomprehensible complexity to our human rules and institutions. We have to realize that nature isn't just humanity's support structure; humanity is a part of nature. Our careless manipulation of it is not only unnatural; it is irrevocably harmful both to nature and, ultimately, to ourselves.

We've now destroyed nearly one-fifth of the Amazon rainforest—more than three times the land area of the entire UK.[12] We lose over 20 million acres of tropical forest per year.[13] There is now estimated to be at least 268,940 tons of plastic floating in our oceans.[14] Rather than biodegrade—the way organic material would—plastic just breaks down into smaller and smaller pieces, devastating the wildlife that ingests it. Coral reefs occupy less than a quarter of 1 percent of the marine environment but house a quarter of known fish species. In the 1970s live coral covered half of the Caribbean's reefs; today it covers 8 percent of them.[15] According to the International Union for Conservation of Nature's latest Red List of Threatened Species, 41 percent of amphibians and 26 percent of mammals are currently under threat of extinction. Precision is difficult, as many species are still undiscovered, but estimates suggest we are losing between five hundred and thirty-six thousand species each year.[16]

One of the most impactful meetings I ever had was when Rohan took me to meet E. O. Wilson at Harvard University. He is one of the first theorists to discuss and advocate for 'biodiversity'—that is, variation among genes within species, species within ecosystems, and ecosystems among each other. As he puts it, we risk losing "'genetic encyclopedias' millions of years in the making,"[17] embodying countless medical, biotechnical, and agricultural opportunities (e.g., 49 percent of cancer-fighting drugs are derived from nature).[18] According to Wilson, we stand to reduce at least half of the earth's remaining plant and animal species to extinction or critical endangerment by the end of the century. Such cataclysms—of which the earth has had five so far, the last one having brought an end to the dinosaurs—take 5 to 10 million years to repair. "We are, in short, flying blind into the environmental future," Wilson says.[19]

To forestall the sixth mass-extinction event of which he speaks, we have to get more serious about conservation. According to a December 2014 assessment by the science journal *Nature*, a loss of 690 species per week, the upper end of estimates, would bring such an event about by the year 2200.[20] Wilson's bold vision—what he calculates is necessary to avoid ruinous biodiversity loss[21]—is to set aside half of the earth for conservation or restoration ("Half Earth"). Crucially it's not just making sure that land already out of civilization's way remains protected (though this is important); it's making sure that all of the world's ecosystems have at least some protected areas where nature can 'do its thing.' In some cases this will require restoration; in others it might mean paying landowners to ensure parts of their land remain undeveloped, but still accessible for light use. It also means threading these protected areas together so that as habitats shift with a changing climate, wildlife is able to migrate— perhaps hundreds or even thousands of miles through accessible 'corridors,' like the White Hawk Project adjoining the Corcovado National Park in Costa Rica.[22] In order to preserve the park's incredible biodiversity—some 2.5 percent of the world's total—the White Hawk Project purchases and maintains land abutting the park in order to create wildlife corridors using conservation easements, which restrict development and land use for ecological benefit.

When our family, along with Rohan and his wife, Kate, vacationed near the park in April 2015, we learned about the White Hawk Project firsthand from Lana Wedmore, our ecolodge's owner and the project's founder. What is so amazing—but equally frustrating—about Lana's work is that compared to the massive sums spent by government (often ineffectively) fighting climate change, she's asking for a pittance. And yet here is a solution that not only contributes to global climate efforts but also conserves land forever and tangibly saves species from extinction— today. Even more tangibly, visiting the Corcovado National Park exposed all of us to the rainforest and showed us firsthand the true value of nature and its protection. This kind of direct exposure to nature has got to be the best way to instill in everyone—especially children—a conservation ethos that lasts a lifetime.

It seems hardly necessary by now to justify why this would be worth-while. The unknown human value that will one day derive from the biodiversity preserved—and stimulated—by a globally connected wil-derness alone makes ambitions like Half Earth and projects like White Hawk easy to justify. But it's also the benefit of having truly natural na-ture (such a phrase would seem ridiculous if it weren't necessary) local to everyone. We would be infusing our modern, sophisticated landscape with pristine nature, side by side, everywhere.

Throughout this book I've discussed how we need to make our world more human. But when it comes to nature, we've already made the world too human. We've distorted our idea of what nature is and should be because we've misunderstood our part in it. So now we need to fun-damentally rethink humanity's relationship with the natural world and move the pendulum back toward the system of our ancestors, in which we benefit from nature while simultaneously giving back to and coexist-ing with it.

NATURAL CAPITAL

Nature isn't just beautiful; it's practical. Nature can help us prevent floods, dampen tidal waves, filter water, and clean the air. Engineers— not just environmentalists—are increasingly recognizing nature as a way to provide essential services we otherwise would trust to machines and concrete and steel. It actually has a term devoted to it: green infra-structure. Nature provides many 'services' to us when left in its natural state. For example, it saves our lives and communities in times of natural disaster. Flooding and storm surges can be softened, if not stopped, by wetlands and marshes that absorb the brunt of the impact. When British authorities built seawalls to protect against annual floods in the Humber Estuary in Yorkshire and in Lincolnshire, they inadvertently killed off the wetlands that had formed natural barriers. So when flood waters hit, the walls held back some water but, without the wetlands to block the storm surge, flooding was actually worse. To solve the problem, seawalls have now been deliberately breached so that the wetlands can return to their natural state, a move that will create around $18 million of net benefit over the next fifty years in terms of saved farmland and property compared to the damage the standing sea wall would have led to.[23] In Boston the Army Corps of Engineers found that annual flooding of the Charles River would cost $17 million a year if not for wetlands protecting the city.[24] Wetlands can be particularly crucial during extreme events: a long-standing rule of thumb holds that for every 2.7 miles of wetlands, a hurricane storm surge can be reduced by as much as a foot.[25] When Hurricane Katrina hit New Orleans in 2005, it found a city built out too far to the ocean's edge, with nineteen hundred square miles of natural wetlands having been destroyed and developed between true land and the Gulf of Mexico.[26] Without these natural shock absorbers, the flooding wasn't just destructive; it was devastating. Thankfully some wetlands were still intact; scientists estimate that if there had been none left, the flood waters would have been three to six feet higher.[27]

Although some environmentalists might scoff at putting a price on nature, not to do so is to completely devalue it and let others take advantage—and destroy—its enormous wealth. Depleting natural resources might not cost money, but it isn't 'free.' Take, for example, the conversion of mangrove swamps in southern Thailand into shrimp farms. One report found that such conversions yield around $1,220 a hectare. But these profits fail to consider the costs of losing the mangroves. After five years the farm is depleted, requiring intensive and expensive rehabilitation. And while they are being used as shrimp farms, the mangrove swamps fail to provide wood for local communities, nurseries for local fish farming, and a barrier against storms. In total, one study found the implicit costs equal $12,392 a hectare, over ten times more than the profits reaped from shrimp farming.[28] Yet because the costs are borne by the 'public' while the profits are earned privately, the decision was a foregone conclusion: profits were made, natural capital was lost, the community suffered. The argument—and a compelling plan—for rigorously accounting for nature is brilliantly set out in *Natural Capital*, the latest book published by economist Dieter Helm (my tutor at Oxford). Simply implementing his approach would make more practical difference than any number of international environmental conferences.

Nature doesn't only mitigate the impacts of future disasters; it also provides us with essential services every day, often cheaper and more reliably than man-made infrastructure can. In Maine about 15 percent of the population, mostly in the greater Portland area, gets its water from Sebago Lake. The lake covers thirty thousand acres, and the area that supplies it is more than fifty miles long.[29] Because of the area's pristine condition, the Portland Water District has long operated under a federal waiver allowing it to draw its water without many of the typical filtration requirements that are otherwise necessary in other geographies. Recently, though, the lake's water quality has deteriorated, as runoff from upstream land development and population growth has increased. The typical approach would be to invest in 'gray' infrastructure, so-called because of the color of the excessive cement usually involved—in this case, 'membrane filtration' technology. An analysis by the World Resources Institute found that this would cost between $102 million and $146 million. Investing instead in conservation and restoration of the surrounding forest ecosystem—green infrastructure—at a cost of between $34 million and $74 million would deliver $70 million in savings.[30] It turns out that natural forest land is just more efficient at keeping our water clean (one study estimates that for every 10 percent increase in forest cover in a source area, there is a corresponding decrease of about 20 percent in water treatment costs[31]). And yet our human habits, Australian ecological economist Robert Costanza estimates, destroy $23 trillion each year of the $142.7 trillion in these 'services' our natural ecosystems provide us—not just clean air and water and storm protection but also waste decomposition, crop pollination, renewable energy sources, and raw materials, to name a few.[32]

DESPITE THESE POWERFUL arguments, the environmental movement is losing. People understand what they can see, hear, touch, and smell. At that level I think most people really do care about the environment, even if they hate green politics and can't stand talk of climate change. I've yet to meet someone who is in favor of dirty air and water, dead forests, or poisoned landscapes. Or someone who doesn't enjoy, if they get the chance, spending time in the mountains, at a lake, or at the beach. Behavior that could be described as 'environmentalist' is really just showing our love of nature. Pretty much everyone is in favor of that. But by branding and politicizing environmentalism, we've made good stewardship a question of saving the entire planet: an unrelatable idea.

So although our local actions do indeed have global impacts, these impacts have to be talked about at the human scale, otherwise their real meaning becomes obscure. Climate change doesn't mean 'global sea-level rise' (though this may happen); it means that farmers lose their crops and livelihoods, entire species of animals and plants are lost forever, and the sea will wipe out centuries-old villages.

The other problem with the big global-environmental argument is that it diffuses responsibility. Elinor Ostrom won the Nobel Prize in economics for demonstrating the tragedy of the commons, in which behavior that benefits the individual at the group's expense leads to everyone doing it until the whole group is out of luck. This phenomenon is exacerbated when problems are made to seem big; the individual actions we take to both create and to solve the problems have the illusion of insignificance. Noble as fighting for 'parts per million' is, it just doesn't mean anything if you're not a scientist. We have to make sure nature is accessible to everyone so everyone can have their own experiences, their own memories to draw from, their own reason to care that we don't destroy it all.

As much as the communications revolution—not to mention high-definition television—has enabled us to more vividly experience exotic ecosystems and animals across the world, there is no substitute for the real thing. The key to making us environmentalists, conservationists, good stewards—or, really, just conscientious human beings—is exposure to what we otherwise wouldn't care about. So the answer to the threat to nature is not a new law, a new government program, an ad campaign, or any of the other traditional levers of bureaucratic action; it's something more human than all of that. It's the simple act of being in nature, walking in nature, playing in nature, getting out into nature, seeing the world's wonder. When you begin to comprehend your place on the planet in the midst of everyone and everything else, it all suddenly comes into perspective. But of course, this theme has been true throughout the book: empathy through human connection and experience.

This is what politicians and conservationists have got wrong. Although often well meaning, their efforts have morphed the environmental movement into Big Green, the bureaucracy and politics of which have needlessly made the environment a contested and partisan issue. The environment should not be a battlefield of Democrats versus Republicans; it's actually about loving the world we live in, our home. People—all people—want blue skies and clean air and safe water, but you'll never convince people to be greener if you make it all about carbon dioxide or a couple of degrees Celsius or Fahrenheit. We have to highlight how nature can actually, tangibly help us in our own daily lives. 'Green' means animals, parks, the countryside. It's about where people want to go on vacation or spend free time with their families. It's about the joy of fresh air and beautiful scenery.

"SHOPPING IS NOT A HOBBY"

Connecting people with nature will become ever more urgent as humanity continues to urbanize. Since 1950 the urban population has increased from 30 percent of the global population to 54 percent today, and it is expected to reach 66 percent by 2050.[33] Cities represent a prosperous and, in some respects, more sustainable future. But for all its modern, hipster vibe, urbanization comes with a significant drawback: the more we live in cities, the further we are from nature and the closer we get to forgetting its importance altogether. We risk what some are calling "nature deficit disorder."[34]

But how do you persuade people to change? At the moment we fail miserably at distilling nature into human terms, resulting in dangerous abstraction. We need to bring people's interaction with nature back to a human, visceral level. Nature must be experienced by the human touch.

But getting people into nature is a big hurdle. I've seen it firsthand. When I grew up, spending time in nature was not the social norm. Now, here in Northern California, where it is very much part of the culture, I've chosen, for the first time in my life, to do strange things for a confirmed urbanite—like go camping. Camping! How horrific. Actually not. It is no exaggeration to say that our children and their friends are never happier than when they are out in the woods or wherever we go in nature. It is cheaper—and better—than any number of toys or trips to theme parks or visitor attractions.

That's why we should start with children. It's not just about a respect for and understanding of the natural world, its importance to us, and the necessity of sustainability and conservation. It also helps child development. Children need to engage in the world if they are to be properly educated. As we saw in Chapter 10, a significant part of their development comes from exploration and adventure, and there is no better place to do that than out in nature.

Many parents understand this but don't know how to go about it. There are too many barriers to getting their children into nature, many of which are simply inherent in our inhuman world today: families live too far away from natural spaces, parents have unrealistic fears of the outdoors, teachers lack enthusiasm for leaving the classroom, technology too easily entertains and distracts.[35] The key is to start the process early, with a proper communication of the interconnection between nature and society. Jason and Scott fondly remember their grandparents sending them the magazines *Your Big Backyard* and *Ranger Rick*, published by the National Wildlife Federation, which, by helping them understand the importance of nature as children, made them lifelong environmentalists. Those magazines worked because they explained nature in children's terms.

The same principle guides author Christiane Dorion, who has developed a creative way to communicate complex environmental and scientific concepts through her pop-up children's books. "Children are naturally interested in the natural world," she explains, so she tries to identify "the questions they are interested in learning about." And it turns out that children are indeed fascinated by the water cycle and weather patterns—just not when described in those words. Instead, Dorion poses questions that children have actually asked her: Where does rain come from? What's inside the earth? How do plants live? She then answers them in surprisingly rich detail while keeping it all age accessible. They might not understand biodiversity loss or climate change, but they come to intuit how small things in their lives connect directly to a wider world.[36]

If applied correctly, technology, like Dorion's books, can play a helpful role too. Researchers at Stanford, MIT, and Harvard are working on various projects to create virtual-reality simulators that put users directly into otherwise inaccessible natural circumstances. One simulation created at Stanford transforms users into a pink coral so they can see what happens to reefs over time. During the simulation sea urchins, sea snails, and fish interact around 'you.' Over the course of thirteen minutes the simulation progresses through a century, and the environment changes around the reef as it is degraded by acidification, an urgent problem currently facing all the world's oceans.[37] Species present at the start disappear, and even the pink coral skeleton that the users embody disintegrates. Early studies suggest that conveying the gravity of human effects on the environment in such a personal way has a significant impact on attitudes, which the researchers confirmed in follow-ups with participants afterward.[38] "One can viscerally experience disparate futures and get firsthand experience about the consequences of human behavior," says Jeremy Bailenson, the director of Stanford's Virtual Human Interaction Lab, which ran the simulation.[39] And with the advent of virtual-reality headsets like Oculus VR, zoos, parks, and schools can increasingly use these technologies to complement their real-world programs.

The studies done around virtual reality prove that we need to empathize with nature to care about it. But it's also pretty ridiculous that we have to reduce nature to a virtual-reality headset. All the book learning in the world won't change the simple fact that children need to touch nature for themselves. It must be palpable, emotional, and experienced firsthand. That's why programs like Vida Verde are so crucial to this effort.

Vida Verde is an educational camp and organic farm in California's Santa Cruz Mountains dedicated to getting children from all backgrounds into nature. "There are thousands of children who live thirty miles from the ocean, and they've never actually seen it," explains Laura Sears, who founded the organization with her husband, Shawn, in 2001. "We've seen kids who come to Vida Verde who've never spent time walking on uneven surfaces." Shawn and Laura bring groups of children from different inner-city schools in the San Francisco area for three days and two nights to their twenty-three-acre property. The children learn experientially, classifying plants and animals on walks, learning about mammals whilst milking the resident goats and learning about birds while collecting hens' eggs, and understanding the sea while running barefoot in the sand (many for the first time in their lives) or exploring rock pools—all in the same lesson, of course. "It's a beautiful thing to let these children start to discover and explore and let their guard down," Laura says, "and just be in this gorgeous environment that they maybe never thought they'd ever get to be in."

"Kids do really well being outside, using all their senses and bodies to learn, not just reading something or hearing it," Shawn explains. Being there and doing it makes it real for them. For the first time they can really connect to the place where they live, and their teachers can use this in the classroom from there on to connect lessons to real life. Teachers report that children engage in their studies as they haven't in the past. Perhaps more importantly than this, nature can be harnessed as a tool for teaching very human lessons about relationships, trying new things, determination, and working together. In one activity, the goat hike, small groups of students use teamwork to herd resident goats across a river, through the thistles, and up a mile-long hill on a steep, sometimes tricky path. "It's a physical challenge. They simply have to work together to make it," says Shawn. "You see students who don't necessarily talk or hang out with each other otherwise doing it because it's needed. People just breaking down and treating each other like human beings—and walking away from the experience with fresh eyes for those around them and new friends."[40] Such programs are so important. Jason and Scott— Northern Californians themselves—remember that when they were sixth graders (they're twins), everyone in their grade went to a place like Vida Verde, where many of them camped for the first time. They spent a week hiking, exploring marshland, running basic experiments in the forest, not to mention growing emotionally by being away from their parents for the first time. Nearly every public school in the region participates in such programs, providing a valuable link to nature for countless schoolchildren.

You can predict the objections. "Well, that's all very well if you live in Northern California in one of the richest and most naturally beautiful places on earth, but what about the real world where you don't have incredible nature on your doorstep? Or incredible wealth to preserve it? Or incredibly rich families who can pay to send their kids to experience it?"

Well, here's the thing: none of this is preordained or determined by geography, finances, or anything else. It's about priorities.

At the moment, across the world, consumerism is the social norm and nature is not. We choose to build Westfield shopping centers. Why? Why do we need more of those? Why do we think it's acceptable for children to spend a weekend afternoon going shopping? As my sister-in-law, Kate Whetstone, once pithily remarked, "Shopping is not a hobby." But for many people in rich countries today, that's exactly what it is. We can change that. The norm has certainly flipped before: when workers spent most of their time in the fields, bronzed by the sun, the elite stayed inside. But with the advent of the factory and then the office cubicle, that norm switched. Once workers' skins grew pale under artificial lights, the rich jumped at any chance they could to develop a tan, setting themselves apart—the 'leisure' class. Now people with money buy homes in the country, houses by the beach, lodges in the mountains, villas on the lake. The rich have made nature fashionable, with eco-tourism and luxury brands and philanthropy. They wouldn't think of keeping their kids inside all the time. But the outdoors shouldn't be a function of fashion; it should be something everyone enjoys from the richest to poorest, that everyone rightly feels entitled to experience as a human, without stigma.

We must choose to make this a priority; we must choose to collectively pay for it; we must choose to require it. Nature should be a fundamental part of our human experience. More than anything else, nature should unify us.

But right now it divides us. The second you suggest that everyone else should get better access to nature, it's suddenly just that—a luxury, a waste of money that we can't afford—because, gosh, what would happen to those SAT scores? Why? Why is nature a necessity for rich people but a luxury for poor people? Why is nature less important for students than math or art or history?

ONE OF THE many reasons I would love to be mayor of a city is to show what can happen when we take a radically different—a revolutionarily different—approach to land use. When it comes to the physical presence of nature in our lives, we could easily incorporate woodlands and wetlands and natural habitats right in the middle of our towns and cities. Not just parks, but real, wild nature. There are some great examples: in Los Angeles I visited the Ballona Wetlands near Playa del Rey. Here, where you'd least expect it—in bustling LA, surrounded by a highway to the east, private homes to the south, a strip mall to the north, and a tourist beach to the west—are six hundred acres of open space that state officials are trying to restore to their former glory. The wetlands here once stretched for miles in either direction up and down the coast but were carved out into developments around fifty years ago. Even in Ballona there is hardly any wetland left. For centuries Berliners have enjoyed the Grunewald forest, covering more than seven thousand acres in the western part of the German capital. In Knoxville, Tennessee, locals recently championed the preservation of one thousand acres of forest along the Tennessee River waterfront. Just three miles from downtown, residents and visitors there can use its more than forty miles of trails to walk, mountain bike, run, or just explore. In London, Hampstead Heath comprises 790 acres of rambling hills and woodland, dearly loved by dogs and visitors alike. And of course, there's New York's Central Park.

But these are exceptions. How about designing a world where they're not?

If we do make space for nature in the midst of our modern world, how do we make sure children grow up in it, not through a once-a-year field trip, but all the time? Well, we know exactly how to do it—we just need to make the choice. There are countless national and local organizations, notably the Scouts, dedicated to giving children fun experiences in nature. We could easily make nature an expectation for every child, just as we expect them to learn math or, now, coding. It's actually more important than either of those or any other academic subject because the kinds of experiences you gain when you spend time in nature, with others, help build your character in ways that are far more useful in the twenty-first century than anything academic.[41] But instead we insist on locking children up in windowless, soulless boxes from eight in the morning for the rest of the day. Madness. But amidst the strange priorities that have infected today's world, the argument I'm making—that we should expect all children to spend time in nature as a basic, substantial part of their education—is more likely to be seen as crazy.

Nature must be made more accessible in another way too. Remember North Carolina park ranger Matthew Browning and the twelve-year-old boy he saw being chastised for playing in nature? The way things stand now, nature is a museum, where we can look but not touch. How do we expect to get excited about nature if we can't engage with it? The typical sheltered life of the twenty-first-century family might make us feel safer, but we are not better off as a result. We cannot survive without nature; we are inextricably linked. Nature is not harmless, but it is far from harmful. We must engage with it, understand it, and raise our children in it. And if we do, not only will we improve everyone's happiness and well-being today, but we will also do something much more significant: we will bring up a generation of people who really understand and respect nature and humanity's place within it.

Because when it comes to the natural world around us, it's time we were a little bit . . . less human.

CONCLUSION

THIS BOOK HAS ranged across many aspects of life. From food to government, the economy to health care. But what about the essence of our humanity—our relationships with one another? How do we make those more human as well?

To be human is to love, to accept, and to empathize with each other, but it seems as if it is just as human to hate, ostracize, and blame. Witness the ethnic, sectarian, and nationalist tensions across the globe today. For as much progress as we've made, we still live in a world of the scapegoat, of the 'other'—whether that's Mexicans being blamed for economic ills in America or all Muslims being blamed for the thoughts and actions of some.

Lack of mutual understanding can lead to grave injustices, civil unrest, and even tragedy—witness here in America the gross disparity between violent deaths afflicting black and white populations. When differences fester, as is happening around the world, we see something worse: terrorism, war, and genocide.

ONE OF THE greatest instances of human suffering today is the global crisis of refugees. Driven mostly from the interminable Syrian civil war as well as instability and chaos in the wider Middle East and strife in Iraq, Afghanistan, Africa, and central Asia, millions are displaced and living in camps, hundreds of thousands of refugees have made their way toward Europe, tens of thousands have crossed through it, and thousands have died in transit.

Some politicians welcome Syrian refugees, but many citizens resist, creating a political crisis on top of a humanitarian one. We have seen the worst of humanity: children drowning on beaches, smugglers leaving their charges to die in trucks and boats—but also immigrants abusing their welcome in disgusting ways. We have seen the best, too: governments inviting refugees in, humanitarians rescuing the distressed, and

townspeople welcoming the tired with food, water, song, applause—
even into their own homes. These good Samaritans exemplify the best
of humanity, a common spirit of empathy, solidarity, and hope. Although
refugees cannot be allowed in without limit, the West has a responsibility to do its part.

THE CONFLICTS IN the Middle East and Africa and the ensuing refugee crisis are not about to end; they are only going to get worse. There will
be more Syrias. National leaders, the foreign-policy establishment, the
NGOs, and the UN must take true responsibility. For over four years the
international community dithered when it came to Syria, letting the
civil war there smolder. Countries across the Middle East are collapsing
upon themselves, the chaos partly the result of either our cack-handed
intervention or the lack of any intervention at all. There is no perfect
solution, and yet somehow the international community waits for one,
imparting half-measures that accomplish nothing. Powerful countries
cannot engage in the world and then retreat from it when their actions
have unintended consequences. Moreover, this fight is not simply a 'conventional' war for land or power; it is a fight against grave evil committed
both in the Middle East and across the world. ISIS, like Boko Haram in
Nigeria or the al-Shabab in Somalia, is a group that is perpetrating un-
speakable barbarism, especially on women and children; a group whose
thirst for brutality is equal to that of the worst twentieth-century dicta-
tors. That kind of terrorism is the nadir of our humanity. That is why the
fight against it is moral, however long and grueling. Although we cannot
be sure of any military campaign's success, sometimes, when fighting to
salvage humanity from itself, the fight is all there is.

We have to create the space for the reform of Islam that is so clearly
necessary. To start, we can take oxygen away from its sources in places
like Saudi Arabia and especially Qatar. That our allies in these countries
also promote the most extreme religious fundamentalism—and even on
occasion its most violent manifestation—should not be allowed to continue just because it is diplomatically convenient. We have to build up
the positive version of Islam. We have to ask ourselves: how do we help
create Islamic societies more like Indonesia, the world's largest Muslim
country, where Nahdlatul Ulama, the world's largest Islamic group, has
launched a campaign against the ideology that ISIS represents? As that
campaign seeks to do, fighting ISIS means delegitimizing Caliphism at
home and abroad.

Then, we need an aggressive effort to advance the basics of a decent human life, an inoculation against extremism: basics that have always and are everywhere underpinned by the institutions of a market economy and a free society: property rights, the rule of law, an independent judiciary, a free press, accountable democratic processes. The lack of these institutions is at the root of many of the problems that beset us.

Reactionaries from Putin in Russia to Erdogan in Turkey have proposed an alternative narrative, erecting authoritarian 'illiberal states.' They posit that not every country should be a democracy or a market economy. But there is no society that doesn't need accountability, representation, or the rule of law. There is no people that doesn't deserve to rule themselves. Living in a liberal society, in the form of democracy and a market economy, is the right of every person. These are the most human ways to order our lives.

So we must double down and insist on them, using every weapon in our military, political, economic, diplomatic, and cultural arsenals. Just because the West invented democracy and markets doesn't make them exclusively ours. It is our human responsibility—not to mention in our own self-interest—to help spread them around the world. We must insist that all people everywhere are accorded the basic human rights due to them. We must incentivize leaders—even the most recalcitrant—to adopt the institutions that are the foundation of true human flourishing, and if they refuse, we must try harder, use more pressure. Never stop until it's done and we ensure that every citizen everywhere enjoys the birthrights we take for granted. It would be impractical to 'take down' every dictatorship or antidemocratic regime, but we at least have a moral imperative to stop shielding them.

Diplomats, economists, and NGO do-gooders have been addressing these issues for years, of course. They have had some successes. But their failures have been glaring. Concerned more with decorum and political correctness than on-the-ground results, they have let down too many people in too many places, allowing their noble intentions to protect them from critical accountability. Our engagement must be based on what actually works, and that means listening to how people—citizens and rulers alike—actually behave and respond to our efforts and then adjusting them until we get it right. Just as such human-centered approaches are vital to the design of—as we've seen in this book—baby incubators or urban spaces, the same care, humility, and empathy must be applied to building the most fundamental of democratic institutions, even when starting from scratch.

Anthropologist Scott Atran has spent years immersing himself among what many would consider our very worst enemies: Western youth who have joined ISIS. Testifying before the UN Security Council, he insists that the key to stopping young people from self-radicalization is to deeply empathize with them. It doesn't mean agreeing with them. It means recognizing that although there is no archetype for an extremist, we will only be able to prevent the arrival of what will almost surely be a next generation of terrorists if we first understand what motivates them to the brink.

Only when we have overcome the blind spot that has brought a seemingly distant war to the hearts of our cities can we create an alternative narrative that engenders the same passion and dedication that leads them to ISIS. We are losing some of our young people at their most vulnerable moments, and as much as we must stop those who prey upon them, we must also work to address the causes of their disillusionment, be they moral, economic, or social. In the West, especially in countries like France and Belgium where young Muslims feel apart from society, Caliphism (through ISIS) provides a way to express agency over their own lives. Yes, we need to humiliate the source of their misplaced inspiration. But more than that, we need to give them an alternative hope.

AS WE WORK to bring marginalized people and societies everywhere into the fold, we must remember that helping others build up their own capacity to help themselves requires tremendous humility. Along with our insistence that all countries are free and fair, we have to listen closely to their people to truly understand what that means for them. We have to be nimble. We have to be respectful. But we do have to be persistent.

Sometimes fulfilling those obligations will come in grand gestures and actions; sometimes, in order to enforce civilized norms and uphold international order, we will need to impose sanctions on other countries—or at the very least on their leaders. But where possible we should look to bolster ways of relating to one another that avoid conflict and reduce strife. Not just economic ties but also things like the informal diplomacy between academics, artists, students, civil-society groups, and tourists in countries around the world, including rogue states like North Korea, Iran, Russia, and China. Exchanges, visits and conferences—personal, human contact—should underpin important international relationships. When world leaders spend time at summits, they don't just negotiate; they also develop rapports that can enhance future relations and nip brewing crises in the bud.

Despite the supposed urgency to discuss other matters, our leaders must never lose sight of what is truly important. In the short term, trade and security cooperation can easily seem like overriding priorities. But for long-term economic success and long-term security, the rule of law, human rights, and the institutions of a market economy and a free society matter more—and Western leaders must remind autocrats of their necessity at every possible moment. We've tried patience with countries like China (and Russia and Saudi Arabia) and yet too often let other considerations get in the way. We are lucky to live in countries that are wealthy, powerful, free, and safe all at the same time. We must not shirk the responsibilities those privileges entail.

GIVEN THE DEPTH and breadth of problems across the globe, supporters of human understanding might look at the world today and sink into despair, wondering whether we have learned anything from the horrors of our past. But the terrible version of ourselves that we see in all those wartorn, chaotic, or even just economically depressed places is not the whole truth about us. It is the anxious us, the ignorant us, the fearful us. And the funny thing is that although rhetorically or theoretically we might blame someone else for our problems—the immigrant or the minority—in practice, on a day-to-day basis, in our real human lives, we do not.

In America successive waves of immigrants have faced racist and xenophobic treatment only to be accepted once they start integrating into society and Americans realize they are perfectly decent people. Proximity and contact are, thus, the ultimate antidotes against insularity and prejudice, a point proven by the steady evolution of public opinion on gay rights. It turns out that once people realize that one of their neighbors, friends, colleagues, or relatives is gay, their homophobia turns into tolerance and then acceptance and then comradeship. It's easy to hate strangers on TV and in faraway parades; it's much harder to hate a group to which your son or daughter belongs. Republicans have traditionally been dead set against gay marriage and other gay rights, but several leading party members have come out in favor of both, almost solely because of their personal experiences. Former vice president Dick Cheney, a stalwart conservative, prominently broke with his boss President George W. Bush on the issue of gay marriage out of concern for his lesbian daughter,

Mary. More recently Republican Senator Rob Portman, a former member of President Bush's cabinet, changed his position on gay marriage when his son came out. He said that learning his son was gay caused him to examine his stance "from a new perspective, and that's of a dad who loves his son a lot and wants him to have the same opportunities that his brother and sister would have—to have a relationship like Jane [Portman's wife] and I have had for over 26 years."[1]

When confronted on their prejudices by their own children, people tend to evolve and overcome them; after all, if you can't empathize with your child, who can you empathize with? Gay people are relatively blessed with the fact that anyone might be gay; even ardent homophobes might end up with a lesbian cousin or a gay nephew. But for those of different ethnic, racial, national, and religious backgrounds, such genetic serendipity is impossible. And although we have come further than ever before in human history, we need to push ourselves to always engage with those who are different.

Being more human with one another is crucial to bridging cultural divides and living in a more peaceful world. If we are to be a successful global society, this is imperative. But it's sometimes much more basic than that. We need to ask ourselves what it is to interact with each other meaningfully on a daily basis. Civility is not just for the advice columns; it is incumbent upon us all to practice it. And in a world in which technology has rapidly changed social interactions, litigating technology's role would be a good start. As we have seen, mobile phones and the Internet have fundamentally altered how we communicate with each other, for good and for bad. Technology helps us learn in our own time, with courses customized to our needs. Mobile phones give parents the comfort of letting their children push the boundaries of independence. And Skype connects distant friends and relatives across oceans, time zones, and continents. Through the advent of big data, we now have more capacity to understand and control our own existences than ever before. But technology has its problems. It can be manipulated by nefarious actors, like terrorists seeking impressionable recruits. It has led to the scourge of preteen and teenage sexting. It is changing our neurology. Perhaps most importantly, it is changing how we live our lives. Too many people, it seems, now live not for the moment but for the 'likes' and 'retweets'; they would too often rather hang out online than in person. Staying connected to others is wonderful, but not if its cost is disconnecting from reality and actual people.

IN TECHNOLOGY AS in so many other areas, you could say, "No, the status quo is human." You could ask, as we did at the beginning of this book: Why is a world designed by humans not already, by definition, 'more human'? Well, in much the same way that all the social-science theories that explain human behavior as rational fail to take into account our own irrationalities, our institutions fail to live up to their own standards too. Sometimes when we created our institutions, we simply didn't know what was or wasn't human. Behavioral science is a rather novel field, and until recently many of us really did believe that people were perfectly rational. But because we weren't—and still aren't—even our 'rational' institutions turn out imperfectly. We fell victim to the hubris—another human trait—that we could outsmart nature, that we could outsmart even ourselves. Cities were built based on how planners believed we should live, not how we actually would. Education systems were designed based on how we once thought children learned and what they needed for success, not on what actually matters now and for the future. That's why it's so important to embrace the science—the human insights—in fields like behavioral economics, neuroscience, psychology, and biology that allows us better to know ourselves, better to pinpoint interventions, and better to help people flourish.

That's not to say that we shouldn't theorize or experiment until we get it right—tinkering is human too, after all—but we should understand the limits of designing any system, product, service, or environment without connecting with the people who will be involved in it on a daily basis as consumers, providers, recipients, residents, patients, or students. We are on the cusp of transcending 'just theory' in many fields simply because we increasingly have easy access to all the data.

We must also remember that everything is interconnected: children don't just need good families, wholesome play, and limits on mobile Internet-enabled devices; they also need livable homes and safe streets, access to nature, and food and schools not made in or designed as factories. For our economy to flourish, we need to not only treat workers as humans, require fair competition, and enable people to fulfill their potential but also plan for the long term, combat poverty at its roots, better educate our future workforce, and lessen the stranglehold of special interests over our regulatory regimes.

As we saw, some themes are woven throughout. Although we must be wary of technology, we must also allow for its near-limitless possibilities. And we must remember that the importance of families pervades every

issue, from education to poverty to jobs to inequality, which is why government should redouble its efforts at early and comprehensive family
interventions.

MORE—OR LESS—HUMAN?

In this book I've argued that more human values, scale, design, products,
and policies are all good things; that we should aspire to make everything
in our lives as human as possible. I've just argued for a revolution in doing so. But although we know what a more human world would mostly
look like, there's an interesting exception emerging, a field in which, as
it gets more human, the result is more *inhuman*.

This is the field of robotics and artificial intelligence. Artificial intelligence (AI), simply defined, is the field of trying to create intelligence
synthetically. We already have many basic versions of it, from IBM's Watson to Apple's Siri to Google's self-driving cars. Perhaps the ultimate expression of AI is the "singularity" hypothesis, which as articulated by fu-
turist Ray Kurzweil predicts "the union of human and machine, in which
the knowledge and skills embedded in our brains will be combined with
the vastly greater capacity, speed, and knowledge-sharing ability of our
own creations."[2]

If this sounds like science fiction, you're right. But excitingly—or
alarmingly, depending on your view—reality is in many ways already
catching up with science fiction. Think about Steven Spielberg's 2002
film *Minority Report*. Although our world doesn't yet resemble his, we
have developed many of the technologies his characters use, like automated cars, facial-recognition software, personalized advertising, predic-
tive crime fighting (they used mutated psychics called precogs; we use
big data and analytics), gesture-based computer interfaces, and even jet
packs.[3] As exciting as that may be, it also means that the future is arriving
sooner than we think. And we have to determine what we want it to look
like.

Technological optimists like Kurzweil and Google's Larry Page believe
that automation and robotics will free us up for more human endeav-
ors. There is certainly a good argument for this. Maybe AI is simply tomorrow's version of a mundane task that can be automated. We don't
fear our washing machines—why fear whatever's coming next? As Rollo
Carpenter, the founder of AI software firm Cleverbot, says, "We cannot
quite know what will happen if a machine exceeds our own intelligence,

so we can't know if we'll be infinitely helped by it, or ignored by it and sidelined, or conceivably destroyed by it . . . I believe we will remain in charge of the technology for a decently long time and the potential of it to solve many of the world's problems will be realized."[4] For some roboticists, replacing people has never been the goal. "There are seven billion people in the world, and almost all of them are very good at being people," says Helen Greiner, cofounder of iRobot, which made the Roomba vacuum-cleaning robot, and CEO of CyPhyWorks. "We're not trying to duplicate people. We're trying to help them; make them more efficient, better at their jobs; empower them to do more with robotic technology."[5] To naturalist and science writer Diane Ackerman, "Surpassing human limits is so human a quest, maybe the most ancient one of all,"[6] and AI is simply the next limit. Indeed, pushing the boundaries of AI might be one of the most human things we can do. In her latest book, *The Human Age,* she writes,

> I find it touchingly poetic to think that as our technology grows more advanced, we may grow more human. When labor, science, manufacturing, sales, transportation, and powerful new technologies are mainly handled by savvy machines, humans really won't be able to compete in those sectors of the economy. Instead we may dominate an economy of interpersonal or imaginative services, in which our human skills shine.[7]

On the other side of the argument, technological pessimists like Elon Musk and Stephen Hawking believe that for every great technological advance, we take a step toward human obsolescence. "With artificial intelligence, we are summoning the demon," Musk says. "You know all those stories where there's the guy with the pentagram and the holy water and . . . he's sure he can control the demon. It doesn't work out."[8] For example, scientists are building robots that can literally feed (power) themselves: engineers at Bristol Robotics Laboratory are building the EcoBot III, which can convert flies into fuel, and the US Defense Department–funded EATR (energetically autonomous tactical robot) uses cameras and sensors to find organic matter like leaves, which it can then pick up and burn as fuel.[9] Perhaps while robots perform mundane tasks, this is perfectly fine, but what happens when we can't stop a robot from overpowering us because we've taught it to power itself? These pessimists fear that, at best, AI will supplant jobs—fueling inequality by leaving the working class with nowhere to go—and challenge the boundary between life and artificiality. But at their worst they fear the very supplanting of humanity as a species. "The development of full artificial intelligence," Hawking warns, "could spell the end of the human race."[10]

We therefore have to ask ourselves real questions about AI's potential impact. In the short term, artificial intelligence could cause inequality on a massive scale, more even than we have seen so far with automation, globalization, and family disparities. It could permanently lock out huge segments of society from the economy. Today robots enhance things we can't do, like compute, position us by using satellites, perform danger-ous tasks, connect to a grid. They are largely unthreatening. But what if computers start to do what we've thought of as essentially human tasks— thinking critically, creating, caring, or applying values and reason? What if computers become more like us?

And what if they become more like us but lack central human qual-ities? "Ultimately," writes Sherry Turkle, whose life's work has involved human interactions with machines, "the question is not whether chil-dren will love their robotic pets more than their animal pets, but rather, what loving will come to mean. [Think of] the young woman who was ready to turn in her boyfriend for a 'sophisticated Japanese robot.' Is there a chance that human relationships will just seem too *hard*?"[11]

Perhaps even more profound a question is: What does it mean if robots don't die? In his 2005 commencement speech at Stanford, Apple founder Steve Jobs spoke of death's great power: "Death is very likely the single best invention of Life. It's Life's change agent."[12] Despite Ray Kurzweil's insistence that humans will achieve immortality through biotechnology and advanced medicine, death is, for now, one of humanity's defining traits. Although human qualities like love and death might be the great divider between humans and artificial intelligence, a dearth of such char-acteristics—particularly if robots have many other unfathomable powers and abilities—might be dangerous. What if, like dystopian visions of the future in film and literature, artificial intelligence overtakes us because it exploits those differences or sees them as weaknesses? If it comes down to it, can humans with hearts beat machines with just brains?

THE DEBATE ABOUT artificial intelligence is about not just the future of humanity but its definition. And yet that debate is cloistered in Silicon Valley and biotech and medicine and nanotech; it is not taking place in public forums, in Congress, in the public eye. We hardly know it is happening—how can we have an opinion about it? As futuristic technol-ogies become more and more available, people will want them. Although not all will result in an artificial intelligence per se, new technologies that merge man and machine carry with them vast implications that need to be considered.

Take the work of Hugh Herr, an MIT scientist and engineer who lost both legs below the knee in a rock-climbing accident. He used that accident as inspiration for what has become his life's work. "I reasoned that a human being can never be broken. Technology is broken. Technology is inadequate. This simple but powerful idea was a call to arms to advance technology for the elimination of my own disability and ultimately the disability of others." At his lab at MIT and in his private company Herr has developed incredibly advanced prosthetics that are customized in every sense of the word.

> I began by developing specialized limbs that allowed me to return to the vertical world of rock and ice climbing. I quickly realized that the artificial part of my body is malleable, able to take on any form, any function, a blank slate through which to create perhaps structures that could extend beyond biological capability. I made my height adjustable. I could be as short as five feet or as tall as I'd like. Narrow, wedged feet allowed me to climb steep rock fissures where the human foot cannot penetrate, and spiked feet enabled me to climb vertical ice walls without ever experiencing muscle leg fatigue. Through technological innovation, I returned to my sport stronger and better. Technology had eliminated my disability and allowed me a new climbing prowess.[13]

Herr recognizes the potential to improve our quality of life across the board. He and others have started to experiment with exoskeletons, applying the same technology that has made him a better climber to perfectly healthy people. And although his work is confined to prosthetic limbs, he sees on the horizon relief for all sorts of disabilities and other physical impairments. "It's not well appreciated," he says, "but over half of the world's population suffers from some form of cognitive, emotional, sensory or motor condition, and because of poor technology, too often, conditions result in disability and a poorer quality of life. Basic levels of physiological function should be a part of our human rights. Every person should have the right to live life without disability if they so choose—the right to live life without severe depression; the right to see a loved one in the case of seeing impaired; or the right to walk or to dance, in the case of limb paralysis or limb amputation." And he is optimistic that this will soon come to pass. "We the people need not accept our limitations, but can transcend disability through technological innovation," he says. "Indeed, through fundamental advances in bionics in this century, we will set the technological foundation for an enhanced human experience, and we will end disability." When Rohan and I met him in Cambridge, Massachusetts, it left a profound impression. And the seed of an idea for a policy response.

Ending disability would be great, but how will we grapple with adding extra ability? What will it mean to compete in sport? How much of a human is it ethical to replace? Should we be allowed to amputate limbs to obtain new, artificial ones?

These are all important questions about the rapidly approaching future in AI, robotics, and biotechnology, questions that bring up an important axiom: Just because we can, should we? Elon Musk, along with other Silicon Valley leaders Reid Hoffman, Peter Thiel, and Sam Altman, came together in late 2015 to launch a nonprofit research institute, OpenAI, dedicated to ensuring artificial intelligence is developed in a measured and responsible manner. "We could sit on the sidelines or we can encourage regulatory oversight," said Musk, "or we could participate with the right structure with people who care deeply about developing AI in a way that is safe and is beneficial to humanity."[14] Similarly Stanford University has announced a century-long study of the effects of AI on society.[15] "Artificial intelligence is one of the most profound undertakings in science, and one that will affect every aspect of human life," says Stanford president John Hennessy. "Given Stanford's pioneering role in AI and our interdisciplinary mindset, we feel obliged and qualified to host a conversation about how artificial intelligence will affect our children and our children's children."[16] Hennessy is right: this is a necessary conversation, but it's one we need to bring out in the open. And although Musk and others are providing a healthy counter to the unquestioning attitude of others in Silicon Valley, they're still in Silicon Valley. Stanford is still Silicon Valley. We need more discussion in America as a whole, and we need it to be more informed and more integrated into daily life and debate. I don't know the answer, but I definitely want to do that most human thing: argue about it.

Britain has provided a precedent for situations such as these. After the world's first baby conceived by *in vitro* fertilization (IVF) was born in 1978, the British government assembled a committee in 1982 to examine the ethical considerations of this new advance. The committee, chaired by philosopher Mary Warnock, delivered a report that managed a consensus on the ethical framework for IVF without judging or making

CONCLUSION 283

moral pronouncements.[17] After the report, the government established the Human Fertilisation and Embryology Authority (HFEA) in 1990, a public body that now independently regulates IVF treatment, human embryo research, and human cloning.[18]

AS WE GRAPPLE with the challenging existential questions that artificial intelligence and robotics present, I think we need to establish in America a body like the HFEA to study it intelligently, carefully, delicately, and, above all, publicly. The HFEA has worked precisely because it has not overstepped its bounds and has avoided moralizing, preaching, or presuming to set political priorities. Similarly any such body for AI could be an impartial arbiter to moderate the discussion among our best minds—not just engineers and scientists but also philosophers, ethicists, doctors, and policymakers—making sure that whatever we do, we walk into the future with the best possible knowledge of its implications.

Even if it is on bionic legs.

THE FIRST STEP

IN THIS BOOK I've discussed many changes. Some we can each start doing individually, like spending more time in nature with our children, and others, businesses can make, like choosing to pay a living wage. But most of the changes proposed in this book are things that will have to come from government—even where the change means government doing less or giving its power away. It still needs government to act. That's not surprising: much of my thinking on the issues in this book has taken place either in or preparing for government. It's also how it should be: in a democracy our political system is the only institution that truly represents us—our wishes, our rights, our aspirations. All governments make rules, limit excess, lock up wrongdoers, preserve what should be protected, and forge ahead where progress is needed. Democracies are different, though, in that their legitimacy stems not from force or birthright but from the authority of our votes. That is democracy's promise—and why democracy must be the solution.

But because of people's almost total lack of confidence these days that our political system in America can really change much of anything, I understand that the arguments in the book could seem out of reach. How are we supposed to transform all of these things? Where do we even start? Well . . .

THE FIRST STEP IS FIXING OUR DEMOCRACY

Americans have long taken great pride in their civic participation. Alexis de Tocqueville, the Frenchman who famously chronicled his travels in the early years of the United States, wrote approvingly of the American commitment to local politics: "The cares of political life engross a most prominent place in the occupation of a citizen in the United States, and almost the only pleasure of which an American has any idea is to take a part in the Government, and to discuss the part he has taken."[1] Indeed, it was that spirit of public-mindedness that inspired Americans to come together in the first place to rebel against British rule in the American Revolution. Although they would debate the nature of their republic for decades after the Revolution, eventually Americans concluded that civil society and participatory democracy were the ultimate manifestation of a proper republic.[2] From the early nineteenth century onward it was citizens gathering together who brought about reforms like universal education, the abolition of slavery, and the emancipation of women.

Although democracy is not uniquely American, its development is. In many countries people have the right to vote or speak their mind, but in America validation and vigorous defense of these principles form an intrinsic part of the national identity, a 'civic religion' of freedom, pluralism, and elected government that ties the nation together. Implicit in the American ethos is that regardless of ethnicity, race, religion, or even history, anyone can be American if they uphold and protect these values.

As befits a people whose revolution represented a grand experiment of popular government, Americans have always had a greater definition of what it means to be a citizen in a democracy. Democracy is voting, yes, but it is much more than that. For a democracy to truly function, the citizenry must be informed, must be represented, and must be involved.

Between partisan gridlock and the power of money in politics, American democracy has in some respects fallen behind compared to its peers. But it also has the opportunity to forge a new path in defining democracy for the twenty-first century, to unleash the promise of a new tradition of civic engagement that echoes the one of which de Tocqueville wrote two centuries ago.

ONE WAY IS to broaden our definition of what it means to be active in our communities.

The Park Slope Food Co-Op is a neighborhood grocery store in Brooklyn, New York. My friend Chloe Wasserman, who lives nearby with her family, first took me there around fifteen years ago, and I fell in love with it instantly. Each of its sixteen thousand members contributes to the community by working in the shop once every four weeks for a total of two hours and forty-five minutes in a squad that almost always works together as a close team. Every member must contribute equally in time but can participate in a variety of tasks. All co-op members are entitled

to play a role in the store's governance. Not only is it a close-knit community, but by saving on labor costs, the co-op can provide its members with
high-quality organic, local food at a 20 to 40 percent discount.

What can a grocery store teach us about civic participation? It shows
us that if you humanize the process, members of a community are happy
to give their time to the common good, working alongside others in all
sorts of areas of life, especially if they get something concrete out of it,
like lower grocery costs. But when it comes to community engagement
through the political system, it's a completely dehumanized process:
an anonymous trip to the polling station once every few years and the
payment of local taxes. That's it. No wonder people feel alienated from
politics.

WE COULD CHANGE that. We could strengthen a neighborhood's social fabric by actively bringing residents into the civic sphere through the concept of 'civic service'. This would be a little like jury duty, except more
predictable and regular. Let's identify useful roles in communities that
could be provided by local residents, and then invite—or even require—
them to give two or three hours of service a month, just like the members
of the Park Slope Food Co-Op. It would help people connect with their
neighbors and increase their sense of belonging and social responsibility.

Civic service is a natural, human complement to neighborhood government. The aim should be to make local service a social norm, make it
easier to do by specifying the time, place, and people to do it with, and offer some kind of tangible incentive, such as perhaps a small discount on
local taxes. Even with a compulsory version of civic service, which might
seem extreme, just as with the Park Slope Food Co-Op, if the benefits are
clear and the social connections strong, people will love it; they will love
being of service and love the engagement with their neighborhood and
their community.

Of course, civic service is an idea that calls for experimentation. In
his terrific book on civic innovation, *Citizenville*, Gavin Newsom writes
about Manor, Texas, which used an innovative gaming and points system to encourage civic service. The authorities there created a mobile
game app in which residents earn points for participation, like submit-
ting ideas to improve the city. A suggestion gets one thousand 'Inno-
bucks,' and its adoption and implementation earns one hundred thousand. These points weren't a real currency, but they did allow residents
to access perks within the city, like police ride-alongs or discounts at

local retailers.[3] Although Newsom concedes that gaming is a strange way to organize a voluntary service system, it is actually an expression of human-centered design. "We have to meet the people where they are," writes Newsom. "And where they are right now is playing games and spending time on social-networking sites."[4] Rather than compete with faceless avatars, Manor's residents competed with their neighbors—for bragging rights over who was the most active citizen.

Let's shift that kind of thinking one step further—not just expressing an opinion about how things should be run but getting involved directly, a couple of hours a month. That's what I mean by civic service. Even if it was compulsory, getting people physically—not just politically—engaged in local services would make them feel more committed. Civic service needn't—and shouldn't—feel like a chore. By meeting people where they are, letting people choose how they serve, and making it enjoyable, local governments can infuse duty with passion.

FOR A SYSTEM of government that has increasingly lost the trust of its own people, simple, human, practical involvement of this kind would be a small step toward rehabilitation. But there's something else we can do. Something you can do.

It goes right back to the first chapter of this book: politics. Fixing our democracy is the first step in moving toward a more human world. We need to take power out of the hands of the big-money donors and the big unions and big businesses and put it back where it belongs—in the hands of the people. End the stranglehold of the political machines on the left and right. Make it easier for more independent and independent-minded candidates to run for office. Give people confidence that it's worth getting involved. Make the representatives we have, actually represent us. As long as the same people control the conversation in city hall, the state house, or Washington, things will stay the same. So we need more grassroots, interactive, accountable politics. We need to make politics more human.

That's where you come in. If you agree with the ideas in this book and want to see them happen, I can tell you exactly what you need to do. You won't necessarily like the answer, but I'm going to tell you anyway.

Of course it means backing candidates for elected office—especially state and local—who are truly committed to change, to overthrowing the systems of governance that have helped precipitate the problems we face today. But the trouble is, there aren't enough such candidates. So, you need to run for office. Run for your city council. Run for mayor. Run for the state legislature.

If that's too scary, run for something more low key—school board or parks commission. But one way or another, get your hands on the levers of power. If enough of us do it, we can really change things. One independent-minded person who wants to see more human politics enacted, on their own, is not going to change anything. But a handful in a city council or state legislature? Now you're talking. A couple of hundred in Congress? That's a revolution.

We can do this. We really can. We can take back our democracy and make the world more human. But it will only happen if you—*yes, you*—take that first step and run for office. I know it's daunting. I know it's off-putting. I know you'll be worried about the kind of people you'll have to deal with, becoming a public figure, having actual responsibility for things. But that's what democracy is. And the trouble is, we've allowed it to be captured by the insiders and the vested interests and the people with money and influence. They're counting on you to be put off by it all, to be put off by the hassle, the complexity, the difficulty. That's their bet—that you don't actually care that much. That you don't really want change.

Prove them wrong.
Take back our democracy.
Make the world more human.

The first step? Right now, go to crowdpac.com/runforoffice.

ACKNOWLEDGMENTS

NUMBER ONE: my amazing wife, Rachel Whetstone, whom I love and respect in equal measure and without whom my recent adventures—moving to California, teaching at Stanford, founding a tech startup—would literally not have been possible. I also appreciate her putting up with days of family disruption during the production of this book—especially Christmas in Beaver Creek, 2014 (Jody and Vivienne, thanks to you too). And of course, Ben and Sonny, who have forever changed how I see the world.

One more thing on Rachel. As everyone who knows us is aware, we have strong opinions and tend to express them. But we try to hold back—in public at least—when it comes to each other's work. When I was in government Rachel had clear views on what we were doing but never aired them. It's the same with me and Uber, where Rachel works today, and I hope you will understand that for the most human of reasons—family harmony!—I'd prefer to express my views in private. Sorry to disappoint, but there are few references to Uber in these pages.

That I have a platform from which to write this book is something I owe to one person above all others: David Cameron. I will always be grateful to him for giving me the incredible honor of working in government. He and Sam are remarkable people and true friends. His strong, steady leadership and remarkable sense of duty were justly rewarded in the British general election of 2015, and I am so immensely proud that he was the first Conservative party leader in well over a century to increase both share of the vote and number of seats in Parliament. As a friend, I'm thrilled he won the majority he so deserved.

There are too many good friends and former colleagues in government to thank here personally, but I want to single out George Osborne, Michael Gove, and Oliver Letwin for their special contribution to my political and policy education; Michael Heseltine, Michael Howard, David Young, and Ken Baker—heroic political figures, all four—for the immense privilege of working with them and the inspiration they have given me; and Andrew Lansley, who helped me take that first, vital step into this strange but fascinating world. I will never be able to thank Maurice Saatchi, Jeremy Sinclair, Bill Muirhead, and the wider Saatchi 'family' enough for all they've done for me personally and in everything I've been able to achieve professionally.

Also essential in developing the ideas in this book: my friend and former business partner Giles Gibbons. Our time working together at the company we founded, Good Business, was a hugely fertile one for my understanding of the social problems addressed in *More Human* and how they might be solved.

Many people helped turn *More Human* into reality. In the UK, Gail Rebuck at Penguin Random House first encouraged me to write this book and helped me hone its theme. In the US, I had heard many great things about PublicAffairs Books, and all those reports were justified and exceeded by my direct experience of the team there. At every stage they have been a pleasure to work with: smart, fun, totally professional. Clive Priddle, Jaime Leifer, Melissa Raymond, Christine Marra, Jane Raese, Josephine Mariea, Sandy Chapman, and Donna Riggs, thank you.

Writing on so many topics has meant reaching out to experts, thinkers, and doers in all of these areas. Jason, Scott, and I feel privileged for having been able to talk to people doing such awe-inspiring work. Many are cited, but some provided feedback and insights without expectation of credit, and I'd like to thank them here.

My first teaching assistant at Stanford, Chelsea Lei, was extremely helpful in constructing an early case study. Sarah Stein Greenberg has proven an indispensable colleague at the Stanford d.school and, along with Mel Kline Lee, Jenny Stefanotti, Stephanie Wade, Sydney Smith-Heimbrock, and Brent Harris, helped us consider the possibilities of human-centered design in government. The enthusiasm of Maya Shankar, who has set up and now leads the White House's own 'nudge' unit, is contagious. Francis Fukuyama at Stanford provided valuable feedback on our government chapter and the history of bureaucracy. Bill Eggers of Deloitte, William Simon of Columbia University, and Paul Verkuil, former chairman of the Administrative Conference of the United States, likewise affirmed our thinking on government reform. Sir Simon Jenkins usefully critiqued our arguments on localism and schooling. Liz Jaff was indispensible in helping us grasp the intricacies of budget scoring.

Lucy Heller of Ark, Sir Anthony Seldon of Wellington College, and Barbara Chow of the William and Flora Hewlett Foundation were insightful and provocative on education. Jamie Heywood's inspiring journey and thoughtfulness were instrumental to our healthcare thesis. Sten Tamkivi and Daniel Vaarik educated us on Estonia's advances in e-health; Jason Oberfest of Mango Health did the same for the intersection of health and mobile devices; Camilla Cavendish helped us understand key aspects of the structure of the NHS. I'm extremely grateful to Liz Kendall MP for pointing us toward the need to discuss end-of-life care. Karen Matsuoka, chief quality officer for Medicaid, and Susan Ridgely of the RAND Corporation gave us a crash course in the many (many) intricacies of the structure of our healthcare system. Patrick Holden of the Sustainable Food Trust, Peter Melchett of the Soil Association, and Patty Lovera of Food and Water Watch helped clarify our thinking on agriculture and food policy. Conversations with Matt Rothe directed us to some of the latest and most interesting innovations in sustainable food. The analytical rigor of agricultural economist Pat Westoff at the University of Missouri is surely second to none. Isabel Oakeshott gave valuable feedback on the food chapter manuscript. Philip Lymbery of Compassion in World Farming provided detailed and timely answers to our numerous questions on factory farm conditions.

John Fingleton, former head of the UK Office of Fair Trading; John Gibson, my former No. 10 colleague now at Nesta; and Christine Varney, former US assistant attorney general for antitrust, proved stimulating sparring partners when discussing competition and helped us create a more rigorous chapter on capitalism. Louise Casey, one of Britain's most inspiring advocates for families and children, helped us set the tone for our poverty chapter; David Robinson of Community Links was similarly inspirational, as was Taryn Gaona, a former teacher and now my children's wonderful nanny. Michael McAfee of PolicyLink gave us a close look at the complexities surrounding the education of a child in poverty. Neil Jameson and Sarah Vero of the Living Wage Foundation, Michael Kelly at KPMG, Conor D'Arcy of the Resolution Foundation, Steve Mobbs of Oxford Asset Management, and Marianne Levine of Politico helped us understand the debate around low pay. There are few who have thought as carefully as Mark Cooper of the Economic Policy Institute on the economics of a higher minimum wage. Sir Charlie Mayfield, chairman of the John Lewis Partnership, provided tremendous insight into the challenges of improving low-paid workers' skills and compensation. Sebastian Thrun, founder and CEO of Udacity, proved extraordinarily thoughtful on the issue of workers and technology as well as artificial intelligence.

James O'Shaughnessey, another former colleague at No. 10, helped us greatly with our arguments in the chapter on spaces. Former Toronto mayor David Crombie, Alan Ricks of MASS Design, Nash Hurley of VITAL Environments, and Carlo Ratti of MIT proved similarly inspirational on architecture and design. Ben Schwegler of the Walt Disney Company, former Pentagon official Paul Stockton, Scott Jacobs of Generate Capital, Teryn Norris formerly of the US Department of Energy, Ryan Satterlee of Accenture, John Thorpe of Thameswey Energy, and Will Dawson and Giles Bristow of Forum for the Future helped us think through our complicated relationship with energy. Sarah Butler-Sloss of the Ashden Trust and David Beach at Stanford provided keen insight and incredibly useful examples and contacts for case studies. Our conversation with children's author Christiane Dorion on teaching nature remains one of the most delightful of the entire writing experience.

A number of people had valuable insights into our themes writ large, including Matthew Taylor of the RSA, Adam Lent of Ashoka, Jim Adams at Stanford, Nick Pearce of IPPR, Geoff Mulgan of Nesta, David Halpern of the Behavioural Insights Team, retired diplomat Sir David Manning, and Nassim Nicholas Taleb of New York University.

A handful of people went above and beyond in their assistance. Richard Young of the Sustainable Food Trust spent a huge amount of time offering technical assistance to help us understand agricultural policies and the effects of antibiotic use on farms. Paul Shapiro of the Humane Society of the United States answered numerous queries on farm animal welfare. Mark Schurman at Herman Miller is as close to a living library on the subject of office design as there can be and was exceptionally generous with his time and knowledge.

Jason and Scott want to thank the ever-perspicacious Todd Johnson of Jones Day, Banny Banerjee of Stanford ChangeLabs, and Paul and Iris Brest of Stanford Law School and the Creative Commons Foundation, respectively, as well as Ed Zhu, Nicholas Chen, and Taylor McAdam. Thanks to Peter, Lisa, and Julianne Cirenza, who welcomed us into their London home during our travels, and Peter, for his astute observations and feedback on the financial sector. Finally, thanks to Paul and Sheri Bade—Mom and Dad—whose support, understanding, guidance, and love is the very human foundation of this, one of our proudest accomplishments.

There are three people who have inspired me personally and professionally in more ways than they know and whose names I'm completely thrilled to see on the jacket of this book: Mike Bloomberg, Arianna Huffington, and Nassim Taleb. They are all major public figures with strong views on many topics—and it's important to point out that the views expressed in this book are entirely mine and not endorsed by them in any specific detail.

I want to thank those who labored through early drafts to give me great feedback: Jenni Russell, who also spent an inordinate amount of effort connecting us with people to talk to; Dieter Helm, my tutor at Oxford, who helped me think through the broad themes of the book as well as the technical aspects of infrastructure and competition; Kate MacTiernan. I'm incredibly grateful to David Crane, Andrew Crutchfield, and Mason Harrison for their friendship, advice, and insightful feedback on the US edition of this book.

Jason and Scott have been a double joy to work with. (Everyone should have twins helping them with their book!) They complemented each other and me in the best ways as they helped me research and write *More Human*, diving into the project head first—and putting up with me for over two years of it. This book couldn't have been produced without them, and I'm so grateful for their hard work.

And then finally, I must thank the person who has been central to this book throughout its life: from the years we spent together developing and working on many of the ideas in *More Human*, to the confidence he gave me that this was a project worth pursuing, to the book's structure and comments on drafts at every stage—my closest friend and former colleague in government, Rohan Silva, to whom this book is dedicated.

NOTES

INTRODUCTION

1. JetBlue has acknowledged and apologized for this incident. The dialogue is not a verbatim transcript but is based on Devereaux's recollection as expressed in various media appearances since the incident. For more, watch her interview at Jennifer Devereaux, interview by Tamron Hall, *NewsNation with Tamron Hall*, MSNBC, June 19, 2014.

2. Hilary Rodham Clinton quoted in: Dan Merica, "Black Lives Matter Video, Clinton Campaign Reveal Details of Meeting," CNN Politics, August 18, 2015, www.cnn.com/2015/08/18/politics/hillary-clinton-black-lives-matter-meeting.

3. "A Deep Dive into Party Affiliation," Pew Research Center, April 7, 2015, www.people-press.org/2015/04/07/a-deep-dive-into-party-affiliation.

4. Tony Blair, *A Journey: My Political Life* (New York: Vintage Books, 2011), xi.

5. Jeremy Rifkin, *The Empathic Civilization: The Race to Global Consciousness in a World in Crisis* (New York: Jeremy P. Tarcher/Penguin, 2009).

6. For more on the nuanced and complicated history of bureaucracy, see Francis Fukuyama, *Political Order and Political Decay* (New York: Farrar, Straus and Giroux, 2014), 15–18, 68–71.

7. Alfred D. Chandler Jr., *The Visible Hand: The Managerial Revolution in American Business* (Cambridge, MA: Harvard University Press, 1977).

8. Michael A. Mitt, David King, Menna Krishnan, Marianna Makri, Mario Schjren, Katsuhiko Shimizu, and Hong Zhu, "Creating Value Through Mergers and Acquisitions: Challenges and Opportunities," in *The Handbook of Mergers and Acquisitions*, ed. David Faulkner, Satu Teerikangas, and Richard J. Joseph (Oxford, United Kingdom: Oxford University Press, 2012), 71–113.

9. Evgeny Morozov, *To Save Everything, Click Here: The Folly of Technological Solutionism* (New York: PublicAffairs, 2013), xii.

10. Since 2007 hourly wages have declined even for workers with a bachelor's or advanced degree. For more, see Elise Gould, *2014 Continues a 35-Year Trend of Broad-Based Wage Stagnation* (Washington, DC: Economic Policy Institute, 2015), www.epi.org/publication/stagnant-wages-in-2014.

CHAPTER 1. POLITICS

1. Francis Fukuyama, *Political Order and Political Decay* (New York: Farrar, Straus and Giroux, 2014), 455–548.

2. According to political scientists Martin Gilens and Benjamin Page, "When a majority of citizens disagrees with economic elites or with organized interests, they generally lose." For more, see Martin Gilens and Benjamin I. Page, "Testing Theories of American Politics: Elites, Interest Groups, and Average Citizens," *Perspectives on Politics* 12, no. 03 (2014): 564–581, 576.

3. "2015 Outside Spending, by Super PAC," *OpenSecrets.org*, September 24, 2015, www.opensecrets.org/outsidespending/summ.php?chrt=V&type=S.

4. "2014 Election Overview," *OpenSecrets.org*, September 24, 2015, www.opensecrets.org/overview.

5. Polly Curtis, "Conservatives Spent Twice as Much as Labour on Election Campaign," *Guardian*, December 2, 2010, www.theguardian.com/politics/2010/dec/02/conservatives-spent-twice-labour-election-campaign.

6. Peter Overby, "Billionaire or Bust: Who Are Rich Backers Lining Up With?" NPR, June 8, 2015, www.npr.org/sections/itsallpolitics/2015/06/08/412763052/billionaire-or-bust-who-are-rich-backers-lining-up-with.

7. Diane Feldman to Michelle Nunn, "The Campaign Plan" (leaked to the National Review, 2014), www.scribd.com/fullscreen/235287519?access_key=key-7XLZhUlmcqs8zb0ft3xs&allow_share=true&escape=false&view_mode=scroll.

8. Ryan Grim and Sabeeka Siddiqui, "Call Time for Congress Shows How Fundraising Dominates Bleak Work Life," Huffington Post, January 8, 2013, www.huffingtonpost.com/2013/01/08/call-time-congressional-fundraising_n_2427291.html.

9. Steve Israel, quoted in Carl Hulse, "Steve Israel of New York, a Top Democrat, Won't Seek Reelection," New York Times, January 5, 2016, http://www.nytimes.com/2016/01/06/us/politics/steve-israel-house-democrat-new-york.html. See also his op-ed on the topic: Steve Israel, "Steve Israel: Confessions of a Congressman," New York Times, January 8, 2016, http://www.nytimes.com/2016/01/09/opinion/steve-israel-confessions-of-a-congressman.html?_r=0.

10. "How Much Do the 1 Percent of the 1 Percent Control Politics?" Crowdpac, April 21, 2015, www.crowdpac.com/blog/the-1-percent-of-the-1-percent.

11. Donald Trump, interview by Chuck Todd, Meet the Press, NBC, August 16, 2015.

12. Tom Steyer, interview by Gwen Ifill, "Why Is a Billionaire Climate Activist Bothering with GOP Primaries?" PBS NewsHour, May 26, 2015, www.pbs.org/newshour/bb/billionaire-climate-activist-bothering-gop-primaries.

13. Full disclosure: Ginsberg is a personal friend and adviser to my political technology startup, Crowdpac.

14. "Prop 87," FollowTheMoney.org, 2013, www.followthemoney.org/entity-details?eid=10246182.

15. Lexington, "How to Win 99.6 % of the Vote," The Economist, October 24, 2014, www.economist.com/news/united-states/21627661-too-many-members-congress-are-running-unopposed-how-win-996-vote.

16. Sanford Levinson, "To End Government Shutdowns, End Partisan Gerrymandering," Al Jazeera America, October 13, 2013, http://america.aljazeera.com/articles/2013/10/13/government-shutdowngerrymanderingdistricts.html.

17. Simon Jackman, Assessing the Current Wisconsin State Legislative Districting Plan (2015), www.thewheelerreport.com/wheeler_docs/files/Exhibit_3.pdf, 69. This paper was written by Jackman, a political scientist, as part of paid expert testimony for the plaintiffs in the 2015 case Whitford v. Nichols. In the suit, several Democratic voters claim that gerrymandering renders their votes meaningless, abrogating their constitutional rights. They are supported by the Wisconsin Fair Elections Project as well as several Democratic and at least one Republican state senator. Although the claimants are mostly Democrats, they do not seek gerrymandering in their favor but rather a neutral redistricting procedure. For more, see Wisconsin Fair Elections Project, www.fairelectionsproject.org.

18. Tom LoBianco and Dan Merica, "Harvard Professor Lawrence Lessig to Launch Long-Shot 2016 Campaign," CNN, September 8, 2015, www.cnn.com/2015/09/06/politics/lawrence-lessig-campaign-finance-reform.

19. Eliza Newlin Carney, "Sarbanes Bill Aims to Draw in Small Donors," Roll Call, February 4, 2014, http://blogs.rollcall.com/beltway-insiders/sarbanes-bill-aims-to-draw-small-donors; "Sarbanes Reintroduces H.R. 20, the Government by the People Act," John Sarbanes.house.gov, January 21, 2015, https://sarbanes.house.gov/media-center/press-releases/sarbanes-reintroduces-hr-20-the-government-by-the-people-act.

20. Ben Kamisar, "Clinton Calls for Constitutional Amendment on Campaign Finance," The Hill, April 14, 2015, http://thehill.com/blogs/ballot-box/presidential-races/238808-clinton-calls-for-constitutional-amendment-on-campaign.

21. Lawrence Lessig, "We the People, and the Republic We Must Reclaim," TED Talk,

February 27, 2013, Long Beach, California, www.ted.com/talks/lawrence_lessig_we_the_people _and_the_republic_we_must_reclaim/transcript?language=en.

CHAPTER 2. GOVERNMENT

1. Alex Singleton, "Obituary: Sir John Cowperthwaite," *Guardian*, February 8, 2006, www .theguardian.com/news/2006/feb/08/guardianobituaries.mainsection.

2. Diane Coyle, "GDP Is a Mirror on the Markets. It Must Not Rule Our Lives," *Guardian*, November 20, 2014, www.theguardian.com/commentisfree/2014/nov/20/gdp-markets-short-term -victorians-value.

3. If that seems like a lot, it is. The ASCE gives America an average infrastructure grade of D+. See *2013 Report Card for America's Infrastructure* (American Society of Civil Engineers, 2013), www.infrastructurereportcard.org.

4. Danielle Kehl, Nick Russo, Robert Morgus, and Sarah Morris, *The Cost of Connectivity 2014: Data and Analysis on Broadband Connectivity in 24 Cities Across the World* (Washington, DC: New America, 2014).

5. Julian Ryall, "Bullet Train at 50: Rise and Fall of the World's Fastest Train," *Telegraph*, October 1, 2014.

6. "Biden Compares La Guardia Airport to 'Third World,'" Associated Press, February 5, 2014.

7. Adam M. Zaretsky, "Should Cities Pay for Sports Facilities?" *Regional Economist*, April 2001, 4–9; Mark S. Rosentraub, *Major League Losers: The Real Cost of Sports and Who's Paying for It* (New York: Basic Books, 1999).

8. Rob Grunewald and Arthur Rolnick, *A Proposal for Achieving High Returns on Early Childhood Development* (Federal Reserve Bank of Minneapolis, 2006).

9. Art Rolnick, phone interview by authors, November 19, 2015.

10. Dieter Helm, interview by authors, Menlo Park, CA, November 21, 2014.

11. Harvard economists Gregory Mankiw and Matthew Weinzierl have shown that tax cuts partially pay for themselves. For more, see N. Gregory Mankiw and Matthew Weinzierl, "Dynamic Scoring: A Back-of-the-Envelope Guide," *Journal of Public Economics* 90, no. 8 (2006): 1415–1433. Meanwhile studies show that infrastructure investment leads to economic gains: *World Economic Outlook October 2014: Legacies, Clouds, Uncertainties* (Washington, DC: International Monetary Fund, 2014), ch. 3.

12. Mankiw and Weinzierl, "Dynamic Scoring."

13. Matt O'Brien, "Paul Ryan Has a Trick Up His Sleeve When It Comes to Taxes. It Won't Work," *Washington Post*, October 14, 2014, www.washingtonpost.com/news/wonk/wp/2014/10/14/paul -ryan-has-a-trick-up-his-sleeve-when-it-comes-to-taxes-it-wont-work; and N. Gregory Mankiw, "Dynamic Scoring in Congress Is Defensible but Slippery," *New York Times*, March 1, 2015, www .nytimes.com/2015/03/01/upshot/a-slippery-new-rule-for-gauging-fiscal-policy.html?_r=0.

14. John K. Delaney, "The House Should Keep 'Dynamic Scoring' Honest," *Washington Post*, January 7, 2015, www.washingtonpost.com/opinions/the-house-should-keep-dynamic-scoring -honest/2015/01/07/48912eae-94fb-11e4-927a-4fa2638cd1b0_story.html.

15. Former Federal Reserve chair Ben Bernanke called current productivity growth in the United States "mediocre," "weak," and "very modest." See Ben Bernanke, interview by Rana Foroohar, *Time*, October 6, 2015, http://time.com/4062889/ben-bernanke-courage-to-act.

16. Anthony King and Ivor Crewe, *The Blunders of Our Governments* (London: Oneworld Publications, 2013), 243.

17. Jane Jacobs, *The Death and Life of Great American Cities* (New York: Vintage Books, 1961), 13.

18. World Health Organization, "Preterm Birth (Fact Sheet 363)," www.who.int/mediacentre/ factsheets/fs363/en.

19. Linus Liang, interview by authors, Stanford, CA, November 20, 2014.

20. "Who Are We?" *Embrace*, 2015, http://embraceglobal.org/who-we-are/our-story.

21. Sadly, Tversky died before their joint work was recognized, so technically Kahneman is the laureate, though he accepted it on behalf of them both. For their seminal paper, see Daniel Kahneman and Amos Tversky, "Choices, Values, and Frames," *American Psychologist* 39, no. 4 (1984): 341.

22. Ronald G. Fryer Jr., Steven D. Levitt, John List, and Sally Sadoff, "Enhancing the Efficacy of Teacher Incentives Through Loss Aversion: A Field Experiment," no. w18237, National Bureau of Economic Research, 2012.

23. David Brooks, "The Character Factory," *New York Times*, August 1, 2014, www.nytimes.com/2014/08/01/opinion/david-brooks-the-character-factory.html.

24. Robert B. Cialdini, Linda J. Demaine, Brad J. Sagarin, Daniel W. Barrett, Kelton Rhoads, and Patricia L. Winter, "Managing Social Norms for Persuasive Impact," *Social Influence* 1, no. 1 (2006): 3–15.

25. Barack Obama, "Remarks by the President in State of the Union Address," White House Office of the Press Secretary, January 25, 2011, www.whitehouse.gov/the-press-office/2011/01/25/remarks-president-state-union-address.

26. Doug Shapiro, Afet Dundar, Xin Yuan, Autumn T. Harrell, and Phoebe K. Wakhungu, *Completing College: A National View of Student Attainment Rates—Fall 2008 Cohort* (Signature Report no. 8) (Hernon, VA: National Student Clearinghouse Center, 2014).

27. David Brooks, "Support Our Students," *New York Times*, January 19, 2015, www.nytimes.com/2015/01/20/opinion/david-brooks-support-our-students.html.

28. This benefit later expanded to full-tuition credits regardless of matter how many credits a student had.

29. Amanda Ripley, "How to Graduate from Starbucks," *Atlantic*, May 2015, 71.

30. Ibid.

31. David Brooks, "Stairway to Wisdom," *New York Times*, May 15, 2014, www.nytimes.com/2014/05/16/opinion/brooks-stairway-to-wisdom.html.

32. Editorial Board, "Mr. Bratton Reverses to Go Forward," *New York Times*, September 12, 2014, www.nytimes.com/2014/09/13/opinion/mr-bratton-reverses-to-go-forward.html.

33. "Measure for Measure," *Economist*, November 30, 2013, www.economist.com/news/united-states/21590954-can-asking-better-questions-reduce-americas-prison-population-measure-measure.

34. US Department of Justice, Civil Rights Division, "Investigation of the Ferguson Police Department," March 4, 2015, 62.

35. Ibid., 2–3.

36. Since his appointment in June 2015 Municipal Court Judge Donald McCullin has rescinded arrest warrants made before December 31, 2014, and moved to reform the pretrial process. See Greg Botelho and Sara Sidner, "Ferguson Judge Withdraws All Arrest Warrants Before 2015," CNN, August 25, 2015, www.cnn.com/2015/08/24/us/ferguson-missouri-court-changes.

37. US Department of Justice, "Investigation of the Ferguson Police Department," 3.

38. Peel, who later served as prime minister, founded the Metropolitan Police in 1829 while he was home secretary. British police officers are affectionately called "bobbies" in his honor. He has been associated with the so-called Peelian Principles, which revolutionized the policing profession by laying down the field's first set of ethical guidelines. Also known as "policing by consent," it is grounded in the idea that the police draws its power, in the words of the British Home Office, from "the common consent of the public." See Home Office, "Freedom of Information Release: Policing by Consent," December 10, 2012, www.gov.uk/government/publications/policing-by-consent.

39. Richard H. Thaler, *Misbehaving: The Making of Behavioral Economics* (New York: W. W. Norton & Company, 2015), 320.

40. Rohan Silva, interview by authors, London, September 17, 2014.

41. Ibid.

42. Lena H. Sun, "Johns Hopkins Team Wins U.S. Award for Improved Suit to Fight Ebola," *Washington Post*, December 13, 2014, www.washingtonpost.com/news/post-nation/wp/2014/12/13 /johns-hopkins-team-wins-u-s-award-for-improved-suit-to-fight-ebola; Julie Hirschfeld Davis, "Adviser Guides Obama into Google Age," *New York Times*, January 4, 2015, www.nytimes.com /2015/01/04/us/politics/her-task-weaning-the-white-house-off-floppy-disks.html.

43. Karen Courington, interview by authors, Menlo Park, CA, July 1, 2015.

44. Charles Murray, "Fifty Shades of Red: A Modest Proposal for Rejecting Rules," *Wall Street Journal*, May 9–10, 2015, C1.

45. Barack Obama, "Remarks by the President in State of the Union Address," 2011.

46. Nicco Mele, *The End of Big: How the Internet Makes David the New Goliath* (New York: St. Martin's Press, 2013), 29.

47. For more, see Peter Schuck, *Why Government Fails So Often: And How It Can Do Better* (Princeton, NJ: Princeton University Press, 2014), 193.

48. For more on the ACA rollout issues, see Jonathan Alter, "Failure to Launch: How Obama Fumbled HealthCare.gov," *Foreign Affairs*, March/April 2014, 39–50.

49. Providence Talks is an early-childhood intervention program in which parents wear devices that record how many words they say on a daily basis and receive regular advice on how better to talk to their children.

50. Shibuya Ward was followed by Tokyo's Setagaya Ward in July 2015. See Hiroko Saito, "Another Ward in Tokyo to Recognize Same-Sex Couples," *Japan Times*, July 30, 2015, www.japan times.co.jp/news/2015/07/30/national/another-ward-in-tokyo-to-recognize-same-sex-couples/ #.VluvZdKrTDd.

51. Jerry Sternin, "The Viet Nam Story," www.positivedeviance.org/about_pd/Monique%20 VIET%20NAM%20CHAPTER%20Oct%2017.pdf.

52. Mauricio Lim Miller, "When Helping Doesn't Help," *Huffington Post*, May 7, 2012, www .huffingtonpost.com/maurice-lim-miller/when-helping-doesnt-help_b_1497038.html.

53. Ibid.

54. Ibid.

55. Anne Stuhldreher and Rourke O'Brien, *The Family Independence Initiative: A New Approach to Help Families Exit Poverty* (Washington, DC: New America Foundation, 2011).

56. David Bornstein, "Out of Poverty, Family-Style," *New York Times*, July 14, 2011, http:// opinionator.blogs.nytimes.com/2011/07/14/out-of-poverty-family-style/?_r=0.

57. Stulhdreher and O'Brien, *The Family Independence Initiative*.

58. Lim Miller, quoted in Bornstein, "Out of Poverty, Family-Style."

CHAPTER 3. SCHOOLS

1. Se-Woong Koo, "An Assault upon Our Children," *New York Times*, August 3, 2014, www.ny times.com/2014/08/02/opinion/sunday/south-koreas-education-system-hurts-students.html.

2. Data from Statistics Korea, as reported in Yewon Kang, "Poll Shows Half of Korean Teenagers Have Suicidal Thoughts," *Wall Street Journal*, March 20, 2014, http://blogs.wsj.com/ korearealtime/2014/03/20/poll-shows-half-of-korean-teenagers-have-suicidal-thoughts.

3. Ibid.

4. Julie Lythcott-Haims, *How to Raise an Adult: Break Free of the Overparenting Trap and Prepare Your Kid for Success* (New York: Henry Holt and Co., 2015), 100–101.

5. In the last six years there have been two major suicide clusters at Palo Alto high schools. From 2009 to 2010 five teens killed themselves by stepping in front of trains. Between October 2014 and May 2015 another four did the same. See "In Palo Alto's High-Pressure Schools, Suicides Lead to Soul-Searching," NPR, May 10, 2015, www.npr.org/2015/05/10/405694832/in -palo-altos-high-pressure-schools-suicides-lead-to-soul-searching.

6. Lythcott-Haims, *How to Raise an Adult*.

7. Julie Lythcott-Haims, interview by authors, Palo Alto, CA, August 5, 2015.

8. All quotes from Jason Pittman are from his interview by authors, Mountain View, CA, November 5, 2014.

9. Jessica Lahey, *The Gift of Failure: How the Best Parents Learn to Let Go So Their Children Can Succeed* (New York: HarperCollins, 2015), 27.

10. Jeff Sandefer, e-mail to authors, September 3, 2014.

11. Jason Tanz, "The Tech Elite's Quest to Reinvent School in Its Own Image," *Wired*, October 26, 2015, www.wired.com/2015/10/salman-khan-academy-lab-school-reinventing-classrooms.

12. Palo Alto High School and Gunn High School, Palo Alto's two public high schools, are widely regarded as being among the best in the nation. Although I am no fan of such ranking systems, Gunn is ranked 38th and Palo Alto High is ranked 56th nationally by *Newsweek*, which puts both above the 99.7th percentile in the United States. For more, see "America's Top Schools 2014," *Newsweek*, www.newsweek.com/high-schools/americas-top-schools-2014.

13. Emerging economies to be sure, but certainly not comparable to two economic superpowers. For the most recent (2012) PISA scores, see "Snapshot of Performance in Mathematics, Reading and Science," PISA, www.oecd.org/pisa/keyfindings/PISA-2012-results-snapshot-Volume-I-ENG.pdf.

14. Jouachim Wuttke, "Uncertainty and Bias in PISA," in *Pisa According to Pisa: Does Pisa Keep What It Promises?*, ed. Stefan Thomas Hopmann, Gertrude Brinek, and Martin Retzl (Vienna, Austria: Lit Verlag, 2007), 241–263.

15. William Stewart, "Is Pisa Fundamentally Flawed?" TES Connect, September 27, 2014, www.tes.co.uk/article.aspx?storycode=6344672.

16. Aleksander P. J. Ellis, Bradford S. Bell, Robert E. Ployhart, John R. Hollenbeck, and D. R. Ilgen, "An Evaluation of Generic Teamwork Skill Training with Action Teams: Effects on Cognitive and Skill-Based Outcomes," *Personnel Psychology* 58, no. 3 (2005): 641–672.

17. Angela L. Duckworth and Martin E. P. Seligman, "Self-Discipline Outdoes IQ in Predicting Academic Performance of Adolescents," *Psychological Science* 16, no. 12 (2005): 939–944.

18. "IBM 2010 Global CEO Study: Creativity Selected as Most Crucial Factor for Future Success," IBM, May 18, 2010, www-03.ibm.com/press/us/en/pressrelease/31670.wss.

19. Tony Wagner and Ted Dintersmith, *More Likely to Succeed: Preparing Our Kids for the Innovation Era* (New York: Simon & Schuster, 2015), 73.

20. Sarah Konrath, Edward H. O'Brien, and Courtney Hsing, "Changes in Dispositional Empathy in American College Students over Time: A Meta-Analysis," *Personality and Social Psychology Review* 15, no. 2 (May 2011): 180–198.

21. Joshua Wolf Shenk, *Powers of Two: How Relationships Drive Creativity* (Boston, MA: Eamon Dolan, 2009).

22. Willem Kuyken, Katherine Weare, Obioha C. Ukoumunne, Rachael Vicary, Nicola Motton, Richard Burnett, Chris Cullen et al., "Effectiveness of the Mindfulness in Schools Programme: Non-Randomised Controlled Feasibility Study," *British Journal of Psychiatry* 203, no. 2 (2013): 126–131.

23. Allyson P. Mackey, Amy S. Finn, Julia A. Leonard, Drew S. Jacoby-Senghor, Martin R. West, Christopher F. O. Gabrieli, and John D. E. Gabrieli, "Neuroanatomical Correlates of the Income-Achievement Gap," *Psychological Science* 26, no. 6 (June 2015): 925–933.

24. Barbara Chow, interview by authors, Menlo Park, CA, June 18, 2015.

25. Richard C. Atkinson and Saul Geiser, "The Big Problem with the New SAT," *New York Times*, May 5, 2015, www.nytimes.com/2015/05/05/opinion/the-big-problem-with-the-new-sat.html.

26. Frank Wu, quoted in Lythcott-Haims, *How to Raise an Adult*, 97.

27. Valerie Strauss, "What One College Discovered When It Stopped Accepting SAT/ACT Scores," *Washington Post*, September 25, 2015, www.washingtonpost.com/news/answer-sheet/wp/2015/09/25/what-one-college-discovered-when-it-stopped-accepting-satact-scores.

28. The Juárez Correa story is heavily adapted from Josh Davis's profile of him in *Wired*. Josh is one of the greatest unearthers of amazing human stories. For the original article, see Joshua Davis, "A Radical Way of Unleashing a Generation of Geniuses," *Wired*, October 15, 2013, www.wired.com/2013/10/free-thinkers.

29. Marjukka Liiten, "Top Favorite: Teaching Profession" (in Finnish), *Helsingin Sanomat*, February 11, 2004, cited in Pasi Sahlberg, *Finnish Lessons: What Can the World Learn from Educational Change in Finland?* (New York: Teachers College Press, 2010), 72.

30. Sahlberg, *Finnish Lessons*, 125.

31. Ibid., 127.

32. Ellen Gamerman, "What Makes Finnish Kids So Smart?" *Wall Street Journal*, February 28, 2008, www.wsj.com/articles/SB120425355065601997. See also Sahlberg, *Finnish Lessons*, 65.

33. OECD, "Education at a Glance: OECD Indicators," www.oecd.org/edu/Education-at-a-Glance-2014.pdf.

34. Anthony Seldon, *An End to Factory Schools: An Education Manifesto 2010–2020* (Surrey, United Kingdom: Centre for Policy Studies, 2010), 9–10.

35. *Vergara v. California—Tentative Decision* (Superior Court of the State of California, County of Los Angeles, June 10, 2014), http://studentsmatter.org/wp-content/uploads/2014/06/Tentative-Decision.pdf.

36. *Asking Students About Teachers* (Measures of Effective Teaching Project, 2012).

37. See, for example, Pearson Learning, www.pearson.com/learning.html; Disney Education Programs, http://dep.disney.go.com; McGraw-Hill Education, www.mheducation.com; Houghton Mifflin Harcourt, www.hmhco.com.

38. Peter Hill and Michael Barber, *Preparing for a Renaissance in Assessment* (London: Pearson PLC, 2014).

39. Editorial Board, "Small Schools Work in New York," *New York Times*, October 18, 2014, www.nytimes.com/2014/10/18/opinion/small-schools-work-in-new-york.html.

40. Rebecca Unterman, *Headed to College: The Effects of New York City's Small High Schools of Choice on Postsecondary Enrollment* (MDRC, 2014), www.mdrc.org/sites/default/files/Headed_to_College_PB.pdf.

41. Institute of Education Sciences, *Numbers and Types of Public Elementary and Secondary Schools from the Common Core of Data: School Year 2010–11* (National Center for Education Statistics, 2012); and US Department of Education, *Digest of Education Statistics, 2013* (National Center for Education Statistics, 2015), ch. 2, https://nces.ed.gov/fastfacts/display.asp?id=84.

42. William T. Harris, "Elementary Education," *North American Review* (1895): 538–546, 15.

43. Barbara Chow, interview by authors, Menlo Park, CA, June 18, 2015.

44. Perhaps one of the reasons there are so many standardized tests is the money they make: Pearson made $85 million per year from 2010 to 2015 just in the state of Texas on test administration. College Board, the private "nonprofit" company responsible for the SAT, makes over three-quarters of a billion dollars in revenue annually. For more, see Matthew M. Chingos, *Strength in Numbers: State Spending on K–12 Assessment Systems* (Washington, DC: Brown Center for Education at the Brookings Institution, 2012); and *Agenda Materials: College Board Forum 2015* (The College Board, November 4–6, 2015).

45. Rob Reich, "Not Very Giving," *New York Times*, September 5, 2013, www.nytimes.com/2013/09/05/opinion/not-very-giving.html.

CHAPTER 4. HEALTH

1. Marshall Allen, "What a New Doctor Learned about Medical Mistakes from Her Mom's Death," ProPublica, January 9, 2013, www.propublica.org/article/what-a-new-doctor-learned-about-medical-mistakes-from-her-moms-death.

2. John T. James, "A New, Evidence-Based Estimate of Patient Harms Associated with Hospital Care," *Journal of Patient Safety* 9, no. 3 (2013): 122–128.

3. Steffie Woolhandler and David U. Himmelstein, "Administrative Work Consumes One-Sixth of US Physicians' Working Hours and Lowers Their Career Satisfaction," *International Journal of Health Services* 44, no. 4 (2014): 635–642.

4. Physicians for a National Health Program, "Administrative Work Consumes One-Sixth of U.S. Physicians' Time and Erodes Their Morale, Researchers Say," press release, October 23, 2014.

5. Dante Morra, Sean Nicholson, Wendy Levinson, David N. Gans, Terry Hammons, and Lawrence P. Casalino, "US Physician Practices versus Canadians: Spending Nearly Four Times as Much Money Interacting with Payers," *Health Affairs* 30, no. 8 (2011): 1443–1450.

6. David U. Himmelstein, Miraya Jun, Reinhard Busse, Karine Chevreul, Alexander Geissler, Patrick Jeurissen, Sarah Thomson et al., "A Comparison of Hospital Administrative Costs in Eight Nations: US Costs Exceed All Others by Far," *Health Affairs* 33, no. 9 (2014): 1586–1594.

7. Woolhandler and Himmelstein, "Administrative Work Consumes."

8. Reid Blackwelder, letter to Edith Ramirez, June 4, 2015, www.aafp.org/dam/AAFP/documents/advocacy/legal/antitrust/LT-FTC-InsuranceMergers-060415.pdf.

9. Jose Guardado, David W. Emmons, and Carol K. Kane, "The Price Effects of a Large Merger of Health Insurers: A Case Study of UnitedHealth-Sierra," *Health Management, Policy and Innovation* 1, no. 3 (2013): 16–35. See also Andrew Ross Sorkin, "Health Care Law Spurs Merger Talks for Insurers," *New York Times*, June 22, 2015, www.nytimes.com/2015/06/23/business/dealbook/health-care-law-spurs-merger-talks-for-insurers.html.

10. "Top Industries (2009)," *OpenSecrets.org*, www.opensecrets.org/lobby/top.php?showYear=2009&indexType=i.

11. Steven Brill, *America's Bitter Pill: Money, Politics, Backroom Deals, and the Fight to Fix Our Broken Healthcare System* (New York: Random House, 2015), 125–126.

12. Peter H. Stone, "Chamber Seeks Cash from Insurers, Financial Firms for New Effort," Center for Public Integrity, December 1, 2010. See also Brill, *America's Bitter Pill*, 144.

13. Abraham Verghese, "A Doctor's Touch," TEDGlobal 2011: The Stuff of Life, Edinburgh, Scotland, September 2011, www.ted.com/talks/abraham_verghese_a_doctor_s_touch?language=en.

14. "Introducing the Vscan Family," GE Healthcare, 2015, https://vscan.gehealthcare.com/introducing-vscan-family.

15. Priit Kruus, Peeter Ross, Riina Hallik, Reelika Ermel, and Ain Aaviksoo, *Wider Implementation of Telemedicine in Estonia* (Tallinn, Estonia: Praxis/Center for Policy Studies, 2014).

16. Responding to author's question at speech: Toomas Ilves, "Evolving into a Genuinely Digital Society," presentation, Green Library, Stanford University, Stanford, CA, May 23, 2014.

17. Ali Parsa, phone interview by authors, October 28, 2014.

18. Jason Oberfest, interview by authors, San Francisco, CA, August 27, 2014.

19. James Heywood, phone interview by authors, October 9, 2014.

20. Nassim Nicholas Taleb, *Antifragile: Things That Gain from Disorder* (New York: Random House Trade Paperbacks, 2014), 338.

21. Alice G. Walton, "Steve Jobs' Cancer Treatment Regrets," *Forbes*, October 24, 2011, www.forbes.com/sites/alicegwalton/2011/10/24/steve-jobs-cancer-treatment-regrets.

22. Mitchell H. Katz, "Failing the Acid Test: Benefits of Proton Pump Inhibitors May Not Justify the Risks for Many Users," *Archives of Internal Medicine* 170, no. 9 (2010): 747–748.

23. Kenneth E. L. McColl, "Effect of Proton Pump Inhibitors on Vitamins and Iron," *American Journal of Gastroenterology* 104 (2009): S5–S9; Nigam H. Shah, Paea LePendu, Anna Bauer-Mehren, Yohannes T. Ghebremariam, Srinivasan V. Iyer, Jake Marcus, Kevin T. Nead et al., "Proton Pump Inhibitor Usage and the Risk of Myocardial Infarction in the General Population," *PloS One* 10, no. 6 (June 2015): e0124653.

24. Taleb, *Antifragile*, 342.

25. Jeanne Whalen, "How Glaxo Marketed a Malady to Sell a Drug," *Wall Street Journal*, October 25, 2006, www.wsj.com/articles/SB116174246339602800.

26. Steven Woloshin and Lisa M. Schwartz, "Giving Legs to Restless Legs: A Case Study of How the Media Helps Make People Sick," *PLoS Medicine* 3, no. 4 (2006): e170.

27. Anita Soni, *Attention-Deficit Hyperactivity Disorder (ADHD) in Children, Ages 5–17: Use and Expenditures, 2007* (Agency for Healthcare Research and Quality, 2007), http://meps.ahrq.gov/data_files/publications/st276/stat276.pdf.

28. Murray Aitken, *Medicines Use and Spending Shifts: A Review of the Use of Medicines in the U.S. in 2014* (IMS Institute for Healthcare Informatics, April 2015); Murray Aitken, *Medicines Use and Spending Shifts: A Review of the Use of Medicines in the U.S. in 2013* (IMS Institute for Healthcare Informatics, April 2014).

29. Michael Anderson, quoted in Alan Schwarz, "Attention Disorder or Not, Pills to Help in School," *New York Times*, October 9, 2012, www.nytimes.com/2012/10/09/health/attention-disorder-or-not-children-prescribed-pills-to-help-in-school.html.

30. Nancy Rappaport, quoted in ibid.

31. Ibid.

32. "Contrast-Enhanced CT Safe for Most Patients," Radiological Society of North America, September 9, 2014, www2.rsna.org/timssnet/media/pressreleases/14_pr_target.cfm?ID=757; E. J. Hall and D. J. Brenner. "Cancer Risks from Diagnostic Radiology," *British Journal of Radiology* 81, no. 965 (May 2008): 362–378; Amy Berrington de González, Mahadevappa Mahesh, Kwang-Pyo Kim, Mythreyi Bhargavan, Rebecca Lewis, Fred Mettler, and Charles Land, "Projected Cancer Risks from Computed Tomographic Scans Performed in the United States in 2007," *Archives of Internal Medicine* 169, no. 22 (2009): 2071–2077.

33. Atul Gawande, "Overkill," *New Yorker*, May 11, 2015, www.newyorker.com/magazine/2015/05/11/overkill-atul-gawande.

34. H. Gilbert Welch, *Less Medicine, More Health: 7 Assumptions That Drive Too Much Medical Care* (Boston, MA: Beacon Press, 2015), 2.

35. Ibid., 113.

36. Charles Edmonds and Grady L. Hallman, "CardioVascular Care Providers: A Pioneer in Bundled Services, Shared Risk, and Single Payment," *Texas Heart Institute Journal* 22, no. 1 (1995): 72.

37. Harold D. Miller, "From Volume to Value: Better Ways to Pay for Health Care," *Health Affairs* 28, no. 5 (2009): 1418–1428. See also John Bertko and Rachel Effros, *Increase the Use of "Bundled" Payment Approaches* (Santa Monica, CA: Rand Corporation, 2010).

38. "Analysis of Bundled Payment," Rand Corporation, www.rand.org/pubs/technical_reports/TR562z20/analysis-of-bundled-payment.html.

39. Victoria Sweet, "The Efficiency of Inefficiency," TEDxMiddlebury, Middlebury, Vermont, March 9, 2013, www.youtube.com/watch?v=VAo8kzp7tSg.

40. Victoria Sweet, *God's Hotel: A Doctor, a Pilgrimage, and a Journey to the Heart of Medicine* (New York: Penguin, 2013), 49–50.

41. Sweet, "The Efficiency of Inefficiency."

42. Francis W. Peabody, "The Care of the Patient," *Journal of the American Medical Association* 88 (1927): 876–882.

43. Sweet, "The Efficiency of Inefficiency."

44. Department of Health and Human Services, *Medicare Atypical Antipsychotic Drug Claims for Elderly Nursing Home Residents* (Office of the Inspector General, May 2011).

45. Although the US government sponsors Medicare for all senior citizens, many also have private medical insurance.

46. Daniel R. Levinson, *Medicare Atypical Antipsychotic Drug Claims for Elderly Nursing Home Residents* (Department of Health and Human Services, May 2011), http://oig.hhs.gov/oei/reports/oei-07-08-00150.pdf.

47. Ina Jaffe and Robert Benincasa, "Nursing Homes Rarely Penalized for Oversedating Patients," NPR, December 9, 2014, www.npr.org/sections/health-shots/2014/12/09/368538773/nursing-homes-rarely-penalized-for-oversedating-patients.

48. The Pathstone story is heavily adapted from Ina Jaffe's reporting for NPR: Ina Jaffe and Robert Benincasa, "This Nursing Home Calms Troubling Behavior Without Risky Drugs," NPR, December 9, 2014, www.npr.org/sections/health-shots/2014/12/09/368539057/this-nursing-home-calms-troubling-behavior-without-risky-drugs.

49. "Woman Dies After Farewell to Horse at Wigan Hospital," BBC News, November 7, 2014, www.bbc.com/news/uk-england-manchester-29951094.

50. "Facts and Figures," Facing Death, Frontline, www.pbs.org/wgbh/pages/frontline/facing-death/facts-and-figures; US Department of Health and Human Services, Health, United States, 2010: With Special Feature on Death and Dying, U.S. Department of Health and Human Services (Centers for Disease Control and Prevention, National Center for Health Statistics, 2010), www.cdc.gov/nchs/data/hus/hus10.pdf, 43.

51. National Audit Office, End of Life Care (London: The Stationery Office, 2008).

52. Dennis McCullough, My Mother, Your Mother: Embracing "Slow Medicine," the Compassionate Approach to Caring for Your Aging Loved Ones (New York: Harper, 2008), 48.

53. Susan Pasternak, "End-of-Life Care Constitutes Third Rail of U.S. Health Care Policy Debate," Medicare NewsGroup, June 3, 2013, www.medicarenewsgroup.com/context/understanding-medicare-blog/understanding-medicare-blog/2013/06/03/end-of-life-care-constitutes-third-rail-of-u.s.-health-care-policy-debate.

54. Ezekiel J. Emanuel, Arlene Ash, Wei Yu, Gail Gazelle, Norman G. Levinsky, Olga Saynina, Mark McClellan et al., "Managed Care, Hospice Use, Site of Death, and Medical Expenditures in the Last Year of Life," Archives of Internal Medicine 162, no. 15 (2002): 1722–1728.

55. Wei Yu, End of Life Care: Medical Treatments and Costs by Age, Race, and Region (Health Services Research and Development study IIR, no. 02-189, 2006).

56. Keshia M. Pollack, Dan Morhaim, and Michael A. Williams, "The Public's Perspectives on Advance Directives in Maryland: Implications for State Legislative and Regulatory Policy," Health Policy 96, no. 1 (2010): 57–63.

57. Chana Joffe-Walt, "The Town Where Everyone Talks About Death," NPR, March 5, 2014, =www.npr.org/sections/money/2014/03/05/286126451/living-wills-are-the-talk-of-the-town-in-la-crosse-wis.

58. Baohui Zhang, Alexi A. Wright, Haiden A. Huskamp, Matthew E. Nilsson, Matthew L. Maciejewski, Craig C. Earle, Susan D. Block et al., "Health Care Costs in the Last Week of Life: Associations with End-of-Life Conversations," Archives of Internal Medicine 169, no. 5 (2009): 480–488.

59. "2011 Minnesota Statutes," The Office of the Revisor of Statutes, www.revisor.mn.gov/statutes/percent20?id=256B.0756&year=2011; Shana F. Sandberg, Clese Erikson, Ross Owen, Katherine D. Vickery, Scott T. Shimotsu, Mark Linzer, Nancy A. Garrett et al., "Hennepin Health: A Safety-Net Accountable Care Organization for the Expanded Medicaid Population," Health Affairs 33, no. 11 (2014): 1975–1984.

60. Story drawn from "Member Spotlight: Ron," Hennepin Health, http://content.govdelivery.com/accounts/MNHENNE/bulletins/be91e8.

61. Sandeep Jauhar, "Bring Back House Calls," New York Times, October 14, 2015, www.nytimes.com/2015/10/15/opinion/bring-back-house-calls.html.

62. Debra Umberson and Jennifer Karas Montez, "Social Relationships and Health a Flashpoint for Health Policy," Journal of Health and Social Behavior 51, no. 1 suppl (2010): S54–S66.

63. For more, see Blue Zones, www.bluezones.com.

64. US Department of Health and Human Services, Health, United States, 2014: With Special Feature on Adults Aged 55–64, US Department of Health and Human Services (Centers for Disease

Control and Prevention, National Center for Health Statistics, 2014), www.cdc.gov/nchs/data/hus/hus14.pdf, 302.

65. "How Does the United States Compare?" *OECD Health Statistics 2014*, OECD, www.oecd.org/unitedstates/Briefing-Note-UNITED-STATES-2014.pdf.

66. David A. Squires, *Explaining High Health Care Spending in the United States: An International Comparison of Supply, Utilization, Prices, and Quality* (Commonwealth Fund May 2012), www.commonwealthfund.org/~/media/files/publications/issue-brief/2012/may/1595_squires_explaining_high_hlt_care_spending_intl_brief.pdf.

67. "OECD Health Statistics 2014—Frequently Requested Data," OECD, www.oecd.org/els/health-systems/oecd-health-statistics-2014-frequently-requested-data.htm.

68. Quotes from *The King's Fund Report* and Joyce Robins (of the charity Patient Concern), quoted in "Hospitals 'Are Medical Factories,'" *BBC News*, December 3, 2008, http://news.bbc.co.uk/2/hi/health/7760764.stm.

69. This original figure came from data analysis reported by the UK Health Care Commission. Subsequent investigations in the public inquiry determined that a specific number couldn't be established with certainty but that the level was much higher than it should have been. The head of the public inquiry explained that although he was asked to conduct individual investigations for everyone who died, he deemed this "impracticable." See Robert Francis, *The Mid Staffordshire NHS Foundation Trust Inquiry: Independent Inquiry into Care Provided by Mid Staffordshire Foundation Trust*, vol. 1, January 2005–March 2009 (London: The Stationery Office, 2010), section C.

70. Henry Taylor, "Who Is the Biggest Employer?" World Economic Forum, June 17, 2015, https://agenda.weforum.org/2015/06/worlds-10-biggest-employers.

CHAPTER 5. FOOD

1. Farm Animal and Field Crop Research Facilities Protection Act, Kan. Stat. Ann. §47-1825–1830; Farm Animal and Research Facilities Protection Act, Mont. Code Ann. §81-30-101–105.

2. Senate File 12, Wis. Stat. Ann. §6-3-414.

3. Mo. Rev. Stat. §578.013.1.

4. Property Protection Act, N.C. Gen. Stat. §99A-1–A-2.

5. Patrick Holden, e-mail to authors, December 23, 2014.

6. See PolitiFact's analysis in Becky Bowers, "Rep. Louise Slaughter Says 80% of Antibiotics Are Fed to Livestock," *Tampa Bay Times*'s PolitiFact.com, October 15, 2013.

7. Antibiotics don't work for every disease on factory farms. Porcine epidemic diarrhea, a virus, emerged and spread so quickly that some workers resorted to pureeing the intestines of dead piglets and feeding them back to the mothers in order to "vaccinate" them. I imagine access to pasture, more humane conditions, and a natural diet would have been equally effective at keeping them healthy, but this almost certainly would have been less profitable. See Nick Kristof, "Is That Sausage Worth This?" *New York Times*, February 20, 2014. See also "Fight Cruelty: Chicken FAQ," ASPCA, 2015, www.aspca.org/fight-cruelty/farm-animal-cruelty/chicken-faq; "Welfare Issues for Meat Chickens," Compassion in World Farming, 2014, www.ciwf.org.uk/farm-animals/chickens/meat-chickens/welfare-issues; and Robert F. Wideman and Rhonda D. Prisby, "Bone Circulatory Disturbances in the Development of Spontaneous Bacterial Chondronecrosis with Osteomyelitis: A Translational Model for the Pathogenesis of Femoral Head Necrosis," *Frontiers in Endocrinology* 3 (February 2012).

8. Tom Frieden, *Antibiotic Resistance Threats in the United States, 2013* (Centers for Disease Control and Prevention, US Department of Health and Human Services, 2013), 11.

9. For more, see Maryn McKenna, "How Your Chicken Dinner Is Creating a Drug-Resistant Superbug," *Atlantic*, July 11, 2012, www.theatlantic.com/health/archive/2012/07/how-your-chicken-dinner-is-creating-a-drug-resistant-superbug/259700; and Cólín Nunan and Richard

Young, "E. coli Superbugs on Farms and Food," *The Use and Misuse of Antibiotics in UK Agriculture* 6 (Bristol, England: Soil Association, 2012).

10. L. Trasande, J. Blustein, M. Liu, E. Corwin, L. M. Cox, and M. J. Blaser, "Infant Antibiotic Exposures and Early-Life Body Mass," *International Journal of Obesity* 37, no. 1 (2013): 16–23; Illseung Cho, Shingo Yamanishi, Laura Cox, Barbara A. Methé, Jiri Zavadil, Kelvin Li, Zhan Gao et al., "Antibiotics in Early Life Alter the Murine Colonic Microbiome and Adiposity," *Nature* 488, no. 7413 (2012): 621–626.

11. To its credit, Perdue, a major chicken manufacturer, announced in late 2014 that it would greatly reduce the use of antibiotics "medically important to humans" on its farms. McDonald's and Foster Farms have made similar moves. Although these are steps in the right direction and should be encouraged, general antibiotic use is still profligate (in at least 95 percent of meat sold in the United States), even among these producers.

12. Although E.coli, mad cow, salmonella, and other such outbreaks are indeed likelier to happen in concentrated animal feedlots than on less dense pastures, food disease is always an inevitability, however humane or sustainable the operation is.

13. James R. Johnson, Michael A. Kuskowski, Kirk Smith, Timothy T. O'Bryan, and Sita Tatini, "Antimicrobial-Resistant and Extraintestinal Pathogenic Escherichia coli in Retail Foods," *Journal of Infectious Diseases* 191, no. 7 (2005): 1040–1049.

14. James Andrews, "17 Months and 634 Illnesses Later, CDC Declares Foster Farms-Linked Salmonella Outbreak Over," *Food Safety News*, July 31, 2014, www.foodsafetynews.com/2014/07/after-17-months-foster-farms-salmonella-outbreak-declared-over/#.Vlu7MNKrTDc.

15. Tanya Basu, "Salmonella Scare Causes Recall of 1.7 Million lbs of Frozen Chicken," *Time*, July 14, 2015, www.foodsafetynews.com/2014/07/after-17-months-foster-farms-salmonella-out break-declared-over/#.Vlu7MNKrTDc.

16. Center for Veterinary Medicine and US FDA, *2012 Retail Meat Report: National Antimicrobial Resistance Monitoring System*, www.fda.gov/downloads/AnimalVeterinary/SafetyHealth/Anti microbialResistance/NationalAntimicrobialResistanceMonitoringSystem/UCM442212.pdf, 21.

17. Ellen K. Silbergeld, Jay Graham, and Lance B. Price, "Industrial Food Animal Production, Antimicrobial Resistance, and Human Health," *Annual Review of Public Health* 29 (2008): 151–169.

18. Michael Greger, quoted in Kathy Freston, "E. Coli, Salmonella and Other Deadly Bacteria and Pathogens in Food: Factory Farms Are the Reason," *Huffington Post*, March 18, 2010, www .huffingtonpost.com/kathy-freston/e-coli-salmonella-and-oth_b_415240.html.

19. Elizabeth Landau and Jason Hanna, "USDA: Recalled Beef May Have Reached 35 States," CNN, March 7, 2014, www.cnn.com/2014/03/07/health/beef-product-recall.

20. Jonathan Safran Foer, *Eating Animals* (New York: Back Bay Books, 2009), 135.

21. Ibid.; "Water in Meat and Poultry," USDA FSIS, www.fsis.usda.gov/wps/portal/fsis /topics/food-safety-education/get-answers/food-safety-fact-sheets/meat-preparation/water-in -meat-and-poultry/CT_Index.

22. Howard Moskowitz, quoted in Michael Moss, "The Extraordinary Science of Addictive Junk Food," *New York Times* Magazine, February 24, 2013, http://www.nytimes.com/2013/02/24/ magazine/the-extraordinary-science-of-junk-food.html.

23. "Yoplait Original 25% Less Sugar," Yoplait USA, www.yoplait.com/products/yoplait -original-style-less-sugar; "REESE'S—Product and Nutrition Information—Peanut Butter Cups," The Hershey Company, www.hersheys.com/reeses/products/reeses-peanut-butter-cups/ milk-chocolate.aspx. And this is after Yoplait's (admirable) efforts to reduce sugar in all of its products by 25 percent.

24. "Nutrition & Ingredient Information on Coca-Cola Products," Coca-Cola Company, www .coca-colaproductfacts.com/en/coca-cola-products/coca-cola.

25. "Caramel Frappuccino Blended Coffee," Starbucks Corporation, www.starbucks.com/ menu/drinks/frappuccino-blended-beverages/caramel-frappuccino-blended-beverage.

26. Larry Hand and Madeline Drexler, "Public Health Takes Aim at Sugar and Salt," *Harvard School of Public Health Review*, Fall 2009.

27. "Nutrition Information," Franchise World Headquarters (Subway), www.subway.com/nutrition/nutritionlist.aspx.

28. "Heinz Ketchup," H.J. Heinz Company, www.heinzketchup.com/Products/Heinz%20Ketchup%2038oz.

29. Manny Fernandez, "Cheese Whatevers, City Has Them by the Handful," *New York Times*, August 4, 2010, www.nytimes.com/2010/08/04/nyregion/04cheez.html.

30. Moss, "The Extraordinary Science of Addictive Junk Food."

31. John Cawley and Chad Meyerhoefer, "The Medical Care Costs of Obesity: An Instrumental Variables Approach," *Journal of Health Economics* 31, no. 1 (2012): 219–230.

32. Y. Claire Wang, Klim McPherson, Tim Marsh, Steven L. Gortmaker, and Martin Brown, "Health and Economic Burden of the Projected Obesity Trends in the USA and the UK," *The Lancet* 378, no. 9793 (2011): 815–825.

33. Tatiana Andreyeva, Joerg Luedicke, and Y. Claire Wang, "State-Level Estimates of Obesity-Attributable Costs of Absenteeism," *Journal of Occupational and Environmental Medicine* 56, no. 11 (2014): 1120–1127.

34. Niman Ranch, profiled in more detail on page 110.

35. Matt Rothe, quoted in Erik Olesund, "How the Tractor Ruined Farming," *Green Grid Radio*, June 28, 2014; and from interview by authors, Stanford, CA, October 24, 2014.

36. *Soil: Protect European Soil from Environmental Damage* (European Environmental Bureau, 2015), www.eeb.org/index.cfm/activities/biodiversity-nature/soil.

37. David Pimentel, "Environmental and Economic Costs of the Application of Pesticides Primarily in the United States," in *Integrated Pest Management: Innovation-Development Process*, ed. Rajinder Peshin (Netherlands: Springer, 2009), 89–111.

38. Daniel J. Sobota, Jana E. Compton, and John A. Harrison, "Reactive Nitrogen Inputs to US Lands and Waterways: How Certain Are We About Sources and Fluxes?" *Frontiers in Ecology and the Environment* 11, no. 2 (2013): 82–90.

39. Christopher Leonard, *The Meat Racket: The Secret Takeover of America's Food Business* (New York: Simon & Schuster, 2014), 122.

40. Ibid., 326.

41. Ibid., 17–46, 115–120.

42. Marcy Lowe and Gary Gereffi, *A Value Chain Analysis of the US Beef and Dairy Industries* (Center on Globalization, Governance & Competitiveness, Duke University, 2009), 29.

43. Leonard, *The Meat Racket*, 209.

44. Memo to Honorable Frank D. Lucas from the Congressional Budget Office, www.cbo.gov/sites/default/files/cbofiles/attachments/hr2642LucasLtr.pdf, 6, table 3.

45. Tamar Haspel, "Farm Bill: Why Don't Taxpayers Subsidize the Foods That Are Better for Us?" *Washington Post*, February 18, 2014, www.washingtonpost.com/lifestyle/food/farm-bill-why-dont-taxpayers-subsidize-the-foods-that-are-better-for-us/2014/02/14/d7642a3c-9434-11e3-84e1-27626c5ef5fb_story.html.

46. Ibid.

47. Ilan Brat and Sarah Nassauer, "Chipotle Suspends Pork Sales at a Third of Its Restaurants," *Wall Street Journal*, January 13, 2015, www.wsj.com/articles/chipotle-suspends-pork-sales-at-a-third-of-its-restaurants-1421194340.

48. Allison Aubry, "Antibiotic-Free Meat Business Is Booming, Thanks to Chipotle," NPR, May 31, 2012, www.npr.org/sections/thesalt/2012/05/31/154084442/antibiotic-free-meat-business-is-booming-thanks-to-chipotle.

49. As defended by the pork industry. See Rick Berman, "Commentary: Playing Chicken with Pork," PORK Network, February 28, 2013, www.porknetwork.com/pork-news/Commentary-Playing-chicken-with- pork-193903501.html?view=all.

50. Paul Willis, phone interview by authors, November 12, 2014.

51. Anya Fernald, phone interview by authors, October 20, 2014.

52. Joel L. Greene, *Lean Finely Textured Beef: The "Pink Slime" Controversy* (Washington, DC: Congressional Research Service, 2012).

53. Geico Insurance, "Free Range Chicken: It's What You Do," YouTube.com, March 8, 2015, www.youtube.com/watch?v=3v1wFKKWMCA.

54. Anders Kelto, "Farm Fresh? Natural? Eggs Not Always What They're Cracked Up to Be," NPR, December 23, 2014, www.npr.org/sections/thesalt/2014/12/23/370377902/farm-fresh-natural-eggs-not-always-what-they-re-cracked-up-to-be.

55. "Cage-Free vs. Battery-Cage Eggs," Humane Society, www.humanesociety.org/issues/confinement_farm/facts/cage-free_vs_battery-cage.html; "The Egg Business," American Egg Board, www.aeb.org/images/PDFs/EggBusiness515.pdf.

56. Jim Perdue, quoted in PerdueChicken, "Jim Perdue, Chairman, Perdue Farms," YouTube .com, July 11, 2011, www.youtube.com/watch?v=2a8x_8liZWA.

57. Nicholas Kristof, "Abusing Chickens We Eat," *New York Times*, December 3, 2014, www .nytimes.com/2014/12/04/opinion/nicholas-kristof-abusing-chickens-we-eat.html.

58. "Settlement Reached in Lawsuit Concerning Perdue Chicken Labeling," Humane Society of the United States, October 13, 2014, www.humanesociety.org/news/press_releases/2014/10/Perdue-settlement-101314.html.

59. Michael Pollan, *Cooked: A Natural History of Transformation* (London: Allen Lane, 2013), 264; Allison Aubrey, "Where's the Whole Grain in Most of Our Wheat Bread?," NPR, April 15, 2014, www .npr.org/sections/thesalt/2014/04/15/301473319/wheres-the-whole-grain-in-most-of-our-wheat -bread.

60. Klaus von Grebmer, Amy Saltzman, Ekin Birol, Doris Weismann, Nilam Prasai, Sandra Yin, Yisehac Yohannes et al., *Global Hunger Index: The Challenge of Hidden Hunger, Synopsis* (International Food Policy Research Institute, 2014), www.ifpri.org/publication/synopsis-2014-global -hunger-index-challenge-hidden-hunger; Catherine Price, "Vitamins Hide the Low Quality of Our Food," *New York Times*, February 15, 2015, www.nytimes.com/2015/02/15/opinion/sunday/vitamins-hide-the-low-quality-of-our-food.html.

61. Leicester City Council, "Council Meat Tests Highlight Labelling Concerns," November 3, 2014, http://news.leicester.gov.uk/newsArchiveDetail.aspx?Id=f2792.

62. Department of State, Department of Commerce, *Action Plan for Implementing the Task Force Recommendations* (Presidential Task Force on Combating IUU Fishing and Seafood Fraud, 2015).

63. Kimberly Warner, Walker Timme, Beth Lowell, and Michael Hirshfield, *Oceana Study Reveals Seafood Fraud Nationwide* (Oceana, February 2013), http://oceana.org/sites/default/files/reports/National_Seafood_Fraud_Testing_Results_FINAL.pdf.

64. Michael Pollan, quoted in Ezra Klein, "Big Food," *Vox*, April 23, 2014, www.vox.com /2014/4/23/5627992/big-food-michael-pollan-thinks-wall-street-has-way-too-much-influence.

65. Kelly Brownell, quoted in Moss, "The Extraordinary Science."

66. Dan Barber, "What Farm-to-Table Got Wrong," *New York Times*, May 17, 2014, www.ny times.com/2014/05/18/opinion/sunday/what-farm-to-table-got-wrong.html.

67. Indeed, although I'm happy to excoriate soft drink companies, it does seem rather unfair to single them out while ignoring all the other junk food in our diets. Dietary Guidelines Advisory Committee, *Scientific Report of the 2015 Dietary Guidelines Advisory Committee* (Washington, DC: USDA and US Department of Health and Human Services, 2015).

68. Lynne Terry, "A Game of Chicken: USDA Repeatedly Blinked When Facing Salmonella Outbreaks Involving Foster Farms," *Oregonian*, May 1, 2015.

69. Jean C. Buzby and Jeffrey Hyman, "Total and Per Capita Value of Food Loss in the United States," *Food Policy* 37, no. 5 (2012): 561–570.

70. For more, visit "Animal Welfare," Jeremy Coller Foundation, .jeremycollerfoundation.org/programmes/animal-welfare.

71. J. Kiley Hamlin, "Moral Judgment and Action in Preverbal Infants and Toddlers Evidence for an Innate Moral Core," *Current Directions in Psychological Science* 22, no. 3 (2013): 186–193; Abraham Sagi and Martin L. Hoffman, "Empathic Distress in the Newborn," *Developmental Psychology* 12, no. 2 (1976): 175.

72. Jeremy Bentham, *An Introduction to the Principles of Morals and Legislation*, ch. 17, para. 122 (1789).

73. Nicky Amos and Rory Sullivan, "The Business Benchmark on Farm Animal Welfare: 2014 Report," *Business Benchmark on Farm Animal Welfare* (2014), 35.

74. *Farm Assurance Schemes & Animal Welfare: How the Standards Compare: 2012* (OneKind and Compassion in World Farming, 2012), www.ciwf.org.uk/media/5231246/standards_analysis_exec_summary.pdf.

75. "Philip Lymbery: Chief Executive," Compassion in World Farming, 2014, www.ciwf.org.uk/about-us/our-staff/philip-lymbery.

76. Foer, *Eating Animals*, 59.

CHAPTER 6. CAPITALISM

1. Priorities USA Action, "Stage," YouTube.com, June 23, 2012, www.youtube.com/watch?v=oLooJwjo3JU.

2. Angei Drobnic Holan and Nai Issa, "In Context: Hillary Clinton and Don't Let Anybody Tell You That Corporations Create Jobs," *Tampa Bay Times*'s Politifact, October 30, 2014, www.politifact.com/truth-o-meter/ article/2014/oct/30/context-hillary-clinton-and-dont-let-anybody-tell.

3. Jonathan Sacks, *The Dignity of Difference: Avoiding the Clash of Civilizations* (Foreign Policy Research Institute, July 2002).

4. David Packard, quoted in James C. Collins and Jerry I. Porras, "Building Your Company's Vision," *Harvard Business Review*, September 1996.

5. Estimates on farming vary and range from as recent as sixty-five hundred to as early as fourteen thousand years ago. For various sources, see Felipe Fernández-Armesto, *The World: A History*, 2nd ed. (London: Prentice Hall, 2010), 31–56; Peter Watson, *Ideas: A History of Thought and Invention, from Fire to Freud* (New York: Harper Perennial, 2005), 53; *Collins Atlas of World History*, ed. Geoffrey Barraclough (Ann Arbor, MI: Arbor Press, 2003), 38. For trade, see Matt Ridley, "When Ideas Have Sex," TED Global 2010, Oxford, England, July 2010, www.ted.com/talks/matt_ridley_when_ideas_have_sex?language=en.

6. Ridley, "When Ideas Have Sex."

7. "Low wage" is defined as 10th percentile, "middle wage" as 50th percentile, and "very high wage" as 95th percentile.

8. Lawrence Mishel, Elise Gould, and Josh Bivens, "Wage Stagnation in Nine Charts," Economic Policy Institute, January 6, 2015.

9. Lawrence Mishel and Alyssa Davis, "Top CEOs Make 300 Times More than Typical Workers," Economic Policy Institute, June 21, 2015.

10. Sam Colt, "Tim Cook's Total Pay for 2014 Was over $100 Million," *Business Insider,* January 24, 2015, www.businessinsider.com/heres-how-tim-cook-raked-in-over-100-million-in-2014-2015-1.

11. Reuters, "A.I.G. Pays Its Ex-Chief $47 Million," *New York Times*, July 2, 2008, www.nytimes.com/2008/07/02/business/02aig.html?_r=0; author calculations from Yahoo Finance; Timothy G. Massad, "Overall $182 Billion Committed to Stabilize AIG During the Financial Crisis Is Now Fully Recovered," Treasury Notes, US Department of the Treasury, www. treasury.gov/connect/blog/Pages/aig-182-billion.aspx.

12. Mishel et al., "Wage Stagnation."

13. Data compiled by Robert Colvile from Income Data Services, FTSE, and Bloomberg. See Robert Colvile, "Yes, CEOs Are Ludicrously Overpaid. And Yes, It's Getting Worse," *Telegraph*, October 13, 2014, www.telegraph.co.uk/comment/columnists/robert-colvile/11158607/Yes-CEOs -are-ludicrously-overpaid.-And-yes-its-getting-worse.html.

14. "SEC Adopts Rule for Pay Ratio Disclosure," US Securities and Exchange Commission, August 5, 2015, www.sec.gov/news/pressrelease/2015-160.html.mes.

15. Gary Cohn, "Overcompensation: Tying Corporate Taxes to CEO Pay," *Capital & Main*, August 6, 2015, http://capitalandmain.com/features/california-expose/overcompensation-tying -corporate-taxes-to-ceo-pay.

16. Nassim Nicholas Taleb, *Black Swan: The Impact of the Highly Improbable Fragility* (New York: Random House, 2010), 182.

17. Rex Nutting, "Transcript of Holder's Admission on Too-Big-to-Jail Banks," *Market Watch*, March 7, 2013, http://blogs.marketwatch.com/thetell/2013/03/07/transcript-of-holders -admission-on-too-big-to-jail-banks.

18. Peter Schroeder and Kevin Cirilli, "Warren, Left Fume over Deal," *The Hill*, December 10, 2014, http://thehill.com/regulation/finance/226638-democrats-balking-at-dodd-frank-changes -in-cromnibus.

19. Matt Fuller, "Republican Champion of Dodd-Frank Changes Goes after Elizabeth Warren," *Roll Call*, January 28, 2015, http://blogs.rollcall.com/218/on-a-controversial-law-subtlety -is-key-for-kevin-yoder; "Rep. Keven Yoder: Top 20 Industries Contributing to Campaign Committee," *OpenSecrets.org*, February 2, 2015, www.opensecrets.org/politicians/industries.php ?cycle=2014&cid=N00031502&type=I&newmem=N.

20. Eric Lipton and Ben Protess, "Banks' Lobbyists Help in Drafting Financial Bills," *New York Times*, May 23, 2013, http://dealbook.nytimes.com/2013/05/23/banks-lobbyists-help-in -drafting-financial-bills.

21. Andy Borowtiz, "Citigroup to Move Headquarters to US Capitol Building," *New Yorker*, December 13, 2013, www.newyorker.com/humor/borowitz-report/citigroup-move-headquarters -u-s-capitol-building.

22. Steven Mufson and Tom Hamburger, "Jamie Dimon Himself Called to Urge Support for the Derivatives Rule in the Spending Bill," *Washington Post*, December 11, 2014, www.washington post.com/news/wonk/wp/2014/12/11/the-item-that-is-blowing-up-the-budget-deal.

23. Eric Lipton, "For Freshmen of the House, Seats of Plenty," *New York Times*, August 11, 2013, www.nytimes.com/2013/08/11/us/politics/for-freshmen-in-the-house-seats-of-plenty.html?_r=0.

24. "About: Secretary of the Treasury Jacob J. Lew," US Department of the Treasury, June 5, 2014, www.treasury.gov/about/Pages/Secretary.aspx.

25. Philip Rucker and Joe Stephens, "White House Economics Aide Summers Discloses Income," *Washington Post*, April 4, 2009, www.washingtonpost.com/wp-dyn/content/article/2009 /04/03/AR2009040303732.html.

26. "Alan Greenspan to Consult for Deutsche Bank Corporate and Investment Bank," *Deutsche Bank*, August 13, 2007, www.db.com/presse/en/content/press_releases_2007_3606.htm.

27. Tom Wheeler, "The Facts and Future of Broadband Competition" (speech), 1776 Headquarters, Washington, DC, September 4, 2014.

28. Applications of Comcast Corp. and Time Warner Cable Inc. for Consent to Assign or Transfer Control of Licenses and Authorizations, Second Amended Modified Joint Protective Order, MB Docket No. 14-57, DA 14-1639, November 12, 2014 ("Second Amended Modified Joint Protective Order").

29. Tim Wu, quoted in Claire Cain Miller, "Why the U.S. Has Fallen Behind in Internet Speed and Affordability," *New York Times*, October 30, 2014, www.nytimes.com/2014/10/31/upshot/ why-the-us-has-fallen-behind-in-internet-speed-and-affordability.html.

30. Nick Russo, Robert Morgus, Sarah Morris, and Danielle Kehl, *The Cost of Connectivity* (Washington, DC: Open Technology Institute at New America Foundation, 2014), 12–13.

31. Jenna Wortham, "What Silicon Valley Can Learn from Seoul," *New York Times Sunday Magazine*, June 7, 2015, www.nytimes.com/2015/06/07/magazine/what-silicon-valley-can-learn -from-seoul.html.

32. Richard Holmes, *Falling Upward: How We Took to the Air: An Unconventional History of Ballooning* (New York: Vintage Books, 2013), 351.

33. Jack Nicas, "Airline Consolidation Hits Smaller Cities Hardest," *Wall Street Journal*, September 10, 2015, www.wsj.com/articles/airline-consolidation-hits-smaller-cities-hardest-1441912457.

34. Darren Booth, "United Raises Most Change Fees by $50, Will Others Follow?" CNBC, April 22, 2013, www.cnbc.com/id/100660764; Genevieve Shaw Brown, "United Raises Second Checked Bag Fee on International Flights," *ABC News*, June 12, 2012, http://abcnews.go.com /blogs/lifestyle/2012/06/united-raises-second-checked-bag-fee-on-international-flights; Thom Patterson, "United Airlines Ends Coach Preboarding for Children," CNN, May 23, 2012, www.cnn .com/2012/05/23/travel/united-children-preboarding.

35. Scott McCartney "Merger Fallout: Some Routes See Huge Fare Increases," *Wall Street Journal*, April 11, 2013, http://blogs.wsj.com/middleseat/2013/04/11/american-airlines-us-air-merger -fallout-some-routes-see-huge-fare-increases.

36. Michael D. Wittman and William S. Swelbar, *Evolving Trends of U.S. Domestic Airfares: The Impacts of Competition, Consolidation, and Low-Cost Carriers* (MIT International Center for Transportation, 2013).

37. US Justice Department Complaint, quoted in James B. Stewart, "For Airlines, It May Be One Merger Too Many," *New York Times*, August 17, 2013, www.nytimes.com/2013/08/17/business /for-airlines-it-may-be-one-merger-too-many.html.

38. Jack Nicas, Brent Kendall, and Susan Carey, "Justice Department Probes Airlines for Collusion," *Wall Street Journal*, July 1, 2015, www.wsj.com/articles/justice-department-probes -airlines-for-collusion-1435775547.

39. The researchers, Gerard Hoberg and Gordon Phillips, applied the widely accepted Herfindahl-Hirschman Index (HHI) to numerous companies and overall industries.

40. For information on many of these mergers, see Theo Francis and Ryan Knutson, "Wave of Megadeals Tests Antitrust Limits in U.S.," *Wall Street Journal*, October 18, 2015, www.wsj.com /articles/wave-of-megadeals-tests-antitrust-limits-in-u-s-1445213306.

41. Mark Liebovich, *This Town: Two Parties and a Funeral—Plus, Plenty of Valet Parking!—in America's Gilded Capital* (New York: Penguin Random House, 2013), 330.

42. Paul Blumenthal and Ryan Grim, "The Inside Story of How Citizens United Has Changed Washington Lawmaking," *Huffington Post*, February 25, 2015, www.huffingtonpost.com /2015/02/26/citizens-united-congress_n_6723540.html.

43. Through 2014. See "Who's Up, Who's Down?," *OpenSecrets.org*, 2015, www.opensecrets .org/lobby/incdec.php. See also Lee Drutman, *The Business of America Is Lobbying: How Corporations Became Politicized and Politics Became More Corporate* (Oxford, United Kingdom: Oxford University Press, 2015).

44. Elizabeth Warren, interview by Michael Krasny, *Forum*, 88.5 KQED FM, May 7, 2014.

45. Allison Fitzgerald, "Koch, Exxon Mobil Among Corporations Helping Write State Laws," *Bloomberg*, July 21, 2011, www.bloomberg.com/news/articles/2011-07-21/koch-exxon-mobil -among-corporations-helping-write-state-laws.

46. John Oliver, "Last Week Tonight with John Oliver: State Legislatures and ALEC" (television, HBO), YouTube.com, www.youtube.com/watch?v=aIMgfBZrrZ8.

47. Fitzgerald, "Koch, Exxon Mobil."

48. "Ag-Gag Laws Silence Whistleblowers," Moyers & Company, July 10, 2013, http://bill moyers.com/2013/07/10/alec-activists-and-ag-gag.

49. John Light, "Frequently Asked Questions About ALEC," Moyers & Company, September 28, 2012, http://billmoyers.com/content/frequently-asked-questions-about-alec.

50. Eric Lipton, "Lobbyists, Bearing Gifts, Pursue Attorneys General," New York Times, October 29, 2014, www.nytimes.com/2014/10/29/us/lobbyists-bearing-gifts-pursue-attorneys-general .html.

51. Eric Lipton, "Energy Firms in Secretive Alliance with Attorneys General," New York Times, December 7, 2014, www.nytimes.com/2014/12/07/us/politics/energy-firms-in-secretive-alliance -with-attorneys-general.html.

52. Eric Lipton, Griff Palmer, and Alicia Parlapiano, "Money Going to Attorneys General," New York Times, October 28, 2014, www.nytimes.com/interactive/2014/10/28/us/politics/money -going-to-state-attorneys-general.html.

53. Lipton, "Lobbyists, Bearing Gifts."

54. Joe Nocera, "Are Our Courts for Sale?" New York Times, October 28, 2014, www.nytimes .com/2014/10/28/opinion/joe-nocera-are-our-courts-for-sale.html.

55. Joe Pinsker, "It's Cheaper to Buy a Judge than a State Senator," Atlantic, November 2, 2014, www.theatlantic.com/business/archive/2014/11/its-cheaper-to-buy-a-judge-than-a-state-senator /382198/.

56. Between 2000 and 2014 $288 million was spent on judicial elections, as opposed to $17 billion on congressional elections in the same period. For more, see AJ Vicens, "How Dark Money Is Taking over Judicial Elections," Mother Jones, October 2014, www.motherjones.com/ politics/2014/10/judicial-elections-dark-money.

57. Ibid. Blankenship's victory was short-lived: the Supreme Court reversed the ruling in 2009, citing the extreme conflict of interest. Perhaps unsurprisingly, Blankenship was separately found guilty in December 2015 of conspiracy to violate mine safety standards in connection with an explosion in a mine he owned that killed twenty-nine of his workers. See Kris Maher, "Ex-Coal CEO Heads to Trial for Alleged Worker-Safety Breaches," Wall Street Journal, September 30, 2015, www .wsj.com/articles/ex-coal-ceo-heads-to-trial-for-alleged-worker-safety-breaches-1443660020.

58. Brian Kelleher Richter, Krislert Samphantharak, and Jeffrey F. Timmons, "Lobbying and Taxes," American Journal of Political Science 53, no. 4 (2009): 893–909.

59. Robert S. Chirnko and Daniel J. Wilson, Can Lower Tax Rates Be Bought? Business Rent-Seeking and Tax Competition Among U.S. States (Federal Reserve Bank of San Francisco, Working Paper 2009-29, 2010).

60. Specifically the firm has an index that tracks the stock prices of these firms. For more, see "The Fury of the Makers," Economist, October 25, 2014, www.economist.com/news/united -states/21627659-big-business-angry-small-firms-are-even-angrier-fury-makers.

61. Christopher Witko, "Campaign Contributions, Access, and Government Contracting," Journal of Public Administration Research and Theory 23, no. 2 (2013): 457–494.

62. Represented Entities, Governmental Affairs Agents and Persons Communicating with the General Public Listed by Expenditures Ranking, Calendar Year 2013 (New Jersey Election Law Enforcement Commission, 2013), www.elec.state.nj.us/pdffiles/Lobby13/l1exp.pdf.

63. Lee Drutman, The Business of America Is Lobbying: How Corporations Became Politicized and Politics Became More Corporate (Oxford, United Kingdom: Oxford University Press, 2015), 13–14.

64. Ibid., 45.

65. "The FACTS About Open Payments Data," US Department of Health and Human Services, http://openpaymentsdata.cms.gov.

66. Figures derived from author calculations. See "City of Hope National Medical Center: Summary Information for Program Year 2014," Open Payments Data, Center for Medicare and Medicaid Services, https://openpaymentsdata.cms.gov/hospital/1128.

67. "Chitranjan Ranawat," Open Payments Data, https://openpaymentsdata.cms.gov/physician /286526.

68. Federal Trade Commission, "Pay-for-Delay: How Drug Company Pay-Offs Cost Consumers Billions," 2010, www.ftc.gov/reports/pay-delay-how-drug-company-pay-offs-cost-consumers-billions-federal-trade-commission-staff.

69. Joe Nation, E-mail correspondence with authors. Stanford, CA, January 20, 2016.

70. Judy Lin, "California's Pension Liability Growing by Billions," *Los Angeles Daily News*, November 14, 2014, http://www.dailynews.com/government-and-politics/20141114/californias-pension-liability-growing-by-billions/. *Pension Tracker,* Stanford Institute for Economic Policy Research, http://www.pensiontracker.org.

71. That we dislike cheating is no surprise, of course, but it's telling that we will, as humans, give up some of our reward in a transaction if it means penalizing someone who has cheated. In repeated versions of the "Ultimatum Game," psychologists allow a participant to divide an amount of money between themselves and a second participant however they choose, with the caveat that if the second person rejects the offer, neither gets anything. Although the economically rational decision would be to accept any offer above 0, it's almost always the case that if the second participant feels short-changed, they are more likely to retaliate by rejecting the money—hurting themselves in order to punish the first participant.

72. Sutirtha Bagchi and Jan Svejnar, "Does Wealth Inequality Matter for Growth? The Effect of Billionaire Wealth, Income Distribution, and Poverty," *Journal of Comparative Economics* 43, no. 3 (August 2015): 505–530.

73. John M. Connor and Robert H. Lande, "Cartels as Rational Business Strategy: Crime Pays," *Cardozo Law Review* 34, no. 427 (2012): 427–489, 430.

74. Stanford, who also served as California governor and represented the state in the US Senate, founded the university in 1885 with his wife, Jane, in honor of their late teenage son, Leland Stanford Jr.

75. Robert Reich, "Big Tech Has Become Way Too Powerful," *New York Times*, September 18, 2015, www.nytimes.com/2015/09/20/opinion/is-big-tech-too-powerful-ask-google.html.

76. US Census Bureau, *Business Dynamics Statistics: Firm Characteristics Data Tables* (Washington, DC: Department of Commerce, 2015), www.census.gov/ces/dataproducts/bds/data_firm.html.

77. "Red Dress Boutique," *SharkTank* Blog, http://sharktankblog.com/business/red-dress-boutique.

78. Rolfe Winkler and Douglas MacMillan, "The Secret Math of Airbnb's $24 Billion Valuation," *Wall Street Journal*, June 17, 2015, www.wsj.com/articles/the-secret-math-of-airbnbs-24-billion-valuation-1434568517.

79. Bastian Lehmann, quoted in Farhad Manjoo, "Amazon Not as Unstoppable as It Might Appear," *New York Times*, December 18, 2014, www.nytimes.com/2014/12/18/technology/personaltech/amazon-not-as-unstoppable-as-it-may-appear.html.

80. Carolyn Said, "Peers Helps Uber, Lyft Drivers Get Back on Road After Accidents," *San Francisco Chronicle*, December 4, 2014, http://sanfrancisco.suntimes.com/sf-business/7/74/42864/peers-helps-uber-lyft-drivers-get-back-on-road-after-accidents.

81. Mark Rogowsky, "After the New Jersey Ban, Here's Where Tesla Can (and Cannot) Sell Its Cars)," *Forbes*, March 15, 2014, www.forbes.com/sites/markrogowsky/2014/03/15/after-the-new-jersey-ban-heres-where-tesla-can-and-cannot-sell-its-cars.

82. "Michigan Becomes 5th US State to Thwart Direct Tesla Car Sales," *Reuters*, October 22, 2014, www.reuters.com/article/2014/10/21/tesla-motors-michigan-idUSL2N0SG2YE20141021.

CHAPTER 7. BUSINESS

1. Mohammed Abdul Ali and Abdul Kader, quoted in Jim Yardley, "Bangladesh Pollution, Told in Colors and Smells," *New York Times*, July 15, 2013, www.nytimes.com/2013/07/15/world/asia/bangladesh-pollution-told-in-colors-and-smells.html.

2. Emily Chang, "China's Famed Pearl River Under Denim Threat," CNN, April 27, 2010, www.cnn.com/2010/WORLD/asiapcf/04/26/china.denim.water.pollution.

3. "Dye Industry: Fact Sheet," Green Cross Switzerland, 2012, www.greencross.ch/nc/en/print/news-info-en/case-studies/environmental-reports/ten-most-dangerous-sources-of-environmental-toxins-2012/2012/dye-industry.html.

4. Sajjad Hussein, "Six Months After Bangladesh Factory Collapse, Workers Remain in Peril," CNN, October 24, 2013, www.cnn.com/2013/10/24/opinion/bangladesh-garment-workers.

5. Mark Spera, quoted in Angela Salazar, "BeGood Clothing's New Line—Organic Cotton and Silk Basics," *SF Gate*, September 12, 2014, www.sfgate.com/style/article/BeGood-Clothing-s-new-line-organic-cotton-and-5629690.php.

6. As reported in Larry Buchannan, Josh Keller, and Haeyoun Park, "Your Contribution to the California Drought," *New York Times*, May 21, 2015, www.nytimes.com/interactive/2015/05/21/us/your-contribution-to-the-california-drought.html?_r=0. For some original figures, see either Mesfin M. Mekonnen and Arjen Y. Hoekstra, "A Global Assessment of the Water Footprint of Farm Animal Products," *Ecosystems* 15, no. 3 (2012): 401–415, or various estimates as assessed by the Pacific Institute.

7. "Water Conservation Tips," *National Geographic*, http://environment.nationalgeographic.com/environment/freshwater/water-conservation-tips.

8. Simon Head, *Mindless: Why Smarter Machines Are Making Dumber Humans* (New York: Basic Books, 2014), 42.

9. Journalist Carole Cadwalladr spent a week working in Amazon's Swansea, Wales, factory. She recounts her experience here: Carole Cadwalladr, "My Week as an Amazon Insider," *Guardian*, November 30, 2013, www.theguardian.com/technology/2013/dec/01/week-amazon-insider-feature-treatment-employees-work.

10. Simon Head, "Worse than Wal-Mart: Amazon's Sick Brutality and Secret History of Ruthlessly Intimidating Workers," *Salon*, February 23, 2014, www.salon.com/2014/02/23/worse_than_wal_mart_amazons_sick_brutality_and_secret_history_of_ruthlessly_intimidating_workers.

11. Jodi Kantor and David Streitfeld, "Amazon's Bruising, Thrilling Workplace," *New York Times*, August 16, 2014, www.nytimes.com/images/2015/08/16/nytfrontpage/scan.pdf.

12. "Full Memo: Jeff Bezos Responds to Brutal NYT story, Says It Doesn't Represent the Amazon He Leads," *GeekWire*, August 16, 2015, www.geekwire.com/2015/full-memo-jeff-bezos-responds-to-cutting-nyt-expose-says-tolerance-for-lack-of-empathy-needs-to-be-zero.

13. Spencer Woodman, "Exclusive: Amazon Makes Even Temporary Warehouse Worker Sign 18-Month Non-Competes," *Verge*, March 26, 2015, www.theverge.com/2015/3/26/8280309/amazon-warehouse-jobs-exclusive-noncompete-contracts.

14. In addition to undercover investigations cited above, you can view video from another by the BBC's *Panorama*, 2013, www.bbc.co.uk/programmes/b03k5kzp. In its response, Amazon also said that it "adhere[s] to all regulations and employment law." Although its response is no longer posted on its website, it is quoted in Matthew Jarvis, "Amazon Response to BBC Panorama Worker Criticism," *PCR*, November 26, 2013, http://www.pcr-online.biz/news/read/amazon-responds-to-bbc-panorama-worker-criticism/032581.

15. Peter Rudegeair, "Pay Gap Between Wall Street CEOs and Employees Narrows," *Wall Street Journal*, April 5, 2015, www.wsj.com/articles/a-pay-gap-narrows-on-wall-street-1428267898.

16. Gretchen Morgenson, "The Boss Actually Said This: Pay Me Less," *New York Times*, December 18, 2005, http://query.nytimes.com/gst/fullpage.html?res=9D01EFDC1630F93BA25751C1A9639C8B63.

17. Will Ashworth, "RiskMetrics Two Years After IPO," *Investopedia*, February 28, 2010, www.investopedia.com/stock-analysis/2010/riskmetrics-two-years-after-ipo-riskmscimhptrifigacas0304.aspx.

18. Almuth McDowall, quoted in Emma Jacobs, "Strategies for Calling Time on Long Hours," *Financial Times*, August 18, 2014.

19. Sir Richard Branson, "Excerpt from: *The Virgin Way: Everything I Know About Leadership*," Virgin.com, September 23, 2014, www.virgin.com/richard-branson/why-were-letting-virgin-staff -take-as-much-holiday-as-they-want.

20. According to a study by conducted by Expedia and the consultancy Northstar. See "Expedia's 2014 Vacation Deprivation Study: Americans and Asian Workers Lag Well Behind Europeans in Vacationing," *PR Newswire*, November 6, 2014, www.prnewswire.com/news-releases/expedias-2014-vacation-deprivation-study-americans-and-asian-workers-lag-well-behind -europeans-in-vacationing-281743231.html.

21. Anne-Marie Slaughter, "Why Women Still Can't Have It All," *Atlantic*, June 13, 2012, www .theatlantic.com/magazine/archive/2012/07/why-women-still-cant-have-it-all/309020.

22. Heather Boushey, "Family Policy: The Foundation of a Middle-Out Agenda," *Democracy* no. 29 (Summer 2013).

23. Peter H. Villanova, John Bernardin, Sue A. Dahmus, and Randi L. Sims, "Rater Leniency and Performance Appraisal Discomfort," *Educational and Psychological Measurement* 53, no. 3 (1993): 789–799.

24. Sam Culbert, quoted in Melissa Dahl, "It's Time to Kill the Performance Review," *New York Magazine*, June 1, 2015, http://nymag.com/scienceofus/2015/05/time-to-revamp-the -performance-review.html.

25. Thomas Krommenacker and Ben Robinson, *Metro Bank: Breaking the Mould but Breaking the Malaise?* (Geneva, Switzerland: Temenos Headquarters SA, 2011), 13.

26. Mary Beth Quirk, "Zappos CSR's Kindness Warms Our Cold Hearts," *Consumerist*, January 17, 2011, http://consumerist.com/2011/01/17/zappos-customer-service-reps-kindness-warms -our-cold-hearts.

27. Armando Roggio, "The Zappos Effect: 5 Great Customer Ideas for Smaller Business," *Practical Ecommerce*, March 21, 2011, www.practicalecommerce.com/articles/2662-The-Zappos -Effect-5-Great-Customer-Service-Ideas-for-Smaller-Businesses.

28. Nathan Vardi, "How 'The Outsiders' Became One of the Most Important Business Books in America," *Forbes*, May 8, 2014, www.forbes.com/sites/nathanvardi/2014/05/08/how -the-outsiders-became-one-of-the-most-important-business-books-in-america.

29. William Thorndike, *The Outsiders: Eight Unconventional CEOs and Their Radically Rational Blueprint for Success* (Cambridge, MA: Harvard University Press, 2012), xii.

30. Ibid., 202.

31. Ibid., 70, 73.

32. Ibid., 23.

33. William Weldon, interview, *Knowledge@Wharton*, June 25, 2008, http://knowledge .wharton.upenn.edu/article/johnson-johnson-ceo-william-weldon-leadership-in-a-decentralized -company.

34. As of 2006. See J. Michael McGinnis, Jennifer Appleton Gootman, and Vivica I. Kraak, eds. *Food Marketing to Children and Youth: Threat or Opportunity?* (Washington, DC: National Academies Press, 2006), 4.

35. Catherine V. Shehan and Jennifer L. Harris, *Trends in Television Food Advertising to Young People: 2014 Update* (UConn Rudd Center for Food Policy and Obesity, 2015).

36. McGinnis, Gootman, and Kraak, *Food Marketing to Children and Youth*.

37. Christina A. Roberto, Jenny Baik, Jennifer L. Harris, and Kelly D. Brownell, "Influence of Licensed Characters on Children's Taste and Snack Preferences," *Pediatrics* 126, no. 1 (2010): 88–93.

38. Jennifer L Harris, Catherine Shehan, Renne Gross, et. al., "Food Advertising Targeted to Hispanic and Black Youth: Contributing to Health Disparities," Rudd Center for Food Policy & Obesity, 2015, 27.

39. Xiaomei Cai and Xiaoquan Zhao, "Click Here, Kids!" *Journal of Children and Media*, 4, no. 2 (2010): 135–154.

40. Jennifer Culp, Robert A. Bell, and Diana Cassady, "Characteristics of Food Industry Web Sites and 'Advergames' Targeting Children," *Journal of Nutrition Education and Behavior*, 42, no. 3 (2010): 197–201.

41. "Advertising to Children and Teens: Current Practices," *Common Sense Media,* Spring 2014, 8.

42. "Eat Brighter!" *Produce Marketing Association,* 2015, http://www.pma.com/events/eat-brighter.

43. Emma Halliwell, Alice Easun, and Diana Harcourt, "Body Dissatisfaction: Can a Short Media Literacy Message Reduce Negative Media Exposure Effects Amongst Adolescent Girls?" *British Journal of Health Psychology* 16, no. 2 (2011): 396–403.

43. Anna Holmes, "Untouched Cover Photos Wanted: $10,000 Reward," *Jezebel,* May 21, 2007.

45. Victoria Rideout, *Advertising to Children and Teens: Current Practices* (San Francisco, CA: Common Sense Media, 2014), 15.

46. Neala Ambrosi Randić, "Perception of Current and Ideal Body Size in Preschool Age Children," *Perceptual and Motor Skills* 90, no. 3 (2000): 885–889.

47. Girl Scouts and the Dove Self-Esteem Fund, "Girls and Body Image," www.girlscouts.org/content/dam/girlscouts-gsusa/forms-and-documents/about-girl-scouts/research/beauty_redefined_factsheet.pdf.

48. Ray Anderson, quoted in Emily Langer, "Ray Anderson, 'Greenest CEO in America,' Dies at 77," *Washington Post,* August 10, 2011, www.washingtonpost.com/local/obituaries/ray-anderson-greenest-ceo-in-america-dies-at-77/2011/08/10/gIQAGoTU7I_story.html.

49. "Press Release: Interface Reports Fourth Quarter and Fiscal Year 2014 Results', *Interface,* February 18, 2015, http://www.interfaceglobal.com/Investor-Relations/Press-Releases.aspx."

50. "Ray Anderson, Interface Chairman and Sustainability Leader, Dies at 77," Environmental Leader, August 9, 2011, http://www.environmentalleader.com/2011/08/09/ray-anderson-interface-chairman-and-sustainability-leader-dies-at-77.

51. Steve Hilton and Giles Gibbons, *Good Business: Your World Needs You* (London: Texere Publishing, 2002): 56–58.

52. Liam Casey, interview by Piers Fawkes, *PSFK 2015,* May 18, 2015.

53. David Bonbright, interview by authors, Palo Alto, CA, October 24, 2014.

54. Elon Musk, "All Our Patent Are Belong to You [sic]," *Tesla Motors,* June 12, 2014, www.teslamotors.com/blog/all-our-patent-are-belong-you.

55. Natasha Jones, "Funding Circle and Santander Announce Partnership to Support Thousands of UK Businesses," *Funding Circle,* June 18, 2014, www.fundingcircle.com/blog/2014/06/funding-circle-santander-announce-partnership-support-thousands-uk-businesses.

56. Mark Kleinman, "Temasek Snaps Up Stake in UK's Funding Circle," *Sky News,* April 2, 2015, http://news.sky.com/story/1457480/temasek-snaps-up-stake-in-uks-funding-circle.

57. "What Is a Benefit Corporation?" *B Lab,* 2015, http://benefitcorp.net.

58. Ainsley O'Connell, "Most Innovative Companies 2015: Revolution Foods," *Fast Company,* 2015, www.fastcompany.com/3039619/most-innovative-companies-2015/revolution-foods.

59. Sarah Perez, "AOL Co-Founder Steve Case Invests $30 Million into School Lunch Company, Revolution Foods," *TechCrunch,* June 5, 2014, http://techcrunch.com/2014/06/05/aol-co-founder-steve-case-invests-30-million-into-school-lunch-company-revolution-foods.

60. "How We Work," Andela, 2015, www.andela.co/how-we-work.

61. Allie Bidwell, "An African Company Pays People to Learn Computer Science," *U.S. News & World Report,* May 14, 2015, www.usnews.com/news/stem-solutions/articles/2015/05/14/andela-an-african-company-paying-people-to-learn-computer-science.

62. Christine Magee, "Backed by Spark Capital, Andela Will Develop a Continent of Tech Talent," *Techcrunch,* June 25, 2015, http://techcrunch.com/2015/06/25/backed-by-spark-capital-andela-will-develop-a-continent-of-tech-talent.

CHAPTER 8. POVERTY

1. David Robinson, interview by authors, London, September 24, 2014.

2. Roughly $8 at 2003 exchange rates.

3. Abdul Durrant, quoted in Nick Cohen, "A Tale of Two Cities," *Guardian*, October 19, 2013, www.theguardian.com/politics/2003/oct/19/socialexclusion.london.

4. Adam Corlett and Laura Gardiner, "Low Pay Britain 2015," Resolution Foundation, October 5, 2015, www.resolutionfoundation.org/publications/low-pay-britain-2015.

5. The Pew study defines "near minimum wage" as between the federal minimum wage and $10.10, the amount to which President Obama unsuccessfully tried to raise the federal minimum wage in 2014. Thus, this figure does not include minimum-wage earners in jurisdictions that have wage floors above $10.10. For more, see Drew Desilver and Steve Schwarzer, "Making More than Minimum Wage, but Less than $10.10 an Hour," Pew Research Center, November 5, 2014, www.pewresearch.org/fact-tank/2014/11/05/making-more-than-minimum-wage-but-less-than-10-10-an-hour.

6. Sendhil Mullainathan, quoted in Maria Konnikova, "No Money, No Time," *New York Times*, June 15, 2014, http://opinionator.blogs.nytimes.com/2014/06/13/no-clocking-out.

7. Sendhil Mullainathan and Eldar Shafir, *Scarcity: Why Having Too Little Means So Much* (New York: Time Books, 2013), 160.

8. Mullainathan, quoted in Konnikova, "No Money, No Time."

9. Johannes Haushofer, quoted in Nicholas Kristof, "It's Not Just About Bad Choices," *New York Times*, June 14, 2015, www.nytimes.com/2015/06/14/opinion/sunday/nicholas-kristof-its-not-just-about-bad-choices.html.

10. Peter Hotez, quoted in Kristof, "It's Not Just About Bad Choices." For the study, see Peter J. Hotez, "Neglected Infections of Poverty in the United States and Their Effects on the Brain," *JAMA Psychiatry* 71, no. 10 (2014): 1099–1100.

11. Kayte Lawton and Matthew Pennycook, *Beyond the Bottom Line: The Challenges and Opportunities of a Living Wage* (London: IPPR and Resolution Foundation, 2013).

12. Oxfam defines low wage as those who would see a wage increase by a minimum wage hike to $10.10 an hour. For their purposes, that equates to workers earning $7.00 to $11.50 an hour. "Working Poor Families in America," OXFAM America, http://policy-practice.oxfamamerica.org/publications/working-poor-families-in-america.

13. Tom MacInnes, Hannah Aldridge, Sabrina Bushe, Peter Kenway, and Adam Tinson, *Monitoring Poverty and Social Exclusion, 2013* (York, United Kingdom: Joseph Rowntree Foundation, 2013).

14. Alfred Deakin, quoted in Marilyn Lake, "Minimum Wage Is More than a Safety Net, It's a Symbol of Australian Values," *The Age* (Melbourne, Australia), April 10, 2014, www.theage.com.au/comment/minimum-wage-is-more-than-a-safety-net-its-a-symbol-of-australian-values-20140409-zqsii.html.

15. Sir Winston Churchill, Hansard House of Commons Debates, April 28, 1909, vol. 4, cols. 342–411.

16. Jonathan Grossman, "Fair Labor Standards Act of 1938: Maximum Struggle for Minimum Wage," *Monthly Labor Review*, June 1978, republished by the US Department of Labor, www.dol.gov/dol/aboutdol/history/flsa1938.htm.

17. Labor economists David Card and Alan Krueger found a minimum wage in one jurisdiction they studied increased hiring by 13 percent. See David Card and Alan B. Krueger, "Minimum Wages and Employment: A Case Study of the Fast Food Industry in New Jersey and Pennsylvania," *National Bureau of Economic Research*, no. w4509, 1993.

18. Desilver and Schwarzer, "Making More than Minimum Wage."

19. Irene Tung, Paul K. Sonn, and Yannet Lathrop, "The Growing Movement for $15," National Employment Law Project, April 13, 2015, http://nelp.org/publication/growing-movement-15.

20. "Policy Basics: The Earned Income Tax Credit," Center on Budget and Policy Priorities, August 20, 2015, www.cbpp.org/research/policy-basics-the-earned-income-tax-credit.

21. Amy Glasmeier, "Living Wage Calculator," MIT, 2015, http://livingwage.mit.edu.

22. Lake, "Minimum Wage Is More than a Safety Net."

23. "Global Powers of Retailing 2015: Embracing Innovation," Deloitte, 2015, www2.deloitte .com/au/en/pages/consumer-business/articles/global-powers-of-retailing.html.

24. Unless otherwise noted, all facts and quotes related to Costco come from Brad Stone, "Costco CEO Craig Jelinek Leads the Cheapest, Happiest Company in the World," *Bloomberg Business*, June 6, 2013, www.bloomberg.com/bw/articles/2013-06-06/costco-ceo-craig-jelinek -leads-the-cheapest-happiest-company-in-the-world.

25. "Costco Wholesale Corp," *MarketWatch*, March 29, 2015, www.marketwatch.com/ investing/stock/cost/financials.

26. William Lazonick, "Profits Without Prosperity," *Harvard Business Review*, September 2014, https://hbr.org/2014/09/profits-without-prosperity.

27. Henry Ford and Samuel Crowther, *The Great Today and Greater Future* (Sydney, Australia: Cornstalk Publishing, 1926; reprint: Whitefish, MT: Kessinger Publishing, 2003), 198–199.

28. Jack Welch, quoted in Francesco Guerrera, "Welch Condemns Share Price Focus," *Financial Times*, March 12, 2009.

29. Paul Polman, quoted in Eric Reguly, "Time to Put an End to the Cult of Shareholder Value," *Globe and Mail* (Toronto, Canada), September 26, 2013, www.theglobeandmail.com/report-on -business/rob-magazine/maybe-its-time-for-ceos-to-put-shareholders-second/article14507016.

30. Cameron Tait, *Work That Pays: The Final Report of the Living Wage Commission* (London, United Kingdom: Living Wage Commission, 2014), 18.

31. Lawton and Pennycook, *Beyond the Bottom Line*, 18.

32. "Joe's Crab Shack Leads Industry in No Tipping Test," Joe's Crab Shack, November 11, 2015, joescrabshack.com/media-center.

33. See Molly Dahl, Thomas DeLeire, and Jonathan Schwabish, "Stepping Stone or Dead End? The Effect of the EITC on Earnings Growth," *National Tax Journal* (2009): 329–346; Nada Eissa and Hilary W. Hoynes, "Behavioral Responses to Taxes: Lessons from the EITC and Labor Supply," in *Tax Policy and the Economy*, vol. 20. ed. James Poterba (Cambridge, MA: MIT Press, 2006): 76–110; and Raj Chetty and John N. Friedman, "New Evidence on the Long-Term Impacts of Tax Credits," *Proceedings: Annual Conference on Taxation and Minutes of the Annual Meeting of the National Tax Association* 104 (2011): 116–124.

34. Jesse Rothstein, *The Unintended Consequences of Encouraging Work: Tax Incidence and the EITC* (Princeton, NJ: Center for Economic Policy Studies, Princeton University, 2008).

35. Although Walmart has recently increased wages a small bit to counter growing turnover, most of its workers are overwhelmingly low paid. See Sruthi Ramakrishnan, "Wal-Mart to Raise Wages for 100,000 U.S. Workers in Some Departments," *Reuters*, June 2, 2015, www.reuters.com/ article/2015/06/02/us-wal-mart-stores-wages-idUSKBN0OI1EW20150602.

36. Krissy Clark, "Part II: 'Save Money, Live Better,'" American Public Media: Marketplace, April 2, 2014.

37. There is no comprehensive study comparing employers of food-stamp recipients. For more, see Katie Sanders, "Alan Grayson Says More Walmart Employees on Medicaid, Food Stamps than Other Companies," *Tampa Bay Times's* PolitiFact, December 6, 2012, www.politifact .com/truth-o-meter/statements/2012/dec/06/alan-grayson/alan-grayson-says-more-walmart -employees-medicaid; and Raz Godelnik, "The Link Between Walmart, Food Stamps and CSR," *Triple Pundit*, April 22, 2014, www.triplepundit.com/2014/04/link-walmart-food-stamps-lack-csr.

38. Kim Souza, "Wal-Mart Downplays SNAP Cuts (Updated)" *City Wire*, October 16, 2013, http://talkbusiness.net/2013/10/wal-mart-downplays-snap-cuts-updated.

39. For more, see Americans for Tax Fairness, *Walmart on Tax Day: How Taxpayers Subsidize*

America's Biggest Employer and Richest Family (Washington, DC: Americans for Tax Fairness, April 2014), www.americansfortaxfairness.org/files/Walmart-on-Tax-Day-Americans-for-Tax-Fairness-1.pdf, 3.

40. According to the Economic Policy Institute, raising the national minimum wage to $12 per hour, which is still below the living wage level in most regions, would lift the wages of 35.1 million workers—more than a quarter of workers in the United States. The average affected worker would earn over $2,000 more each year.

Raising the wage to $10.10 would still mean that 1.7 million American workers would no longer rely on public assistance programs, including not only EITC but also food stamps, home energy subsidies, and other cash assistance programs. This would reduce government spending by $7.6 billion per year, not counting savings from eliminating much of the bureaucracy now needed to administer those interventions. Meanwhile such a raise would provide 27 million workers—20.5 percent of US wage earners—with $31.8 billion in additional wages. A living wage would also increase government revenue from payroll and income tax revenue. See David Cooper, *EPI Briefing Paper #405: Raising the Minimum Wage to $12 by 2020 Would Lift Wages for 35 Million American Workers* (Washington, DC: Economic Policy Institute, 2015); David Cooper, "Raising the Minimum Wage to $10.10 Would Save Safety Net Programs Billions and Help Ensure Businesses Are Doing Their Fair Share," Economic Policy Institute, October 16, 2014.

41. *An Unhealthy Dose of Stress: The Impact of Adverse Childhood Experiences and Toxic Stress on Childhood Health and Development* (Center for Youth Wellness).

42. Paul Tough, "The Poverty Clinic," *New Yorker*, March 21, 2008, www.newyorker.com/magazine/2011/03/21/the-poverty-clinic, 25–32.

43. This story is drawn from Jane Ellen Stevens, "The Adverse Childhood Experiences Study—The Largest, Most Important Public Health Study You Never Heard of Began in an Obesity Clinic," *ACES Too High News*, October 3, 2012, http://acestoohigh.com/2012/10/03/the-adverse-childhood-experiences-study-the-largest-most-important-public-health-study-you-never-heard-of-began-in-an-obesity-clinic.

44. Nadine Burke Harris, "The Chronic Stress of Poverty: Toxic Stress to Children," *The Shriver Report*, January 12, 2014, http://shriverreport.org/the-chronic-stress-of-poverty-toxic-to-children-nadine-burke-harris; Vincent J. Felitti, Robert F. Anda, Dale Nordenberg, David F. Williamson, Alison M. Spitz, Valerie Edwards, Mary P. Koss et al., "The Relationship of Adult Health Status to Childhood Abuse and Household Dysfunction," *American Journal of Preventive Medicine* 14 (1998): 245–258.

45. Those who suffer from toxic stress are 2.2 times as likely to suffer from ischemic heart disease, 2.4 times as likely to have a stroke, 1.9 times as likely to suffer from cancer, 1.6 times as likely to suffer from diabetes, 12.2 times as likely to attempt suicide, 10.3 times as likely to use injection drugs, and 7.4 times as likely to be an alcoholic. For more, see "An Unhealthy Dose of Stress." For the original study, see Felitti et al., "The Relationship of Adult Health Status."

46. As defined by the American Academy of Pediatrics. For more, see Sara B. Johnson, Anne W. Riley, Douglas A. Granger, and Jenna Riis, "The Science of Early Life Toxic Stress for Pediatric Practice and Advocacy," *Pediatrics* 131, no. 2 (2013): 319–327.

47. Nadine Burke Harris, interview by authors, San Francisco, CA, October 6, 2014.

48. This reflects the federal government only, not inclusive of state, local, and broader economic costs, which are not insignificant. Journalist Mike Konczal wrote a detailed breakdown of government poverty statistics in Mike Konczal, "No, We Don't Spend $1 Trillion on Welfare Each Year," *Washington Post*, January 24, 2014, www.washingtonpost.com/news/wonk/wp/2014/01/12/no-we-dont-spend-1-trillion-on-welfare-each-year.

49. "Excessive Drinking Costs U.S. $223 Billion," Centers for Disease Control and Prevention, April 17, 2014, www.cdc.gov/features/alcoholconsumption. Although this figure is from a 2006 study, it is the most recently done on the subject and is still used by the CDC.

50. *National Drug Threat Assessment 2011* (Washington, DC: US Department of Justice National Drug Intelligence Center, August 2011).

51. Harry J. Holzer, Diane Whitmore Schanzenbach, Greg J. Duncan, and Jens Ludwig, "The Economic Costs of Childhood Poverty in the United States," *Journal of Children and Poverty* 14, no. 1 (2008): 41–61.

52. These are based on 2007 numbers, including economic losses to victims and criminal justice expenditures, including those on police, corrections, and other legal proceedings. See a discussion of these statistics in Kathryn E. McCollister, Michael T. French, and Hai Fang, "The Cost of Crime to Society: New Crime-Specific Estimates for Policy and Program Evaluation," *Drug Alcohol Dependence* 108, no. 1 (2010): 98–109.

53. One study estimates that each year's cohort of high school dropouts will lose out on approximately $154 billion over their lifetimes. For more, see *The High Cost of High School Dropouts: What the Nation Pays for Inadequate High Schools* (Washington, DC: Alliance for Excellent Education, November 2011), and *Dropouts, Diplomas, and Dollars: U.S. High Schools and the Nation's Economy* (Washington, DC: Alliance for Excellent Education, August 2008).

54. Veronica Engert, Franziska Plessow, Robert Miller, Clemens Kirschbaum, and Tania Singer, "Cortisol Increase in Empathic Stress Is Modulated by Emotional Closeness and Observation Modality," *Psychoneuroendocrinology* 45 (2014): 192–201.

55. Michael Weinstein, quoted in Kathryn Peterson, "All in One Place," *Stanford Social Innovation Review* 13, no. 1 (2015): 17–18.

56. *Harlem Children's Zone*, HCZ.org, 2015.

57. Michael McAfee, e-mail to authors, September 4, 2014.

58. Department for Communities and Local Government, "Tackling Troubled Families," British Government, December 15, 2011, www.gov.uk/ government/news/tackling-troubled-families.

59. "Troubled Families," Local Government Association, January 29, 2015, www.local.gov.uk/ community-budgets/-/journal_content/56/10180/3691966/ARTICLE.

60. Louise Casey, phone interview by authors, November 7, 2014.

61. "Troubled Families: Progress Information at December 2014 and Families Turned Around at February 2015," Department for Communities and Local Government, March 10, 2015, www .gov.uk/government/publications/troubled-families-programme-progress-information-at -december-2014-and-families-turned-around-at-february-2015.

62. Richard Reeves, "Bringing Up Baby," *New Statesman*, January 29, 2009.

63. See Nicholas Kristof, "The Way to Beat Poverty," *New York Times*, September 12, 2014, www.nytimes.com/2014/09/14/opinion/sunday/nicholas-kristof-the-way-to-beat-poverty.html, which discusses the study or the study itself: Lynn A. Karoly, M. Rebecca Kilburn, and Jill S. Cannon, *Early Childhood Interventions: Proven Results, Future Promise* (Santa Monica, CA: RAND Corporation, 2005).

64. Robert Gordon, "Investing in What Works: Voluntary Home Visiting Programs," White House, September 28, 2011.

65. See Harriet J. Kitzman, David L. Olds, Robert E. Cole, Carole A. Hanks, Elizabeth A. Anson, Kimberly J. Arcoleo, Dennis W. Luckey et al., "Enduring Effects of Prenatal and Infancy Home Visiting by Nurses on Children: Follow-Up of a Randomized Trial Among Children at Age 12 Years," *Archives of Pediatrics & Adolescent Medicine* 164, no. 5 (2010): 412–418; David L. Olds, Charles R. Henderson, and Harriet Kitzman, "Does Prenatal and Infancy Nurse Home Visitation Have Enduring Effects on Qualities of Parental Caregiving and Child Health at 25 to 50 Months of Life?" *Pediatrics* 93, no. 1 (1994): 89–98; David L. Olds, Charles R. Henderson Jr., Robert Cole, John Eckenrode, Harriet Kitzman, Dennis Luckey, Lisa Pettitt et al., "Long-Term Effects of Nurse Home Visitation on Children's Criminal and Antisocial Behavior: 15-Year Follow-Up of a Randomized Controlled Trial," *JAMA* 280, no. 14 (1998): 1238–1244; David L. Olds, Charles R. Henderson, Robert Tatelbaum, and Robert Chamberlin, "Improving the Delivery of Prenatal

Care and Outcomes of Pregnancy: A Randomized Trial of Nurse Home Visitation." *Pediatrics* 77, no. 1 (1986): 16–28; Edward Rodrigue and Richard V. Reeves, "Home Visiting Programs: An Early Test for the 114th Congress," Brookings, February 5, 2015.

66. Kristof, "It's Not Just About Bad Choices."

CHAPTER 9. INEQUALITY

1. Sebastian Thrun, interview by authors, Mountain View, CA, November 11, 2014.

2. Chad Stone, Danilo Trisi, Arloc Sherman, and Brandon Debot, "A Guide to Statistics on Historical Trends in Income Inequality," Center on Budget and Policy Priorities, October 26, 2015, www.cbpp.org/research/poverty-and-inequality/a-guide-to-statistics-on-historical-trends-in -income-inequality.

3. Ibid.

4. Emmanuel Saez, "Striking It Richer," January 25, 2015, http://eml.berkeley.edu/~saez/saez -UStopincomes-2013.pdf.

5. From April 2014 through February 2015 it hovered between 62.7 and 62.9 percent. John Cassidy, "The New Job Figures and Secular Stagnation," *New Yorker*, April 3, 2015, www.new yorker.com/news/john-cassidy/the-new-job-figures-and-secular-stagnation.

6. Jaison R. Abel and Richard Deitz, "The Class of 2015 Might Have a Little Better Luck Finding a Good Job," Liberty Street Economics, Federal Reserve Bank of New York, May 15, 2015, http://libertystreeteconomics.newyorkfed.org/2015/05/the-class-of-2015-might-have-a-little -better-luck-finding-a-good-job.html#.VmCEroTI6jQ.

7. During the Depression, when it hit up to 45 percent. Historically the long-term unemployed make up between 10 and 20 percent of the overall unemployed, a figure that still stands at almost 27 percent. See US Bureau of Labor Statistics, "Productivity and Costs, Second Quarter 2015, Revised," Bureau of Labor Statistics, September 2, 2015, www.bls.gov/news.release/prod2.nr0.htm. See also Gilliam B. White, "What 27 Weeks of Unemployment Does to the American Worker," *Atlantic*, March 6, 2015, www.theatlantic.com/business/archive/2015/03/what-27-weeks-of -unemployment-does-to-the-american-worker/387031; Tomaz Cajner and David Ratner, "The Recent Decline in Long-Term Unemployment," FEDS Notes, July 21, 2014, www.federalreserve.gov/ econresdata/notes/feds-notes/2014/the-recent-decline-in-long-term-unemployment-20140721 .html; Alan B. Krueger, Judd Cramer, and David Cho, *Are the Long-Term Unemployed on the Margins of the Labor Market?* (Brookings Papers on Economic Activity, Spring 2014), www.brookings .edu/~/media/Projects/BPEA/Spring%202014/2014a_Krueger.pdf, 229–299.

8. Tyler Cowen, quoted in Derek Thompson, "A World Without Work," *Atlantic*, July/August 2015, www.theatlantic.com/magazine/archive/2015/07/world-without-work/395294.

9. "Nonfarm Business Sector: Labor Share," Federal Reserve Bank of St. Louis, February 9, 2015, https://research.stlouisfed.org/fred2/series/PRS85006173.

10. Loukas Karabarbounis and Brent Neiman, "The Global Decline of the Labor Share," *Quarterly Journal of Economics* 129, no. 1 (2014): 61–103.

11. Emmanuel Saez and Gabriel Zucman, "The Explosion in U.S. Wealth Inequality Has Been Fueled by Stagnant Wages, Increasing Debt, and a Collapse in Asset Values for the Middle Classes," *LSE*, October 29, 2014, http://blogs.lse.ac.uk/usappblog/2014/10/29/the-explosion-in-u-s-wealth -inequality-has-been-fuelled-by-stagnant-wages-increasing-debt-and-a-collapse-in-asset-values -for-the-middle-classes. See their paper at Emmanuel Saez and Gabriel Zucman, *Wealth Inequality in the United States Since 1913: Evidence from Capitalized Income Tax Data*, no. w20625 (National Bureau of Economic Research, 2015), http://gabriel-zucman.eu/files/SaezZucman2014.pdf.

12. Saez and Zucman, "Wealth Inequality."

13. Tyler Cowen, "Automation Alone Isn't Killing Jobs," *New York Times*, April 6, 2014, www .nytimes.com/2014/04/06/business/automation-alone-isnt-killing-jobs.html?_r=0.

14. Krueger et al., *Are the Long-Term Unemployed*.

15. Jaison R. Abel, Richard Deitz, and Yaqin Su, "Are Recent College Graduates Finding Good Jobs?" *Current Issues in Economics and Finance* 20, no. 1 (2014).

16. Carl Benedikt Frey and Michael A. Osborne, "The Future of Employment: How Suscepti-ble Are Jobs to Computerisation?" September 17, 2013, www.oxfordmartin.ox.ac.uk/downloads/academic/The_Future_of_Employment.pdf.

17. David Graeber, quoted in Thomas Frank, "David Graeber: 'Spotlight on the Financial Sector Did Make Apparent Just How Bizarrely Skewed Our Economy Is in Terms of Who Gets Rewards,'" *Salon*, June 1, 2014, www.salon.com/2014/06/01/help_us_thomas_piketty_the_1s _sick_and_twisted_new_scheme.

18. Clayton Christensen, "The Capitalist's Dilemma," lecture, RSA, London, September 23, 2013.

19. Laurence Chandy and Geoffrey Gertz, *Poverty in Numbers: The Changing State of Global Poverty from 2005 to 2015* (Brookings Institution, 2011), www.brookings.edu/~/media/research/files/papers/2011/1/global%20poverty%20chandy/01_global_poverty_chandy.pdf.

20. See Steve Hilton, "I Run a Silicon Valley Startup—but I Refuse to Own a Cellphone," *Guardian*, January 11, 2016, http://www.theguardian.com/technology/2016/jan/11/steve-hilton -silicon-valley-no-cellphone-technology-apps-uber.

21. Robert Caro, *The Years of Lyndon Johnson*, vol. 1: *The Path to Power* (New York: Vintage, 1981; reprint: London: Pimlico, 2003), 504.

22. Ibid., 513.

23. Rohan Silva, "Could a Robot Do My Job?" BBC Panorama, September 18, 2015, http://www.bbc.co.uk/programmes/b06cn1wv.

24. Matthias J. Koepp, Roger N. Gunn, Andrew D. Lawrence, Vincent J. Cunningham, Alain Dagher, Tasmin Jones, David J. Brooks, C. J. Bench et al., "Evidence for Striatal Dopamine Re-lease During a Video Game," *Nature* 393, no. 6682 (1998): 266–268.

25. Richard M. Ryan and Edward L. Deci, "Self-Determination Theory and the Facilitation of Intrinsic Motivation, Social Development, and Well-Being," *American Psychologist* 55, no. 1 (2000): 68.

26. Sebastian Thrun, interview by authors, Mountain View, CA, November 11, 2014.

27. For up to two years as long as the worker's unemployment insurance contribution has been paid.

28. "Flexicurity," Denmark: The Official Website of Denmark, http://denmark.dk/en/society/welfare/flexicurity.

29. Thomas Bredgaard and Arthur Daemmrich, "The Welfare State as an Investment Strategy: Denmark's Flexicurity Policies," July 2012, http://ilera2012.wharton.upenn.edu/RefereedPapers /BredgaardThomas%20ArthurDaemmrich.pdf.

30. "OECD Income Distribution Database: Gini, Poverty, Income, Methods, and Concepts," OECD, June 19, 2014, www.oecd.org/social/income-distribution-database.htm.

31. Leo Mirani, "The Secret to the Uber Economy: Wealth Inequality," *Quartz*, December 16, 2014, http://qz.com/312537/the-secret-to-the-uber-economy-is-wealth-inequality.

32. Leon Feinstein, "Very Early," *CentrePiece*, Summer 2003, http://cep.lse.ac.uk/pubs/down load/CP146.pdf.

33. Morris Kleiner, *Reforming Occupational Licensing Practices* (Washington, DC: Brookings Institute: Hamilton Project, 2015), 5.

34. Reihan Salam, "The Upper Middle Class Is Ruining America," *Slate*, January 30, 2015, www.slate.com/articles/news_and_politics/politics/2015/01/the_upper_middle_class_is_ ruining_all_that_is_great_about_america.html.

35. "America's Elite: An Hereditary Meritocracy," *The Economist*, January 24, 2015, www .economist.com/news/briefing/21640316-children-rich-and-powerful-are-increasingly-well -suited-earning-wealth-and-power.

36. "America's New Aristocracy," *The Economist*, January 24, 2015, www.economist.com/news/leaders/21640331-importance-intellectual-capital-grows-privilege-has-become-increasingly.

37. A fellow British export to America now at Brookings, Richard Reeves is a brilliant analyst of economic and societal trends. For his masterly survey of some of how some of them affect America, see: Richard Reeves, "Stuck," *Esquire,* December/January 2015/2016, http://www.brookings.edu/~/media/Blogs/brookings-now/2015/11/Future-of-America-Esquire-Dec-2015.pdf.

38. Betty Hart and Todd R. Risley, "The Early Catastrophe: The 30 Million Word Gap by Age 3," *American Educator* 27, no. 1 (2003): 4–9.

39. Katherine Harmon, "How Important Is Physical Contact with Your Infant?" *Scientific American*, May 6, 2010, www.scientificamerican.com/article/infant-touch.

40. Melissa S. Kearney and Phillip B. Levine, *Early Childhood Education by MOOC: Lessons from Sesame Street*, no. w21229 (National Bureau of Economic Research, 2015), www.nber.org/papers/w21229.

41. Susan L. Brown, "Family Structure and Child Well-Being: The Significance of Parental Cohabitation," *Journal of Marriage and Family* 66 (2004), 351–367.

42. Terry-Ann Craigie, Jeanne Brooks-Gunn, and Jane Waldfogel, *Family Structure, Family Stability and Early Child Wellbeing*, no. 1275 (2010), http://crcw.princeton.edu/workingpapers/WP10-14-FF.pdf.

43. Richard Fry, "New Census Data Show More Americans Are Tying the Knot, But Mostly It's the College-Educated," FactTank, Pew Research Center, February 6, 2014, www.pewresearch.org/fact-tank/2014/02/06/new-census-data-show-more-americans-are-tying-the-knot-but-mostly-its-the-college-educated.

44. Robert Rector, "Marriage: America's Greatest Weapon Against Child Poverty," Heritage Foundation, September 5, 2012, www.heritage.org/research/reports/2012/09/marriage-americas-greatest-weapon-against-child-poverty, chart 2.

45. Andrew J. Cherlin, Elizabeth Talbert, and Suzumi Yasutake, *Changing Fertility Regimes and the Transition to Adulthood: Evidence from a Recent Cohort* (Boston, MA, Annual Meeting of the Population Association of America, May 3, 2014), http://krieger.jhu.edu/sociology/wp-content/uploads/sites/28/2012/02/Read-Online.pdf.

46. Ibid.

47. Cherlin, quoted in Olga Khazan, "The Luxury of Waiting for Marriage to Have Kids," *Atlantic*, June 17, 2014, www.theatlantic.com/business/archive/2014/06/why-poor-women-dont-wait-for-marriage-to-give-birth/372890.

48. Jean M. Twenge, Keith W. Campbell, and Craig A. Foster, "Parenthood and Marital Satisfaction: A Meta-Analytic Review," *Journal of Marriage and the Family* 65 (2003), 574–583.

49. Dan Gilbert, quoted in Kate Devlin, "Marriage Without Children the Key to Bliss," *Telegraph*, May 9, 2008, www.telegraph.co.uk/news/1941195/Marriage-without-children-the-key-to-bliss.html.

50. Niko Matouschek and Imran Rasul, "The Economics of the Marriage Contract Theories and Evidence," *Journal of Law and Economics* 51, no. 1 (2008): 59–110.

51. John Hayward and Guy Brandon, "Cohabitation: An Alternative to Marriage?" Jubilee Centre, June 2011, www.jubilee-centre.org/cohabitation-alternative-marriage-john-hayward-guy-brandon.

52. Ellen C. Perrin, Benjamin S. Siegel, James G. Pawelski, Mary I. Dobbins, Arthur Lavin, Gerri Mattison, John Pascoe et al., "Promoting the Well-Being of Children Whose Parents Are Gay or Lesbian," *Pediatrics* 131, no. 4 (2013): e1374–e1383.

53. Dan Gilbert, quoted in Devlin, "Marriage Without Children."

54. Shawn Grover and John F. Helliwell, *How's Life at Home? New Evidence on Marriage and the Set Point for Happiness*, no. w20794 (National Bureau of Economic Research, 2014), http://faculty.arts.ubc.ca/jhelliwell/papers/w20794.pdf.

55. Shawn Grover, quoted in Claire Cain Miller, "Study Finds More Reasons to Get and Stay

Married," *New York Times*, January 8, 2015, www.nytimes.com/2015/01/08/upshot/study-finds -more-reasons-to-get-and-stay-married.html.

56. John F. Helliwell, quoted in ibid.

57. For example, President George W. Bush's Healthy Marriage Initiative. See US Department of Health and Human Services, *The Community Healthy Marriage Initiative Evaluation: Impacts of a Community Approach to Strengthening Families* (Washington, DC: Office of Planning, Research and Evaluation, 2012).

58. Ronald Mincy, quoted in Suzy Hansen, "The Myth of the Deadbeat Dad," *Salon*, August 9, 2001, www.salon.com/2001/08/09/black_fathers.

59. Rose Marie Kreider, *Living Arrangements of Children, 2004* (US Department of Commerce, Economics and Statistics Administration, US Census Bureau, 2008).

60. Cynthia C. Harper and Sara S. McLanahan, "Father Absence and Youth Incarceration," *Journal of Research on Adolescence* 14 (September 2004): 369–397.

61. Specifically, girls raised by single mothers. See Jay D. Teachman, "The Childhood Living Arrangements of Children and the Characteristics of Their Marriages," *Journal of Family Issues* 25 (January 2004): 86–111.

62. Kimberly S. Howard, Jennifer E. Burke Lefever, John G. Borkowski, and Thomas L. Whitman, "Fathers' Influence in the Lives of Children with Adolescent Mothers," *Journal of Family Psychology* 20, no. 3 (2006): 468.

63. Christine Winquist Nord and Jerry West, *Fathers' and Mothers' Involvement in Their Children's Schools by Family Type and Resident Status*, NCES 2001-032. (Washington, DC: US Department of Education, National Center for Education Statistics, 2001), http://nces.ed.gov/pubs2001 /2001032.pdf.

64. Brooke Conroy Bass, "Preparing for Parenthood? Gender, Aspirations, and the Reproduction of Labor Market Inequality," *Gender & Society* 29, no. 3 (2015): 362–385.

65. Slaughter, "Why Women Still Can't Have It All."

66. Liza Mundy, "Daddy Track: The Case for Paternity Leave," *Atlantic*, January/February 2014, www.theatlantic.com/magazine/archive/2014/01/the-daddy-track/355746.

67. US Census Bureau, *Maternity Leave and Employment Patterns of First-time Mothers: 1961– 2008* (Washington, DC: Department of Commerce, 2011).

68. Heather Boushey and Sarah Jane Glynn, *The Effects of Paid Family Medical Leave on Employment Stability and Economic Stability* (Washington, DC: Center for American Progress, 2012), www.americanprogress.org/wp-content/uploads/issues/2012/04/pdf/BousheyEmployment Leave1.pdf, 3.

69. According to the OECD, children whose families eat their main meal together are less likely to be truant in school. See *Who Are the School Truants?* (PISA in Focus, January 2014), www .oecd.org/pisa/ pisaproducts/pisainfocus/PISA-in-Focus-n35-(eng)-FINAL.pdf.

70. Eileen Appelbaum and Ruth Milkman, *Leaves That Pay: Employer and Worker Experiences with Paid Family Leave in California* (Washington, DC: Center for Economic and Policy Research, 2011), www.cepr.net/documents/publications/paid-family-leave-1-2011.pdf.

71. Mundy, "Daddy Track," 16.

72. Indeed, feeling overwhelmed and unprepared is common for parents. See Susanne N. Biehle and Kristin D. Mickelson, "Preparing for Parenthood: How Feelings of Responsibility and Efficacy Impact Expectant Parents," *Journal of Social and Personal Relationships* 28, no. 5, (2011): 668–683.

73. Octavius Black, quoted in Amelia Gentleman, "Do We Need Parenting Classes?" *Guardian*, March 31, 2012, www.theguardian.com/lifeandstyle/2012/mar/31/do-we-need-parenting-classes.

74. Staci R. Eisenberg, Megan H. Bair-Merritt, Eve R. Colson, Timothy C. Heeren, Nicole L. Geller, and Michael J. Corwin, "Maternal Report of Advice Received for Infant Care," *Pediatrics* 136, no. 2 (2015): e315–e322.

75. Geoff Lindsay, Mairi Ann Cullen, Stephen Cullen, Vaso Totsika, Ioanna Bakopoulou, Susan Goodlad, Richard Brind et al., *CANparent Trial Evaluation: Final Report Research Report* (Department for Education, University of Warwick, 2014), www.gov.uk/government/uploads/system /uploads/attachment_data/file/332182/RR357_-_CANparent_trial_evaluation_final_report_ _09_07_14_.pdf.

76. Geoff Colvin, *Humans Are Underrated: What High Achievers Know That Brilliant Machines Never Will* (New York: Portfolio/Penguin, 2015).

CHAPTER 10. CHILDHOOD

1. Lenore Skenazy, "Free-Range Kids: FAQ," Free Range Kids, https://freerangekids.wordpress .com/faq.

2. David Ball in Tim Gill, *No Fear: Growing Up in a Risk Averse Society* (London: Calouste Gulbenkian Foundation, 2007), 26–27.

3. Gill, *No Fear*, 37–38.

4. David Yearley in ibid., 25–26.

5. David Ball in ibid., 29; and National Highway Traffic Safety Administration, *Traffic Safety Facts* (DOT HS 812 124, February 2015), www-nrd.nhtsa.dot.gov/Pubs/812124.pdf. See also David J. Ball, "Policy Issues and Risk–Benefit Trade-offs of 'Safer Surfacing' for Children's Playgrounds," *Accident Analysis & Prevention* 36, no. 4 (2004).

6. "Stressed Parents: Cancel That Violin Class," *The Economist*, July 26, 2014, www.economist .com/news/united-states/21608793-helicopter-moms-and-dads-will-not-harm-their-kids-if-they -relax-bit-cancel-violin.

7. A Department of Justice report found that only 3 percent of murdered children under age five were killed by a stranger; 63 percent were killed by a parent. See Alexia Cooper and Erica L. Smith, *Homicide Trends in the United States, 1980–2008* (Washington, DC: US Department of Justice, November 2011), www.bjs.gov/content/pub/pdf/htus8008.pdf, 7.

8. Jay Griffiths, *A Country Called Childhood* (Berkeley, CA: Counterpoint, 2014), 57.

9. Noreen C. McDonald, "Active Transportation to School: Trends Among U.S. Schoolchildren, 1969–2001," *American Journal of Preventive Medicine* 32, no. 6 (June 2007): 509–516.

10. Donna St. George, "'Free Range' Parents Cleared in Second Neglect Case After Kids Walked Alone," *Washington Post*, June 22, 2015, www.washingtonpost.com/local/education/free-range -parents-cleared-in-second-neglect-case-after-children-walked-alone/2015/06/22/82283c24 -188c-11e5-bd7f-4611a60odd8e5_story.html.

11. Ellen B. H. Sandseter, "Children's Risky Play from an Evolutionary Perspective: The Anti-Phobic Effects of Thrilling Experiences," *Evolutionary Psychology* 9, no. 2, (2001): 257–284.

12. Paul Hocker, interview by authors, London, September 26, 2014.

13. James Siegal, "Kids First: What's Good for Kids Is Good for Cities," *Medium*, March 4, 2015, https://medium.com/@kaboom/kids-first-what-s-good-for-kids-is-good-for-cities-73811301165f.

14. Annie Murphy Paul, "School of Hard Knocks: 'How Children Succeed,' by Paul Tough," *New York Times Sunday Book Review*, August 26, 2012, www.nytimes.com/2012/08/26/books /review/how-children-succeed-by-paul-tough.html.

15. "Women CEOs of the S&P 500," *Catalyst*, November 18, 2015, www.catalyst.org/know ledge/women-ceos-sp-500.

16. Emma Rush and Andrea La Nauze, *Corporate Paedophilia: Sexualisation of Children in Australia* (Canberra: Australia Institute, 2006).

17. Samantha M. Goodin, Alyssa Van Denburg, Sarah K. Murnen, and Linda Smolak, "'Putting On' Sexiness: A Content Analysis of the Presence of Sexualizing Characteristics in Girls' Clothing," *Sex Roles* 65, no. 1–2 (2011): 1–12.

18. APA Task Force on the Sexualization of Girls, *Report of the APA Task Force on the Sexual-ization of Girls* (Washington, DC: American Psychological Association, 2010), www.apa.org/pi/women/programs/girls/report.aspx.

19. Barbara L. Fredrickson, Tomi-Ann Roberts, Stephanie M. Noll, Diane M. Quinn, and Jean M. Twenge, "That Swimsuit Becomes You: Sex Differences in Self-Objectification, Restrained Eating, and Math Performance," *Journal of Personality and Social Psychology* 75, no. 1 (July 1998), 269–284.

20. Kathrine D. Gapinski, Kelly D. Brownell, and Marianne LaFrance, "Body Objectification and 'Fat Talk': Effects on Emotion, Motivation, and Cognitive Performance," *Sex Roles* 48, nos. 9–10 (2003): 377–388.

21. Beverley Turner, "Pubic Hair Is Back Ladies. The Men Don't Care and the Women Can't Be Bothered," *Telegraph*, November 15, 2013, www.telegraph.co.uk/women/womens-life/104523 27/Pubic-hair-is-back-ladies.-The-men-dont-care-and-the-women-cant-be-bothered.html; Heidi Stevens, "Your 11-Year-Old Daughter Wants to Shave. Everywhere," *Chicago Tribune*, July 10, 2012, http://articles.chicagotribune.com/2012-07-10/features/sc-fam-0710-tween-wax-20120710 _1_hair-removal-daughter-body.

22. "When Do Parents Give in to Kids' Pleas for Devices?" *eMarketer*, August 21, 2015, www.emarketer.com/Article/Do-Parents-Give-Kids-Pleas-Devices/1012887.

23. *Pearson Student Mobile Device Survey 2014: Grades 4 through 12 Conducted by Harris Poll* (New York: Pearson, May 2014), www.pearsoned.com/wp-content/uploads/Pearson-K12-Student -Mobile-Device-Survey-050914-PUBLIC-Report.pdf, 9.

24. "One in Ten British Kids Own a Mobile Phone by the Age of Five," *uSwitch*, August 2013, www.uswitch.com/mobiles/news/2013/08/one_in_ten_british_kids_own_mobile_phone_by_ the_age_of_five; Ofcom, *Children and Parents: Media Use and Attitudes Report* (2014), http://stakeholders.ofcom.org.uk/market-data-research/other/research-publications/childrens/children-parents-oct-14, 29 and 32.

25. Hilda K. Kabali, Matilde M. Irigoyen, Rosemary Nunez-Davis, Jennifer G. Budacki, Sweta H. Mohanty, Kristin P. Leister, and Robert L. Bonner Jr., "Exposure and Use of Mobile Media Devices by Young Children," *Pediatrics* 136, no. 6 (December 2015): 1044–1050.

26. "The Digital Divide: How the Online Behavior of Teens Is Getting Past Parents," McAfee, June 2012, www.mcafee.com/us/resources/misc/digital-divide-study.pdf.

27. *2014 Teen Internet Safety Survey* (Atlanta, GA: Cox Communications, 2014), www.cox.com /wcm/en/aboutus/datasheet/takecharge/tween-internet-safety-survey.pdf.

28. Jane D. Brown and Kelly L. L'Engle, "X-Rated Sexual Attitudes and Behaviors Associated with US Early Adolescents' Exposure to Sexually Explicit Media," *Communication Research* 36, no. 1 (2009): 129–151.

29. Patricia Romito and Lucia Beltramini, "Watching Pornography: Gender Differences, Violence and Victimization: An Exploratory Study in Italy," *Violence Against Women* 17, no. 10 (October 2011): 1077801211424555.

30. "Young People Sexual Relationships," IPPR, www.ippr.org/assets/media/publications/attachments/youngpeoplesexrelationships.jpg.

31. Michael Flood, "The Harms of Pornography Exposure Among Children and Young People," *Child Abuse Review* 18, no. 6 (2009): 384–400.

32. Tori DeAngelis, "Web Pornography's Effect on Children," *American Psychological Association Monitor* 38, no. 10 (November 2007): 50.

33. David Finkelhor, Richard Ormrod, and Mark Chaffin, *Juveniles Who Commit Sex Offenses Against Minors* (Washington, DC: US Department of Justice, December 2009), www.ncjrs.gov/pdffiles1/ojjdp/227763.pdf.

34. Wesley Johnson, "Children, Some Age Five, Commit Thousands of Child Sex Offences," *Telegraph*, March 4, 2013, www.telegraph.co.uk/news/uknews/crime/9905727/Children-some -aged-five-commit-thousands-of-child-sex-offences.html.

35. Gail Dines, quoted in Martin Daubney, "Experiment That Convinced Me Online Porn Is the Most Pernicious Threat Facing Children Today: By Ex Lads' Mag Editor Martin Daubney," *Daily Mail*, September 25, 2013.

36. Todd G. Morrison, Shannon R. Ellis, Melanie A. Morrison, Anomi Bearden, and Rebecca L. Harriman, "Exposure to Sexually Explicit Material and Variations in Body Esteem, Genital Attitudes, and Sexual Esteem Among a Sample of Canadian Men," *Journal of Men's Studies* 14, no. 2 (Spring 2006): 209–222.

37. Daubney, "Experiment That Convinced Me."

38. "2015 Year in Review," *Pornhub Insights*, January 6, 2016, www.pornhub.com/insights/ 2015-year-in-review.

39. Daubney, "Experiment That Convinced Me."

40. Sally Kalson, "Sexting . . . and Other Stupid Teen Tricks," *Pittsburgh Post-Gazette*, March 29, 2009, www.post-gazette.com/opinion/sally-kalson/2009/03/29/Sexting-and-other-stupid -teen-tricks/stories/200903290190.

41. Donald Lowe, quoted in Hanna Rosin, "Why Kids Sext," *Atlantic*, November 2014, www .theatlantic.com/magazine/archive/2014/11/why-kids-sext/380798, 67.

42. Amanda Lenhart, "Mobile Access Shifts Social Media Use and Other Online Activities," Pew Research Center, April 9, 2015, www.pewinternet.org/2015/04/09/mobile-access-shifts -social-media-use-and-other-online-activities.

43. Rosin, "Why Kids Sext," 68.

44. Kassondra Cloos and Julie Turkewitz, "Hundreds of Nude Photos Jolt Colorado School," *New York Times*, November 6, 2015, www.nytimes.com/2015/11/07/us/colorado-students-caught -trading-nude-photos-by-the-hundreds.html?_r=0.

45. Jeff R. Temple, Jonathan A. Paul, Patricia van den Berg, Vi Donna Le, Amy McElhany, and Brian W. Temple, "Teen Sexting and Its Association with Sexual Behaviors," *Archives of Pediatrics & Adolescent Medicine* 166, no. 9 (2012): 828–833.

46. "Physical Activity Guidelines for Children and Young People," NHS Choices, www.nhs .uk/Livewell/fitness/Pages/physical-activity-guidelines-for-young-people.aspx.

47. Brian Verdine, quoted in Allison Bond, "Blocks, Puzzles Help Kids Prep for School," *Reuters*, March 20, 2014, www.reuters.com/article/2014/03/20/us-puzzles-kids-idUSBREA2J1LN 20140320.

48. Anna V. Sosa, "Association of the Type of Toy Used During Play with the Quantity and Quality of Parent-Infant Communication," *JAMA Pediatrics* (2015): 1–6.

49. Marsha Gerdes, quoted in Bond, "Blocks, Puzzles Help Kids Prep for School."

50. Brian N. Verdine, Roberta M. Golinkoff, Kathryn Hirsh Pasek, Nora S. Newcombe, An- drew T. Filipowicz, and Alicia Chang, "Deconstructing Building Blocks: Preschoolers' Spatial Assembly Performance Relates to Early Mathematical Skills," *Child Development* 85, no. 3 (2014): 1062–1076.

51. Pooja S. Tandon, Chuan Zhou, Paula Lozano, and Dimitri A. Christakis, "Preschoolers' Total Daily Screen Time at Home and by Type of Child Care," *Journal of Pediatrics* 158, no. 2 (2011): 297–300. See also "Zero to Eight: Children's Media Use in America 2013," Common Sense Media, Fall 2013.

52. "Touch Screens," Michael Cohen Group LLC, February 17, 2014, www.mcgrc.com/wp -content/uploads/2015/03/MCGRC_Digital-Kids-Presentation_022014.pdf.

53. Sherry Turkle, "Connected, But Alone?" TED Talk, April 2012, www.ted.com/talks/ sherry_turkle_alone_together?language=en.

54. Sherry Turkle, *Alone Together: Why We Expect More from Technology and Less from Each Other* (New York: Basic Books, 2011), 268.

55. "The Dos and Don'ts of Using Your Phone at a Party," *Huffington Post*, September 26, 2014, www.huffingtonpost.com/2014/09/26/dinner-party-etiquette-phones-at-dinner_n_5884418 .html.

56. Sherry Turkle, quoted in Catherine de Lange, "Sherry Turkle: 'We're Losing the Raw, Human Part of Being with Each Other,'" *Guardian*, May 5, 2013, www.theguardian.com/science/2013/may/05/rational-heroes-sherry-turkle-mit.

57. "The Common Sense Census: Media Use by Tweens and Teens," Common Sense Media Kids Action, Fall 2015, www.commonsensemedia.org/research/the-common-sense-census-media-use-by-tweens-and-teens.

58. Katie Rogers, "The Vault Apps That Keep Sexts a Secret," *New York Times*, November 6, 2015, www.nytimes.com/2015/11/07/us/the-vault-apps-that-keep-sexts-a-secret.html.

59. Justin Higginbottom, "Growing Number of Children with Cellphones Adds Pressure to Purchase," *Deseret News*, April 22, 2012, www.deseretnews.com/article/765570742/Growing-number-of-children-with-cellphones-adds-pressure-to-purchase.html?pg=all.

60. See Steve Hilton, "I Run a Silicon Valley Startup—but I Refuse to Own a Cellphone," *Guardian*, January 11, 2016, http://www.theguardian.com/technology/2016/jan/11/steve-hilton-silicon-valley-no-cellphone-technology-apps-uber.

CHAPTER 11. SPACES

1. Will Hunter, "The Best Office in the World? Selgas Cano's New Work Space in London," *Architectural Review*, January 29, 2015, www.architectural-review.com/buildings/the-best-office-in-the-world-selgas-canos-new-work-space-in-london/8677631.article.

2. José Selgas and Lucia Cano, quoted in "Future of Work," *Courier* 5 (August 2014), 5.

3. Interview with Rohan Silva.

4. Sir Winston Churchill, Hansard House of Commons Debate, October 28, 1943, vol. 393, cols. 403–473.

5. Yuichi Shoda, "Individual Differences in Social Psychology: Understanding Situations to Understand People, Understanding People to Understand Situations," in *The Sage Handbook of Methods in Social Psychology*, ed. Carol Sansone, Carolyn C. Morf, and Abigail T. Panter (Thousand Oaks, CA: Sage Publications, 2004), 119–121.

6. Robert Fulford, *Accidental City: The Transformation of Toronto* (Canada: MacFarlane, Walter & Ross, 1995), 77.

7. Jane Jacobs, *The Death and Life of Great American Cities* (New York: Vintage Books, 1961), 4.

8. As characterized by the author; Napoleon III, quoted in Colin Jones, *Paris: A History* (New York: Penguin Books, 2004), 301.

9. David Pinkney, *Napoleon III and the Rebuilding of Paris* (Princeton, NJ: Princeton University Press, 1972), 18.

10. Maxime Du Camp, quoted in Jones, *Paris*, 304.

11. Jones, *Paris*, 301.

12. Georges-Eugène Haussmann, quoted in Friedrich Lenger, *European Cities in the Modern Era, 1850–1914*, trans. Joel Golb (Leiden, Netherlands: Koninklijke Brill NV, 2012), 22.

13. Christopher Caldwell, "Revolting High Rises," *New York Times Magazine*, November 27, 2005, www.nytimes.com/2005/11/27/magazine/revolting-high-rises.html.

14. Fulford, *Accidental City*, 85.

15. Nadine Kalinauskas, "St. Lawrence Market in Toronto Named World's Best Food Market by National Geographic," *Shine On*, 5 April 2012, https://ca.shine.yahoo.com/blogs/shine-on/st-lawrence-market-toronto-named-world-best-food-145127435.html.

16. Jacobs, *Death and Life*, 50.

17. Dave LeBlanc, "35 Years on, St. Lawrence Is a Template for Urban Housing," *Globe and Mail*, February 6, 2013, www.theglobeandmail.com/life/home-and-garden/architecture/35-years-on-st-lawrence-is-a-template-for-urban-housing/article8296990.

18. David Crombie, phone interview by authors, September 17, 2014.

19. Amanda Burden, "How Public Spaces Make Cities Work," TED Talk, April 2014, www.ted.com/talks/amanda_burden_how_public_spaces_make_cities_work?language=en. Background information from interview with Amanda Burden, New York, October 16, 2015.

20. Janette Sadik-Khan, "New York's Streets? Not So Mean Anymore," TED Talk, September 2013, New York, New York, www.ted.com/talks/janette_sadik_khan_new_york_s_streets_not_so_mean_any_more?language=en. Background information from e-mail to authors, October 25, 2015.

21. Laura Dudnick, "In SF's Surging Real Estate Market, How Do Teachers Stack Up?," *San Francisco Examiner*, June 7, 2015, http://archives.sfexaminer.com/sanfrancisco/in-sfs-surging-real-estate-market-how-do-teachers-stack-up/Content?oid=2932447.

22. Enrico Moretti and Per Thulin, "Local Multipliers and Human Capital in the United States and Sweden," *Industrial and Corporate Change* 22, no. 1 (2013): 339-362.

23. Kim-Mai Cutler, "How Burrowing Owls Lead to Vomiting Anarchists (Or SF's Housing Crisis Explained)," *TechCrunch*, April 14, 2014, http://techcrunch.com/2014/04/14/sf-housing.

24. Laxmaiah Manchikanti, "Epidemiology of Low Back Pain," *Pain Physician* 3, no. 2 (2000): 167–192; Alois Stutzer and Bruno S. Frey, "Stress That Doesn't Pay: The Commuting Paradox," *Scandinavian Journal of Economics* 110, no. 2 (2008): 339–366; Michael P. Johnson, "Environmental Impacts of Urban Sprawl: A Survey of the Literature and Proposed Research Agenda," *Environment and Planning A* 33, no. 4 (2001): 717–735.

25. "Why Plants in the Office Make Us More Productive," *ScienceDaily*, September 1, 2014, www.sciencedaily.com/releases/2014/09/140901090735.htm.

26. Mohamed Boubekri, Ivy N. Cheung, Kathryn J. Reid, Chia-Hui Wang, and Phyllis C. Zee, "Impact of Windows and Daylight Exposure on Overall Health and Sleep Quality of Office Workers: A Case-Control Pilot Study," *Journal of Clinical Sleep Medicine: JCSM: Official Publication of the American Academy of Sleep Medicine* 10, no. 6 (2014): 603.

27. Carlo Ratti, phone interview by authors, October 13, 2014.

28. Judith Heerwagen, "Green Buildings, Organizational Success and Occupant Productivity," *Building Research & Information* 28, nos. 5–6 (2000): 353–367.

29. Kimberly Bradley, "Model Factories: Fagus-GreCon," *Monocle* 69, no. 7 (December 2013–January 2014): 133–134.

30. Christine Congdon, Donna Flynn, and Melanie Redman, "Balancing 'We' and 'Me': The Best Collaborative Spaces Also Support Solitude," *Harvard Business Review*, October 2014, https://hbr.org/2014/10/balancing-we-and-me-the-best-collaborative-spaces-also-support-solitude.

31. "Power of Place," *Steelcase 360°*, no. 68 (2014): 17.

32. Kaisa Nuikkinen, "Vision of the Helsinki City School Building Program: Healthy and Safe School Building," presentation at the American Institute for Architects' Schools in a Flat World conference, Helsinki, Finland, September 11, 2008.

33. Kees Keizer, Siegwart Lindenberg, and Linda Steg, "The Spreading of Disorder," *Science* 322, no. 5908 (2008): 1681–1685.

34. Anthony A. Braga and Brenda J. Bond, "Policing Crime and Disorder Hot Spots: A Randomized Controlled Trial," *Criminology* 46, no. 3 (2008): 577–607.

35. Keizer et al., "Spreading of Disorder."

36. OECD, *Road Safety Annual Report 2015* (OECD Publishing, 2015), DOI: 10.1787/irtad-2015-en.

37. Ibid., 436. See also "Why Sweden Has So Few Road Deaths," *The Economist*, February 26, 2014, www.economist.com/blogs/economist-explains/2014/02/economist-explains-16.

38. "Vision Zero Initiative: Traffic Safety by Sweden," Swedish Government and Business Sweden, www.visionzeroinitiative.com/en.

39. "Why Sweden Has So Few Road Deaths."

40. "Cycling Facts and Figures," IAmsterdam, 2015, www.iamsterdam.com/en/media-centre

/city-hall/dossier-cycling/cycling-facts-and-figures; Amanda Buck, "Transparency: The Most Dangerous Cities for Walking," *GOOD Magazine*, September 3, 2010, http://magazine.good.is/infographics/transparency-the-most-dangerous-cities-for-walking.

41. Statistics Netherlands, "Traffic Deaths Down Again," April 18, 2011, www.cbs.nl/en-GB/menu/themas/gezondheid-welzijn/publicaties/artikelen/archief/2011/2011-029-pb.htm; Ben Fried, "The Origins of Holland's 'Stop Murdering Children' Street Safety Movement," StreetsBlog Network, February 20, 2013, http://streetsblog.net/2013/02/20/the-origins-of-hollands-stop-murdering-children-street-safety-movement.

42. "Amsterdam Children Fighting Cars in 1972," Bicycle Dutch, https://bicycledutch.wordpress.com/2013/12/12/amsterdam-children-fighting-cars-in-1972.

43. "Jan Gehl: Biography," Project for Public Spaces, www.pps.org/reference/jgehl.

44. Richard Rogers, "Forward," in Jan Gehl, *Cities for People* (Washington, DC: Island Press, 2010), ix.

45. Jan Gehl, quoted in Ellie Violet Bramley, "Is Jan Gehl Winning His Battle to Make Our Cities Liveable?" *Guardian*, December 8, 2014, www.theguardian.com/cities/2014/dec/08/jan-gehl-make-cities-liveable-urban-rethinker.

46. Jan Gehl, quoted in "Interview with Jan Gehl," American Society for Landscape Architects, www.asla.org/ContentDetail.aspx?id=31346.

47. Bramley, "Is Jan Gehl Winning His Battle?"

48. *Towards a Fine City for People* (Copenhagen, Denmark: Gehl Architects, June 2004), http://issuu.com/gehlarchitects/docs/issuu_270_london_pspl_2004/0.

CHAPTER 12. NATURE

1. Matthew Browning, quoted in Emma Marris, "Let Kids Run Wild in the Woods," *Slate*, May 25, 2014, www.slate.com/articles/health_and_science/science/2014/05/kid_play_zones_in_parks_leave_no_trace_inhibits_fun_and_bonding_with_nature.html.

2. Edward O. Wilson, *Biophilia* (Cambridge, MA: Harvard University Press, 1984), 85.

3. David Hancocks, "Bringing Nature into the Zoo: Inexpensive Solutions for Zoo Environments," *International Journal for the Study of Animal Problems* 1, no. 3 (1980): 170–177.

4. Roger S. Ulrich, Robert F. Simons, Barbara D. Losito, Evelyn Fiorito, Mark A. Miles, and Michael Zelson, "Stress Recovery During Exposure to Natural and Urban Environments," *Journal of Environmental Psychology* 11, no. 3 (1991): 201–230; Chen-Yen Chang and Ping-Kun Chen, "Human Response to Window Views and Indoor Plants in the Workplace," *HortScience*, 40, no. 5 (2005): 1354–1359; Terry Hartig, Gary W. Evans, Larry D. Jamner, Deborah S. Davis, and Tommy Gärling, "Tracking Restoration in Natural and Urban Field Settings," *Journal of Environmental Psychology* 23, no. 2 (2003): 109–123.

5. Maria Bodin and Terry Hartig, "Does the Outdoor Environment Matter for Psychological Restoration Gained Through Running?" *Psychology of Sport and Exercise* 4, no. 2 (2003): 141–153.

6. Roger S. Ulrich, "View Through a Window May Influence Recovery Surgery," *Science*, New Series 224, no.4647 (April 27, 1984): 420–421.

7. "The Great Smog of 1952," Met Office, June 10, 2014, www.metoffice.gov.uk/education/teens/case-studies/great-smog.

8. Louis Bainbridge to James T. Duff, October 31, 1948, in "The Donora Smog Disaster October 30–31, 1948," Pennsylvania Historical & Museum Commission, www.portal.state.pa.us/portal/server.pt/community/documents_from_1946_-_present/20426/donora_smog_disaster/999079.

9. Jonathan H. Adler, "Fables of the Cuyahoga: Reconstructing a History of Environmental Protection," *Fordham Environmental Law Journal* 14 (2002): 89–146.

10. 'Theodore Roosevelt," in *The National Parks: America's Best Idea*, PBS, 2009, www.pbs.org/nationalparks/people/historical/roosevelt.

11. E. F. Schumacher, *Small Is Beautiful: A Study of People as If People Mattered* (New York: Harper Perennial, 2010), 14.

12. Rhett Butler, "Brazil," Mongabay.com, July 13, 2014, http://rainforests.mongabay.com /20brazil.wtm; "Coordenaçã-Geral de Observção da Terra—OBT: Projecto Prodes: Monitora-menot da Floresta Amazônica Brasileira por Satélite" (in Portuguese), Ministério da Ciêcia e Technologia e Inovação e Minstério do Melo Ambiente, 2014, www.obt.inpe.br/prodes/index .php.

13. "Measuring the Daily Destruction of the World's Rainforests," *Scientific American*, November 19, 2009, www.scientificamerican.com/article/earth-talks-daily-destruction.

14. Jenna R. Jambeck, Roland Geyer, Chris Wilcox, Theodore R. Siegler, Miriam Perryman, Anthony Andrady, Ramani Narayan, and Kara Lavender Law, "Plastic Waste Inputs from Land into the Ocean," *Science* 347, no. 6223 (2015): 768–771.

15. "Coral Reefs: Facts and Figures," IUCN, March 20, 2013, www.iucn.org/media/facts_ and_figures/?12680/Coral-reefs---Facts-and-figures.

16. Richard Monastersky, "Life: A Status Report," *Nature* 516 (December 11, 2014): 159–161.

17. Edward O. Wilson, quoted in "Edward O. Wilson: 'The Loss of Biodiversity Is a Tragedy,'" UNESCO Media Services, September 2, 2010, www.unesco.org/new/en/media-services/single -view/news/edward_o_wilson_the_loss_of_biodiversity_is_a_tragedy/#.Vlxh4dKrTDc.

18. David J. Newman and Gordon M. Cragg, "Natural Products as Sources of New Drugs over the 30 Years from 1981 to 2010," *Journal of Natural Products* 75, no. 3 (2012): 311–335.

19. Edward O. Wilson, "My Wish: Build the Encyclopedia of Life," TED Talk 2007, 2007, www .ted.com/talks/e_o_wilson_on_saving_life_on_earth?language=en.

20. Monastersky, "Life."

21. Tony Hiss, "Can the World Really Set Aside Half of the Planet for Wildlife?" *Smithsonian Magazine*, September 2014, www.smithsonianmag.com/ist/?next=/science-nature/can-world -really-set-aside-half-planet-wildlife-180952379.

22. I encourage you to learn more about their amazing work at www.whitehawkproject.org.

23. Daniela Russi, Patrick ten Brink, Andrew Farmer, Tomas Badura, David Coates, Johannes Förster, Ritesh Kumar et al., *The Economics of Ecosystems and Biodiversity for Water and Wetlands: Executive Summary* (Institute for European Environmental Policy & Ramsar Secretariat, 2013), www.teebweb.org/publication/the-economics-of-ecosystems-and-biodiversity-teeb-for-water -and-wetlands, 50.

24. Environmental Protection Agency, Office of Water, *Wetlands: Protection Life and Property from Flooding* (May 2006), http://water.epa.gov/type/wetlands/ outreach/upload/Flooding.pdf.

25. There has been debate in the scientific community about the validity of this number, as there have been some instances in which the presence of intact wetlands do not reduce storm surge. For a thoughtful analysis, see Jeffrey Masters, "Storm Surge Reduction by Wetlands," *Weather Underground*, www.wunderground.com/hurricane/surge_wetlands.asp?MR=1. We acknowledge that the impact wetlands can have on reducing storm surges can't be generalized to all scenarios, but the benefit they have had and can have in many others is undeniable. See also Corps of Engineers, US Army Engineer District, New Orleans, *Interim Survey Report, Morgan City, Louisiana and Vicinity*, no. 63 (New Orleans, LA: US Army Engineer District, November 1963).

26. Robert G. Dean, "New Orleans and the Wetlands of Southern Louisiana," *Bridge* 36, no. 1 (2006): 35–42.

27. Donald F. Boesch, Leonard Shabman, L. George Antle, John W. Day Jr., Robert G. Dean, Gerald E. Galloway, Charles G. Groat et al., *A New Framework for Planning the Future of Coastal Louisiana after the Hurricanes of 2005* (Cambridge, MD: University of Maryland Center for Environmental Science, 2006), http://ian.umces.edu/pdfs/ian_report_333.pdf, 16.

28. Edward B. Barbier, "Valuing Ecosystem Services as Productive Inputs," *Economic Policy* 22, no. 49 (2007): 178–229.

29. "Sebago Lake," Portland Water District, www.pwd.org/environment/sebago/sebago.php.

30. John Talberth, Erin Gray, Evan Branosky, and Todd Gartner, *Insights from the Field: Forests for Water* (Washington, DC: Water Resources Institute, 2012), http://pdf.wri.org/insights_from_the_field_forests_for_water.pdf.

31. Caryn Ernst, *Protecting the Source: Land Conservation and the Future of America's Drinking Water* (San Francisco: The Trust for Public Land, 2004).

32. Robert Costanza, Rudolf de Groot, Paul Sutton, Sander van der Ploeg, Sharolyn J. Anderson, Ida Kubiszewski, Stephen Farber et al., "Changes in the Global Value of Ecosystem Services," *Global Environmental Change* 26 (2014): 152–158.

33. United Nations, Department of Economic and Social Affairs, Population Division, *World Urbanization Prospects: The 2014 Revision, Highlights* (ST/ESA/SER.A/352), http://esa.un.org/unpd/wup/highlights/wup2014-highlights.pdf, 1.

34. The term was coined by the writer Richard Louv in his book *Last Child in the Woods: Saving Our Children from Nature-Deficit Disorder* (Chapel Hill, NC: Algonquin Books, 2005).

35. *Reconnecting Children with Nature: Findings of the Natural Childhood Inquiry* (The National Trust, 2012), www.nationaltrust.org.uk/document-1355773744553.

36. Christiane Dorion, interview by authors, London, September 26, 2014.

37. Jeremy Bailenson, "Virtual Reality Could Make a Real Difference in Environment," *San Francisco Chronicle*, August 15, 2014, www.sfgate.com/opinion/article/Virtual-reality-could-make-real-difference-in-5691610.php.

38. Sun Joo Grace Ahn, Jeremy N. Bailenson, and Dooyeon Park, "Short- and Long-Term Effects of Embodied Experiences in Immersive Virtual Environments on Environmental Locus of Control and Behavior," *Computers in Human Behavior* 39 (2014): 235–245.

39. Jeremy Bailenson, quoted in Amy Westervelt, "Can't Picture a World Devastated by Climate Change? These Games Will Do It for You," *Smithsonian Magazine*, July 21, 2014, www.smithsonianmag.com/science-nature/cant-picture-world-devastated-climate-change-these-games-will-do-it-you-180952104.

40. Shawn and Laura Sears, interview (San Gregorio, CA) and e-mail correspondence with authors, October 2014.

41. Outdoor play, studies show, is pivotal for a child's development and well-being. See Peter Gray, "The Decline of Play and the Rise of Psychopathology in Children and Adolescents," *American Journal of Play* 3, no. 4 (2011): 443–463.

CONCLUSION

1. Rob Portman, "Rob Portman Commentary: Gay Couples Also Deserve Chance to Get Married," *Columbus Dispatch*, March 15, 2013, www.dispatch.com/content/stories/editorials/2013/03/15/gay-couples-also-deserve-chance-to-get-married.html.

2. See, for instance, Ray Kurzweil, *The Singularity Is Near: When Humans Transcend Biology* (New York: Viking, 2005).

3. Michael Howard, "The Movie That Accurately Predicted the Future of Technology," Esquire.com, September 23, 2014, www.esquire.com/entertainment/movies/a30140/minority-report-tech-is-real-now.

4. Rory Cellan-Jones, "Stephen Hawking Warns Artificial Intelligence Could End Mankind," BBC News, December 2, 2014, www.bbc.com/news/technology-30290540.

5. "She, Robot: A Conversation with Helen Greiner," *Foreign Affairs* 94, no. 1 (January–February 2015), 21.

6. Diane Ackerman, *The Human Age: The World Shaped by Us* (New York: W. W. Norton & Co., 2014), 225.

7. Ibid., 221–222.

8. Matt McFarland, "Elon Musk: 'With Artificial Intelligence We Are Summoning the Demon,'" *Washington Post*, October 24, 2014, www.washingtonpost.com/news/innovations/wp/2014/10/24/elon-musk-with-artificial-intelligence-we-are-summoning-the-demon.

9. Susannah F. Locke, "Robots That Eat Bugs and Plants for Power," *Popular Science*, October 9, 2009, www.popsci.com/military-aviation-amp-space/article/2009-09/robots-eat-bugs-and-plants-power.

10. Stephen Hawking, quoted in Cellan-Jones, "Stephen Hawking Warns."

11. Sherry Turkle, "Authenticity in the Age of Digital Companions," *Interaction Studies* 8, no. 3 (2007), 514.

12. Steve Jobs, "Stanford Commencement Address," Stanford University, Stanford, CA, June 14, 2005.

13. Hugh Herr, "The New Bionics That Let Us Run, Climb and Dance," TED Talk, March 2014, www.ted.com/talks/hugh_herr_the_new_bionics_that_let_us_run_climb_and_dance?language=en.

14. Elon Musk, quoted in John Markoff, "Artificial-Intelligence Research Center Is Founded by Silicon Valley Investors," *New York Times*, December 11, 2015, www.nytimes.com/2015/12/12/science/artificial-intelligence-research-center-is-founded-by-silicon-valley-investors.html.

15. Chris Cesare, "Stanford to Host 100-Year Study on Artificial Intelligence," *Stanford News*, December 16, 2014, http://news.stanford.edu/news/2014/december/ai-century-study-121614.html; John Markoff, "Study to Examine Effects of Artificial Intelligence," *New York Times*, December 16, 2014, www.nytimes.com/2014/12/16/science/century-long-study-will-examine-effects-of-artificial-intelligence.html.

16. Cesare, "Stanford to Host 100-Year Study."

17. Mary Warnock, *A Question of Life: The Warnock Report on Human Fertilisation and Embryology* (London: Her Majesty's Stationery Office, 1984).

18. Fertilisation, Human, and Embryology Act, Chapter 37 (London: Her Majesty's Stationery Office, 1990).

P.S. THE FIRST STEP

1. Alexis de Tocqueville, *Democracy in America*, vol. 1 (New York: A.S. Barnes & Co., 1851), 271.

2. Johann N. Neem, *Creating a Nation of Joiners; Democracy and Civil Society in Early National Massachusetts* (Cambridge, MA: Harvard University Press, 2008), 173.

3. Gavin Newsom, *Citizenville: How to Take the Town Square Digital and Reinvent Government* (New York: Penguin Press, 2013), 113–118.

4. Ibid., 121.

BIBLIOGRAPHY

"2011 Minnesota Statutes." The Office of the Revisor of Statutes. www.revisor.mn.gov/statutes/percent2o?id=256B.0756&year=2011.

2014 Teen Internet Safety Survey. Atlanta: Cox Communications, 2014. www.cox.com/wcm/en/aboutus/datasheet/takecharge/tween-internet-safety-survey.pdf.

"2015 Year in Review." *Pornhub Insights*, January 6, 2016. www.pornhub.com/insights/2015-year-in-review.

"6-Inch Low Fat Subs: Nutritional Information." Subway. www.subway.co.uk/assets/pdf/subway-nutritional-values-uk.pdf.

Abel, Jaison R., and Richard Deitz. "The Class of 2015 Might Have a Little Better Luck Finding a Good Job." Liberty Street Economics, Federal Reserve Bank of New York, May 15, 2015. http://libertystreeteconomics.newyorkfed.org/2015/05/the-class-of-2015-might-have-a-little-better-luck-finding-a-good-job.html#.VmCEroTI6jQ.

Abel, Jaison R., Richard Deitz, and Yaqin Su. "Are Recent College Graduates Finding Good Jobs?" *Current Issues in Economics and Finance* 20, no. 1 (2014). www.newyorkfed.org/medialibrary/media/research/current_issues/ci20-1.pdf.

"About: Secretary of the Treasury Jacob J. Lew." US Department of the Treasury, June 5, 2014. www.treasury.gov/about/Pages/Secretary.aspx.

Ackerman, Diane. *The Human Age: The World Shaped by Us.* New York: W. W. Norton & Company, 2014.

Adler, Jonathan H. "Fables of the Cuyahoga: Reconstructing a History of Environmental Protection." *Fordham Environmental Law Journal* 14 (2002): 89–146.

"Advance Care Planning: National Guidelines." *Concise Guidance to Good Practice*, no. 12. London: Royal College of Physicians, 2009.

"Advertising to Children and Teens: Current Practices." *Common Sense Media,* Spring 2014.

Agenda Materials: College Board Forum 2015. College Board, November 4–6, 2015. http://media.collegeboard.com/digitalServices/pdf/forum-agenda.pdf.

"Ag-Gag Laws Silence Whistleblowers." *Moyers & Company*, July 10, 2013. http://billmoyers.com/2013/07/10/alec-activists-and-ag-gag.

Ahn, Sun Joo Grace, Jeremy N. Bailenson, and Dooyeon Park. "Short-and Long-Term Effects of Embodied Experiences in Immersive Virtual Environments on Environmental Locus of Control and Behavior." *Computers in Human Behavior* 39 (2014): 235–245.

Aitken, Murray. *Medicines Use and Spending Shifts: A Review of the Use of Medicines in the U.S. in 2014.* IMS Institute for Healthcare Informatics, April 2015.

"Alan Greenspan to Consult for Deutsche Bank Corporate and Investment Bank." *Deutsche Bank*, August 13, 2007. www.db.com/presse/en/content/press_releases_2007_3606.htm.

Allen, Marshall. "What a New Doctor Learned About Medical Mistakes from Her Mom's Death." *ProPublica*, January 9, 2013. www.propublica.org/article/what-a-new-doctor-learned-about-medical-mistakes-from-her-moms-death.

"Almere, Holland." The Self-Build Portal, 2015. www.selfbuildportal.org.uk/homeruskwartier-district-almere.

Alter, Jonathan. "Failure to Launch: How Obama Fumbled HealthCare.gov." *Foreign Affairs*, March/April 2014. www.foreignaffairs.com/articles/united-states/2014-02-12/failure-launch.

Ambrosi-Randić, Neala. "Perception of Current and Ideal Body Size in Preschool Age Children." *Perceptual and Motor Skills* 90, no. 3 (2000): 885–889.

333

American Society of Civil Engineers. "Failure to Act: The Impact of Infrastructure Investment on America's Economic Growth." 2013. www.asce.org/uploadedFiles/Issues_and_Advocacy/Our_Initiatives/Infrastructure/Content_Pieces/failure-to-act-economic-impact-summary-report.pdf.

"America's Elite: An Hereditary Meritocracy." *Economist*, January 24, 2015. www.economist.com/news/briefing/21640316-children-rich-and-powerful-are-increasingly-well-suited-earning-wealth-and-power.

"America's New Aristocracy." *The Economist*, January 24, 2015. www.economist.com/news/leaders/21640331-importance-intellectual-capital-grows-privilege-has-become-increasingly.

"America's Top Schools 2014." *Newsweek*. www.newsweek.com/high-schools/americas-top-schools-2014.

Amos, Nicky, and Rory Sullivan. *The Business Benchmark on Farm Animal Welfare: 2014 Report*. Business Benchmark on Farm Animal Welfare, 2014. www.bbfaw.com/wp-content/uploads/2015/02/BBFAW_2014_Report.pdf.

"Amsterdam Children Fighting Cars in 1972." Bicycle Dutch. https://bicycledutch.wordpress.com/2013/12/12/amsterdam-children-fighting-cars-in-1972.

An Unhealthy Dose of Stress: The Impact of Adverse Childhood Experiences and Toxic Stress on Childhood Health and Development. Center for Youth Wellness. www.centerforyouthwellness.org/download/document/203/CYW%20White%20Paper_An%20Unhealthy%20Dose%20of%20Stress_National%20Final.pdf.

"Analysis of Bundled Payment." Rand Corporation. www.rand.org/pubs/technical_reports/TR562z20/analysis-of-bundled-payment.html.

Andrews, James. "17 Months and 634 Illnesses Later, CDC Declares Foster Farms-Linked Salmonella Outbreak Over." *Food Safety News*, July 31, 2014. www.foodsafetynews.com/2014/07/after-17-months-foster-farms-salmonella-outbreak-declared-over/#.Vlu7MNKrTDc.

Andreyeva, Tatiana, Joerg Luedicke, and Y. Claire Wang. "State-Level Estimates of Obesity-Attributable Costs of Absenteeism." *Journal of Occupational and Environmental Medicine* 56, no. 11 (2014): 1120–1127.

"Animal Welfare." Jeremy Coller Foundation. www.jeremycollerfoundation.org/programmes/animal-welfare.

"Antimicrobial Resistance—Why the Irresponsible Use of Antibiotics in Agriculture Must Stop." Alliance to Save Our Antibiotics, June 2014. www.soilassociation.org/LinkClick.aspx?fileticket=G9q4uEb5deI%3D&tabid=1841.

APA Task Force on the Sexualization of Girls. *Report of the APA Task Force on the Sexualization of Girls*. Washington, DC: American Psychological Association, 2010.

Appelbaum, Eileen, and Ruth Milkman. *Leaves That Pay: Employer and Worker Experiences with Paid Family Leave in California*. Washington, DC: Center for Economic and Policy Research, 2011.

Applications of Comcast Corp. and Time Warner Cable Inc. for Consent to Assign or Transfer Control of Licenses and Authorizations. "Second Amended Modified Joint Protective Order." MB Docket no. 14-57, DA 14-1639, November 12, 2014.

Archer, Tom, and Ian Cole. "Still Not Plannable? Housing Supply and the Changing Structure of the Housebuilding Industry in the UK in 'Austere' Times." *People, Place and Policy* 8, no. 2 (2014): 93–108.

Ashworth, Will. "Risk Metrics Two Years after IPO." *Investopedia*, February 28, 2010. www.investopedia.com/stock-analysis/2010/riskmetrics-two-years-after-ipo-riskmscimhptrifigacas0304.aspx.

Asking Students About Teachers. Measures of Effective Teaching Project, 2012.

Atkinson, Richard C., and Saul Geiser. "The Big Problem with the New SAT." *New York Times*, May 5, 2015. www.nytimes.com/2015/05/05/opinion/the-big-problem-with-the-new-sat.html.

Aubrey, Allison. "Antibiotic-Free Meat Business Is Booming, Thanks to Chipotle." NPR, May 31, 2012. www.npr.org/sections/thesalt/2012/05/31/154084442/antibiotic-free-meat-business-is-booming-thanks-to-chipotle.

————. "Where's the Whole Grain in Most of Our Wheat Bread?" NPR, April 15, 2014. www.npr.org/sections/thesalt/2014/04/15/301473319/wheres-the-whole-grain-in-most-of-our-wheat-bread.

Bagchi, Sutirtha, and Jan Svejnar. "Does Wealth Inequality Matter for Growth? The Effect of Billionaire Wealth, Income Distribution, and Poverty." *Journal of Comparative Economics* 43, no. 3 (2015): 505–530.

Bailenson, Jeremy. "Virtual Reality Could Make a Real Difference in Environment." *San Francisco Chronicle*, August 15, 2014. www.sfgate.com/opinion/article/Virtual-reality-could-make-real-difference-in-5691610.php.

Bainbridge, Louis. Louis Bainbridge to James T. Duff, October 31, 1948. In "The Donora Smog Disaster October 30–31, 1948." Pennsylvania Historical & Museum Commission. www.portal.state.pa.us/portal/server.pt/community/documents_from_1946__present/20426/donora_smog_disaster/999079.

Ball, David J. "Policy Issues and Risk-Benefit Trade-offs of 'Safer Surfacing' for Children's Playgrounds." *Accident Analysis & Prevention* 36, no. 4 (2004): 661–670.

Ballona Wetlands Restoration Project. 2014. http://ballonarestoration.org.

Banham, John, Kate Faulkner, Roger Graef, and Mavis McDonald. *Building the Homes and Communities Britain Needs*. Future Homes Commission, Royal Institute of British Architects, 2012.

Barber, Dan. "What Farm-to-Table Got Wrong." *New York Times*, May 17, 2014. www.nytimes.com/2014/05/18/opinion/sunday/what-farm-to-table-got-wrong.html.

Barbier, Edward B. "Valuing Ecosystem Services as Productive Inputs." *Economic Policy* 22, no. 49 (2007): 178–229.

"Barclays Appoints Hector Sants." Barclays, December 12, 2012. www.barclays.com/news/2012/12/barclays-appoints-hector-sants.html.

Barnett, Alina, Sandra Batten, Adrian Chiu, Jeremy Franklin, and Maria Sebastia-Barriel. "The UK Productivity Puzzle." *Bank of England Quarterly Bulletin* Q2 (2014): 114–128.

Basu, Tanya. "Salmonella Scare Causes Recall of 1.7 Million lbs of Frozen Chicken." *Time*, July 14, 2015. www.foodsafetynews.com/2014/07/after-17-months-foster-farms-salmonella-outbreak-declared-over/#.Vlu7MNKrTDc.

"BBC Poll: One in Five 'Disillusioned' with Westminster." *BBC News*, October 31, 2014. www.bbc.com/news/uk-politics-29857784.

Bennett, Drake. "The Dunbar Number, from the Guru of Social Networks." *Bloomberg Business*, January 10, 2013. www.bloomberg.com/bw/articles/2013-01-10/the-dunbar-number-from-the-guru-of-social-networks.

Bentham, Jeremy. *An Introduction to the Principles of Morals and Legislation*. 1789.

Berman, Rick. "Commentary: Playing Chicken with Pork." *PORK Network*, February 28, 2013. www.porknetwork.com/pork-news/Commentary-Playing-chicken-with-pork-193903501.html.

Berrington de González, Amy, Mahadevappa Mahesh, Kwang-Pyo Kim, Mythreyi Bhargavan, Rebecca Lewis, Fred Mettler, and Charles Land. "Projected Cancer Risks from Computed Tomographic Scans Performed in the United States in 2007." *Archives of Internal Medicine* 169, no. 22 (December 2009): 2017–2077.

Bertko, John, and Rachel Effros. *Increase the Use of "Bundled" Payment Approaches*. Santa Monica, CA: Rand Corporation, 2010.

"Bevolkingsontwikkeling; regio per maand" (in Dutch). *CBS Statline*, June 26, 2014.

"Biden Compares La Guardia Airport to 'Third World.'" *New York Times*, February 6, 2014. www.nytimes.com/2014/02/07/nyregion/biden-compares-la-guardia-airport-to-third-world.html?_r=0.

Bidwell, Allie. "An African Company Pays People to Learn Computer Science." *U.S. News & World Report*, May 14, 2015. www.usnews.com/news/stem-solutions/articles/2015/05/14/andela-an -african-company-paying-people-to-learn-computer-science.

Biehle, Susanne N., and Kristin D. Mickelson. "Preparing for Parenthood: How Feelings of Responsibility and Efficacy Impact Expectant Parents." *Journal of Social and Personal Relationships* 28, no. 5 (2011): 668–683.

Blackwelder, Reid. Letter to Edith Ramirez, June 4, 2015. www.aafp.org/dam/AAFP/documents/ advocacy/legal/antitrust/LT-FTC-InsuranceMergers-060415.pdf.

Blair, Tony. *A Journey: My Political Life*. New York: Vantage Books, 2011.

Bloomberg View. "Why Should Taxpayers Give Big Banks $83 Billion a Year?" *Bloomberg View*, February 20, 2013. www.bloombergview.com/articles/2013-02-20/why-should-taxpayers-give-big -banks-83-billion-a-year.

———. "Small Schools Work in New York." *New York Times*, October 18, 2014. www.nytimes .com/2014/10/18/opinion/small-schools-work-in-new-york.html.

Blumenthal, Paul, and Ryan Grim. "The Inside Story of How Citizens United Has Changed Washington Lawmaking." *Huffington Post*, February 25, 2015. www.huffingtonpost.com/2015/02/26/ citizens-united-congress_n_6723540.html.

Blundell, Richard, Alan Duncan, Julian McCrae, and Costas Meghir. "The Labour Market Impact of the Working Families' Tax Credit." *Fiscal Studies* 21, no. 1 (2000): 75–104.

Bodin, Maria, and Terry Hartig. "Does the Outdoor Environment Matter for Psychological Restoration Gained Through Running?" *Psychology of Sport and Exercise* 4, no. 2 (2003): 141–153.

Boesch, Donald F., Leonard Shabman, L. George Antle, John W. Day Jr., Robert G. Dean, Gerald E. Galloway, Charles G. Groat et al. *A New Framework for Planning the Future of Coastal Louisiana After the Hurricanes of 2005*. Cambridge, MD: University of Maryland Center for Environmental Science, 2006.

Bond, Allison. "Blocks, Puzzles Help Kids Prep for School and Life." *Reuters*, March 20, 2014. www.reuters.com/article/2014/03/20/us-puzzles-kids-idUSBREA2J1LN20140320.

Booth, Darren. "United Raises Most Change Fees by $50, Will Others Follow?" CNBC, April 22, 2013. www.cnbc.com/id/100660764.

Bornstein, David. "Out of Poverty, Family-Style." *New York Times*, July 14, 2011. http://opinionator .blogs.nytimes.com/2011/07/14/out-of-poverty-family-style/?_r=0.

Borowitz, Andy. "Citigroup to Move Headquarters to US Capitol Building." *New Yorker*, December 13, 2013. www.newyorker.com/humor/borowitz-report/citigroup-move-headquarters-u-s -capitol-building.

Boseley, Sarah. "Mid Staffordshire NHS Trust Fined for 'Avoidable and Tragic Death.'" *Guardian*, April 28, 2014. www.theguardian.com/society/2014/apr/28/mid-staffordshire-nhs-trust -fined-gillian-astbury.

Botelho, Greg, and Sara Sidner. "Ferguson Judge Withdraws All Arrest Warrants Before 2015." CNN, August 25, 2015. www.cnn.com/2015/08/24/us/ferguson-missouri-court-changes.

Boubekri, Mohamed, Ivy N. Cheung, Kathryn J. Reid, Chia-Hui Wang, and Phyllis C. Zee. "Impact of Windows and Daylight Exposure on Overall Health and Sleep Quality of Office Workers: A Case-Control Pilot Study." *Journal of Clinical Sleep Medicine: JCSM: Official Publication of the American Academy of Sleep Medicine* 10, no. 6 (2014): 603.

Boushey, Heather. "Family Policy: The Foundation of a Middle-Out Agenda." *Democracy* no. 29 (Summer 2013). http://democracyjournal.org/magazine/29/family-policy-the-foundation-of -a-middle-out-agenda.

Boushey, Heather, and Sarah Jane Glynn. *The Effects of Paid Family Medical Leave on Employment Stability and Economic Stability*. Washington, DC: Center for American Progress, 2012. www .americanprogress.org/wp-content/uploads/issues/2012/04/pdf/BousheyEmploymentLeave1 .pdf.

Bowers, Becky. "Rep. Louise Slaughter Says 80% of Antibiotics Are Fed to Livestock." *Tampa Bay Times*'s PolitiFact.com, October 15, 2013. www.politifact.com/truth-o-meter/statements/2013/oct/15/louise-slaughter/rep-louise-slaughter-says-80-antibiotics-are-fed-l/

Bradley, Kimberly. "Model Factories: Fagus-GreCon." *Monocle*, 69, no. 7 (December 2013–January 2014): 133–134.

Bradshaw, Tim. "Airbnb Valued at $13 B Ahead of Staff Stock Sale." *Financial Times*, October 23, 2014. www.ft.com/cms/s/0/99312b96-5b05-11e4-8625-00144feab7de.html#axzz3sLWpwtyb.

Braga, Anthony A., and Brenda J. Bond. "Policing Crime and Disorder Hot Spots: A Randomized Controlled Trial." *Criminology* 46, no. 3 (2008): 577–607.

Bramley, Ellie Violet. "Is Jan Gehl Winning His Battle to Make Our Cities Liveable?" *Guardian*, December 8, 2014. www.theguardian.com/cities/2014/dec/08/jan-gehl-make-cities-liveable-urban-rethinker.

Branson, Sir Richard. "Excerpt from: The Virgin Way: Everything I Know About Leadership." Virgin.com, September 23, 2014. www.virgin.com/richard-branson/why-were-letting-virgin-staff-take-as-much-holiday-as-they-want.

Brat, Illan, and Sarah Nassauer. "Chipotle Suspends Pork Sales at a Third of Its Restaurants." *Wall Street Journal*, January 13, 2015. www.wsj.com/articles/chipotle-suspends-pork-sales-at-a-third-of-its-restaurants-1421194340.

Bredgaard, Thomas, and Arthur Daemmrich. *The Welfare State as an Investment Strategy: Denmark's Flexicurity Policies*. July 2012. http://ilera2012.wharton.upenn.edu/RefereedPapers/BredgaardThomas%20ArthurDaemmrich.pdf.

Brill, Steven. *America's Bitter Pill: Money, Politics, Backroom Deals, and the Fight to Fix Our Broken Healthcare System*. New York: Random House, 2015.

British Government. *Number of Individual Income Taxpayers by Marginal Rate, Gender and Age, 1990–91 to 2014–15*. www.gov.uk/government/uploads/system/uploads/attachment_data/file/404149/Table_2.1.pdf.

Brooks, David. "The Character Factory." *New York Times*, August 1, 2014. www.nytimes.com/2014/08/01/opinion/david-brooks-the-character-factory.html.

———. "Out of Poverty, Family-Style." *New York Times*, July 14, 2011. http://opinionator.blogs.nytimes.com/2011/07/14/out-of-poverty-family-style.

———. "Support Our Students." *New York Times*, January 19, 2015. www.nytimes.com/2015/01/20/opinion/david-brooks-support-our-students.html.

———. "Stairway to Wisdom." *New York Times*, May 15, 2014. www.nytimes.com/2014/05/16/opinion/brooks-stairway-to-wisdom.html.

Brown, Jane D., and Kelly L. L'Engle. "X-Rated Sexual Attitudes and Behaviors Associated with US Early Adolescents' Exposure to Sexually Explicit Media." *Communication Research* 36, no. 1 (2009): 129–151.

Brown, Susan L. "Family Structure and Child Well-Being: The Significance of Parental Cohabitation." *Journal of Marriage and Family* 66, no. 2 (2004): 351–367.

Buchannan, Larry, Josh Keller, and Haeyoun Park. "Your Contribution to the California Drought." *New York Times*, May 21, 2015. www.nytimes.com/interactive/2015/05/21/us/your-contribution-to-the-california-drought.html?_r=0.

Buck, Amanda. "Transparency: The Most Dangerous Cities for Walking." *GOOD Magazine*, September 3, 2010. http://magazine.good.is/infographics/transparency-the-most-dangerous-cities-for-walking.

"Building Blocks." *The Economist*, December 22, 2014. www.economist.com/news/finance-and-economics/21568717-regional-deals-are-only-game-town-supporters-free-trade-are-they-any.

Building in a Small Island? Why We Still Need the Brownfield First Approach. Kemsing, Kent: Green Balance (for the Campaign to Protect Rural England), 2011.

Burden, Amanda. "How Public Spaces Make Cities Work." TED Talk, April 2014. www.ted.com/talks/amanda_burden_how_public_spaces_make_cities_work?language=en.

Butler, Rhett. "Brazil." Mongabay.com, July 13, 2014. http://rainforests.mongabay.com/20brazil.htm.

Buzby, Jean C., and Jeffrey Hyman. "Total and Per Capita Value of Food Loss in the United States." *Food Policy* 37, no. 5 (2012): 561–570.

Cadwalladr, Carole. "My Week as an Amazon Insider." *Guardian*, November 30, 2013. http://www.theguardian.com/technology/2013/dec/01/week-amazon-insider-feature-treatment-employees-work.

"Cage-Free vs. Battery-Cage Eggs." Humane Society. www.humanesociety.org/issues/confinement_farm/facts/cage-free_vs_battery-cage.html

Cai, Xiaomei, and Xiaoquan Zhao. "Click Here, Kids!" *Journal of Children and Media*, 4, no. 2 (2010). www.federalreserve.gov/econresdata/notes/feds-notes/2014/the-recent-decline-in-long-term-unemployment-20140721.html.

Cajner, Tomaz, and David Ratner. "The Recent Decline in Long-Term Unemployment." FEDS Notes, July 21, 2014. www.federalreserve.gov/econresdata/notes/feds-notes/2014/the-recent-decline-in-long-term-unemployment-20140721.html.

Caldwell, Christopher. "Revolting High Rises." *New York Times Magazine*, November 27, 2005. www.nytimes.com/2005/11/27/magazine/revolting-high-rises.html.

"Campylobacter." Food Standards Agency. www.food.gov.uk/science/microbiology/campylobacterevidenceprogramme.

Card, David, and Alan B. Krueger. *Minimum Wages and Employment: A Case Study of the Fast Food Industry in New Jersey and Pennsylvania*, no. w4509. National Bureau of Economic Research, 1993.

Caro, Robert. *The Years of Lyndon Johnson*, vol. 1: *The Path to Power*. New York: Vintage, 1981; reprint: London: Pimlico, 2003.

Carr, Nicholas. *The Shallows: What the Internet Is Doing to Our Brains*. New York: W. W. Norton & Company, 2010.

Casciani, Dominic. "Secret Life of the Office Cleaner." *BBC News*, September 19, 2005.

Casey, Liam. Interview by Piers Fawkes. PSFK 2015, May 18, 2015.

Cassidy, John. "The New Job Figures and Secular Stagnation." *New Yorker*, April 3, 2015. www.newyorker.com/news/john-cassidy/the-new-job-figures-and-secular-stagnation.

Cawley, John, and Chad Meyerhoefer. "The Medical Care Costs of Obesity: An Instrumental Variables Approach." *Journal of Health Economics* 31, no. 1 (2012).

Cellan-Jones, Rory. "Stephen Hawking Warns Artificial Intelligence Could End Mankind." *BBC News*, December 2, 2014. www.bbc.com/news/technology-30290540.

Census Bureau (US). *Business Dynamics Statistics: Firm Characteristics Data Tables*. Washington, DC: Department of Commerce, 2015. www.census.gov/ces/dataproducts/bds/data_firm.html.

———. *Maternity Leave and Employment Patterns of First-Time Mothers: 1961–2008*. Washington, DC: Department of Commerce, 2011.

"Census Shows Rise in Foreign-Born." *BBC News*, December 11, 2012.

Center for Medicare and Medicated Services, Open Payments Data. "City of Hope National Medical Center: Summary Information for Program Year 2014." https://openpaymentsdata.cms.gov/hospital/1128.

Cesare, Chris. "Stanford to Host 100-Year Study on Artificial Intelligence." *Stanford Report*, December 16, 2014. http://news.stanford.edu/news/2014/december/ai-century-study-121614.html.

Chandler, Alfred D. Jr. *The Visible Hand: The Managerial Revolution in American Business*. Cambridge, MA: Harvard University Press, 1977.

Chandy, Laurence, and Geoffrey Gertz. *Poverty in Numbers: The Changing State of Global Poverty from 2005 to 2015*. Washington, DC: Brookings Institution, 2011.

Chang, Chen-Yen, and Ping-Kun Chen. "Human Response to Window Views and Indoor Plants in the Workplace." *HortScience* 40, no. 5 (2005): 1354–1359.

Chang, Emily. "China's Famed Pearl River Under Denim Threat." CNN, April 27, 2010. www.cnn .com/2010/WORLD/asiapcf/04/26/china.denim.water.pollution.

Cherlin, Andrew J., Elizabeth Talbert, and Suzumi Yasutake. "Changing Fertility Regimes and the Transition to Adulthood: Evidence from a Recent Cohort." In *Annual Meeting of the Population Association of America*. Boston, MA, May 3, 2014.

Chetty, Raj, and John N. Friedman. "New Evidence on the Long-Term Impacts of Tax Credits." Proceedings: Annual Conference on Taxation and Minutes of the Annual Meeting of the National Tax Association 104, 2011.

Chew, Jesslyn. "Marriages Benefit When Fathers Share Household Parenting Responsibilities, MU Researchers Say." *University of Missouri News Bureau*, April 8, 2013. http://munews .missouri.edu/news-releases/2013/0408–marriages-benefit-when-fathers-share-household -parenting-responsibilities-mu-researcher-says.

Chingos, Matthew M. "Agenda Materials: College Board Forum 2014." The College Board, October 27–29, 2013.

———. *Strength in Numbers: State Spending on K-12 Assessment Systems*. Washington, DC: Brown Center for Education at the Brookings Institution, 2012.

Chirnko, Robert S., and Daniel J. Wilson. *Can Lower Tax Rates Be Bought? Business Rent-Seeking and Tax Competition Among U.S. States*. Federal Reserve Bank of San Francisco, Working Paper 2009-29, 2010.

Cho, Illseung, Shingo Yamanishi, Laura Cox, Barbara A. Methé, Jiri Zavadil, Kelvin Li, Zhan Gao et al. "Antibiotics in Early Life Alter the Murine Colonic Microbiome and Adiposity." *Nature* 488, no. 7413 (2012): 621–626.

Christensen, Clayton. "The Capitalist's Dilemma." Lecture, RSA. London, September 23, 2013.

Chu, Jenny, Jonathan Faasse, and P. Raghavendra Rau. "Do Compensation Consultants Enable Higher CEO Pay?" *New Evidence from Recent Disclosure Rule Changes*, September 23, 2014.

Churchill, Sir Winston. Hansard House of Commons Debate, April 28, 1909, vol. 4, cols. 342–411.

———. Hansard House of Commons Debate, October 28, 1943, vol. 393, cols. 403–73.

Cialdini, Robert B., Linda J. Demaine, Brad J. Sagarin, Daniel W. Barrett, Kelton Rhoads, and Patricia L. Winter. "Managing Social Norms for Persuasive Impact." *Social Influence* 1, no. 1 (2006): 3–15.

Citizens UK. "Living Wage Week 2013." YouTube.com, November 3, 2013. www.youtube.com/ watch?v=7XzoylCLBgE.

Clark, Krissy. "Part II: 'Save Money, Live Better.'" American Public Media: Marketplace, April 2, 2014. www.marketplace.org/2014/04/02/wealth-poverty/secret-life-food-stamp/part-ii-save -money-live-better.

Cloos, Kassondra, and Julie Turkewitz. "Hundreds of Nude Photos Jolt Colorado School." *New York Times*, November 6, 2015. www.nytimes.com/2015/11/07/us/colorado-students-caught -trading-nude-photos-by-the-hundreds.html.

Coca-Cola Company. "Nutrition & Ingredient Information on Coca-Cola Products." www .coca-colaproductfacts.com/en/coca-cola-products/coca-cola.

Cohen, Nick. "A Tale of Two Cities." *Observer*, October 19, 2013. www.theguardian.com/politics /2003/oct/19/socialexclusion.london.

Cohn, Gary. "Overcompensation: Tying Corporate Taxes to CEO Pay." *Capital & Main*, August 6, 2015. http://capitalandmain.com/features/california-expose/overcompensation-tying-cor porate-taxes-to-ceo-pay.

Collins Atlas of World History. Edited by Geoffrey Barraclough. Ann Arbor, MI: Arbor Press, 2003.

Collins, James C., and Jerry I. Porras. "Building Your Company's Vision." *Harvard Business Review*, September 1996. https://hbr.org/1996/09/building-your-companys-vision.

Collinson, Patrick. "Self-Build: It's Time to Go Dutch." *Guardian*, November 25, 2011. www
.theguardian.com/money/2011/nov/25/self-build-go-dutch.

Colt, Sam. "Tim Cook's Total Pay for 2014 Was over $100 Million." *Business Insider,* January
24, 2015. www.businessinsider.com/heres-how-tim-cook-raked-in-over-100-million-in-2014
-2015-1.

Colvile, Robert. "Yes, CEOs Are Ludicrously Overpaid. And Yes, It's Getting Worse." *Telegraph*, October 13, 2014. www.telegraph.co.uk/comment/columnists/robert-colvile/11158607/Yes-CEOs
-are-ludicrously-overpaid.-And-yes-its-getting-worse.html.

Colvin, Geoff. *Humans Are Underrated: What High Achievers Know That Brilliant Machines Never
Will.* New York: Portfolio/Penguin, 2015.

"The Common Sense Census: Media Use by Tweens and Teens." Common Sense Media Kids
Action, Fall 2015. www.commonsensemedia.org/research/the-common-sense-census-media
-use-by-tweens-and-teens.

Competition Commission. *Market Investigation into the Supply of Groceries in the UK.* London: UK
Competition Commission, 2008.

Comptroller and Auditor General. *The Criminal Justice System: Landscape Review.* London: National Audit Office, 2014.

Congdon, Christine, Donna Flynn, and Melanie Redman. "Balancing 'We' and 'Me': The Best
Collaborative Spaces Also Support Solitude." *Harvard Business Review*, October 2014. https://
hbr.org/2014/10/balancing-we-and-me-the-best-collaborative-spaces-also-support-solitude.

Connor, John M., and Robert H. Lande. "Cartels as Rational Business Strategy: Crime Pays."
Cardozo Law Review 34, no. 427 (2012): 427–489, 430.

Conroy Bass, Brooke. "Preparing for Parenthood? Gender, Aspirations, and the Reproduction of
Labor Market Inequality." *Gender & Society* 29, no. 3 (2015): 362–385.

"Consumers Face 'Lost Decade' as Spending Squeeze Bites." *BBC News*, September 29, 2014.
www.bbc.com/news/business-29406079.

"Contrast-Enhanced CT Safe for Most Patients." Radiological Society of North America, September 9, 2014. www2.rsna.org/timssnet/media/pressreleases/14_pr_target.cfm?ID=757.

Cooper, Alexia, and Erica L. Smith. *Homicide Trends in the United States, 1980–2008.* Washington, DC: US Department of Justice, November 2011. www.bjs.gov/content/pub/pdf/htus8008
.pdf, 7.

Cooper, David. *EPI Briefing Paper #405: Raising the Minimum Wage to $12 by 2020 Would Lift Wages
for 35 Million American Workers.* Washington, DC: Economic Policy Institute, 2015.

———. *Raising the Minimum Wage to $10.10 Would Save Safety Net Programs Billions and Help
Ensure Businesses Are Doing Their Fair Share.* Washington, DC: Economic Policy Institute, October 16, 2014.

"Coordenaçã-Geral de Observção da Terra—OBT: Projecto Prodes: Monitoramenot da Floresta
Amazônica Brasileira por Satélite" (in Portuguese). Ministério da Ciêcia e Technologia e Inovação e Minstério do Melo Ambiente, 2014. www.obt.inpe.br/prodes/index.php.

"Coral Reefs: Facts and Figures." IUCN, March 20, 2013. www.iucn.org/media/facts_and_
figures/?12680/Coral-reefs---Facts-and-figures.

Corlett, Adam, and Laura Gardiner. "Low Pay Britain 2015." *Resolution Foundation*, October 5,
2015. www.resolutionfoundation.org/publications/low-pay-britain-2015.

Corlett, Adam, and Matthew Whittaker. *Low Pay Britain 2014.* London: Resolution Foundation,
2014.

Corps of Engineers, US Army Engineer District, New Orleans. *Interim Survey Report, Morgan City,
Louisiana and Vicinity,* no. 63. New Orleans, LA: US Army Engineer District, 1963.

Cost of Outcomes Associated with Low Levels of Adult Numeracy in the UK. National Numeracy and
Pro Bono Economics, 2014.

Costanza, Robert, Rudolf de Groot, Paul Sutton, Sander van der Ploeg, Sharolyn J. Anderson, Ida

Kubiszewski, Stephen Farber, and R. Kerry Turner. "Changes in the Global Value of Ecosystem Services." *Global Environmental Change* 26 (2014): 152–158.

Costco Wholesale Corp. *Marketwatch*, March 29, 2015. www.marketwatch.com/investing/stock/cost/financials.

Coughlan, Sean. "Is Five Too Soon to Start School?" *BBC News*, February 8, 2008. http://news.bbc.co.uk/2/hi/uk_news/education/7234578.stm.

Council Regulation (EC). 1999/74 of July 19, 1999, Laying Down Minimum Standards for the Protection of Laying Hens [1999]. OJ L203/53. http://eur-lex.europa.eu/legal-content/EN/TXT/?uri=uriserv%3Al12067.

Cowen, Tyler. "Automation Alone Isn't Killing Jobs." *New York Times*, April 6, 2014. www.nytimes.com/2014/04/06/business/automation-alone-isnt-killing-jobs.html.

Coyle, Diane. *GDP: A Brief but Affectionate History*. Princeton, NJ: Princeton University Press, 2014.

————. "GDP Is a Mirror on the Markets. It Must Not Rule Our Lives." *Guardian*, November 20, 2014. www.theguardian.com/commentisfree/2014/nov/20/gdp-markets-short-term-victorians-value.

Cragg, Gordon M. "Natural Products as Sources of New Drugs Over the 30 Years from 1981 to 2010." *Journal of Natural Products* 75, no. 3 (2012): 311–335.

Craigie, Terry-Ann, Jeanne Brooks-Gunn, and Jane Waldfogel. *Family Structure, Family Stability and Early Child Wellbeing*, no. 1275. 2010. http://crcw.princeton.edu/workingpapers/WP10-14-FF.pdf.

Culp, Jennifer, Robert A. Bell, and Diana Cassady. "Characteristics of Food Industry Web Sites and 'Advergames' Targeting Children." *Journal of Nutrition Education and Behavior* 42, no. 3 (2010): 197–201.

Cutler, Kim-Mai. "How Burrowing Owls Lead to Vomiting Anarchists (Or SF's Housing Crisis Explained)." *TechCrunch*, April 14, 2014. http://techcrunch.com/2014/04/14/sf-housing.

"Cycling Facts and Figures." IAmsterdam, 2015. www.iamsterdam.com/en/media-centre/city-hall/dossier-cycling/cycling-facts-and-figures.

Dahl, Melissa. "It's Time to Kill the Performance Review." *New York Magazine*, June 1, 2015. http://nymag.com/scienceofus/2015/05/time-to-revamp-the-performance-review.html.

Dahl, Molly, Thomas DeLeire, and Jonathan Schwabish. "Stepping Stone or Dead End? The Effect of the EITC on Earnings Growth." *National Tax Journal* (April 2009). http://ftp.iza.org/dp4146.pdf.

Daubney, Martin. "Experiment That Convinced Me Online Porn Is the Most Pernicious Threat Facing Children Today: By Ex Lads' Mag Editor Martin Daubney." *Daily Mail*, September 25, 2013.

Davis, Joshua. "How a Radical New Teaching Method Could Unleash a Generation of Geniuses." *Wired*, October 15, 2013. www.wired.com/2013/10/free-thinkers.

de Lange, Catherine. "Sherry Turkle: "We're Losing the Raw, Human Part of Being with Each Other." *Guardian*, May 5, 2013. www.theguardian.com/science/2013/may/05/rational-heroes-sherry-turkle-mit.

de Ruiter, Jan, Gavin Weston, and Stephen M. Lyon. "Dunbar's Number: Group Size and Brain Physiology in Humans Reexamined." *American Anthropologist* 113, no. 4 (2011): 557–568.

de Tocqueville, Alexis. *Democracy in America*, vol. 1. New York: A. S. Barnes & Co., 1851.

Dean, Robert G. "New Orleans and the Wetlands of Southern Louisiana." *Bridge* 36, no. 1 (2006): 35–42.

DeAngelis, Tori. "Web Pornography's Effect on Children." *American Psychological Association Monitor* 38, no. 10 (November 2007): 50.

Delaney, John K. "The House Should Keep 'Dynamic Scoring' Honest." *Washington Post*, January 7, 2015. www.washingtonpost.com/opinions/the-house-should-keep-dynamic-scoring-honest/2015/01/07/48912eae-94fb-11e4-927a-4fa2638cd1b0_story.html.

Department for Communities and Local Government. *Troubled Families: Progress Information at December 2014 and Families Turned Around at February 2015*. British Government, March 10, 2015.

———. *Tackling Troubled Families*. British Government, December 15, 2011. www.gov.uk/gov ernment/news/tackling-troubled- families.

Department of Education (UK). *CANparent Trial Evaluation: Final Report Research*. By Geoff Lindsay, Mairi Ann Cullen, Stephen Cullen, Vaso Totsika, Ioanna Bakopoulou, Susan Goodlad, Richard Brind, et al. University of Warwick, 2014. www.gov.uk/government/uploads/system /uploads/attachment_data/file/332182/RR357_-_CANparent_trial_evaluation_final_report __09_07_14_.pdf.

Department for Education (US). *Barriers to Participation in Education and Training*. By Thomas Spielhofer, Sarah Golden, Kelly Evans, Helen Marshall, Ellie Mundy, Marco Pomati, and Ben Styles. National Foundation for Education Research. 2010.

———. *Digest of Education Statistics, 2013* (National Center for Education Statistics, 2015). https://nces.ed.gov/fastfacts/display.asp?id=84.

Department of Health and Human Services (US). *The Community Healthy Marriage Initiative Evaluation: Impacts of a Community Approach to Strengthening Families*. Washington, DC: Office of Planning, Research and Evaluation, 2012.

———. "The FACTS About Open Payments Data." US Department of Health and Human Services. http://openpaymentsdata.cms.gov.

———. *Health, United States, 2010: With Special Feature on Death and Dying, U.S. Department of Health and Human Services*. Centers for Disease Control and Prevention, National Center for Health Statistics, 2010. www.cdc.gov/nchs/data/hus/hus10.pdf.

———. *Health, United States, 2014: With Special Feature on Adults Aged 55–64, US Department of Health and Human Services*. Centers for Disease Control and Prevention, National Center for Health Statistics, 2014. www.cdc.gov/nchs/data/hus/hus14.pdf.

———. Office of the Inspector General. *Medicare Atypical Antipsychotic Drug Claims for Elderly Nursing Home Residents*. Office of the Inspector General, May 2011.

Department of Justice (US), Civil Rights Division. "Investigation of the Ferguson Police Department." March 4, 2015. www.justice.gov/sites/default/files/opa/press-releases/attachments/ 2015/03/04/ferguson_police_department_report.pdf.

Department of State (US), Department of Commerce. *Action Plan for Implementing the Task Force Recommendations*. Presidential Task Force on Combating IUU Fishing and Seafood Fraud, 2015.

Desilver, Drew, and Steve Schwarzer. "Making More than Minimum Wage, but Less than $10.10 an Hour." Pew Research Center, November 5, 2014. www.pewresearch.org/fact-tank/2014/11/ 05/making-more-than-minimum-wage-but-less-than-10-10-an-hour.

Devereaux, Jennifer. *NewsNation with Tamron Hall*. MSNBC, June 19, 2014.

Devlin, Kate. "Marriage Without Children the Key to Bliss." *Telegraph*, May 9, 2008. www .telegraph.co.uk/news/1941195/Marriage-without-children-the-key-to-bliss.html.

Diep, Francie. "Watch a Spray-On Solar Getting Made." *Popular Science*, December 9, 2014. www .popsci.com/watch-spray-solar-cell-getting-made.

"The Digital Divide: How the Online Behavior of Teens Is Getting Past Parents." McAfee, June 2012. www.mcafee.com/us/resources/misc/digital-divide-study.pdf.

"The Dos and Don'ts of Using Your Phone at a Party." *Huffington Post*, September 26, 2014. www .huffingtonpost.com/2014/09/26/dinner-party-etiquette-phones-at-dinner_n_5884418.html.

Drobnic Holan, Angie, and Nai Issa. "In Context: Hillary Clinton and Don't Let Anybody Tell You That Corporations Create Jobs." *Tampa Bay Times*'s Politifact, October 30, 2014. www. politifact .com/truth-o-meter/article/2014/oct/30/context-hillary-clinton-and-dont-let-anybody-tell-.

Dropouts, Diplomas, and Dollars: U.S. High Schools and the Nation's Economy. Washington, DC: Alliance for Excellent Education, August 2008.

Drutman, Lee. *The Business of America Is Lobbying: How Corporations Became Politicized and Politics Became More Corporate.* Oxford, United Kingdom: Oxford University Press, 2015.

Duckworth, Angela L., and Martin E. P. Seligman. "Self-Discipline Outdoes IQ in Predicting Academic Performance of Adolescents." *Psychological Science* 16, no. 12 (2005): 939–944.

Dudnick, Laura. "In SF's Surging Real Estate Market, How Do Teachers Stack Up?" *San Francisco Examiner*, June 7, 2015. http://archives.sfexaminer.com/sanfrancisco/in-sfs-surging-real-estate-market-how-do-teachers-stack-up/Content?oid=2932447.

Dunbar, Robin I. M. "Neocortex Size as a Constraint on Group Size in Primates." *Journal of Human Evolution* 22, no. 6 (1992): 469–493.

"Dye Industry: Fact Sheet." Green Cross Switzerland, 2012. www.greencross.ch/nc/en/print/news-info-en/case-studies/environmental-reports/ten-most-dangerous-sources-of-environmental-toxins-2012/2012/dye-industry.html.

Edmonds, Charles, and Grady L. Hallman. "CardioVascular Care Providers: A Pioneer in Bundled Services, Shared Risk, and Single Payment." *Texas Heart Institute Journal* 22, no. 1 (1995): 72–76.

"Edward O. Wilson: 'The Loss of Biodiversity Is a Tragedy.'" UNESCO Media Services, September 2, 2010. www.unesco.org/new/en/media-services/singleview/news/edward_o_wilson_the_loss_of_biodiversity_is_a_tragedy/#.U7x4hxZbuuc.

"The Egg Business." American Egg Board. www.aeb.org/images/PDFs/EggBusiness515.pdf.

Eisenberg, Staci R., Megan H. Bair-Merritt, Eve R. Colson, Timothy C. Heeren, Nicole L. Geller, and Michael J. Corwin. "Maternal Report of Advice Received for Infant Care." *Pediatrics* 136, no. 2 (2015): e315–e322.

Eissa, Nada, and Hilary W. Hoynes. "Behavioral Responses to Taxes: Lessons from the EITC and Labor Supply." *Tax Policy and the Economy.* Edited by James Poterba, vol. 20. Cambridge, MA: MIT Press, 2006.

Elkin, David. Interview with Neal Conan. "Can You Make Your Baby Smarter, Sooner?" *Talk of the Nation.* NPR, October 28, 2009. www.npr.org/templates/story/story.php?storyId=114247630.

Ellicott, Claire. "NHS Hospital Scandal Which Left 1,200 Dead Could Happen Again, Warn Campaigners." *Daily Mail*, November 9, 2010. www.dailymail.co.uk/news/article-1327766/Mid-Staffordshire-NHS-hospital-scandal-left-1-200-dead-happen-again.html.

Ellis, Aleksander P. J., Bradford S. Bell, Robert E. Ployhart, John R. Hollenbeck, and D. R. Ilgen. "An Evaluation of Generic Teamwork Skill Training with Action Teams: Effects on Cognitive and Skill-Based Outcomes." *Personnel Psychology* 58, no. 3 (2005): 641–672.

Ellyatt, Wendy, Al Aynsley-Green, Richard Layrd, Guy Claxton, John Freeman, David Whitebread, Barry Sheerman et al. "The Government Should Stop Intervening in Early Education" (signed letter to the editor). *Telegraph*, September 11, 2013. www.telegraph.co.uk/comment/letters/10302844/The-Government-should-stop-intervening-in-early-education.html.

Emanuel, Ezekiel J., Arlene Ash, Wei Yu, Gail Gazelle, Norman G. Levinsky, Olga Saynina, Mark McClellan et al. "Managed Care, Hospice Use, Site of Death, and Medical Expenditures in the Last Year of Life." *Archives of Internal Medicine* 162, no. 15 (2002): 1722–1728.

Engert, Veronica, Franziska Plessow, Robert Miller, Clemens Kirschbaum, and Tania Singer. "Cortisol Increase in Empathic Stress Is Modulated by Emotional Closeness and Observation Modality." *Psychoneuroendocrinology* 45 (2014): 192–201.

"English Mayoral Elections and Referendums." *BBC News*, May 4, 2012. www.bbc.com/news/uk-england-17854687.

Environmental Protection Agency, Office of Water. *Wetlands: Protecting Life and Property from Flooding.* 2006. http://water.epa.gov/type/wetlands/outreach/upload/Flooding.pdf.

Ernst, Caryn. *Protecting the Source: Land Conservation and the Future of America's Drinking Water.* San Francisco, CA: The Trust for Public Land, 2004.

Evans, Stephen. "Mislabelled Fish Slip into Europe's Menus." *BBC News*, April 2, 2013. www.bbc.com/news/world-europe-21993684.

"Excessive Drinking Costs U.S. \$223 Billion." Centers for Disease Control and Prevention, April 17, 2014. www.cdc.gov/features/alcoholconsumption.

"Expedia's 2014 Vacation Deprivation Study: Americans and Asian Workers Lag Well Behind Europeans in Vacationing." *PR Newswire*, November 6, 2014. www.prnewswire.com/news-releases/expedias-2014-vacation-deprivation-study-americans-and-asian-workers-lag-well-behind-europeans-in-vacationing-281743231.html.

Fackler, Martin. "District in Tokyo Plans to Extend Rights of Gay Couples." *New York Times*, February 13, 2015. www.nytimes.com/2015/02/13/world/asia/tokyo-ward-plans-to-extend-rights-of-gay-couples.html.

"Facts and Figures." Facing Death. *Frontline*. www.pbs.org/wgbh/pages/frontline/facing-death/facts-and-figures.

Farm Animal and Field Crop Research Facilities Protection Act, Kan. Stat. Ann. §47-1825–1830.

Farm Animal and Research Facilities Protection Act, Mont. Code Ann. §81-30-101–105.

Farm Assurance Schemes & Animal Welfare: How the Standards Compare: 2012. Edinburgh and Surrey, United Kingdom: OneKind and Compassion in World Farming, 2012.

Federal Trade Commission. "Pay-for-Delay: How Drug Company Pay-Offs Cost Consumers Billions." 2010. www.ftc.gov/reports/pay-delay-how-drug-company-pay-offs-cost-consumers-billions-federal-trade-commission-staff.

Feinstein, Leon. "Very Early." *CentrePiece*, Summer 2003. http://cep.lse.ac.uk/pubs/download/CP146.pdf.

Felitti, Vincent J., Robert F. Anda, Dale Nordenberg, David F. Williamson, Alison M. Spitz, Valerie Edwards, Mary P. Koss, et al. "The Relationship of Adult Health Status to Childhood Abuse and Household Dysfunction." *American Journal of Preventive Medicine* 14 (1998): 245–258.

Fernandez, Manny. "Cheese Whatevers, City Has Them by the Handful." *New York Times*, August 4, 2010. www.nytimes.com/2010/08/04/nyregion/04cheez.html.

Fernández-Armesto, Felipe. *The World: A History*, 2nd ed. London: Prentice Hall, 2010.

Fertilisation, Human, and Embryology Act. "Chapter 37." Her Majesty's Stationery Office: London, 1990.

"Fight Cruelty: Chicken FAQ." ASPCA, 2015. www.aspca. org/fight-cruelty/farm-animal-cruelty/chicken-faq.

Finkelhor, David, Richard Ormrod, and Mark Chaffin. *Juveniles Who Commit Sex Offenses Against Minors*. Washington, DC: US Department of Justice, December 2009. www.ncjrs.gov/pdf files1/ojjdp/227763.pdf.

Fitzgerald, Alison. "Koch, Exxon Mobil Among Corporations Helping Write State Laws." *Bloomberg*, July 21, 2011. www.bloomberg.com/news/articles/2011-07-21/koch-exxon-mobil-among-corporations-helping-write-state-laws.

"Flexicurity." Denmark: The Official Website of Denmark. http://denmark.dk/en/society/welfare/flexicurity.

Flood, Michael. "The Harms of Pornography Exposure Among Children and Young People." *Child Abuse Review* 18, no. 6 (2009): 384–400.

Foer, Jonathan Safran. *Eating Animals*. New York: Back Bay Books, 2009.

Ford, Henry, and Samuel Crowther. *Great Today and Greater Future*. Sydney, Australia: Cornstalk Publishing, 1926; reprint: Whitefish, MT: Kessinger Publishing, 2003.

Forgacs, Ian, and Aathavan Loganayagam. "Overprescribing Proton Pump Inhibitors." *BMJ* 336, no. 7634 (2008): 2–3.

Francis, Pope. *Evangelli Gaudium: Apolistic Exhortation on the Proclamation of the Gospel in Today's World*. Vatican City: Libreria Editrice Vaticana, 2013.

Francis, Robert. *The Mid Staffordshire NHS Foundation Trust Inquiry: Independent Inquiry into Care Provided by Mid Staffordshire Foundation Trust, January 2005–March 2009*, vol. 1. London: The Stationery Office, 2010.

Francis, Theo, and Ryan Knutson. "Wave of Megadeals Tests Antitrust Limits in U.S." *Wall Street Journal*, October 18, 2015. www.wsj.com/articles/wave-of-megadeals-tests-antitrust-limits-in -u-s-1445213306.

Frank, Thomas. "David Graeber: 'Spotlight on the Financial Sector Did Make Apparent Just How Bizarrely Skewed Our Economy Is in Terms of Who Gets Rewards.'" *Salon*, June 1, 2014. www .salon.com/2014/06/01/help_us_thomas_piketty_the_1s_sick_and_twisted_new_scheme.

Fredrickson, Barbara L., Tomi-Ann Roberts, Stephanie M. Noll, Diane M. Quinn, and Jean M. Twenge. "That Swimsuit Becomes You: Sex Differences in Self-Objectification, Restrained Eating, and Math Performance." *Journal of Personality and Social Psychology* 75, no. 1, (July 1998): 269–284.

Freston, Kathy. "E. Coli, Salmonella and Other Deadly Bacteria and Pathogens in Food: Factory Farms Are the Reason." *Huffington Post*, March 18, 2010. www.huffingtonpost.com/kathy -freston/e-coli-salmonella-and-oth_b_415240.html.

Frey, Carl Benedikt, and Michael A. Osborne. "The Future of Employment: How Susceptible Are Jobs to Computerisation?" 2013. www.oxfordmartin.ox.ac.uk/downloads/academic/The_ Future_of_Employment.pdf.

Fried, Ben. "The Origins of Holland's 'Stop Murdering Children' Street Safety Movement." StreetsBlog Network, February 20, 2013. http://streetsblog.net/2013/02/20/the-origins-of -hollands-stop-murdering-children-street-safety-movement.

Frieden, Tom. *Antibiotic Resistance Threats in the United States, 2013.* Centers for Disease Control and Prevention, US Department of Health and Human Services, 2013.

Fry, Richard. "New Census Data Show More Americans Are Tying the Knot, But Mostly It's the College-Educated." FactTank, Pew Research Center, February 6, 2014. www.pewresearch .org/fact-tank/2014/02/06/new-census-data-show-more-americans-are-tying-the-knot-but -mostly-its-the-college-educated.

Fryer, Ronald G. Jr., Steven D. Levitt, John List, and Sally Sadoff. *Enhancing the Efficacy of Teacher Incentives Through Loss Aversion: A Field Experiment,* no. w18237. National Bureau of Economic Research, 2012.

"FTSE 100 Directors' Total Earnings Jump by 21% in a Year." *Thomson Reuters* and *IDS*, October 13, 2014. www.incomesdata.co.uk/wp-content/uploads/2014/10/IDS-FTSE-100-directors-pay -20141.pdf.

Fukuyama, Francis. *Political Order and Political Decay.* New York: Farrar, Straus and Giroux, 2014.

Fulford, Robert. *Accidental City: The Transformation of Toronto.* Canada: MacFarlane, Walter & Ross, 1995.

"Full Memo: Jeff Bezos Responds to Brutal NYT Story, Says It Doesn't Represent the Amazon He Leads." *GeekWire*, August 16, 2015. www.geekwire.com/2015/full-memo-jeff-bezos-responds -to-cutting-nyt-expose-says-tolerance-for-lack-of-empathy-needs-to-be-zero.

Fuller, Matt. "Republican Champion of Dodd-Frank Changes Goes After Elizabeth Warren." *Roll Call*, January 28, 2015. http://blogs.rollcall.com/218/on-a-controversial-law-subtlety-is-key-for -kevin-yoder.

"The Future of Jobs." *The Economist*, January 18, 2014. www.economist.com/news/briefing/2159 4264-previous-technological-innovation-has-always-delivered-more-long-run-employment -not-less.

Gamerman, Ellen. "What Makes Finnish Kids So Smart?" *Wall Street Journal*, February 28, 2008. www.wsj.com/articles/SB120425355065601997.

Gapinski, Kathrine D., Kelly D. Brownell, and Marianne LaFrance. "Body Objectification and 'Fat Talk': Effects on Emotion, Motivation, and Cognitive Performance." *Sex Roles* 48, nos. 9–10 (2003): 377–388.

Gawande, Atul. "Overkill." *New Yorker*, May 11, 2015. www.newyorker.com/magazine/2015/05/11/ overkill-atul-gawande.

Geico Insurance. "Free Range Chicken: It's What You Do." YouTube.com, March 8, 2015. www
   .youtube.com/watch?v=3v1wFKKWMCA.

Gentleman, Amelia. "Do We Need Parenting Classes?" *Guardian*, March 31, 2012. www.theguard
   ian.com/lifeandstyle/2012/mar/31/do-we-need-parenting-classes.

Gilens, Martin, and Benjamin I. Page. "Testing Theories of American Politics: Elites, Interest
   Groups, and Average Citizens." *Perspectives on Politics* 12, no. 03 (2014).

Gill, Tim. *No Fear: Growing Up in a Risk Averse Society*. London: Calouste Gulbenkian Foundation,
   2007.

Girl Scouts and the Dove Self-Esteem Fund. "Girls and Body Image." www.girlscouts.org/content
   /dam/girlscouts-gsusa/forms-and-documents/about-girl-scouts/research/beauty_redefined_
   factsheet.pdf.

Glasmeier, Amy. "Living Wage Calculator." MIT, 2015. http://livingwage.mit.edu.

Global Powers of Retailing 2015: Embracing Innovation. Deloitte. 2015. www2.deloitte.com/au/en/
   pages/consumer-business/articles/global-powers-of-retailing.html.

Godelnik, Raz. "The Link Between Walmart, Food Stamps and CSR." *Triple Pundit*, April 22,
   2014. www.triplepundit.com/2014/04/link-walmart-food-stamps-lack-csr.

Goodin, Samantha M., Alyssa Van Denburg, Sarah K. Murnen, and Linda Smolak. "'Putting On'
   Sexiness: A Content Analysis of the Presence of Sexualizing Characteristics in Girls' Clothing." *Sex Roles* 65, no. 1–2 (2011): 1–12.

Gordon, Robert. "Investing in What Works: Voluntary Home Visiting Programs." White House,
   September 28, 2011.

Gray, Peter. "The Decline of Play and the Rise of Psychopathology in Children and Adolescents."
   American Journal of Play 3, no. 4 (2011): 443–463.

"The Great Smog of 1952." Met Office, June 10, 2014. www.metoffice.gov.uk/education/teens/
   case-studies/great-smog.

Green, Duncan. "Robert Chambers: Why Don't All Developments Do Immersions?" *People,
   Spaces, Deliberation* (The World Bank), September 6, 2012. http://blogs.worldbank.org/public
   sphere/node/6091.

Greene, Joel L., *Lean Finely Textured Beef: The "Pink Slime" Controversy* (Washington, DC: Congressional Research Service, 2012).

Griffiths, Jay. *A Country Called Childhood*. Berkeley, CA: Counterpoint, 2014.

Grossman, Jonathan. "Fair Labor Standards Act of 1938: Maximum Struggle for Minimum Wage."
   Monthly Labor Review, June 1978, republished by the US Department of Labor. www.dol.gov/
   dol/aboutdol/history/flsa1938.htm.

Grover, Shawn, and John F. Helliwell. *How's Life at Home? New Evidence on Marriage and the Set
   Point for Happiness*, no. w20794. National Bureau of Economic Research, 2014.

"Grunewald." Visit Berlin. www.visitberlin.de/en/spot/grunewald.

Grunewald, Rob, and Arthur Rolnick. *A Proposal for Achieving High Returns on Early Childhood
   Development* (Federal Reserve Bank of Minneapolis, 2006).

Guardado, Jose, David W. Emmons, and Carol K. Kane. "The Price Effects of a Large Merger of
   Health Insurers: A Case Study of UnitedHealth-Sierra." *Health Management, Policy and Innovation* 1, no. 3 (2013): 16–35.

Guerrera, Francesco. "Welch Condemns Share Price Focus." *Financial Times*, March 12, 2009.

Hall, E.J., and D. J. Brenner. "Cancer Risks from Diagnostic Radiology." *British Journal of Radiology*
   81, no. 965 (May 2008).

Halliwell, Emma, Alice Easun, and Diana Harcourt. "Body Dissatisfaction: Can a Short Media
   Literacy Message Reduce Negative Media Exposure Effects Amongst Adolescent Girls?" *British Journal of Health Psychology* 16, no. 2 (2011): 396–403.

Hamlin, J. Kiley. "Moral Judgment and Action in Preverbal Infants and Toddlers Evidence for
   an Innate Moral Core." *Current Directions in Psychological Science* 22, no. 3 (2013): 186–193.

Hancocks, David. "Bringing Nature into the Zoo: Inexpensive Solutions for Zoo Environments." *International Journal for the Study of Animal Problems* 1, no. 3 (1980): 170–177.

Hand, Larry, and Madeline Drexler. "Public Health Takes Aim at Sugar and Salt." *Harvard School of Public Health Review*, Fall 2009. www.hsph.harvard.edu/news/magazine/sugar-and-salt.

Hansen, Suzy. "The Myth of the Deadbeat Dad." *Salon*, 9 August 2001.

Harlem Children's Zone, HCZ.org, 2015.

Harmon, Katherine. "How Important Is Physical Contact with Your Infant?" *Scientific American*, May 6, 2010. www.scientificamerican.com/article/infant-touch.

Harper, Cynthia C., and Sara S. McLanahan. "Father Absence and Youth Incarceration." *Journal of Research on Adolescence* 14 (September 2004): 369–397.

Harris, Jennifer L., Catherine Shehan, Renne Gross, et. al. "Food Advertising Targeted to Hispanic and Black Youth: Contributing to Health Disparities." *Rudd Center for Food Policy & Obesity*, 2015.

Harris, Nadine Burke. "The Chronic Stress of Poverty: Toxic Stress to Children." *Shriver Report*, January 12, 2014.

Harris, William T. "Elementary Education." *North American Review* (1895).

Hart, Betty, and Todd R. Risley. "The Early Catastrophe: The 30 Million Word Gap by Age 3." *American Educator* 27, no. 1 (2003) .

Hartig, Terry, Gary W. Evans, Larry D. Jamner, Deborah S. Davis, and Tommy Gärling. "Tracking Restoration in Natural and Urban Field Settings." *Journal of Environmental Psychology* 23, no. 2 (2003) .

Haspel, Tamar. "Farm Bill: Why Don't Taxpayers Subsidize the Foods That Are Better for Us?" *Washington Post*, February 18, 2014. www.washingtonpost.com/lifestyle/food/farm-bill-why-dont-taxpayers-subsidize-the-foods-that-are-better-for-us/2014/02/14/d7642a3c-9434-11e3-84e1-27626c5ef5fb_story.html.

Hayward, John, and Guy Brandon. "Cohabitation: An Alternative to Marriage?" Jubilee Centre, 2011. www.jubilee-centre.org/cohabitation-alternative-marriage-john-hayward-guy-brandon.

Head, Simon. *Mindless: Why Smarter Machines Are Making Dumber Humans.* New York: Basic Books, 2014.

———. "Worse than Wal-Mart: Amazon's Sick Brutality and Secret History of Ruthlessly Intimidating Workers." *Salon*, February 23, 2014. www.salon.com/2014/02/23/worse_than_wal_mart_amazons_sick_brutality_and_secret_history_of_ruthlessly_intimidating_workers.

Heckman, James J. "Skill Formation and the Economics of Investing in Disadvantaged Children." *Science* 312, no. 5782 (2006): 1900–1902.

Heerwagen, Judith. "Green Buildings, Organizational Success and Occupant Productivity." *Building Research & Information* 28, no. 5–6 (2000): 353–367.

"Heinz Ketchup." H.J. Heinz Company. www.heinzketchup.com/Products/Heinz%20Ketchup%20380z.

Hennepin Health. "Member Spotlight: Ron." http://content.govdelivery.com/accounts/MN HENNE/bulletins/be91e8.

Herr, Hugh. "The New Bionics That Let Us Run, Climb, and Dance." TED Talk 2014: The Next Chapter. Vancouver, Canada. March 2014. www.ted.com/talks/hugh_herr_the_new_bionics_that_let_us_run_climb_and_dance?language=en.

Hershey Company. "REESE'S—Product and Nutrition Information—Peanut Butter Cups." www.hersheys.com/reeses/products/reeses-peanut-butter-cups/milk-chocolate.aspx.

Higginbottom, Justin. "Growing Number of Children with Cellphones Adds Pressure to Purchase." *Deseret News* (Salt Lake City, UT), April 22, 2012. www.deseretnews.com/article/765570742/Growing-number-of-children-with-cellphones-adds-pressure-to-purchase.html?pg=all.

Higginson, Irene J., Ilora G. Finlay, Danielle M. Goodwin, Kerry Hood, Adrian G. K. Edwards, Alison Cook, Hannah-Rose Douglas et al. "Is There Evidence That Palliative Care Teams Alter

End-of-Life Experiences of Patients and Their Caregivers?" *Journal of Pain and Symptom Management* 25, no. 2 (2003): 150–168.

The High Cost of High School Dropouts: What the Nation Pays for Inadequate High Schools. Washington, DC: Alliance for Excellent Education, November 2011.

Hill, Peter, and Michael Barber. *Preparing for a Renaissance in Assessment.* London: Pearson PLC, 2014.

Hilton, Steve. "I Run a Silicon Valley Startup—but I Refuse to Own a Cellphone." *Guardian,* January 11, 2016, http://www.theguardian.com/technology/2016/jan/11/steve-hilton-silicon-valley-no-cellphone-technology-apps-uber.

Hilton, Steve, and Giles Gibbons. *Good Business: Your World Needs You.* London: Texere Publishing, 2002.

Himmelstein, David U., Miraya Jun, Reinhard Busse, Karine Chevreul, Alexander Geissler, Patrick Jeurissen, Sarah Thomson et al.. "A Comparison of Hospital Administrative Costs in Eight Nations: US Costs Exceed All Others by Far." *Health Affairs* 33, no. 9 (2014): 1586–1594.

Hirschfeld Davis, Julie. "Adviser Guides Obama into Google Age." *New York Times,* January 4, 2015. www.nytimes.com/2015/01/04/us/politics/her-task-weaning-the-white-house-off-floppy-disks.html.

Hiss, Tony. "Can the World Really Set Aside Half of the Planet for Wildlife?" *Smithsonian Magazine,* September 2014. www.smithsonianmag.com/science-nature/can-world-really-set-aside-half-planet-wildlife-180952379.

Hitt, Michael A., David King, Menna Krishnan, Marianna Makri, Mario Schijven, Katsuhiko Shimizu, and Hong Zhu. "Creating Value Through Mergers and Acquisitions: Challenges and Opportunities." In *The Handbook of Mergers and Acquisitions.* Edited by David Faulkner, Satu Teerikangas, and Richard J. Joseph, 71–113. Oxford, United Kingdom: Oxford University Press, 2012.

Holmes, Anna. "Untouched Cover Photos Wanted: $10,000 Reward." *Jezebel,* May 21, 2007.

Holzer, Harry J., Diane Whitmore Schanzenbach, Greg J. Duncan, and Jens Ludwig. "The Economic Costs of Childhood Poverty in the United States." *Journal of Children and Poverty* 14, no. 1 (2008).

Home Office. "Freedom of Information Release: Policing by Consent." December 10, 2012. www.gov.uk/government/publications/policing-by-consent.

Hood, Andrew, and Paul Johnson. What Is Welfare *Spending?* Institute for Fiscal Studies, November 4, 2014. www.ifs.org.uk/publications/7424.

"Hospitals 'Are Medical Factories.'" *BBC News,* December 3, 2008. http://news.bbc.co.uk/2/hi/health/7760764.stm.

Hopkirk, Elizabeth. "The Netherlands' Almere Leads the Way on Self-Build Communities." *bdonline,* June 6, 2011. www.bdonline.co.uk/the-netherlands-almere-leads-the-way-on-self-build-communities/5019196.article.

Hotez, Peter J. "Neglected Infections of Poverty in the United States and Their Effects on the Brain." *JAMA Psychiatry* 71, no. 10 (2014): 1099–1100.

Houghton Mifflin Harcourt. www.hmhco.com.

House of Commons Committee of Public Accounts. *Department of Health: The National Programme for IT: – the NHS.* Twentieth Report of Session 2006–07, HC 390. London: The Stationery Office, 2007.

How Taxpayers Subsidize America's Biggest Employer and Richest Family. Washington, D.C.: Americans for Tax Fairness, April 2014.

"How We Work." Andela, 2015. www.andela.co/how-we-work.

Howard, Kimberly S., Jennifer E. Burke Lefever, John G. Borkowski, and Thomas L. Whitman. "Fathers' Influence in the Lives of Children with Adolescent Mothers." *Journal of Family Psychology* 20, no. 3 (2006): 468.

Howard, Michael. "The Movie That Accurately Predicted the Future of Technology." *Esquire*, September 23, 2014. www.esquire.com/entertainment/movies/a30140/minority-report-tech-is-real-now.

Hulse, Carl. "Steve Israel of New York, a Top Democrat, Won't Seek Reelection." *New York Times*, January 5, 2016. http://www.nytimes.com/2016/01/06/us/politics/steve-israel-house-democrat-new-york.html. See also his op-ed on the topic.

Hunter, Will. "The Best Office in the World? Selgas Cano's New Work Space in London." *Architectural Review*, January 29, 2015. www.architectural-review.com/buildings/the-best-office-in-the-world-selgas-canos-new-work-space-in-london/8677631.article.

Hussein, Sajjad. "Six Months After Bangladesh Factory Collapse, Workers Remain in Peril." CNN, October 24, 2013. www.cnn.com/2013/10/24/opinion/bangladesh-garment-workers.

"IBM 2010 Global CEO Study: Creativity Selected as Most Crucial Factor for Future Success." IBM, May 18, 2010. www-03.ibm.com/press/us/en/pressrelease/31670.wss.

Ilves, Toomas. "Evolving into a Genuinely Digital Society." Speech at Green Library, Stanford University, Stanford, CA, May 23, 2014.

"In Palo Alto's High-Pressure Schools, Suicides Lead to Soul-Searching." NPR, May 10, 2015. www.npr.org/2015/05/10/405694832/in-palo-altos-high-pressure-schools-suicides-lead-to-soul-searching.

Institute of Education Sciences. *Numbers and Types of Public Elementary and Secondary Schools from the Common Core of Data: School Year 2010–11*. National Center for Education Statistics, 2012.

"Interface Reports Fourth Quarter and Fiscal Year 2014 Results." *Interface*, Press Release, February 18, 2015. www.interfaceglobal.com/Investor-Relations/Press-Releases.aspx.

"Interview with Jan Gehl." American Society for Landscape Architects. www.asla.org/Content Detail.aspx?id=31346.

"Introducing the Vscan Family." GE Healthcare, 2015. https://vscan.gehealthcare.com/introducing-vscan-family.

Israel, Steve. "Steve Israel: Confessions of a Congressman." *New York Times*, January 8, 2016. http://www.nytimes.com/2016/01/09/opinion/steve-israel-confessions-of-a-congressman.html?_r=0.

Jacobs, Emma. "Strategies for Calling Time on Long Hours." *Financial Times*, August 18, 2014. www.ft.com/intl/cms/s/2/510c5bd6-198a-11e4-8730-00144feabdc0.html

Jacobs, Jane. *The Death and Life of Great American Cities*. New York: Vintage Books, 1961.

Jaffe, Ina, and Robert Benincasa. "Nursing Homes Rarely Penalized for Oversedating Patients." NPR, December 9, 2014. www.npr.org/sections/health-shots/2014/12/09/368538773/nursing-homes-rarely-penalized-for-oversedating-patients.

———. "Old and Overmedicated: The Real Drug Problem in Nursing Homes." NPR, December 8, 2014. www.npr.org/sections/health-shots/2014/12/08/368524824/old-and-overmedicated-the-real-drug-problem-in-nursing-homes.

———. "This Nursing Home Calms Troubling Behavior Without Risky Drugs." NPR, December 9, 2014. www.npr.org/sections/health-shots/2014/12/09/368539057/this-nursing-home-calms-troubling-behavior-without-risky-drugs.

Jambeck, Jenna R., Roland Geyer, Chris Wilcox, Theodore R. Siegler, Miriam Perryman, Anthony Andrady, Ramani Narayan, and Kara Lavender Law. "Plastic Waste Inputs from Land into the Ocean." *Science* 347, no. 6223 (2015): 768–771.

James, John T. "A New, Evidence-Based Estimate of Patient Harms Associated with Hospital Care." *Journal of Patient Safety* 9, no. 3 (2013): 122–128.

"Jan Gehl: Biography." Project for Public Spaces. www.pps.org/ reference/jgehl.

Jarvis, Matthew. "Amazon Response to BBC Panorama Worker Criticism." *PCR*, November 26, 2013. www.pcr-online.biz/news/read/amazon-responds-to-bbc-panorama-worker-criticism/032581.

Jauhar, Sandeep. "Bring Back House Calls." *New York Times*, October 14, 2015. www.nytimes .com/2015/10/15/opinion/bring-back-house-calls.html.

Jobs, Steve. "Stanford Commencement Address." Speech, Stanford University, Stanford, CA, June 14, 2005.

"Joe's Crab Shack Leads Industry in No Tipping Text." Joe's Crab Shack, November 11, 2015. Joes crabshack.com/media-center.

Joffe-Walt, Chana. "The Town Where Everyone Talks About Death." NPR, March 5, 2014. www .npr.org/sections/money/2014/03/05/286126451/living-wills-are-the-talk-of-the-town-in-la -crosse-wis.

Johnson, James R., Michael A. Kuskowski, Kirk Smith, Timothy T. O'Bryan, and Sita Tatini. "Antimicrobial-Resistant and Extraintestinal Pathogenic Escherichia coli in Retail Foods." *Journal of Infectious Diseases* 191, no. 7 (2005): 1040–1049.

Johnson, Michael P. "Environmental Impacts of Urban Sprawl: A Survey of the Literature and Proposed Research Agenda." *Environment and Planning* A33, no. 4 (2001): 717–735.

Johnson, Nathanael J. "Swine of the Times." *Harper's Magazine*, May 2006. http://harpers.org/ archive/2006/05/swine-of-the-times.

Johnson, Sara B., Anne W. Riley, Douglas A. Granger, and Jenna Riis. "The Science of Early Life Toxic Stress for Pediatric Practice and Advocacy." *Pediatrics* 131, no. 2 (2013): 319–327.

Johnson, Susan R. "Teaching Our Children to Write, Read, and Spell: A Developmental Approach Looking at the Relationship of Children's Foundational Neurological Pathways to Their Higher Capacities for Learning." You and Your Child's Health, May 7, 2007. www .youandyourchildshealth.org/youandyourchildshealth/articles/teaching%20our%20 children.html.

Johnson, Wesley. "Children, Some Age Five, Commit Thousands of Child Sex Offenses." *Telegraph*, March 4, 2013. www.telegraph.co.uk/news/uknews/crime/9905727/Children-some -aged-five-commit-thousands-of-child-sex-offences.html.

Jones, Colin. *Paris: A History.* New York: Penguin Books, 2004.

Jones, Natasha. "Funding Circle and Santander Announce Partnership to Support Thousands of UK Businesses." *Funding Circle*, June 18, 2014. www.fundingcircle.com/blog/2014/06/ funding-circle-santander-announce-partnership-support-thousands-uk-businesses.

Kabali, Hilda K., Matilde M. Irigoyen, Rosemary Nunez-Davis, Jennifer G. Budacki, Sweta H. Mohanty, Kristin P. Leister, Robert L. Bonner Jr. "Exposure and Use of Mobile Media Devices by Young Children." *Pediatrics* 136, no. 6 (December 2015): 1044–1050.

Kahneman, Daniel, and Amos Tversky. "Choices, Values, and Frames." *American Psychologist* 39, no. 4 (1984): 341–350.

Katz, Mitchell H. "Failing the Acid Test: Benefits of Proton Pump Inhibitors May Not Justify the Risks for Many Users." *Archives of Internal Medicine* 170, no. 9 (2010): 747–748.

Kalinauskas, Nadine. "St. Lawrence Market in Toronto Named World's Best Food Market by National Geographic." *Shine On*, April 5, 2012. https://ca.shine.yahoo.com/blogs/shine-on/st -lawrence-market-toronto-named-world-best-food-145127435.html.

Kalson, Sally. "Sexting . . . and Other Stupid Teen Tricks." *Pittsburgh Post-Gazette*, March 29, 2009. www.post-gazette.com/opinion/sally-kalson/2009/03/29/Sexting-and-other-stupid-teen -tricks/stories/200903290190.

Kang, Yewon. "Poll Shows Half of Korean Teenagers Have Suicidal Thoughts." *Wall Street Journal*, March 20, 2014. http://blogs.wsj.com/korearealtime/2014/03/20/poll-shows-half-of -korean-teenagers-have-suicidal-thoughts.

Kantor, Jodi, and David Streitfeld. "Amazon's Bruising, Thrilling Workplace." *New York Times*, August 16, 2014. www.nytimes.com/images/2015/08/16/nytfrontpage/scan.pdf.

Karabarbounis, Loukas, and Brent Neiman. "The Global Decline of the Labor Share." *Quarterly Journal of Economics* 129, no. 1 (2014): 61–103.

Karabell, Zachary. *The Leading Indicators: A Short History of the Number That Rule Our World.* New York: Simon & Schuster, 2014.

Karoly, Lynn A., M. Rebecca Kilburn, and Jill S. Cannon. *Early Childhood Interventions: Proven Results, Future Promise.* Santa Monica, CA: RAND Corporation, 2005.

Kearney, Melissa S., and Phillip B. Levine. *Early Childhood Education by MOOC: Lessons from Sesame Street*, no. w21229. National Bureau of Economic Research, 2015. www.nber.org/papers/w21229.

Kehl, Danielle, Nick Russo, Robert Morgus, and Sarah Morris. *The Cost of Connectivity 2014: Data and Analysis on Broadband Connectivity in 24 Cities Across the World.* Washington, DC: New America, 2014.

Keizer, Kees, Siegwart Lindenberg, and Linda Steg. "The Spreading of Disorder." *Science* 322, no. 5908 (2008): 1681–1685.

Kelleher Richter, Brian, Krislert Samphantharak, and Jeffrey F. Timmons. "Lobbying and Taxes." *American Journal of Political Science* 53, no. 4 (2009): 893–909.

Kelto, Anders. "Farm Fresh? Natural? Eggs Not Always What They're Cracked Up to Be." NPR, December 23, 2014. www.npr.org/sections/thesalt/2014/12/23/370377902/farm-fresh-natural-eggs-not-always-what-they're-cracked-up-to-be.

Kennedy, Jack, Tim Moore, and Annabel Fiddes. *Living Wage Research for KPMG: Structural Analysis of Hourly Wages and Current Trends in Household Finances, 2014 Report.* Henley on Thames, England: Markit, 2014.

Kennedy, Robert F. "Speech at the University of Kansas." Speech, University of Kansas, Lawrence, KA, March 18, 1968.

Khazan, Olga. "The Luxury of Waiting for Marriage to Have Kids." *Atlantic*, June 17, 2014. www.theatlantic.com/business/archive/2014/06/why-poor-women-dont-wait-for-marriage-to-give-birth/372890.

Khimm, Suzy. "How Paying No Federal Income Tax Helps the Poor Get Off Welfare and into Work." *Washington Post*, September 18, 2012. www.washingtonpost.com/news/wonk/wp/2012/09/18/how-paying-no-federal-income-taxes-helps-the-poor-get-off-welfare-and-into-work.

King, Anthony, and Ivor Crewe. *The Blunders of Our Governments.* London: Oneworld Publications, 2013.

"KitKat Collection: 4 Finger Milk Nutritional Information." *Société des Produits Nestlé S.A*, 2015. www.kitkat.co.uk/content/ kitkatcollection/FourFinger.

Kitzman, Harriet J., David L. Olds, Robert E. Cole, Carole A. Hanks, Elizabeth A. Anson, Kimberly J. Arcoleo, Dennis W. Luckey et al. "Enduring Effects of Prenatal and Infancy Home Visiting by Nurses on Children: Follow-Up of a Randomized Trial Among Children at Age 12 Years." *Archives of Pediatrics & Adolescent Medicine* 164, no. 5 (2010): 412–418.

Klein, Ezra. "Big Food." *Vox*, April 23, 2014. www.vox.com/2014/4/23/5627992/big-food-michael-pollan-thinks-wall-street-has-way-too-much-influence.

Kleiner, Morris. *Reforming Occupational Licensing Practices.* Washington, DC: Brookings Institute, Hamilton Project, 2015.

Kleinman, Mark. "Temasek Snaps Up Stake in UK's Funding Circle." *Sky News*, April 2, 2015. http://news.sky.com/story/1457480/temasek-snaps-up-stake-in-uks-funding-circle.

Koepp, Matthias J., Roger N. Gunn, Andrew D. Lawrence, Vincent J. Cunningham, Alain Dagher, Tasmin Jones, David J. Brooks et al. "Evidence for Striatal Dopamine Release During a Video Game." *Nature* 393, no. 6682 (1998): 266–268.

Konczal, Mike. "No, We Don't Spend $1 Trillion on Welfare Each Year." *Washington Post*, January 24, 2014. www.washingtonpost.com/news/wonk/wp/2014/01/12/no-we-dont-spend-1-trillion-on-welfare-each-year.

Konnikova, Maria. "No Money, No Time." *New York Times*, June 15, 2014. http://opinionator.blogs.nytimes.com/2014/06/13/no-clocking-out.

Konrath, Sarah, Edward H. O'Brien, and Courtney Hsing. "Changes in Dispositional Empathy in American College Students over Time: A Meta-Analysis." *Personality and Social Psychology Review* 15, no. 2 (May 2011): 180–198.

Koo, Se-Woong. "An Assault upon Our Children." *New York Times*, August 3, 2014. www.nytimes .com/2014/08/02/opinion/sunday/south-koreas-education-system-hurts-students.html.

Kramer, Miriam. "Elon Musk: Artificial Intelligence Is Humanity's 'Biggest Existential Threat.'" *Live Science*, October 27, 2014. www.livescience.com/48481-elon-musk-artificial-intelligence -threat.html.

Kreider, Rose Marie. *Living Arrangements of Children, 2004.* US Department of Commerce, Economics and Statistics Administration, US Census Bureau, 2008.

Kristof, Nicholas. "Abusing Chickens We Eat." *New York Times*, December 3, 2014. www.nytimes .com/2014/12/04/opinion/nicholas-kristof-abusing-chickens-we-eat.html.

_____. "Is That Sausage Worth This?" *New York Times*, February 20, 2014. www.nytimes.com /2014/02/20/opinion/kristof-is-that-sausage-worth-this.html.

_____. "It's Not Just About Bad Choices." *New York Times*, June 14, 2015. www.nytimes.com /2015/06/14/opinion/sunday/nicholas-kristof-its-not-just-about-bad-choices.html.

_____. "Oklahoma! Where the Kids Learn Early." *New York Times*, November 10, 2013. www .nytimes.com/2013/11/10/opinion/sunday/kristof-oklahoma-where-the-kids-learn-early .html?_r=0.

_____. "The Way to Beat Poverty." *New York Times*, September 12, 2014. www.nytimes.com /2014/09/14/opinion/sunday/nicholas-kristof-the-way-to-beat-poverty.html.

Krommenacker, Thomas, and Ben Robinson, *Metro Bank: Breaking the Mould but Breaking the Malaise?* Geneva, Switzerland: Temenos Headquarters SA, 2011.

Krueger, Alan B, Judd Cramer, and David Cho. *Are the Long-Term Unemployed on the Margins of the Labor Market?* Brookings Papers on Economic Activity, 2014: 229–280.

Kruus, Priit, Peeter Ross, Riina Hallik, Reelika Ermel, and Ain Aaviksoo. *Wider Implementation of Telemedicine in Estonia* (English Summary of the Study's Results). Tallinn, Estonia: Praxis/ Center for Policy Studies, 2014.

Kurzweil, Ray. *The Singularity Is Near: When Humans Transcend Biology.* New York: Viking, 2005.

Kuyken, Willem, Katherine Weare, Obioha C. Ukoumunne, Rachael Vicary, Nicola Motton, Richard Burnett, Chris Cullen, et al. "Effectiveness of the Mindfulness in Schools Programme: Non-Randomised Controlled Feasibility Study." *British Journal of Psychiatry* 203, no. 2 (2013): 126–131.

Lahey, Jessica. *The Gift of Failure: How the Best Parents Learn to Let Go So Their Children Can Succeed.* New York: HarperCollins, 2015.

Lake, Marilyn. "Minimum Wage Is More than a Safety Net, It's a Symbol of Australian Values." *The Age* (Melbourne, Australia), April 10, 2014. www.theage.com.au/comment/minimum -wage-is-more-than-a-safety-net-its-a-symbol-of-australian-values-20140409-zqsii.html.

Landau, Elizabeth, and Jason Hanna. "USDA: Recalled Beef May Have Reached 35 States." CNN, March 7, 2014. www.cnn.com/2014/03/07/health/beef-product-recall.

Langer, Emil. "Ray Anderson, 'Greenest CEO in America,' Dies at 77." *Washington Post*, August 10, 2011. www.washingtonpost.com/local/obituaries/ray-anderson-greenest-ceo-in-america-dies -at-77/2011/08/10/gIQAGoTU7I_story.html.

Larsson, Stefan. "What Doctors Can Learn from Each Other." TED@BCG Singapore, Singapore, October 2013. www.ted.com/talks/stefan_larsson_what_doctors_can_learn_from_ each_other?language=en.

Lawrence, Felicity, Andrew Wasley, and Radu Ciorniciuc. "Revealed: The Dirty Secret of the UK's Poultry Industry." *Guardian*, July 23, 2014. www.theguardian.com/world/2014/jul/23 /-sp-revealed-dirty-secret-uk-poultry-industry-chicken-campylobacter.

Lawton, Kayte, and Matthew Pennycook. *Beyond the Bottom Line: The Challenges and Opportunities of a Living Wage.* London: IPPR and Resolution Foundation, 2013.

Lazonick, William. "Profits Without Prosperity." *Harvard Business Review*, September 2014. https://hbr.org/2014/09/profits-without-prosperity.

Leadbeater, Charles, and Jake Garber. *Dying for Change*. London: Demos, 2010.

"Lean In Collection." Getty Images. www.gettyimages.com/creative/frontdoor/leanin.

LeBlanc, Dave. "35 Years On, St. Lawrence Is a Template for Urban Housing." *Globe and Mail* (Canada), February 6, 2013. www.theglobeandmail.com/life/home-and-garden/architecture /35-years-on-st-lawrence-is-a-template-for-urban-housing/article8296990.

Leicester City Council. "Council Meat Tests Highlight Labelling Concerns." March 11, 2014. www.leicester.gov.uk/news/news-story-details?nId=81297.

Lenger, Friedrich. *European Cities in the Modern Era, 1850–1914*. Translated by Joel Golb. Leiden, Netherlands: Koninklijke Brill NV, 2012.

Lenhart, Amanda. "Mobile Access Shifts Social Media Use and Other Online Activities." Pew Research Center, April 9, 2015. www.pewinternet.org/2015/04/09/mobile-access-shifts -social-media-use-and-other-online-activities.

Leonard, Christopher, *The Meat Racket: The Secret Takeover of America's Food Business*. New York: Simon & Schuster, 2014.

Lessig, Lawrence. "We the People, and the Republic We Must Reclaim." TED 2013, Long Beach, CA, February 2013. www.ted.com/talks/lawrence_lessig_we_the_people_and_the_republic _we_must_reclaim?language=en.

Levine, Marianne. "LA Becomes Latest, Biggest to Approve $15 Minimum Wage." *Politico*, May 19, 2015.

Levinson, Daniel R. *Medicare Atypical Antipsychotic Drug Claims for Elderly Nursing Home Residents*. Department of Health and Human Services, May 2011. http://oig.hhs.gov/oei/reports/ oei-07-08-00150.pdf.

Liebenwein, Sylva, Heiner Barz, and Dirk Randoll. "Zusammenfassung zentraler Befunde: Waldorfschule aus Schülersicht" (in German). In *Bildungserfahrungen an Waldorfschulen*. Edited by Sylva Liebenwein, Heiner Barz, and Dirk Randoll, 5–12. Wiesbaden, Germany: VS Verlag für Sozialwissenschaften, 2012.

Liebovich, Mark. *This Town: Two Parties and a Funeral—Plus, Plenty of Valet Parking!—in America's Gilded Capital*. New York: Penguin Random House, 2013.

Light, John. "Frequently Asked Questions About ALEC." *Moyers & Company*, September 28, 2012. http://billmoyers.com/content/frequently-asked-questions-about-alec.

Liiten, Marjukka. "Top Favorite: Teaching Profession" (in Finnish). *Helsingin Sanomat*, February 11, 2004. Cited in Sahlberg, Pasi. *Finnish Lessons: What Can the World Learn from Educational Change in Finland?* New York: Teachers College Press, 2010.

Lim Miller, Mauricio. "When Helping Doesn't Help." *Huffington Post*, May 7, 2012. www.huffington post.com/maurice-lim-miller/when-helping-doesnt-help_b_1497038.html.

Lin, Judy. "California's Pension Liability Growing by Billions." *Los Angeles Daily News*, November 14, 2014. http://www.dailynews.com/government-and-politics/20141114/californias-pension -liability-growing-by-billions/.

Lipton, Eric. "Energy Firms in Secretive Alliance with Attorneys General." *New York Times*, December 7, 2014. www.nytimes.com/2014/12/07/us/politics/energy-firms-in-secretive-alliance -with-attorneys-general.html.

———. "For Freshmen of the House, Seats of Plenty." *New York Times*, August 11, 2013.

———. "Lobbyists, Bearing Gifts, Pursue Attorneys General." *New York Times*, October 29, 2014. www.nytimes.com/2014/10/29/us/lobbyists-bearing-gifts-pursue-attorneys-general .html.

Lipton, Eric, and Ben Protess. "Banks' Lobbyists Help in Drafting Financial Bills." *New York Times*, May 24, 2013. http://dealbook.nytimes.com/2013/05/23/banks-lobbyists-help-in-draft ing-financial-bills.

Lipton, Eric, Griff Palmer, and Alicia Parlapiano. "Money Going to Attorneys General." *New York*

Times, October 28, 2014. www.nytimes.com/interactive/2014/10/28/us/politics/money-going
-to-state-attorneys-general.html.

"Living Wage Employers." Living Wage Foundation, March 2015. www.livingwage.org.uk/
employers.

"Local Elections." France in the United States, Embassy of France in the United States. December
20, 2013. www.ambafrance-us.org/spip.php?article518.

Local Government Boundary Commission for England. *Counties Pivot Data*. 2014. www.lgbce
.org.uk/ data/ assets/excel_doc/0006/22839/NEW-Copy-of-Counties-Pivot- Table-2014.xlsx.

Locke, Susannah F. "Robots That Eat Bugs and Plants for Power." *Popular Science*, October 9,
2009. www.popsci.com/military-aviation-amp-space/article/2009-09/robots-eat-bugs-and
-plants-power.

Lorber, Janie. "Former IRS Official Demands Investigation of ALEC." *Roll Call*, July 1, 2012. www
.rollcall.com/news/-215876-1.html.

Louv, Richard. *Last Child in the Woods: Saving Our Children from Nature-Deficit Disorder*. Chapel
Hill, NC: Algonquin Books, 2005.

Lowe, Marcy, and Gary Gereffi, *A Value Chain Analysis of the US Beef and Dairy Industries*. Center
on Globalization, Governance & Competitiveness, Duke University, 2009.

Lowe, Simon. "Plotting a New Course to Improved Governance." In *Corporate Governance Review,
2014*. Grant Thornton UK LLP, 2014. www.grant-thornton.co.uk/Global/Publication_pdf/
Corporate-Governance-Review-2014.pdf

Lythcott-Haims, Julie. *How to Raise an Adult: Break Free of the Overparenting Trap and Prepare Your
Kid for Success*. New York: Henry Holt and Co., 2015.

MacInnes, Tom, Hannah Aldridge, Sabrina Bushe, Peter Kenway, and Adam Tinson. *Monitoring
Poverty and Social Exclusion, 2013*. York, England: Joseph Rowntree Foundation, 2013.

Mackey, Allyson P., Amy S. Finn, Julia A. Leonard, Drew S. Jacoby-Senghor, Martin R. West,
Christopher F. O. Gabrieli, and John D. E. Gabrieli. "Neuroanatomical Correlates of the Income-Achievement Gap." *Psychological Science* 26, no. 6 (June 2015): 925–933.

Mafi, John N., Ellen P. McCarthy, Roger B. Davis, and Bruce E. Landon. "Worsening Trends in
the Management and Treatment of Back Pain." *JAMA Internal Medicine* 173, no. 17 (2013):
1573–1581.

Magee, Christine. "Backed by Spark Capital, Andela Will Develop a Continent of Tech Talent." *Techcrunch*, June 25, 2015. http://techcrunch.com/2015/06/25/backed-by-spark-capital
-andela-will-develop-a-continent-of-tech-talent.

Maher, Kris. "Ex-Coal CEO Heads to Trial for Alleged Worker-Safety Breaches." *Wall Street Journal*, September 30, 2015. www.wsj.com/articles/ex-coal-ceo-heads-to-trial-for-alleged-worker
-safety-breaches-1443660020.

Manchikanti, Laxmaiah. "Epidemiology of Low Back Pain." *Pain Physician* 3, no. 2 (2000):
167–192.

Manchin, Stephen. *Real Wages and Living Standards*. London: London School of Economics and
Political Science Centre for Economic Performance, 2015. http://cep.lse.ac.uk/pubs/down
load/EA024.pdf.

Manjoo, Farhad. "Amazon Not as Unstoppable as It Might Appear." *New York Times*, December
18, 2014. www.nytimes.com/2014/12/18/technology/personaltech/amazon-not-as-unstoppa
ble-as-it-may-appear.html.

Mankiw, Gregory N. "Dynamic Scoring in Congress Is Defensible but Slippery." *New York Times*,
March 1, 2015. www.nytimes.com/2015/03/01/upshot/a-slippery-new-rule-for-gauging-fiscal
-policy.html?_r=0.

Mankiw, Gregory N., and Matthew Weinzierl. "Dynamic Scoring: A Back-of-the-Envelope
Guide." *Journal of Public Economics* 90, no. 8 (2006): 1415–1433.

Manning, Alan. "The UK's National Minimum Wage." *CentrePiece*, Autumn 2009. http://cep.lse
.ac.uk/pubs/download/cp290.pdf.

Markoff, John. "Artificial-Intelligence Research Center Is Founded by Silicon Valley Investors." *New York Times*, December 11, 2015. www.nytimes.com/2015/12/12/science/artificial-intelli gence-research-center-is-founded-by-silicon-valley-investors.html.

Marris, Emma. "Let Kids Run Wild in the Woods." *Slate*, May 25, 2014. www.slate.com/articles/ health_and_science/science/2014/05/kid_play_zones_in_parks_leave_no_trace_inhibits_ fun_and_bonding_with_nature.html.

Massad, Timothy G. "Overall $182 Billion Committed to Stabilize AIG During the Financial Cri-sis Is Now Fully Recovered." *Treasury Notes (U.S. Department of the Treasury)*, September 11, 2012. www.treasury.gov/connect/blog/Pages/aig-182–billion.aspx.

Masters, Jeffrey. "Storm Surge Reduction by Wetlands." *Weather Underground*. www.wunder ground.com/hurricane/surge_wetlands.asp?MR=1.

Matouschek, Niko, and Imran Rasul. "The Economics of the Marriage Contract Theories and Evidence." *Journal of Law and Economics* 51, no. 1 (2008): 59–110.

McCartney, Scott. "Merger Fallout: Some Routes See Huge Fare Increases." *Wall Street Journal*, April 11, 2013. http://blogs.wsj.com/middleseat/2013/04/11/american-airlines-us-air-merger -fallout-some-routes-see-huge-fare-increases.

McColl, Kenneth E. L. "Effect of Proton Pump Inhibitors on Vitamins and Iron." *American Journal of Gastroenterology* 104, suppl. 2 (2009): S5–9.

McCollister, Kathryn E., Michael T. French, and Hai Fang. "The Cost of Crime to Society: New Crime-Specific Estimates for Policy and Program Evaluation." *Drug Alcohol Dependence* 108, no. 1 (2010): 98–109.

McCullough, Dennis. *My Mother, Your Mother: Embracing "Slow Medicine": The Compassionate Approach to Caring for Your Aging Loved Ones*. New York: Harper, 2008.

McDonald, Noreen C. "Active Transportation to School: Trends Among U.S. Schoolchildren, 1969–2001." *American Journal of Preventive Medicine* 32, no. 6 (June 2007): 509–516.

McFarland, Matt. "Elon Musk: 'With Artificial Intelligence We Are Summoning the Demon.'" *Washington Post*, October 24, 2014. www.washingtonpost.com/news/innovations/wp/2014/10 /24/elon-musk-with-artificial-intelligence-we-are-summoning-the-demon.

McGinnis, J. Michael, Jennifer Appleton Gootman, and Vivica I. Kraak, eds. *Food Marketing to Children and Youth: Threat or Opportunity?* Washington, DC: National Academies Press, 2006.

McGraw-Hill Education. www.mheducation.com.

McKenna, Maryn. "How Your Chicken Dinner Is Creating a Drug-Resistant Superbug." *Atlan-tic*, July 11, 2012. www.theatlantic.com/health/archive/2012/07/how-your-chicken-dinner-is -creating-a-drug-resistant-superbug/259700.

McVeigh, Tracy. "Scandal of NHS 'Death Factories.'" *Observer*, August 11, 2002. www.theguardian .com/society/2002/aug/11/health.politics.

"Measure for Measure." *The Economist*, November 30, 2013. www.economist.com/news/united -states/21590954-can-asking-better-questions-reduce-americas-prison-population-measure -measure.

"Measuring the Daily Destruction of the World's Rainforests." *Scientific American*, November 19, 2009. www.scientificamerican.com/article/earth-talks-daily-destruction.

Mekonnen, Mesfin M., and Arjen Y. Hoekstra. "A Global Assessment of the Water Footprint of Farm Animal Products." *Ecosystems* 15, no. 3 (2012): 401–415.

Mele, Nicco. *The End of Big: How the Internet Makes David the New Goliath*. New York: St. Martin's Press, 2013.

Memo to Honorable Frank D. Lucas from the Congressional Budget Office. www.cbo.gov/sites/ default/files/cbofiles/attachments/hr2642LucasLtr.pdf, 6, table 3.

Meyerson, Harold. "How Workers Lost the Power Struggle—and Their Pay Raises." *Washington Post*, October 8, 2014. www.washingtonpost.com/opinions/harold-meyerson-workers-lose-the -power-struggle--and-their-pay-raises/2014/10/08/bbe3b0a2-4ee2-11e4-babe-e91da079cb8a_ story.html.

"Michigan Becomes 5th US State to Thwart Direct Tesla Car Sales." *Reuters*, October 22, 2014. www.reuters.com/article/2014/10/21/tesla-motors-michigan-idUSL2N0SG2YE20141021.

Miller, Claire Cain. "Study Finds More Reasons to Get and Stay Married." *New York Times*, January 8, 2015. www.nytimes.com/2015/01/08/upshot/study-finds-more-reasons-to-get-and-stay-married.html.

———. "Why the U.S. Has Fallen Behind in Internet Speed and Affordability." *New York Times*, October 30, 2014. www.nytimes.com/2014/10/31/upshot/why-the-us-has-fallen-behind-in-internet-speed-and-affordability.html.

Miller, Dana D., and Stefano Mariani. "Smoke, Mirrors, and Mislabeled Cod: Poor Transparency in the European Seafood Industry." *Frontiers in Ecology and the Environment* 8, no. 10 (2010): 517–521.

Miller, Harold D. "From Volume to Value: Better Ways to Pay for Health Care." *Health Affairs* 28, no. 5 (2009).

Mirani, Leo. "The Secret to the Uber Economy: Wealth Inequality." *Quartz*, December 16, 2014. http://qz.com/312537/the-secret-to-the-uber-economy-is-wealth-inequality.

Mishel, Lawrence, and Alyssa Davis. "Top CEOs Make 300 Times More than Typical Workers." Economic Policy Institute, June 21, 2015.

Mishel, Lawrence, Elise Gould, and Josh Bivens. "Wage Stagnation in Nine Charts." Economic Policy Institute, January 6, 2015.

Monaghan, Angela. "UK Housebuilders Counter Ed Miliband's Land-Hoarding Claim." *Guardian*, December 16, 2013. www.theguardian.com/business/2013/dec/16/uk-housebuilders-ed-miliband-land-hoarding.

Monastersky, Richard. "Life: A Status Report." *Nature* 516 (December 11, 2014): 159–161.

Monk, Ed. "The Ultimate DIY Investment." *This Is Money*, November 8, 2013. www.thisismoney.co.uk/money/mortgageshome/article-2491020/The-ultimate-DIY-investment-Novices-urged-self-build-solve-housing-shortage--make-30–cent-profit-bargain.html.

Moretti, Enrico, and Per Thulin. "Local Multipliers and Human Capital in the United States and Sweden." *Industrial and Corporate Change* 22, no. 1 (2013): 339–362.

Morgenson, Gretchen. "The Boss Actually Said This: Pay Me Less." *New York Times*, December 18, 2005. http://query.nytimes.com/gst/fullpage.html?res=9D01EFDC1630F93BA25751C1A9639C8B63.

Morozov, Evgeny. *To Save Everything, Click Here: The Folly of Technological Solutionism*. New York: PublicAffairs, 2013.

Morra, Dante, Sean Nicholson, Wendy Levinson, David N. Gans, Terry Hammons, and Lawrence P. Casalino. "US Physician Practices versus Canadians: Spending Nearly Four Times as Much Money Interacting with Payers." *Health Affairs* 30, no. 8 (2011): 1443–1450.

Morrison, Todd G., Shannon R. Ellis, Melanie A. Morrison, Anomi Bearden, and Rebecca L. Harriman. "Exposure to Sexually Explicit Material and Variations in Body Esteem, Genital Attitudes, and Sexual Esteem Among a Sample of Canadian Men." *Journal of Men's Studies* 14, no. 2 (Spring 2006): 209–222.

Moss, Michael. "The Extraordinary Science of Addictive Junk Food." *New York Times Magazine*, February 24, 2013. www.nytimes.com/2013/02/24/magazine/the-extraordinary-science-of-junk-food.html.

Moyer, Virginia A. "Vitamin, Mineral, and Multivitamin Supplements for the Primary Prevention of Cardiovascular Disease and Cancer: US Preventive Services Task Force Recommendation Statement." *Annals of Internal Medicine* 160, no. 8 (2014): 558–564.

Mufson, Steven, and Tom Hamburger. "Jamie Dion Himself Called to Urge Support for the Derivatives Rule in the Spending Bill." *Washington Post*, December 11, 2014. www.washingtonpost.com/news/wonk/wp/2014/12/11/the-item-that-is-blowing-up-the-budget-deal.

Mullainathan, Sendhil, and Eldar Shafir. *Scarcity: Why Having Too Little Means So Much*. New York: Time Books, 2013.

"Müller Fruit Corner Strawberry." Müller Dairy. 2012. www.mullerdairy.co.uk/nutrition -information/fruit-corner.

Mundy, Liza. "Daddy Track: The Case for Paternity Leave." *Atlantic*, January/February 2014. www .theatlantic.com/magazine/archive/2014/01/the-daddy-track/355746.

Murray, Charles. "Fifty Shades of Red: A Modest Proposal for Rejecting Rules." *Wall Street Journal*, May 9–10, 2015, C1. http://online.wsj.com/public/resources/documents/print/WSJ_ -C001-20150509.pdf.

Musk, Elon. "All Our Patent Are Belong to You [sic]." Tesla Motors, June 12, 2014. www.tesla motors.com/blog/all-our-patent-are-belong-you.

National Audit Office. *End of Life Care*. London: The Stationery Office, 2008.

National Drug Threat Assessment 2011. Washington, DC: US Department of Justice National Drug Intelligence Center, August 2011.

National Highway Traffic Safety Administration, *Traffic Safety Facts*. DOT HS 812 124, February 2015. www-nrd.nhtsa.dot.gov/Pubs/812124.pdf.

Neem, Johann N. *Creating a Nation of Joiners; Democracy and Civil Society in Early National Massa-chusetts*. Cambridge, MA: Harvard University Press, 2008.

Nelson, Fraser. "Milburn: How I Can Help Gordon Brown." *Spectator*, May 19, 2007. http://new .spectator.co.uk/2007/05/milburn-how-i-can-help-brown.

Neumark, David, and William Wascher. *Minimum Wages, the Earned Income Tax Credit, and Employment: Evidence from the Post-Welfare Reform Era*. IZA Discussion Papers, no. 26100, 2007.

New Jersey Election Law Enforcement Commission. *Represented Entities, Governmental Affairs Agents and Persons Communicating with the General Public Listed by Expenditures Ranking, Cal-endar Year 2013*.

Newman, David J., and Gordon M. Cragg. "Natural Products as Sources of New Drugs over the 30 Years from 1981 to 2010." *Journal of Natural Products* 75, no. 3 (2012): 311–335.

Newsom, Gavin. *Citizenville: How to Take the Town Square Digital and Reinvent Government*. New York: Penguin Press, 2013.

New York Times. "Mr. Bratton Reverses to Go Forward." *New York Times*, September 13, 2014. www.nytimes.com/2014/09/13/opinion/mr-bratton-reverses-to-go-forward.html.

Nicas, Jack. "Airline Consolidation Hits Smaller Cities Hardest." *Wall Street Journal*, September 10, 2015. www.wsj.com/articles/airline-consolidation-hits-smaller-cities-hardest-1441912457.

Nicas, Jack, Brent Kendall, and Susan Carey. "Justice Department Probes Airlines for Collusion." *Wall Street Journal*, July 1, 2015. www.wsj.com/articles/justice-department-probes-airlines -for-collusion-1435775547.

Nicholls, Dana, and Peggy Syvertson. *Sensory Integration*. Baltimore, MD: New Horizons for Learning, Johns Hopkins School of Education, 2012.

"No Quick Fix: Exposing the Depth of Britain's Drug and Alcohol Problem." Part of *Breakdown Britain II*. London: Centre for Social Justice, 2013.

Nocera, Joe. "Are Our Courts for Sale?" *New York Times*, October 28, 2014. www.nytimes.com /2014/10/28/opinion/joe-nocera-are-our-courts-for-sale.html.

"Nonfarm Business Sector: Labor Share." Federal Reserve Bank of St. Louis, February 9, 2015. https://research.stlouisfed.org/fred2/series/PRS85006173.

Nuikkinen, Kaisa. "Vision of the Helsinki City School Building Program: Healthy and Safe School Building." Presentation at the American Institute for Architects' Schools in a Flat World con-ference, Helsinki, Finland, September 11, 2008.

Nunan, Cólin, and Richard Young. "E.coli Superbugs on Farms and Food." In *Use and Misuse of Antibiotics in UK Agriculture*, 6. Bristol, England: Soil Association, 2012.

"Nutrition Information." Franchise World Headquarters (Subway). www.subway.com/nutrition/ nutritionlist.aspx.

Nutting, Rex. "Transcript of Holder's Admission on Too-Big-To-Jail Banks." *Market Watch*, March 7,

2013. http://blogs.marketwatch.com/thetell/2013/03/07/transcript-of-holders-admission-on-too-big-to-jail-banks.

Obama, Barack. "Remarks by the President in State of the Union Address." White House Office of the Press Secretary, January 25, 2011. www.whitehouse.gov/the-press-office/2011/01/25/remarks-president-state-union-address.

_____. "Remarks by the President in State of the Union Address." US Capitol, Washington DC, January 20, 2015.

O'Brien, Matt. "Paul Ryan Has a Trick Up His Sleeve When It Comes to Taxes. It Won't Work." *Washington Post*, October 14, 2014. www.washingtonpost.com/news/wonk/wp/2014/10/14/paul-ryan-has-a-trick-up-his-sleeve-when-it-comes-to-taxes-it-wont-work.

O'Connell, Ainsley. "Most Innovative Companies 2015: Revolution Foods." *Fast Company*, 2015. www.fastcompany.com/3039619/most-innovative-companies-2015/revolution-foods.

OECD. "Consumer Prices." OECD, March 30, 2015. https://stats.oecd.org/index.aspx?queryid =221.

_____. *Education at a Glance 2014: OECD Indicators*. Paris: OECD Publishing, 2014. www.oecd.org/edu/Education-at-a-Glance-2014.pdf

_____. "OECD Health Statistics 2014—Frequently Requested Data." OECD. www.oecd.org/els/health-systems/oecd-health-statistics-2014-frequently-requested-data.htm.

_____. "How Does the United States Compare?" OECD Health Statistics, 2014. www.oecd.org/unitedstates/Briefing-Note-UNITED-STATES-2014.pdf.

_____. *OECD Income Distribution Database: Gini, Poverty, Income, Methods, and Concept*. Paris: OECD Publishing, 2014. www.oecd.org/social/ income-distribution-database.htm.

_____. *PISA 2012 Database Tables*. Paris: OECD Publishing, 2012. www.oecd.org/pisa/keyfindings/PISA-2012–results-snapshot-Volume-I-ENG.pdf.

_____. *Road Safety Annual Report 2014*. Paris: OECD Publishing, 2014.

Ofcom. *Children and Parents: Media Use and Attitudes Report*. 2014. http://stakeholders.ofcom.org.uk/market-data-research/other/research-publications/childrens/children-parents-oct-14.

Office for National Statistics. *Annual Survey of Hours and Earnings, 2014 Provisional Results*. London: Office for National Statistics, 2014. www.ons.gov.uk/ons/rel/ ashe/annual-survey-of-hours-and-earnings/2014–provisional-results/stb-ashe-statistical-bulletin-2014.html.

_____. *Divorces in England and Wales, 2012: Number of Divorces, Age at Divorce and Marital Status Before Marriage, Table 3a*. London: Office for National Statistics, 2012. www.ons.gov.uk/ons/rel/vsob1/divorces-in-england-and-wales/2012/stb-divorces-2012.html.

_____. *Underemployed and Overemployed: – the UK, 2014*. London: Office for National Statistics, 2014. www.ons.gov.uk/ons/dcp171776_387087.pdf.

_____. *Labour Market Statistics, March 2015: Unemployment by Age and Duration*. London: Office for National Statistics, 2015. www.ons.gov.uk/ons/publications/re-reference-tables.html ?edition=icm%3A77-35368#tab-Unemployment-economic-inactivity-tables.

_____. *Marriages in England and Wales (Provisional), 2012*. London: Office for National Statistics, 2014. www.ons.gov.uk/ons/dcp171778_366530.pdf.

_____. *UK National Population Projections—Principals and Variants, 2012–2087*. London: Office for National Statistics. www.ons.gov.uk/ons/interactive/uk-national-population-projections---dvc3/index.html.

_____. *2011 Census: Key Statistics for England and Wales, March 2011*. London: Office for National Statistics, 2012. www.ons.gov.uk/ons/rel/census/2011–census/key- statistics-for-local-authorities-in-england-and-wales/stb-2011–census-key-statistics-for-england-and-wales.html#tab---Religion.

_____. *Trends in the United Kingdom Housing Market, 2014* (calculated from Table 6). London: Office for National Statistics, 2014. www.ons.gov.uk/ons/rel/hpi/house-price-index-guidance/trends-in-the-uk-housing-market-2014/housing-trends-article.html?format=print.

Ofgem. *The Revenues, Costs and Profits of the Large Energy Companies in 2013.* 2013. www.ofgem
.gov.uk/sites/default/files/docs/2014/10/css_2013_summary_document_3.pdf.

———. *Supply Market Indicator for January 2015.* January 29, 2015.

Olds, David L., Charles R. Henderson Jr., Robert Cole, John Eckenrode, Harriet Kitzman, Dennis
Luckey, Lisa Pettitt et al. "Long-Term Effects of Nurse Home Visitation on Children's Criminal
and Antisocial Behavior: 15-Year Follow-Up of a Randomized Controlled Trial." *JAMA* 280, no.
14 (1998): 1238–1244.

Olds, David L., Charles R. Henderson, and Harriet Kitzman. "Does Prenatal and Infancy Nurse
Home Visitation Have Enduring Effects on Qualities of Parental Caregiving and Child Health
at 25 to 50 Months of Life?" *Pediatrics* 93, no. 1 (1994): 89–98.

Olds, David L., Charles R. Henderson, Robert Tatelbaum, and Robert Chamberlin. "Improving
the Delivery of Prenatal Care and Outcomes of Pregnancy: A Randomized Trial of Nurse
Home Visitation." *Pediatrics* 77, no. 1 (1986): 16–28.

Olesund, Erik. "How the Tractor Ruined Farming." *Green Grid Radio*, June 28, 2014. http://green
gridradio.org/2014/06/28/s4e7-how-the-tractor-ruined-farming.

Oliver, John. "State Legislatures and ALEC (HBO)." *Last Week Tonight with John Oliver.* HBO, 2014.

"One in Ten British Kids Own a Mobile Phone by the Age of Five." *uSwtich*, August 2013. www
.uswitch.com/mobiles/news/2013/08/one_in_ten_british_kids_own_mobile_phone_by_
the_age_of_five.

"Outdoor Knoxville." Legacy Parks Foundation, 2014. www.outdoorknoxville.com/urban
-wilderness.

Overby, Peter. "Conservative Group's Charity Status Draws Questions." NPR, April 19, 2012.
www.npr.org/2012/04/19/150984876/conservative-group-criticized-for-tax-exempt-status.

Panorama. Television. BBC, 2013.

Papadopoulos, Linda. *Sexualisation of Young People Review.* 2010. http://webarchive.national
archives.gov.uk/+/http:/www.homeoffice.gov.uk/documents/sexualisation-of-young-people
.pdf.

Parliament of the United Kingdom. *Agricultural Incomes and Subsidies.* 2012 data.

Pasternak, Susan. "End-of-Life Care Constitutes Third Rail of U.S. Health Care Policy Debate."
Medicare NewsGroup, June 3, 2013. www.medicarenewsgroup.com/context/understanding
-medicare-blog/understanding-medicare-blog/2013/06/03/end-of-life-care-constitutes-third
-rail-of-u.s.-health-care-policy-debate.

Patterson, Thom. "United Airlines Ends Coach Preboarding for Children." CNN, May 23, 2012.
www.cnn.com/2012/05/23/travel/united-children-preboarding.

Paul, Annie Murphy. "School of Hard Knocks: 'How Children Succeed,' by Paul Tough." *New York
Times Sunday Book Review*, August 26, 2012. www.nytimes.com/2012/08/26/books/review/
how-children-succeed-by-paul-tough.html.

Peabody, Francis W. "The Care of the Patient." *Journal of the American Medical Association* 88
(1927): 876–82.

Pearson Learning. www.pearson.com/learning.html

Pearson Student Mobile Device Survey 2014: Grades 4 through 12 Conducted by Harris Poll. New York:
Pearson, May 2014. www.pearsoned.com/wp-content/uploads/Pearson-K12-Student-Mobile
-Device-Survey-050914-PUBLIC-Report.pdf.

People Who Abuse Children (An NSPCC Research Briefing). NSPCC, 2014. www.nspcc.org.uk/global
assets/documents/information-service/research-briefing-people-who-abuse-children.pdf.

PerdueChicken. "Jim Perdue, Chairman, Perdue Farms." YouTube.com, July 11, 2011. www.youtube
.com/watch?v=2a8x_8liZWA.

Perez, Sarah. "AOL Co-Founder Steve Case Invests $30 Million into School Lunch Company, Rev-
olution Foods." *TechCrunch*, June 5, 2014. http://techcrunch.com/2014/06/05/aol-co-founder
-steve-case-invests-30-million-into-school-lunch-company-revolution-foods.

Perrin, Ellen C., Benjamin S. Siegel, James G. Pawelski, Mary I. Dobbins, Arthur Levin, Gerri Mattson, John Pascoe et al. "Promoting the Well-Being of Children Whose Parents Are Gay or Lesbian." *Pediatrics* 131, no. 4 (2013): e1374–31383.

"Philip Lymbery: Chief Executive." Compassion in World Farming, 2014. www.ciwf.org.uk/about-us/our-staff/philip-lymbery.

"Physical Activity Guidelines for Children and Young People." NHS Choices. www.nhs.uk/Livewell/fitness/Pages/physical-activity-guidelines-for-young-people.aspx.

Pilgrim, Tanya. "The End of the Supermarket Sweep?" *Pennington Manches*, October 8, 2012. www.penningtons.co.uk/news-publications/archive-news/2012/the-end-of-the-supermarket-sweep.

Pension Tracker. *Stanford Institute for Economic Policy Research.* http://www.pensiontracker.org.

Peshin, Rajinder, ed. "Environmental and Economic Costs of the Application of Pesticides Primarily in the United States." In *Integrated Pest Management: Innovation-Development Process.* Netherlands: Springer, 2009.

Peterson, Kathryn. "All in One Place." *Stanford Social Innovation Review* 13, no. 1 (2015): 17–18.

Pinkney, David. *Napoleon III and the Rebuilding of Paris.* Princeton, NJ: Princeton University Press, 1972.

Pinsker, Joe. "It's Cheaper to Buy a Judge than a State Senator." *Atlantic*, November 2, 2014. www.theatlantic.com/business/archive/2014/11/its-cheaper-to-buy-a-judge-than-a-state-senator/382198/.

PISA. "Snapshot of Performance in Mathematics, Reading and Science." www.oecd.org/pisa/keyfindings/PISA-2012-results-snapshot-Volume-I-ENG.pdf.

"PISA Interactive Data Selection—Variable ST42Q03 ('Math Anxiety—Get Very Tense')." OECD, 2012. http://pisa2012.acer.edu.au/interactive.php.

"Policy Basics: The Earned Income Tax Credit." Center on Budget and Policy Priorities, August 20, 2015. www.cbpp.org/research/policy-basics-the-earned-income-tax-credit.

Pollack, Keshia M., Dan Morhaim, and Michael A. Williams. "The Public's Perspectives on Advance Directives in Maryland: Implications for State Legislative and Regulatory Policy." *Health Policy* 96, no. 1 (2010): 57–63.

Pollan, Michael. *Cooked: A Natural History of Transformation.* London: Allen Lane, 2013.

———. *In Defense of Food: An Eater's Manifesto.* New York: Penguin Press, 2008.

Porter, Eduardo. "A Relentless Widening of Disparity in Wealth." *New York Times*, March 12, 2014. www.nytimes.com/2014/03/12/business/economy/a-relentless-rise-in-unequal-wealth.html.

Portman, Rob. "Gay Couples Also Deserve Chance to Get Married." *Columbus Dispatch*, March 15, 2013. www.dispatch.com/content/stories/editorials/2013/03/15/gay-couples-also-deserve-chance-to-get-married.html.

"Poultry Processors and Retailers Respond to the Campylobacter Claims." *Guardian*, July 23, 2014. www.theguardian.com/world/2014/jul/23/-sp-poultry-processors-retailers-respond-campylobacter-claims.

"Power of Place." *Steelcase 360°*, no. 68, 2014.

"Press Release." Resolution Foundation, October 1, 2014. www.resolutionfoundation.org/media/press-releases/a-record-1–2–million-workers-to-benefit-from-first-real-terms-minimum-wage-rise-for-six-years-today.

"Preterm Birth (Fact Sheet 363)." World Health Organization, November 2014. www.who.int/mediacentre/factsheets/fs363/en/

Price, Catherine. "Vitamins Hide the Low Quality of Our Food." *New York Times*, February 15, 2015. www.nytimes.com/2015/02/15/opinion/sunday/vitamins-hide-the-low-quality-of-our-food.html.

Priorities USA Action. "Stage." YouTube.com, June 23, 2012. www.youtube.com/watch?v=0LooJwjo3JU.

Property Protection Act, N.C. Gen. Stat. §99A-1–A-2.

Purvis, Andrew. "Running on Empty Carbs." *Guardian*, March 22, 2009. www.theguardian.com/lifeandstyle/2009/mar/22/obesity-children-eating-habits.

Quirk, Mary Beth. "Zappos CSR's Kindness Warms Our Cold Hearts." *Consumerist*, January 17, 2011. http://consumerist.com/2011/01/17/zappos-customer-service-reps-kindness-warms-our-cold-hearts.

Ramakrishnan, Sruthi. "Wal-Mart to Raise Wages for 100,000 U.S. Workers in Some Departments." *Reuters*, June 2, 2015. www.reuters.com/article/2015/06/02/us-wal-mart-stores-wages-idUSKBN0OI1EW20150602.

Ramesh, Randeep. "Give Each NHS Hospital Patient a Single Consultant, Says Jeremy Hunt." *Guardian*, January 23, 2014. www.theguardian.com/politics/2014/jan/23/nhs-patients-single-consultant-continuity-jeremy-hunt.

Randle, Henry W. "Suntanning: Differences in Perceptions Throughout History." *Mayo Clinic Proceedings* 72, no. 5 (1997): 461–466.

Rankin, Jennifer. "Fewer Women Leading FTSE Firms than Men Called John." *Guardian*, March 6, 2015. www.theguardian.com/business/2015/mar/06/johns-davids-and-ians-outnumber-female-chief-executives-in-ftse-100.

"Ray Anderson, Interface Chairman and Sustainability Leader, Dies at 77." *Environmental Leader*, August 9, 2011. www.environmentalleader.com/2011/08/09/ray-anderson-interface-chairman-and-sustainability-leader-dies-at-77.

Rayner, Jay. "Booths: The Honest Supermarket." *Guardian*, November 12, 2011. www.theguardian.com/business/2011/nov/13/supermarkets-big-competition-booths.

Reconnecting Children with Nature: Findings of the Natural Childhood Inquiry. The National Trust, 2012.

Rector, Robert. "Marriage: America's Greatest Weapon Against Child Poverty." Heritage Foundation, September 5, 2012. www.heritage.org/research/reports/2012/09/marriage-americas-greatest-weapon-against-child-poverty, chart 2.

"Red Dress Boutique." SharkTank Blog. http://sharktankblog.com/business/red-dress-boutique.

Redlawsk, David P., Caroline J. Tolbert, and Todd Donovan. *Why Iowa?: How Caucuses and Sequential Elections Improve the Presidential Nominating Process.* Chicago: University of Chicago Press, 2011.

Reeves, Richard. "Bringing Up Baby." *New Statesman*, January 29, 2009. www.newstatesman.com/ideas/2009/01/parents-children-parenting.

Reguly, Eric. "Time to Put an End to the Cult of Shareholder Value." *Globe and Mail* (Toronto, Canada), September 26, 2013. www.theglobeandmail.com/report-on-business/rob-magazine/maybe-its-time-for-ceos-to-put-shareholders-second/article14507016.

Reich, Robert. "Big Tech Has Become Way Too Powerful." *New York Times*, September 18, 2015. www.nytimes.com/2015/09/20/opinion/is-big-tech-too-powerful-ask-google.html.

———. "Not Very Giving." *New York Times*, September 5, 2013. www.nytimes.com/2013/09/05/opinion/not-very-giving.html.

Reilly, Brendan M. "Physical Examination in the Care of Medical Inpatients: An Observational Study." *Lancet* 362, no. 9390 (2003): 1100–1105.

"Rep. Kevin Yoder: Top 20 Industries Contributing to Campaign Committee." *OpenSecrets.org*, February 2, 2015. www.opensecrets.org/politicians/industries.php?cycle=2014&cid=N00031502&type=I&newmem=N.

Research, Development and Statistics Directorate. *Reducing Homicide: A Review of the Possibilities.* By Fiona Brookman and Mike Maguire. London: Home Office, 2003.

Reuters. "A.I.G. Pays Its Ex-Chief $47 Million." *New York Times*, July 2, 2008. www.nytimes.com/2008/07/02/business/02aig.html?_r=0.

Ridley, Matt. *The Rational Optimist: How Prosperity Evolves.* New York: Harper Perennial, 2010.

_____. "When Ideas Have Sex." TEDGlobal 2010, Oxford, England, July 2010. www.ted.com/talks/matt_ridley_when_ideas_have_sex?language=en.

Rideout, Victoria. *Advertising to Children and Teens: Current Practices*. San Francisco, CA: Common Sense Media, 2014.

Rifkin, Jeremy. *The Empathetic Civilization: The Race to Global Consciousness in a World in Crisis*. New York: Jeremy P. Tarcher/Penguin, 2009.

Ripley, Amanda. "How to Graduate from Starbucks." *Atlantic*, May 2015. www.theatlantic.com/magazine/archive/2015/05/the-upwardly-mobile-barista/389513.

"Robert Rubin." Council on Foreign Relations. www.cfr.org/staff/b292.

Robert-Hughes, Rebecca. *The Case for Space: The Size of England's New Homes*. Edited by Will Fox and Anna Scott-Marshall. London: Royal Institute of British Architects, 2011.

Roberto, Christina A., Jenny Baik, Jennifer L. Harris, and Kelly D. Brownell. "Influence of Licensed Characters on Children's Taste and Snack Preferences." *Pediatrics* 126, no. 1 (2010): 88–93.

Robinson, David. *Out of the Ordinary: Learning from the Community Links Approach to Social Regeneration*. London: Community Links, 2010.

Rodrigue, Edward, and Richard V. Reeves. "Home Visiting Programs: An Early Test for the 114th Congress." Brookings, February 5, 2015. www.brookings.edu/blogs/social-mobility-memos/posts/2015/02/05-home-visiting-funding-reeves.

Rogers, Katie. "The Vault Apps That Keep Sexts a Secret." *New York Times*, November 6, 2015. www.nytimes.com/2015/11/07/us/the-vault-apps-that-keep-sexts-a-secret.html?_r=0.

Rogers, Richard. Foreword to Jan Gehl. In *Cities for People*. Washington, DC: Island Press, 2010.

Roggio, Armando. "The Zappos Effect: 5 Great Customer Ideas for Smaller Business." *Practical Ecommerce*, March 21, 2011. www.practicalecommerce.com/articles/2662-The-Zappos-Effect-5-Great-Customer-Service-Ideas-for-Smaller-Businesses.

Rogowsky, Mark. "After the New Jersey Ban, Here's Where Tesla Can (and Cannot) Sell Its Cars." *Forbes*, March 15, 2014. www.forbes.com/sites/markrogowsky/2014/03/15/after-the-new-jersey-ban-heres-where-tesla-can-and-cannot-sell-its-cars.

Romito, Patricia, and Lucia Beltramini. "Watching Pornography: Gender Differences, Violence and Victimization: An Exploratory Study in Italy." *Violence Against Women* (2011): 1077801211424555.

Rosentraub, Mark S. *Major League Losers: The Real Cost of Sports and Who's Paying for It*. New York: Basic Books, 1999.

Rosin, Hanna. "Hey! Parents, Leave Those Kids Alone." *Atlantic*, April 2014. www.theatlantic.com/magazine/archive/2014/04/hey-parents-leave-those-kids-alone/358631.

_____. "Why Kids Sext." *Atlantic*, November 2014. www.theatlantic.com/magazine/archive/2014/11/why-kids-sext/380798.

Rothstein, Jesse. *The Unintended Consequences of Encouraging Work: Tax Incidence and the EITC*. Center for Economic Policy Studies. Princeton, NJ: Princeton University, 2008.

Rucker, Philip, and Joe Stephens. "White House Economics Aide Summers Discloses Income." *Washington Post*, April 4, 2009. www.washingtonpost.com/wp-dyn/content/article/2009/04/03/AR2009040303732.html.

Rudegeair, Peter. "Pay Gap Between Wall Street CEOs and Employees Narrows." *Wall Street Journal*, April 5, 2015. www.wsj.com/articles/a-pay-gap-narrows-on-wall-street-1428267898.

Rush, Emma, and Andrea La Nauze. *Corporate Paedophilia: Sexualisation of Children in Australia*. Canberra City: Australia Institute, 2006.

Russell, Jenni. "Let's Put Character Above Exam Results." *Sunday Times*, June 5, 2011. www.thesundaytimes.co.uk/sto/comment/columns/article641455.ece.

Russi, Daniela, Patrick ten Brink, Andrew Farmer, Tomas Badura, David Coates, Johannes Förster, Ritesh Kumar et al. *The Economics of Ecosystems and Biodiversity for Water and Wetlands: Executive Summary*. Institute for European Environmental Policy & Ramsar Secretariat, 2013.

Russo, Nick, Robert Morgus, Sarah Morris, and Danielle Kehl. *The Cost of Connectivity*. Washington, DC: Open Technology Institute at New America Foundation, 2014.

Ryall, Julian. "Bullet Train at 50: Rise and Fall of the World's Fastest Train." *Telegraph*, October 1, 2014. www.telegraph.co.uk/news/worldnews/asia/japan/11133241/Bullet-train-at-50-rise-and-fall-of-the-worlds-fastest-train.html.

Ryan, Richard M., and Edward L. Deci. "Self-Determination Theory and the Facilitation of Intrinsic Motivation, Social Development, and Well-Being." *American Psychologist* 55, no. 1 (2000): 68–78.

Sacks, Jonathan. *The Dignity of Difference: Avoiding the Clash of Civilizations*. Philadelphia, PA: Foreign Policy Research Institute, July 2002.

Sadik-Khan, Janette. "New York's Streets? Not So Mean Anymore." TED Talk, New York, NY, September 2013. www.ted.com/talks/janette_sadik_khan_new_york_s_streets_not_so_mean_any_more?language=en. Background information from e-mail to author, October 25, 2015.

Saez, Emmanuel. "Striking It Richer." January 25, 2015. http://eml.berkeley.edu/~saez/saez-UStopincomes-2013.pdf.

Saez, Emmanuel, and Gabriel Zucman. "The Explosion in U.S. Wealth Inequality Has Been Fueled by Stagnant Wages, Increasing Debt, and a Collapse in Asset Values for the Middle Classes." *LSE*, October 29, 2014. http://blogs.lse.ac.uk/usappblog/2014/10/29/the-explosion-in-u-s-wealth-inequality-has-been-fuelled-by-stagnant-wages-increasing-debt-and-a-collapse-in-asset-values-for-the-middle-classes.

_____. *Wealth Inequality in the United States Since 1913: Evidence from Capitalized Income Tax Data*, no. w20625. National Bureau of Economic Research, 2015. http://gabriel-zucman.eu/files/SaezZucman2014.pdf.

Sagi, Abraham, and Martin L Hoffman. "Empathic Distress in the Newborn." *Developmental Psychology* 12, no. 2 (1976): 175–176.

Sahlberg, Pasi. *Finnish Lessons: What Can the World Learn from Educational Change in Finland?* New York: Teachers College Press, 2010.

Said, Carolyn. "Peers Helps Uber, Lyft Drivers Get Back on Road After Accidents." *San Francisco Chronicle*, December 4, 2014. http://sanfrancisco.suntimes.com/sf-business/7/74/42864/peers-helps-uber-lyft-drivers-get-back-on-road-after-accidents.

St. George, Donna. "'Free Range' Parents Cleared in Second Neglect Case After Kids Walked Alone." *Washington Post*, June 22, 2015. www.washingtonpost.com/local/education/free-range-parents-cleared-in-second-neglect-case-after-children-walked-alone/2015/06/22/82283c24-188c-11e5-bd7f-4611a60dd8e5_story.html.

Saito, Hiroko. "Another Ward in Tokyo to Recognize Same-Sex Couples." *Japan Times*, July 30, 2015. www.japantimes.co.jp/news/2015/07/30/national/another-ward-in-tokyo-to-recognize-same-sex-couples/#.VluvZdKrTDd.

Salam, Reihan. "The Upper Middle Class Is Ruining America." *Slate*, January 30, 2015. www.slate.com/articles/news_and_politics/politics/2015/01/the_upper_middle_class_is_ruining_all_that_is_great_about_america.html.

Salazar, Angela. "BeGood Clothing's New Line—Organic Cotton and Silk Basics." *SF Gate*, September 12, 2014. www.sfgate.com/style/article/BeGood-Clothing-s-new-line-organic-cotton-and-5629690.php.

Sandberg, Shana F., Clese Erikson, Ross Owen, Katherine D. Vickery, Scott T. Shimotsu, Mark Linzer, Nancy A. Garrett, et al. "Hennepin Health: A Safety-Net Accountable Care Organization for the Expanded Medicaid Population." *Health Affairs* 33, no. 11 (2014).

Sanders, Katie. "Alan Grayson Says More Walmart Employees on Medicaid, Food Stamps than Other Companies." *Tampa Bay Times*'s PolitiFact, December 6, 2012. www.politifact.com/truth-o-meter/statements/2012/dec/06/alan-grayson/alan-grayson-says-more-walmart-employees-medicaid.

Sanders, Michael, and Elspeth Kirkman. *I've Booked You a Place. Good Luck: A Field Experiment Applying Behavioural Science to Improve Attendance at High-Impact Recruitment Events*, no. 13/334. Bristol, England: Department of Economics, University of Bristol, 2014.

Sandseter, Ellen B. H. "Children's Risky Play from an Evolutionary Perspective: The Anti-Phobic Effects of Thrilling Experiences." *Evolutionary Psychology* 9, no. 2 (2001): 257–284.

Schroeder, Peter, and Kevin Cirilli. "Warren, Left Fume over Deal." *The Hill*, December 10, 2014. http://thehill.com/regulation/finance/226638-democrats-balking-at-dodd-frank-changes-in -cromnibus.

Schuck, Peter. *Why Government Fails So Often: And How It Can Do Better*. Princeton, NJ: Princeton University Press, 2014.

Schumacher, E. F. *Small Is Beautiful: A Study of People as If People Mattered*. New York: Harper Perennial, 2010.

Schwarz, Alan. "Attention Disorder or Not, Pills to Help in School." *New York Times*, October 9, 2012. www.nytimes.com/2012/10/09/health/attention-disorder-or-not-children-prescribed -pills-to-help-in-school.html.

Scientific Report of the 2015 Dietary Guidelines Advisory Committee. Dietary Guidelines Advisory Committee. Washington, DC: USDA and US Department of Health and Human Services, 2015.

"Seafood Fraud." Oceana. http://oceana.org/sites/default/files/euo/OCEANA_fish_label_english .pdf.

"Sebago Lake." Portland Water District. www.pwd.org/environment/sebago/sebago.php.

"SEC Adopts Rule for Pay Ratio Disclosure." US Securities and Exchange Commission, August 5, 2015. www.sec.gov/news/pressrelease/2015-160.html.mes.

Seldon, Anthony. *An End to Factory Schools: An Education Manifesto 2010–2020*. Surrey, England: Centre for Policy Studies, 2010.

Service, Owain, Michael Hallsworth, David Halpern, Felicity Algate, Rory Gallagher, Sam Nguyen, Simon Ruda et al. *EAST: Four Simple Ways to Apply Behavioural Insights*. London: The Behavioural Insights Team, 2014.

"Settlement Reached in Lawsuit Concerning Perdue Chicken Labeling." Humane Society of the United States, October 13, 2014. www.humanesociety.org/news/press_releases/2014/10/ Perdue-settlement-101314.html.

Seymour, Philip H. K., Mikko Aro, and Jane M. Erskine. "Foundation Literacy Acquisition in European Orthographies." *British Journal of Psychology* 94, no. 2 (2003): 143–174.

Shah, Nigam H., Paea LePendu, Anna Bauer-Mehren, Yohannes T. Ghebremariam, Srinivasan V. Iyer, Jake Marcus, Kevin T. Nead, et al. "Proton Pump Inhibitor Usage and the Risk of Myocardial Infarction in the General Population." *PloS One* 10, no. 6 (June 2015): e0124653.

Shapiro, Doug. Afet Dundar, Xin Yuan, Autumn T. Harrell, and Phoebe.K. Wakhungu. *Completing College: A National View of Student Attainment Rates—Fall 2008 Cohort* (Signature Report no. 8). Hernon, VA: National Student Clearinghouse Center, 2014.

Shaw Brown, Genevieve. "United Raises Second Checked Bag Fee on International Flights." *ABC News*, June 12, 2012. http://abcnews.go.com/blogs/lifestyle/2012/06/united-raises-second -checked-bag-fee-on-international-flights.

"She, Robot: A Conversation with Helen Greiner." *Foreign Affairs* 94, no. 1 (Jan/Feb 2015): 16–22.

Shehan, Catherine V., and Jennifer L. Harris. *Trends in Television Food Advertising to Young People: 2014 Update*. Hartford, CT: UConn Rudd Center for Food Policy and Obesity, 2015.

Shenk, Joshua Wolf. *Powers of Two: How Relationships Drive Creativity*. Boston, MA: Eamon Dolan, 2014.

Shoda, Yuichi. "Individual Differences in Social Psychology: Understanding Situations to Understand People, Understanding People to Understand Situations." In *The Sage Handbook of Methods in Social Psychology*. Edited by Carol Sansone, Carolyn C. Morf, and Abigail T. Panter, 119–121. Thousand Oaks, CA: Sage Publications, 2004.

Siegal, James. "Kids First: What's Good for Kids Is Good for Cities." *Medium*, March 4, 2015. https://medium.com/@kaboom/kids-first-what-s-good-for-kids-is-good-for-cities-73811301165f.

Silbergeld, Ellen K., Jay Graham, and Lance B. Price. "Industrial Food Animal Production, Anti-microbial Resistance, and Human Health." *Annual Review of Public Health* 29 (2008): 151–169.

Silva, Rohan. "Could a Robot Do My Job?" BBC Panorama, September 18, 2015. http://www.bbc.co.uk/programmes/b06cn1wv.

Singleton, Alex. "Obituary: Sir John Cowperthwaite." *Guardian*, February 8, 2006. www.theguardian.com/news/2006/feb/08/guardianobituaries.mainsection.

"Sir James Crosby Resigns from FSA." *BBC News*, February 11, 2009. www.theguardian.com/business/2009/feb/11/banking-hbos.

"Sir Jeremy Heywood, Cabinet Secretary and Head of the Civil Service: Biography." British Government. www.gov.uk/government/people/jeremy-heywood.

Skenazy, Lenore. "Free Range Kids: FAQ." Free Range Kids. https://freerangekids.wordpress.com/faq.

Slaughter, Anne-Marie. "Why Women Still Can't Have It All." *Atlantic*, June 13, 2012. www.theatlantic.com/magazine/archive/2012/07/why-women-still-cant-have-it-all/309020.

Snowdon, Christopher. *Who's Killing the British Pub? Institute for Economic Affairs*. London: Institute for Economic Affairs, 2014.

Sobota, Daniel J., Jana E. Compton, and John A. Harrison. "Reactive Nitrogen Inputs to US Lands and Waterways: How Certain Are We About Sources and Fluxes?" *Frontiers in Ecology and the Environment* 11, no. 2 (2013): 82–90.

Soil Association 2014 Organic Market Report Reveals Growth in Organic Sales for the First Time in Four Years. Soil Association, March 13, 2014. www.soilassociation.org/news/newsstory/article id/6650/soil-association-2014–organic-market-report-reveals-growth-in-organic-sales-for -the-first-time-in-fo.

Soil: Protect European Soil From Environmental Damage. European Environmental Bureau, 2015. www.eeb.org/index.cfm/activities/biodiversity-nature/soil.

Soni, Anita. *Attention-Deficit Hyperactivity Disorder (ADHD) in Children, Ages 5–17: Use and Expenditures, 2007*. Rockville, MD: Agency for Healthcare Research and Quality, 2007. http://meps.ahrq.gov/data_files/publications/st276/stat276.pdf.

Soper, Spencer. "Amazon Workers Cool After Company Took Heat for Hot Warehouse." *Morning Call*, June 3, 2012. www.articles.mcall.com/2012-06-03/business/mc-amazon-warehouse-air -conditioning-20120602_1_warehouse-workers-air-conditioning-breinigsville-warehouse.

Sorkin, Andrew Ross. "Health Care Law Spurs Merger Talks for Insurers." *New York Times*, June 22, 2015. www.nytimes.com/2015/06/23/business/dealbook/health-care-law-spurs-merger -talks-for-insurers.html.

Souza, Kim. "Wal-Mart Downplays SNAP Cuts (Updated)." *City Wire*, October 16, 2013. http://talkbusiness.net/2013/10/wal-mart-downplays-snap-cuts-updated.

"Spare5—Preview Addition." *CNET*. http://download.cnet.com/Spare5–Preview-Edition/3000 -31709_4–76156057.html.

Squires, David A. *Explaining High Health Care Spending in the United States: An International Comparison of Supply, Utilization, Prices, and Quality*. New York: Commonwealth Fund, May 2012. www.commonwealthfund.org/~/media/files/publications/issue-brief/2012/may/1595_ squires_explaining_high_hlt_care_spending_intl_brief.pdf.

"Stafford Hospital: Q&A." *BBC News*, March 25, 2013. www.bbc.com/news/health-21275826.

"Stafford Hospital: The Victims of the Hospital Scandal." *BBC News*, February 6, 2013. www.bbc.com/news/uk-england-stoke-staffordshire-21339330.

Statistics Netherlands. *Traffic Deaths Down Again*. April 18, 2011. www.cbs.nl/en-GB/menu/themas/gezondheid-welzijn/publicaties/artikelen/archief/2011/2011–029–pb.htm

Steadman, Ian. "Dutch City Gives Residents a Self-Build Affordable Housing Catalogue." *Wired*, April 18, 2013. www.wired.co.uk/news/archive/2013-04/18/dutch-architecture-plans.

Steenhuysen, Julie. "Overuse of Heartburn Drugs Is Risky: Study." *Reuters*, May 10, 2010. www
.reuters.com/article/2010/05/10/us-heartburn-drugs-idUSTRE6495YS20100510.

Sternin, Jerry. "The Viet Nam Story." www.positivedeviance.org/about_pd/Monique%20VIET
%20NAM%20CHAPTER%20 Oct%2017.pdf.

Stevens, Heidi. "Your 11-Year-Old Daughter Wants to Shave. Everywhere." *Chicago Tribune*, July
10, 2012. http://articles.chicagotribune.com/2012-07-10/features/sc-fam-0710-tween-wax
-20120710_1_hair-removal-daughter-body.

Stevens, Jane Ellen Stevens. "The Adverse Childhood Experiences Study—The Largest, Most
Important Public Health Study You Never Heard of Began in an Obesity Clinic." *ACES Too
High News*, October 3, 2012. http://acestoohigh.com/2012/10/03/the-adverse-childhood
-experiences-study-the-largest-most-important-public-health-study-you-never-heard-of
-began-in-an-obesity-clinic.

Stewart, James B. "For Airlines, It May Be One Merger Too Many." *New York Times*, August 17, 2013.
www.nytimes.com/2013/08/17/business/for-airlines-it-may-be-one-merger-too-many.html.

Stewart, William. "Is Pisa Fundamentally Flawed?" *TES Connect*, September 27, 2014. www.tes
.co.uk/article.aspx?storycode=6344672.

Stone, Brad. "Costco CEO Craig Jelinek Leads the Cheapest, Happiest Company in the World."
BloombergBusiness, June 6, 2013. www.bloomberg.com/bw/articles/2013-06-06/costco-ceo
-craig-jelinek-leads-the-cheapest-happiest-company-in-the-world.

Stone, Chad, Danilo Trisi, Arloc Sherman, and Brandon Debot. "A Guide to Statistics on Historical Trends in Income Inequality." Center on Budget and Policy Priorities, October 26, 2015.
www.cbpp.org/research/poverty-and-inequality/a-guide-to-statistics-on-historical-trends
-in-income-inequality.

Stone, Peter H. "Chamber Seeks Cash from Insurers, Financial Firms for New Effort." Center
for Public Integrity, December 1, 2010. www.publicintegrity.org/2010/12/01/2282/chamber
-seeks-cash-insurers-financial-firms-new-effort.

Strauss, Valerie. "What One College Discovered When It Stopped Accepting SAT/ACT Scores."
Washington Post, September 25, 20015. www.washingtonpost.com/news/answer-sheet/wp
/2015/09/25/what-one-college-discovered-when-it-stopped-accepting-satact-scores.

"Stressed Parents: Cancel That Violin Class." *The Economist*, July 26, 2014. www.economist.com/
news/united-states/21608793-helicopter-moms-and-dads-will-not-harm-their-kids-if-they
-relax-bit-cancel-violin.

Stuhldreher, Anne, and Rourke O'Brien. *The Family Independence Initiative: A New Approach to
Help Families Exit Poverty*. Washington, DC: New America Foundation, 2011.

Stutzer, Alois, and Bruno S. Frey. "Stress That Doesn't Pay: The Commuting Paradox." *Scandinavian Journal of Economics* 110, no. 2 (2008): 339–366.

Suggate, Sebastian P., Elizabeth A. Schaughency, and Elaine Reese. "Children Learning to Read
Later Catch Up to Children Reading Earlier." *Early Childhood Research Quarterly* 28, no. 1
(2013): 33–48.

Sun, Lena H. "Johns Hopkins Team Wins U.S. Award for Improved Suit to Fight Ebola." *Washington Post*, December 13, 2014. www.washingtonpost.com/news/post-nation/wp/2014/12/13/
johns-hopkins-team-wins-u-s-award-for-improved-suit-to-fight-ebola.

"Survey of Self-Build Intentions." Ipsos-Mori, March 12, 2013. www.ipsos-mori.com/research
publications/researcharchive/3171/Survey-of-selfbuild-intentions.aspx.

Sweet, Victoria. *God's Hotel: A Doctor, a Pilgrimage, and a Journey to the Heart of Medicine*. New
York: Penguin, 2013.

———. "The Efficiency of Inefficiency." TEDxMiddlebury, Middlebury, VT, March 9, 2013.
http://tedxtalks.ted.com/video/The-Efficiency-of-Inefficiency.

Tait, Cameron. *Work That Pays: The Final Report of the Living Wage Commission*. London: Living
Wage Commission, 2014.

Talberth, John, Erin Gray, Evan Branosky, and Todd Gartner. *Insights from the Field: Forests for Water*. Washington, DC: Water Resources Institute, 2012.

Taleb, Nassim Nicholas. *Antifragile: Things That Gain from Disorder*. New York: Random House Trade Paperbacks, 2014.

———. *Black Swan: The Impact of the Highly Improbable Fragility*. New York: Random House, 2010.

Tandon, Pooja S., Chuan Zhou, Paula Lozano, and Dimitri A. Christakis. "Preschoolers' Total Daily Screen Time at Home and by Type of Child Care." *Journal of Pediatrics* 158, no. 2 (2011): 297–300.

Tanz, Jason. "The Tech Elite's Quest to Reinvent School in Its Own Image." *Wired*, October 26, 2015. www.wired.com/2015/10/salman-khan-academy-lab-school-reinventing-classrooms.

Taylor, Henry. "Who Is the Biggest Employer?" *World Economic Forum*, June 17, 2015. https://agenda.weforum.org/2015/06/worlds-10-biggest-employers.

Teachman, Jay D. "The Childhood Living Arrangements of Children and the Characteristics of Their Marriages." *Journal of Family Issues* 25 (January 2004): 86–111.

Temple, Jeff R., Jonathan A. Paul, Patricia van den Berg, Vi Donna Le, Amy McElhany, and Brian W. Temple. "Teen Sexting and Its Association with Sexual Behaviors." *Archives of Pediatrics & Adolescent Medicine* 166, no. 9 (2012): 828–833.

Terry, Lynne. "A Game of Chicken: USDA Repeatedly Blinked When Facing Salmonella Outbreaks Involving Foster Farms." *Oregonian*, May 1, 2015. www.oregonlive.com/usda-salmonella.

"Tesco's Travails: Supermarket Sweep." *The Economist*, April 21, 2012. www.economist.com/node/21553049.

Thaler, Richard H. *Misbehaving: The Making of Behavioral Economics*. New York: W. W. Norton & Company, 2015.

Thaler, Richard H., and Shlomo Benartzi. *The Behavioral Economics of Retirement Savings Behavior*. Washington DC: AARP Public Policy Institute, 2007.

Thaler, Richard H., and Cass R. Sunstein. *Nudge: Improving Decisions About Health, Wealth, and Happiness: Revised and Expanded Edition*. New York: Penguin Books, 2009.

"Theodore Roosevelt." In *The National Parks: America's Best Idea*. PBS, 2009. www.pbs.org/nationalparks/people/historical/roosevelt.

Thompson, Derek. "A World Without Work." *Atlantic*, July/August 2015. www.theatlantic.com/magazine/archive/2015/07/world-without-work/395294.

Thorndike, William. *The Outsiders: Eight Unconventional CEOs and Their Radically Rational Blueprint for Success*. Boston, MA: Harvard University Press, 2012.

Timmins, Nicholas. "NHS Electronic Records Are Two Years Late." *Financial Times*, May 29, 2006. www.ft.com/intl/cms/s/0/d8aca40c-ef49-11da-b435-0000779e2340.html.

"Top Industries (2009)." *OpenSecrets.org*. www.opensecrets.org/lobby/top.php?showYear=2009&indexType=i.

"Touch Screens." Michael Cohen Group LLC, February 17, 2014. www.mcgrc.com/wp-content/uploads/2015/03/MCGRC_Digital-Kids-Presentation_022014.pdf

Tough, Paul. "The Poverty Clinic." *New Yorker*, March 21, 2008. www.newyorker.com/magazine/2011/03/21/the-poverty-clinic.

Towards a Fine City for People. Copenhagen, Denmark: Gehl Architects, 2004. http://issuu.com/gehlarchitects/docs/issuu_270_london_pspl_2004/0.

Trasande, L., J. Blustein, M. Liu, E. Corwin, L. M. Cox, and M. J. Blaser. "Infant Antibiotic Exposures and Early-Life Body Mass." *International Journal of Obesity* 37, no. 1 (2013): 16–23.

"Troubled Families." Local Government Association, January 29, 2015. www.local.gov.uk/community-budgets/-/journal_content/56/10180/3691966/ARTICLE.

Tung, Irene, Paul K. Sonn, and Yannet Lathrop. "The Growing Movement for $15." *National Employment Law Project*, April 13, 2015. http://nelp.org/publication/growing-movement-15.

Turkle, Sherry. *Alone Together: Why We Expect More from Technology and Less from Each Other.* New York: Basic Books, 2011.

———. "Authenticity in the Age of Digital Companions." *Interaction Studies* 8, no. 3 (2007): 501–517.

———. "Connected, But Alone?" TED, April 2012. www.ted.com/talks/sherry_turkle_alone_together?language=en.

Turner, Beverley. "Pubic Hair Is Back Ladies. The Men Don't Care and the Women Can't Be Bothered." *Telegraph*, November 15, 2013. www.telegraph.co.uk/women/womens-life/10452327/Pubic-hair-is-back-ladies.-The-men-dont-care-and-the-women-cant-be-bothered.html.

Twenge, Jean M., Keith W. Campbell, and Craig A. Foster. "Parenthood and Marital Satisfaction: A Meta-Analytic Review." *Journal of Marriage and the Family* 65 (2003): 574–583.

Twentyman, Jessica. "Tesco CIO Sharpens Focus on the Digital Customer Experience." *I-CIO*, October 2013. www.i-cio.com/strategy/big-data/item/tesco-cio-sharpens-focus-on-the-digital-customer-experience.

Ueda, Kenichi, and Beatrice Weder di Mauro. "Quantifying Structural Subsidy Values for Systemically Important Financial Institutions." *Journal of Banking and Finance* 37, no. 10 (2013): 3830–3842.

Ulrich, Roger S., Robert F. Simons, Barbara D. Losito, Evelyn Fiorito, Mark A. Miles, and Michael Zelson. "Stress Recovery During Exposure to Natural and Urban Environments." *Journal of Environmental Psychology* 11, no. 3 (1991): 201–230.

Ulrich, Roger S. "View Through a Window May Influence Recovery Surgery." *Science*, New Series 224, no. 4647 (April 27, 1984): 420–421.

Umberson, Debra, and Jennifer Karas Montez. "Social Relationships and Health a Flashpoint for Health Policy." *Journal of Health and Social Behavior* 51, no. 1 suppl (2010): S54–S66.

UNICEF. "Child Poverty in Perspective: An Overview of Child Well-Being in Rich Countries." *Innocenti Report Card* 7. Florence, Italy: UNICEF Innocenti Research Centre, 2007.

United Nations, Department of Economic and Social Affairs, Population Division. *World Urbanization Prospects: The 2014 Revision, Highlights.* ST/ESA/SER.A/352.

Unterman, Rebecca. *Headed to College: The Effects of New York City's Small High Schools of Choice on Postsecondary Enrollment.* New York: MDRC, 2014. www.mdrc.org/sites/default/files/Headed_to_College_PB.pdf.

US Bureau of Labor Statistics. "Productivity and Costs, Second Quarter 2015, Revised." Bureau of Labor Statistics, September 2, 2015. www.bls.gov/news.release/prod2.nro.htm.

The Use of Medicines in the United States: Review of 2011. Parsippany, NJ: IMS Institute for Healthcare Informatics, 2011.

Vangelova, Luba. "How the English Language Is Holding Kids Back." *Atlantic*, February 9, 2015.

Vardi, Nathan. "How 'The Outsiders' Became One of the Most Important Business Books in America." *Forbes*, May 8, 2014. www.forbes.com/sites/nathanvardi/2014/05/08/how-the-outsiders-became-one-of-the-most-important-business-books-in-america.

Verdine, Brian N., Roberta M. Golinkoff, Kathryn Hirsh Pasek, Nora S. Newcombe, Andrew T. Filipowicz, and Alicia Chang. "Deconstructing Building Blocks: Preschoolers' Spatial Assembly Performance Relates to Early Mathematical Skills." *Child Development* 85, no. 3 (2014): 1062–1076.

Vergara v. California—Tentative Decision. Superior Court of the State of California, County of Los Angeles, June 10, 2014. http://studentsmatter.org/wp-content/uploads/2014/06/Tentative-Decision.pdf.

Verghese, Abraham. "A Doctor's Touch." TEDGlobal 2011: The Stuff of Life, Edinburgh, Scotland, September 2011. www.ted.com/talks/abraham_verghese_a_doctor_s_touch?language=en.

Villanova, Peter H., John Bernardin, Sue A. Dahmus, and Randi L. Sims. "Rater Leniency and Performance Appraisal Discomfort." *Educational and Psychological Measurement* 53, no. 3 (1993): 789–799.

"Vision Zero Initiative: Traffic Safety by Sweden." Swedish Government and Business Sweden. www.visionzeroinitiative.com/en/.

von Grebmer, Klaus, Amy Saltzman, Ekin Birol, Doris Weismann, Nilam Prasai, Sandra Yin, Yisehac Yohannes et al. *Global Hunger Index: The Challenge of Hidden Hunger, Synopsis.* Bonn, Germany, Washington, DC, Dublin, Ireland: International Food Policy Research Institute, October 2014.

Wagner, Tony, and Ted Dintersmith, *More Likely to Succeed: Preparing Our Kids for the Innovation Era.* New York: Simon & Schuster, 2015.

Wainwright, Oliver. "Right to Build: Nick Boles Tells Councils to Offer Land for Self-Builds 'Or Be Sued.'" *Guardian*, May 7, 2014. www.theguardian.com/artanddesign/architecture -design-blog/2014/may/07/right-to-nick-boles-councils-self-build-sued.

Walker, Tim. "How Finland Keeps Kids Focused Through Free Play." *Atlantic*, June 30, 2014. www .theatlantic.com/education/archive/2014/06/how-finland-keeps-kids-focused/373544.

Walton, Alice G. "Steve Jobs' Cancer Treatment Regrets." *Forbes*, October 24, 2011. www.forbes .com/sites/alicegwalton/2011/10/24/steve-jobs-cancer-treatment-regrets.

Wang, Y. Claire, Klim McPherson, Tim Marsh, Steven L. Gortmaker, and Martin Brown. "Health and Economic Burden of the Projected Obesity Trends in the USA and the UK." *The Lancet* 378, no. 9793 (2011): 815–825.

Warner, Kimberley, Walker Timme, Beth Lowell, and Michael Hirshfield. *Oceana Study Reveals Seafood Fraud Nationwide.* Oceana, 2013. http://oceana.org/sites/default/files/reports/National _Seafood_Fraud_Testing_Results_FINAL.pdf.

Warnock, Mary. *A Question of Life: The Warnock Report on Human Fertilisation and Embryology.* London: Her Majesty's Stationery Office, 1984.

Warren, Elizabeth. *Forum.* By Michael Krasny. *Forum*, 88.5 KQED FM, May 7, 2014.

"Water Conservation Tips." *National Geographic.* http://environment.nationalgeographic.com/ environment/freshwater/water-conservation-tips.

Watson, Peter. *Ideas: A History of Thought and Invention, from Fire to Freud.* New York: Harper Perennial, 2005.

Watson, Robert, Steve Albon, R. Aspinall, M. Austen, B. Bardgett, I. Bateman, P. Berry et al. *UK National Ecosystem Assessment: Synthesis of the Key Findings.* Cambridge, England: UNEP-WCMC, 2011.

Wei Yu, *End of Life Care: Medical Treatments and Costs by Age, Race, and Region.* Health Services Research and Development study IIR, no. 02-189, 2006.

Welch, H. Gilbert. *Less Medicine, More Health: 7 Assumptions That Drive Too Much Medical Care.* Boston, MA: Beacon Press, 2015.

Weldon, William. Interview, Knowledge@Wharton, June 25, 2008. http://knowledge.wharton.u penn.edu/article/johnson-johnson-ceo-william-weldon-leadership-in-a-decentralized-company.

"Welfare Issues for Meat Chickens." Compassion in World Farming, 2014. www.ciwf.org.uk/ farm-animals/chickens/meat-chickens/welfare-issues.

Westervelt, Amy. "Can't Picture a World Devastated by Climate Change? These Games Will Do It for You." *Smithsonian Magazine*, July 21, 2014. www.smithsonianmag.com/science-nature/ cant-picture-world-devastated-climate-change-these-games-will-do-it-you-180952104.

Whalen, Jeanne. "How Glaxo Marketed a Malady to Sell a Drug." *Wall Street Journal*, October 25, 2006. www.wsj.com/articles/SB116174246339602800.

"What Have the Immigrants Ever Done for Us?" *The Economist*, November 8, 2014. www.econ omist.com/news/britain/21631076-rather-lot-according-new-piece-research-what-have -immigrants-ever-done-us.

"What Is a Benefit Corporation?" B Lab, 2015. http://benefitcorp.net.

"What Is the Living Wage?" *BBC News*, November 2, 2014. www.bbc.com/news/business-20204594.

Wheeler, Tom, "The Facts and Future of Broadband Competition" (speech). 1776 Headquarters, Washington, DC, September 4, 2014.

"When Do Parents Give into Kids' Pleas for Devices?" *eMarketer*, August 21, 2015. www.emar
    keter.com/Article/Do-Parents-Give-Kids-Pleas-Devices/1012887.

White, Gilliam B. "What 27 Weeks of Unemployment Does to the American Worker." *Atlantic*,
    March 6, 2015. www.theatlantic.com/business/archive/2015/03/what-27-weeks-of-unemploy
    ment-does-to-the-american-worker/387031.

"Who Are the School Truants?" PISA in Focus, January 2014. www.oecd.org/pisa/ pisaproducts/
    pisainfocus/PISA-in-Focus-n35-(eng)-FINAL.pdf.

"Who Are the Working Poor?" UC Davis Center for Poverty Research, July 2014. http://poverty
    .ucdavis.edu/faq/who-are-working-poor.

"Who Are We?" Embrace, 2015. http://embraceglobal.org/who-we-are/our-story.

"Who's Up, Who's Down?" *Open Secrets.org*, 2015. http://www.opensecrets.org/lobby/incdec.php.

"Why Plants in the Office Make Us More Productive." *ScienceDaily*, September 1, 2014. www
    .sciencedaily.com/releases/2014/09/140901090735.htm.

"Why Sweden Has So Few Road Deaths." *The Economist*, February 26, 2014. www.economist
    .com/blogs/economist-explains/2014/02/economist-explains-16.

"Why Waldorf Works: Frequently Asked Questions." Association of Waldorf Schools of North
    America. www.whywaldorfworks.org/02_W_Education/faq_about.asp.

Wideman, Robert F., and Rhonda D. Prisby. "Bone Circulatory Disturbances in the Development
    of Spontaneous Bacterial Chondronecrosis with Osteomyelitis: A Translational Model for the
    Pathogenesis of Femoral Head Necrosis." *Frontiers in Endocrinology* 3 (February 2012): 183.

Wildman, Charlotte. "The 'Chicago of Great Britain': Growth and Urban Regeneration in Liver-
    pool." In *The History Boys: Lessons from Local Government's Past*. Edited by Simon Parker and
    Joe Manning, 29–38. London: New Local Government Network, 2013.

Wilen, Holden. "State House Passes Minimum Wage Increase." *Sentinel Newspapers*, April 21,
    2014. www.thesentinel.com/mont/newsx/state/item/192-state-house-passes-minimum-wage
    -increase.

Wilson, Edward O. *Biophilia: The Human Bond with Other Species*. Cambridge, MA: Harvard Uni-
    versity Press, 1984.

———. "My Wish: Build the Encyclopedia of Life." TED Talk 2007, 2007. www.ted.com/talks/e
    _o_wilson_on_saving_life_on_earth?language=en.

Winkler, Rolf, and Douglas MacMillan. "The Secret Math of Airbnb's $24 Billion Valuation."
    Wall Street Journal, June 17, 2015. www.wsj.com/articles/the-secret-math-of-airbnbs-24
    -billion-valuation-1434568517.

Winquist Nord, Christine, and Jerry West, *Fathers' and Mothers' Involvement in Their Children's
    Schools by Family Type and Resident Status*, NCES 2001-032. Washington, DC: US Depart-
    ment of Education, National Center for Education Statistics, 2001. http://nces.ed.gov/pubs
    2001/2001032.pdf.

Wintour, Patrick. "Government 'Is Starting to Help 120,000 Troubled Families.'" *Guardian*,
    October 29, 2014. www.theguardian.com/society/2014/oct/28/government-help-troubled
    -families-local-authority-figures.

Witko, Christopher. "Campaign Contributions, Access, and Government Contracting." *Journal of
    Public Administration Research and Theory* 23, no. 2 (2013).

Wittman, Michael D., and William S. Swelbar. *Evolving Trends of U.S. Domestic Airfares: The Im-
    pacts of Competition, Consolidation, and Low-Cost Carriers*. MIT International Center for Trans-
    portation, 2013.

Woloshin, Steven, and Lisa M. Schwartz. "Giving Legs to Restless Legs: A Case Study of How the
    Media Helps Make People Sick." *PLoS Medicine* 3, no. 4 (2006): e170.

"Woman Dies After Farewell to Horse at Wigan Hospital." *BBC News*, November 7, 2014. www
    .bbc.com/news/uk-england-manchester-29951094.

"Women CEOs of the S&P 500." *Catalyst*, November 18, 2015. www.catalyst.org/knowledge/
    women-ceos-sp-500.

Woodman, Spencer. "Exclusive: Amazon Makes Even Temporary Warehouse Worker Sign 18-Month Non-Competes." *Verge*, March 26, 2015. www.theverge.com/2015/3/26/8280309/amazon-warehouse-jobs-exclusive-noncompete-contracts.

Woods, Lucy. "Friday Focus: Solar's Future Fantasies." *PV Tech*, December 13, 2013. www.pv-tech.org/friday_focus/friday_focus_solars_future_fantasies.

Woolhandler, Steffie, and David U. Himmelstein. "Administrative Work Consumes One-Sixth of US Physicians' Working Hours and Lowers Their Career Satisfaction." *International Journal of Health Services* 44, no. 4 (2014): 635–642.

Working Paper: Uprating the UK Living Wage in 2014. Centre for Research in Social Policy, Loughborough University, 2014.

"Working Poor Families in America." OXFAM America. http://policy-practice.oxfamamerica.org/publications/working-poor-families-in-america.

World Bank. *Long-Term Unemployment (% of Total Unemployment).* 2015. http://data.worldbank.org/indicatorSL.UEM.LTRM.2S?order=wbapi-data-value-last&sort=asc.

World Economic Outlook October 2014: Legacies, Clouds, Uncertainties. Washington, DC: International Monetary Fund, 2014.

Wortham, Jenna. "What Silicon Valley Can Learn from Seoul." *New York Times Sunday Magazine*, June 7, 2015. www.nytimes.com/2015/06/07/magazine/what-silicon-valley-can-learn-from-seoul.html.

Wuttke, Joachim. "Uncertainty and Bias in PISA." In *Pisa According to Pisa: Does Pisa Keep What It Promises?* Edited by Stefan Thomas Hopmann, Gertrude Brinek, and Martin Retzl, 241–263. Vienna, Austria: Lit Verlag, 2007.

Yardley, Jim. "Bangladesh Pollution, Told in Colors and Smells." *New York Times*, July 15, 2013. www.nytimes.com/2013/07/15/world/asia/bangladesh-pollution-told-in-colors-and-smells.html.

"Yoplait Original 25% Less Sugar." Yoplait USA. www.yoplait.com/products/yoplait-original-style-less-sugar.

Young People Sexual Relationships. IPPR. www.ippr.org/assets/media/publications/attachments/youngpeoplesexrelationships.jpg.

Zaretsky, Adam M. "Should Cities Pay for Sports Facilities?" *Regional Economist*, April 2001.

"Zero to Eight: Children's Media Use in America 2013." Common Sense Media, Fall 2013. www.commonsensemedia.org/file/zero-to-eight-2013pdf-0/download.

Zhang, Baohui, Alexi A. Wright, Haiden A. Huskamp, Matthew E. Nilsson, Matthew L. Maciejewski, Craig C. Earle, Susan D. Block et al.. "Health Care Costs in the Last Week of Life: Associations with End-of-Life Conversations." *Archives of Internal Medicine* 169, no. 5 (2009): 480–488.

LIST OF INTERVIEWS AND CORRESPONDENCE

Bonbright, David. Interview by authors. Palo Alto, CA, October 24, 2014.

Burden, Amanda. Interview by authors. New York, NY, October 16, 2015.

Casey, Louise. Interview by authors. November 7, 2014.

_____. Interview by authors. Menlo Park, CA, November 28, 2014.

Cavendish, Camilla. Interview by authors. September 8, 2014.

_____. Interview by authors. London. September 25, 2014.

Chow, Barbara. Interview by authors. Menlo Park, CA, June 18, 2015.

Courington, Karen. Inveriew by authors. Menlo Park, CA, July 1, 2015.

Crombie, David. Interview by authors. Menlo Park, CA, September 17, 2014.

Dorion, Christiane. Interview by authors. London, September 26, 2014.

Fernald, Anya. Phone interview by authors. October 20, 2014.

Fukuyama, Francis. Interview by authors. Stanford, CA, July 31, 2014.

Harris, Nadine Burke. Interview by authors. San Francisco, CA, October 6, 2014.

Heller, Lucy. Interview by authors. October 15, 2014.

Helm, Dieter. Interview by authors. Menlo Park, CA, November 21, 2014.

Heywood, James. Phone interview by authors. October 9, 2014.

Hocker, Paul. Interview by authors. London. September 26, 2014.

Holden, Patrick. Interview by authors. Belvedere, CA, October 3, 2014.

_____. E-mail to authors. December 23, 2014.

Jacobson, Niclas. Interview by authors. November 6, 2014.

Jameson, Neil. Interview by authors. London, September 25, 2014.

Kelly, Mike. Interview by authors. London, September 25, 2014.

Liang, Linus. Interview by authors. Stanford, CA, November 20, 2014.

Letwin, Oliver. Interview by authors. London, September 26, 2014.

Lovera, Patty. Phone interview by authors. July 1, 2015.

Lymbery, Philip. E-mail to authors. March 29, 2015.

Lythcott-Haims, Julie. Interview by authors. Palo Alto, CA, August 5, 2015.

Manzoni, Niccolo, and Rosie Wardle. Interview by authors. February 5, 2015.

Matsuoka, Karen. Interview by authors. Menlo Park, CA, June 19, 2015.

Mayfield, Charlie. Interview by authors. October 22, 2014.

McAfee, Michael. E-mail to authors, September 4, 2014.

Melchett, Peter. Interview by authors. October 15, 2014.

Nation, Joe. E-mail correspondence with authors. Stanford, CA, January 20, 2016.

Oakeshott, Isabel. E-mail to authors. March 14, 2015.

Oberfest, Jason. Interview by authors. San Francisco, CA, August 27, 2014.

O'Shaughnessy, James. Interview by authors. November 19, 2014.

Parsa, Ali. Phone interview by authors. October 28, 2014.

Pittman, Jason. Interview by authors. Mountain View, CA, November 5, 2014.

Ratti, Carlo. Interview by authors. October 13, 2014.

Ricks, Alan. Interview by authors. October 8, 2014.

Robinson, David. Interview by authors. London, September 24, 2014.

Rolnick, Art. Phone interview by authors. November 19, 2015.

Rothe, Matt. Interview by authors. Stanford, CA, October 24, 2014.

Sandefer, Jeff. E-mail to authors. September 3, 2014

Schwegler, Ben. Interview by authors. August 20, 2014.

Sears, Shawn and Laura. Interview by and email to authors. October 2014.

Seldon, Anthony. Interview by authors. October 17, 2014.

Silva, Rohan. Interview by authors. London, September 17, 2014.

Stein-Greenberg, Sarah. Interview by authors. October 23, 2014.

Stockton, Paul. Interview by authors. October 1, 2014.

Tamkivi, Sten. Interview by authors. Palo Alto, CA, August 28, 2014.

Tatham, Ken. Interview by authors. December 16, 2014.

Thomas, Jeff and Rachael. Interview by authors. October 9, 2014.

Thrun, Sebastian. Interview by authors. Mountain View, CA, November 11, 2014.

Vaarik, Daniel. Interview by authors. Menlo Park, CA, December 2, 2014.

Verkuil, Paul. Phone interview by authors. July 16, 2015.

Westoff, Pat. Phone interview by authors. July 17, 2015.

Willis, Paul. Interview by authors. Menlo Park, CA, November 12, 2014.

INDEX

ABOUT THE AUTHORS

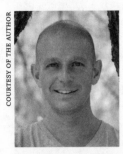

STEVE HILTON is cofounder and CEO of Crowdpac, a Silicon Valley political tech startup, and a visiting professor at Stanford University. He was formerly senior adviser to Prime Minister David Cameron and played a leading role in the modernization of the Conservative Party and in the implementation of its government reform program. Steve is a graduate of New College, Oxford University, where he studied philosophy, politics, and economics. He now lives in California with his wife and young family.

SCOTT BADE works on the communications team of Michael Bloomberg and Bloomberg Philanthropies. He previously researched international security at Stanford University's Freeman Spogli Institute of International Studies. Scott graduated from Stanford University and lives in New York.

JASON BADE lectures on social problem solving at Stanford Law School and is active in the impact investing space. He often advises startups and social entrepreneurs on strategy and human-centered design. Jason graduated from Stanford University and lives in California.

PublicAffairs is a publishing house founded in 1997. It is a tribute to the standards, values, and flair of three persons who have served as mentors to countless reporters, writers, editors, and book people of all kinds, including me.

I. F. Stone, proprietor of *I. F. Stone's Weekly*, combined a commitment to the First Amendment with entrepreneurial zeal and reporting skill and became one of the great independent journalists in American history. At the age of eighty, Izzy published *The Trial of Socrates*, which was a national bestseller. He wrote the book after he taught himself ancient Greek.

Benjamin C. Bradlee was for nearly thirty years the charismatic editorial leader of *The Washington Post*. It was Ben who gave the *Post* the range and courage to pursue such historic issues as Watergate. He supported his reporters with a tenacity that made them fearless and it is no accident that so many became authors of influential, best-selling books.

Robert L. Bernstein, the chief executive of Random House for more than a quarter century, guided one of the nation's premier publishing houses. Bob was personally responsible for many books of political dissent and argument that challenged tyranny around the globe. He is also the founder and longtime chair of Human Rights Watch, one of the most respected human rights organizations in the world.

.   .   .

For fifty years, the banner of Public Affairs Press was carried by its owner Morris B. Schnapper, who published Gandhi, Nasser, Toynbee, Truman, and about 1,500 other authors. In 1983, Schnapper was described by *The Washington Post* as "a redoubtable gadfly." His legacy will endure in the books to come.

Peter Osnos, *Founder and Editor-at-Large*